ENSITIVE SYSTEMS:

emistry and Application
Nonsilver Halide Photographic Processes

WILEY SERIES ON PHOTOGRAPHIC SCIENCE
AND TECHNOLOGY AND THE GRAPHIC ARTS

EDITOR
WALTER CLARK
Kodak Research Laboratories

Light-Sensitive Systems:
Chemistry and Application
of Nonsilver Halide Photographic Processes
JAROMIR KOSAR

Light-Sensitive Systems:

Chemistry and Application
of Nonsilver Halide Photographic Processes

Jaromir Kosar

Director of Research and Development
Ulano Companies, Brooklyn, New York

John Wiley & Sons, Inc., New York | London | Sydney

Library of Congress Catalog Card Number: 65-22427
Printed in the United States of America

To my father and mother,
to my wife, and
to our children

Foreword

Photography has become one of the most important means of scientific and technical observation, record, measurement, and information storage. The uses are growing rapidly. The need for a clear understanding of its basic principles, its applications, its potential, and its limitations is more and more evident. Proper preparation and interpretation of photographs can be vital to the successful outcome of experiments and the effectiveness of records. The scope of photography is very broad. By definition it embraces all means of producing visible images on sensitive surfaces directly or indirectly by the action of light or other form of radiant energy. All photosensitive systems which can be used for photography fall within the scope of this series.

This series will therefore be devoted to a wide range of applications of photography to assist the scientist, technologist, engineer, teacher, or other user in the wise selection of his materials and methods, to define the limitations of the methods, to utilize the capabilities fully, and to design photographic methods for special purposes. Historical perspective will be included where desirable, the approach will be tutorial and practical, and the underlying principles will be elaborated to the fullest extent. The objective of the series is to lead to a better understanding of and a rational and effective use of the techniques, and to the most reliable interpretation of the results.

Since the quality of printed illustrations in books, journals, magazines, and newspapers, in black-and-white and color, depends on the proper understanding and carrying out of the intermediate photographic steps, some books on the graphic arts will be included.   The place of photography is well established in the field of business, and it is vital to all aspects of public enlightenment.   Special technical aspects involved, as in television, motion pictures, and other audiovisual arts, may be dealt with in the series.

WALTER CLARK

Preface

Nonsilver halide light-sensitive systems are now receiving worldwide attention, a natural consequence of the growing influence of photography in daily life. Although some of these systems have been known for more than a century, information about nonsilver halide photosensitive materials has until recently been confined to scattered items in journals and patents, and, unlike silver halide photographic chemistry, has not been organized into a monograph. This book attempts to fill that gap by providing an essentially complete review of the literature through December 1964, covering major journals and patents. Historical developments have been included in order to provide a complete background, but I have concentrated on contributions published since 1945. In view of the great number of developments each year it is impossible for a single author to cover the entire field authoritatively, and it would be foolhardy to claim that no important contribution has been overlooked.

Patents, with all their well-known limitations, are frequently the sole source of forthcoming developments, and much in this book is the result of an intensive survey of domestic and foreign patents. It must not be forgotten that the processes described in them are not necessarily commercially successful; they are included to show the direction that research aims and techniques are taking in particular fields.

The organization of this book was largely guided by my own interest in photographic chemistry. The vast amount of notes on the published information, accumulated during a ten-year period, has been brought into a systematic order and grouped according to the chemical origin of the individual systems. The first three chapters describe light-sensitive inorganic compounds and their application in reproduction fields. Chapters 4 and 5 are concerned with systems in which the images are produced as a result of the formation of very large molecules, either by crosslinking of unsaturated compounds or by polymerization.   Light-sensitive diazonium salts and diazotype processes are the subject of Chapter 6.   The seventh chapter deals with the application of diazo, azido, and related compounds in presensitized printing plates.   Chapter 8 covers the photochemical formation and destruction of dyes; subjects such as photochromism, leuco dyes, and photographic bleach-out processes are described.   The last chapter is on thermographic processes.   Electrostatic processes were not included because their natures are more physical than chemical; besides, at least two books devoted to this subject are in preparation at this time.

The dual purpose of this book is to give the reader a basic under-standing of a wide variety of light-sensitive systems, and to provide means for using knowledge of the past to solve present problems.   There is a need for this, since photographic chemistry, despite its importance, is almost completely neglected in academic curricula.   It is hoped that this book will also be of value to those concerned with the photographic industry and will be helpful to anyone who needs a reasonably complete record of what has been done in the field of nonsilver halide light-sensitive systems.   Since, in any discussion of so vast a subject, errors of fact or interpretation are inescapable, I would be grateful to any reader who reveals an error to me, and especially grateful to the reader who offers criticism and suggestions for improvement.

A great deal of the inspiration for this book came from two professional societies of which I am a proud member.   These are the Society of Photo-graphic Scientists and Engineers and the Royal Photographic Society of Great Britain.   Their publications, "Abstracts of Photographic Science and Engineering" and "Photographic Abstracts" have been invaluable.

It is a privilege to express my thankful appreciation to all those who made this book possible.   I wish to acknowledge my special indebtedness to my former employers, Keuffel & Esser Company, for the encouragement I received from them.   Particularly, I would like to thank Robert Gold and Pearl Schwartz for many helpful discussions and for editorial assis-tance.   Special thanks are due to Walter Clark and his associates at the Eastman Kodak Company for their suggestions and to Lloyd Varden of Columbia University for valued criticism.   Grateful thanks also go to John McGraw of Lafayette College and to Steven Levinos of the Photo and Repro Division, General Aniline & Film Corporation, for their valuable contributions.   I also thank many other friends who have made material available to me.

Last, but not least, I would like to thank my wife for her secretarial help and all the members of my family for their patience and understanding.

JAROMIR KOSAR

Beechhurst, New York
May, 1965

Contents

CHAPTER 1.   INORGANIC COMPOUNDS

1.1   *Introduction*, 1

    1.1a   Radiant Energy, 1
    1.1b   Photochemical Laws, 3
    1.1c   Energy Requirements, 9

1.2   *Inorganic Compounds*, 12

    1.2a   Hydrogen Compounds, 12
    1.2b   Alkali Metal Halides, 13
    1.2c   Alkaline-Earth Metal Halides, 14
    1.2d   Copper Salts, 14
    1.2e   Mercury Salts.   Photothermographic Substances, 15
    1.2f   Zinc, Cadmium and Lead Compounds, 17
    1.2g   Thallium Halide Emulsions, 18
    1.2h   Silver Compounds.   Endothermic Systems, 18
    1.2i   Tungstic and Molybdic Acids, 21
    1.2j   Photosensitive Glass, 22
    1.2k   Transition Metal Complexes, 25

1.3   *Photographic Iron Processes*, 27

    1.3a   Blueprint, 28
    1.3b   Brownprint, 37
    1.3c   Tanning Processes, 39

CHAPTER 2.   DICHROMATED COLLOIDS 46

2.1   *Dichromated Colloid Layers*, 46
    2.1a   Historical Review, 46
    2.1b   Carbon Printing, 47
    2.1c   Other Processes, 49
    2.1d   Collotype, 50

2.2   *Composition of Sensitizing Solution*, 51
    2.2a   Chromates and Dichromates, 52
    2.2b   Organic Colloids (General), 54
    2.2c   Gelatin, 55
    2.2d   Process Glue, 62
    2.2e   Albumins, 62
    2.2f   Casein, 62
    2.2g   Natural Gums, 63
    2.2h   Starch and Its Derivatives, 64
    2.2i   Other Colloids, 65
    2.2j   Synthetic Resins, 65
    2.2k   Polyvinyl Alcohol, 66

2.3   *Photochemical Hardening of Dichromated Layers*, 67

2.4   *The Validity of Photochemical Laws.   Spectral Sensitivity*, 71

2.5   *Factors Affecting the Light Sensitivity*, 74
    2.5a   Effect of the Dichromate Concentration, 74
    2.5b   Effect of pH, 78
    2.5c   Thickness of the Coating, 80
    2.5d   Moisture Content, 81

2.6   *Dark Reaction*, 82
    2.6a   Sensitizing Solution, 82
    2.6b   Sensitized Layer, 86
    2.6c   Mechanism of the Dark Reaction, 88
    2.6d   Stability of Chromates, 90

2.7   *Methods for Increasing the Sensitivity*, 91
    2.7a   Desensitizing of Dichromated-Colloid Layers, 94

2.8   *Sensitometry of Dichromated-Colloid Layers*, 95

CHAPTER 3.   PHOTOMECHANICAL PRINTING PROCESSES 103

3.1   *Photographic Resist*, 103

3.2   *Photoengraving*, 104

3.3 *Photogravure,* 107

3.4 *Silk-Screen Process,* 112

3.5 *Wash-Off Process,* 114

3.6 *Reversal Images,* 118

3.7 *Photolithography,* 119

    3.7a Surface Plates, 120
    3.7b Deep-Etch Plates, 124
    3.7c Bimetallic and Trimetallic Plates, 127
    3.7d Plastic and Paper Litho Plates, 128

CHAPTER 4. UNSATURATED COMPOUNDS   137

4.1 *Introduction,* 137

4.2 *Cinnamic Acid and Its Derivatives.* *Kodak Photo-Resist,*
    140

4.3 *Chalcone-Type Compounds,* 149

4.4 *Stilbene Compounds,* 151

CHAPTER 5. PHOTOPOLYMERIZATION PROCESSES   158

5.1 *Introduction,* 158

5.2 *Photopolymerization Initiators,* 160

    5.2a Carbonyl Compounds, 160
    5.2b Organic Sulfur Compounds, 167
    5.2c Peroxides, 170
    5.2d Redox Systems, 173
    5.2e Azo and Diazo Compounds, 175
    5.2f Halogen Compounds, 180
    5.2g Photoreducible Dyes, 184
    5.2h Other Initiators, 187

CHAPTER 6. DIAZOTYPE PROCESSES   194

6.1 *Diazo Compounds,* 194

6.2 *Classification of Diazo Compounds,* 201

6.3 *Coupling and Coupling Components,* 215

6.4   *Positive Processes*, 249

6.4a   Principle, 249
6.4b   Dry Development, 253
6.4c   Semiwet Development, 255

6.5   *Thermal Development*, 259

6.6   *Negative Process*, 267

6.6a   Autocoupling, 267
6.6b   Diazosulfonates, 269
6.6c   Diazobiguanides, 270
6.6d   Auto-oxidation, 271
6.6e   The Metal-Diazonium Process, 272
6.6f   Vesicular Process, 276

6.7   *Reflex Copying*, 282

6.8   *Manufacture of Diazotype Material*, 292

6.8a   Formulation of the Sensitizing Solution, 292
6.8b   Preparation of the Base Material, 296
6.8c   Coating, 300

6.9   *Applications*, 302

CHAPTER 7.   PRESENSITIZED PRINTING PLATES   321

7.1   *Diazo Sensitizers*, 321

7.2   *Aromatic Azido Compounds*, 330

7.3   *p-Quinone Diazides*, 336

7.4   *o-Quinone Diazides*, 339

7.5   *Other Sensitizers*, 352

7.6   *Wipe-On Plates*, 353

CHAPTER 8.   PHOTOCHEMICAL FORMATION AND
             DESTRUCTION OF DYES   358

8.1   *Photochemical Formation of Dye Images*, 358

8.2   *Light-Sensitive Leuco Dyes*, 370

8.3   *Photochromism*, 380

8.4   *Bleach-Out Process*, 387

CHAPTER 9.   THERMOGRAPHY   402

9.1   *Recording Papers,* 402

9.2   *Thermographic Copying Papers,* 403
    9.2a   Single Component Papers, 403
    9.2b   Chemical Papers, 404
    9.2c   Copying of Colored Originals, 413
    9.2d   Applications, 414

AUTHOR INDEX   421

SUBJECT INDEX   439

1

Inorganic Compounds

1.1 INTRODUCTION

1.1a *Radiant Energy*

It has been known for many years that light is able to bring about chemical changes. Reactions of many types, e.g., oxidations and reductions, decompositions, additions, polymerizations, and dimerizations, can be initiated by exposure to light of suitable wavelength, or light can exhibit an accelerating effect on reactions that proceed in the dark at a very low rate. The term light, as used here, includes not only the visible part of the spectrum but also ultraviolet and infrared radiations, which lie outside the limits of the visible spectrum. The visible spectrum occupies no more than a very limited range of electromagnetic radiations, differing only in wavelength (Table 1.1), and can be subdivided into a number of bands of characteristic color as follows:

violet	395–455 mμ
blue	455–490 mμ
green	490–570 mμ
yellow	570–590 mμ
orange	590–650 mμ
red	650–750 mμ

The energy represented by electromagnetic waves has been termed radiant energy. This energy is emitted or absorbed in definite units called "quanta." All quanta are not of the same magnitude and the amount of energy ϵ carried by each is proportional to the frequency ν of the light which it constitutes. This proportionality is given by the expression

$$\epsilon = h\nu \tag{1}$$

TABLE *1.1.*   Electromagnetic Spectrum

Radio broadcast	> 100 m
Short radio waves	0.1 cm – 100 m
Infrared	0.75 μ –1000 μ
Visible light	3950 Å –7500 Å
Ultraviolet	50 Å –3950 Å
X-rays	0.1 Å – 50 Å
γ-rays	0.001 Å– 0.1 Å
Cosmic rays	< 0.001 Å

which is the fundamental equation of the Quantum Theory. Here $h = 6.62 \times 10^{-27}$ erg-sec and is known as Planck's constant.

Einstein gave to a single quantum of radiant energy the name "photon." The absolute magnitude of a photon increases directly with the frequency. Since the frequency is equal to the velocity of light c (3.00 × 10¹⁰ cm/sec) divided by the wavelength λ, the energy of a photon can also be expressed

$$\epsilon = \frac{hc}{\lambda} \tag{2}$$

This equation shows that for each wavelength there is a corresponding definite amount of energy. The energy of a green light, for example, is:

$$\epsilon = \frac{6.62 \times 10^{-27} \times 3 \times 10^{10}}{4.9 \times 10^{-5}} = 4.05 \times 10^{-12} \text{ erg} = 2.54 \text{ ev}$$

Light quanta of short wavelength have more energy than those of long wavelength; ultraviolet rays are more powerful than violet rays, which, in turn, are stronger than blue and green radiation; blue and green radiation is more energetic than red or infrared radiation. Inasmuch as we are interested only in electromagnetic radiations with energies ranging from 1.5 ev to 4 ev, it might be of interest to note that radiations of much higher energy are available. Of these, two are important: X-rays with energies up to 500 ev and γ-rays with energies approaching one million ev.

Since a single molecule can absorb one quantum of energy, the energy absorbed by one mole will be

$$E_{ergs} = \epsilon N = Nh\nu \tag{3}$$

where N is Avogadro's number (= 6.02 × 10²³).

Since 1 cal = 4.18 × 10⁷ ergs, we get

$$E_{kcal} = \frac{Nh}{4.18 \times 10^7 \times 10^3} \nu \tag{4}$$

The energy of an Avogadro's number of photons is called an "einstein," the value of which is given in kilo-calories. Introducing the numerical values of N and h, we get

$$E_{\text{kcal}} = \frac{6.02 \times 10^{23} \times 6.62 \times 10^{-27}}{4.18 \times 10^7 \times 10^3} \times \nu = 9.53 \times 10^{-14} \times \nu \quad (5)$$

According to equation 2, ν can be substituted by c/λ, and by expressing the wavelength in angstrom units equation 5 can be written

$$E_{\text{kcal}} = Nh\frac{c}{\lambda} = \frac{9.53 \times 10^{-14} \times 3 \times 10^{10} \times 10^8}{\lambda} = \frac{286,000}{\lambda} \quad (6)$$

This equation enables us to express radiant energy in kilo-calorie units and is useful in comparing thermal requirements of chemical reactions with radiation energies (Table 1.2); luminous radiations can cause a chemical reaction only if they possess an amount of energy at least equal to that required by the chemical process.

For most thermal reactions that proceed at measurable speeds the activation energy is between 10 and 80 kcal per mole, and any reaction with a heat of activation less than about 16 kcal per mole will proceed rapidly at room temperature. From this it follows that such reactions are not suitable for photographic processes since these reactions will take place in the dark. Energy of 16 kcal corresponds to a wavelength of 18,000 Å, which must be considered as the upper limit for spectral sensitization of light-sensitive systems.

1.1b *Photochemical Laws*

An einstein of photons of visible light has an energy ranging from 40 to 70 kcal, and the energy of an einstein of ultraviolet radiation is even higher. Hence, absorption of light provides sufficient energy to initiate most chemical reactions. It does not necessarily follow, however, that the reaction will occur merely because the required energy has been provided. According to the Grotthus-Draper law only radiations which are absorbed by the reacting systems can result in a photochemical reaction.

The absorption of energy is accompanied by the elevation of one or more electrons from ground level to an excited state.

The quantity of energy required for the transportation of a peripheral electron to a higher energy level is related to the energies of the electron in the two orbits and is expressed by the Einstein-Bohr law, according to which the difference in energy between the ground state E_1 and the excited state E_2 is directly proportional to the frequency

$$E_2 - E_1 = h\nu \quad (7)$$

TABLE *1.2.* Energy Corresponding to Different Wavelengths

Å	3000	3600	3950	4550	4900	5750	5900	6500	7500	9000
	ultraviolet		violet	blue	green	yellow	orange	red		infrared
Energy per photon — eV	4.13	3.44	3.15	2.72	2.53	2.15	2.10	1.90	1.65	1.39
Energy per photon — ergs × 10^{-12}	6.60	5.51	4.97	4.32	4.01	3.42	3.33	3.02	2.62	2.20
Energy per einstein — kcal	95.0	79.6	71.8	62.3	57.8	49.3	48.0	43.6	37.8	31.8

When a definite quantity of energy is absorbed by the system complete removal of an electron from the sphere of influence of the positive nucleus will result. This process is called ionization, and the energy required for the electron removal corresponds to the ionization potential of the particular atom. For most atoms the ionizing energy is too high to be supplied by visible or ultraviolet light and ionization is only rarely involved in photochemical reactions. Usually, photochemical reactions take place when the molecule is merely excited to a higher energy level.

The electrons affected by the absorption of light do not remain in the excited state but may relax to a lower energy level by losing the energy acquired by re-emission of radiation of the same or longer wavelength, as in fluorescence or phosphorescence; or some of the energy may be converted into heat by collisions of the molecules, which cause a temperature rise of the reaction system. The energy-rich molecules may, in certain cases, lose energy by collision with other atoms or molecules and thereby initiate a chemical reaction, or, dissociation of the molecule may occur, yielding free atoms or radicals of great chemical reactivity. These may undergo further reaction, either by themselves or with another molecule, which leads to the formation of a more stable product. The excited molecule can also transfer its excess energy to another molecule which is thereby made chemically reactive. Such reactions are called "sensitized reactions" and the original excited molecule is called the "sensitizer." Two examples are the mercury-sensitized photodecomposition of ammonia and the dye sensitization of silver halide emulsions.

The relation between the quantity of the reaction product and the amount of radiation is expressed in the Bunsen-Roscoe law, which states that the quantity of the radiation product is proportional to the product of the intensity of the incident light and the exposure time. To obtain a given yield the required exposure time t is inversely proportional to the light intensity I that is used

$$I \times t = \text{constant} \tag{8}$$

Photographic systems, in general, do not obey this law under all conditions; additional variants include the characteristics of the reaction system, the exposure time, and the temperature of the material at the time of exposure. Schwartzchild corrected these anomalies by introducing into equation 8 an exponent p

$$I \times t^p = \text{constant} \tag{9}$$

The equivalence between absorbed quanta and molecules of absorbing reactant is postulated in Einstein's Law of Photochemical Equivalence. According to the photoequivalent relation, the radiant energy which must be absorbed in order to decompose one gram-molecule of a photolyte, is as we have already seen, $Nh\nu$; in other words, each molecule engaged in a photochemical reaction absorbs one quantum of actinic radiation. Hence, for the photochemical equivalent ω we obtain the reciprocal of equations 4 and 6

$$\omega = \frac{4.18 \times 10^7 \times 10^3}{Nh\nu} = \frac{\lambda}{286,000} \tag{10}$$

Einstein's law thus assumes that the extent of photochemical decomposition is independent of concentration, temperature, or any factors other than the energy of the absorbed radiation; in other words, the theoretical photochemical equivalent ω is constant for all decompositions involving only one specific wavelength. The effective photochemical equivalent γ differs from ω in general because any primary photochemical decomposition is followed by secondary reactions.

The quantum yield of any photochemical reaction is the ratio of the number of molecules that have reacted to the number of quanta absorbed

$$\phi = \frac{\gamma}{\omega} = \frac{\text{number of molecules reacted}}{\text{number of quanta absorbed}} \tag{11}$$

In a reaction in which only one product is formed it is possible to speak of either the quantum yield of the formation of that compound or the quantum yield of disappearance of the starting material. In such a case the value of one quantum yield is equivalent to the value of the other. In reactions which produce two different compounds the two quantum yields do not have to be equivalent and it is necessary to specify the compound for which the yield is given. At this point it should be emphasized that the quantum yield as just described applies to the primary process only and that in photographic processes the effect of the exposure to light is often multiplied by a secondary reaction. The number of molecules produced, however, does not constitute exact measure of the light sensitivity of the process, since the size and optical absorption of the molecules formed play a role.

In order to calculate quantum efficiency it is first necessary to know the number of molecules reacting per unit time and the number of quanta absorbed in the same interval. The first step, the determination of the number of molecules that have reacted, should not present any difficulties and chemical or physical analytical methods can be used. The analysis, however, must be quite sensitive since the actual extent of chemical reaction is usually very small. The second step, the calculation of the number of absorbed photons, requires considerable skill. For this determination we have to know the energy of the radiation entering the system, the amount of radiation which is reflected by the media and by the vessels containing the photosensitive chemicals, and the energy which is transmitted by the system. Knowing the entire quantity of the absorbed energy and the energy of one quantum, we can then calculate the number of quanta absorbed. Instruments suitable for measuring radiant energy include photoelectric cells, thermopiles, and bolometers, all of which must be calibrated by some photochemical reaction of known quantum yield. One of the best "chemical actinometers" is a solution of an uranyl salt and oxalic acid; uranyl ion UO_2^{2+} becomes excited on absorption of light and decomposes oxalic acid into carbon monoxide, carbon dioxide, and water. The quantity of residual acid is determined by simple titration. The quantum yield of this reaction is 0.50.

Einstein's law implies that the quantum yield of photochemical reactions must always be equal to one. This is true, however, only for the primary process, the process in which the radiation is absorbed. The secondary process is usually much more complicated, and, because of the complications the over-all quantum yield differs from the unity in most photochemical reactions and can vary from a very small fraction up to several thousand.

If the quantum yield is less than one it is obvious that some of the absorbed quanta were ineffective. This can happen if some of the molecules lose the absorbed energy before they can take part in the chemical reaction. The energy loss can be attributed to deactivating collisions of the molecules or to emission of radiation of the same or longer wavelengths. If recombination of dissociated compounds predominates, the quantum yield is also very small. In any case low quantum yield does not mean that more than one quantum of energy must be absorbed by one molecule to bring it into reaction.

The photolysis of hydrogen iodide is an example of a chemical reaction in which the quantum yield is two. It was suggested that the reaction proceeds through the following steps:

$$HI + h\nu = H\cdot + I\cdot \tag{12}$$

$$H\cdot + HI = H_2 + I\cdot \tag{13}$$

$$I\cdot + I\cdot = I_2 \tag{14}$$

Here photochemical decomposition occurs in the primary reaction (12). After absorbing one quantum hydrogen iodide is dissociated into activated hydrogen atom and activated iodide atom. Activated hydrogen reacts with another molecule of HI to yield a hydrogen molecule and activated iodine atom. Two activated iodine atoms then combine into an iodine molecule. Because the concentration of HI is high compared to the hydrogen concentration, reaction (13) occurs much more often than the reaction between two activated hydrogens. The possibility of reaction between HI and I is eliminated by the fact that this reaction, being endothermic, requires considerable energy. Consequently, the chain reaction cannot be propagated, and the over-all effect is the formation of one molecule of hydrogen and one molecule of iodine per quantum absorbed

$$2HI + h\nu = H_2 + I_2 \tag{15}$$

The photolysis of HBr is similar; light of wavelengths smaller than 2900 Å is necessary to rupture the hydrogen–bromine bond. If, on the other hand, the atoms or radicals formed by the primary process react with others to form new atoms or radicals, chain reactions may take place. Then the quantum yield is much greater than one, occasionally reaching thousands and millions, depending on the length of the chain.

One example of a chain reaction is the classical photochemical union of hydrogen and chlorine. In the dark the mixture of these two elements is quite stable; however, they combine in a weak diffused light, explosively on exposure to intense light. The chlorine molecule absorbs a photon and is dissociated into two activated chlorine atoms

$$Cl_2 + h\nu = Cl\cdot + Cl\cdot \tag{16}$$

This is followed by a chain reaction, and a new activated chlorine atom is formed for each one entering into reaction

$$Cl\cdot + H_2 = HCl + H\cdot \tag{17}$$

$$H\cdot + Cl_2 = HCl + Cl\cdot \tag{18}$$

Both these reactions occur very rapidly and continue until two activated chlorine atoms combine accidentally

$$Cl\cdot + Cl\cdot = Cl_2 \tag{19}$$

In the hydrogen-chlorine reaction at least one million molecules of hydrogen chloride can be formed by each quantum absorbed. The reaction is highly exothermic and is accompanied by a large decrease in free energy. The light acts here as a catalyst.

The quantum yield of the hydrogen-bromine combination is very much smaller. The reaction

$$Br\cdot + H_2 = HBr + H\cdot \tag{20}$$

requires much more energy per mole than does the reaction with chlorine. The photochemical union of hydrogen and iodine does not take place at all, since this reaction is still more endothermic.

1.1c   *Energy Requirements*

Photosynthesis of all hydrogen halides does not occur under the same conditions. Although the hydrogen-chlorine reaction proceeds explosively on exposure to visible light, the hydrogen-bromine system requires exposure to strong sunlight at 196°C. Light has no permanent effect on a hydrogen-iodine mixture; hydrogen iodide is formed very slowly and only on heating in the presence of a catalyst. These results are in agreement with the observation that the heat of formation of hydrogen halides decreases with an increase in molecular weight (Table 1.3).

TABLE *1.3*. Dissociation Energy and Heat of Formation of Hydrogen Halides

Dissociation Energy kcal/mole	Hydrogen Halide	Heat of Formation, kcal/mole at 25.0°C
135	HF	− 64.2
102	HCl	− 22.06
87	HBr	− 8.66
71	HI	6.20

The difference between the heat of formation of hydrogen fluoride and that of hydrogen chloride explains the explosive reaction of hydrogen with fluorine in the dark.

Since the heat of formation determines, to a large extent, the stability of a compound, it is not surprising to note that the light sensitivity of hydrogen halides increases from fluoride to iodide. The decomposition of hydrogen chloride requires ultraviolet light of wavelength 2000 Å, and hydrogen bromide decomposes very rapidly and completely under the same conditions. Hydrogen iodide is decomposed readily by blue and violet light. Hydrogen fluoride is very stable and does not decompose.

The quantum energy of the light employed must be large enough to break the bond between the hydrogen and the halogen. The energy requirements for the photolysis of hydrogen halides can be obtained by subtracting the dissociation energy of molecular hydrogen and molecular halogen which is released during the reaction from the dissociation energy of hydrogen halides:

$$2D_{\mathrm{HF}} - D_{\mathrm{H_2}} - D_{\mathrm{F_2}} = 2(135) - 104 - 41 = 125 \text{ kcal/mole} \quad (21)$$

$$2D_{\mathrm{HCl}} - D_{\mathrm{H_2}} - D_{\mathrm{Cl_2}} = 2(102) - 104 - 57 = 43 \text{ kcal/mole} \quad (22)$$

$$2D_{\mathrm{HBr}} - D_{\mathrm{H_2}} - D_{\mathrm{Br_2}} = 2(87) - 104 - 47 = 25 \text{ kcal/mole} \quad (23)$$

$$2D_{\mathrm{HI}} - D_{\mathrm{H_2}} - D_{\mathrm{I_2}} = 2(71) - 104 - 36 = 2 \text{ kcal/mole} \quad (24)$$

In crystalline compounds, where many types of bonds may be involved, the situation is more complex (1); the energy required to overcome forces in ionic crystals holding the crystal particles in order has to be taken into consideration. The crystal energy U of NaCl-type compounds can be calculated (2) as follows:

$$U = -\Delta H^\circ f + S + \tfrac{1}{2}D + I - E \qquad (25)$$

where $\Delta H^\circ f$ = standard heat of formation
$\quad\quad S$ = heat of sublimation
$\quad\quad D$ = heat of dissociation
$\quad\quad I$ = ionization energy
$\quad\quad E$ = electron affinity

This energy is equivalent to the energy liberated when one gram mole of the NaCl-type compound is formed from free ions. Conversely, for the reaction

$$AB \longrightarrow A + B$$

to proceed, it is necessary that the absorbed energy split the lattice into ions A^+ and B^-. During this process energy corresponding to the crystal energy U and to the electron affinity E of B is needed, whereas energy equivalent to the sum of the ionization energy, heat of the sublimation, and heat of dissociation is absorbed.

Taking the cycle as a whole, the energy requirement for the photochemical decomposition of crystalline compound AB is given by

$$\mathscr{E} = U_{AB} + E_B - I_A - D_B - S_A \qquad (26)$$

This energy is equivalent to the heat of formation (3) and is dependent on the size, charge, and configuration of the ions involved. Theoretically, it is possible to open or break any desired bond by exposing the compound to radiation of selected wavelength and sufficient intensity. As in decomposition by heat, it can be expected that the light sensitivity of compounds within the same family will increase as their heat of formation decreases.

Compounds which are dissociated only at high temperature will be affected only by the very rapid vibration of the extreme ultraviolet.

In the foregoing formula the ionization energy and the heat of sublimation are related to the positive ions, whereas dissociation energy and electron affinity are associated with the negative ions. The crystal energy, of course, is dependent on both the positive and the negative ions.

In a comparison of the light sensitivity of a series of compounds having the same negative ion we need not be concerned with the values for electron affinity and dissociation energy, since they will be the same for all the compounds in question. The heat of sublimation is of little importance since its value changes only negligibly with the size of the positive ion. Thus, only the ionization energy and the crystal energy have to be considered. The ionization energy is less for ions of larger radii and therefore the light sensitivity of crystalline inorganic compounds will increase when the positive ion is replaced by another ion of equal charge but smaller radius. Under these conditions the crystal energy will not increase sufficiently to counterbalance the effect of the ionic radii.

Since the radius of the ion decreases and the ionization energy increases for each subsequent electron to be removed, it can be expected that the light sensitivity will increase when the charge of the positive ion is increased. If, on the other hand, the positive ion in a series of compounds remains the same and the anion is changed, the heat of sublimation and the ionization energy remain constant, and the heat of dissociation, electron affinity, and crystal energy become of interest. In monovalent ions changes in the difference $D - E$ are very small and can be neglected. The crystal energy is the predominant factor, and, because its value decreases when the radius of the negative ion increases, replacement of a small monovalent ion by a larger one of the same charge will be reflected in increased light sensitivity.

When the radius of the negative ion is kept approximately the same and the charge is changed, compounds having in their molecule a negative ion of a higher charge will be, as a rule, more sensitive to light than equivalent compounds having a negative ion of a lower charge.

The influence of the ionization energy on the light sensitivity is obvious in compounds containing a positive ion with an 18-electron configuration. The ionization energy of such ions is much higher than that of ions of equal size but of rare-gas configuration. The effect of the higher ionization energy on the light sensitivity is only partly counteracted by the higher crystal energy, and thus the light sensitivity is expected to increase when a noble-gas ion is substituted by one of 18-electron configuration.

To summarize, the light sensitivity of inorganic compounds can be expected to increase when

1. the positive ion is replaced by another ion of equal charge but smaller radius;
2. the charge of the positive ion is increased and the radius remains the same;
3. the negative ion is substituted by another ion of equal charge but larger radius;
4. the charge of the negative ion is decreased and the radius is unchanged;
5. a noble-gas ion is substituted by one with 18-electron configuration.

Unfortunately, the energies required for the decomposition of the majority of inorganic compounds cannot be calculated, since data for the heat of sublimation, heat of dissociation, and electron affinity are not known for most of the elements, or their values are inaccurate. In addition, the relation between the heat of formation and light sensitivity is not always so simple as in some of the examples mentioned, in which certain assumptions had to be made to arrive at satisfactory results. This is especially true for compounds containing highly charged ions, which cannot be considered as completely rigid spheroids. Forces other than those due to the electric charges are involved. Furthermore, as a result of strong polarization, the energy with which the electrons are held in the ion is changed, with consequent shift in absorption spectra.

As a result of these shortcomings, we are, in general, unable to predict accurately whether a given compound will be changed by exposure to light or if one compound will be more light-sensitive than another. Our knowledge of molecular excitation, of the properties of activated molecules, and of some other relevant matters is at present much too meager, and the time is still to come when numerous photochemical phenomena can be clarified.

1.2   INORGANIC COMPOUNDS

1.2a   *Hydrogen Compounds*

Among the large number of inorganic light-sensitive compounds described in the literature (4, 5, 6), hydrogen halides have already been mentioned, and it has been shown that quantum-energy requirements for the photochemical decomposition of these compounds depend on the size of the halogen ion. The heat of formation of the iodides is nearly always smaller than that of the other halides, and consequently less energy suffices for their decomposition. The law of the inverse stability of inorganic compounds toward light in relation to the decrease in their heat of formation has also been observed in the group H_2O, H_2S, H_2Se, and H_2Te. Hydrogen sulfide is less stable than water because of the larger radius of its negative ion; hydrogen selenide and telluride are still less stable. This is in agreement with the heat of formation, which is the lowest for tellurides. Another example can be found in the series H_3N, H_3P, H_3As, and H_3Sb. Ammonia decomposes in a few hours when illuminated by ultraviolet light, whereas the decomposition of phosphine is evident even in a few minutes. Arsine also decomposes readily when exposed to ultraviolet rays. As the stability of hydrides of the fifth subgroup decreases from nitrogen to antimony, stibine would be expected to be photolyzed much more easily than arsine. Bismuth hydride is very unstable and is decomposed even in the dark. Table 1.4 gives the heat of formation in kilo-calories/mole of some hydrogen compounds.

TABLE *1.4.*   Heat of Formation of Hydrogen Compounds

HF	-64.2	H_2O	-57.8	H_3N	-11.04
HCl	-22.06	H_2S	-4.82	H_3P	2.21
HBr	-8.66	H_2Se	20.5	H_3As	41.0
HI	6.20	H_2Te	36.9	H_3Sb	81.8

1.2b   *Alkali Metal Halides*

Since the coulomb energy of the outer electrons is less in ions of larger radius, the ionization energy decreases with the size of the ion and the heat of formation of the compound increases accordingly. It can be expected that halides of alkali metals will be affected by light to a lesser degree than will hydrogen halides. This is so, and alkali metal halides can hardly be considered light-sensitive. They are, however, changed by X-rays or ultraviolet radiation in the sense that the absorption of a photon removes an electron from the halide ion, which is transferred to the positive ion. The neutralized atoms of the alkali metal form colloidal particles which absorb visible light and cause discoloration of the crystal.

The color of the alkali metal halide crystal is more or less intense, depending on the size of the colloidal particles dispersed in the lattice. The modern theory of solid state chemistry interprets the discoloration of alkali halides as the formation of anion vacancies in the crystal lattice. These vacancies, also called color centers, absorb radiation in the visible part of the spectrum and thus impart color to the crystal (7). The intensity of the discoloration is then proportional to the number of the vacancies present in the crystal. The research on photo-chemical reactions in alkali halide crystals has been reviewed by Pohl (8), Martienssen (9), and Symons and Doyle (10). The energy required for the photolytic decomposition of alkali-metal halides is not known. From the values for heats of formation and from the absorption maxima, however, we can conclude that the decomposition of lithium fluoride will require the highest, and rubidium iodide the lowest, energy. It is observed that the heat of formation of alkali metal fluorides decreases from lithium to cesium. This is always the case when comparatively large positive ions of low charge combine with small negative ions. For this reason cesium fluoride is less stable than lithium fluoride. This discrepancy disappears in compounds having positive ions with a charge of two or greater. Thus, strontium iodide decomposes more rapidly than barium iodide.

1.2c *Alkaline-Earth Metal Halides*

From the general formula for the heat of formation it follows that when a positive ion is replaced by one with the same structure but with a higher charge, the heat of formation decreases and the susceptibility of the compound to decomposition by light increases. Consequently, compounds containing divalent or trivalent positive ions will be affected by light much more readily than will compounds of univalent positive ions. Although alkali-metal iodides show only very limited light sensitivity, iodides of some alkaline-earth metals are decomposed by radiation of proper wavelength. Potassium iodide decomposes much more slowly when exposed to ultraviolet rays than do strontium or barium iodide.

1.2d *Copper Salts*

Now let us investigate the way in which the light sensitivity is influenced when a positive ion with a rare-gas configuration is replaced by one of equal size and charge, but having 18-electron configuration. Because of the greater ionization energy of the 18-electron ion a decrease in the heat of formation is to be expected. Although the size of Na^+ ions and Cu^+ ions is nearly equal, cuprous chloride darkens on exposure to visible light, and sodium chloride remains unchanged. The cuprous chloride probably decomposes as follows (11):

$$2CuCl \xrightarrow{hv} Cu + CuCl_2 \qquad (27)$$

The photolysis of cupric salts involves two separate processes, the photochemical reduction of the cupric to the cuprous state and later the deposition of a metallic copper according to the reaction (27).

The light sensitivity of copper salts has been known for many years and is only of academic interest. More recently, Wojtczak (12) prepared a light-sensitive composition by successively adding to copper acetate a solution of ascorbic acid and acetic acid. On exposure to light this composition changes from yellow to black. The quantum yield of this photo-oxidation has been studied (13) in the region of 280 to 640 mμ and varied from 2.5 to 16, with a maximum in the vicinity of 400 mμ. This reaction is reversible in the dark. By mixing cuprous chloride or bromide with gelatin, agar-agar, or polyvinyl alcohol, this investigator obtained an emulsion that could be sensitized to tungsten light with crystal violet (14).

In another formulation (15) a copper emulsion was sensitized to infrared radiation with ions forming easily oxidized and reduced systems, such as Co, Cr, Se, UO_2, and hydroquinone. The latent image can be developed with an alkaline solution of glycol, and the unexposed emulsion is dissolved in an aqueous solution of sodium chloride. Photosensitive material analogous to silver salts was prepared by Schwab and Nissl (16) by reducing a cupric salt dissolved in a conventional binder solution with sulfur dioxide. Cupric salts are easily reduced to the cuprous state when exposed to light in the presence of anthraquinone sulfonic acid or its alkali-metal salts (17) or in the presence of sodium hydrosulfite (18). To a limited extent, copper salts have been used as photosensitizers or catalysts for other photochemical reactions.

1.2e *Mercury Salts. Photothermographic Substances*

For photographic application mercury salts seem to be more suitable than corresponding copper salts. In the literature (4) the sensitivity of both mercurous and mercuric compounds to light has been reported. Mercurous iodide darkens upon exposure to light; this is probably due to the reaction

$$Hg_2I_2 \xrightarrow{h\nu} Hg + HgI_2 \tag{28}$$

Photographic characteristics of HgI-gelatin emulsion were investigated by Suzuki and Nagae (19), who found that the black print-out image fades away with time. They did not succeed in finding a suitable developing and fixing agent.

Gelatino-mercury iodide emulsion is made more sensitive by incorporating therein allylthiourea, allyl isothiocyanate, allylselenourea, or the corresponding tellurium compounds (20). The complex $2HgS \cdot HgI_2$ was studied by Takei (21, 22), who observed microscopic black spots after irradiation, which he attributed to colloidal mercury. A mixture of mercurous iodide and silver iodide has been described (23) as being highly light-sensitive.

Blackening of papers impregnated with yellow mercuric oxide, sodium iodide, and sodium thiosulfate can be intensified by conventional photographic developers (24). Also, addition of certain organic dyes to this system affects the degree of blackening.

Mercurous nitrate, which is soluble only in an acid solution, is converted by the action of light into a basic salt which can be reduced with a solution containing a ferrous salt and oxalic or tartaric acid into metallic mercury. Basic mercurous tartrate forms, on exposure to light, a latent image developable in ferrous tartrate solution. Mercurous citrate, mercurous oxalate, and mercury ammonium oxalate also show definite photosensitivity. By prolonged exposure, print-out images can be obtained without heating or chemical development. The unexposed sections can be dissolved either in sodium chloride or sodium thiosulfate solution, or converted into less sensitive compounds. Vanselow and Leermakers (25) recommended overcoating the sensitive layer with polyvinylbutyral, which is relatively transparent to ultraviolet light until it is heat-treated during the developing process of the image. As a rule, basic salts are more light-sensitive than normal salts and oxalates are usually more so than citrates. Addition of oxalic acid to mercuric chloride increases its sensitivity. In one patent (26), ammonium oxalate and ferric oxalate were added to mercuric chloride and the solution applied to paper. After the exposure, the image is developed in ammonia vapor.

The light sensitivity of mercury oxalates has been investigated thoroughly in connection with photothermographic systems. Substances are considered photothermographic if they can be decomposed by heat in areas previously exposed to the action of visible or ultraviolet light (27,28,29); during the exposure nuclei of a new solid phase, such as metal or metal oxide, are formed on the molecular aggregates and catalyze the thermal decomposition of mercurous oxalate. This process is very slow; somewhat higher sensitivity is produced either by adding an excess of potassium oxalate or by using a coprecipitated mixture of silver and mercurous oxalate (30). The increased sensitivity in the latter is due to the catalytic effect of the metallic mercury formed by the exposure to light on the thermal decomposition of silver oxalate (31). Van der Meulen and Gilman (32) obtained higher sensitivity by addition of silver iodide and mercury iodide. According to Formstecher (33), the reaction between mercurous iodide and silver iodide is reversible and takes place as follows:

$$\underset{\text{green}}{\text{HgI}} + \underset{\text{yellow}}{\text{AgI}} \underset{\text{dark}}{\overset{\text{light}}{\rightleftharpoons}} \underset{\text{red}}{\text{HgI}_2} + \underset{\text{black}}{\text{Ag}} \tag{29}$$

On the basis of sensitometric and X-ray-diffraction studies (34), van der Meulen and Gilman concluded that the increase in spectral sensitivity is probably caused by the efficient photolysis of a mercurous iodide/silver iodide mixture to form mercuric iodide and mercury, which catalyzes the thermal decomposition of mercurous oxalate. The emulsions of mercurous oxalate are especially sensitive to ultraviolet, but the addition of certain dyes, such as acriflavin or some of the phthalein and cyanine dyes, increases the spectral range in a similar manner as in silver halide emulsions (35,36). It is interesting to note that Acridine Yellow, which does not affect the spectral sensitivity of silver halide emulsions, is an efficient optical sensitizer for mercurous oxalate; this is apparently related to different dye absorption by silver bromide and mercurous oxalate. The spectral sensitivity of compositions containing mercurous iodide is extended to the visible range, even without dye sensitization.

Besides mercurous and mercuric oxalates, the following mercury compounds have photothermographic properties: mercurous phosphate, carbonate, formate, sulfate, halide, chromate, tungstate, molybdate, and so forth. From these salts, mercurous chloride hydrazine and mercurous azide are the fastest and mercurous tungstates and chromates are the slowest. Mercurous and mercuric orthoarsenites are described by Sheppard and Vanselow (38) as having photothermographic properties.

1.2f *Zinc, Cadmium, and Lead Compounds*

Zinc and cadmium compounds are considerably less sensitive to light than mercury compounds; this fact is in agreement with the rules discussed above. Mercuric sulfide blackens on exposure to light much faster than do zinc or cadmium sulfide. Zinc oxide is used as a photoconductor in electrophotographic processes and is known to accelerate bleaching of dyes on exposure to light. Cadmium compounds have about the same light sensitivity as the corresponding zinc compounds.

Lead compounds, in general, are also less light-sensitive; lead sulfide, which is oxidized by light to lead sulfate, is used in infrared-sensitive photoconductive cells (39). Emulsions containing lead iodide as the light-sensitive substance were prepared by Weyde (40), Schoen (41), and Wojciak (42,43), and suggested by Dawood and Forty (44) for print-out recording processes. Before illumination the lead iodide is yellow, but after illumination the color depends on the colloid employed. The introduction of sodium thiosulfate increases the sensitivity of the colloidal lead iodide (45). In the presence of gelatin, first a double salt, NaPb-thiosulfate, is formed and reacts with the lead iodide; the final product is lead sulfide which creates the image. It is a print-out image and only fixing is necessary.

Thin evaporated films of lead iodide are unaffected by light at room temperature and become sensitive to green light when heated to 180°C; they decompose into molecular iodine and metallic lead (46). Bis-(tricyclohexyllead) was used by Peters (47) for print-out material; lead oxalate, lead arsenite, and lead formate form the sensitive component in a photothermographic composition (37,48). In another patent (49), lead acetate was used as the light-sensitive medium. After exposure to ultraviolet light and subsequent treatment with a solution of silver nitrate, the images are made visible with a ferrous sulfate developer.

1.2g　Thallium Halide Emulsions

At this point, mention should be made of thallous chloride, which resembles mercurous and silver chloride in becoming dark on exposure to light. Thallous bromide and iodide also tend to darken in the light, and, when precipitated in the presence of gelatin, they have the ability to register an invisible latent image. Similarly, as in silver halide emulsions, the latent image may be developed by means of a physical developer containing silver.

Efforts to develop latent images with conventional developers were negative. Farrer (50) overcame this inconvenience by treating the exposed thallous bromide emulsion with silver nitrate, thereby converting thallium bromide, which constitutes the latent image, into the corresponding silver image. After washing, the silver latent image can be developed with a metol-hydroquinone developer. The fixing is done in the usual way. The conduction band of thallium bromide lies at a higher level, and, therefore, light quanta richer in energy have to be imparted to the electrons to raise them to this level. This is the reason why thallium bromide has its sensitivity range in ultraviolet.

The light sensitivity of thallous bromide emulsions is low compared to silver halide emulsions and can be markedly increased by addition of bromide acceptors, such as sodium nitrite, to the emulsion (51,52), or by addition of silver nitrate, gold chloride, palladium chloride, or ruthenium chloride (53). The effect of rhodium chloride on the speed of thallium bromide emulsions was most pronounced. Analogous to silver bromide emulsions, the presence of thallous iodide in thallous bromide emulsions also increases its sensitivity. Contrary to findings with silver emulsions, however, fine-grained thallous bromide emulsions seem to be faster than coarse-grained ones. Thallic oxalate dispersed in gelatin was used as a light-sensitive medium by Sheppard and Dietz (54).

1.2h　Silver Compounds.　Endothermic Systems

The replacement of a positive ion having a rare-gas configuration by one of equal size and charge, but with an 18-electron configuration, has an effect on the color of the compound and thus also on its absorption of light. Although the size of a potassium ion and that of a silver ion is nearly equal, potassium halides are colorless, and the color of the corresponding silver salts increases with increasing molecular weight:

$AgCl$—colorless　　—maximum absorption at 248 mμ

$AgBr$—light yellow—maximum absorption at 319 mμ

AgI —yellow　　 —maximum absorption at 438 mμ

The extra field of the subgroup ions causes a strong polarization of negative ions, with consequent modification of the electronic structure. This produces a change in the absorption spectra. Since the bromide and iodide ions are more strongly polarized than the chloride ions, silver bromide and silver iodide absorb light of longer wavelength and thus can be considered more light-sensitive than silver chloride. During the exposure to light, however, the surface of silver iodide crystals becomes opaque; this is responsible for the slower photolysis of silver iodide relative to that of silver bromide and chloride (55). It should also be kept in mind that silver bromide and silver iodide respond less to ultraviolet light than does silver chloride.

The increasing light sensitivity of silver halides with the size of the negative ion is also in agreement with the decreasing heat of formation of these compounds. As we have already seen, the substitution of one negative ion by another influences to a marked degree only the crystal energy, and since the crystal energy decreases when the radius of the negative ion increases, chlorides have larger heats of formation than bromides and iodides (Table 1.5).

TABLE *1.5*. Heat of Formation of Silver Halides

Silver Halide	Heat of Formation
AgF	−48.5
AgCl	−30.36
AgBr	−23.78
AgI	−14.91

Silver fluoride is an unusual case; here the polarization of the fluoride ion is much smaller than that of the larger halide ions. In addition, the magnitude of the coulomb forces in silver fluoride is quite high, which is reflected in the value for the heat of formation. Silver fluoride is not light-sensitive, and, unlike the other silver halides, it is of no importance in photography.

We shall not attempt to describe here the photographic process based on the light sensitivity of silver halides; that is outside the scope of this book. We will, however, discuss the light sensitivity of silver compounds other than halides.

Light-sensitive emulsions with properties similar to those of silver halides were prepared by precipitating silver tungstate or silver molybdate in gelatin solution. The silver tungstate emulsions are sensitive to γ-rays from Co^{60}, and the sensitivity increases when excess sodium tungstate is used (56). The sensitivity of silver molybdate emulsions was reported to be dependent on the quality of gelatin (57) and on the acid used in preparation; citric acid and tartaric acid increased the sensitivity, and oxalic and acetic acids decreased the sensitivity. Silver molybdate emulsions have very low sensitivity to X-rays and γ-rays; they respond to wavelengths ranging from ultraviolet to 4072 Å. The long-wave limit of sensitivity of the silver salts investigated by Kawasaki (58) was 4072 Å for benzoate, 4405 Å for salicylate, 3828 Å for anthranilate, 3625 Å for sulfosalicylate, 4405 Å for cinnamate, and 3856 Å for phthalate. The mixed emulsions of silver tungstate and silver molybdate show higher sensitivity than single emulsions, and almost equal that of silver chloride (59). The sensitivity ranges up to 4529 Å. On exposure to light, a latent image is formed which can be developed by conventional methods. Latent images can be formed also by exposing suspensions of silver titanate in gelatin to light (60).

The use of silver oxalate in photothermographic compositions has already been described above in connection with light-sensitive mercury salts. Levy and Schulze found that the following are also suitable for photothermographic systems: silver succindiamidoxime (61), silver salts of thiosemicarbazide (62), silver salts of benzamidoxime (63), silver salts of malondiamidoxime and glutardiamidoxime (64), and silver salts of organic sulfinates, for example, silver *p*-toluene sulfinate and silver benzene sulfinate (65). These compounds are dispersed in organic colloids, or, preferably, in polyvinyl chloride, in order to obtain photographic material which can be desensitized to further action of light by application of heat (66). The light sensitivity can be modified by the addition of wetting agents which may either increase or decrease the response of the photothermographic silver salts to light (67); for instance, the light sensitivity of silver thiosemicarbazide is increased by the addition of sodium 2-ethylhexene sulfonate, but decreased by the addition of sodium heptadecyl sulfate. The sensitivity of silver succindiamidoxime and that of silver sulfinates is improved by adding to the composition, for example, sodium lauryl sulfate, sodium decyl sulfate, or sodium dioctyl phosphate (68).

The quantum yield of all photographic systems based on the light sensitivity of silver salts, including gelatin silver halide emulsions, is smaller than one; photochemical changes induced by the action of light are usually increased by a development process and quantum yields of the order of 10^{10}, taking into account the subsequent treatment of the silver halide photographic layer after exposure, have been reported (69). Many attempts to employ endothermic compounds that would, upon exposure to a flash of light of short duration and adequate intensity, trigger a chain reaction with a quantum yield greater than one, were unsuccessful mainly because of the poor stability and explosive nature of suitable compounds (70). Eggert (71,72,73) avoided the danger of explosion by embedding the labile compounds, e.g., silver azide, silver fulminate, silver carbide, silver imide, and silver amide in fibrous material. Silver azide emulsions were also studied by Tomoda (74). Especially suitable is nitrogen iodide NI_3, prepared by placing hardened filter paper, previously soaked in an iodine/potassium iodide solution, in aqueous ammonia. After drying, the brown-black paper is exposed under a transparency to a flash of light of high intensity, obtained from a gaseous discharge lamp, yielding immediately a direct-positive image composed of the undecomposed ammonia complex of nitrogen iodide (NI_3NH_3). This image can be converted with a solution of silver nitrate into a silver iodide image, which can be reduced later with an alkaline solution of sodium stannite to metallic silver. When properly exposed, such material has an effective speed of about one thousand times that of blueprint and diazotype papers. The light sensitivity and the quantum yield of this process depend a great deal on the intensity of the radiation and any attempts to increase the susceptibility of these compounds to detonation under the action of light would inevitably create a thermal instability. It is obvious that for this reason the explosive materials do not offer a real prospect of obtaining highly sensitive photographic layers.

1.2i *Tungstic and Molybdic Acids*

Tungstic and molybdic acids and their salts form, in the presence of organic reducing agents, e.g., glucose, light-sensitive systems. A photographic paper based on this phenomenon was patented by Sheppard and Eberlin (75). Cochran (76) employed the reaction product of a mixture of oxalic acid and the sodium salts of molybdic and tungstic acids; material of this type is sensitive to radiations of wavelengths between 3550 and 3750 Å, with the maximum at 3663 Å. More recently, Chalkley (77) found that heteropolyacids such as silicotungstic or silicomolybdic and phosphotungstic or phosphomolybdic acids are particularly suitable for photographic processes. The basic reaction taking place during the exposure may be illustrated by (78):

$$H_3PW_{12}O_{40} + H + light \longrightarrow H_4PW_{12}O_{40} \qquad (30)$$

phosphotungstic   phosphotungstous
acid (colorless)   acid (black)

This reaction is reversible and thus the image formed by light will fade in the dark. Faded material can be printed on again. The phototropic images can be made permanent by various toning procedures based on the reducing power of the phosphotungstous acid (79); silver toning, gold toning, and Prussian blue toning are examples. In another patent, Chalkley (80) describes a color process based on the fact that phosphotungstic acid forms, with the leucobases of some dyes, colorless and insoluble phosphotungstates; upon exposure to actinic radiation these compounds undergo intramolecular oxidation and reduction and the resulting products are the phosphotungstites of the dyes. The black phosphotungstite ion is oxidized in the air to a colorless phosphotungstate ion, thereby exposing the bright color of the dye.

1.2j   *Photosensitive Glass*

A number of new products and processes have resulted from the discovery that certain metallic ions dissolved in glass can, by exposure to actinic radiation, be reduced to colloidal metal particles which act as color formers or as nucleating agents for crystallization of supersaturated phases.

Photosensitive glass in which a permanent photographic image can be reproduced after exposure and development (81,82) is made by mixing conventional silicate-glass components with a reducing agent and an ionic compound of copper or silver and melting the mixture at a high temperature (83,84,85,86,87). Especially suitable are glasses containing approximately 5 per cent of alkali-metal oxide and about the same amount of barium oxide. Superior results are obtained by the use of gold salts together with palladium salts (88); palladium salts act as color modifiers. In order to increase the spectral sensitivity, about 0.05 per cent of cerium oxide is added. Fluorides, chlorides, and sodium oxide refine the properties of the glass; in particular, they prevent discoloration during melting (89). Introduction of Sb_2O_3 to photosensitive glass eliminates bubbles (90). Compounds of Fe, Pb, U, V, As, Mn, etc., inhibit photosensitivity. All other substances which may be present in the glass are of no importance as long as they do not absorb actinic radiation.

For exposure, X-rays (91) and β-rays (92) can be used; if the glass contains cerium ions, any source of ultraviolet light in the band between 300 and 350 mμ is suitable.

During the exposure, metallic ions of copper, silver, gold, or palladium, dissolved in the glass, are reduced to metallic atoms, for example:

$$Ag^+ + e = Ag \tag{31}$$

The electrons required are supplied by those set free by radiation. According to Stookey (93), silver and copper act as their own sensitizers and the reaction proceeds as follows:

$$2Ag^+ + h\nu = Ag^2 + Ag \tag{32}$$

and

$$2Cu^+ + h\nu = Cu^2 + Cu \tag{33}$$

In the presence of a cerium compound, the reaction is

$$Ce^{3+} + h\nu = Ce^{4+} + e \tag{34}$$

The quantum absorbed is used to transform tervalent cerium ion into tetravalent, with the liberation of an electron. This is the primary photochemical process. Because the glass is rigid at room temperature, the electrons are trapped in centers adjacent to the parent ions. The changes in ionic structure originated by the exposure can take place only when the viscosity of the glass is reduced by heating, which permits the capture of the electrons by metal ions:

$$Au^+ + e = Au \tag{35}$$

Atoms of the metal formed by the photoreduction are allowed to migrate in the glass until the aggregates become large enough to be visible. It is not necessary to develop the exposed glass immediately after the exposure; development can be completed at any time, provided the glass is protected from further exposure to actinic radiation.

It is believed that during the development step the formation of metal atoms is followed by growth of colloidal metal particles (94), which are the coloring agents (95,96,97). The intensity of the coloring is proportional to the metal content (98), and thus the density of the developed image will be dependent on the concentration of the metallic salts in the glass, on the exposure time, and on the duration and temperature of development (99). The average development temperature is 580 to 650°C and the average development time is between 10 and 60 minutes. The developing time can be shortened by adding to the glass melt thermoreducing compounds of multivalent elements such as antimony and tin (100). Orange and red colors, which are produced by strong exposure, are developed more rapidly than blue and purple.

Depending on the duration of the exposure and on the wavelength of the radiation, the image penetrates the glass to different depths. Since longer wavelengths penetrate deeper into the glass, the images prepared under such conditions are distributed throughout the thickness of the glass plate, provided the exposure has been of sufficiently long duration. On short exposure, the image may be confined so near the surface of the glass as to be substantially two-dimensional.

When the developed image is cooled to room temperature, the light-sensitive components remain inactive unless the glass is again heated to a high temperature. During the cooling period, the atoms present in the photosensitive glass, as well as in the regular glass, do not arrange themselves into crystalline patterns and the glass appears amorphous. By introducing metal particles of colloidal size, one may nucleate the crystallization of another phase. It was found by Stookey (101,102,103,104, 105) that trace quantities of colloidal metal particles formed by reduction through the effect of radiation may serve also as nucleating agents for the growth of nonmetallic crystals such as lithium or barium silicate, within the glass, to produce an opalescent effect. The colloidal size of the metallic particles necessary for causing lithium metasilicate glass to crystallize is of the order of 80 Å in diameter (106), and consists of about 100,000 atoms of gold (107). In photosensitive glass, obviously, the crystallization is confined to the exposed parts so that after exposure and carefully controlled development a three-dimensional image consisting of microscopic light-diffusing crystals is obtained. The necessary nuclei are provided by photoreduced metallic ions (108).

The practical application of this type of glass is based on the differing physical and optical properties of the image areas from those of the surrounding glass. Especially important is the difference in the rate of solution in dilute hydrofluoric acid, which is about fifty times faster in the exposed areas. This effect is explained by the enormous increase in surface area in the crystalline glass; it has been found that the average crystal is 4 μ in diameter, which gives about ten billion crystals per cubic centimeter. Prolonged exposures will produce metal particles too small to cause nucleation at the development temperature, and, consequently, the glass will etch poorly (109).

This type of glass is sold in finished form by Corning Glass Works under the trade name " Fotoform " as a chemical machining type of photosensitive glass. Because of the highly precise nature of this process (110), accuracy is very high and such glass can be used advantageously for the preparation of accurately dimensioned glass forms of intricate shape, such as fine-mesh screens, printed circuit boards, etc. (111). Screens of one million holes per square inch and aperture masks for color-television picture tubes with 360,000 aperture holes accurately spaced and accurately pointing towards the electron gun have been produced.

The most suitable glass for chemical machining is essentially a lithium silicate containing potassium oxide and aluminum oxide. As light-sensitive substances, cerium salts and silver compounds are used.

The etched glass can be transformed into crystalline material by re-exposing and reheating, which gives the product superior hardness, toughness, strength, and thermal shock endurance. Because of its high electrical resistance this type of glass is of great importance in electronic design and engineering.

Photosensitive glasses activated with silver ions are also capable of responding to γ-ray radiation, and have been suggested as a means of measuring total γ-ray dosage (112). They are essentially potassium-barium-aluminum phosphate glasses containing silver (113,114,115). During the exposure to γ-rays, elemental silver is produced, which is, after subsequent irradiation with ultraviolet light, detected by the emission of visible light, the intensity of which is directly proportional to the γ-ray dosage.

Another method of producing images in glass was disclosed by Stookey and his co-workers (116,117,118,119). This process, unrelated to the one just described, consists of transferring a silver image prepared by conventional photographic means on the surface of the glass, covering the image with a special paste of ferric sulfate and yellow ochre in a liquid binder, and heating the sandwich, preferably in an oxidizing atmosphere containing sulphur dioxide, to a temperature just below the softening point of the glass. During this process, silver ions produced by oxidation migrate into the glass by means of an ion exchange with the alkali-metal ions present in the glass. When the glass is heated in a reducing atmosphere of hydrogen, carbon monoxide, methane, or a mixture of hydrogen and nitrogen, silver ions are reduced back to metallic silver, which forms the image. This process, called "photostaining," can be applied to all glasses containing alkali-metal ions, such as soda-lime-silicate or boro-silicate types; it has been suggested as a method for manufacturing accurate scales, reticles, dials, microphotographic records, etc. The image is two-dimensional, permanent, dimensionally stable, and scratch-resistant.

1.2k *Transition Metal Complexes*

It has been known for almost two hundred years that certain compounds of transition metals are reduced when exposed to light. Ferric chloride is known to be reduced in the presence of an electron donor to ferrous chloride (120). Ferric salts of organic acids, e.g., oxalic, citric, and tartaric, are likewise reduced on exposure to actinic radiation (121). The oxalate decomposition takes place as follows:

$$Fe_2(C_2O_4)_3 \xrightarrow{h\nu} 2FeC_2O_4 + 2CO_2 \tag{36}$$

Oxalates are most sensitive and are followed by tartrates; citrates are more stable. The ease with which these salts are affected by light decreases with increasing molecular weight.

From the photochemical point of view, much more important than the simple salts of transition metals are their complex salts corresponding to the general formula $(M_x)RCOO_yA_z$ where M is a metal of variable valence, R is an organic radical, A an alkali metal or ammonia, and x, y, and z are integers. Examples are ferric ammonium citrate, ferric ammonium oxalate, etc. These compounds possess comparatively high light sensitivity and have found applications in many photographic processes. Related trioxalato-complexes of cobalt (122,123) and manganese (124) have a certain photoactivity also, and respond to the action of light sufficiently to be useful for photographic purposes (125). Certain trivalent cobalt salts, e.g., hexamine cobaltic chloride $Co(NH_3)_6Cl_3$, oxidize, through a photochemical reaction induced by light, sulfides of heavy metals to a white sulfate (126). Particularly useful are the sulfides of lead, copper, nickel, mercury, and silver. Trivalent Mn^3 in alkaline tartrate solution has been found light sensitive (127); it is most probably present as hydroxo-tartarato-manganate. Bis(aromatic . hydrocarbon) iron compounds are photosensitive also and have been suggested for making photographic paper (128).

The most thoroughly studied reaction is the photochemical decomposition of the ferric complexes in the ultraviolet and visible region of the spectrum; Allmand and Webb (129) proposed that upon exposure to light an activated complex ion is formed which reacts with an inactive ferrioxalate anion as follows:

$$[Fe^{3+}(C_2O_4)_3]^{3-} \longrightarrow (C_2O_4)^{2-}[Fe(C_2O_4)_2]^- \qquad (37)$$

$$(C_2O_4)^{2-}[Fe(C_2O_4)_2]^- + [Fe^{3+}(C_2O_4)_3]^{3-} \longrightarrow$$
$$2[Fe(C_2O_4)_2]^{2-} + (C_2O_4)^{2-} + 2CO_2 \quad (38)$$

More recently, Parker and Hatchard (130) observed that irradiation of a ferrioxalate solution frozen at the temperature of liquid oxygen produces an orange-brown substance identified as free oxalate radical $C_2O_4^-$ or CO_2^-. If the existence of free radicals is taken into consideration, the photodecomposition of the ferrioxalate ion takes place in the following stages:

$$[Fe^{3+}(C_2O_4)_3]^{3-} \xrightarrow{h\nu} [Fe^{3+}(C_2O_4)_3]^{3-*} \longrightarrow$$

trioxalato-ferric ion   excited ion

$$\left[C_2O_4 - Fe \begin{array}{c} C_2O_4 \\ \diagup \\ \diagdown \\ C_2O_4 \end{array} \right]^{3-} \longrightarrow C_2O_4^- + [Fe^{2+}(C_2O_4)_2]^{2-}$$

metastable state   oxalate radical   dioxalato-ferrous ion

(39)

$$C_2O_4^- + [Fe^{3+}(C_2O_4)_3]^{3-} \longrightarrow (C_2O_4)^{2-} + [Fe^{3+}(C_2O_4)_3]^{2-}$$

oxalate   trioxalato-ferric   oxalate   dioxalato-ferric ion
radical   ion   ion   attached to oxalate radical

$$\longrightarrow [Fe^{2+}(C_2O_4)_2]^{2-} + 2CO_2 \quad (40)$$

dioxalato ferrous ion

The quantum yields are nearly constant in the short wavelength region of the spectrum but decrease with increasing wavelength (131). Hnatek (132) estimated that the quantum yield decreases with increasing intensity and duration of the exposure. Quantum yield of the ferrioxalate actinometer at 365 mμ was found to be 1.26 $\pm$ 0.03 (133).

Transition metal salts also act as sensitizers in numerous reactions; photolysis of oxalic acid (5) and photo-oxidation of water (134) and of thiourea (135), to name a few examples.

1.3 PHOTOGRAPHIC IRON PROCESSES

A number of photographic printing processes, based on the light sensitivity of iron salts, have been developed in the past; because of long exposure times and elaborate processing, many of these processes are now obsolete, and only about two are still used at the present time. These will be discussed in more detail. Photographic iron processes may be classified as follows:

1. Processes in which the original ferric salts or the reduced ferrous salt react with another substance to form a colored reaction product.
2. Processes in which the ferrous salt reduces another metallic salt to form a metallic image.
3. Processes based on the ability of ferric salts to render gelatin and other organic colloids insoluble.

To the first group belongs the blueprint process, which is a negative process and gives white lines on a blue background. Blue color is formed as a result of a reaction between the ferrous salt and the ferricyanide. When the opposite is wanted—blue lines on a white background, the paper is sensitized with a ferric salt and after exposure is treated with a solution of potassium ferrocyanide. The product resulting from the reaction of the ferrous salt with ferrocyanide is white, and the reaction product of ferrocyanide with the unchanged ferric salt forms a blue precipitate of ferric ferrocyanide. The positive prints of the original are washed in water and fixed in a weak solution of sulfuric or hydrochloric acid.

Another process belonging to this group is the ferro-gallic process, based on the reaction of the ferrous salt with gallic or tannic acid. The reaction product is purplish-black. For sensitizing, simple ferric salts, such as ferric chloride or ferric sulfate, may be used. Development of exposed paper is carried out in a bath containing a solution of gallic acid to which a small quantity of oxalic acid has been added in order to obtain clean whites. Paper containing, in the light-sensitive layer, both the soluble ferric salt and tannic acid, was suggested by Omoto (136). A positive-working modification of this process has also been patented (137). White images on a black background can also be prepared by coating a black base with a transparent gelatin solution containing ferric ammonium citrate and a small amount of glucose (138). The sensitivity can be increased by addition of a dicarboxylic acid containing at least ten carbon atoms (139). After exposure to ultraviolet light, the image is developed by heating the material to 80 to 100°C.

At this point mention should be made, also, of a process patented by Kögel (140,141), in which the photoreduced iron salts react with β-naphthoquinone sulfonic acid, isonitrosoacetylacetone, isonitrosopropionylacetone or nitroso-β-naphthol and form colored images. Schmidt (142) recommended replacing the latter compounds with ω-isonitroso-ω-cyano-2,4-dimethylacetophenone or similar compounds, corresponding to the general formula,

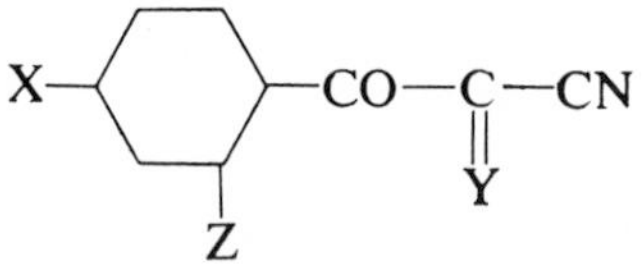

$$X-\underset{Z}{\underbrace{\bigcirc}}-CO-\underset{Y}{\overset{|}{C}}-CN$$

where X stands for methyl, Z for hydrogen or methyl, and Y for an isonitroso group.

1.3a   *Blueprint*

Since blueprinting was first developed by Sir John Herschel in the middle of the last century, this process has been used almost exclusively for copying line originals, giving white lines on blue background. As base material, paper is usually used; however, cloth (143,144), film, metal (145), glass cloth (146), etc., were employed also.

In order to withstand frequent washing and rough handling, blueprint papers are made with a special kind of paperstock containing 25, 50, or 100 per cent ragstock, free from chemical impurities. The paper base must first be properly sized with animal glue, gelatin, or some other material, and calendered so that the surface which is to receive the coating is not excessively absorbent or too hard. The function of the sizing is to prevent the solution from penetrating too deeply into the paper. The right degree of penetration by the sensitizing solution is obtained, it is claimed, by sizing the paper base with a gelatin size containing magnesium hydroxide and a gelatin hardener (147), or with an aqueous dispersion of a water-dispersible polymeric adhesive containing a water insoluble hydrous zirconium compound (148).

Uniform penetration of the sensitizing solution into the paper is of great importance. If the solution penetrates too deeply, the light-sensitive chemicals are partially concealed in the paper matrix, and longer exposures are necessary. In addition, washing of the exposed print must be prolonged. If, on the other hand, the paper surface is too hard, not enough sensitizing solution is accepted by the surface and the density of the final image is low. The penetration of the sensitizing solution can be controlled either by adjusting the viscosity of the sensitizing solution with a gel-forming colloidal clay such as bentonite (149), or by means of a precoat. Satisfactory results have been obtained with precoats containing colloidal dispersions of silica (150), or with colloidal silicates of metals of the second and third groups of the periodic system, such as magnesium, calcium, and zinc silicate (151).

The composition of blueprint sensitizing solutions varies widely. In general it consists of an aqueous solution of potassium ferricyanide, ferric ammonium citrate, or some other complex ferric salt and a polybasic acid such as citric or oxalic. In many instances, alkali metal salts, for example, sodium citrate or potassium oxalate, are added to the solution in order to obtain coatings with desired properties. If stock solutions are prepared for future use, a small amount of sodium formate may be required to prevent mold. Ferric salts are, in general, used in excess over the quantity which is equivalent to the ferricyanide salt, to insure sufficient light sensitivity of the coating. Some of the ferric salts are listed in Table 1.6. Potassium ferricyanide, commonly known as "red potash," can be replaced by ammonium nitro-ferricyanide (152) or diammonium sodium ferricyanide (153); according to this patent, diammonium sodium ferricyanide possesses the property of improving the intensity and keeping qualities of the blue pigment. An alkali-metal ferrocyanide (154) can be substituted for part of the ferricyanide to give faster printing (155). The ferrocyanide, however, reduces the ferric salt present in the coating; this results in poor washing-out of the unexposed parts of the print and in poor stability of the sensitized paper unless the sensitizing solution is buffered to neutral, alkaline, or slightly acid pH with a hydrolyzable alkali-metal phosphate (156,157). Addition of peroxide-type oxidizing agents was recommended by Crowley and Goodyear (158, 159). When diguanidine disodium ferrocyanide is employed instead of alkali-metal ferrocyanide (160), the sacrifice in latitude and stability is less pronounced. To improve the washing-out

TABLE *1.6* Blueprint Sensitizers

Ferric Salt	Molecular Weight	Printing Speed	Washing, Keeping	Latitude	Remarks
Ferric ammonium citrate—green 14.5–16% Fe; 7.5% NH_3; 75% hydrated citric acid		slow	fair	good	excess gives a gloss on paper; hygroscopic
Ferric ammonium citrate—brown 16.5–18.5% Fe; 9% NH_3; 65% hydrated citric acid		very slow			not satisfactory in blueprint
Ferric potassium citrate 16% Fe; 65% citric acid		slow	good	short	higher concentration improves keeping
Ferric ammonium oxalate $(NH_4)_3Fe(C_2O_4)_3 \cdot 3H_2O$	428.08	fast	poor	excellent	
Ferric sodium oxalate $Na_3Fe(C_2O_4)_3 \cdot 4\text{-}1/2H_2O$	469.97	slow	good	short	solubility in water is limited
Ferric potassium oxalate $K_3Fe(C_2O_4)_3 \cdot 3H_2O$	491.25	fast	good		very low solubility in water
Ferric ammonium tartrate $Fe_2O_3(C_4H_4O_6)_2 \cdot 2NH_3 \cdot 9H_2O$	652.05	fast	poor	good	
Ferric citrate $FeC_6H_5O_7 \cdot 5H_2O$	335.03	slow	good	good	must be used with other iron salts
Ferric oxalate $Fe_2(C_2O_4)_3 \cdot 6H_2O$	484.00	fast	fair	excellent	
Ferric chloride $FeCl_3 \cdot 6H_2O$	270.30	very fast	poor	good	is used together only with other iron salts

of the soluble salts from the unexposed areas Jahoda (161) recommended adding potassium sodium hexametaphosphate known as "plastic metaphosphate" to the sensitizing solution. Whitlock and Kienast (162) advised the use of sugar for the same purpose.

The primary controller of the printing speed is potassium ferricyanide; with other factors equal, the more ferricyanide the slower the speed of the paper, and vice versa (163). Empirical formulas for the relationship between the amount of potassium ferricyanide and the sensitivity have been given by Tomoda (164).

The presence of organic acids, for instance tartaric acid or oxalic acid, also extends the sensitivity threshold of layers sensitized with organic iron salts, and increases the maximum density of the printed area. Citric acid and acetic acid have little effect (165). In general it can be said that the acids exert an effect proportional to their strength, which determines their effect on the hydrogen ion concentration of the solution. Among other acids, maleic, fumaric, and itaconic have been claimed as suitable (166).

The desire to obtain blueprint paper of higher sensitivity is reflected in a number of patents; among compounds which were suggested as sensitizers are the following: vanadium pentoxide (167), guanidine carbonate (168), quaternary ammonium compounds such as trimethylbenzylammonium hydroxide (169) and potassium dichromate (170). It was also found that blueprint papers requiring shorter exposures can be obtained when the paper is precoated prior to sensitizing with a certain type of wetting agent, for example dioctyl sulfosuccinate (171) or the guanidine salt of dioctylsulfonic acid ester (172). About 25 per cent increase in speed is claimed by addition of polyvinyl alcohol (173).

The influence of the composition of the sensitizing solution on the sensitometric qualities of blueprint papers was investigated by Hnatek (174) and by Tomoda and Kawasaki (175). Tomoda and Kawasaki demonstrated that the decomposition of ammonium ferric oxalate does not obey the Bunsen-Roscoe reciprocity law and that sodium nitrite added to the sensitizing solution increases the contrast of blueprint paper.

Coating of the sensitizing solution and subsequent drying of the paper is done entirely automatically, by specially designed machines, for example the one patented by Cazares (176), in which the paper passes between a series of pulling rollers and over a hard rubber roller. This roller revolves in a pan containing the sensitizing solution and, as it revolves it carries a thin film of the solution, which is transferred to the under surface of the paper while being moved in a horizontal plane. Approximately three feet from this roller is a glass or stainless steel bar, and, as the paper passes in a substantially vertical plane over this bar, excess solution is wiped from the paper surface and runs down by gravity over the paper and back into the coating tray. The sensitized paper, upon leaving the coating machine, enters a heated enclosure where it is dried at a temperature of about 200 to 230°F before being rolled. The lower the temperature at which paper is dried, the yellower the color, the better the washing, and, to some extent, the better the keeping quality. Later, the sensitized paper is re-rolled, measured, and cut into the desired lengths. Obviously, the whole operation of coating, drying, re-rolling, and cutting has to be done in subdued light. Commercial blueprint paper contains 60 to 75 grams of iron salts per 100 square meters.

As stated previously, blueprint paper is generally used for the reproduction of engineering and architectural drawings. When the light-sensitive blueprint coating is exposed to actinic radiation while in contact with the original, the light passes through the transparent sections of the sheet, and, in these portions, the ferric compound is reduced to ferrous salt, which reacts with the ferricyanide to produce a deep blue color. The main reaction taking place during the exposure can be characterized by the following equation:

$$Fe_2(C_2O_4)_3 \xrightarrow{h\nu} 2Fe(C_2O_4) + 2CO_2 \qquad (41)$$

Potassium ferricyanide is much less sensitive to light than the ferric oxalate, and is reduced to ferrocyanide only if the exposure to light is considerably prolonged. Besides potassium ferrocyanide, ferric hydroxide and cyanogen are formed on prolonged exposures (177). Potassium ferrocyanide reacts then with ferrous oxalate to give ferrous ferrocyanide, which is white and makes the image appear lighter in color

$$K_4[Fe(CN)_6] + 2FeC_2O_4 \longrightarrow Fe_2[Fe(CN)_6] + 2K_2C_2O_4 \quad (42)$$

When the exposure is completed, the print is washed in clean water; during this procedure the unreduced salts dissolve out of the unexposed areas, and the ferrous oxalate reacts with the potassium ferricyanide:

$$3Fe(C_2O_4) + 2K_3[Fe(CN)_6] \longrightarrow Fe_3[Fe(CN)_6]_2 + 2K_2C_2O_4 \quad (43)$$

The developed print contains no chemicals in areas which were protected from the light; where it was struck by light, the image formed, consisting of blue-colored insoluble ferrous ferricyanide, also known as Turnbull's blue. According to Suzuki (178), Turnbull's blue is formed during the exposure as the result of an electron transfer in the ferric oxalate.

After being washed, the print is treated with a developing solution, washed again in water, and finally dried. The developing solution consists of an oxidizing agent, which oxidizes the ferrous ferrocyanide to a deep blue ferric ferrocyanide or Prussian blue:

$$3Fe_2[Fe(CN)_6] \longrightarrow Fe_4[Fe(CN)_6] \qquad (44)$$

Murray (179) is of the opinion that the bulk of the blue pigment is not formed by the reaction between potassium ferricyanide and ferrous salt, but by the oxidation in light of ferrous ferrocyanide; the latter is probably formed by a secondary reaction between Prussian blue and ammonium ferrous oxalate.

Rakos (180) studied the photochemical process of blueprinting by a magnetic method, and came to the conclusion that during the exposure to ultraviolet light, weakly paramagnetic Prussian blue and diamagnetic potassium ferrocyanide are formed first, followed later by strongly paramagnetic Turnbull's blue. According to Mukaibo and Tsujimura (181), both blue compounds change, with excess exposure, to a colorless substance of unknown composition. The blue color of the image thus consists of a mixture of ferric ferrocyanide and ferrous ferricyanide.

As the oxidizing component of the developing solution, potassium dichromate is generally used, but other compounds, for instance hydrogen peroxide (182), urea peroxide (183), and alkali-metal bromates (184) are also suitable.

Excess oxidizing agents must generally be washed off the surface by a water wash, after which the paper is ready for drying. Water containing large quantities of calcium ions may weaken the blue image because of the formation of yellowish basic iron salts. This effect can be remedied by acidifying the final wash water with a little hydrochloric acid.

The blueprint image is water-insoluble, but may be dissolved and removed by alkali-metal hydroxides; on this property are based the marking and retouching solutions (185) with which blueprints can be quickly and easily corrected. Another correcting fluid consists of a solution of potassium oxalate (186), which reduces the blue ferrous ferricyanide to white ferrous ferrocyanide.

Commercially, blueprints are exposed and developed continuously on one of the machines designed for this purpose (187,188); the sensitized paper is carried automatically, after exposure to a suitable source of light, through a water-wash arrangement consisting of a tube with nozzles that direct sprays of water against the surface of the paper; thereafter, the paper travels through a developing bath and again through a wash bath, and finally over a series of heated rollers where it is dried before being wound on a removable roller.

Depending on the composition of the blueprint sensitizer (189), it may happen that when water is applied to the exposed material the blue color runs, more or less, into the white background, giving it a bluish cast and causing the white lines to appear narrower than the lines on the original tracing. This effect is called "bleeding" and can be partially eliminated either by coating the light-sensitive ferric salts and potassium ferricyanide in separate operations (190), or by exposing the sensitized paper for a shorter time so that no excess of ferrous salts is formed. An increase in ferricyanide concentration would be impractical because the excess of ferricyanide would greatly reduce the printing speed. Another means of preventing "bleeding" consists of applying an acid solution of a ferrocyanide, a reducing agent, and an aliphatic polyhydroxyl compound (191) immediately after exposure, then giving it the customary water wash, treating it with dichromate and final water rinse. The migration of the ferrous ion can also be stopped by washing the paper, prior to the usual washing, with a solution of a ferric salt, which reacts with the ferrocyanide in the exposed portions to form insoluble ferric ferrocyanide (192). According to another patent (193), the running of the color can be eliminated by applying water to the side of the sheet opposite the one having the light-sensitive coating.

Instead of the usual developing just described, blueprints can be processed either by a semidry process or by stabilization of the unexposed parts of the sheet against further action of light. In the stabilization of the unexposed parts of the sheet, the exposed sheet is treated with a solution of a substance capable of forming with the ferricyanides present in the unexposed parts, insoluble and light-insensitive compounds. Among the suitable agents are solutions of nickel, zinc, manganese, cadmium and cobalt salts (194), and chlorides, sulfates or nitrates of alkaline-earth metals, aluminum, zirconium, cerium, and uranium in the presence of hexamethylene tetramine (195). In another patent (196), addition of phosphoric acid to the foregoing solution is recommended. In all these instances, yellow lines on a blue background are obtained.

In the semidry method of development, a thin film of the neutral or weakly acid solution of a ferric salt, potassium ferrocyanide, or potassium ferricyanide, or both, and sodium nitrite (197) is used for sensitizing. Sodium nitrite is essential if white lines are to be secured; if left out, the unexposed portions are blue or green and such prints would be unusable. The image is developed and fixed by a special developer containing a soluble magnesium salt, zinc, nickel, or cobalt salt, and an oxidizing agent (198). The developer is applied to the exposed paper in a machine designed for this purpose, in which the liquid developer is carried out of a shallow trough on the surface of a roller; by changing the speed the amount of the applied developer can be controlled. As the unreacted salts remain in the paper, prints developed by the "semidry" method tend to fade on exposure to light, and are thus less stable than blueprints developed by the general method of washing. It has been claimed that some improvement is obtained when the exposed blueprint sheet is wetted with water or water vapor prior to the development just described (199).

In order to provide more compact processing equipment, a monobath developing process for blueprints was suggested by Fujiyama (200). The developing solution contains, in addition to hydrogen peroxide and ammonia, an organic acid and zinc phosphate which decolorizes the unexposed areas. A small amount of an ultraviolet absorber prevents discoloration of the developed print. A two-bath developing method for blueprints was described by the same author (201).

The quality of blueprint paper is determined not only by the printing speed of the sensitized material and by the whiteness of the lines in the finished print, but also by the depth and brilliance of the blue color and the keeping quality of the unexposed sheet. Also, in order to obtain a satisfactory print it is necessary for the sensitized paper to have good printing latitude.

Unfortunately, it is impossible to incorporate all these desirable properties into a single product, since each of them is affected by changes in the others. In general, it can be said that increased sensitivity is associated with loss in latitude and shelf life, and vice versa. Any changes made in order to increase the density of the blue color will be reflected in higher contrast. Obviously a compromise has to be made when the sensitizing solution is formulated. If a standard is assumed for any one property, the sensitizing solution should be so formulated in order to give the most desirable properties. Printing speeds have been standardized by commercial usage, and, therefore, criteria for concomitant properties are the best color, good latitude, quick washing, and acceptable shelf life.

Good quality, freshly coated blueprint paper is lemon-yellow; in storage it gradually turns greenish yellow, green, and finally, blue. When this stage is reached the paper is practically useless. Papers sensitized with a ferricyanide-ferrocyanide combination are bluish directly after coating. The chemical changes which take place during storage in the absence of light are quite complex and cannot be expressed by simple chemical equations. Probably the most important factor is the reduction of ferric salts, which leads to the formation of insoluble blue compounds. These reactions are accelerated by adverse environmental conditions, especially heat and moisture; for this reason blueprint paper is usually kept in a dry, cold atmosphere, and even under such conditions it can be stored only for a few weeks. Various means are known for improving the keeping quality of blueprint papers. In the past it has been found advisable to use acids, such as phosphoric or oxalic, or alkali oxalates (202). More stable coatings can also be obtained by addition of ammonium nitrate (203) or oxidizing substances such as potassium dichromate or ammonium persulfate (204). In general, oxidizing agents decrease the light sensitivity and the oxalates, when not completely removed by washing, worsen the fading of the prints. To improve the shelf life, Hinkel (205) added to the sensitizing solution an hydroxyalkylamine salt of a polybasic acid, e.g., trihydroxyethylamine oxalate, which dissolves basic ferrous salts of organic acids assumed to be present in the background of the prints after exposure. Extraordinary stability, it is claimed, is achieved by the substitution of ferric guanidine oxalate for the usual ferric ammonium oxalate (206). If not available, the same improvement can be obtained when ferric oxalate and guanidine oxalate in approximately stoichiometrical amounts are added to the blueprint solution to form ferric guanidine oxalate (207). The increase in shelf life is, supposedly, not associated with lower sensitivity. Vallen and van den Dolder (208) found that fluorides capable of liberating fluoride ions in aqueous solutions do enhance the keeping of blueprint papers without affecting the printing speed significantly.

The brilliance and depth of the blue color is of major importance, and many efforts have been made to increase it. Crowley and Goodyear obtained an intense blue by incorporating into the sensitizing solution either an alkali-metal nitrate (209,210) or salts of an aliphatic nitrogen base, e.g., salts of ethanolamine (211). Beeber and Gold (212) increased the intensity of the blue pigment by dispersing in the sensitizing solution finely divided silica. In order to prevent "feathering" when prints are written on with inks, a synthetic latex is included. Polyvinyl acetate latex was used by Warman and Milborne (213). When low density is caused by underexposure, the image can be intensified in a 1 per cent solution of sulfuric acid or by immersion of the exposed paper in an alkaline solution of potassium ferrocyanide and a reducing agent such as sodium sulfite (214). On the other hand, overexposed prints can be reduced in a solution of ammonium dichromate and chrome alum.

When exposed to strong light, all blueprints fade because the blue ferrous ferricyanide is reduced to white ferrous ferrocyanide. The extent to which this reduction takes place depends on the composition of the sensitizing solution used and on the degree of washing. Insufficient removal of the unreacted salts is always accompanied by rapid fading; however, traces of dichromate work in the opposite direction and improve the light fastness of the blue pigment. Faded blueprints regain their color when stored for a period of time in a cool dark place or when treated with a dilute solution of hydrogen peroxide.

The blue color of the blueprint can be converted into dark green by treating the print with an acid solution of potassium ferricyanide and an uranium salt (215). Prussian blue also forms an excellent mordant for dye bases or dye intermediates, which may be coupled to produce a dye (216). In general, any dye base which may be coupled to form a dye may be used; diazo dye bases (for example, diazotized aniline) are especially suitable and are introduced into the sensitized layer by imbibition of their aqueous solution. By applying an appropriate coupler, e.g., resorcinol for magenta, *m*-aminophenol for cyan, and phenol for yellow, the mordanted dyebase is converted into a color image, and the remaining Prussian blue is removed with a weak solution of sodium hydroxide. Dye images can also be formed by treating the base carrying the blueprint image with a leuco sulfuric acid ester of a vat dye and an oxidizing agent. Prussian blue catalyzes the oxidation of the leuco ester; upon removal of the blue image, the colored dye image remains (217).

1.3b *Brownprint*

In the second group of processes using iron salts as the light-sensitive components, are included photographic printing systems based on the ability of ferrous compounds to reduce salts of platinum, gold, palladium, copper, mercury, and silver to the corresponding metals. It should be pointed out that these metal salts act as image formers only, and their light sensitivity is of secondary importance. Now, if a paper is sensitized with ferric oxalate and a reducible metal salt, exposed to light, and washed in water or potassium oxalate solution, an image is formed which consists of finely divided metal. The reactions taking place are as follows:

$$Fe^{3+} + e \xrightarrow{h\nu} Fe^{2+} \tag{45}$$

$$Fe^{2+} + M^{+} \longrightarrow Fe^{3+} + M \quad (M = metal) \tag{46}$$

Suitable salts include potassium chloroplatinite, sodium chloropalladite, sodium chloroaurate, silver nitrate, etc. A number of photographic printing processes have been derived from this principle. These processes are, with few exceptions, of historical interest only and are no longer commercially available. Platinotype (218), palladiotype (219), an iron-gold system (220), and iron-mercury systems (221,226) are examples of these obsolete processes.

The only process still commercially available is the iron-silver system, at present used chiefly for making negatives of tracings for subsequent wash-off or blueprint reproductions. Papers of this type, known as brownprints, sepia prints, or "van Dyke" prints (222), are made by coating on a base material (223), usually heavily sized high-rag-content paper, an aqueous solution of silver nitrate, the light-sensitive ferric salt of an organic acid, and an alkali metal salt of a polycarboxylic acid; the salt of a polycarboxylic acid acts as a solvent for the ferrous salts which, eventually, are formed during the exposure to light. The strong reducing action of the dissolved ferrous salt is used to develop the silver image. Tartaric acid is added to redissolve the precipitated silver salt (224). In order to increase the sensitivity, Süs (166) recommended maleic acid, fumaric acid, or some other aliphatic unsaturated polycarboxylic acid. In order to obtain black images, uranium nitrate (225) or a soluble mercury salt (226) may be incorporated in the sensitizing solution. According to Schmidt (142), the ω-isonitroso-ω-cyano compound of an aryl methyl ketone gives good contrast in brownprints.

In practice, sensitized brownprint paper is exposed under a tracing to a carbon-arc or mercury-vapor lamp; during the exposure, ferric ammonium oxalate is reduced by the action of light to insoluble ferrous ammonium oxalate, which is a potent reducing agent and reduces a portion of the silver nitrate to metallic silver. When the exposure is prolonged, or when silver nitrate is used in excess, some of the silver compound is decomposed by light to metallic silver, giving the print a shiny appearance. The color change of the sensitive coating during the exposure is gradual, but not intense. By dipping the exposed sheet in water, the light-brown color in the exposed regions changes to deeper brown, resulting from the reduction of silver nitrate by ferrous oxalate:

$$3FeC_2O_4 + 3AgNO_3 \longrightarrow Fe_2(C_2O_4)_3 + 3Ag + Fe(NO_3)_3 \quad (47)$$

Unexposed and thus unchanged ferric ammonium oxalate, together with water soluble reaction products, goes into solution. The developed sheet is fixed in a 2 per cent solution of sodium thiosulfate, which dissolves the unexposed silver salt. Kienast (227) recommended for fixing brownprints, a solution containing besides hypo, a wetting agent and ammonium oxalate, which is a powerful solvent for any undissolved trivalent and bivalent iron salts left in the sheet after the first water wash. After the print has been left in the fixing solution for a short time, it is given a final water wash and then dried.

Although the brownprint image does not appear very opaque, when compared with the silver images of silver halide photographic materials, it absorbs nearly all the radiations to which blueprint paper and wash-off material are sensitive. The images are substantially grainless; resolution of 1000 lines per millimeter is possible (228). Exposed iron-silver paper can also be developed by treatment with an acidic solution of a reducing agent and hydroquinone or metol (229). If necessary, the silver image can be further intensified by means of a physical developer, e.g., a solution which contains, in addition to silver nitrate, a photographic developing agent and citric acid (230,231,232).

Brownprint is a negative-working process and the prints usually consist of white lines on a dark brown background. When it is necessary to make changes, the area to be corrected is bleached with a suitable bleaching solution, e.g., sodium hyposulfite or chlorinated water; after corrections are made with a specially prepared ink (233), the entire bleached area is repainted with coloring substance similar to the background color. While still wet, dilute acetic acid is applied; this reacts with the ink and removes the coloring substance from the surface of the paper so that the redrawn lines appear white on the colored background.

One disadvantage of the brownprint process is the poor keeping quality of the sensitized paper; this is due not only to the reduction of ferric salts in the dark, but also to the formation of nitrogen oxides, which attack the light-sensitive layer and the supporting material. Kosar (234) found that the tendency of brownprint material to be deteriorated is minimized by substitution of the silver nitrate with a water-insoluble silver salt such as silver carbonate, silver citrate, or silver tartrate.

Iron-silver systems have been suggested also for sensitizing lenticular films (235) and for producing colored pictures through bleaching and redeveloping of the silver image with color developers in the presence of a coupler (236). In such applications it may be necessary to include water-soluble or organic-solvent-soluble binders (237).

In the past, silver-iron printing papers were employed also for producing continuous-tone prints. This process was named "Kallitype" (238,239, 240); its attractive feature was the possibility of toning the prints with toning baths such as those used for printing-out papers (241). A modification of the Kallitype process was adapted by Fichter, Dickerson, and Sprague (242) for the preparation of molded photosurface terrain models.

1.3c *Tanning Processes*

Ferric salts are able to render gelatin and some other organic colloids insoluble. On exposure to light, the ferric salts are reduced to the ferrous state. In these areas, gelatin becomes more soluble and can be removed by washing with warm water. As a result a relief image is obtained which can be used for silk-screen printing or for lithographic printing plates (243,244). Another process involving the photoreduction of ferric salts and resulting in relief images was patented by Martinez (245). Closely related to these processes is a method of offset duplicating known as the "True-to-Scale Process" (246). This process uses blueprint paper which, after the exposure, is pressed face down on the surface of a moist jelly consisting principally of gelatin and ferrous sulfate.   The unreacted ferricyanide diffuses from the unexposed areas into the gelatin, where it reacts with the ferrous salt to make the gelatin insoluble and ink-accepting.   When greasy duplicating ink of any desired color is applied to this surface, the ink adheres only to the parts corresponding to the lines of the image.   The ink can be transferred to ordinary paper by pressing it onto the gelatin. By repeating the inking and transfer of the ink, about twenty-five additional copies of satisfactory quality can be made.   Since wetting and drying are not involved, the copies are free from distortion; this is the most distinctive feature of this process.   A similar process was patented by Fuchs (247).

REFERENCES

1. L. Pauling. *Phys. Rev.*, **34**, 954–963 (1929).
2. G. M. Barrow. *Physical Chemistry*, McGraw-Hill Book Co., New York, 1961.
3. A. E. Van Arkel. *Molecules and Crystals*, Interscience Publishers, New York, 1956.
4. J. M. Eder. *Ausführliches Handbuch der Photographie*, IV, 4, Wilhelm Knapp, Halle, 1929.
5. N. D. Dhar. *The Chemical Action of Light*, Blackie & Son, Ltd., London, 1931.
6. C. Ellis and A. A. Wells. *The Chemical Action of Ultraviolet Rays*, Reinhold Publishing Corp., New York, 1941.
7. N. B. Hannay. *Inter. Sci. and Techn.*, October 1963, pp. 65–70.
8. R. W. Pohl. *Phys. Z.*, **39**, 36 (1938).
9. W. Martienssen. In *Progress in Photography 1951–1954*, edited by D. A. Spencer, pp. 59–71, Focal Press Ltd, London, 1955.
10. M. C. R. Symons and W. T. Doyle. *Quart. Rev. (London)*, **14**, 62 (1962).
11. G. H. Hecht and G. Müller. *Z. Physik. Chem.*, **202**, 403 (1953).
12. J. Wojtczak. *Roczniki Chem.*, **31**, 343–345 (1957).
13. J. Wojtczak. *Acta Chem. Scand.*, **15**, 888–896 (1961).
14. J. Wojtczak. *Zeszyty Nauk. Uniw. Poznan. Mat. Chem.*, No. 1, 32–39 (1957).
15. J. Wojtczak. *Roczniki Chem.*, **34**, 999–1010 (1960).
16. M. Schwab and F. Nissl. Ger. pat. 950,428/1956.
17. A. Schoen. U.S. pat. 2,504,593/1950.
18. J. Wojtczak. *Poznan. Towarz. Przyjaciol Nauk, Wydzial Mat. Przyrod. Prace Komisji Mat. Przyrod.*, **7**, 25–41 (1959).
19. S. Suzuki and T. Nagae. *Kogyo Kagaka Zasshi*, **66**, 1419–1423 (1963).
20. S. E. Sheppard and J. H. Hudson. U.S. pat. 1,602,589/1926.
21. K. Takei. *Bull. Chem. Soc. Japan*, **28**, 403–408 (1955).
22. K. Takei. *Nippon Kagaku Zasshi*, **73**, 202–204 (1952); *ibid.*, **77**, 830(1956).
23. P. A. van der Meulen and P. B. Gilman, Jr. U.S. pat. 2,874,047/1959.
24. W. Wojciak. *Poznan. Towarz. Przyjaciol Nauk, Wydzial Mat. Przyrod. Prace Komisji Mat. Przyrod.*, **9**, 27–35 (1962).
25. W. Vanselow and J. A. Leermakers. U.S. pat. 2,732,304/1956.
26. S. C. Slifkin. U.S. pat. 2,459,136/1949.

27. S. E. Sheppard and W. Vanselow. U.S. pat. 1,939,232/1933.
28. S. E. Sheppard and W. Vanselow. U.S. pat. 1,976,302/1934.
29. S. E. Sheppard and W. Vanselow. U.S. pat. 2,095,839/1937.
30. L. Suchow and S. L. Herch. U.S. pat. 2,700,610/1955.
31. J. Y. MacDonald. *J. Chem. Soc.*, **1936**, 832–838.
32. P. A. van der Meulen and P. B. Gilman, Jr. U.S. pat. 2,933,389/1960.
33. F. Formstecher. *Phot. Korr.*, **63**, 129 (1927).
34. P. B. Gilman, Jr., P. A. Vaughan and P. A. van der Meulen. *Phot. Sci. Eng.*, **3**, 215–220 (1959).
35. P. A. van der Meulen and R. H. Brill. *Phot. Sci. Eng.*, **2**, 121–127 (1958).
36. F. Frankenburger and G. Rössler. U.S. pat. 1,738,530/1929.
37. P. A. van der Meulen and R. C. Countryman. *Phot. Eng.*, **4**, 104–112 (1953).
38. S. E. Sheppard and W. Vanselow. U.S. pat. 2,019,737/1935.
39. J. V. Morgan. U.S. pat. 3,026,218/1962.
40. E. Weyde. U.S. pat. 2,084,420/1937.
41. A. Schoen. U.S. pat. 2,414,839/1947.
42. W. Wojciak. *Bull. Amis. Sci. Letters Poznan*, Ser. B, **14**, 295–305 (1958).
43. W. Wojciak. *Poznan. Towarz. Przyjaciol Nauk, Wydzial Mat. Przyrod. Prace Komisji Mat. Przyrod.*, **7**, 29–41 (1958).
44. R. I. Dawood and A. J. Forty. *Phil. Mag.*, **8**, 1003–1008 (1963).
45. W. Wojciak and J. Giebel. *Poznan Towarz. Przyjaciol Nauk, Wydzial Mat. Przyrod. Prace Komisji Mat. Przyrod.*, **7**, 9–23 (1959).
46. A. J. Forty, R. I. Dawood, and M. R. Tubbs. *J. Sci. Instr.*, **41**, 274–276 (1964).
47. R. A. Peters. U.S. pat. 2,967,105/1961.
48. Kodak-Pathé. Fr. pat. 728,099/1931.
49. J. H. de Boer and C. J. Dippel. U.S. pat. 2,057,016/1936.
50. W. J. G. Farrer. *Phot. J.*, **76**, 486–492 (1936).
51. J. A. Thom. *Phot. J.*, **86B**, 100–108 (1946).
52. J. A. Thom. *Sci. Ind. Phot.*, **17**, 193–204 (1946).
53. E. Brauer and H. J. Wehran. *Phot. Korr.*, **93**, 67–70 (1957).
54. S. E. Sheppard and H. J. Dietz. U.S. pat. 1,880,503/1932.
55. G. Burley. *J. Res. Nat. Bur. Std.*, **A67**, 301–307 (1963).
56. Y. Tomoda, M. Kawasaki, T. Otsu, and Y. Takahashi. *Tokyo Kogyo Shikensko Hokoku*, **55**, 1–8 (1960).
57. Y. Tomoda and M. Kawasaki. *Nippon Shashin Gakkai Kaishi*, **21**, 138–142 (1958).
58. M. Kawasaki. *Nippon Shashin Gakkai Kaishi*, **25**, 82–88 (1962).
59. Y. Tomoda, N. Nakamura, and M. Kawasaki. *Tokyo Kogyo Shikensko Hokoku*, **53**, 261–268 (1958).
60. G. D. Patterson and H. M. Stark. U.S. pat. 2,757,069/1956.
61. M. Levy and H. Schulze. U.S. pat. 2,759,819/1956.
62. M. Levy. U.S. pat. 2,739,893/1956.
63. M. Levy and H. Schulze. U.S. pat. 2,758,028/1956.
64. M. Levy and H. Schulze. U.S. pat. 2,799,582/1957.
65. M. Levy. U.S. pat. 2,887,381/1959.
66. M. Levy. U.S. pat. 2,835,577/1958.
67. M. Levy. U.S. pat. 2,756,146/1956.
68. M. Levy and N. A. Kidd. U.S. pat. 2,841,494/1958.
69. V. I. Sheberstov. *Zh. nauchn. Prikl. Fotogr. Kinematogr.*, **7**, 141–142 (1962).
70. E. Roederer. *Z. Anorg. Chem.*, **226**, 145–167 (1936).

71. J. Eggert.   *Sci. Inds. Phot.*, **23A**, 227–236 (1952).
72. J. Eggert.   *Fundamental Mechanisms of Photographic Sensitivity*, pp. 94–98, Butterworth's Scientific Publications, London, 1951.
73. J. Eggert.   U.S. pat. 2,703,283/1955.
74. Y. Tomoda.   *Nippon Shashin Gakkai Kaishi*, **22**, 78–82 (1959).
75. S. E. Sheppard and L. W. Eberlin.   U.S. pat. 1,934,451/1933.
76. T. R. Cochran.   U.S. pat. 2,427,443/1947.
77. L. Chalkley.   *J. Opt. Soc. Am.*, **44**, 699–702 (1954).
78. L. Chalkley.   *J. Phys. Chem.*, **56**, 1084–1086 (1952).
79. L. Chalkley.   U.S. pat. 2,981,622/1961.
80. L. Chalkley.   U.S. pat. 2,895,892/1959.
81. Anon.   *Chem. Week*, **91**, 85–86 (1962).
82. F. Reinhart.   *Glas-Email-Keramo-Tech.*, **7**, 153–156, 208–210 (1956).
83. R. H. Dalton.   U.S. pat. 2,326,012/1945.
84. R. H. Dalton.   U.S. pat. 2,422,472/1947.
85. S. D. Stookey.   U.S. pat. 2,515,937/1950.
86. S. D. Stookey.   U.S. pat. 2,515,938/1950; Can. pat. 442,273/1947.
87. W. H. Armistead.   U.S. pat. 2,515,936/1950; Can. pat. 442,272/1947.
88. S. D. Stookey.   U.S. pat. 2,515,942/1950; Brit. pat. 597,089/1943; Can. pat. 444,616/1947.
89. G. Miyake, S. Kuwayama, and M. Yagi.   Japan. pat. 5022/1962 and 5023/1962.
90. S. D. Stookey.   U.S. pat. 2,515,275/1950.
91. V. A. Borgman and V. G. Chistoserdov.   *Opt. i Spectroskopiya*, **13**, 233–235, 421–424 (1962).
92. K. H. Sun and N. J. Kreidl.   *The Glass Industry*, **33**, 511–514, 546, 589–594, 614, 651–653, 674 (1952).
93. S. D. Stookey.   *Ind. Eng. Chem.*, **41**, 856–861 (1949).
94. M. Tashiro and N. Soga.   *Kogyo Kagaku Zasshi*, **65**, 337–346 (1962).
95. C. Gottfried.   *Glastech. Ber.*, **6**, 177–183 (1928).
96. L. Riedel and E. Zschimmer.   *Keram. Rundschau*, **37**, No. 12, 14, 16, 32, 34, 37 (1929).
97. H. P. Rooksby.   *J. Soc. Glass Technol.*, **16**, 171–81 (1932).
98. G. Mie.   *Annalen der Physik*, IV, 25, 377 (1908).
99. K. Riess, W. C. Bosch and T. T. Reboul.   *Am. J. Phys.*, **16**, 399–403 (1948).
100. S. D. Stookey.   *J. Am. Ceram. Soc.*, **32**, 246–249 (1949).
101. S. D. Stookey.   *Ind. Eng. Chem.*, **45**, 115–118 (1953).
102. S. D. Stookey.   U.S. pat. 2,515,939/1950.
103. S. D. Stookey.   U.S. pat. 2,515,940/1950.
104. S. D. Stookey.   U.S. pat. 2,515,941/1950.
105. S. D. Stookey.   U.S. pat. 2,515,943/1950.
106. R. D. Maurer.   *J. Chem. Phys.*, **31**, 444–448 (1959).
107. S. D. Stookey.   *Chem. Eng. News*, 116–125, June 19 (1961).
108. R. D. Maurer.   *J. Appl. Phys.*, **29**, 1–8 (1958).
109. F. W. Schuler.   *Chem. Eng. Progress*, **52**, 210–212 (1956).
110. N. Lazar.   *Product Engineering*, July 11, 1960, 66–70.
111. M. Byer.   *Material and Methods*, **43**, 134–137 (1956).
112. S. D. Stookey.   *Ind. Eng. Chem.*, **46**, 174–176 (1954).
113. W. A. Weyl, J. H. Schulman, R. J. Ginther, and L. W. Evans.   *Trans. Electrochem. Soc.*, **95**, 70–79 (1949).

114. J. H. Schulman, R. J. Ginther, C. C. Klick, and E. W. Claffy. *The Glass Industry*, **32**, 234A (1951).
115. J. H. Schulman, R. J. Ginther, and L. W. Evans. U.S. pat. 2,524,839/1950.
116. S. D. Stookey. U.S. pat. 2,732,298/1956.
117. H. G. Ross and F. W. Schuler. U.S. pat. 2,904,432/1959.
118. S. D. Stookey. U.S. pat. 2,911,749/1959.
119. Corning Glass Works. Ger. pat. 965,266/1957.
120. A. C. McCloskey. U.S. pat. 1,213,925/1917.
121. J. Rzymkowski. *Sci. Ind. Phot.*, **22**, 125–127 (1951).
122. T. B. Copestake and N. Uri. *Proc. Roy. Soc. (London)*, **A228**, 252–263 (1955).
123. A. W. Adamson and A. H. Sporer. *J. Am. Chem. Soc.*, **80**, 3865–3870 (1958).
124. G. H. Cartledge and W. P. Ericks. *J. Am. Chem. Soc.*, **58**, 2061–2065 (1936).
125. J. L. Lambert. *U.S. Govt. Res. Rep.* 31,455 (1959).
126. K. C. D. Hickman and L. A. Staib. U.S. pat. 1,962,307/1934.
127. N. Tanaka, Y. Kikuchi, and Y. Usvi. *Z. Physik. Chem.* **37**, 133–134 (1963).
128. L. Parts, R. L. Pruett, and W. R. Myers. U.S. pat. 3,101,360/1963.
129. A. J. Allmand and W. W. Webb. *J. Chem. Soc.*, **1929**, 1518–1531, 1531–1537.
130. C. A. Parker and C. G. Hatchard. *J. Phys. Chem.*, **63**, 22–26 (1959).
131. G. B. Porter, J. G. W. Doering, and S. Karanka. *J. Am. Chem. Soc.*, **84**, 4027–4029 (1962).
132. A. Hnatek. *Phot. Korr.*, **92**, 3–8 (1956).
133. J. Lee and H. H. Seliger. *J. Chem. Phys.*, **40**, 519–523 (1964).
134. G. V. Buxton, S. P. Wilford, and R. J. Williams. *J. Chem. Soc.*, **1962**, 4957–4962.
135. K. G. Mathai and E. Rabinowitch. *J. Phys. Chem.*, **66**, 663–664 (1962).
136. R. Omoto. U.S. pat. 1,805,592/1931.
137. J. Boettner and T. Dicke. U.S. pat. 557,047/1896.
138. W. Zindler. Brit. pat. 922,595/1963; Fr. pat. 1,227,855/1960; Ger. pat. 1,096,195/1960.
139. W. Zindler. Brit. pat. 935,428/1963.
140. G. Kögel. U.S. pat. 1,776,155/1930; Brit. pat. 302,282/1928.
141. G. Kögel. *Brit. J. Phot.*, **76**, 763 (1929).
142. M. P. Schmidt. U.S. pat. 2,264,334/1941.
143. A. L. Lippert and W. P. Hall. U.S. pat. 2,121,205/1938.
144. E. N. Mason and D. J. Norman. Brit. pat. 573,975/1945.
145. M. H. Dickerson. U.S. pat. 2,935,403/1960.
146. A. Eichorn. U.S. pat. 2,848,327/1958.
147. H. H. Hanson. U.S. pat. 2,866,707/1958.
148. S. M. Beekman and J. F. Cipriand. U.S. pat. 2,964,403/1960.
149. C. A. Crowley and J. B. Mullen. U.S. pat. 2,317,521/1943.
150. E. Jahoda. U.S. pat. 2,433,515/1947.
151. O. Süs, W. Neugebauer, H. Böttger, F. Enderman, and W. Schäfer. U.S. pat. 2,813,792/1957.
152. R. B. West. U.S. pat. 625,527/1899.
153. R. B. Barnes, G. P. Ham, and L. P. Moore. U.S. pat. 2,238,301/1941.
154. J. Holden. Brit pat. 418,369/1934.
155. E. N. Mason and Sons, Ltd. Brit. pat. 462,554/1937.
156. A. P. Reynolds. U.S. pat. 2,093,738/1937.
157. A. P. Reynolds. U.S. pat. 2,126,504/1938.
158. C. A. Crowley and G. H. Goodyear. U.S. pat. 2,323,798/1943.

159. C. A. Crowley and G. H. Goodyear.   U.S. pat. 2,323,799/1943.
160. R. B. Barnes, G. P. Ham, and L. P. Moore.   U.S. pat. 2,221,628/1940.
161. E. Jahoda.   U.S. pat. 2,517,111/1950.
162. D. E. Whitlock and J. F. Kienast.   U.S. pat. 2,209,548/1940.
163. Y. Tomoda.   *J. Japan Tech. Assoc. Pulp Paper Ind.*, **4**, No. 5, 20–22 (1950).
164. Y. Tomoda.   *J. Chem. Soc. Japan, Ind. Chem. Sec.*, **54**, 34–36 (1951).
165. A. Hnatek.   *Phot. Korr.*, **91**, 111–115 (1955).
166. O. Süs.   U.S. pat. 2,025,675/1935.
167. G. W. Miles.   U.S. pat. 1,518,997/1924.
168. G. P. Ham.   U.S. pat. 2,165,166/1939.
169. G. P. Ham.   U.S. pat. 2,172,319/1939.
170. W. O. Wilson.   U.S. pat. 2,398,986/1946.
171. G. P. Ham and R. B. Barnes.   U.S. pat. 2,209,917/1940.
172. R. B. Barnes.   U.S. pat. 2,199,368/1940.
173. H. J. Brunk.   U.S. pat. 3,140,950/1964.
174. A. Hnatek.   *Phot. Korr.*, **87**, 37–38, 40–42, 44–45 (1951).
175. Y. Tomoda and M. Kawasaki.   *Rept. Gov. Chem. Ind. Res. Inst. Tokyo*, **47**, 31–36, 145–150, 348–354 (1952).
176. J. L. Cazares.   U.S. pat. 1,625,349/1927.
177. R. Schwarz and K. Tede.   *Ber.*, **60B**, 69–72 (1927).
178. S. Suzuki.   *J. Chem. Soc. Japan, Ind. Chem. Sec.*, **55**, 755–757 (1952).
179. H. D. Murray.   *Chem. Ind.*, 645–646 (1940).
180. M. Rakos.   *Sb. Ved. Prac. Vysokej Skoly Tech. Kosiciach*, **4**, No. 1, 29–38 (1960).
181. T. Mukaibo and S. Tsujimura.   *Chem. Soc. Japan, Ind. Chem. Sec.*, **56**, 224–225 (1953).
182. K. Ono.   Japan pat. 128, 662.
183. J. S. Reichert.   U.S. pat. 1,998,883/1935.
184. W. M. Hinman.   U.S. pat. 2,135,872/1938.
185. J. R. Fisher.   U.S. pat. 2,466,799/1949.
186. O. D. Lantz.   U.S. pat. 2,931,724/1960.
187. W. L. Sullivan.   U.S. pat. 2,179,026/1939.
188. H. J. Brunk.   U.S. pat. 2,287,763/1942.
189. C. A. Crowley and G. H. Goodyear.   U.S. pat. 2,350,991/1944.
190. H. J. Brunk and M. Dickason.   U.S. pat. 2,196,788/1940.
191. C. A. Crowley and G. H. Goodyear.   U.S. pat. 2,093,421/1937.
192. H. J. Brunk.   U.S. pat. 1,861,298/1932.
193. H. J. Brunk.   U.S. pat. 2,145,752/1939.
194. H. D. Murray.   U.S. pat. 2,014,692/1935.
195. L. R. Harper and D. W. Powell.   Brit. pat. 427,746/1935.
196. L. R. Harper and D. W. Powell.   Brit. pat. 461,893/1947.
197. J. Holden.   U.S. pat. 2,158,422/1939; RE pat. 21,240/1939; Brit. pat. 494,572/1938.
198. J. Holden.   U.S. pat. 2,189,264/1940.
199. J. Holden.   U.S. pat. 2,346,872/1944; Brit. pat. 536,567/1941.
200. C. Fujiyama.   Japan pat. 38–5498/1963.
201. C. Fujiyama.   Japan pat. 38–5497/1963.
202. E. Bertsch.   U.S. pat. 1,500,433/1924.
203. C. A. Crowley and G. H. Goodyear.   U.S. pat. 2,113,423/1938.
204. G. P. Ham and R. B. Barnes.   U.S. pat. 2,166,546/1939.

205. G. A. Hinkel. U.S. pat. 2,188,900/1940; Brit. pat. 539,066/1941.
206. R. B. Barnes. U.S. pat. 2,218,969/1940.
207. R. B. Barnes, L. P. Moore and G. P. Ham. U.S. pat. 2,237,084/1941.
208. M. M. P. Vallen and J. M. H. van den Dolder. U.S. pat. 2,443,844/1948; Dutch pat. 54,927/1943.
209. C. A. Crowley and G. H. Goodyear. U.S. pat. 2,137,015/1938.
210. C. A. Crowley and G. H. Goodyear. U.S. pat. 2,130,071/1938.
211. C. A. Crowley and G. H. Goodyear. U.S. pat. 2,130,070/1938.
212. A. R. A. Beeber and R. M. Gold. U.S. pat. 2,852,377/1958.
213. H. Warman and D. S. Milborne. U.S. pat. 2,874,911/1959; Ger. pat. 1,088,806/1960.
214. R. E. Kwech. U.S. pat. 1,877,246/1932.
215. R. Fritsche. U.S. pat. 1,712,428/1929.
216. H. P. Husch. U.S. pat. 2,444,567/1948.
217. A. Schoen. U.S. pat. 2,611,701/1952.
218. C. N. Bennett. *Home Photographer*, 7, 289, 312 (1939).
219. C. B. Neblette. *Photography, its Principles and Practice*, 4th edition, p. 695, D. van Nostrand Co., New York, 1942.
220. R. Fairthorne. *Miniature Camera Mag.*, 6, 389 (1942).
221. R. B. West. U.S. pat. 674,227/1901.
222. H. Denstman. *Reprographics*, 2(1), 6 (1964).
223. R. J. Scanlan. U.S. pat. 2,495,661/1950.
224. W. Schröter. U.S. pat. 585,452/1897.
225. F. I. Rubricius. U.S. pat. 1,126,872/1915.
226. G. W. Leighton and C. S. Babcock. U.S. pat. 1,225,146/1917.
227. J. F. Kienast. U.S. pat. 2,578,075/1951.
228. C. Rossi. U.S. pat. 2,689,792/1954; Can. pat. 548,960/1957.
229. S. C. &. P. Harding Ltd. and W. P. Leuch. Brit. pat. 557,361/1943.
230. H. Jonker, R. J. H. Alink, and T. W. van Rijssel. U.S. pat. 2,738,272/1956.
231. H. Jonker, R. J. H. Alink, and T. W. van Rijssel. U.S. pat. 2,929,709/1960.
232. N. N. Tumanov. U.S.S.R. pat. 105,728.
233. E. Devores. U.S. pat. 2,484,019/1949.
234. J. Kosar. U.S. pat. 3,038,803/1962.
235. E. Gretener and C. Rossi. U.S. pat. 2,829,051/1958.
236. M. P. L. Martinez. U.S. pat. 2,886,435/1959.
237. R. J. H. Alink. U.S. pat. 2,291,130/1942; Brit. pat. 538,245/1941; Dutch pat. 57,651/1945.
238. L. P. Clerc. *Photography, Theory and Practice*, Pitman and Sons, Ltd., London, 1954.
239. A. E. Fletcher. *Brit. J. Phot.*, 88, 445–446 (1941).
240. S. Blumann. *Brit. J. Phot.*, 89, 30 (1942); *Brit. J. Phot.*, 90, 22 (1943).
241. H. V. Schieren. *Am. Phot.*, 37, No. 10, 18–19 (1943).
242. H. L. Fichter, M. H. Dickerson, and R. H. Sprague. *Phot. Sci. Eng.*, 3, 299–301 (1959).
243. V. M. Perikov. *Poligr. Prvizv.*, No. 213, 21–33 (1940).
244. P. C. Smethurst. *Process. Engr. Monthly*, 54, 142–145 (1947).
245. M. Martinez. U.S. pat. 1,944,293/1934.
246. E. Brown. *Brit. J. Phot.*, 86, 719–721 (1939).
247. W. Fuchs. Brit. pat. 556,705/1943.

2

Dichromated Colloids

2.1 DICHROMATED-COLLOID LAYERS

It has long been known that water soluble chromates and dichromates, when mixed with certain organic substances of animal or vegetable origin such as gelatin, fish glue, gum arabic, or shellac, and dried, produce films which are considerably affected by light. If such a film is subjected to suitable radiation and filtered through a negative, the film becomes hardened and less soluble in areas which were exposed to the radiation, so that when washed with an appropriate solvent, only those areas which have been exposed to light remain on the supporting material. These residual parts form a relief image, whose physical and chemical properties differ from the original layer.

For instance, dichromated gelatin, which is soluble in water before exposure to light, becomes insoluble after the exposure, or substances such as sugar, dextrin, or gum, treated with dichromate, lose their tackiness when exposed to actinic radiation (1,2).

2.1a *Historical Review*

Since the light sensitivity of dichromates in the presence of organic matter was discovered by Suckow (1830), this field has been the subject of numerous investigations, and forms the basis not only of many photo-mechanical processes but also a number of color printing methods are derived from it (3,4).

First to suggest using this phenomenon for photographic purposes was Scot Mungo Ponton (1839). He impregnated a sheet of paper with a solution of potassium dichromate and exposed it under an object to light. After removing the unreduced dichromate by washing, a brown image resulting from chemical reaction between the dichromate and the size of the paper remained. This was about the time when Frenchman Louis Jacques Mandé Daguerre made his first photographs in Paris and William Henry Fox Talbot laid the foundation for negative-positive photography.

The next few years were rich in photographic discoveries, and many improvements were suggested. Becquerel sized paper with dichromated starch. On exposure to sun, the exposed starch became insoluble, forming an intense colored image after washing and treatment with an iodine solution; the visible image consisted of the deep blue starch-iodine complex. Later he found that the reduction products of dichromates have a hardening effect also on other organic substances, for example, gelatin, casein, albumen.

Since he was interested in photography, Fox Talbot put these discoveries to practical use and in 1852 patented a photoengraving process, called by him "photoglyphy." This etching process consisted of coating steel or copper plates with a solution of gelatin and potassium dichromate. When exposed to daylight under an object, like leaves of plants, the exposed sections became water-insoluble and only the nonimage parts could be removed by washing in warm water, laying bare the metal plate at these points. The image portions, serving as resist, protected the metal from the action of platinic chloride, or later, ferric chloride, etching solution, which engraved the areas uncovered by the tanned gelatin. The action of the etching solution was controlled by the addition of small amounts of water.

After etching, the light-hardened gelatin stencil was removed leaving an intaglio image in metal, which accepted printing ink. By placing a black gauze between the original and an emulsion, thereby laying the foundation for later screen processes, Talbot obtained halftones. This method, later modified by a Czech, Karel Václav Klič, is used to this day in the production of photogravure plates.

2.1b *Carbon Printing*

In 1855, French engineer and chemist Alphons Louis Pointevin, to whom we also owe the first method of photolithography, added powdered carbon to the sensitized gelatin solution, making an advance in the direction of obtaining visible and permanent images. After the exposure, the carbon particles remained imbedded in the tanned gelatin. Since that time, this now-classical method of printing has been called "carbon printing," and was the beginning of the many processes still practiced at the present time. In its simplest form, a paper tissue is coated with a moderately hard and pigmented gelatin and sensitized shortly before use by a solution of potassium or ammonium dichromate. By changing the concentration of dichromate, the contrast of the image could be varied to a certain degree. After drying and exposure to light, the tissue is soaked in water for a short time and then the unexposed, and thus not hardened, parts are washed away with warm water. Symmes pointed out that drying is not necessary (5).

The hardening of the gelatin by exposure to light starts at the surface, the lower parts remaining soluble for a longer time; this causes, as pointed out by Laborde in 1857, the halftones and highlights to be reproduced very poorly or lost completely. Attempts have been made to eliminate this difficulty by exposing the sensitized material through the support. In this case, the hardening starts from the support and the image adheres to the base material. Since the paper support was only slightly transparent, the exposure time was extremely long—a serious disadvantage and the reason why carbon printing was not generally accepted. A slight improvement was obtained by transparentizing the paper with paraffin oil after sensitizing.

The solution to this problem in carbon printing was the transfer of the exposed coating on another paper support with a gelatin layer, originally suggested by Fargier (1860) and perfected by Sir Joseph Swan (1864), who showed that more delicate tones could be retained by introducing single and double transfer. This was the first successful, practical, and relatively easy method of producing carbon prints.

In order to give the tissue more pliancy, Swan also suggested the addition of sugar to the coating solution. This practice is used to this day, although it can be replaced by other polyalcohols, such as glycerin.

The pigments in the gelatin sheet can be any color desired. They are usually carbon, or of inorganic origin (titanium oxide, chrome green and chrome yellow, Prussian blue, ultramarine, red and yellow ochre, aluminum sodium silicate, and sodium pentasulfide [6]), but mixing with insoluble organic dyes, such as certain azo dyes or phthalocyanine dyes or dyes laked with alumina, kaolin, or phosphotungstic acid in various proportions, is possible, in order to obtain the right color for artistic effects. From this point of view, the carbon process is a most flexible printing process, giving a wide choice of color and contrast, according to the personal taste of the photographer (7). The pigments and dyes used for carbon printing must, of course, be resistant to light, and they must be readily dispersible in gelatin solution. Certain pigments may be found to react with dichromate, causing spontaneous insolubilization without any exposure. In addition, for natural-color photography it would be necessary to use pigments and dyes of desired spectral characteristics

(8,9). As a rule, the images are made in yellow, magenta, and cyan and then superimposed in register with one another.

Since the first basic experiments in carbon printing, there has been no basic change in the process. The fundamental reactions involved, however, have been varied and combined into many modifications. Scores of people have worked out countless improvements based on the ideas of the pioneers, and within a few years after the first experiments the patent offices overflowed with applications related to this—for that time—revolutionary process. Davies in 1864 simplified the process by using a waterproof surface for transfer, and Sawyer, ten years later, preferred a flexible support.

2.1c *Other Processes*

About the time that Davies simplified the carbon printing process, Marion introduced his "Mariotype"; this variation of carbon printing consisted of pressing, after the exposure, dichromate-sensitized paper on a separate pigmented gelatin layer. After leaving this sandwich in intimate contact for several hours, the insolubilized pigmented gelatin adhered to the image while the unhardened parts were washed away with warm water. In 1894 V. Artigue of Paris introduced his "velour charbon" process, designed to do away with the necessity of transferring the printed tissue to a temporary support for development. In 1899 Thomas Manly modified mariotype in his "Ozotype" process. He exposed a sheet of dichromated transfer paper under a negative to get a visible image and applied it to a sheet of carbon tissue previously soaked in an acid solution of hydroquinone. After drying and subsequent soaking in cold water, the image was developed by dissolving away the untanned gelatin as in the carbon process.

In 1905, T. Manly found that silver images could be used to reduce dichromates and made pigment images directly from bromide prints. In this process, called the "Ozobrome" process, a sheet of pigmented paper sensitized with an acid solution containing a dichromate, potassium ferricyanide, and soluble bromide, is pressed into intimate contact with the silver image on a bromide paper.

The chemical actions responsible for hardening are still, as in all dichromated colloid processes, somewhat obscure. By placing the sensitized tissue in contact with the wet bromide print, the sensitizer diffuses to the surface of the bromide print, where the silver image is bleached by the combined action of ferricyanide and bromide:

$$K_3Fe(CN)_6 + KBr + Ag = AgBr + K_4Fe(CN)_6 \qquad (1)$$

The amount of reduced ferricyanide is proportional to the quantity of silver present in the bromide print. The ferrocyanide formed by this action migrates back into the pigmented tissue where it is re-oxidized by the dichromate with the consequent formation of a trivalent chromium compound which hardens gelatin areas corresponding to image areas on the bromide print. The chemical changes are complicated, and, needless to say, any disturbance will cause serious difficulties.

After a certain time, the tissue is stripped from the bromide print and transferred to a temporary support (waxed celluloid) and washed in hot water to remove the untanned sections and leave a colored image in relief. After drying and rewetting in cold water, the image is squeegeed to a sheet of damp gelatin-coated paper. In the same way, in the case of multicolor reproduction, the second and third monochrome image is applied to complete the tricolor print from a set of separation negatives.

The Ozotype and Ozobrom processes are forerunners of the present day carbro process which possesses all the tone-rendering advantages of carbon printing without its slow speed. It is also of interest to note that the principles of carbon printing are widely employed in several photo-mechanical methods.

The discoveries of E. H. Farmer (1894), C. Welborne Piper (1907), and E. F. Mortimer (1911) led to the development of the bromoil process, which, utilizing the same material and procedure as the carbro process, is based on the fact that tanned gelatin sections will absorb printing inks, and the unexposed and unhardened portions will repel the ink. Similar to the bromoil is the oleotype. Instead of incorporating the pigment in the gelatin, the hardened image is made visible by application of a greasy ink which is, as in the bromoil process, repelled by the swollen, unexposed gelatin and clings only to the hardened and the least swollen parts of the image. The ink image on the original plate can then be transferred to a sheet of paper and in this way multiple copies can be made.

In another application, the tanned image is made visible by powdering the surface of an exposed dichromated gelatin coating with resin pigments which will stick only to the unhardened parts of the image. This process was called resinotype. To the same category belongs also the pinatype and the hydrotype processes using water solution of dyes to make the image visible. These methods were employed chiefly for producing multicolor transparencies.

2.1d   *Collotype*

In 1855 Alphonse Pointevin introduced another photomechanical printing process, based on the formation of reticulation grains of very fine wrinkles over the whole surface of dichromated gelatin. This reticulation appears during closely controlled drying at elevated temperatures (20 to 40°C). The wrinkles are so fine that they cannot be distinguished by the naked eye. During the exposure to a continuous-tone laterally reversed negative, the gelatin is hardened in proportion to the amount of light passing through the negative. According to the degree of hardening, the exposed parts accept different quantities of ink, and the unexposed portions, by being kept moist with water and glycerin, repel the ink. Thus the process is based on the antipathy between grease and water. The least tanned highlight areas absorb more of the glycerin-water solution than do the shadows and will accept less lithographic ink, which is applied with a gelatin roller. In sections of intermediate tanning, the quantity of ink absorbed will be less than that absorbed by fully exposed parts, in direct ratio to the amount of actinic light which has passed through the negative (10).

This procedure provides a plate for printing, and up to 2000 impressions can be obtained from one plate. The durability of the dichromated-gelatin image can be increased by the hardening of the gelatin layer with dialdehydes or ketoaldehydes (11).

The Collotype process, which has been known also as heliotype, lichtdruck, photogelatin, etc., was made commercially practicable by the German photographer Joseph Albert (1825–1886) in 1873 and called albertype. Constant research and introduction of better equipment have improved this method of printing to such a degree that it has become an important commercial process.

Collotype reproduces delicate details and the atmosphere of the original picture with remarkable fidelity, and is mainly used for fine art reproductions. Although it is very difficult to control, its capacity for giving depth of color is unsurpassed by any other printing method and for its screenless appearance it is claimed to be the ideal color reproduction process.

All dichromated-colloid processes are considerably less sensitive to light than silver halide emulsions and require relatively long exposures to strong actinic light. Nevertheless, because of the superior quality of their tone rendition, they have received much attention in the past, both before and after the turn of the century, and in many instances are used even at the present time.

2.2 COMPOSITION OF SENSITIZING SOLUTION

The sensitizing solution for dichromated-colloid layers consists of an organic colloid dissolved in a solvent, usually water; to this solution, a soluble chromate or dichromate is added. The extent of the photochemical hardening process of the coated layers can be controlled by the composition of the sensitizing solution.

2.2a Chromates and Dichromates

All chromates or dichromates soluble in water produce together with organic colloids solutions capable of forming photosensitive layers. Most commonly used for sensitizing colloids is ammonium dichromate $(NH_4)_2Cr_2O_7$. It forms bright orange-red monoclinic crystals which, when heated to 180°C, decompose violently into chromic trioxide, nitrogen, and water:

$$(NH_4)_2Cr_2O_7 = Cr_2O_3 + N_2 + 4H_2O \qquad (2)$$

If heated to 225°C, the decomposition becomes self-sustaining with spectacular swelling and evolution of heat.

Ammonium dichromate is a flammable solid which can explode in contact with many substances. The crystals are unaffected by exposure to air and light and are odorless. An aqueous saturated solution contains 30.8 grams per 100 cc at 15°C and 89 grams per 100 cc at 30°C. The high solubility of ammonium dichromate in water permits high concentrations in the presence of colloids without crystallization taking place when the coating is dried. This might be one reason for the slightly higher sensitivity of solutions sensitized with the ammonium salt. Another possible reason for the general assumption that ammonium dichromate gives the greatest printing speed is the fact that layers containing the ammonium salt have a lower pH than layers prepared with potassium or sodium dichromate. The pH of the ammonium dichromate solution is about 4.5.

Next in sensitivity is potassium dichromate, $K_2Cr_2O_7$, which forms large garnet-red crystals with a bitter, metallic taste. Potassium dichromate may be obtained by adding the requisite amount of sulphuric acid to a saturated solution of potassium chromate. On cooling the potassium dichromate crystallizes out. The crystals are soluble in water and insoluble in alcohol.

The potassium salt is preferred for sensitizing the carbon-gelatin tissue used in photogravure, whereas ammonium dichromate was found to be superior in photolithography, where it is used with albumin or gum arabic, and in photoengraving, mixed with fish glue.

Little use seems to be made of sodium dichromate, $Na_2Cr_2O_7 \cdot 2H_2O$. This salt is generally considered unsatisfactory for sensitizing purposes because of its delinquescent nature. It forms reddish to bright orange crystalline fragments, which are monoclinic. On prolonged heating, they lose the water of crystallization. Sodium dichromate is more easily soluble and cheaper than potassium salt, but is more difficult to purify.

Commercial samples of dichromates often contain free acid, and, consequently, give a more acid reaction than the pure dichromates. Even when pure dichromates are used, the pH of different samples may vary and cause changes in the speed and keeping quality of the sensitized layers. Howard and Wensley (12) in their investigation on the sensitizing of carbon tissue, found that on adjusting the strength of ammonium dichromate to 2.5 per cent, it had the same speed, contrast, and keeping quality as 3.5 per cent potassium dichromate. Sodium dichromate appeared to be equivalent to potassium salt in all respects, and the investigators expressed a doubt that the hygroscopic qualities of the sodium salt matter as much as some people suppose. Cox and Howard came to similar conclusions (13); their results are summarized in Table 2.1.

TABLE *2.1.* Comparative Sensitivities of Chromates and Dichromates in Different Colloids

	Albumin	Gum Arabic	Process Glue
Ammonium dichromate	100	100	100
Ammonium chromate	100	72	100
Potassium dichromate	20	46	65
Potassium chromate	0	0	12
Sodium dichromate	28	100	100
Sodium chromate	0	0	12

Chromates and dichromates, like all chromium compounds, are poisonous. Dermal contact with their solutions at the strength normally used in the photographic or printing industry can cause painful skin sores. Since the chromate and dichromate ions can be absorbed through the skin and act as a protein precipitant, it is irritant in action and can produce dermatitis and local ulceration to a serious degree. The first symptoms of this injury, commonly called "chromic poisoning," are shown by irritation of the skin between the fingers, on the roots of the nails, in the creases of the knuckles, and on the hairy parts of the back of the hands and forearms. This is followed by the formation of watery pimples. Sometimes people become sensitive to dichromate solutions after handling them for a long time without any difficulties. In more serious lesions, ulcers are formed on the hands and forearms; these are known as "chrome holes." The ulcers penetrate deep into the skin, but are not painful and interfere with work only when they occur on the knuckles. If the person avoids further contact with the solutions, the ulcers heal in a few weeks with a permanent scar. At least one case has been reported (14) where the rash of dermatitis disappeared completely in three days after injection of 30/1000 units of penicillin into the hip.

Persons who have been exposed to splashes of chromium compounds should wash the affected areas as soon as possible with adequate quantities of water and carbolic soap, and follow by washing with hydrogen peroxide, which decomposes the dichromate. Sometimes reducing agents, such as sodium bisulfite, are recommended to reduce chromates to less toxic trivalent compounds (15,16).

2.2b *Organic Colloids (General)*

It is known that not all grades of gelatin or other colloids can be used. It is necessary that the colloids have certain properties, which may vary according to the application, but, generally, it is required that the colloid be easily oxidized by dichromates and form, after drying, a continuous flexible film without excessive hygroscopicity. In addition, the film must not be tacky when subjected to high relative humidity and must transmit actinic radiation to a high degree. The solubility of the colloid in the particular solvent is also of importance. Many grades of gelatin are not usable because of their limited solubility in water (17,18), since the difference in solubility between exposed and unexposed parts of the sensitive layer is of vital importance for the quality of the print.

Elöd and Berczeli (19) investigated the effect of the micellar size and of the decomposition products of gelatin on light sensitivity and found that less soluble gelatins have a higher light sensitivity. Rapid solution rate and high light sensitivity seem to be mutually exclusive. Figure 2.1, taken from Elöd and Berczeli's work, shows the influence of the disintegration of the polypeptide chain on the light sensitivity. It can be assumed that the light-hardening ability of a particular colloid will increase with the size of the molecule and decrease by introducing solubilizing groups into the same molecule.

Generally we can say that colloids which can be hardened by the action of actinic light in the presence of dichromates contain in their molecule one, or a combination, of the following polar groups:

hydroxy-	—OH
carboxy-	—COOH
cabonyl-	=CO
amino-	—NH$_2$

All the organic colloids react with dichromates in a more or less similar manner and are used for one or another of the various photoreproduction

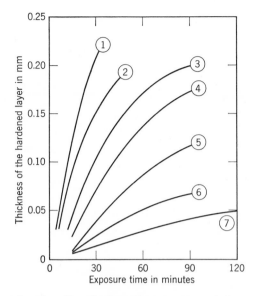

*Figure 2.1. The effect of gelatin disintegration on light sensitivity
(reference 19).*

1. Untreated
2. Heated to 100°C
3. Disintegrated for 1 hr
4. Disintegrated for 2 hr
5. Disintegrated for 3 hr
6. Disintegrated for 6 hr
7. Disintegrated for 12 hr

processes for which their respective qualities render them particularly suitable.

According to their chemical composition, organic colloids used in photomechanical printing processes can be divided in two general groups—proteins and carbohydrates. To the first group belong gelatin, animal glues, albumin, casein, etc., and gum arabic and starch and its derivatives are carbohydrates. Because of their importance, some of these will be discussed in more detail in the hope that it will contribute to the understanding of the complex reactions taking place during the photochemical process.

2.2c *Gelatin*

Gelatin is a product of animal origin derived from collagen by treating waste skin, bones, and connective tissue of animals with calcium hydroxide from one to six months.   The pH of the liquor is approximately 12. Under this treatment, the bulk of the material undergoes irreversible hydrolysis to form gelatin having its isoelectric point at pH 4.9 to 5.0. Gelatin can also be prepared by soaking skins in a dilute acid, e.g., hydrochloric, sulfuric, or phosphoric, for one to two months.   Skins are then washed in water and loaded into cook tanks.   From the liquors obtained, about 50 to 75 per cent water is removed by evaporation.   The gelatin solution that remains is chilled, the gelatin gel is dried, and, when the moisture content is reduced to about 10 per cent, the gelatin is broken down to the required particle size or pulverized.   Acid processing yields gelatin of somewhat different properties; here the amide group $-CONH_2$ is largely unaffected.

Gelatin is generally regarded as a complex chain of amino and imino acids linked together in a partially ordered fashion by polypeptide bonds (20):

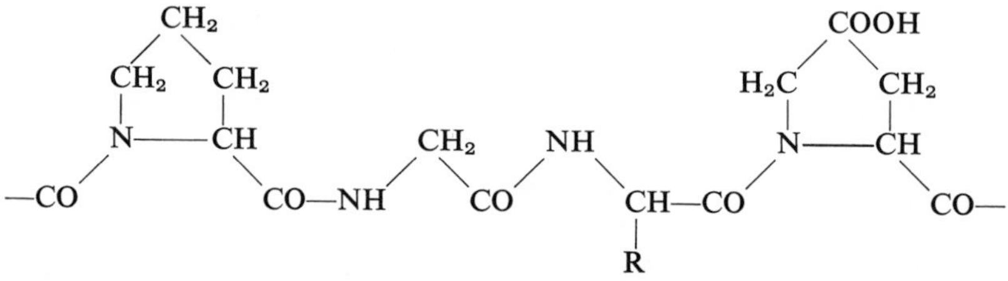

R represents a side chain, such as $-CH_2CH_3$, $-COOH$, or $-NH_2$ of a dibasic or diamino amino acid.

According to the latest chemical analysis (21), about every third residue is glycine, every ninth, hydroxyproline, and every twelfth in a hundred is proline.   Tyrosine, hystidine, and sulfur-containing amino acids are present only in small amounts.

glycine: $NH_2 \cdot CH_2 \cdot COOH$

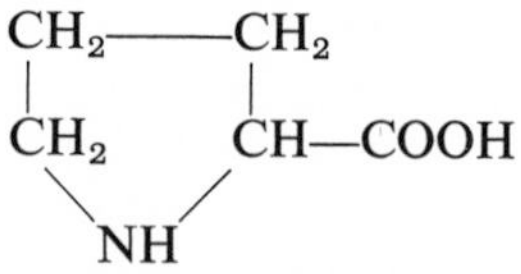

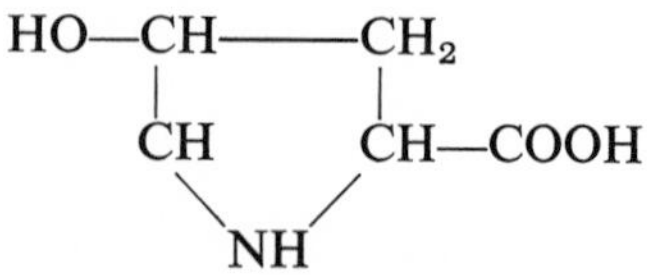

Most gelatins also contain traces of other compounds which may make them suitable for a particular use, as is the case of gelatins used in the preparation of silver halide photographic emulsions. These foreign components may be present in the original material or they are introduced during the manufacturing process in order to obtain required properties.

Gelatin is a natural product and it can be expected that there will be certain chemical differences not only between different types of gelatin but also between different batches of the same type, and that the detailed structure and composition of the polypeptide chain will vary from species to species.

The structural protein in the skin furnishing the gelatin is collagen. The molecular structure of collagen is extremely complicated; however, the essential features have been fairly well established and are generally accepted as being substantially correct (22,23,24). Because of the unbalanced forces on the two sides of the chain and the tendency for a given group always to seek the same environment for maximum stability, the chain takes the form of a helix. Three single helical polypeptide chains wind slowly around each other forming a triple helix. The three chains are held together by the hydrogen bonds formed between an ⟩NH of one chain and a ⟩CO of another chain, as ⟩NH·········O=C⟨ . The hydrogen bond is not a covalent bond, as hydrogen has only one valence. It is simply a force of attraction set up by a hydrogen atom resonating between two strongly electronegative atoms. The hydrogen bond is not strong, but there are many of them. The hydrogen crossbonds can be ruptured by the action of hydrogen peroxide without forming gelatin and making the collagen dispersible in water (25).

The triple helix is called the protofibril of collagen. The protofibrils are held together by bonds formed between the side chains of the amino acid residues. That is, these side chains probably stick out as a fringe from the protofibril, possibly as a result of the compact close packing of the three helical chains. The chief type of bond between protofibrils is possibly due to hydroxyproline, that is a hydrogen bond

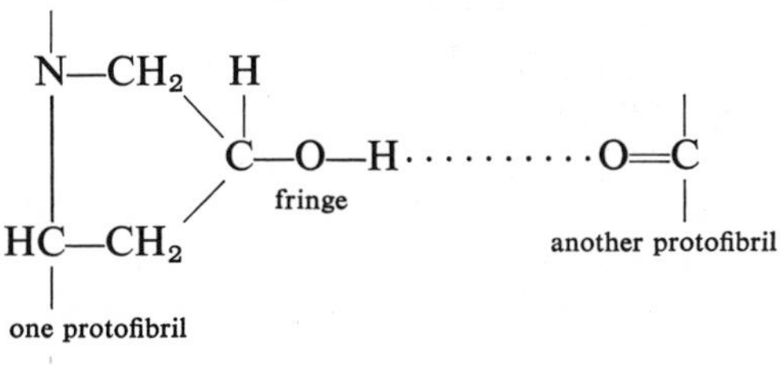

$$
\begin{array}{l}
\mathrm{N-CH_2 \quad H} \\
\qquad\qquad \mathrm{C-O-H\cdots\cdots\cdots O{=}C} \\
\qquad\qquad\quad \text{fringe} \\
\mathrm{HC-CH_2} \qquad\qquad \text{another protofibril} \\
\text{one protofibril}
\end{array}
$$

Other possible types are

the salt linkage $\longrightarrow$ —NH$_3{}^+$ $^-$OOC—

and the ester linkage $\longrightarrow$ $\overset{\displaystyle H}{\underset{\displaystyle }{\diagdown}}\overset{\displaystyle }{\underset{\displaystyle }{\text{C—O—C—}}}\overset{\displaystyle O}{\underset{\displaystyle }{\parallel}}$

These protofibrils, running parallel, form the collagen fibrils which in turn make the fibers. As the five-membered ring of hydroxyproline is highly rigid, its linkage, along with the other possible types, is likely to keep the distance between neighboring protofibrils highly uniform and also make the repeat spacing along the fiber axis exactly the same. It should not be overlooked that the position of these active valence centers between protofibrils is fairly well fixed by the rigidity of the hydrogen-bond structure within the triple helix.

The protofibrils are linear polymers of a unit monomer, designated tropocollagen, which is a macromolecule having the dimensions of 14 × 2800 Å and a molecular weight of about 360,000. Each macromolecule consists of three helical chains winding around each other, each chain having a molecular weight of about 120,000; the three chains are held together by hydrogen bonds.

When collagen fibers are heated or treated with certain chemicals, such as nickel nitrate or potassium thiocyanate, the fibers shrink in the direction of the fiber axis to about one-fourth of the original length. If the chemical treatment becomes more and more drastic, or if the heat-shrunken collagen is heated in water, gelatin is produced. The chemical compositions of collagen and that of gelatin are practically identical. It is believed that during the shrinking process, the crosslink bonds between the protofibrils break first. This results in disorientation of the protofibril lattice, whereupon the protofibrils fold and twist. Finally, the individual chains of the triple chains are separated and some cleavage of the peptide links occurs. The helical structure of the collagen is destroyed, leaving polypeptide chains of irregular shape.

When gelatin is prepared from collagen by cold-lime treatment, followed by neutralization and extraction with water at elevated temperature, it appears most probable that the lime treatment first produces hydrolytic cleavage of the macromolecules making up the protofibrils, followed in the hot water treatment by the breaking of the crosslink bonds between the protofibril segments and the separation of the individual chains of the triple chains. It is questionable whether the crosslink bonds would break in the cold treatment. The conversion of collagen to gelatin is irreversible.

Air-dried gelatin contains 8 to 15 per cent moisture, depending on the conditions under which it was dried. As for dried gelatin in contact with water vapor, the absorbed moisture is a function of the relative humidity of the environment and of some other factors.

The moisture taken up at a fixed relative humidity depends on the pH of the original sol before gelation and drying. It rises rapidly with the pH of the sol from pH 2 to pH 5, and then levels off. This is in contrast to gelatin swelling in aqueous solution; in this case, the swelling increases sharply with increasing pH, drops to a minimum at the isoelectric point and rises again, however, more slowly, at higher alkalinity.

It is generally believed (26) that the polar side chains of amino acid residues such as tyrosine, lysine, arginine, and glutamic acid, provide much of the attraction for the water molecules and thus the number and availability of the polar groups determines the amount of water a protein is able to absorb. The hydrogen-bond-forming capacity of the carbonyl and imido groups is sufficiently saturated in $\diagdown$ NH $\cdots\cdots\cdots$ O$=$C $\diagup$ linkages and the residual attraction of these groups for water is negligible (27,28).

According to Mellon, Korn, and Hoover (29), the moisture is held by different forces depending on the relative humidity. Within the region between 0 and 6 per cent relative humidity, water molecules are held to the polar groups by hydrogen bonding:

$$
\begin{array}{ccc}
\text{R} & & \text{R} \\
| & & | \\
\text{H—N—H}^+ & & ^+\text{H—N—H} \\
| & & | \\
\text{H} & & \text{H} \\
 & \text{O} & \\
 & \diagup \diagdown & \\
 & \text{H} \quad \text{H} &
\end{array}
$$

Similar attachment was described by Pauling (28); one molecule is first bound tightly to two cooperating polar groups:

$$
\begin{array}{cccc}
\text{H} & \text{H} & \text{H} & \text{H} \\
| & | & | & | \\
\text{H—N} & \text{N} & \text{N} & \text{N—H} \\
\diagdown & \diagup\!\!= & = \!\!\diagdown & \diagup \\
\text{C} & \text{H} & \text{H} & \text{C} \\
| & \diagdown\diagup & | \\
\text{NH} & \text{O} & \text{HN} \\
\diagup & & \diagdown
\end{array}
$$

A second water molecule is added, giving a total of one water molecule per polar group. Additional water molecules attach themselves, and, as the relative humidity increases, the absorption continues and a complete layer of water is sandwiched into each space between the protein layers. Cassie (30) has shown that local sites for absorption are not limited to the surface layer of the protein, but that they can be distributed through the lattice, exhibiting changes in cellular dimensions.

Above 70 per cent relative humidity, the amount of water absorbed on the amino groups increases rapidly due to the condensation of water molecules on water molecules previously attached to the amino groups. At 95 per cent relative humidity six or seven water layers have been introduced between each layer and each neighboring layer. All the water absorbed in this step is held by hydrogen bonds of about the same strength, equivalent to water-to-water hydrogen bonds. The sorption of water at high relative humidities depends, however, on the prior sorption on active sorptive groups (31).

When placed in water below 20°C, gelatin swells up and the swelling continues until the gelatin dissolves. In solution, gelatin is in the colloidal state and exhibits the Tyndall effect. The gelatin molecules are of various lengths, and have molecular weights ranging possibly from some lower limit, say 20,000, up to about 120,000. These chains, which are probably still in the helical condition, are in constant motion with kinetic energy of translation and internal vibration energy.

The viscosity of gelatin solution depends upon concentration, temperature, pH, and other factors. With aging, the viscosity of a gelatin solution generally decreases, due probably to hydrolysis. The temperature is, however, an important factor. At low temperatures, the viscosity increases with the time; at higher temperatures, the viscosity first rises, then drops. To explain this behavior, Sheppard and Houck (32) assumed the coexistence of two opposing processes—gelation and hydrolysis. At low temperature the gelation predominates over hydrolysis and the viscosity increases; at higher temperature, the gelation rate first exceeds the hydrolytic action, whereas the latter effect becomes greater at the end. At still higher temperatures, the viscosity shows a steady drop, in which case the hydrolytic process predominates all the way.

On standing, if the conditions are right, a gelatin sol will set to a gel. The average kinetic energy of the molecules must not be too large. In the randomness of movement, certain active points or groups will be at the proper distance and orientation to react, in time. One such combination may be the beginning of the formation of a matrix. The active point may amount to partial alignment of small sections of two peptide chains. The gelatin network is of such a type that the individual molecular chains are bound together by secondary attractive forces localized at widely separated points. Secondary forces are assumed because the bonds can be dissociated by a small increase in temperature. That the loci of attraction are far apart is inferred from the mechanical properties and stability of gels.

As the gel stands, more and more active points of attraction may be formed and it is conceivable that some hydrogen or covalent bonds may be formed. This is evident from the contraction and consequent syneresis that occurs with gelatin gels on standing.

The higher the concentration of the gelatin, the more rapid the formation of a gel. The lower the concentration, the lower the setting point. If the concentration is less than 1 per cent, the sol will not gel. Pouradier (33) has shown that the sol-gel transformation takes place according to

$$\text{GEL} \underset{30°C}{\overset{40°C}{\rightleftarrows}} \text{SOL}$$

The setting and melting points do not coincide. Above 40°C, a gelatin sol will not gel regardless of concentration. The kinetic energy of the gelatin molecules may be large enough to overcome any attractive forces which would lead to gel formation regardless of the proximity of the molecules.

The melting point of a gel likewise varies with the concentration of gelatin. It increases as the concentration increases and tends toward a limiting value between 30 and 35°C. It also increases slightly with the aging of the gel.

This dependence of the setting and melting points on the concentration of gelatin would indicate the existence of a larger probability for the setting up of attractive forces, or bonds, with the greater proximity of the molecular chains in the more concentrated solutions. With an approach toward equilibrium, more bonds are formed in the gel matrix, which would account, on standing, for a slight rise in the melting point.

For a given concentration of gelatin, the setting point is lower than the melting point. The melting point for a given concentration of gelatin is highest at the isoelectric point, which is about pH 4.8 for lime gelatin. This is due to more compact packing of the chain.

Another very important property of gelatin is the ability to become insolubilized and hardened. The hardening of gelatin can be produced by heat (34,35), by ultraviolet radiation (36) and by certain chemicals. Insolubilization in the first two methods is not the same as in the third. Insolubilization by heat and ultraviolet light probably involves the rupture of certain bonds, resulting in a rearrangement to a more stable structure. In hardening with formaldehyde it is believed (37) that the following structure is set up between amino groups on separate gelatin chains:

$$-NH_2 + CH_2O + NH_2- \longrightarrow -NH-CH_2-NH- + H_2O \quad (3)$$

The group —NH—CH$_2$—NH— would serve as a crosslink, which would increase the rigidity of the gel and raise the melting point.

Chromic ion, Cr^{3+}, insolubilizes gelatin by formation of a coordinated complex between the chromic ion and the carboxylate group —COO$^-$. The chromium complex constitutes a crosslink between the chains which again gives more rigidity to the gelatin, makes it less soluble, and raises the melting point.

2.2d   *Process Glue*

Process glue is a refined product obtained from the skins of dried codfish and cusk in the preparation of boneless salt fish.   It is, like gelatin, an organic colloid of complex protein structure with similar distribution of amino acids and related products; it contains, however, much less proline and hydroxyproline.   The pH is generally between 6.5 and 7.2.   Process glue, or fish glue, as it is sometimes called, is a brown viscous liquid containing 40 to 50 per cent solids, and is used very often in the formulation of the sensitizing solution for photolithographic plates.

2.2e   *Albumins*

Albumins belong to the class of proteins which contain, in addition to carbon, hydrogen, oxygen, and nitrogen, a small amount of sulfur and yield only amino acids upon cleavage by enzymes or acids.   Albumins are widely distributed in animal and vegetable tissues and form yellow, transparent, amorphous lumps or scales, or yellowish powder.   In water, albumin swells at first, then gradually dissolves; on heating the solution to 60 to 70°C, the albumin coagulates.   If the solutions are not used within a few days, antiseptic agents and preservatives have to be added to prevent attack by bacteria and molds.   Pyridyl mercuric acetate or thymol is very effective (38).   Others, like sodium benzoate or pentachlorophenol, can also be used.

In the presence of dichromates, albumins can be hardened by the action of ultraviolet light, and are used in the preparation of sensitizing solutions. For sensitizing lithographic plates, egg albumin is generally used (39). Blood albumin was suggested by Van Deusen (40).

2.2f   *Casein*

Casein is a globular amphoteric heterogeneous protein, composed of at least 19 amino acids.   It is the principal protein of cow's milk, probably present as neutral calcium caseinate.   Casein is a phosphoprotein and contains 0.85 per cent organic phosphorus and about the same amount of sugar.

Most authorities agree that casein consists of chainlike compounds united through the peptide linkage:

$$-CO-\!\!-NH-CH-CO-\!\!-NH-CH-COOH$$

$$\qquad\qquad R \qquad\qquad\qquad R$$

where R can vary according to the individual amino acid.

Senti (41) has represented a polypeptide chain typical of those formed in casein by

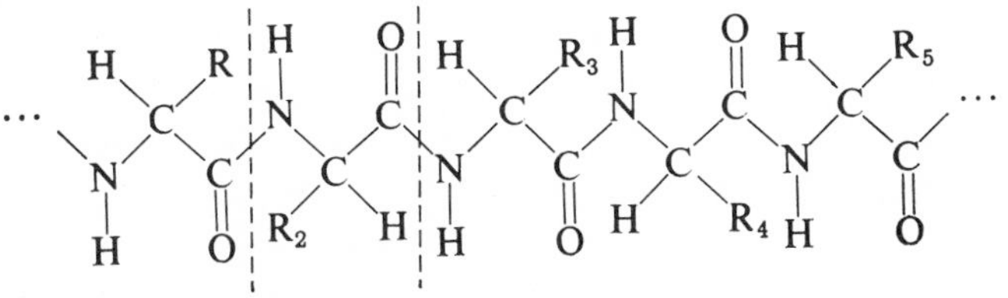

The α-amino acid residue is enclosed by the dotted line; the side group R may be —H, —CH$_3$, —CH$_2$, —C$_6$H$_5$(CH$_2$)$_4$NH$_2$, —CH$_2$COOH, etc. The molecular weight of casein ranges from about 75,000 to about 375,000.

Casein forms a white amorphous powder very sparingly soluble in water and in nonpolar organic solvents; it is soluble in aqueous solutions of alkalies and in salt solutions such as those of sodium oxalate and sodium acetate. From solution, it can be precipitated with metallic salts. Casein is not coagulated by heat.

Casein is used in the lithographic industry as a substitute for albumin in sensitizing surface plates. Especially suited for this purpose is casein obtained from an ammoniacal solution of the raw casein by fractionating out undesirable portions with nitric acid (42). Another casein derivative was proposed by Danehy (43,44) for making lithographic printing plates. Lupo (45) suggested casein for the preparation of pigmented contact printing emulsions.

2.2g *Natural Gums*

Natural gums have been known and used for many years and still find important applications in the photomechanical field. They are carbohydrates of complex irregular structure, in which hexose, pentose, and uronic acid units are linked with one another. Butler and Cretcher (46)

obtained on hydrolysis, *l*-arabinose, *d*-galactose, and *l*-rhamnose, along with *d*-glucuronic acid.

Natural resins are formed as decomposition products in many plants, particularly in plants growing in very dry regions. They can be grouped according to their plant origin, but only a few of them are of any importance in photomechanical printing. The most important is gum arabic, an exudation of an acacia tree of tropical Africa. The best qualities are known as "kordofan" from Sudan, "senegal" from West Africa, and "mogodor" from Morocco.

Gum arabic forms a white or yellowish powder, easily soluble in cold water, insoluble in alcohols and other organic solvents. Since it is a natural material, its properties, especially the viscosity of the solution, vary not only from batch to batch, but also with age. These variations make the sensitizing properties inconsistent. Harrison (47) suggested addition of urea to control the increase in viscosity of dichromated gum arabic solutions and their tendency to gel with age. Satisfactory results can be obtained also with arabic acid, the active constituent of the gum, prepared by passing gum arabic solution over an ion exchange resin (48,49,50), which replaces the calcium and magnesium ions with hydrogen ions.

Gum arabic is also a major ingredient of etches, gums, and deep-etch coatings. It has good adherence to metal; this is due to the presence of free carboxyl groups, which form a comparatively firm bond between the gum and the metal.

2.2h   *Starch and Its Derivatives*

Starch is a high-polymeric material of definite chemical composition; it is a compound of carbon, hydrogen, and oxygen in the ratio $C_6H_{10}O_5$. At one time it was believed that starch forms a linear chain similar to cellulose. Investigations of Kerr and Severson (51,52) disclosed that starch actually occurs in two structural forms: one, a linear chain of perhaps 500 to 1000 glucose units, now generally termed amylose, the other, a branched chain polymer called amylopectin. While in cellulose the glucose units are joined together by β-1,4-linkages with an oxygen bridge on one side of the glucose, starch has α-1,4-couplings with the oxygen bridge on the opposite side of the glucose unit.

This difference in the spatial arrangement of the atoms in the molecule is responsible for the difference in properties. While the rigid rodlike molecule gives cellulose high structural strength and water insolubility, the α-1,4-linkage makes the starch molecule very flexible and more reactive. Starches of different origin such as corn, rice, tapioca, wheat, or potato contain different proportions of amylose and amylopectin.

Starch dissolves hardly at all in cold water or alcohol, but quite well in hot water. It forms a viscous liquid which gels on cooling. This phenomenon can be explained by the strong affinity of the OH-groups in one molecule for those in another molecule. In concentrated starch solution, straight linear chains line up parallel to each other and the hydroxyl groups bind them fast together by hydrogen bonding, forming aggregates that are insoluble in water.

The tendency to form association through hydrogen bonds can be decreased or completely eliminated by introducing substituent groups along the chain, which reduces the linearity of the amylose molecules. The modification of starch can take place through reactions on the hydroxyl groups or by depolymerization at the bonds between glucose units (53). So, by methylation of starch, methyl groups can take the place of the hydrogens, giving, when the methylation is complete, trimethyl starch.

Starch can be hydrolyzed with dilute acids to glucose:

$$(C_6H_{10}O_5)_x + xH_2O \longrightarrow xC_6H_{12}O_6 \tag{4}$$

By interrupting the acid hydrolysis of starch, dextrin is produced, the properties of which are determined by the extent to which the hydrolysis, molecular rearrangements, and repolymerization of small fragments to larger molecules, have taken place.

Dextrin forms a white or yellow amorphous powder, soluble in water, insoluble in alcohol. It is used instead of gum arabic or gelatin, in combination with dichromates, as a photosensitive resist for printing plates.

Dextran, a partially hydrolyzed product of microbial action on sugar, has been suggested for the same application (54).

2.2i   *Other Colloids*

Many of these colloids are not satisfactory for use in certain photo-engraving processes employing the etching of metals by acids, because of the permeability of the hardened image to aqueous solutions of acids and other etching reagents used in etching, and substances like shellac (55,56,57) or zein must be used.

2.2j   *Synthetic Resins*

In the last few decades, many synthetic materials have been introduced to the trade such as nitrocellulose (58), cellulose acetate (59), mixed cellulose esters of polybasic organic acids, e.g., cellulose acetate phthalate, cellulose acetate citrate or cellulose acetate succinate (60), sodium carboxymethyl cellulose (61,62), polyvinylpyrrolidone (61), polyvinyl butyral (63), halogenated polyvinyl alcohol (64), other vinyl polymers and copolymers (65,66,67), and urea-formaldehyde resins (68). Polyamide condensation polymers for the production of printing forms were suggested by Freundorfer and Hoerner (69,70). Dichromated vinyl methyl ether/maleic anhydride polymer PVM/MA and the dimethylamine salt of the vinyl acetate/maleic acid copolymer are claimed to be particularly suitable for printing plates (71). Most attention, however, was given to polyvinyl alcohol.

2.2k *Polyvinyl Alcohols*

Polyvinyl alcohols are water-soluble resins prepared from polyvinyl acetates or other vinyl esters by replacement of acetate groups by hydroxyl groups (72). They are usually obtained in the form of a powder having the formula:

$$\cdots\cdots\left[-CH_2-CH-CH_2-CH\cdots\atop \qquad\ \ \ OH\qquad\quad\ OH\right]_n\cdots$$

By varying the conditions in the manufacturing cycle, it is possible to produce a series of polyvinyl alcohols differing markedly in physical and chemical properties. The principal factors governing these properties are the degree of polymerization and the degree of hydrolysis. In general, the degree of polymerization ranges from a compound having the foregoing formula with $n = 20$ to one of $n = 350$. This range can be subdivided into compounds having low molecular weight ($n = 20 - 100$), medium molecular weight ($n = 100 - 200$), and high molecular weight ($n = >200$). There is, however, no sharp line of division between them. Within each molecular-weight range, polyvinyl alcohols of various degree of hydrolysis can be obtained. Those which are hydrolyzed approximately 99 per cent are referred to as "completely hydrolyzed," and those whose acetyl groups have been replaced with hydroxyl radicals to a lesser extent are classified as "partially hydrolyzed" grades.

Polyvinyl alcohols are, in general, soluble in water, or in water-alcohol mixtures. They are easily sensitized by dichromates (73,74,75,76,77) and are used for sensitizing lithographic plates, silk screens, and as photoresists for letterpress printing. In general, it can be said that the high-molecular-weight modifications have a greater degree of light sensitivity than those with low molecular weight.

In contrast to dichromated colloids such as fish glue, gelatin, and albumin, dichromated polyvinyl alcohol solutions are attacked neither by bacteria nor fungi; but they are subject to molding. With aging, the viscosity of a dichromated polyvinyl alcohol solution decreases, apparently due to the oxidation of polyvinyl alcohol, and it is believed that during such oxidation depolymerization is taking place. Films prepared from aged solutions are less sensitive to light and show a marked decrease in acid resistance. A small amount of phenol stabilizes the solutions against a decrease in viscosity (78).

2.3 PHOTOCHEMICAL HARDENING OF DICHROMATED LAYERS

Although the process of hardening dichromated colloid layers has been the subject of considerable investigation during the last hundred years, it is certainly remarkable that the fundamental theory of the hardening and the mechanism of the reactions resulting from the light exposure have yet to be explained satisfactorily.

In a chiefly qualitative study of dichromated gelatin, Eder (79,80) came to the conclusion that dichromates in the presence of oxidizable organic matter are decomposed through a series of complicated reactions into neutral chromates and a chromic chromate, $mCrO_3 \cdot nCr_2O_3$, which, by subsequent washing was further decomposed into chromic acid and green chromium oxide. The neutral chromate and chromic acid are supposedly carried away by water, and the chromium oxide combines with the gelatin to form an insoluble complex.

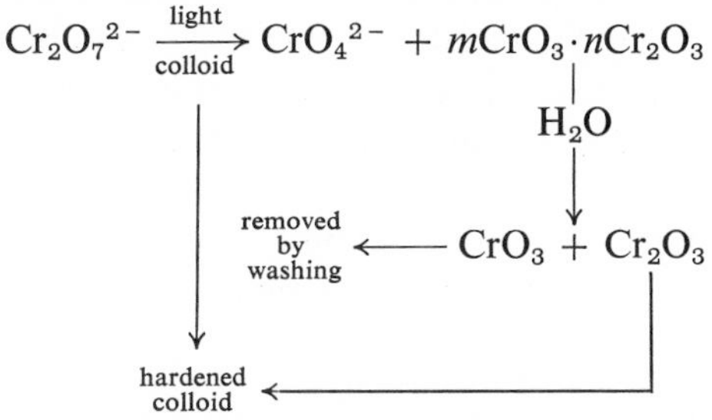

$$Cr_2O_7^{2-} \xrightarrow[\text{colloid}]{\text{light}} CrO_4^{2-} + mCrO_3 \cdot nCr_2O_3$$

$$\downarrow H_2O$$

$$\text{removed by washing} \longleftarrow CrO_3 + Cr_2O_3$$

$$\downarrow \text{hardened colloid} \longleftarrow$$

(5)

Popovitski (81) identified the reaction product as $4Cr_2O_3 \cdot 3CrO_3$, which was obtained by the following process:

$$16K_2Cr_2O_7 = 16K_2CrO_4 + 8Cr_2O_3 + 12O_2 \tag{6}$$

$$6K_2Cr_2O_7 = 6K_2CrO_4 + 6CrO_3 \tag{7}$$

A different approach to identifying the hardening action was the assumption (82, 83) that the liberated oxygen reacts with the gelatin and forms a water-insoluble "oxyglutin"

$$K_2Cr_2O_7 + H_2O \xrightarrow{\text{light}} Cr_2O_3 + 2KOH + 3O \tag{8}$$

$$\text{gelatin} + 3O \longrightarrow \text{"oxyglutin"} \tag{9}$$

This theory was abandoned after it was learned that oxidized colloids retained their solubility and light sensitivity in the presence of dichromates. The oxidation of the colloid is only a side reaction and has no effect on the hardening.

Eder also found that the exposed parts of a dichromated gelatin film became more completely insoluble when subsequently kept in the dark before development, although the unexposed parts did not. This after-effect was studied by Abney (84), Hardy and Perrin (85), and demonstrated earlier by Mayer (86); he observed a continuous increase of electrical resistance of dichromated films for some time after the exposure. Also, according to Stötzer (87), plates developed six hours after the exposure were equivalent to plates exposed 15 to 20 per cent longer and developed immediately after exposure. Biltz and Eggert (88), on the basis of their quantum-yield measurements, concluded that the afterhardening of exposed plates is comparable to the dark reaction of unexposed plates. The reason for the "afterhardening" effect is not in the catalytical action of the already hardened colloid on the unhardened, but in the aging of the layer, with, consequently, a higher degree of crosslinking.

More recently, Ammann (89) found that through the light reduction of dichromates in the presence of organic substances, a compound of tri- and sexivalent chromium in the ratio 2 : 1 is formed. Eder himself was not certain if the brown product on the exposed areas had a definite chemical composition. It was found by later workers (90) that the ratio of chromic acid to chromic oxide is more or less dependent on the original dichromate concentration, and the brown color is considered a simple mixture of the reduced chromium compound with the unreacted orange dichromate.

Another explanation of the hardening of dichromated colloids by the action of light came from Biltz and Eggert (88), who summarized the hardening by the following reactions:

$$3(NH_4)_2Cr_2O_7 + 6H\cdot + h\nu = (CrO)_2CrO_4 + 6NH_4OH \qquad (10)$$

$$(CrO)_2CrO_4 + 2 \text{ gelatin} = \text{absorption complex} \qquad (11)$$

The second equation supports the assumption of Wintgen and Löwenthal (91), who explained the loss of the gelatin's ability to absorb water by the association of a negatively charged gelatin miscelle with a positively charged chromium ion.

The foregoing interpretation gives an acceptable explanation of the rising pH during the exposure because of the OH^--ion formation, and the increase in the electrical resistance of the film is accounted for by the reduction in the number of hydrogen ions.

This theory is, however, hardly acceptable for other colloids, such as polyvinyl alcohol or methylcellulose, as was pointed out by Smethurst (92), who suggested formation of crosslinkages between the molecular chains of the colloid during the hardening. He proposed

$$H^+ + HCrO_4{}^- + h\nu = CrO_3 + H_2O \tag{12}$$

as a possible explanation of the photochemical reaction.

Another proposal came from Asperger (93). Stiehler (94), in his investigation of the absorption spectra of exposed dichromated-colloid solutions, observed increasing pH value during the exposure; this effect he explained by the following reaction:

$$Cr_2O_7{}^{2-} + 14H^+ + 6e = 2Cr^{3+} + 7H_2O \tag{13}$$

All tanning theories suggest that the hardening of dichromated colloids is, in principle, the same as the chromium tanning of leather (95), and explain more or less satisfactorily the effects of concentration of both dichromate and colloid and the influence of pH, temperature, and moisture on the printing speed. Biltz and Eggert, in addition, give a convincing explanation of the stability of dichromated-colloid solutions to light. According to them, the chromate or dichromate ions in the solution combine with water molecules, producing hydrated ions. Because of the high dipole moment of water, we can reasonably assume that there is a tight bond between the ions and water molecules. If we assume that the least distance at which the ion and dipole can approach each other is equal to the sum of the radii of the two, and that, on the average, each dichromate ion combines with n dipoles, then the energy necessary to break the bond between them is equal to (96):

$$H_{\text{ergs}} = \left(\frac{e\mu}{r^2}\right)_n \cdot 2N \tag{14}$$

where H = hydration energy
μ = dipole moment of water = $1.84 \cdot 10^{-18}$
e = charge of the ion
r = sum of the radii

How high this energy really is, we do not know, but it must be well above 150 kcal per mole, which is more than the light energy can supply.

In the air-dried layer, not enough water is present to cause hydration of the chromate or dichromate ions, but it is present in sufficient amount to keep the dichromate molecule in a dissociated state. By complete dehydration of the layer, i.e., by removing all water, the dichromate crystallizes out, and an ionic reaction is excluded. Before any action of the light on the system can take place, the crystal energy has to be overcome.

The tanning theory has never succeeded in explaining the most remarkable feature, i.e., that colloids containing only very minute amounts of dichromates can be completely hardened, provided that the exposure to actinic radiation is sufficiently long. Some investigators (97,98) are of the opinion that, in such cases, the gelatin micelles are not hardened completely through, and that the hardening took place only on the surface of each gelatin micelle. Smethurst (99), to explain the hardening of colloids containing very small amounts of dichromate by prolonged exposure, suggested that each dichromate ion reacts more than once with the surrounding colloid molecules in a process similar to optical sensitization.

The idea that the dichromate ion might act as a photosensitizer was first proposed by Galinsky (100) on the grounds of observations made by Brintzinger and Maurer (101). They prepared insoluble gelatin films merely by exposure to ultraviolet light. Galinsky concluded that the first action of light is to produce a change in the protein molecule, followed by fixation of chromium with the gelatin by prolonged exposure.

That gelatin can be hardened by exposure to light in the presence of dyes such as erythrosine or auramine, both known as optical sensitizers of silver halide gelatin emulsions, was reported as early as 1916 by Meisling (102) and applied a year later by Warburg (103). This process failed in practice because of the low degree of sensitivity and because of the necessity of exposing the layers in a moist state.

Sheppard and Houck (33) showed that the hardening of gelatin is the result of intramolecular changes resulting from the energetic reactions, and demonstrated that gelatin on prolonged heating at sufficiently elevated temperature progressively loses its solubility in warm water. They proved that the insolubilization of gelatin by exposure to ultraviolet light follows the same reaction course as the hardening by heat, although at greater velocity than at the highest temperature studied (116°C).

Although the tanning theory has certain limitations and fails to give a satisfactory explanation for many phenomena, there is no doubt that during the exposure the hexavalent chromium ion is reduced to a lower valency, which subsequently forms a complex with two or more colloid molecules. Whether these lower chromium oxides have the formula of a chromium oxychromate as postulated by Eggert and Biltz, or the formula of a chromic chromate as suggested by Eder, is a subject of discussion, and, in either case, no positive proof was presented. Also, the question as to whether the chromium ion forms a part of the final complex is not definitely answered. Stiehler, in the reported study (94), came to the conclusion that the strong differences in the course of the absorption refer to a decided trivalent chromium-colloid compound. The theory that the photohardening of dichromated-colloid layers is initiated by photo-reduction of Cr^{6+} to Cr^{3+}, is supported also by the work of Suzuki and Aisaka (104), who measured the electrical resistance of dichromated-gelatin solution irradiated by γ-rays.

2.4   THE VALIDITY OF PHOTOCHEMICAL LAWS. SPECTRAL SENSITIVITY

According to the Grothus-Draper law, only radiation that is absorbed by a system can produce a photochemical reaction in that system.   In other words, production of a chemical change by actinic radiation requires the absorption of this radiation.   In dichromated-colloid layers, the photosensitive components, that is, the dichromates, are efficient absorbers of ultraviolet, violet, and blue radiation; the maximum absorption by ammonium and potassium dichromates is at 3670 and 3575 Å, respectively.

O'Brien (105) studied the spectral sensitivity of several resins, both synthetic and natural, containing alkali dichromates.   He found that the spectral sensitivity curve of each dichromated colloid almost coincided with the spectral absorption curve of the corresponding dichromate. Figure 2.2 shows the spectral sensitivity of two commercial sensitized shellac photoengraving resist layers.   The parallelism between these curves and the absorption curve of ammonium dichromate clearly demonstrates the validity of the Grothus-Draper law for dichromated colloids.

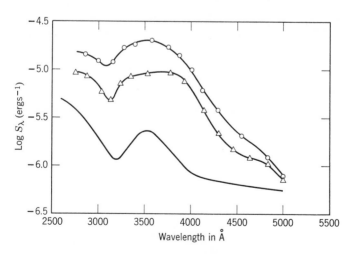

Figure 2.2.   Spectral sensitivity of two commercial shellac-base photoresists, on a logarithmic scale, compared to absorption of ammonium dichromate (reference 105).

It is not certain that colloid layers follow the Bunsen-Roscoe reciprocity law.   According to this law, in a photochemical reaction the yield of product is a function of the total radiant energy absorbed, i.e., of the product of the light intensity and the exposure time.   To obtain a given yield, the required exposure time, t, is inversely proportional to the light intensity, I, that is used.   Silver halide emulsions obey a modified form of this equation, Schwarzschild's law, which holds at low intensities.   For nonpigmented dichromated gelatin, Bouček (106) and others (107,108,109) found the Schwarzschild coefficient p to be nearly one.   For certain dichromated colloids, including polyvinyl alcohol and dextrin, p equals one except for lower concentrations of dichromate, where it is slightly smaller (110).

As we have seen in a previous page, the light hardening of a dichromated colloid includes two steps.   First, light reduces the dichromate to a chromium(III) compound; the reduced compound is then adsorbed on the colloid, thereby affecting the physical properties of the colloid.   The nature of the linkage between the colloid molecule and the chromium compound is not yet known exactly.

The quantum yield of the reduction, that is, the reciprocal of the number of quanta required to reduce a single dichromate group, was calculated by Biltz and Eggert (88) to be 0.5.   In other words, two light quanta are required to reduce one dichromate group.   With prolonged exposure, however, the quantum yield decreases because the colored reaction product absorbs actinic radiation (Figure 2.3).   In addition, Biltz and Eggert obtained 0.3 for the quantum yield of gelatin insolubilization by assuming that the gelatin molecule is either completely nonhardened or completely hardened (nonswelling), and neglecting any intermediate

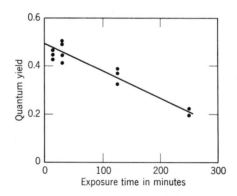

Figure 2.3.   Quantum yield of dichromated colloid layers (reference 88).

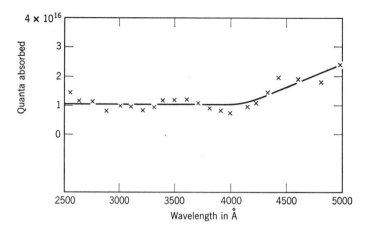

Figure 2.4.   Quantum yield of dichromated colloid layers (reference 105).

stages.   This means that approximately three light quanta are required to harden one gelatin molecule.

The quantum yield of threshold hardening was found by O'Brien (105) to be nearly constant for wavelengths shorter than approximately 4100 Å, but, above this limit, to decrease with increasing wavelength (Figure 2.4). This is explained by the smaller energy of the longer wave quantum; this reduces the probability of its absorption by a photosensitive molecule. It is apparent that the number of quanta that must be absorbed in order to tan a certain thickness of film depends upon both the spectral sensitivity and the absorption factor of the film in the vicinity of wavelength λ. The same relationship was observed by Shklover (111).

The spectral sensitivity of a dichromated-colloid film is not uniform throughout the visible region.   Cartwright (112) found the sensitivity to be maximum between 3500 and 4500 Å.   Sensitivity to the equal-energy spectrum was found by Reed and Dorst (113) to be greatest in the far ultraviolet.   From a maximum at 2100 Å it decreases rapidly near 3200 Å, and then rises to a weaker maximum at 3550 Å where the sensitivity is about one-fifth of the first maximum (Figure 2.5).   Beyond this second peak, in the visible violet, the sensitivity falls off rapidly, and in the blue and green, more slowly, finally falling to zero in the green-yellow, at approximately 5800 Å.   At wavelengths above 6000 Å, dichromated colloids may be considered insensitive.

In a comprehensive study of the same problem, Koch, Byers, and Rossel (114) obtained curves similar to the curve of Reed and Dorst. Similarly, Feldmann (109) observed a practical degree of sensitivity

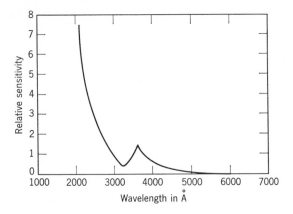

Figure 2.5.   Spectral sensitivity of dichromated colloids (reference 113).

between 3000 and 4500 Å, with a maximum at 3600 Å.   Since, ordinarily, printing is through glass which does not transmit wavelengths shorter than 3400 Å, it is necessary to use thin glass and light sources having high intensity in the region of 3500 Å.

Apparently the spectral sensitivity of dichromated-colloid layers is influenced little, if at all, by the nature of the colloid.   Jorgensen (115) showed that observed shifts are due to differences in the spectral absorption of individual colloids.

2.5   FACTORS AFFECTING THE LIGHT SENSITIVITY

The amount of light exposure that a dichromated-colloid layer needs to reach the desired degree of hardening is given by the sensitivity of that coating to actinic radiation.   Although the chemistry of the light-hardening process has been studied for many years, the reactions taking place are so complex that we cannot express them by chemical equations.   We have learned, however, enough about these processes, and in the following pages we will discuss the factors which do affect the light sensitivity of dichromated-colloid layers, so that we can control and adjust them to the specific requirements.

2.5a   *Effect of the Dichromate Concentration*

The concentration of dichromate ion in the sensitizing solution has a marked influence on the sensitivity of the coated layer.   Although only very small amounts (0.5 per cent) of dichromate are necessary for the

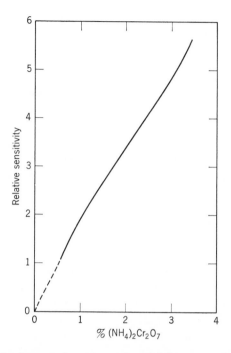

Figure 2.6.   Relation between the concentration of dichromate and relative sensitivity.

photochemical hardening of dichromated colloids, the sensitivity increases almost proportionally with the dichromate concentration. Figure 2.6 shows the relationship between the dichromate concentration and the thickness of hardened colloid layer, for constant exposure time. In practical applications a commonly used ratio of dichromate to colloid is 1:3 by weight. In numerous formulations, however, the ratio ranges from 1:20 to 1:2. The limit of dichromate concentration in the layer is determined by the concentration that causes formation of crystals in the dried film; with the dichromate crystals on the surface, hardening no longer occurs. Besides that, coatings having recrystallized dichromate on the surface are useless for purposes of reproduction, because the crystals quickly dissolve or chip off. Layers with recrystallized dichromates on the surface can be made usable by dipping them, for a short time, in pure water or in a 2 per cent dichromate solution (116). Treatment with diluted alcohol also gives satisfactory results (117).

To prevent the recrystallization, it was recommended that ferric oxalate be incorporated into the layer (118). Furthermore, to combat the tendency of the dichromate to crystallize out, Liesegang (119) proposed adding gelatose to the dichromated gelatin; gelatose was prepared by heating a 20 per cent gelatin solution for several days.

During the exposure, dichromate ion is reduced to a compound of lower valency, which is subsequently fixed onto the colloid molecule. The relationship between the various dichromate:albumin ratios and the quantity of reduced dichromate for a given exposure time, is shown in Figure 2.7. The quantity of reduced dichromate increases with the increase in dichromate:colloid ratio, up to about 0.5. Beyond this point, the amount of reduced dichromate decreases, probably because of the light-filtering action of Cr_2O^{2-} ion. At very low dichromate concentrations, the exposure necessary to produce a satisfactory image is needlessly long.

Figure 2.8 illustrates the effect of exposure time on the amount of reduced dichromate at various dichromate concentrations. The quantity of reduced dichromate increases with the exposure time and the concentration. The rate, however, decreases as the exposure progresses. This might indicate that the reaction follows the law of mass action, which states that the quantity of components reacting in a given time is directly proportional to the quantity of reactants present. However, we also have to take into consideration the following fact. During the exposure, as the film becomes tanned, a color change is taking place in the exposed areas, with the consequent appearance of a brown, detailed image on the surface. The intensity of this print-out image increases with the exposure time and dichromate concentration in the layer. The spectral absorption of light by the dichromated-colloid layer in question

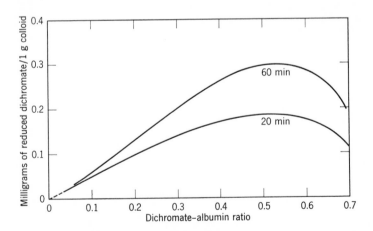

Figure 2.7. Relation between quantity of reduced dichromate and various dichromate-albumin ratios for 20- and 60-min exposures.

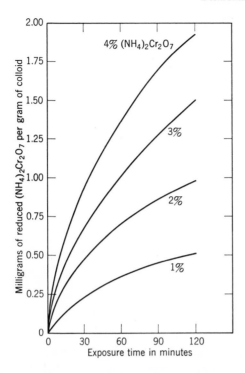

Figure 2.8. Effect of exposure time on the amount of reduced dichromate at various concentrations.

will be higher in the previously exposed parts than in the unexposed areas, as was demonstrated by Koch, Byers, and Rossell (114) and as illustrated in Figure 2.9. The absorption of wavelengths longer than 400 mμ thus effectively blocks deeper penetration of actinic radiation into the layer and hinders, to some extent, the tanning reaction.

If we imagine the sensitized layer as being composed of a number of individual strata, a, b, c, and d, of identical composition, then, during the first stage of the exposure, the dichromate is decomposed in the exposed parts of the upper stratum a. In these areas a brownish print-out image is formed which absorbs a certain percentage of actinic radiation and permits only the remaining part to penetrate into stratum b, situated directly under stratum a. As the exposure proceeds, the same situation is repeated in the remaining strata so that less and less light can penetrate into the coating near the supporting base. In extreme cases, it can happen that the well-tanned image on the surface will be washed off during the development, simply because the brown product hindered the reaction

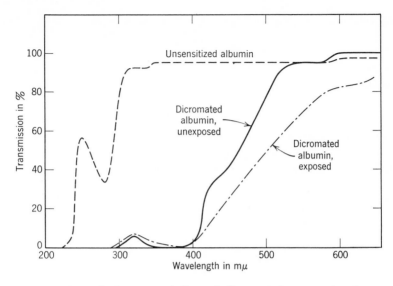

Figure 2.9.   Spectral absorption of films of albumin and unexposed and exposed dichromated albumin (reference 114).

in underlying layers, and the colloid stratum adjacent to the support had never received sufficient radiation.   Although light absorption by the brown reaction-product increases with increasing exposure, the reaction rate of the photochemical hardening decreases with the reaction time, and can, under some circumstances, approach zero.

2.5b   *Effect of pH*

In solution, chromate and dichromate ions are in equilibrium, and the following reactions may take place:

$$2HCrO_4^- \longrightarrow Cr_2O_7^{2-} + H_2O \qquad (15)$$

$$H_2CrO_4 \longrightarrow H \qquad + HCrO_4^- \qquad (16)$$

$$HCrO_4^- \longrightarrow H \qquad + CrO_4^{2-} \qquad (17)$$

Reaction 15 describes the equilibrium between acid chromate and dichromate ions in the presence of water.   This equation is not directly dependent on the pH.   Equations 16 and 17 involve the hydrogen ion concentration, and therefore the concentration of $HCrO_4^-$ is directly related to pH.

Since the hardening of dichromated colloids depends initially on the $HCrO_4^-$-ion concentration (120), it is obvious that the hydrogen-ion concentration has a great effect on the speed, contrast, and keeping quality of the sensitized layers.

The addition of an alkali to the dichromated-colloid solution decreases the concentration of $HCrO_4^-$ ions, and the color of the solution gradually changes from orange to lemon-yellow:

$$Cr_2O_7^{2-} + 2OH^- = 2CrO_4^{2-} + H_2O \qquad (18)$$

If so much alkali is added to the sensitizing solution that all dichromate is converted into a monochromate, the light sensitivity of the dried layer drops to about 25 per cent, which makes a longer exposure necessary to print a given image from a given negative. The higher the pH of the layer, the longer the required exposure. Photochemically speaking, the chromates are thus slower than dichromates. This is so with solutions in which the pH has been raised with nonvolatile alkalies, such as alkali metal carbonates or hydroxides. If the pH was adjusted with ammonia, it was found that beyond a slight initial fall in sensitivity as the pH was raised to about 7, no further marked reduction took place even when an excess of ammonia was used. This behavior can be explained by the volatility of ammonia. During the coating and drying period, a large proportion of the added ammonia is lost, leaving a light-sensitive layer similar to that obtained from a solution of much lower pH. The rate

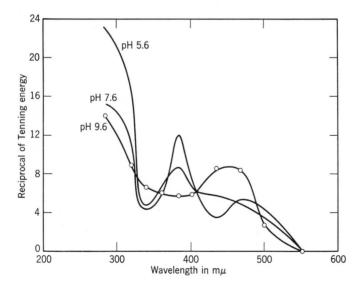

Figure 2.10. Spectral sensitivity of films of dichromated albumin from solutions at pH 9.6, pH 7.6, and pH 5.6 (reference 114).

at which the ammonia leaves the coating is increased by application of moderate heat, which shortens the standing time before exposure. The addition of ammonia changes the physical properties of dichromated-colloid solutions somewhat (increased density and decreased viscosity), but the changes are very small so that they do not have any significant effect on the coating (113).

The light absorption of chromate and dichromate ions is different, and it can be expected that the spectral sensitivity of dichromated-colloid layers will be influenced by pH variations.   Koch and his co-workers (114) demonstrated that over-all sensitivity of dichromated albumin in the spectral range from 2850 to 6000 Å is greatest for pH 5.6 and intermediate for pH 7.6, and solutions having pH value of 9.6 produced the least sensitive coating.   Figure 2.10 shows the spectral sensitivity of films of dichromated albumin from solutions at these pH values.   The curves show that films prepared from solutions having pH 5.6 and 7.6 have sensitivity peaks between 3600 and 4000 Å, and the peak for a solution of pH 9.6 is between 4000 and 5000 Å.   This sensitivity peak, however, cannot be utilized under practical conditions, although a tanned image can be produced with excessive exposure times.

2.5c   *Thickness of the Coating*

The principal solid materials present in the sensitizing solution are the colloids and the dichromates.   By increasing the solids, the viscosity of the solution increases proportionally (121) and thicker layers are produced. Since the insolubilization of the layer starts at the surface and goes progressively deeper into the coating, thicker layers require longer exposures to reach the water-insoluble state right down to the supporting base. For the same reason thicker layers have better shelf life than thinner coatings.   The maximum allowable thickness is limited because the exposed upper layer acts as a filter which absorbs a certain percentage of the actinic light necessary to render the underlayers of the coating insoluble to the grain of the plate.   To shorten the exposure time the dichromated-colloid coatings should be made as thin as possible.   The thickness of the coating is further influenced by the nature and treatment of the plate, type, and speed of the whirler, or the coating speed, and can vary with different methods of drying (122).   The effect of the relative humidity on the thickness of the coating is negligible if a heated whirler is used.   Further, it is important to keep the thickness, both within the layer and from coating to coating, constant; this can be controlled by measuring the solution density, maintaining a uniform speed for the whirler, and applying a given volume of the solution over a given area.

2.5d *Moisture Content*

The reduction of dichromate ion during the exposure to actinic radiation is an ionic reaction, and it is not surprising to learn that the presence of a certain amount of moisture in the coated and dried layer is necessary for the hardening reaction. During the drying operation, most of the water evaporates, but, although the coating appears perfectly dry, a small quantity of moisture remains in the layer. Gelatin and other colloids used in these processes lose or acquire moisture slowly, according to the state of the surrounding atmosphere; the amount of moisture in the layer varies with the relative humidity. The amount of water left in the layer has, of course, a great influence on the light sensitivity of the coating, retarding or accelerating the hardening process, and exposure times have to be changed to compensate for the effects caused by changes in relative humidity. When the humidity is high, the sensitivity to light is also high, the speed of light hardening being almost double with an increase of 30 per cent in relative humidity, as can be deduced from Figure 2.11. On the other hand, completely dehydrated or fully swollen coatings do not show any light sensitivity at all (123).

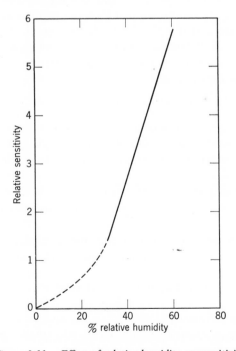

Figure 2.11. Effect of relative humidity on sensitivity.

On the basis of experiments that were repeated many times, Watter (108) came to the conclusion that the moisture content in pigment papers does not affect light sensitivity, and explained the printing-speed differences by increased rates of the dark reaction and afterhardening.

Just to demonstrate the difference in opinions on the effects of relative humidity, we can also mention the work of Romer, Luczak, and Starostka (124). After eliminating the changes in the dark-reaction rates, they found that samples conditioned at low relative humidity were more sensitive than those conditioned at high humidity. The difference was most marked when the low relative humidity preceded the high, confirming that high relative humidity speeds up image afterhardening.

2.6 DARK REACTION

2.6a *Sensitizing Solution*

Solutions of alkali metal or ammonium dichromates and solutions of oxidizable proteins or carbohydrates, when kept separately, do not change on standing and are not affected by light or air. As soon as they are mixed together, however, a reaction takes place, changing the color of the solution from yellow to a reddish-brown that increases in intensity with the age of the solution. Because this reaction takes place in the dark, it is called the "dark reaction" to distinguish it from the photochemical or light reaction.

The reaction responsible for this effect, with the intermediate steps omitted, can be expressed as:

$$Cr_2O_7{}^{2-} + 6H^+ \longrightarrow Cr^{3+} + CrO_4{}^{2-} + 3H_2O \qquad (19)$$

The mixture of green chromic ion, yellow chromate ion, and unreacted dichromate forms the brownish color of the aged solution. Jorgensen (125) used this color change for checking the usefulness of aged dichromate-colloid solutions.

Under normal conditions, this reaction is relatively slow, probably because of the low ionic mobility and oriented water molecules around the colloid particles.

The chromate and dichromate ions in the solution are in equilibrium; the equilibrium is dependent on the hydrogen-ion concentration:

$$Cr_2O_7{}^{2-} \underset{H^+}{\overset{OH^-}{\rightleftharpoons}} 2CrO_4{}^{2-} \qquad (20)$$

In a solution having a pH above 7.0, the equilibrium is shifted to the right and the dichromate concentration is very small. Since the rate of the hardening reaction is given by dichromate-ion concentration, it is evident that the pH of the solution will influence the useful life of the sensitizing solution to a marked degree.

The foregoing reaction also explains why sensitizing solutions in which the pH has been adjusted with ammonia are more stable than solutions prepared only from dichromates and colloid.

The effect of pH on the useful life of the sensitizing solution is demonstrated in Figure 2.12. From this chart it can be seen that a solution of pH 7 or lower will keep only for a day or two, and the keeping quality increases very fast with increasing pH, so that if enough ammonia is added to the solution to raise the pH to 9, the mixture will keep under average conditions for many months.

During the oxidation-reduction process that is taking place in the solution, the pH rises because of the consumption of hydrogen ions. The increase of pH is, in the beginning, rapid, and after a certain time slows down, depending on the original pH value. The slowing down period is connected with the shifted $Cr_2O_7^{2-} \longrightarrow CrO_4^{2-}$ equilibrium to the right. The curves in Figure 2.13 show the increasing pH, during storage, of 2 per cent gelatin (A); 8 per cent photoengraving glue (B), and 10 per cent gum arabic (C) solutions containing 5 per cent ammonium dichromate.

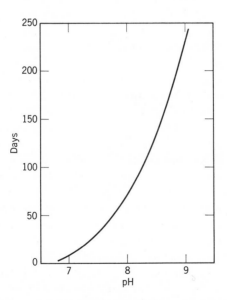

Figure 2.12. The effect of pH on the useful life of dichromated glue solution at room temperature.

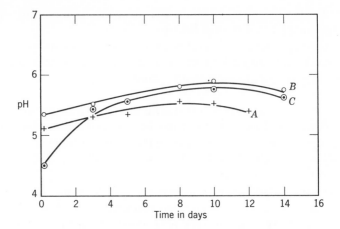

Figure 2.13. Variation in pH during aging of dichromated (A) gelatin solution, (B) glue solution, (C) gum-arabic solution.

During the aging, a change in physical properties of the sensitizing solution, such as increased viscosity, can be noticed. Adams (126) investigated the effect of increasing viscosity on the deterioration of the sensitizing solution and showed the relation of the pH to the rate of dark reaction.   Figure 2.14 shows the increasing viscosity during the aging, and the curves in Figure 2.15 demonstrate the increased reaction rate with increasing dichromate concentration.   Adams concluded that at a pH of 8 or higher, the reduction of hexavalent chromium is almost nonexistent, and thus the deterioration of solutions in that pH region is practically eliminated.   According to Murray and White (127), the keeping quality of a sensitizing solution is improved considerably by subjecting it to a heat of about 260°F and to approximately twenty pounds of pressure. The increasing viscosity during the aging can be accounted for by the attractive action of the chromic ions for parts of the peptide chain.   This attractive action increases with increasing concentration of chromic ions, until enough forces are present to cause gelation of the solution.

Coating solutions that have undergone aging produce layers which are already partially insolubilized and thus require less light to complete the hardening.   For this reason they seem to be more light-sensitive.

Layers obtained from considerably aged solutions are almost insoluble and useless for practical purposes.   They probably retain some light sensitivity, however, and, if such plates are exposed to actinic radiation under a negative and drastic development methods are used, an image may be obtained.

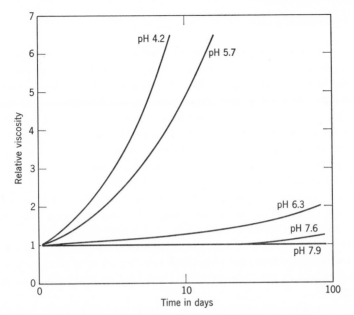

Figure 2.14.   *Variation in viscosity during aging of dichromated solutions.   Reprinted
with the permission of Percy Lund, Humphries & Co. Ltd. (reference 126).*

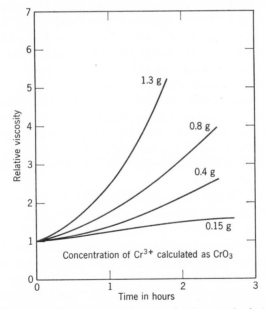

Figure 2.15.   *Variation in viscosity during aging of dichromated solutions.   Reprinted
with permission of Percy Lund, Humphries & Co., Ltd. (reference 126).*

2.6b   Sensitized Layer

When a freshly prepared solution is coated on a plate and dried, an oxidation-reduction reaction starts.   As the sensitive layer ages, the layer becomes more and more insoluble.   A sensitized layer hardens completely in the dark after a few days, depending on the temperature and relative humidity.   Watter (107) was able to keep pigment papers sensitized with ammonium dichromate for 70 days in the ice box, and for only three days at room temperature.   The difference in solubility between the exposed and unexposed parts becomes smaller, finally, so small that development without damaging the image is no longer possible.   The degree to which the dark reaction has progressed affects the exposure time necessary to reach the required degree of hardening.   The partial aging then can be compared to an over-all pre-exposure, so that shorter exposure is required to harden the sections of the layer completely.   This is due to the fact that the prior decomposition has hardened the colloid to some extent, and so less energy in the form of light is required to bring about complete insolubility.

The importance of controlled atmospheric humidity during drying and storage of sensitized plates can be related to the ionic character of the dark reaction.   For example, the dark reaction can proceed in air-dried layers or in layers dried with gentle warming, since such layers will always contain some water.   On the other hand, after being dried at a temperature high enough to dehydrate the coating, the dark reaction does not occur and consequently the shelf life is very good.   Reed and Dorst (113) studied the effect of relative humidity on the dark reaction rate of dichromated-albumin sensitized aluminum plates at room temperature.   They aged the sensitized plates in containers within which the relative humidity was controlled with the help of saturated salt solutions inside the jars.   The plates were removed at certain time intervals and dyed with methyl violet after development.   Figure 2.16 shows the relationship between relative humidity and the aging time required for the layers to reach the maximum dye absorption.

Protein layers absorb water very easily (128); their moisture content is a function of the relative humidity of the surrounding air.   The control of relative humidity during drying, storage, and handling is of importance.   Also, under controlled conditions, the sensitized material is serviceable only for a limited period and should be used as soon as possible after coating.   Overcoating of the sensitized layer with a varnish (129) or a waxy material (130) is only partially successful and is generally not used.

The marked influence of temperature on the rate of the dark reaction had already been observed by Lumiere and Seyewitz (131) and had been

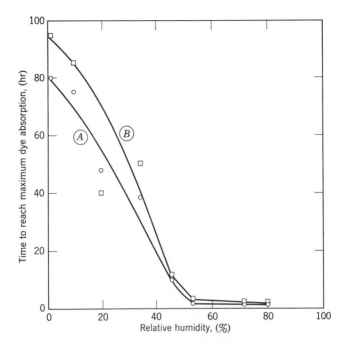

Figure 2.16. Relation between relative humidity and the time required for albumin coatings to reach maximum dye absorption in the absence of light (reference 90).

(A) *Coating solution without ammonia (pH 5.6 chlorphenol red)*
(B) *Coating solution with ammonia (pH 8.1 phenol red)*

further investigated by Bekk (132). The pronounced effect of temperature is, however, not surprising, since an increase in temperature almost invariably increases the rate of chemical reactions. In many cases, an increase of 10°C in temperature doubles or more than doubles the rate of reaction. The Lithographic Technical Foundation (90) investigated the influence of temperature on the thermal decomposition of deep-etch coatings on zinc plates, and showed that in the temperature range between 25 and 42°C, each rise of 10°C increased the dark reaction rate about threefold, provided the relative humidity was kept constant.

The same institution reported that the thermal reaction on dichromated-albumin and gum-arabic deep-etch plates, can almost be stopped when the plates are stored at 38°F (3.3°C) and 72 per cent relative humidity. However, a small drop in gamma can be expected after sensitized materials have been stored at low temperature for a prolonged period (133).

An increase in the initial concentration of reactants also results in acceleration of the dark reaction. During the course of a thermal reaction, the rate for any given initial concentration does not remain constant, but is highest at the beginning and decreases with time as the reactants are consumed. It would be expected that the rate of the dark reaction would decrease with time, since the concentration of dichromate in the layers would also be decreasing. For the hardening of a colloid, however, only very small amounts of chromic ions are necessary, and the decrease of dichromate-ion concentration during the decomposition process is insignificant in any practical formulation.

The nature of the constituent colloid also affects the insolubilization; since this influence has been insufficiently stressed in the past, there are not many facts known. Presumably, a colloid with a higher pH will give coatings with better keeping qualities than one with a lower pH, provided no pH adjustments have been made. Also, it is known that as the solubility of the constituent colloid decreases, it can be expected that the shelf life of the coating will shorten also. Colloids composed of larger molecules are believed to become insolubilized faster than those of smaller molecules. To draw any positive conclusions from the physical characteristics of the colloids, however, would be very difficult.

2.6c   *Mechanism of the Dark Reaction*

The pronounced effect of the layer's moisture content, temperature, pH, and, to some extent, the influence of the dichromate-colloid ratio on the rate of the thermal reaction, together with the observation that a layer dehydrated immediately after the coating and kept in this condition in the dark will remain fresh without any sign of hardening for a long period of time, suggests the following mechanism for the dark reaction. When a dichromate is dissolved in water, it is dissociated according to the equation

$$Cr_2O_7^{2-} + H_2O \longrightarrow 2HCrO_4^- \longrightarrow 2H^+ + 2CrO_4^{2-} \qquad (21)$$

When this solution, together with the colloid, is coated on a plate and dried, the pH of the layer drops because of the formation of chromic acid and chromate:

$$2HCrO_4^- \longrightarrow H_2CrO_4 + CrO_4^{2-} \qquad (22)$$

At this time, the aging taking place is represented by an oxidation-reduction process. Chromic acid is reduced to trivalent chromium, and the colloid is oxidized:

$$2H_2CrO_4 + 6H^+ + 3e \longrightarrow 2Cr^{3+} + 5H_2O + 3O \qquad (23)$$

The oxidation of the colloid can be illustrated as follows:

$$=CHOH + O \longrightarrow =C=O + H_2O \tag{24}$$

During the oxidation-reduction process, water is formed as a reaction product; this is probably responsible for the syneresis taking place in dichromated gels. At this point, it should be remembered that the oxidation of the colloid is not responsible for the hardening, and that the oxidation products are only of secondary importance.

If the pH is in the neighborhood of 7 or higher, the equilibrium

$$Cr_2O_7^{2-} \rightleftharpoons 2CrO_4^{2-} \tag{25}$$

is shifted to the right and chromic acid cannot be formed; this explains the excellent keeping of solutions with adjusted pH.

The common practice of adding ammonia to solutions of dichromated colloids in order to improve the shelf life of the sensitizing solution does not have any effect on the keeping quality of the sensitized plate. As soon as the plate is coated, ammonia starts to evaporate, and as a result of the evaporation the pH drops to the acid side. Green and Howard (134) report a pH decrease from 8.3 before coating to pH 5.9 after coating. Similar results have been reported by the Lithographic Technical Foundation; their investigation shows that the pH, varying from 7.2 to 9.2, fell, within one hour after coating, to pH 4.9 to 5.0; this indicates that apparently all the excess ammonia that had been added to the solution, evaporated during the coating, drying and one-hour aging.

If a solid alkali (sodium hydroxide or carbonate) is used for adjusting the pH of the coating solution, the alkalinity of the dried layer is not changed, and remains the same during the aging period. The very good keeping of such layers can be explained by the neutralization of chromic acid with the nonvolatile alkali

$$H_2CrO_4 + Na_2CO_3 = H_2CO_3 + Na_2CrO_4 \tag{26}$$

Because, at such a high pH the concentration of $HCrO_4^-$-ions is very small, the sensitivity to light is low.

The hardening of dichromated colloids is a chemical process, the rate of which depends on the composition of the sensitizing solution, the nature of the reactants, the pH, and, to no lesser degree, on the conditions under which the layer was dried and stored.

The composite effect of these factors on the rate of hardening in the dark can be expressed by the following equation (135):

$$\text{Reaction rate} = \frac{kT}{h} \cdot \frac{f(C_1 \cdot C_2 \cdots)}{f(C_A \cdot C_B \cdots)} \cdot e^{-\frac{E}{RT}} \tag{27}$$

where k, h, e, R = physical constants

T = absolute temperature

C_1, C_2 = functions of the concentration of the reaction products

$C_A C_B$ = functions of the concentration of the reactants (colloid, dichromate, moisture content, pH, etc.)

E = energy of activation

From this equation, it can be seen that, for a given dichromate-colloid concentration, the rate of thermal decomposition will be low when the pH is high and the temperature and relative humidity are low.   For this reason, many plate-making rooms are air-conditioned in order to keep the temperature around 70°F and the relative humidity below 50 per cent.

If the value of one of these three factors (pH, T, RH) is favorable for a low dark-reaction rate, this factor dominates, and the shelf life of the coating will be good.   For instance, when the pH of the coating is high, the dark reaction will be slow, even at high temperature and high relative humidity.   On the other hand, coatings with a low pH value can be stored for long periods of time at low temperatures.

2.6d   *Stability of Chromates*

The poor shelf life of dichromated-colloid layers can be explained also by the molecular instability of the hexavalent chromium compounds. These compounds may be arranged in a series of increasing complexity, in which the oxygens are regarded as being successively replaced by CrO_4^{2-}-ions (136).

Me_2CrO_4	chromates
$Me_2CrO_3 \cdot CrO_4$	dichromates
$Me_2CrO_2 \cdot (CrO_4)_2$	trichromates
$Me_2CrO \cdot (CrO_4)_3$	tetrachromates

In this series of compounds, the stability decreases with increasing molecular weight; in the presence of water, chromates and dichromates are stable, and the trichromates and tetrachromates decompose immediately into lower chromates and chromic acid:

$$Me_2CrO_2 \cdot (CrO_4)_2 + 2H_2O \longrightarrow Me_2CrO_4 + 2H_2CrO_4 \qquad (28)$$

The poor storage properties of layers sensitized with pyridine dichromate (137,138) can be explained by the tendency of the compound to split into pyridine and dichromic acid; dichromic acid rapidly hardens the colloid.

$$C_5H_5N \cdot H_2CrO_3 \cdot CrO_4 \longrightarrow C_5H_5N + H_2Cr_2O_7 \qquad (29)$$

2.7 METHODS FOR INCREASING THE SENSITIVITY

One of the chief drawbacks of dichromated-colloid processes is their low sensitivity to light. The printing speed of dichromated-colloid layers is very low, about that of printing-out papers. The sensitivity, as we have already seen, can be influenced to a limited extent by the composition of the sensitizing solution.

In the past, many efforts have been made to increase the sensitivity by the addition of various agents, either to the colloid mixtures themselves, or to the sensitizing or developing baths. Their action is either to promote the reduction of the dichromate ion to chromic ion, which then hardens the colloid, or to partially tan the colloids themselves.

Before we discuss ways of increasing the sensitivity, we must mention that all these methods have also been found to accelerate the dark reaction. On account of this, the storage life of both the sensitizing solution and the sensitized coating is radically shortened, and hence, methods of accelerating the light reaction have not yet come into general use.

Among the first agents suggested for this purpose was manganese sulfate (139), but later it was found by Eder (140) that this addition did not improve the sensitivity, although in contrast to previous findings, it did improve the storage stability of the sensitized layer.

After a study of dichromate processes, Valenta (141) and Eder (142) noticed that some substances decreased the speed, and others increased it; it was reported that the addition of cupric chloride to dichromated glue considerably increased the sensitivity of the layer. This effect was later confirmed by Cherney (143). Eder reported that an addition of about one-tenth per cent cupric chloride increased the sensitivity three to four times, and Tritton (144) obtained only a twofold increase in speed. Copper sulfate and cobalt chloride were not as good. In all cases, the keeping quality of the sensitized tissues was greatly lowered, and it was suggested that these salts be used, not in the sensitizing solutions, but as developers for exposed dichromated-colloid layers. A considerable increase in sensitivity by incorporation of soluble copper, cobalt, nickel, and the rare earths salts into the colloid layer, while in an unsensitized state, was reported by Sharp (145).

Tritton (146) was more successful with salts of cerium and lanthanum, and stated that an increase in sensitivity could be obtained by the addition of metallic salts, the hydroxides of which are precipitated at a pH slightly higher than that of the colloid solution. If the pH of the solution is lower than, or equal to, the pH at which the hydroxide precipitates, there will be a tendency for the hydroxide to be deposited in the gelatin and harden it. Since cerium and lanthanum hydroxides precipitate at pH 8.0 and 8.5, respectively (147), presumably the salts of these two elements do not tan the gelatin at all, but increase the printing speed three and four times, respectively (148).   Lobel and Dubois (149,150) reported that the presence of thorium chloride as an impurity in the cerium chloride may prevent the sensitizing action.

The use of magnesium chloride with an acid salt was patented in England by Wadhams and co-workers (151), who disclosed several sensitizing formulas for obtaining higher sensitivity.   They claim that nickel chloride also gives satisfactory results, and ferric and cupric chlorides are unsuitable. The same patent suggests aniline hydrochloride, which is blackened by light as much as dichromate, provided that magnesium chloride is present. The effect of ammonium nitrate was reported by John (152).

According to Zechnall (153), the light sensitivity of dichromated colloids is increased only by the addition of metallic salts that form insoluble chromates, but do not form a precipitate on contact with a dichromate. During the exposure, the dichromates are converted into neutral chromates, which then react with the metallic salt to precipitate insoluble chromate. The metallic salt does not, itself, contribute to the tanning of the colloid, but reacts with the chromate and this way increases the tanning action.

The effect of organic bases was studied by Hauberrisser (154); he suggested the addition of aniline, methylamine, and other compounds containing amino groups, for sensitizing purposes.   In all instances this increased printing speed, but at the same time considerably reduced keeping qualities.

Maillet (138) introduced the use of pyridine dichromate as a sensitizing agent for colloids used in photomechanical printing processes.   This sensitizer is obtained by the direction action of chromic acid on pyridine; by varying the proportions, salts of different sensitivities are obtained. Instead of pyridine, other organic bases like pyperidine, quinoline, quinoxaline, etc., can be used.   These salts may be separated and crystallized or added to the colloid in the dissolved stage.   Pure pyridine dichromate —$Cr_2O_7H_2 \cdot C_5H_5N \cdot 11H_2O$—forms water-soluble orange-red crystals; impure crystals are brown or black, with an unpleasant odor.   They are also not completely soluble in water.

The particular combination of pyridine and chromic acid adopted by Maillet, was called "Pyrax."   The exposure of the "Pyrax"-sensitized layers was reduced to one third, compared with ammonium dichromate. Cotton (155) concluded comparative tests with pyridine dichromate and ammonium dichromate.   According to his results (Figure 2.17), plates sensitized with "Pyrax" needed only 62.5 per cent of the exposure of a plate sensitized with ammonium dichromate, to achieve the same result.   In Cotton's opinion, much of this difference was due to the fact that the

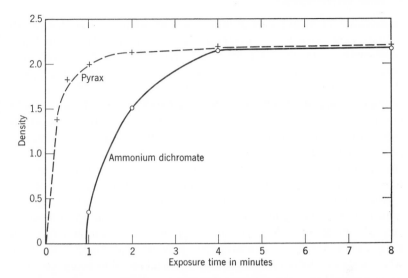

Figure 2.17. Sensitivity of "Pyrax" sensitized layers (reference 155).

resistance to ultraviolet light of the solution sensitized with "Pyrax," was much less than that of the solution sensitized with ammonium dichromate.

This process, in spite of certain advantages, did not find wide acceptance because of poor storage qualities.

Another way to increase the sensitivity of dichromated colloids is the addition of a reducing agent to the sensitizing bath, with consequent reduction of the dichromate ion to chromic ion; this results in the tanning of the colloid. Reducing agents, for example, sodium sulfite, reduce the dichromate immediately and, therefore, are unsuitable. Only mild reducing agents can be employed and even among these, selection must be made very carefully. Weingarten (156) suggested potassium ferrocyanide, which has mild reducing properties, but the results were unreliable.

While the addition of reducing agents to the sensitizing solution has a deteriorative effect on dichromated layers, even in the absence of light, better results can be obtained by developing the exposed material in a solution containing a mild reducing agent. For this purpose, hydroquinone and phloroglucinol have been suggested; resorcinol and thiourea work also, and increase the sensitivity up to fifty times (153).

Gorodnitzky (157) claims an increase in sensitivity of five times, after a thirty-minute hypersensitizing of the dichromated-colloid layer with mercury vapor, and ten times after a one-hour treatment.

Since dichromated-colloid layers are sensitive only to blue, violet, and ultraviolet light, it was only logical, during the time that the optical sensitization of silver halide emulsions was becoming known, that investigations were carried out on sensitizing dichromated colloids to longer wavelengths with the help of sensitizing dyes. G.O.'t Hooff (158) describes a procedure for the color sensitization of dichromated colloid. A dichromated-gelatin layer is bathed with a solution of a dye (for example, malachite green, ethyl cyanine, pinatype green D, ethyl violet, erythrosine, rose bengal). According to his results, the plate gained sensitivity to orange and red light. For sensitizing, Seymour (159) used silver iodide having turquoise blue adsorbed on it. G.O.'t Hooff's sensitizing method did not find wide application, because it was necessary to expose the plates wet to assure maximum sensitivity increase.

More recently, Oster and Oster (160,161) investigated the photoreduction of a variety of metal ions, and found that this photoreduction can take place in visible light in the presence of photoreducible dyes. During the exposure, the dye (methylene blue) is reduced to the leuco form, which serves as the reducing agent for the metal ion, thus being reoxidized to the normal form; the source of electrons is a chelating agent (ethylenediaminetetraacetic acid). By this method, dichromated-colloid layers are sensitized to the entire visible spectrum. This has been confirmed by Kerutskite and co-workers (162), who improved the sensitivity of dichromated-gelatin coating by incorporating triethanolamine and a spectral sensitizer like rose bengal, rhodamine B, eosin and erythrosin. By using arc-lamp exposure, the different dyes increased the tanning threshold sensitivity two to five times. Sensitization to red light with methylene blue was reported earlier by Jacobson and Wagner (163).

In spite of all these efforts to increase the sensitivity of dichromated-colloid systems, no method has been worked out which would find general application. It is the nature of the process that the optimum conditions for high sensitivity and good keeping quality are antagonistic, and it is natural that between these two extreme sets of conditions, only a compromise can be achieved.

2.7a *Desensitizing of Dichromated-Colloid Layers*

Dichromated-colloid layers are very slow, and it is usually not of interest to decrease the sensitivity. However, because the depressed sensitivity is accompanied by increased keeping quality, which in some cases might be desirable, a few methods of desensitizing will be mentioned. We have seen already that a higher pH decreases the sensitivity and increases the storage life of dichromated layers. A similar effect is produced by a lower concentration of dichromate, or by replacement of ammonium dichromate by the sodium salt.

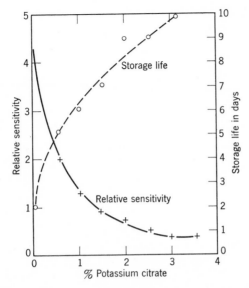

Figure 2.18. Effect of K-citrate on the sensitivity and storage life of dichromated colloid layers.

Probably the most controllable and efficient way to decrease the light sensitivity is the addition of salts that form complexes with the chromium. For this purpose, alkali metal citrates are generally used. Figure 2.18 shows the effect of potassium citrate on the light sensitivity and storage life of dichromated-gelatin layers.

2.8   SENSITOMETRY OF DICHROMATED-COLLOID LAYERS

Modern sensitometry dates from Hurter and Driffield's observation in 1890 that in an exposed and developed photographic emulsion the mass of reduced, metallic silver is proportional to exposure. This enabled them to characterize photographic sensitivities by studying these optical densities (D) as a function of the exposures producing them (E). On plotting D against log $10E$, they obtained the curves that have become standard for characterizing photographic emulsions sensitometrically.

Although the sensitometry of gelatin/silver halide photoemulsions has been studied extensively, that of dichromate-colloid layers has been studied hardly at all and a search of the literature discloses only a few papers. Work in this field is complicated by the great number of variable factors that influence the sensitivity of dichromated-colloid layers. The sensitometry of papers coated with dichromated gelatin containing dispersed carbon black, was studied by Richter (164) and Keilich (165). Hardy and Perrin (166) used silver bromide positive plates sensitized with a dichromate solution, and Bouček (107,167) made his sensitometric measurements on unpigmented dichromated layers.

When a dichromated-colloid layer is exposed to light through a photographic step tablet, the thickness of the hardened dichromate layer formed underneath each step reflects the depth to which the printing light has penetrated. When the layer is pigmented or dyed, the relative thickness of each hardened area is proportional to its transmission optical density. A plot of the measured density of each step against the logarithm of the exposure producing it, resembles the Hurter-Driffield characteristic curves for silver halide/gelatin photoemulsions; thus, within the linear portion the thickness of the hardened colloid is a linear function of the logarithm of the exposure time and the intensity of the printing illumination.

The slope (gamma), or steepness, of the linear portion of the curve is given by the ratio of any specific density increment, $(D_2 - D_1)$, to the difference between the logarithms of the respective exposures producing the two densities ($\log E_2 - \log E_1$):

$$\gamma = \frac{D_2 - D_1}{\log E_2 - \log E_1} \tag{31}$$

Where the printing illumination is constant, and only the exposure time (t) is varied, the equation becomes

$$\gamma = \frac{D_2 - D_1}{\log t_2 - \log t_1} \tag{32}$$

and its gamma is a measure of the contrast of a photoemulsion. Within the linear range of the characteristic curve, a given increase in exposure produces, in low-contrast photosensitive material, only a small increase in density, but a much larger change in high-contrast photosensitive material. Where t is the exposure time at which the straight-line portion of the characteristic curve, extended downward, intercepts the horizontal ($\log t$) axis (D is then zero), this represents the minimum correct exposure for this photosensitive material. This value for t_1 is known as the "inertia," and provides a measure of the photoemulsion speed.

The straight-line portion in the characteristic curve for a dichromated-colloid layer is longer than in a silver halide/gelatin characteristic-curve, and often extends over a relative-exposure scale of one to one hundred. As a result, dichromated-colloid reproductions are remarkably faithful and are especially suitable for positives; even today, in certain fields, they cannot be replaced by conventional gelatin/silver halide materials.

The specific form of the characteristic curve—and the degree of contrast, which is related to this—is determined by the spectral properties of the printing light and by the optical absorption of the photosensitive layer. Cartwright (113) prepared characteristic curves for dichromated gelatin exposed with two separate light sources: enclosed arc light (200 volts, 10 amps) and tungsten (1000 watts). These curves are shown in Figure 2.19. The ultraviolet rich arc light produces a less steep curve than does the tungsten light because shorter rays are scattered and absorbed in the top layer of the photoemulsion, and rays of longer wavelength penetrate more deeply, and produce prints of higher contrast (or, in other words, a thicker insolubilized layer). Monochromatic light produces a straight-line characteristic curve without either toe or shoulder (168). This is shown in Figure 2.20. Monochromatic light of short wavelength (366 mμ) produces a less tilted line than does monochromatic light of longer wavelengths (405 and 436 mμ). Radiation containing multiple wavelengths produces a slightly curved line.

The dichromate concentration influences not only the sensitivity (speed) of the coating, but also the contrast of the resulting print. In general, at lower concentrations the contrast and inertia are greater (hence, the speed is lower). Figure 2.21 shows sensitometric curves obtained by Watter (108) for papers sensitized with ammonium dichromate solutions (0.25 per cent, 1 per cent, and 5 per cent). At higher dichromate concentrations, the sensitivity increases, but the contrast decreases considerably because of light absorption in the upper layers. The use of sodium and potassium dichromates in varying proportions affects the contrast of the developed print slightly (169); a relatively high concentration of sodium dichromate tends to produce softer contrast. In addition, the spectral character of the light source strongly influences the extent to which

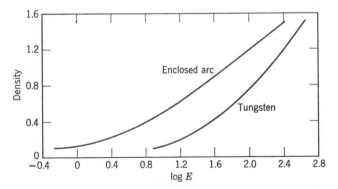

Figure 2.19. Characteristic curves for dichromated gelatin layer exposed with two different light sources (reference 112).

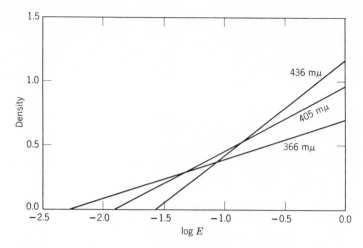

Figure 2.20. Characteristic curves for dichromated-colloid layers exposed with monochromatic light of different wavelengths (reference 168).

dichromate concentration affects speed and contrast. Dichromate concentration has practically no effect in the presence of tungsten light, but ultraviolet and violet rays are relatively more highly absorbed at higher dichromate concentrations. A similar effect is produced by the addition of dyes that absorb actinic radiation (113,166,170).

One additional factor affecting the print contrast is the pH of the sensitizer bath. For example, gelatin films sensitized in a solution of low hydrogen-ion concentration yield prints having higher contrast because the low-density areas have not been light-hardened.

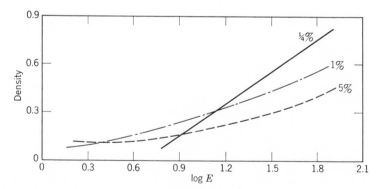

Figure 2.21. Effect of the dichromate concentration on the characteristic curve (reference 107).

REFERENCES

1. K. Smith and R. Zerbst. U.S. pat. 2,370,330/1945.
2. W. B. Hislop. *Process Engr. Monthly*, **48**, 328 (1941).
3. F. Fiedler. *Deut. Kamera Almanach*, **30**, 169–179 (1940).
4. E. M. Symmes. *Am. Phot.*, **38**, No. 8, 23 (1944).
5. E. M. Symmes. U.S. pat. 2,381,234/1945.
6. J. Sury. U.S. pat. 1,571,103/1926.
7. J. Crawford. U.S. pat. 2,244,905/1941.
8. H. C. J. Deeks. U.S. pat. 1,430,061/1922.
9. J. M. Lupo, Jr. U.S. pat. 2,716,060/1955.
10. P. C. Smethurst. *Phot. J.*, **92 B**, 115–123 (1952).
11. H. H. Lerner. U.S. pat. 3,012,886/1961.
12. H. L. Howard and G. C. Wensley. *Process Engr. Monthly*, **66**, 235–242 (1959).
13. R. S. Cox and H. L. Howard. *Process Engr. Monthly*, **66**, 10–13 (1959).
14. J. T. Rigley. *Process Engr. Monthly*, **54**, 145 (1947).
15. B. J. Slater. *N.Y. State J. Med.*, **36**, 1731 (1936).
16. B. J. Slater. *J. Am. Med. Assoc.*, **96**, 633 (1931).
17. F. Fairbrother. *Biochem. J.*, **18**, 647 (1924).
18. J. Knaggs, A. B. Manning and S. B. Schreiver. *Biochem. J.*, **17**, 423 (1923).
19. E. Elöd and H. Berczeli. *Kolloid-Z.*, **75**, 66–73 (1936).
20. W. T. Astbury. *J. Intern. Soc. Leather Trade's Chemists*, **24**, 69 (1940).
21. C. B. Anfinsen, Jr., M. L. Anson, K. Bailey, and J. T. Edsall. *Advances in Protein Chemistry*, Vol. 16, p. 31, Academic Press, New York, 1961.
22. A. Rich and F. H. C. Crick. *Nature*, **176**, 915–916 (1955).
23. P. M. Cowan, S. McGavin, and A. C. T. North. *Nature*, **176**, 1062–1064 (1955).
24. G. N. Ramachanran. *Nature*, **177**, 710–711 (1956).
25. H. L. Keil and E. F. Cavanaugh. U.S. pat. 3,073,702/1963.
26. O. L. Sponsler, J. D. Bath, and J. W. Ellis. *J. Phys. Chem.*, **44**, 996–1006 (1940).
27. D. J. Lloyd and H. Phillips. *Trans. Faraday Soc.*, **29**, 132–148 (1933).
28. L. Pauling. *J. Am. Chem. Soc.*, **67**, 555–557 (1945).
29. E. F. Mellon, A. H. Korn, and S. R. Hoover. *J. Am. Chem. Soc.*, **69**, 827–831 (1947).
30. A. B. D. Cassie. *Trans. Faraday Soc.*, **41**, 450–458 (1945).
31. E. F. Mellon, A. H. Korn, and S. R. Hoover. *J. Am. Chem. Soc.*, **70**, 3040–3044 (1948).
32. S. E. Sheppard and R. C. Houck. *J. Phys. Chem.*, **36**, 2319–2324 (1932).
33. J. Pouradier. *Sci. Ind. Phot.*, **19**, 81–91 (1948).
34. F. Hofmester. *Z. Physiol. Chem.*, **2**, 299 (1878).
35. S. E. Sheppard and R. C. Houck. *J. Phys. Chem.*, **36**, 2885–2900 (1932).
36. H. Brintzinger and K. Maurer. *Kolloid-Z.*, **41**, 6 (1927).
37. F. Blum. *Z. Physiol. Chem.*, **22**, 127 (1896).
38. E. F. Dell. U.S. pat. 2,229,052/1941.
39. L. L. Pries. U.S. pat. 2,858,214/1958.
40. C. H. van Deusen. U.S. pat. 2,434,727/1948.
41. F. R. Senti. *Am. Dyestuff Reptr.*, **36**, 230 (1947).
42. T. R. Caton. U.S. pat. 2,921,852/1960.
43. J. P. Danehy. U.S. pat. 2,324,197/1943.
44. J. P. Danehy and J. P. Newland. U.S. pat. 2,324,198/1943.

45. J. Milupo, Jr. U.S. pat. 2,716,061/1955.
46. C. L. Butler and L. W. Cretcher. *J. Am. Chem. Soc.*, **52**, 4509–4511 (1930).
47. A. P. Harrison. *Tappi*, **44**, 854–857 (1961).
48. W. H. Wood. U.S. pat. 2,645,578/1953.
49. W. H. Wood. U.S. pat. 2,663,639/1953.
50. R. A. C. Adams. U.S. pat. 2,694,057/1954.
51. R. W. Kerr and G. M. Severson. *J. Am. Chem. Soc.*, **65**, 193–198 (1943).
52. R. W. Kerr. *Arch. Biochem.*, **7**, 377 (1945).
53. W. T. Ritter, R. O. Ragan, and R. F. Trant. U.S. pat. 2,916,376/1959.
54. Powers Chemco Inc. U.S. pat. 2,942,974/1960; Brit. pat. 764,380/1956; Ger. pat. 1,071,481/1959.
55. C. Eckardt. U.S. pat. 2,824,000/1958.
56. W. Krohe. Ger. pat. 932,646/1955; Ger. pat. 934,141/1955.
57. S. Takagaki. Japan pat. 29-2891/1954.
58. R. S. Colt. U.S. pat. 2,448,861/1948.
59. A. Miller. U.S. pat. 2,020,901/1935.
60. M. W. Seymour. U.S. pat. 2,043,905/1936.
61. F. F. Frost. U.S. pat. 2,624,673/1953.
62. D. A. Newman and A. T. Schlotzhauer. U.S. pat. 2,808,778/1957.
63. T. T. Boersma. U.S. pat. 2,819,164/1958; Ger. pat. 972,998/1959; Dutch pat. 83,171/1956.
64. W. H. Wood. U.S. pat. 2,199,865/1940; Brit. pat. 501,069/1937.
65. C. A. Brown. U.S. pat. 3,004,851/1961.
66. J. O. Printy and E. W. Wagner. U.S. pat. 2,990,281/1961.
67. Harris-Intertype Corp. Brit. pat. 864,033/1961; Ger. pat. 1,056,931/1959.
68. H. Prüfer and K. Dulik. U.S. pat. 1,964,136/1934.
69. R. Freundorfer and H. Hoerner. U.S. pat. 3,060,027/1962.
70. H. Hoerner. U.S. pat. 3,102,030/1963; Brit. pat. 906,465/1962.
71. The Printing, Packaging and Allied Trades Research Assoc. Fr. pat. 1,321,933/1963.
72. W. O. Herrmann and W. Haehnel. U.S. pat. 1,672,156/1928.
73. A. F. Greiner. U.S. pat. 2,174,629/1939.
74. W. C. Toland and E. Bassist. U.S. pat. 2,302,816/1942.
75. W. C. Toland and E. Bassist. U.S. pat 2,302,817/1942.
76. W. G. Mullen. U.S. pat. 2,444,205/1948.
77. C. A. Brown. U.S. pat. 2,830,899/1958.
78. C. A. Brown. U.S. pat. 2,742,358/1956.
79. J. M. Eder. *Phot. Korr.*, **15**, 32, 48, 75, 98, 117, 144 (1878).
80. J. M. Eder. *Brit. J. Phot.*, **25**, 150 (1878).
81. A. Popovitski. *J. Russ. Phys. Chem. Ges.*, **55**, 1 (1924).
82. M. Schiel. *Atelier Phot.*, **33**, 26 (1926).
83. F. Schönerer. *Phot. Rundschau*, **63**, 120, 138 (1926).
84. W. de W. Abney. *Instruction in Photography*, Iliffe Sons, Ltd., 1905.
85. A. C. Hardy and F. H. Perrin. *J. Franklin Inst.*, **205**, 197–219 (1928).
86. I. H. Mayer. *Z. Phys. Chem.*, **66**, 33 (1909).
87. K. Stötzer. *Reproduction*, p. 112, 1935.
88. M. Biltz and J. Eggert. *Wiss. Voröff, AGFA*, **3**, 294–302 (1933).
89. H. Ammann. *Z. Wiss. Phot.*, **36**, 33–58 (1937).
90. G. W. Jorgensen and M. H. Bruno. *The Sensitivity of Bichromated Coatings*, LTF, New York, 1954.

91. R. Wintgen and H. Löwenthal. *Kolloid-Z.*, **34**, 289–295 (1924).
92. P. C. Smethurst. *Sci. Ind. Phot.*, **18**, 23 (1947).
93. S. Asperger. *Arhiv Kemiju*, **20**, 46–60 (1948).
94. H. Stiehler. *Intern. Bull.*, January 1956, pp. 12–15.
95. E. Stiasny. *Gerbereichemie*, T. Steinkopff, Dresden, 1931.
96. A. E. van Arkel. *Molecules and Crystals in Inorganic Chemistry*, p. 178, Interscience Publishers, New York, 1956.
97. E. Elöd, T. Schachowskoy and T. de Chezeaulx-Meyer. *Kolloid-Z.*, **98**, 341–348 (1942).
98. A. Küntzel. *Kolloid-Z.*, **91**, 152–191 (1940); **97**, 99–104 (1941); **100**, 274–282 (1942).
99. P. C. Smethurst. *The Process Engr. Monthly*, **53**, 114–115, 142–143, 198–199, 229, 254–255 (1946).
100. A. Galinsky. *Biochem. J.*, **24**, 1706–1715 (1930).
101. H. Brintzinger and K. Maurer. *Kolloid-Z.*, **41**, 46 (1927).
102. A. A. Meisling. *Dansk Fotografish Tidssk.*, **38**, 65, 73 (1916).
103. J. C. Warburg. *Phot. J.*, **57**, 169 (1917).
104. S. Suzuki and K. Aisaka. *Bull. Soc. Sci. Phot. Japan*, **12**, 13–14 (1962).
105. O'Brien, Jr. *J. Opt. Soc. Am.*, **42**, 101–103 (1952).
106. J. Bouček. *Procédé*, **36**, 100 (1935).
107. O. Watter. *Phot. Korr.*, **71** (1935); Beilage des Juni-Heftes, Diss. Berlin, 1935.
108. W. Feldmann. *Untersuchungen über die Sensitometrie der Chromat-Schichten*, Diss., Hannover, 1936.
109. A. Heigl. *Deut. Drucker*, **48**, 449–452 (1942).
110. E. Rupp. *Fachhefte für Chemigraphie*, p. 137, 1950.
111. F. Ya. Shklover. *Zh. Nauchn. Prikl. Fotogr. Kinematogr.*, **3**, 191–196 (1958).
112. M. Cartwright. *Phot. J.*, **63**, 265–277 (1923).
113. R. F. Reed and P. W. Dorst. *Res. Bull.* 6, p. 97, LTF, New York, 1945.
114. R. W. Koch, D. J. Byers, and R. E. Rossell. *Proceedings of the Fourth Annual Tech. Meeting*, TAGA, pp. 105–119 (1952).
115. G. W. Jorgensen. *Research Progress* 14, LTF, New York, 1949.
116. N. Lebedenko. Fr. pat. 646,484/1928.
117. C. Roehrich. U.S. pat. 1,936,525/1933.
118. K. Herberts and Co. Fr. pat. 874,015/1942.
119. R. E. Liesegang. *La Photographie des Colleurs*, p. 288, 1908.
120. E. J. Bowen. *J. Chem. Soc.*, **1932**, 2031.
121. M. H. Bruno and A. Wahl. *National Lithographer* 53, July and August, 1946.
122. F. C. Cox. *Proceedings of the Third Annual Meeting*, TAGA, p. 9 (1951).
123. A. V. Frost, E. A. Galashin. *Zhur. Fiz. Khim.*, **28**, 1668–1671, 1954.
124. W. Romer, M. Luczak, and B. Starostka. *J. Phot. Soc.*, **9**, 274–276 (1961).
125. G. W. Jorgensen. *Modern Lithography*, **19**, 11, p. 35 (1951).
126. R. A. C. Adams. *The Penrose Annual*, **46**, 135 (1952).
127. J. J. Murray and L. A. White. U.S. pat. 2,000,453/1935.
128. E. F. Mellon, A. H. Korn, and S. Hoover. *J. Am. Chem. Soc.*, **69**, 827–31 (1947).
129. F. E. Ives. U.S. pat. 1,240,344/1917.
130. G. S. Rowell. U.S. pat. 1,992,965/1935.
131. A. Lumiere and A. Seyewetz. *Bull. Soc. Franc. Phot.*, **2**, 21, p. 541 (1905).
132. J. Bekk. *Klimschs. Jahrb. f.d. Graph. Gewerbe*, **28**, 119 (1935).
133. F. Henrici. *Chemigraphie*, p. 26, 1949.

134. L. P. Green and H. L. Howard. *Process Engr. Monthly*, **65**, 207–210 (1958).

135. G. W. Jorgensen and M. H. Bruno. *Phot. Eng.*, **7**, 1, 12–22 (1956).

136. J. R. Partington. *Textbook of Inorganic Chemistry*, p. 937, Macmillan and Co., Ltd., London, 1947.

137. G. Maillet. U.S. pat. 2,025,996/1935; Ger. pat. 601,658/1933; Fr. pat. 770,593/1934; Brit. pat. 417,643/1934; G. Maillet. *Procédé*, **36**, 16 (1935).

138. G. Maillet. *Bull. Soc. Franc. Phot.*, **22**, 202–204 (1935).

139. W. Weissenberger. *Phot. Korr.*, **25**, 463–467 (1888).

140. J. M. Eder. *Phot. Korr.*, **51**, 327 (1914).

141. E. Valenta. *Phot. Korr.*, **51**, 327–329 (1914).

142. J. M. Eder. *Procédé*, **20**, 132 (1919).

143. I. Cherney. *Photo-Kino. Chem. Ind. USSR*, No. 4, 28–30 (1935).

144. F. J. Tritton. *Phot. J.*, **69**, 281–285 (1929).

145. F. W. Sharp. U.S. pat. 1,994,289/1935.

146. F. J. Tritton. *Modern Lithography and Offset Printer*, **25**, No. 8, 178–180 (1929).

147. H. T. S. Britton. *J. Chem. Soc.*, **127**, 2142–2147 (1925).

148. F. W. Sharp and The Autotype Co., Ltd. Ger. pat. 528,638/1931; Brit. pat. 413,428/1934.

149. L. Lobel and M. Dubois. *Bull. Soc. Franç. Phot.*, **19**, 57–62 (1932).

150. L. Lobel and M. Dubois. *Kino Tech.*, **13**, 270–271 (1931).

151. W. H. Wadhams, A. Ziehm, H. A. Sonderman, and P. Worthe. Brit. pat. 228,377/1925.

152. R. John. U.S. pat. 1,875,292/1932.

153. A. Zechnall. *Über die Empfindlichkeitssteigerung von lightempfindlichen Bichromat-Fischleimschichten*, Diss., Darmstadt 1932.

154. G. Hauberrisser. *Phot. Korr.*, **44**, 225 (1907).

155. L. J. Cotton. *Process Engr. Monthly*, **43**, 309–313 (1936).

156. A. Weingarten. U.S. pat. 1,564,161/1925.

157. M. A. Gorodnitzky. *Polygrafitschaskoje Proiswodstwo*, **6** (1948).

158. G. O.'t Hooff. *Z. Wiss. Phot.*, **25**, 394–400 (1928).

159. M. W. Seymour. U.S. pat. 1,984,090/1934.

160. G. K. Oster and G. Oster. *J. Am. Chem. Soc.*, **81**, 5543–45 (1959).

161. G. K. Oster and G. Oster. U.S. pat. 3,074,794/1963.

162. M. K. Kerutskite, L. M. Ryabova, B. A. Shashlov, and V. I. Shebertsov. *Zh. Nauchn. i Prikl. Fotogr. i Kinematogr.*, **8** (4), 303–304 (1963).

163. K. Jacobson and E. Wagner. *Atelier Phot.*, **37**, 98–100 (1930).

164. V. Richter. *Z. Wiss. Phot.*, **23**, 61 (1925).

165. K. H. Keilich. *Z. Wiss. Phot.*, **37**, 195–218 (1938).

166. A. C. Hardy and F. H. Perrin. *J. Franklin Inst.*, **205**, 197–219 (1928).

167. J. Bouček. *Sb. České Vysoké Školy Techn. v Brně*, **9**, 30–36 (1935).

168. K. H. Keilich. *Z. Wiss. Phot.*, **37**, 195–218 (1938).

169. F. De. Lesseps. Brit. pat. 384,770/1932.

170. M. W. Seymour. U.S. pat. 1,984,090/1934.

3

Photomechanical Printing Processes

Dichromated colloid layers play an important role in the history of photographic processes. They form the base of many photographic and photomechanical processes, and, in spite of many disadvantages, dichromated colloids are still used at the present time. It is certainly very interesting to note that the tremendous progress made in the field of synthetic chemistry in the last years has not, in many instances, succeeded in offering to the trade a material which would do the job so well.

3.1 PHOTOGRAPHIC RESIST

Organic colloids sensitized with dichromates are very suitable for preparing photographic resists such as are needed in the production of fine lines, scales, and graticules (1,2,3), in manufacturing of fine metal grids (4), or for decorating and marking glass, ceramics, metals, and plastics (5,6,7,8). Yaeger and Lappala (9) used saponifiable scribe-coat layers sensitized with dichromated colloids for producing color separations required for map printing. In the last ten years, dichromated gelatin, glue, or polyvinyl alcohol (10) found an application in the expanding field of printed-circuit manufacture, although other types of photoresist have been quickly adopted by this industry (11,12,13).

The term "photoresist" refers to a protective stencil formed by selective insolubilization of a suitable material sensitive to light, so as to protect the underlaying surface against the action of physical, electrical, or chemical attack. During the exposure to actinic radiation, the light-sensitive material usually becomes less soluble, and the unexposed sections can be easily removed by a solvent, leaving a relief image on the support.

The application of dichromated colloids in the photomechanical printing field is by far the most important. Leaving aside manual and mechanical details, we will discuss the chemistry of these processes only; those seeking more information we refer to the trade literature (14,15,16,17,18).

3.2 PHOTOENGRAVING

Photoengraving is the oldest of the photomechanical processes and is concerned with the preparing of etched-relief and intaglio-metal printing plates. Originally the image on the metal was obtained by manual design. The first photoengraving was made in 1826 by Joseph Nicephore Nièpce on a pewter plate sensitized with Syrian asphalt, but these early attempts only established the basic principles of the process; real progress started with the introduction of the photographic negative, permitting an accurate and faithful reproduction of the original.

Photoengraving plates are prepared by sensitizing a metal plate with a dichromated solution, which, after the exposure to actinic radiation under suitable negative and development, acts as a resist to the etching acid.

Zinc was the first metal used in photoengraving, but other metals, such as copper, magnesium, or specially prepared alloys became popular also. Magnesium, for its light weight, high strength, and ease of processing is used very widely. In more recent years, bimetallic plates consisting of two or more different metals were introduced. All these metals have their advantages and disadvantages, and are used according to the nature of the work invoived. The plates are usually bought in large sheets and are cut by the engraver to the designed size.

After being polished with a pumice, the plates are coated on one side with a dichromated-colloid solution which is poured over the plate and dried in a whirling device in order to spread the enamel evenly over the surface; the speed of the whirler determines the thickness of the coating. The enameled plate is dried during the whirling. For zinc plates, dichromated albumen is used, and dichromated glue, alone or in combination with egg albumen (19), is preferred for sensitizing copper plates. For better hardening, β-hydroxy-butyric aldehyde (20) can be added. A small amount of alcohol (21) or a wetting agent (22) improves the wetting and flowing properties of the glue without interfering with the photosensitive characteristics of the material. Gum arabic is sometimes chosen for halftone color etching. The most simple and popular is, however, "cold-top enamel," a mixture of shellac, ammonium dichromate, and water, rendered alkaline (to a pH value of about 9.0) by ammonia, borax, or a carbonate (23,24,25,26). In order to prevent undercutting it was recommended that the metal plate be sensitized with a light-sensitive, semipermeable resist, e.g., dichromated gelatin. This layer is overcoated with a relatively thin, light-senstive, nonpermeable resist, such as shellac dissolved in ammonia and containing ammonium chromate (27).

With the progress of organic chemistry, new synthetic materials have been introduced for photomechanical processes. Polyvinyl alcohol, which may serve as an example, is used for sensitizing magnesium, and is the preferred photoresist for the Dow Etch process (28,29). Cold-top enamel does not adhere very well to magnesium unless specially treated (30).

The sensitized plate is next placed, together with the negative, in a vacuum printing frame and exposed to light, usually an electric-arc. The time of exposure varies with the atmospheric conditions, as mentioned before, with the intensity of the light, and with the density of the negative. It will obviously vary also with each sensitizer. The sensitized coating on the plate becomes hardened and insoluble wherever it is exposed to light. It is most important that the exposure be adequate to ensure that the colloid is insolubilized right down to the metal. Otherwise, there would be a tendency for the image to lift during development because the colloid dissolves below the hardened surface.

The plate is next rolled over with a greasy etching ink and developed by soaking in clean water and gentle rubbing of the surface with absorbent cotton until the unhardened areas are washed away. Those parts which have become insoluble by the action of light remain on the plate and act as an etching resist. Before the etching operation, the dried plate, for the purpose of increasing the acid resistance of the image, is powdered with topping powder which adheres to the ink. The surplus powder is removed and the plate is heated to fuse the resin. The acid resistivity of glue enamel is increased by heating the plate until the image acquires a chocolate-brown color. Both powdering and burning-in are not required when cold enamel has been used for sensitizing. In this case, the plate is ready for etching directly after development in alcohol.

Before starting the etching, the back side of the plate and the margins have to be protected from the action of the etchant by being covered with a varnish. At this stage, the plate is ready for etching, which can be described as the removal of metal from the nonprinting areas. Etching is usually done by a chemical method. To achieve this, the plate is placed in the etching bath for a short time, to get the "flat bite," then washed and dried by heat. Powdered dragon's blood, or some other suitable gum or resin, is applied in four directions so that after melting the resin all sides of the etched lines or dots will be protected from the etching solution. In this way, it is possible to etch deeply without the danger of undercutting the lines, the fundamental problem of the photoengraver. This operation is repeated as often as necessary to achieve the necessary printing depth.

One powdering may be sufficient for coarse halftone work, five or more powderings and etchings may be needed to reach 0.035 inch in some line work.   In order to prevent, or at least to reduce, the undercutting of the lines during the etching operation, it was suggested (31,32) that two images, one on top of the other, be prepared; the upper image was to be slightly larger or out-of-register with respect to the lower one.   Etching is carried out as usual until the undercutting of the top image approaches the first image.

Zinc is most satisfactory etched with nitric acid.   Etching with solutions of successively decreasing strengths produces, instead of deep pits, dish-shaped cells which carry the ink better and give clearer impressions in printing (33).   Lateral underetching of the edges at exposed-unexposed interfaces can be prevented by using a solution containing in addition to nitric acid a film-forming agent, a surface-active wetting agent, and an agent, e.g., gelatin, which prevents film formation at small insulated areas (34).

For copper, ferric chloride has been used almost exclusively.   It can be replaced with a cheaper solution, however, containing hydrochloric acid and cupric chloride (35).   Ammonium or sodium persulfate was suggested also (36).   Electrolytic etching, however, is supposed to be more economical (37).

Magnesium is treated with diluted nitric acid, alone or in combination with dioctyl sodium sulfosuccinate and some other organic chemicals, and a film-forming agent, as described in the Dow Etch process (38,39), covered by a number of patents (40,41,42,43).   In this process, the necessity for powdering plates is eliminated and the etching in stages is reduced to a single operation.   The process has gained wide acceptance in the photoengraving field and is carried out automatically in special etching machines.   The etching solution employed is essentially a two-phase system, containing diluted nitric acid and a wetting agent in the water phase, and diethylbenzene in the oily phase.   It etches vertically into the metal plate with practically no horizontal or side etching.   This action is explained by the formation of an acid-resistant film on the side walls of the relief.   This film is destroyed in nonresist areas of the plate by the large amount of heat generated during the etching.   Since some heat on the sides of resist areas is conducted away by the metal under the resist, the temperature at this area is significantly lower and the film is not dissolved.   As the etching action continues, the acid-resisting film is continuously formed on the bare metal, thereby preventing the etchant from undercutting the resist areas.   A similar approach for preventing undercutting in etching copper plates was taken by Photo-Engravers Research, Inc. (44) and is based on the gelatinous film formation on the surface of a copper plate etched in a ferric chloride solution containing thiourea (45). In another variety, a passivating agent is added to the ferric chloride solution. The passivating agents are formamide disulfite and its salts (46), and are added in a concentration of 0.6 to 3 grams per liter, to an etching solution containing 200 to 460 grams of ferric chloride. An increase in the rate of vertical etch can be accomplished by the addition of small amounts of isopropanol amines. Finely divided inert powders, such as magnesium silicate, incorporated in the foregoing etching bath do affect the reduction in area loss (47). An etching emulsion consisting of diluted nitric acid, a petroleum solvent and an alkyl-aryl-sulfonate wetting agent was recommended by Sherer and Ruzicka (48). This single-step etching process is equivalent to the conventional three to five steps.

It has been also proposed to etch photoengraving plates by use of a sand blast (49,50), but this is generally unsatisfactory. The line etching process is also occasionally used for color work. Each color requires a separate plate, which is processed in the usual way.

When a full-tone subject has to be reproduced, halftone engraving has to be employed. For this purpose, negatives are exposed behind a half-tone screen, so that the continuous tones in the original are represented by a large number of separate dots of varying size and uniform density on the developed image. The fineness of the screen is largely governed by the tone of gray required and by the quality of the printing paper. Each halftone dot represents a minute portion of the entire picture. Copper plates sensitized with dichromated glue are used almost exclusively. Processing is about the same as in the line etching. Ferric chloride is used as the etchant. The same procedure is used in the etching of halftone colorplates, with the difference that four separation negatives have to be used. The loss of saturation produced by dividing the image into dots is compensated for by a supplementary black printing which fills in the empty space.

Recently a new method for producing engraved plates or cylinders has been introduced (51), which dispenses altogether with etching. In this process, an apparatus is used which is equipped with an optical-electronic device which scans the grey tones of the original. The registered impulses are then electronically transferred to an electromagnetic engraving system which engraves the appropriate dots straight onto the plate.

3.3 PHOTOGRAVURE

Photogravure is a photomechanical intaglio-printing process. In this method the image is etched below the surface of a plate or cylinder, deeply into the areas representing the shadows and less deeply into the highlights.

The ink is held in little pits and cannot be squeezed out at the sides. With this process it is possible to deposit on the printing surface various thicknesses of ink according to the depth of the etched cavities.

In photogravure the most common printing surfaces are copperized cylinders or thin copper plates which can be attached to the cylinders of rotary presses.   For this reason, the process is also called rotogravure. The construction and the size of the cylinders vary, depending on the design of the rotogravure press and on the type of work produced.

The first step in the preparation of a gravure form is the sensitizing of the carbon tissue.   Carbon tissue, sometimes called "pigment paper," which serves after development as a resist during the etching, essentially consists of a paper support of sufficient strength, coated with a mixture of medium-hard gelatin and red-brown iron oxide.   This layer may also contain other materials to render the tissue more pliable and to improve the working qualities of the tissue.

In spite of all the disadvantages connected with the instability of dichromated colloid layers, no other light-sensitive material has been found, up to the present time, which would do the job so well.   The only exception, perhaps, is Rotofilm (Du Pont) consisting of a fine grain orthochromatic gelatino-silver halide emulsion coated on a "stripping" type film (52,53), such as polyethylene terephthalate film with a gelatin-polyvinyl pyrrolidone stripping layer (54).   Another material designed to replace pigment paper is that introduced by Gevaert under the name of "Rotargo" (55).

A simple solution of potassium dichromate serves as a sensitizer for carbon tissue.   The concentration of dichromate ranges from 2.5 to 5 per cent.   The time of immersion varies with the temperature, the pH, and the strength of the bath.   The water content of the gelatin before sensitizing is also most important.   In general practice gravure tissues are immersed in the dichromate bath for three minutes.   However, de Goeij (56) suggested that pigment paper, in order to have reproducible properties, should be acclimated to a certain relative humidity and temperature before sensitizing, and sensitized in a weaker solution for a longer time if anything like comparable properties are to be achieved.

Sensitized tissue is then "squeezed" on a ferrotype plate in order to remove all moisture and air bubbles which may be trapped between the plate and tissue, and uniformly dried.   As soon as it is dry, it becomes detached from the plate.

Sensitized and dried pigment paper is then exposed, under the assembly of continuous-tone gravure positives, to carbon-arc lamps, resulting in differential hardening of the gelatin coating.   All the tones of the positive are represented on the exposed tissue by different thicknesses of hardened gelatin. After the exposure, the positives are removed and the exposed tissue is given another exposure, this time through a specially ruled screen, which breaks up the tones of the photograph and forms on the etched cylinder a pattern of raised lines preventing a doctor blade from wiping the thin intaglio ink out of the etched areas during the printing. The usual ruling of the screen is 150 to 175 lines to the inch, and differs from cross-line halftone screens in that the opaque squares are wider than the transparent lines. When it is necessary to etch a picture and type simultaneously, Wolfson recommended providing the picture part with a special screen (57).

The exposure time varies, as in all dichromated-colloid coatings, not only with the composition of the sensitized tissue, but also with the age of the tissue and with atmospheric conditions (58). Following the exposure, the carbon tissue is ready for transfer to the copper cylinder, which previously has been made chemically clean and free from grease. This is done either by the "dry-lay" technique or by a "wet" method. Transfer of the tissue is, in principle, a very simple operation; however, it requires close attention and much experience. Perhaps the most serious problem, particularly in multicolor work, is to produce a set of plates all having the same image size. To improve the dimensional stability of the carbon tissue under changing conditions of temperature and humidity, Sandford and Howe (59) suggested, prior to exposure, placing a dimensionally stable backing sheet, coated with a pressure-sensitive adhesive, against the paper backing of the carbon tissue.

The next operation is known as developing, and involves immersing the cylinder on which the carbon tissue has been transferred in warm water. Gelatin which has been hardened during the exposure does not dissolve in warm water and remains on the cylinder, and the unexposed, and thus soluble, gelatin is washed from the print. The backing paper is stripped off at the moment it starts to become detached at the ends, and development continues till completion. The time required for the removal of the backing sheet from the gelatin layer can be reduced by applying a benzole acetone mixture to the back of the carbon paper prior to development (60). The cylinder, with all that is left of the gelatin film, is cooled and dried. All other parts of the printing surface which are not to be etched are protected with an acid-resistant turpentine-benzol-asphalt varnish. This operation is called "staging."

When ready the printing surface is subjected to the action of ferric chloride solutions of varying concentrations which penetrate the carbon-paper resist to the same degree that the light has hardened the gelatin. In other words, the rate of penetration depends on the thickness of the resist (61,62). As illustrated in Figure 3.1, thinner parts of the resist are

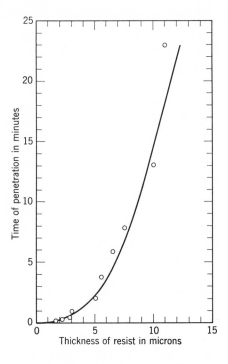

Figure 3.1.   Relation of resist thickness to penetration time (reference 63).

penetrated more rapidly by the mordant solution, with the result that underlying areas are etched first and proportionately to greater depths and, consequently, are able not only to hold more ink but also deposit more ink on the paper to be printed than areas attacked at a later stage.   Thus, a thin gelatin layer gives dark tones, and a thick layer, highlights.   Dugan (63), in his study on single-solution etching, calculated that the time of penetration varies as the third power of the thickness.   In other words, if the thickness of the resist is doubled, the time of penetration becomes eight times as long.   The rate of diffusion is, of course, also influenced by the temperature and relative humidity and is accelerated by both factors. The depth to which the copper plate is etched depends on printing conditions, the color of the ink, and on the characteristics of the printed surface.

In order to obtain smoother etching, Dugan (64) and Thode (65) recommend the addition of ferric sulfate to the ferric chloride solution. The rate of penetration can be further controlled by addition of copper to the fresh etching solution (66).

The chemistry of copper etching with ferric chloride was studied by Cartwright (67). He showed that in the initial action, cuprous chloride is formed on the surface of the copper plate:

$$FeCl_3 + Cu = FeCl_2 + CuCl \tag{1}$$

Cuprous chloride is insoluble in water and would remain as a white solid on the plate if no adequate amount of ferric chloride were present. However, ferric chloride oxidizes cuprous chloride almost immediately to soluble cupric chloride, which diffuses out through the gelatin.

$$FeCl_3 + CuCl = CuCl_2 + FeCl_2 \tag{2}$$

Because of this reaction, the reddish-brown ferric chloride solution acquires a darker color as the etching progresses, and, eventually, may become green as the concentration of cupric chloride increases. When the etching solution is stored in open containers, some of the ferrous chloride is oxidized back to the ferric salt, and some is converted into ferric hydroxide—an insoluble compound precipitating out in the used solution (65):

$$12FeCl_2 + 6H_2O + 3O_2 = 8FeCl_3 + 4Fe(OH)_3 \tag{3}$$

During the etching, black particles are sometimes formed on the surface of the resist, most probably as the result of air oxidation:

$$2CuCl_2 + 3FeCl_2 + O = CuCl \cdot CuO + 3FeCl_3 \tag{4}$$

The insoluble $CuCl \cdot CuO$ eventually dissolves in the excess of ferric chloride and hydrochloric acid

$$CuCl \cdot CuO + FeCl_3 + 2HCl = 2CuCl_2 + FeCl_2 + H_2O \tag{5}$$

The reason why ferric chloride is so suitable for etching copper plates is the fact that during the etching no gaseous products are formed.

After the etching has been completed, the action of ferric chloride is stopped by washing the plate or cylinder with water. The varnish is removed with a suitable solvent, and the resist scrubbed off with a soft brush and water. Sometimes it may be necessary to use a weak caustic soda solution to remove all remaining traces of gelatin.

The printing itself is mechanical. As the etched cylinder rotates in the printing press, sufficient ink is applied by an inking device so that all the etched cavities are filled with ink. The excess ink is scraped from the surface with a fine steel doctor blade. The etched parts of the cylinder, which represent the tones of the design, retain ink which is subsequently transferred to the paper or other surface as it passes between the printing and impression cylinder. The ink sinks immediately into the paper pores and, because of slight sidewise diffusion, the screen structure disappears almost completely, particularly in the deep-color areas. By this method of printing, the original photographs or artwork are reproduced with excellent tone values and details.

Rotogravure is best suited for publication printing where high printing speed and very good quality are of importance. It is used for mass editions of illustrated magazines, book illustrations, and newspaper supplements. Because the ink dries very rapidly, the printing work is usually dry when it leaves the press and successive color impressions can be made without delay. The rotogravure process is widely employed for wallpaper and textile printing. It has also been successfully applied to security and stamp printing. In recent years, the growing packaging industry has adopted rotogravure for printing wrapping material, cartons, and labels.

3.4   SILK-SCREEN PROCESS

The silk-screen process is the youngest photomechanical mass-printing technique employing dichromated colloids. It is the modern form of the stencil printing used by Chinese and Japanese many centuries ago. In its simplest form, it consists of producing a design on bolting silk stretched over a rigid wooden or metal frame by covering the areas which are to remain unprinted with a material impervious to the ink used for printing. The printing operation is performed by scraping the ink with a rubber squeegee, held at about a 60-degree angle, from one end of the frame to the other, and filling the open areas of the stencil with the ink. While the stencil is kept in intimate contact with the printing surface, the ink is forced through the open parts of the screen mesh and adheres to the flat, curved, or irregularly shaped surface beneath. After drying, the next color may be applied from another stencil to produce a multicolored print.

Bolting silk is usually used as the carrier or support for the stencil; however, other fabrics, such as nylon, rayon, cotton organdy, and metal screens are used also. The metal cloth of copper, phosphor bronze, or stainless steel is required in those cases where ceramic inks are used. They provide, also, higher accuracy, longer screen life, and greater control over ink thickness.

Many methods have been designed for preparing silk-screen stencils. Stencils can be prepared either on the screen itself or produced independently of the screen. The introduction of new plastic-base hand-cut films makes the job simpler. These hand methods are easy and rapid but they are not recommended for the reproduction of fine and complicated subjects, and, in such cases, it is advisable to make the stencils photographically by impregnating the screen with dichromated gelatin and exposing it to light by contact printing under a line or halftone positive. After the exposure, the image is developed by removing the gelatin from the unexposed areas with warm water (68).

An approximately 10 per cent gelatin solution containing potassium dichromate is used for sensitizing (69). Polyvinyl alcohol or glue can replace gelatin (70). Modified polyvinyl alcohol and polyvinyl acetate (71) are superior to gelatin in heat resistance and particularly suitable for decoration of glass by vitreous enamels. A combination of fish glue with egg albumen was suggested by Keel (72). A small amount of glycerin or some other plasticizing agent for gelatin can be added to make the stencil more flexible. The acidity of the sensitizing solution, if necessary, is reduced with sodium carbonate. Because of the high gelatin content, the temperature of the solution at the time of application has to be at least 100°F. The condensation products of diazodiphenylamine and aldehydes are also suitable sensitizers (73).

In the recent progress of organic chemistry, polymers are starting to take their place in various printing processes. For silk screening, N-alkoxymethylated polyamides obtained by the polycondensation of a ω,ω'-diamine and a ω,ω'-dicarboxylic acid was suggested (74). Another example of this trend is N-alkoxymethylated poly-ϵ-caprolactam (75). These polymers may be sensitized by a dichromate, a diazonim compound, or an azide, e.g., 4-azido-β-methylstyrene-2-sulfonic acid sodium salt or 4-(4'-azido-β-methylstyryl) pyridine.

Another method of producing photostencils for screen printing entails the transfer to the screen of processed images on carbon tissues or on other film prepared for this purpose (76). This can be further exemplified by the heat transfer of unexposed sections of a photopolymerizable composition containing thermoplastic resin, to the silk screen while the polymerized portions remain on the support and form a relief image (77).

The low sensitivity and other disadvantages of dichromated-colloid layers were reponsible for the development and introduction of the Ektagraph process by Eastman Kodak and the Screen process by Du Pont, both utilizing gelatin/silver halide emulsions coated on stripping films (78,79). Paper, films, or metal supports carrying a layer of synthetic polyamide sensitized with an azide-type compound, have been suggested for similar reasons (80).

In these methods the mesh of the screen does not interfere with the formation of the gelatin coating, and therefore they are especially suitable for the reproduction of very fine and delicate details. Improvements in photographic methods for stencil production permit precision registration of multicolor halftones.

The silk-screen process was originally developed to cover the need for printing on surfaces other than paper. Since that time, however, it has been adapted for printing on almost any surface. Screen printing has long been used in the textile industry for printing fabrics, and, as another example, in the ceramic industry, for decorative purposes. Because this process is very economical, it is frequently used for printing jobs requiring a limited number of impressions, such as posters, catalogues, dials, scales, maps, book covers, and signs. As the surface to be printed need not be of a certain thickness or a regular shape, the silk-screen process is well suited for printing on all types of irregular surfaces, such as bottles, machine parts, furniture, toys, and other objects which could not be run through a printing press.

For special effects, glitter finishes, fluorescent inks, or special beading for light reflection are available and find application in the printing of outdoor signs. Many electronic plants are producing printed circuits with the screen process. Because of the versatility of the process and the quality of the work, the application of screen printing has increased tremendously in recent years.

As compared with other printing processes, screen printing has the disadvantage of being relatively slow, unsuitable for reproducing subjects with delicate gradation of tone and fine detail and for very long runs.

3.5   WASH-OFF PROCESS

The light sensitivity of dichromated colloids also forms the basis of a major industrial reproduction process—the wash-off process. This process is used mainly to make duplicates of engineering drawings which serve as second originals or from which prints can be made by some ordinary reproduction method.

This photosensitive material is made by coating tracing paper or tracing cloth with a colloid layer containing glue, gelatin, or polyvinyl alcohol, a dichromate and a silver halide. For preparing such a sensitizing solution, silver nitrate and potassium chloride, in separate funnels, are allowed to run slowly into a glue-water mixture under constant stirring. After the silver chloride precipitation is complete, ammonium dichromate solution is added. Sodium hexametaphosphate can be added to improve the wash-off (81).

When tracing cloth is used as the base material, it is necessary to waterproof the tracing cloth first, so that the water in the sensitizing solution will not attack the starch which is used in the base cloth. The necessary waterproofing may be accomplished in the usual manner, by coating the tracing cloth with a nitrocellulose lacquer, an alkyd resin lacquer or other lacquer (82). Waterproofed tracing paper (83) or dimensionally stable flexible material, such as that patented by Spechler

(84), are also suitable. In order to improve the adhesion of the light-sensitive layer to the base material it is necessary to apply a gelatin subbing on top of the waterproofing layer.

After coating and drying, the sensitized material is exposed to carbon-arc light under a negative, usually a brown-print, in a special printing frame which provides heavy pressure to ensure perfect contact between the negative image and sensitive layer. Ordinarily vacuum-printing frames are used in which the pressure is secured by means of a rubber sheet applied against the edges of the glass plate, thus constituting an air-tight enclosure within which a partial vacuum is produced with a vacuum pump. The pump is driven by an electric motor, which is automatically switched off by means of an electric contact in the pressure gauge.

During the exposure the colloid layer loses its property of dissolving again in cold water in the parts acted on by light but retains it in the parts protected from the light, so that if a sheet of material coated with this type of emulsion is exposed through a negative a hardened positive is formed which can be developed by washing in running tap water to remove the unexposed background areas. The print-out silver image is then intensified by development in an ordinary photographic developer containing, for example, hydroquinone, sodium carbonate, and sodium sulfite.

A black image on a clear background is obtained, which is distinguished by excellent absorption power for short wavelength and visible light.

The reaction between the hydroquinone of the developer and the silver chloride present in the emulsion is the same as in standard photographic development and can be represented by the equation

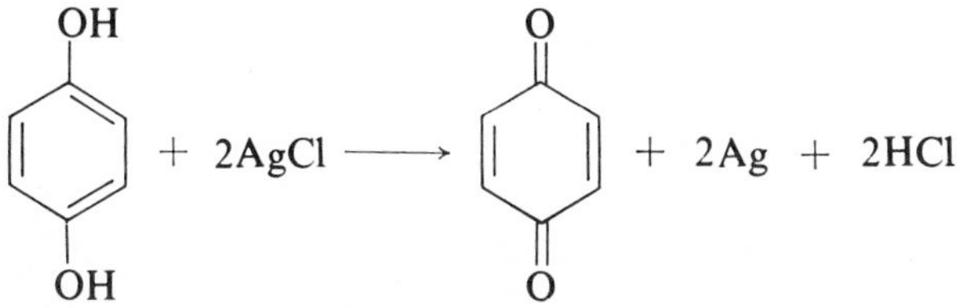

$$\text{(hydroquinone)} + 2AgCl \longrightarrow \text{(quinone)} + 2Ag + 2HCl \tag{6}$$

The hydrogen chloride is neutralized with the sodium carbonate, and the sodium sulfite converts the quinone to a stable, unreactive sulfonic acid salt:

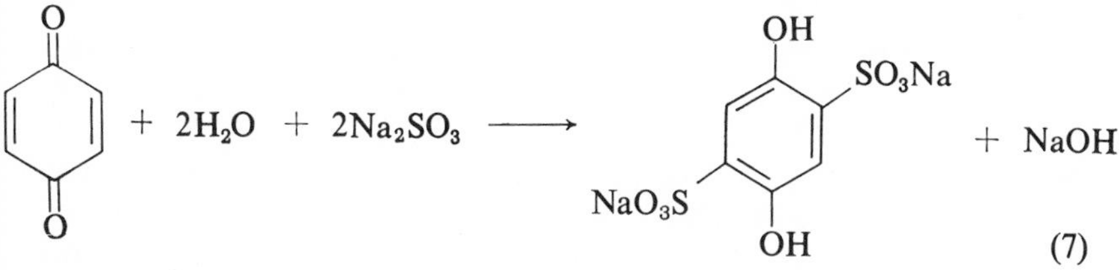

$$\text{(quinone)} + 2H_2O + 2Na_2SO_3 \longrightarrow \text{(sulfonic acid salt)} + NaOH \tag{7}$$

To get a clear, clean background it is often desirable to bleach the print in a solution of Farmer's reducer, which is a mixture of potassium ferricyanide and sodium thiosulfate.

Potassium ferricyanide oxidizes metallic silver while being reduced to potassium ferrocyanide by a reduction in the valence of the ferric ion. The electron is provided by the silver, which passes from the metallic state to the ionic, being converted to water-insoluble silver ferrocyanide which is simultaneously dissolved by sodium thiosulfate.

The reactions taking place are as follows:

$$4K_3Fe(CN)_6 + 4Ag \longrightarrow 3K_4Fe(CN)_6 + Ag_4Fe(CN)_6 \qquad (8)$$

$$Ag_4Fe(CN)_6 + 8Na_2S_2O_3 \longrightarrow Na_4Fe(CN)_6 + 4Na_3Ag(S_2O_3)_2 \quad (9)$$

or summed up:

$$[Fe^{3+}(CN)_6]^{3-} + Ag \longrightarrow [Fe^{2+}(CN)_6]^{4-} + Ag^+ \qquad (10)$$

It must be remembered that in this process the silver chloride is used only as a source of black metallic silver for visual contrast, rather than for its light sensitivity. The use of silver halide is preferred over the incorporation of pigments (85) such as carbon black or dyes (86,87), because such substances would act as a filter by absorbing a large portion of the light required for the photochemical reaction. This would necessitate a greatly increased exposure time. The use of silver salt is also preferred over the method of dyeing the relief image with a suitable dye (88), such as naphthol or naphthaline black. The image density achieved by such a method is far from satisfactory. Griggs (89) incorporated lead sulfite in an aqueous mixture of dichromated colloid. After the exposure and washing away of the soluble parts, the print is then treated with a sulfiding agent, such as 2 to 5 per cent sodium sulfide solution or with hydrogen sulfide solution or gas. The result is the transformation in the image areas of the lead sulfite to lead sulfide, leaving an opaque black relief image of high density. In a process patented by Wagner (90), the silver image is obtained by immersing, for a few minutes, the developed relief image in a bath containing ammoniacal silver nitrate and a reducing agent, e.g., glucose and formaldehyde.

Photosensitive material sensitized with colloid layers containing dichromates and silver halide has the disadvantage, like all dichromated-colloid layers, of having a poor shelf life. For this reason, it is necessary to use these materials within a short time after the sensitizing solution has been coated on the base, even if they are stored under conditions of low temperature and low humidity. When stored for a longer period of time, a black layer of finely divided silver forms over the whole surface of the print after development; this makes it impossible to distinguish any detail of the image. The black areas are very difficult to remove without damaging the image and usually the material has to be discarded.

Attempts have been made to incorporate antifogging agents into the developing solution in order to prevent fog formation in the unexposed parts of the print during storage. Neugebauer and Reichel (91) advised the use of

6-nitrobenzimidazole

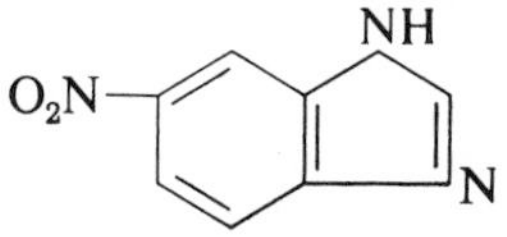

6-nitrobenzotriazole

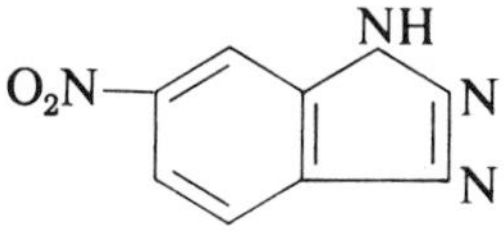

or 6-nitrobenzopyrazole

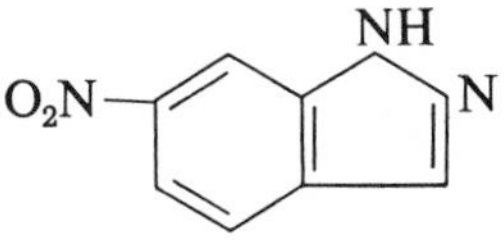

but other antifogging agents, such as

benzotriazole

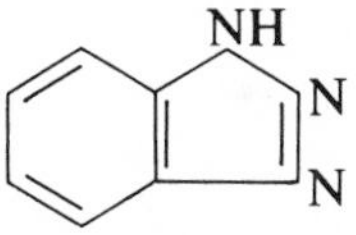

or the sulfonation product of 6-nitrobenzimidazole will give equally favorable results.

The action of antifogging agents on silver halide grains is not fully understood, but according to Sheppard and Hudson (92) these compounds form irreducible complexes with silver halide, which do tend to insulate the large nuclei such as are assumed to produce fog and prevent development.

There are innumerable organic compounds described as "antifoggants," "fog inhibitors," or "stabilizers" in patents taken out by manufacturers of photographic materials in recent years.

If, for example, 0.15 per cent 6-nitrobenzimidazole or 0.2 per cent benzotriazole is added to a soda-alkaline-hydroquinone developing solution, the unexposed areas of the aged material developed therewith are free from silver fog, even if the photosensitive layer on the material is so decomposed that it would have given an almost entirely black print.

Because the colloid layer of the aged material is insoluble and cannot be removed by washing, it is necessary to dissolve the unexposed silver halide by treatment with an acid fixing solution.

The reaction between sodium thiosulfate and silver chloride forms an insoluble compound $NaAg(S_2O_3)$, which immediately reacts with another molecule of thiosulfate to form $Na_3[Ag(S_2O_3)_2]$; this complex is very soluble in water and can be removed by washing. The reactions are ionic and can be expressed by the following equations:

$$Ag^+ + S_2O_3^{2-} \longrightarrow (AgS_2O_3)^- \tag{11}$$

$$(AgS_2O_3)^- + S_2O_3^{2-} \longrightarrow [Ag(S_2O_3)_2]^{3-} \tag{12}$$

or, summarized,

$$Ag^+ + 2S_2O_3^{2-} \longrightarrow [Ag(S_2O_3)_2]^{3-} \tag{13}$$

It is important to note that the antifogging agents must be added to the developing solution. Addition of these compounds to the photosensitive layer is not effective, apparently because of the presence of dichromates.

There the colloid layer is insolubilized and forms a continuous film similar to silver halide emulsion material, and the main advantage of the wash-off process, namely, the easy erasure of the relief image with a wet eraser rather than a chemical eradicator, is lost.

3.6   REVERSAL IMAGES

An interesting variation of dichromated-colloid processes is the method for preparing reversal relief images from a layer of dichromated hydrophilic colloid containing an aqueous dispersion of a water-insoluble, soft, synthetic resin capable of drying to a continuous film. This mixture, after being coated on a support somewhat thicker than is customary with the conventional dichromated colloids, is dried and exposed through a positive to a high-intensity light. The exposure is somewhat less than is required for the ordinary process. The development is carried out by immersing the exposed material in warm water to which a small amount of ammonia has been added to promote the swelling of the exposed areas. After a few seconds, the material is washed with a stream of warm water to remove the exposed portions of the layer completely. The unexposed areas adhere to the support and form the positive relief image. This action is directly opposite to that obtained with the regular dichromate process, in which the image is produced in the exposed sections. The image is quite delicate when wet, but on drying becomes very durable; it can be hardened to form a satisfactory resist for acids, alkalies, or electrolytic etching.

The essential components of this process are dichromated hydrophilic colloids, such as gelatin, fish glue, gum arabic, or polyvinyl alcohol, and an aqueous dispersion of a water-insoluble resin. A number of resins are useful, and the following are mentioned in patents: acrylate resins such as polymethyl or polyethyl acrylate, polystyrene, polyvinyl and neoprene latexes, plasticized cellulose nitrate dispersions (88). Saran latex and an aqueous colloidal dispersion of polyvinyl-chloride/polyvinyl-acetate co-polymer (93), natural rubber latex (94), copolymers of ethyl or methyl acrylate and acrylonitrile (49), or water-insoluble cellulose derivatives compatible with the hydrophilic colloid binder (95). To improve the washing away of the exposed parts and obtain a clean image, sodium hexametaphosphate is added to the dichromated colloid (81). In order to improve the visibility of the image, white (96) or colored pigments can be incorporated into the coating. Water-insoluble azo dyes are used when transparent colored images have to be made (86). The coloring power of the insoluble dyes in the coated layer is comparatively low, with little effect on the light absorption during the exposure; the full brilliance of the dye is brought out by exposing the developed image to the vapor or a solvent for the dye.

The resolving power of this reversal material is high or low, depending on the degree of dispersion of the solid constituents. It is claimed that the addition of a small amount of polyvinyl acetate stabilizers to the dispersion of gelatin and acrylate resin, by decreasing the tendency of this composition to agglomerate, improves the resolution greatly (97).

The exact mechanism of this process is not completely clear. It appears, however, that the partially tanned gelatin changes its volume as the result of swelling during the development, and breaks up the continuous film of the resin in the exposed areas, which are then washed away in the second stage of development.

3.7 PHOTOLITHOGRAPHY

Photolithography is the process of printing from specially prepared surfaces, some areas of which are capable of accepting lithographic ink, although other areas, when moistened with water, will not accept the ink. The areas which accept ink form the printed image, and the ink-rejecting areas form the background.

Photolithography is a planographic printing process, which means that the printing and nonprinting sections are at the same level, and therefore the object of lithographic plate making is to form on a plate an image or design that will be ink-receptive and to treat the background areas in such a manner that they will take water and repel ink.

Standard types of photolithographic plates are surface plates and deep-etch plates.   The difference between these two types is in the kind of image produced.   The image on the surface plates is formed by hardened colloid, and the image portions on the deep-etch plates consist of an oleophilic lacquer which fills the chemically etched areas.   Surface plates are less expensive and are generally used for less exacting short runs. For more exacting jobs, particularly those calling for a wide range of tone values, deep-etch plates are preferred.

3.7a   *Surface Plates*

Photolithographic printing plates are usually of zinc or aluminum; the choice is determined by the kind of work being printed, and by personal preference.   Other metals, such as stainless steel of nickel-chromium type or alloys of copper and nickel (monel metal) have also been suggested, and are mainly used for special types of work.   The plates must be thin and flexible enough to wrap snugly around the cylinder, the thickness varying according to the press size from 0.006 to 0.025 inch.   Lithographic plates can also be prepared by vacuum deposition of metals on polystyrene supports (98); it is claimed that metal deposited by vacuum deposition is more resistant to etching.

The initial step in the preparation of surface plates is the graining operation, giving the surface of the metal a uniform rough texture consisting of microscopic hills and valleys, which serve as storage places for water in background areas and as anchorage centers for the image. Graining is an entirely mechanical operation, usually carried out by firms specializing in such work, and involving the rotation of steel, glass, or even wood marbles, over the surface of the plate covered with natural or artificial abrasives.   Sufficient water is added to the abrasive to form a suspended mud.   Another method involves directing an aqueous dispersion of the abrasive against the surface of the plate by means of compressed air.   Sandblasting, both wet and dry, and chemical graining (99) have also been suggested.   Uniform surfaces, suitable for receiving a light-sensitive coating, can also be prepared by etching the aluminum plate in an alkaline and subsequently in an acid bath and electrolyzing it with alternating current in diluted oxalic, sulfuric, or hydrochloric acid (100).

The grained surface is treated with a weak acid solution to remove any residue of dirt, grease, or metal oxide which might be left on the plate in order to assure good anchorage of the sensitizing solution and of the desensitizing gum to the metal.   For this purpose, hydrochloric, hydrofluoric, citric, or acetic acid is used.   Other acids, such as phosphoric acid (101), sulfuric acid, or a nitric acid potassium alum mixture were suggested, also as dictated by the nature of the metal. This operation is called "counter-etching."

To prevent oxidation or corrosion of the metal during periods of high humidity, the grained and counter-etched zinc plates are treated with a so-called Cronak solution before applying the light-sensitive coating. This procedure consists of a short immersion of the plate in a water solution of ammonium dichromate and sulfuric acid. After drying, a very thin brownish film—a basic chromate of the general formula $Cr_2O_3 \cdot CrO_3 \cdot XH_2O$—is formed on the grained surface; the depth of color depends on the dichromate concentration and on the length of time the solution acted on the plate. This treatment, developed by the New Jersey Zinc Co. (102) and modified for lithographic use at the Army Map Service and at LTF, is called Cronaking and can be expressed by the following reaction:

$$3Zn + 14H^+ + Cr_2O_7{}^{2-} \longrightarrow 2Cr^{3+} + 3Zn^{2+} + 7H_2O \qquad (14)$$

The advantages of Cronaking are numerous. Besides the prevention of oxidation, the Cronak plates are easily developed and can be used for longer runs than bare zinc plates.

Aluminum plates are treated with Brunak solution, developed by Bruno and Hartsuch of LTF (103). It is similar to Cronak solution, and contains ammonium dichromate and hydrofluoric acid. Sometimes aluminum plates for use in planographic printing are treated with an alkali-metal silicate which is hardened with 5 per cent calcium nitrate solution (104,105) or with a solution of citric or tartaric acid (106). Or it can be coated with a hydrophilic layer, consisting of three components: a phosphate glass, a silicate, and a silicomolybdate (107). Treatment with steam in the presence of ammonia, ethanolamine, or aliphatic amine to produce a film of hydrated alumina (108) is also suitable. Good hydrophilic properties are also obtained by overcoating a base plate, first, with a modified melamine aldehyde resin, and second, with a layer of acrylic (109), or by applying methacrylic acid directly from a hot aqueous solution (110). Hydrophilic surfaces on anodized aluminum are obtainable by immersing the plate, immediately after anodizing, in a hot solution of gum arabic and drying it in a steam enclosure in order to allow the hydrocolloid to seal the surface (111). A surface physically similar to lithographic "stone" can be obtained by spraying a solution of ammonium zirconyl carbonate on the metal plate, heated to 300 to 600°F (112). In another patent, treatment with a 1 per cent solution of potassium zirconium fluoride at 150°F for 3 minutes is recommended (113).

Other surface treatments, such as the Phosphate and Nital treatments were developed to avoid poisonous chromium compounds. The Nital solution consists of diluted nitric acid to which a small amount of ammonium aluminum sulfate has been added; in contact with zinc it produces on the surface a layer of amorphous aluminum hydroxide, which is an excellent base for the sensitizing solution. The use of a perhalogenated fatty acid (trifluoro- or trichloroacetic acid) for cleaning and counter-etching was recommended by Wood and Adams (114).

Before applying the sensitizer, lithographic plates are treated, in most instances, with a gum arabic dichromate solution acidified with phosphoric acid or with a solution of cellulose gum, phosphoric acid, and magnesium nitrate, to provide a very thin film on the surface of the plate.

At this stage the plates are ready for surface-coating, with the purpose of covering the plate with a light-sensitive composition which, after being dried and exposed to actinic radiation under a negative, becomes insoluble in the image areas of the plate, and, at the same time, ink-receptive. Requirements for a successful light-sensitive coating include particularly that the material in solution form be homogeneous and have a viscosity and solids content that permit easy application to the plate and solidification to a layer of proper thickness. The sensitizing solution consists, usually, of a mixture of egg albumen, ammonium dichromate, and a small amount of ammonia. For this reason, surface plates are also called albumin plates. Albumin has certain advantages for printing plates, but it has also many disadvantages, such as inhomogeneity and poor stability in solutions. Better adhesion and tougher coating is obtained by the addition of about 5 per cent of ethanedial CHO—CHO (based on the weight of dry albumin) to the solution and adjustment of the pH to 9.0 with ammonia (115). Addition of some fatty substances, such as dried milk, dried whole egg, or natural soybean powder, to the sensitizing solution supposedly improves the ink-receptivity of the image areas for long periods of time (116). If the albumin solution is not to be used promptly, an antiseptic, such as pyridyl mercuric acetate, phenol, pentachlorophenol, methyl-*p*-hydroxy benzoate, sodium benzoate, or thymol (117) has to be added.

Egg albumen can be replaced by casein (118,119), a casein-gelatin combination (120), blood albumin (121,122), water-soluble caseinate (123), alginates (124), or other colloids (125) or their mixtures. To increase the receptivity of printing ink to hardened polyvinyl alcohol images (126), different addenda were recommended (127). Phosphates are sometimes added to expedite the removal of unexposed film from the metal (128,129).

The sensitized plate is next exposed through a film negative to the light of an arc lamp or other source of actinic radiation, which decomposes the dichromate and causes it to exert a tanning or hardening effect upon the albumin.

Dichromated-colloid images are very sensitive to variations in the relative humidity and, to counteract this, exposed plates are sometimes protected with nonblinding lacquers; these contain, usually, synthetic vinyl resins, which are very ink-receptive and adhere very well to the colloid images. Then the coating is covered with a fatty or greasy developing ink, which is a mixture of a greasy nondrying binder, carbon black, and a volatile solvent, such as turpentine. The evenly distributed ink makes the printing image visible on the developed plate and repels the desensitizing gum which is applied later. When a greasy ink which transmits the radiation is chosen, it can be applied to the sensitive layer prior to the exposure (130).

The next step in the preparation of lithographic surface plates is to soak the inked plate in lukewarm water and remove the unexposed and unhardened portions of the colloid layer from the background or nonimage areas of the plate by rubbing the surface with wads of absorbent cotton. The unhardened albumin particles are carried away, leaving bare metal in the nonimage areas.

It is recommended that printing plates sensitized with polyvinyl alcohol be developed with an aqueous dispersion of about 1 per cent of hematin, hematoxylin, catechin, etc., to improve the hardness of the exposed portions of the coating (29).

The mechanical operation of washing, however, does not remove the albumin or casein coating completely from the nonimage areas of the plate, and, to clean these perfectly from the almost invisible film of residual colloid, zinc plates have to be subjected either to post-Cronak treatment or post-Nital treatment. The Brunak treatment is performed on aluminum plates, and it is believed that during this operation the residual coating trapped inside the aluminum oxide layer is released. The introduction of this operation was responsible for tremendous improvement in the quality of albumin plates, and is one of the greatest advancements in surface plate making.

After this operation, we have a plate with image areas consisting of insoluble albumin covered with a thin layer of developing ink and with bare metal in the background areas. So that these areas will not pick up ink during the run on the press, they must be protected or "desensitized" with a thin, invisible, but tightly adhering film of gum arabic, cellulose gum (Na-carboxymethylcellulose), or some other water-receptive "desensitizing" agent, having in their molecule at least one —COOH or —OH group (131,132,133). Uhlig and Rebenstock (134) recommended, for the purpose of strengthening the image, treatment with an emulsion containing, in the water phase, gum arabic or some other water-soluble colloid, and, in the oil phase, a low molecular-weight phenol-formaldehyde resin dissolved in an organic solvent. A method for testing the quality of desensitizers was devised by Albrecht and Watter (135). The desensitizing solution, sometimes also called the etching solution, contains, in addition to the hydrophilic colloid, certain acids, such as phosphoric acid, in order to increase the number of carboxyl groups in the gum molecule to insure good anchorage of the film to the surface of the metal. The presence of a small amount (0.001 per cent) of fluoride ions in the gum arabic phosphoric acid mixture further increases the ink repellence (136). More recently, a hydrophilic colloid containing finely dispersed barium, calcium, or strontium hydroxide, was suggested (137). To reduce the attack on the metal by the acid, inorganic salts, such as phosphates, nitrates, or dichromates are added to the etch solution. Electrolytic deposition of water-receptive layers was patented by Strecker (138). Sometimes the plate etch solution contains tanning agents. Chromic salt or tannic acid is usually used (139). These materials harden the gum, leaving a more durable film of desensitizing gum on the metal surface. In order to protect the nonimage areas from accidental damage during inspection, an additional coating of gum arabic is applied. This operation is called gumming, and improves the hydrophilic characteristics of surface plates.

At this stage, the plate is ready for printing. However, to prevent ink receptivity in the image areas and to protect the surface from contamination, the developing ink can be removed and replaced with a thin light-tan layer of asphaltum, which is removed by the pressman just prior to printing. This is the final step in preparing a surface plate.

3.7b   *Deep-Etch Plates*

Using the albumin plates described in the preceding paragraph, the printing is of the image areas, which accept the lithographic ink. There is, however, yet another method of planographic printing utilizing the light hardening of dichromated colloids. In this process, which is sometimes called "deep-etch" or "intaglio offset," the printing is of an image in direct contact with the grained metal. Contrary to albumin plates, deep-etch plates are made by a reversal procedure, during plate making, employing a line or halftone positive. It is a lengthier operation, but sharper images and greater durability of the plates justify the extra effort necessary.

The first two steps, graining and counter-etching of zinc or aluminum plates, are identical with the albumin process. Also the pretreatment with Cronak or Brunak solutions is sometimes recommended. Stainless steel plates, which are handled very much like aluminum plates, do not need pretreatment. Pre-etching is not always necessary, however advisable. For sensitizing, a slightly alkaline dichromated solution of glue, gum arabic, or a mixture of albumin and ammonium arabate (140) are used. Both are hardened by the action of light; however, in contrast with albumin, the hardened image does not accept the ink so willingly.

Also, gum arabic derivatives, particularly those treated with diammonium hydrogen phosphate (141) or ion exchange resins (142,115,143) to remove calcium and magnesium ions present, are finding wide application.

Another water-soluble polysaccharide forming a base for deep-etch plate coating, is arabinogalactan (144). Arabinogalactan is a complex, highly branched polysaccharide produced under pressure by the extraction of larchwood with hot water (145). Dextrans (146) are reported to have better stability than gum or glue solutions, and are particularly suited for the production of deep-etch offset plates because of the ease with which the stencil can be removed, after having served its purpose, with the aid of chromium complexing agents.

Among other colloids, polyvinyl alcohol (147) is quite suitable if special precautions are taken during development. Since the light-exposed areas are relatively soft, an aqueous solution of chromic acid is used for additional hardening. For better image visibility, dyes can be added to the sensitizing solution. Characteristics of dichromated coatings containing different colloids were compared by Albrecht and Watter (148).

Long lasting printing surfaces are produced by subcoating the metal plate with a composition containing gum arabic, potassium dichromate, phosphoric acid, and lithium bromide. This layer is light-hardened prior to sensitizing with a mixed gum arabic, ammonium dichromate, and gelatin solution (149). After processing, the sublayer is removed with a ferric perchlorate solution acidified with citric or nitric acid.

After exposure to a line or halftone positive, a stop-out solution consisting mainly of shellac and alcohol is applied to areas which have to be protected from the action of the developer and deep-etch solution. For development, a concentrated aqueous solution of calcium chloride, acidified with some lactic acid, is used; this solution dissolves the unhardened dichromated gum from the image areas of the plate, but does not attack the hardened gum as water alone would do. More effective than calcium chloride, it is supposed, is magnesium chloride in combination with malic acid (150) or glycol and glycol acetate (151). Straub (152) preferred to develop the image by rubbing the exposed plate with an aqueous solution of glycerol and acetic acid. Another satisfactory slow developer which does not result in loss of detail contains calcium chloride, zinc chloride, and hydroxyacetic acid (153). This operation is very much influenced by atmospheric conditions, and it is recommended that more concentrated developers be used when the temperature and humidity are high.

For etching aluminum plates, ferric chloride is added to the developing formula (154) or commercial deep-etch solutions are used. A small quantity of a salt of one of the platinum-group metals may be substituted for ferric chloride to prevent the darkening of the aluminum. When the developed image appears sharp and clean, "deep-etch" solution is poured over the entire surface of the plate and allowed to react for about one minute, depending on the degree of etching desired. The deep-etch solution has to be formulated in such a way that it will dissolve enough metal in the image areas to make them slightly depressed (0.0003 to 0.0006 inch) and, at the same time, will not dissolve any of the hardened colloid protecting the nonimage sections of the plate. This is accomplished by making the ferric solution quite acid with hydrochloric acid, and adding enough calcium chloride to prevent the dissolving of the hardened colloid. Chemical reactions taking place during the etching operation can be expressed by the following equations:

$$Zn + HCl \longrightarrow ZnCl_2 + H_2 \tag{15}$$

$$Zn + 2FeCl_3 \longrightarrow ZnCl_2 + 2FeCl_2 \tag{16}$$

Aluminum and zinc plates can be also etched with a solution of hydrofluoric acid containing a small amount of a copper salt, ferric chloride, and zinc chloride (155).

As soon as the deep-etch operation has been completed, the salts have to be removed from the plate by repeated washing with anhydrous alcohol or a mixture of 99 per cent isopropyl alcohol and cellosolve (ethylene glycol monoethylether C_2H_5—O—CH_2CH_2OH). When the plate is dry, deep-etch lacquer and developing ink are applied. The deep-etch lacquer, usually containing a vinyl polymer, adheres tightly to the deep-etch areas and forms a strongly ink-receptive surface at the image areas. Because of their tendency not to be wet by water, vinyl lacquers are preferred to the nitrocellulose lacquer originally used.

The deep-etch developing ink, because of its color, renders the image more visible, and, because of its oleophilic nature, improves the ink acceptance of the printing areas and prevents them from being covered with gum during the desensitizing and gumming operation. The hardened gum forming the background areas must now be removed from the nonprinting areas of the plate by soaking the plate in warm water and scrubbing the stencil off with a brush. If removal is a problem, a solution of citric or sulfuric acid can be used. The last operation—desensitizing of the plate with acidified gum arabic—is the same as with albumin plates.

3.7c   *Bimetallic and Trimetallic Plates*

In the preceding pages we have seen that a lithographic plate has two surfaces, a water-receptive ink-repellent surface and an ink-receptive water-repellent surface. The surface of the latter was a light-hardened dichromated-colloid, while the water-receptive portion of the plate was a hydrophilic metal, such as chromium, aluminum and zinc, or impregnated paper or plastic.

The image and nonimage areas can also be formed of two different metals with different affinities for lithographic ink, one of which forms the nonimage areas and the other, the image areas. According to the number of metals involved, these plates are called bimetallic or trimetallic plates. The first bimetallic plate was suggested by Murray at the beginning of this century, and many systems have been disclosed since then. A comprehensive review was given by Mertle (156). In all the variations, bimetallic plates consist of two metals, one of which forms the printing areas, and the other, the nonprinting areas. The latter metal has to be water-receptive; aluminum, stainless steel, or, preferably, chromium is used. Lead, nickel, or zinc are also used for some processes (157). As image metal, copper is most often selected because of its excellent affinity for greasy inks and its high resistance to abrasion. The image and nonimage metals are usually electroplated on a third metal, such as steel, and are called trimetallic plates.

A ferrous metal base, overlaid with a wear-resistant metal, such as chromium, was suggested by Geese (158,159) in order to reduce the price of chromium-plated copper plates. The image areas of these plates, obtained after etching, are made more ink-receptive by treating the bare steel with a solution of ammonium chloride, ferric chloride, cupric chloride, and bismuth oxychloride.

In principle, there are two methods of obtaining a metallic printing area on the background of another metal. In the first instance, the preparation is identical with that of conventional plates; the difference is in depositing the second metal in the nonimage areas by electroplating (160,161). The plate is then finished in the usual manner. Because of the expensive electroplating equipment required, this method did not find wide application and plates with a second metal electroplated over the base metal were made available. In the case where an image metal is on top of the nonimage metal, an acid-resistant positive image has to be formed and the image metal etched away from nonimage areas. In another variation, when the nonimage metal forms the upper layer, an acid-resistant negative image is required and the nonimage metal is etched away in order to expose the image metal in the positive-image areas. In both methods, the protective resist is removed prior to printing. To prevent damage on the nonimage metal during the development, Leekley (162) formulated a special developer containing, in addition to the usual calcium chloride and lactic acid, a certain amount of urea.

In instances where copper is used as the image metal, and chromium as the nonimage metal, these two metals are usually electroplated on a third metal, which serves as a base, and can be steel, aluminum, or zinc. This type of plate is, for all practical purposes, equivalent to bimetallic plates. The thickness of the metals plated on each other is of importance and has to be very accurate. A method for determining the thickness of both the chromium and the copper plating was described by Shapiro and Colberg (163).

The advantage of bi- and trimetallic plates is in their durability, compared to conventional deep-etch plates in which the copper printing areas are much tougher than the lacquer coatings. Bi- and trimetallic plates also show the widest difference obtainable between the ink and water receptivity of image and nonimage areas; the boundaries between these two are very sharp. For these two reasons, bi- and trimetallic plates are used for long runs and high-quality work.

3.7d   *Plastic and Paper Litho Plates*

The lithographic plate itself that supports the light-sensitive coating is commonly made of aluminum, zinc, or other metal. Many efforts, however, have been made in the past to use flexible synthetic materials as substitutes, and printing surfaces made of nonmetallic substances have a long history. They date back to the "stone paper" patented by the inventor of lithography, Alois Senefelder, at the beginning of the nineteenth century. Although Senefelder's idea did not find any practical application, it pointed out to others a possible way to replace cumbrous litho stone or metal plates in lithographic printing (164,165).

The first practical plastic support for a lithographic image was celluloid, either as a support for a "stone-like" coating or as a litho printing surface (166,167).

Among the first so-called plastic plates offered to the litho trade were sheets of cellulose ester sensitized by incorporation of a chromate (168,169), which, after the exposure to light, acts as a resist against subsequent saponification of the sheet. Because of the hydrolysis, cellulose acetate is reconverted, in the printing areas, to cellulose, which is wettable with water and repels greasy inks. Ostwald's proposal to use cellulosic supports induced much research and was the forerunner of commercial presensitized printing plates.

In another system, the chemically treated cellulose sheet is sensitized in such a manner that the exposed sections of the plate become ink-receptive (170,171). Mention has to be made, also, of Westcott's patent (172), comprising a cellulosic plate with a printing surface of dense translucent amyloid (acid-treated) parchment. Cellulose base sheet coated with carboxymethylcellulose belongs to the same category (173). Graining of cellulose acetate sheets by sand blasting was introduced by Caton in his "K–Tin" plastic plate (174).

A similar approach was taken by the Eastman Kodak Company in their Ektalith process, designed for the economical production of tricolor photolitho halftone reproductions from color film transparencies (175, 176,177,178,179). In this process, uniformly hydrolyzed cellulose acetate sheets, strengthened by aluminum foil to improve dimensional stability, are sensitized with 5 per cent dichromate solution, containing 3 per cent ammonia and a small amount of a wetting agent. Other sensitizers, such as silver salts or ferric compounds, can also be employed (180,181,182). During the exposure, the exposed areas of the cellulose are oxidized; this process provides weak links in the cellulose chain. These areas can be removed with a solution of alkali, or alkali containing an oxidizing agent, and this uncovering of the underlying cellulose acetate surface, which is not wettable with water, thus forms the ink-receptive printing areas. The unexposed areas of the plate, when moist, repel the ink. This technique provides a comparatively quick method for the preparation of printing plates (183).

The first commercially available plastic plates were Lithomat plates, consisting of a plastic-treated paper base, and Photomat plates, comprised of a fiber base impregnated with a synthetic resin and bearing a polyvinyl alcohol layer. The polyvinyl alcohol layer was sensitized with a dichromate solution. These plates were quickly followed by the Plastolith variety of Bassist and Toland (184,185,186,187,188,189,190,191,192), comprised of a waterproofed paper laminated with polyvinyl alcohol or urea-formaldehyde resin and sensitized with dichromated polyvinyl alcohol. In one process, polyvinyl alcohol serves as the ink-receptive area, in another as the water-receptive area (193,194,195). The ink-receptive area is prepared by coating polyvinyl alcohol with dichromated albumin, drying, exposing, and developing in the usual way. In another patent, polyvinyl alcohol is insolubilized with N,N'-ethylene-dimethylol cyclic urea (196). In cases like this where the hydrophilic colloid is insolubilized by a cross-linking agent, the presence of colloidal silica improves the oleo-hydrophilic characteristics of the surface (197).

Casein-clay coatings on a flexible paper support were patented independently by Simons (198,199), by Shepherd (200), and later by Salzberg

(201).   Water-resistant paper having a heavy casein layer subsequently overcoated with polyvinyl alcohol (202) or oxy-cellulose (203) is another variety.   The use of casein was not, by any means, new in lithography. Berger (204) and De Nagy and Pepe (205) proposed a casein coating subsequently hardened with formaldehyde, on rigid supports, such as stone or wood.

In the last decade, many other materials were suggested for use in the lithographic industry.   Newman (206,207) suggested coating a high-wet-strength paper support with carboxymethylcellulose, carboxymethyl-hydroxyethylcellulose (208), or polysaccharide-carboxyether (209). Oransky (210) used, for the same purpose, the hydroxyethyl ether of starch hardened with a urea-formaldehyde or melamine formaldehyde resin (211). Chlorinated starch with a thermosetting resin capable of crosslinking with the hydrophilic colloid, was suggested by McKnight and Perkins (212).   Mazanek and Paquin (213) obtained a lithographic surface by coating a paper support with the reaction product of a starch component (e.g., an oxidized starch, the ester of a starch acetate, or an acid-modified starch) and a urea-formaldehyde condensate; the layer is then overcoated with an aqueous solution of aluminum chloride or sodium aluminate, which acts as a catalyst in the reaction between the two components.

Clay-polystyrene-latex layer on a paper base, overcoated with a casein-dimethylolurea pigment mixture, followed by a coating of a water-soluble cellulose derivative (e.g., hydroxyethyl-cellulose), was suggested by Brinnick (214).   A styrene-butadiene copolymer was used in similar formulation by Richard (215).   Ensink (216) recommended waterproofed sheets of paper, coated with an insolubilized alginate; alkali-metal alginates used in this process are water-soluble and are insolubilized, either by incorporating metal salts, such as aluminum or zinc chloride directly into the solution, or by treating the alginate coating with such metal salts in a later stage.

To impact both oleophilic and hydrophilic characteristics to the plate, the paper base is impregnated with a mixture of a hydrophobic film-forming polymer (Acryloid B-72) with a nonionic hydrophilic surfactant (Carbowax) dispersed in an organic solvent.   The plate is then over-coated with a silica-starch or silica-casein layer (217).

An insoluble hydrophilic-oleophilic surface suitable for offset printing can be obtained by coating water-soluble methylolated polyacrylamide, mixed with suitable clay or pigment, on a base and crosslinking by heating (218).   Printing properties are greatly improved by rubbing the surface against rotating brushes or by buffing (219,220).   In order to desensitize the areas which do not bear an image, it was suggested that the plates be treated with solutions of a high-molecular-weight, anionic, colloidal polyelectrolyte, such as a polyacrylic acid (221).

Marked improvement in the ability of the coating to resist penetration by aqueous lithographic solutions, and the consequent better holdup of such solution upon the surface in order to repel printing ink, is achieved by addition of water-soluble salts of bivalent metals (222) or multivalent metal salts, such as aluminum or zirconium acetate in conjunction with alkali metal or ammonium formate or acetate (223).

In many instances, it may prove necessary to coat the other side of the paper plate with a film-forming composition to cause a counter-curl equal in effect to the curl produced by the planographic surfacing material. In one such composition, Neuman (224) used for the back-coating an aqueous dispersion of a coagulable colloid, e.g., 5 per cent solution of casein, drying the paper sheet and treating the surface with a coagulant solution, such as solution of chromic acid, ferric chloride, or aluminum sulfate. When lithographic paper plates have to be preserved for further use, it is advisable to treat the plate before storage with a solution containing gum arabic, potassium alum, and sodium sulfite (225).

In order to improve the strength and dimensional stability, it may be required to laminate the paper plate or a film-containing printing plate to a metal element, either with the help of an acrylic adhesive (226) or a thermoplastic material (227), which provides the bond between the two surfaces. A plastic printing plate of excellent dimensional stability can also be prepared by spraying a glass-fiber fabric with a polyester resin, styrene, and a peroxide catalyst (228).

REFERENCES

1. A. Schoen and L. L. Patterson.   U.S. pat. 2,393,821/1946.
2. E. E. Loening.   Brit. pat. 573,798/1945.
3. P. C. Smethurst.   *Phot. J.*, **84**, 147–151 (1944).
4. D. C. Gresham and E. E. Loening.   U.S. pat. 2,459,129/1929; Brit. pat. 523,798/1940.
5. K. Smith and R. Zerbst.   U.S. pat. 2,370,330/1945.
6. H. C. Staehle.   U.S. pat. 2,472,128/1949.
7. A. E. Charlton.   U.S. pat. 2,900,255/1959.
8. A. E. Charlton.   U.S. pat. 2,942,972/1960.
9. L. L. Yaeger and R. P. Lappala.   U.S. pat. 3,023,099/1962.
10. Master Etching Mach. Co.   Brit. pat. 928,890/1963.
11. E. E. Loening.   *Perspective*, **2**, 257–263, 1960.
12. B. C. Sher and H. F. Fruth.   U.S. pat. 3,031,344/1962.
13. L. M. Minsk, J. G. Smith, W. P. van Deusen, and J. F. Wright.   *J. Appl. Polymer Sci.*, **2**, 302–307 (1959).
14. The Lithographer's Manual, edited by Victor Strauss, Wactwin Publishing Co., New York, 1958.

15. H. M. Cartwright and R. MacKay. *Rotogravure*, MacKay Publishing Co., Inc., Lyndon, Kentucky.
16. J. S. Mertle and G. L. Monsen. *Photomechanics and Printing*, Mertle Publishing Co., Chicago, Illinois, 1957.
17. P. Eisler. *Technology of Printed Circuits*, Heywood & Co., Ltd., London, 1959.
18. R. Reed. *Offset Platemaking*, Lithographic Technical Foundation, Inc., New York, 1957.
19. W. W. MacDonald. U.S. pat. 2,526,759/1950.
20. A. B. Davis. U.S. pat. 1,703,512/1929.
21. J. J. Murray and L. A. White. U.S. pat. 2,000,453/1935; Brit. pat. 439,093/1935.
22. N. Drey. Brit. pat. 517,686/1940.
23. T. Freundorfer and R. Freundorfer. U.S. pat. 1,552,428/1925.
24. C. E. Tebbs and J. Helfrich. U.S. pat. 1,579,898/1926.
25. J. Helfrich. U.S. pat. 1,883,161/1931.
26. M. Thimann. U.S. pat. 2,005,060/1935.
27. P. Bayer. U.S. pat. 3,031,302/1962.
28. R. S. Cox and R. V. Cannon. *The Penrose Annual*, **44**, 116–118 (1950).
29. C. A. Brown. U.S. pat. 2,830,899/1958.
30. J. Strauss. U.S. pat. 3,043,693/1962.
31. J. H. Gibson. U.S. pat. 2,331,772/1943.
32. K. M. Iversen and B. E. Blandhoel. U.S. pat. 2,692,828/1954.
33. R. Kaulen. Brit. pat. 814,165/1959.
34. R. F. Paterson and Y. Yamada. Ger. pat. 1,095,849/1960.
35. O. D. Black and L. H. Cuttler. *Ind. Eng. Chem.*, **50**, 1539–1540 (1958).
36. R. W. Jones. *Graphic Technology*, **1**, 59–62 (1962).
37. W. B. Hislop and W. J. C. Hislop. *Graphic Technology*, **1**, 32–35 (1961).
38. J. A. Easley. *TAGA Proceedings*, 76–84 (1954).
39. J. A. Easley. *TAGA Proceedings*, part A, 7–14 (1957); *TAGA Proceedings*, part B, 182–183 (1957).
40. J. A. Easley and H. E. Swayze. U.S. patents 2,640,763–767/1953.
41. J. A. Easley, W. E. Eden, and H. E. Swayze. U.S. pat. 2,669,048/1954.
42. J. A. Easley and M. H. Fishaber. U.S. pat. 3,023,138/1962.
43. J. A. Easley and C. W. Hopkins. U.S. pat. 2,979,387/1961.
44. P. F. Borth and M. C. Rogers. *TAGA Proceedings*, 1–8 (1961).
45. R. W. Jones. U.S. pat. 2,746,848/1956.
46. P. M. Daugherty and H. C. Vaughn. U.S. pat. 3,033,725/1962.
47. J. W. Bradley, L. W. Elston, and W. H. Burrows. U.S. pat. 3,033,793/1962.
48. A. I. Sherer and J. Ruzicka. U.S. pat. 3,074,836/1963.
49. H. C. Staehle. U.S. pat. 2,548,565/1951.
50. H. C. Staehle. U.S. pat. 2,604,388/1952.
51. D. J. Kyte. *Printing Technol.*, **6**, 51–64 (1962).
52. M. R. Boyer and A. W. Grumbine. U.S. pat. 2,650,877/1953.
53. M. R. Boyer and A. W. Grumbine. U.S. pat. 2,650,878/1953.
54. F. P. Alles. U.S. pat. 2,976,147/1961.
55. W. P. Jaspert. *Gravure*, **8**, 46–47 (1962).
56. H. J. A. de Goeij. *J. Phot. Sci.*, **3**, 124–128/1955.
57. K. Wolfson. U.S. pat. 2,431,359/1947.
58. G. S. Baldwin. *Process Engr. Monthly*, **63**, 90–91 (1956).
59. R. S. Sandford and G. T. Howe. U.S. pat. 2,892,711/1954.
60. L. Hughes. U.S. pat. 1,761,125/1930.

61. M. Cartwright.   *Phot. J.*, **63**, 265–277 (1942).
62. R. B. Fisheden.   *Phot. J.*, **55**, 143 (1935).
63. J. M. Dugan.   *TAGA Proceedings*, 19–28 (1960).
64. J. M. Dugan.   *TAGA Proceedings*, 117 (1953).
65. W. Thode.   *G.T.A. Bull.*, **9(2)**, 174 (1960).
66. A. E. Rupp.   *Printing Technol.*, **4(1)**, 24–40 (1960).
67. H. M. Cartwright.   *Proc. 7th International Congress of Phot.*, 393–406 (1928).
68. T. T. Baker.   *Am. Ann. Phot.*, **60**, 145–148 (1946).
69. W. A. Leeds and N. J. Sweet.   U.S. pat. 2,924,520/1956.
70. Etablissement Tiflex.   Fr. pat. 1,251,342/1960.
71. A. B. Chismar and E. W. Kmetz.   U.S. pat. 3,100,150/1963.
72. G. I. Keel.   U.S. pat. 1,597,899/1926.
73. Kalle A.G.   Belg. pat. 621,176/1962.
74. M. K. Reichel and W. Neugebauer.   U.S. pat. 3,143,416/1964; Kalle A.G. Belg. pat. 595,628/1960; Brit. pat. 942,824/1963.
75. M. K. Reichel and W. Neugebauer.   U.S. pat. 3,143,417/1964; Kalle A.G. Belg. pat. 595,627/1960.
76. J. F. Hansman and M. J. Jurisch.   U.S. pat. 2,590,857/1952.
77. E. I. du Pont.   Brit. pat. 905,700/1962.
78. E. C. Yackel.   U.S. pat. 2,685,510/1954.
79. F. P. Jankowski.   U.S. pat. 3,031,324/1962.
80. Kalle A.G.   Fr. pat. 1,268,922/1961.
81. R. S. Bryce.   U.S. pat. 2,544,877/1951.
82. K. Murck.   U.S. pat. 1,989,879/1935.
83. W. M. Hinman and W. G. Hollmann.   U.S. pat. 2,253,562/1941.
84. D. S. Spechler.   U.S. pat. 2,943,936/1960.
85. W. N. Baker and A. R. Baker.   U.S. pat. 1,704,356/1929.
86. H. C. Staehle.   U.S. pat. 2,544,903/1951.
87. D. J. Janet, Jr.   U.S. pat. 2,704,253/1955.
88. V. D. Potapov and M. S. Ulanov.   USSR pat. 57,603/1943.
89. W. H. Griggs.   U.S. pat. 2,484,451/1949.
90. F. Wagner.   Ger. pat. 1,056,932/1959.
91. W. Neugebauer and M. K. Reichel.   U.S. pat 2,656,271/1953.
92. S. E. Sheppard and H. Hudson.   *Photo. J.*, **67**, 359 (1927).
93. H. C. Staehle and L. E. Martinson.   U.S. pat. 2,675,315/1954.
94. H. C. Staehle.   U.S. pat. 2,533,530/1950.
95. H. C. Staehle.   Brit. pat. 573,771/1945.
96. H. C. Staehle.   Can. pat. 439,291/1947.
97. W. H. Griggs and W. F. Fowler.   U.S. pat. 2,500,028/1950.
98. W. H. Wood.   U.S. pat. 2,760,432/1956.
99. Algraphy Ltd. and R. A. C. Adams.   Brit. pat. 879,767/1961; Brit. pat. 879,768/1961.
100. R. A. C. Adams.   U.S. pat. 3,073,765/1963.
101. B. Cohn.   U.S. pat. 2,882,153/1954.
102. E. J. Wilhelm.   U.S. pat. 2,035,380/1936.
103. Modern Lithographer, 51–53 (1948).
104. C. H. van Dusen.   U.S. pat. 2,732,796/1956.
105. B. Cohn.   U.S. pat. 2,882,154/1959.
106. R. Gumbinner.   U.S. pat. 2,992,715/1961.
107. P. Chebiniak.   U.S. pat. 3,030,210/1962; Brit. pat. 882,856/1961.

108. Kalle A.G. Brit. pat. 912,130/1962.
109. Lithoplate, Inc. Brit. pat. 918,599/1963.
110. E. F. Deal. U.S. pat. 3,064,562/1962.
111. R. A. C. Adams. Brit. pat. 781,814/1957.
112. S. W. Brandstreet and J. S. Griffith. U.S. pat. 2,814,988/1957.
113. Polychrome Corp. Brit. pat. 884,110/1961.
114. W. H. Wood and D. N. Adams. U.S. pat. 2,830,536/1958.
115. W. H. Wood and D. N. Adams. U.S. pat. 2,663,639/1953.
116. V. L. Gregory. U.S. pat. 2,690,395/1953.
117. E. F. Dell. U.S. pat. 2,229,052/1941.
118. C. D. Hallam and A. Haigh. *Process Engr. Monthly*, **49**, 180 (1942).
119. T. R. Caton. U.S. pat. 2,921,852/1960.
120. A. W. Buck and J. W. Miller. U.S. pat. 2,387,056/1945.
121. I. A. Pakovich and V. S. Raikhlin. *Poligr. Proizv.*, No. 1, 8–11 (1941).
122. C. H. van Dussen. U.S. pat. 2,434,727/1948.
123. V. L. Gregory and L. R. MacDonnel. U.S. pat. 2,677,611/1954.
124. A. Ensink. Belg. pat. 560,829/1957.
125. F. H. Frost and F. E. Brinnick. U.S. pat. 2,624,673/1953.
126. K. Mizuta. Japan pat. 34-5462/1959.
127. C. Dangelmajer. U.S. pat. 2,184,288/1937. F. M. Meigs and C. Dangelmajer.
     U.S. pat. 2,184,310/1937. C. Dangelmajer. U.S. pat. 2,184,289/1937.
     F. M. Meigs. U.S. pat. 2,184,311/1937.
128. F. H. Frost and F. E. Brinnick. U.S. pat. 2,624,672/1953.
129. L. L. Pries. U.S. pat. 2,858,214/1958.
130. W. C. Toland and E. Bassist. U.S. pat. 2,311,888/1943.
131. F. J. Tritton. *J. Soc. Chem. Ind.*, 299, and 307 (1932).
132. R. F. Reed, P. W. Dorst, and H. Horning. *LTF Bull.* 3.
133. W. H. Wood. U.S. pat. 2,589,313/1952.
134. F. Uhlig and A. Rebenstock. Ger. pat. 1,143,710/1963.
135. J. Albrecht and O. Watter. *Druck-und Werbe-Kunst*, p. 407, 1939.
136. H. H. Borchers, E. A. Hausmann, and D. Osswald. Ger. pat. 1,165,617/1964;
     Fr. pat. 1,269,919/1959; Can. pat. 684,794/1962; Brit. pat. 955,687/1964.
137. W. and G. Ritzerfeld. U.S. pat. 3,016,824/1962.
138. O. Strecker. Ger. pats.: 120,061/1900; 148,048/1900; 152,593/1900; 642,782/
     1933.
139. A. K. Schwerin, H. D. Evans, and W. E. Burrows. Brit. pat. 891,898/1962.
140. W. H. Wood. U.S. pat. 2,328,371/1943.
141. G. R. Hodgkins and R. Timmerman. U.S. pat. 2,950,195/1960.
142. W. H. Wood. U.S. pat. 2,645,578/1953.
143. D. N. Adams. U.S. pat. 2,694,057/1954.
144. W. H. Wood. U.S. pat. 2,297,932/1942.
145. C. Douglas. *Tappi*, **46**, 544–548 (1963).
146. G. S. Schwarz. U.S. pat. 2,942,974/1960; Brit. pat. 764,380/1956.
147. O. Watter. *Druck-und Werbe-Kunst*, 250 (1941).
148. J. Albrecht and O. Watter. *Der Graphische Betrieb*, **18**, 3 (1943).
149. W. C. Huebner. U.S. pat. 3,070,008/1962.
150. W. H. Wood. U.S. pat. 2,265,829/1941.
151. W. Krohe. Brit. pat. 817,686/1959.
152. E. Straub. U.S. pat. 1,656,843/1928.
153. P. J. Whyzmuzis and W. O. Kaupp. U.S. pat. 2,564,414/1951.

154. W. H. Wood. U.S. pat. 2,270,712/1942.
155. A. R. C. Adams. Brit. pat. 790,565/1958.
156. J. S. Mertle. *National Lithographer*, Vol. 54, pp. 28–29, July 1947; pp. 26–27, August 1947; pp. 28, 29, 90, September 1947; pp. 34–35, October 1947; pp. 38–39, November 1947; pp. 36–37, December 1947. Vol. 55, pp. 36–37, January 1948; pp. 34–35, February 1948; pp. 30, 31, 75–76, April 1948; pp. 44, 45, 94, 95, May 1948.
157. V. D. Glushko, Y. N. Berezyuk, and S. D. Kazimin. U.S.S.R. pat. 141,872/ 1961.
158. C. F. Gees. U.S. pat. 2,907,273/1959.
159. C. F. Gees. U.S. pat. 2,907,656/1959.
160. C. F. Gees and D. B. Lytle. U.S. pat. 2,678,299/1954.
161. H. T. Holsapple. U.S. pat. 2,726,200/1955.
162. R. M. Leekely. U.S. pat. 2,678,275/1954.
163. R. Shapiro and K. H. Colberg. *Anal. Chem.*, **34**, 435–436 (1962).
164. G. S. Christie. Brit. pat. 19,007/1902.
165. Capitain and von Hertline. Ger. pat. 52,868/1889.
166. T. Köhler. Ger. pat. 112,615/1900.
167. O. E. Krell. *Graphische Rundschau*, **5**, 59 (1903).
168. H. Miller. U.S. pat. 2,020,901/1935.
169. U. Ostwald. U.S. pat. 1,943,486/1934; Ger. pat. 572,055/1933; Brit. pat. 385,274/1932.
170. A. Ehrenthalier. Ger. pat. 648,333/1937.
171. A. Keller. Ger. pat. 637,799/1934.
172. W. B. Westcott. U.S. pat. 2,205,998/1940; Brit. pat. 496,421/1938.
173. C. H. van Dusen. U.S. pat. 2,542,784/1951.
174. T. R. Caton. U.S. pat. 2,304,541/1942.
175. R. S. Colt. U.S. pat. 2,448,861/1948.
176. G. F. Nadeau and C. B. Starck. U.S. pat. 2,635,962/1953.
177. W. Clark. *Modern Lithography*, **18**, 40–41 (1950).
178. W. Clark. *Printing Equipment Engineer*, **47**, November 1950.
179. W. Clark. *Penrose Annual*, 45, 132–33 (1951).
180. W. O. Kenyon and C. C. Unruh. U.S. pat. 2,548,537/1951.
181. W. O. Kenyon and J. A. Cathcart. U.S. pat. 2,568,503/1951.
182. G. F. Nadeau and C. B. Starck. U.S. pat. 2,685,511/1954.
183. H. C. Staehle and C. F. Amering. U.S. pat. 2,484,431/1949.
184. E. Bassist and W. C. Toland. U.S. pat. 2,280,985/1942.
185. E. Bassist and W. C. Toland. U.S. pat. 2,230,981/1941.
186. E. Bassist and W. C. Toland. U.S. pat. 2,230,982/1941.
187. E. Bassist and W. C. Toland. U.S. pat. 2,280,986/1942.
188. E. Bassist and W. C. Toland. U.S. pat. 2,302,816/1942.
189. E. Bassist and W. C. Toland. U.S. pat. 2,302,817/1942.
190. E. Bassist and W. C. Toland. U.S. pat. 2,301,770/1942.
191. E. Bassist and W. C. Toland. U.S. pat. 2,312,852/1943.
192. E. Bassist and W. C. Toland. U.S. pat. 2,312,854/1943.
193. W. C. Toland, A. P. Reynolds, and M. H. Hamilton. U.S. pat. 2,532,865/1950.
194. W. C. Toland, A. P. Reynolds, and M. H. Hamilton. U.S. pat. 2,532,866/1950.
195. C. A. Brown. U.S. pat. 2,550,326/1951.
196. Oxford Paper Co. Brit. pat. 879,628/1961.
197. G. H. Perkins. U.S. pat. 3,055,295/1962.

198. F. L. Simons. U.S. pat. 2,132,443/1938.
199. F. L. Simons. U.S. pat. 2,156,100/1939.
200. J. V. R. Shepherd. U.S. pat. 2,154,219/1939.
201. H. K. Salzberg. U.S. pat. 3,017,826/1962.
202. W. G. Mullen. U.S. pat. 2,405,513/1946.
203. Addressograph-Multigraph Corp. Brit. pat. 844,085/1960.
204. D. Berger. Ger. pat. 161,528/1905.
205. D. de Nagy and L. Pepe. Brit. pat. 413,680/1934.
206. D. A. Newman. U.S. pat. 2,570,262/1951.
207. D. A. Newman. U.S. pat. 2,953,088/1960.
208. F. E. Brinnick and R. L. Oransky. U.S. pat. 2,778,735/1957.
209. D. A. Newman. U.S. pat. 2,941,466/1960.
210. R. C. Oransky. U.S. pat. 2,724,665/1955.
211. R. C. Oransky. U.S. pat. 2,876,134/1959; Brit. pat. 788,282/1957.
212. G. S. McKnight, Jr. and G. H. Perkins. U.S. pat. 3,017,827/1962.
213. J. B. Mazanek and L. J. Paquin. U.S. pat. 3,115,829/1963; Belg. pat. 598,192/1960; Brit. pat. 923,712/1963.
214. F. E. Brinnick. U.S. pat. 2,778,301/1957.
215. L. E. Richard. U.S. pat. 3,020,839/1962.
216. A. L. Ensink. U.S. pat. 2,835,576/1958; Brit. pat. 826,077/1957.
217. J. F. Thurlow. U.S. pat. 3,016,823/1962.
218. Oxford Paper Co. U.S. pat. 2,930,317/1960; Brit. pat. 834,332/1960.
219. S. V. Worthen and C. H. van Deusen, Jr. U.S. pat. 2,707,359/1955.
220. F. H. Frost. U.S. pat. 2,534,588/1953.
221. A. B. Dick Co. Belg. pat. 624,440/1963.
222. S. V. Worthen. U.S. pat. 2,534,650/1950.
223. S. V. Worthen. U.S. pat. 2,635,537/1953.
224. D. A. Newman. U.S. pat. 3,031,958/1962; Can. pat. 643,939/1962.
225. E. D. Osinski and G. W. Bucklin. U.S. pat. 2,463,554/1949.
226. E. W. Taylor and H. C. Staehle. U.S. pat. 3,003,413/1961.
227. Ditto, Inc. Brit. pat. 910,248/1962.
228. Koch Processes Ltd. Brit. pat. 908,600/1962.

4

Unsaturated Compounds

4.1 INTRODUCTION

A large number of compounds with one or more ethylene linkages undergo cis-trans isomerization, when irradiated with ultraviolet light. The stereoisomeric forms differ from each other in their properties to such a degree that they can be used for photographic purposes. A well-known example of such compounds is afforded by maleic (the cis form) and fumaric (the trans form) acids (1,2):

$$
\begin{array}{cc}
\text{HC·COOH} & \text{HC·COOH} \\
\| \quad \xrightarrow{\ h\nu\ } & \| \\
\text{HC·COOH} & \text{HOOC·CH} \\
\text{maleic acid} & \text{fumaric acid}
\end{array}
\tag{1}
$$

Cis-trans isomerization is not limited to substituted alkylenes alone, and was observed also in other unsaturated compounds (3), azo compounds, and oximes (4,5).

The absorption of light can result also in molecular rearrangement, as is the case with o-nitrobenzaldehyde, which, when irradiated by light of 3130 to 4360 Å, gives o-nitrosobenzoic acid (6,7).

Certain substances with at least one double bond in their molecule possess the ability, when exposed to actinic radiation, of changing their physicochemical properties, for instance swelling and solubility in solvents. This change is attributed to the rupture of the double bonds by the absorbed light, followed by the creation of new linkages. The effect of this process is the formation of ring structures or crosslinks, so that more complex molecules, often with a three-dimensional network, are formed, and, obviously, have properties differing from those of the original substances.

As early as 1826, Nièpce obtained a photograph by exposing a glass plate coated with bitumen to outdoor illumination for twelve hours. Bitumen is a complex unsaturated hydrocarbon polymeric mixture which, owing to the formation of crosslinks in the structure, loses its solubility on prolonged exposure to short wavelength radiation.   The illuminated sections of the plate were rendered less soluble, or even insoluble, in solvents such as oil of lavender.   This process, widely used in the last century for the preparation of printing plates, was soon replaced by dichromated colloids.   Dichromates, however, were unsuitable for sensitizing water-insoluble resins, and many attempts have been made to find sensitizers of more acceptable characteristics.   Beebe, Murray, and Herlinger (8,9,10,11) have suggested iodine compounds, such as iodoform or colloidal lead-iodide for sensitizing drying oils and natural or synthetic resins.   A similar process was proposed by Clement (12).   The in-solubilization of unsaturated cellulose esters by ultraviolet light was reported by Malm and Fordyce (13).   In another patent, a condensation product of furfural and acetone was disclosed as a light-sensitive composi-tion (14).   The condensation product of formaldehyde and cyclopentanone was suggested as a sensitizer for cellulose ethyl ether or an acrylate resin, by van Deusen (15).   Schröter and Rieger (16,17) prepared light-sensitive derivatives of polyvinyl alcohol and cellulose by attaching to the molecule a heterocyclic group having at least three linear joined benzene rings. The 9-anthracene-aldehyde acetal of 50 per cent acylated polyvinyl alcohol is an example:

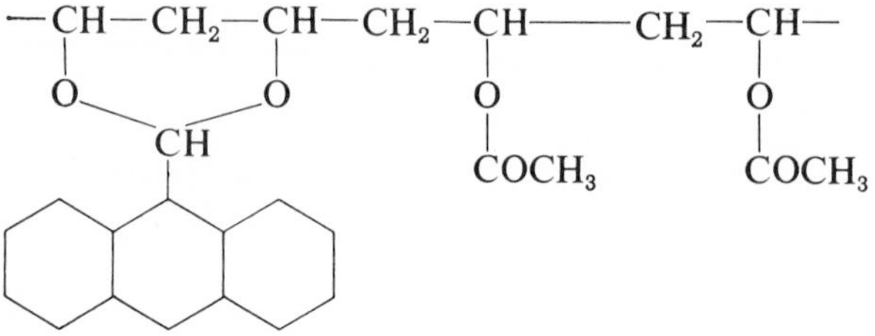

This substance, when strongly illuminated, becomes insoluble in benzene; this effect is attributed to a cross-linking reaction equivalent to the di-merization of anthracene.

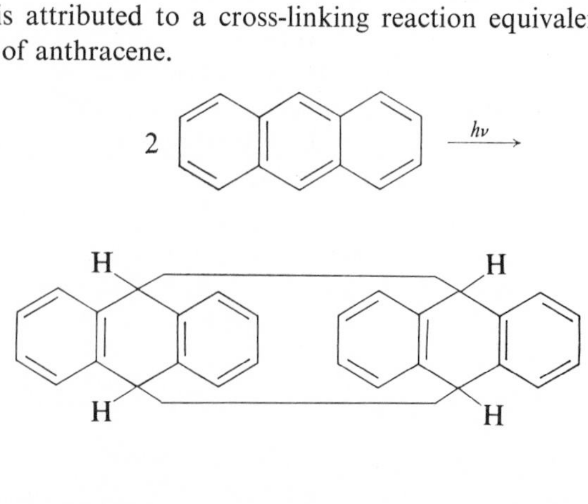

(2)

The energy of activation for the dimerization of acethracene was calculated to be 1.75 kcal per mole (18). A similar effect was observed with sym-meso-di-substituted anthracenes, e.g., the 1,4-butane-diol and the 1,6-hexanediol derivatives of 9,10-anthrylene-dipropionic acid (19) which form, upon exposure to ultraviolet light, three-dimensional lattices. Both compositions were suggested for photomechanical processes. Schönberg and Mustafa (20) found that a solution of *o*-phthalaldehyde in benzene exposed to sunlight forms a colorless crystalline dimer which reduces ammoniacal silver nitrate solution:

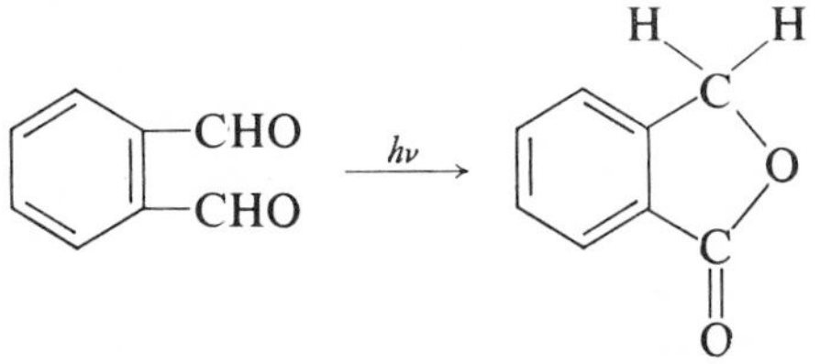

(3)

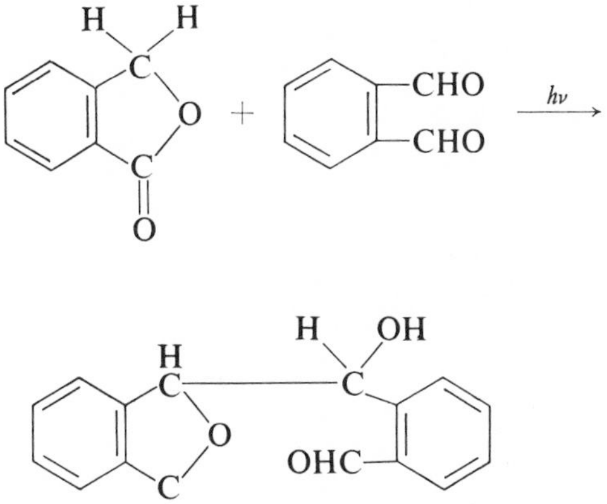

(4)

In this process the visible image is formed from the aromatic 1,2-dialdehyde that has not been acted on by the light. It is essential, in order to obtain clean background, that all the aldehyde in the exposed areas be destroyed. The optional sensitizing agents include benzoin, benzophenone, anthraquinone-2-sulfonic acid, phenanthraquinone, etc., whose primary effect is to absorb radiation in a spectral region where the phthalaldehyde itself has low absorbance and to transfer it to the aldehyde. As developers, ammonium salts are generally used, but urea and acetamide can act as thermal developers at higher temperature.

Crosslinking of polyethylene or paraffin wax by irradiation with ultraviolet light of 170 to 300 mμ was reported by Oster (21).

Insolubilization of polymeric substances on exposure to light in the presence of nitrophenols was disclosed by Kalle A.G. (22). Sagura and Unruh (23) prepared light-sensitive resins useful for the preparation of lithographic plates, by reacting maleic anhydride copolymers with hydroxy-alkyl derivatives of rhodamine compounds, such as 3-(2-hydroxyethyl)-rhodamine and 3-(2-hydroxyethyl)-5-(4-dimethylamino-benzylidene)-rhod-amine.

Because of their low light sensitivity these systems have not found many practical applications and are only of academic interest. If, however, the dimerization is part of a polymeric system, doubling of the molecular size brings a change in the solubility, which is reflected in higher sensitivity. Among the best known systems are processes giving cyclo-butane derivatives (24).

4.2 CINNAMIC ACID AND ITS DERIVATIVES. KODAK PHOTO RESIST

Dimerization of cinnamic acid under the action of ultraviolet light was first observed by Berthram and Kursten (25) and further investigated by Stobbe (26) and Stoermer and Laage (27). The two —C=C— double bonds add to one another, and because of the unsymmetrical structure of cinnamic acid the addition may take place in two different ways:

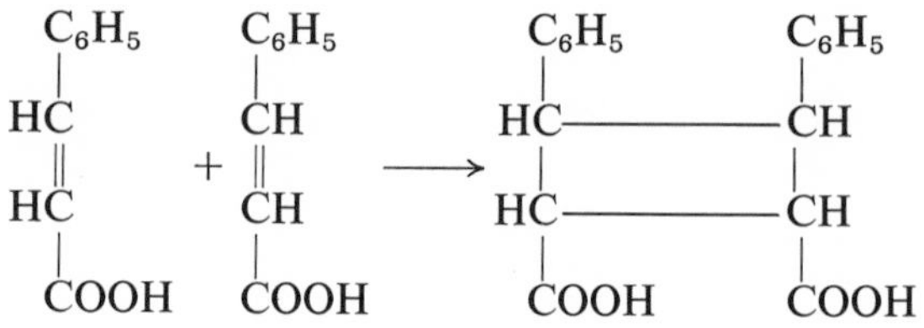

$$
\begin{array}{ll}
\underset{\substack{| \\ \mathrm{HC} \\ \| \\ \mathrm{HC} \\ | \\ \mathrm{COOH}}}{\mathrm{C_6H_5}} + \underset{\substack{| \\ \mathrm{CH} \\ \| \\ \mathrm{CH} \\ | \\ \mathrm{COOH}}}{\mathrm{C_6H_5}} \longrightarrow \underset{\substack{| \\ \mathrm{HC}\text{——}\mathrm{CH} \\ | \qquad | \\ \mathrm{HC}\text{——}\mathrm{CH} \\ | \qquad | \\ \mathrm{COOH} \quad \mathrm{COOH}}}{\mathrm{C_6H_5} \qquad \mathrm{C_6H_5}} & \text{β-isotruxillic acid} \qquad (5)
\end{array}
$$

$$
\begin{array}{ll}
\underset{\substack{| \\ \mathrm{HC} \\ \| \\ \mathrm{HC} \\ | \\ \mathrm{COOH}}}{\mathrm{C_6H_5}} + \underset{\substack{| \\ \mathrm{CH} \\ \| \\ \mathrm{CH} \\ | \\ \mathrm{C_6H_5}}}{\mathrm{COOH}} \longrightarrow \underset{\substack{| \\ \mathrm{HC}\text{——}\mathrm{CH} \\ | \qquad | \\ \mathrm{HC}\text{——}\mathrm{CH} \\ | \qquad | \\ \mathrm{COOH} \quad \mathrm{C_6H_5}}}{\mathrm{C_6H_5} \qquad \mathrm{COOH}} & \text{α-truxillic acid} \qquad (6)
\end{array}
$$

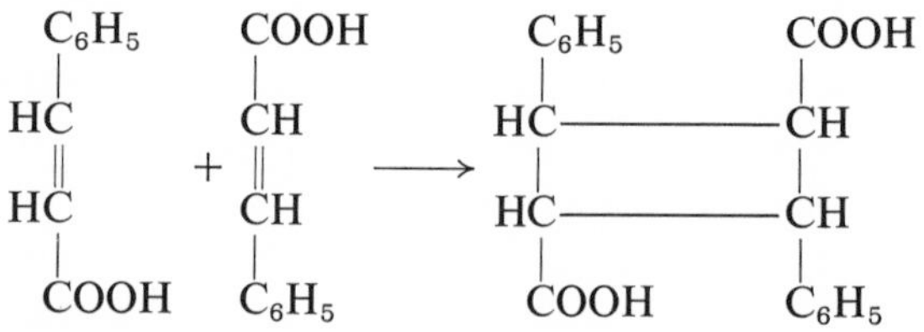

Stobbe and his co-workers (28,29,30,31,32), also studied the light sensitivity of organic compounds containing the cinnamoyl group $C_6H_5 \cdot CH{=}CH \cdot CO{-}$. Dicinnamal-acetone $C_6H_5CH{=}CH \cdot CH{=}CH \cdot CO \cdot CH{=}CH \cdot$

$CH=CH \cdot C_6H_5$ was suggested as a sensitizer for resinous material by Murray (33) and later by Van Deusen (15). The sensitivity of these unsaturated keto compounds can be considerably increased by adding optical sensitizers (34). The shelf life of material sensitized with light-sensitive unsaturated ketones, e.g., cinnamylidene methyl ethyl ketone and cinnamylidene acetophenone, can be considerably improved by addition of certain quinones and thiazine dyes (35). Unsaturated aromatic or hetero-cyclic aldehydes, e.g., 2-nitrocinnamaldehyde, 4-nitrocinnamalde-hyde, and 4-methoxycinnamaldehyde are light-sensitive also (36). Ultra-violet sensitivity of cinnamoyl polystyrene resins was disclosed by Allen and Van Allan (37). Cinnamoyl-polystyrene resins are made by the acylation of polystyrene with cinnamoyl chloride. Since acylation pro-ceeds only to a limited extent before insolubilization occurs, a copolymer of the following general structure is obtained:

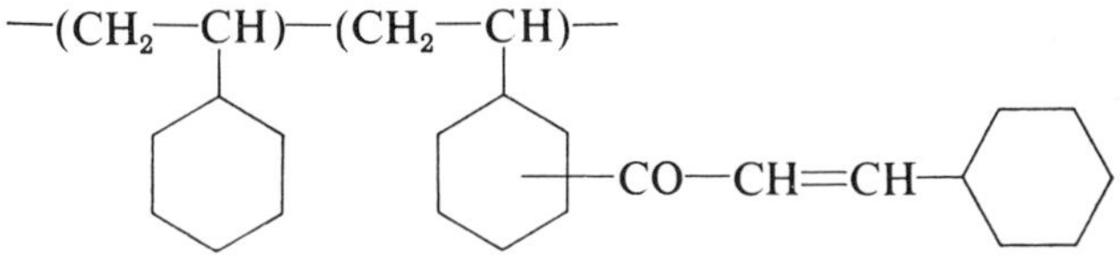

If, as in this example, the cinnamic acid is a pendant group on a polymeric chain, then under the influence of ultraviolet radiation crosslinking between the chains ensues.

The Kodak Photo Resist (KPR and KMER) is based on this principle. When coated on a plate and dried, the coating becomes insoluble in areas exposed to ultraviolet radiation. During the development, the nonexposed sections of the plate are removed with solvents, e.g., with trichlorethylene, leaving a resist pattern tightly adhering to almost any metal, glass, or ceramic.

Eastman Kodak Company has not released much information on the chemical composition of the photoresists, but from the patents assigned to this company in that field, we can assume that the light-sensitive component is polyvinyl cinnamate or a closely related compound. These are obtained by esterification of a polymeric material having hydroxyl groups in their molecule with a cinnamic acid halide (38,39,40). Hydroxy-allylated, partially allylated, or esterified cellulose or polyvinyl alcohol are also suitable. Addition of a less fully esterified polyvinyl cinnamate to the coating mixture supposedly improves the processing latitude of exposed fully esterified cinnamate coating (41).

Inami and Moritomo (42) investigated the photohardening of polyvinyl cinnamate and concluded that the hardening is due to the crosslinking reaction of the $C=C$ double bond of the cinnamate group.

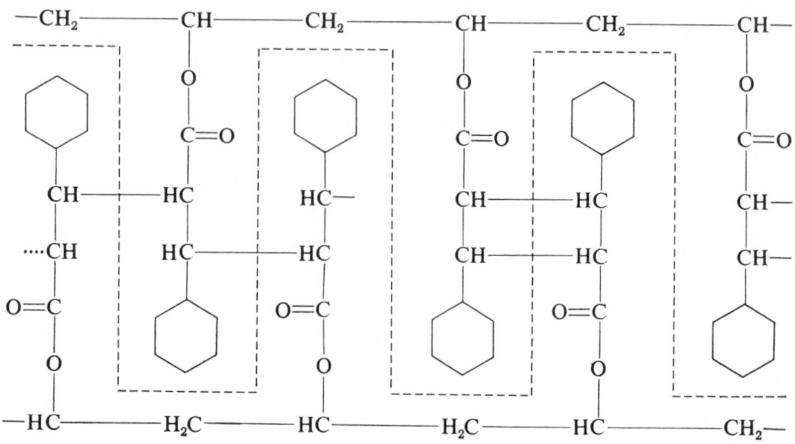

crosslinked polyvinyl cinnamate

Whereas original formulations showed no higher sensitivity than earlier described polymers (43), it was found that polyvinyl cinnamate and similar compounds can be sensitized to ultraviolet radiation and visible light with nitroaryl compounds (44,45), anthrones (46), quinones (47), diaminobenzophenone imides, diaminodiphenyl methanes, diamino-diphenyl ketones, and diaminodiphenyl carbinols (48). Triphenyl-methane dyes (49) and cyanine dyes (50) are also claimed as sensitizers. Tsunoda and Nozoki (51) reported a 50- to 100-times speed increase of polyvinyl cinnamate with nitrofluorenes, benzoylacenaphthenes, and diphthaloylnaphthalenes.

The result of sensitization, the peak sensitivity, and the extension of sensitivity of a number of sensitizers just described are given in Table 4.1. The initial speed of the polyvinyl cinnamate is represented by a speed value of 2, and dichromated shellac would have a speed value of approximately 30.

The light sensitivity of polyvinyl cinnamate coatings can also be, supposedly, increased by incorporating finely divided radiation transmitting pigments, e.g., aluminum stearate (52).

The spectral sensitivity (53), graphically illustrated in Figure 4.1, is not uniform through the entire range of the spectrum. As the curve shows, the first maximum is in the near ultraviolet at 320 mμ; from this point, the sensitivity decreases to 360 mμ, and rises to a second maximum at about 420 mμ. Beyond this second peak, in the violet-blue, the

TABLE *4.1.* Polyvinyl Cinnamate Sensitizers (reference 41)

Sensitizer	Sensitivity Value	Maximum Sensitivity, mμ	Extension of Sensitivity, mμ	Reference
None	2.2	320	340	43
Hydrocarbons				
Naphthalene	2.6			
Anthracene	7.7			43
Phenanthrene	14.0			
Chrysene	18.0			
Nitro Compounds				
Nitrobenzene	8.0			
o-Nitrodiphenyl-ether	10.0			
o-Nitroanisol	20.0			
p-Nitrobromo-benzene	20.0			43
β-Nitrostyrene	30.0			44
p-Dinitrobenzene	40.0			
m-Nitroanisole	50.0			
p-Nitroanisole	60.0			
m-Nitrophenol	70.0			
p-Nitrodiphenyl	200.0	360	380	
5-Nitro-2-amino-toluene	200.0			
Amino Compounds				
m-Nitroaniline	50.0			
p-Nitroaniline	100.0	370	400	43
2,4,6-Trinitro-aniline	300.0			44
2,6-Dichloro-4-nitroaniline	300.0	380	410	
4-nitro-2-chloro-aniline	300.0			
Anthrones				
4-Cyclohexyl-benzanthrone	3.0			
Pyranthrone	7.0			
Anthrone	31.0			43

Sensitizer	Sensitivity Value	Maximum Sensitivity, $m\mu$	Extension of Sensitivity, $m\mu$	Reference
None	2.2	320	340	43
Anthrones—(*continued*)				
3-Keto-1,2-diaza-benzanthrone	40.0			46
2-Keto-3-aza-benzanthrone	55.0			
Dianthrone	80.0			
1,9-Benzanthrone	90.0	320	330	
1-Cyano-2-keto-3-methyl-6-bromo-3-azabenzanthrone	200.0			
1-Carbethoxy-2-keto-3,4-dimethyl-6-bromo-3-aza-benzanthrone	400.0			
2-Keto-3-methyl-1,3-diazabenzan-throne	500.0			
3-Methyl-1,3-diaza-1,9-benzan-throne	100.0	470	490	
Quinones				
Benzoquinone	2.2			
Tolu-*p*-quinone	5.0			
2,6-Dichloro-quinone	9.0			
1,2-Naphtho-quinone	20.0			43
2,3-Benzanthra-quinone	60.0			47
9,10-Anthra-quinone	99.0	320	420	
β-Chloroanthra-quinone	200.0			
β-Phenylanthra-quinone	300.0			
1,2-Benzanthra-quinone	500.0	420	470	

Sensitizer	Sensitivity Value	Maximum Sensitivity, mμ	Extension of Sensitivity, mμ	Reference
None	2.2	320	340	43
Ketones				
Acetophenone	2.6			
Benzophenone	20.0			
4,4′-Diaminodiphenyl ketone	35.0			
Benzil	50.0			
Dibenzalacetone	60.0			43
p,p′-Dimethylaminobenzophenone	510.0			
p,p′-Tetramethyldiaminobenzophenone	640.0	380	420	48
p,p′-Tetramethyldiaminodiphenyl ketone	650.0			
p,p′-Tetraethyldiaminodiphenyl ketone	740.0			
Aldehydes				43
Benzaldehyde	6.8			
9-Anthraldehyde	35.0			
Triphenylmethane Dyes				
Rhoduline blue 6GA	2.0			
Methyl violet	3.0			49
Victoria blue	5.0			
Malachite green	10.0			
Crystal violet-XC	15.0			
Cyanine Dyes				
3,3′-Di(*p*-nitrophenyl)thiacarbocyanine iodide	4.0			
3,3′-diethyl-4,5,4′,5′-dibenzothiacarbocyanine bromide	7.0			

Sensitizer	Sensitivity Value	Maximum Sensitivity, mμ	Extension of Sensitivity, mμ	Reference
None	2.2	320	340	43
Cyanine Dyes—(*continued*)				
3,3'-di(*p*-nitro-benzyl)oxacarbo-cyanine iodide	11.0			50
3,3'-dilauryloxa-cyanine perchlorate	40.0			
1',3-diethyl-6-nitrothia-2'-cyanine iodide	50.0			
3,3'-diethyl-4,5,4',5'-dibenzo-thiacyanine iodide	200.0			

sensitivity falls off rapidly and reaches zero at approximately 465 mμ; it is obvious that for the exposure, carbon arcs, mercury-vapor lamps, or other high-energy light sources are most useful.

Kodak Photo Resist was originally developed for making printing plates (54,55).   Because of its interesting properties, however, it is used in the manufacture of printed circuits (55), semiconductor devices, stencils (56), name plates, etc.   Photosensitive resists of this type are utilized in chemical milling and in the etching of decorative designs on metals and glass and in decorating ceramic objects (57).

Polymeric cinnamic acid esters are stable in the absence of light, in solution, or coated on a support.   It was found, however, that when

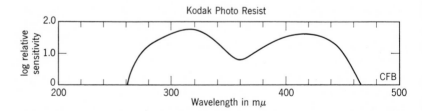

Figure 4.1.   Spectral sensitivity of Kodak Photo Resist.   Reproduced, with permission, from the copyrighted Kodak publication, Kodak Photosensitive Resists for Industry *(reference 53).*

coated on zinc plates and aged for about 24 hours, the exposed parts could not be completely removed by the solvent developer so that the printing ink adheres to these areas and decreases the quality of the photolithographic plate.   This condition, called "scumming," can be reduced or completely prevented by adding to the sensitizing solution an insolubilizing inhibitor having reducing properties (58).   Hydroquinone is an example.   Further improvement, it is claimed, results from the incorporation of triethanol-amine (59).   For removing the thin film of crosslinked polymer from the surface of the plate, ethylene glycol mono-methyl ether can be used.   An oil-in-water emulsion for developing, densensitizing, and coloring the image areas in one single operation was formulated by Adams (60). The solvent phase contains a water-insoluble solvent with a boiling point between 100 to 200°C, e.g., xylene, and waxoline red; the aqueous phase consists of gum arabic, phosphoric acid, and an anionic wetting agent.

Material sensitized with polyvinyl cinnamate was also suggested for a color-reproduction process in which the developed sheets are dyed with appropriate cyan, magenta, and yellow dyes (61).

To avoid using organic solvents required for the removal of the un-exposed portions of the light-sensitive layer, polymers containing a substantial number of carboxyl groups in the molecule were prepared (62). As examples, only polyvinyl cinnamate succinate and phthalate will be mentioned.   These substances can be coated from and processed with aqueous alkaline solutions.   Polymers in which the light-sensitive cinna-mate group is attached to a polymeric backbone by means of isocyanate groups forming urethanes, may be cast from dilute aqueous acid solution to give light-sensitive films (63,64).

Continuing research in this field has resulted in the synthesis of other light-sensitive polymeric materials, such as that obtained by the esterifi-cation of a styrene/maleic-anhydride copolymer with cinnamamide (65). Unruh and Smith, who are responsible for the synthesis of the above compounds found also that the N-(cinnamoylphenyl) urethane derivatives of hydroxyl-containing polymers are about 280 times more sensitive than unsensitized polyvinyl cinnamate.   This type of polymer can be further sensitized with Michler's ketone or with 2-benzoylmethylene-1-methyl-β-naphthothiazoline (66).

Polymers with a sensitivity up to 6000 times that of polyvinyl cinnamate were prepared by Merrill and Smith (67) by esterifying partially hydrolyzed cellulose acetate with a 3- or 4-(α-cyano-cinnamido-) phthalic anhydride. The reaction product of vinyl-acetate/maleic-anhydride, or similar copolymer with ethyl 4-aminocinnamate is also sensitive to light (68).

Ethylene/vinyl-cinnamate copolymers (69) or polymers obtained by heating styrene/maleic-anhydride copolymer with monoesters of ethylene glycol and cinnamic acid (70) are also useful as resists in graphic arts. For the same application de Waile and Croker (71) recommended epoxy resins esterified with cinnamoyl chloride. By etherifying the epoxy resin with sorbitol before esterification, resins of much higher light sensitivity, it is claimed, are obtainable (72). Instead of sorbitol, the epoxy resins can be esterified with tartaric acid to form a compound containing hydroxyl groups which are then esterified with cinnamoyl chloride. This product is superior to resins made directly from epoxy resins and cinnamic acid. Condensation product of di-*p*-phenylol-2:2-propane with epichlorohydrin reacted with sorbitol and esterified with cinnamic acid or cinnamoyl chloride is useful for sensitizing lithographic plates (73).

Soluble polyamides, such as that obtained by reacting γ,γ'-diamino-propylether with cinnamic acid-*p*-carboxyl acid dimethylester, were recommended for sensitizing metal and glass plates (74). Photosensitive diamides of cinnamylidenemalonic acid coated on a support such as paper or aluminum are used for preparation of printing plates (75); their sensitivity can be increased with methyl-2-(N-methylbenzothiazoly-lidene) dithioacetate.

Light-sensitive cinnamylidene arylvinylacetophenone polymers were utilized in a photographic transfer process (76); the light-sensitive layer, exposed under a line or halftone negative, is moistened with methyl ethyl ketone and placed in contact with a paper-receiving sheet in order to transfer a portion of the unexposed area; to increase the visibility of the transferred image, dyes or pigments are added to the light-sensitive composition. The condensation product of ethylene glycol with cinnamyl-idenemalonic acid (77) and *p*-formylcinnamic acid acetal of polyvinyl alcohol have been suggested for use in photography and for the prepara-tion of printing plates (78). Polymers formed by the condensation of 1,4-butane-diol and cinnamylidene malonic acid are useful as a resist in the deep-etch lithographic plate process (79). Cinnamylidenemalonic acid substituted with azido or nitro groups can be used for the same purpose (80). Another reproduction process utilizing the photosensitizing pro-perties of a polyester prepared by condensation of phthalic anhydride, adipic acid, and cinnamic acid was patented by Schellenberg and Bayer (81). Because of the crosslinking of —CH=CH—CO— groups bonded to the aromatic nucleus, the sections exposed to ultraviolet radiation become insoluble in acetone and thus a solvent wash results in a photographic image of the original transparency. Images which can be fixed on ceramics can be prepared by using poly-tetramethylene cinnamalidenemalonate as sensitizer; after the exposure to ultraviolet light, the unexposed areas are softened by heating to 150 to 190°C to make them accept carbon black or other pigments suitable for enameling (82). Polymeric quaternary ammonium salts obtained by the reaction of polyvinyl sulfonates such as polyvinylbenzene sulfonate, polyvinyltoluene solfonate, and polyvinylmethyl sulfonate with pyridine and pyridine derivatives possess good light sensitivity (83). For example, by reacting 2-furfuraldehyde with the reaction product of 4-picoline with a *p*-toluene sulfonic acid ester of polyvinyl alcohol, a polymer, containing units of the formula

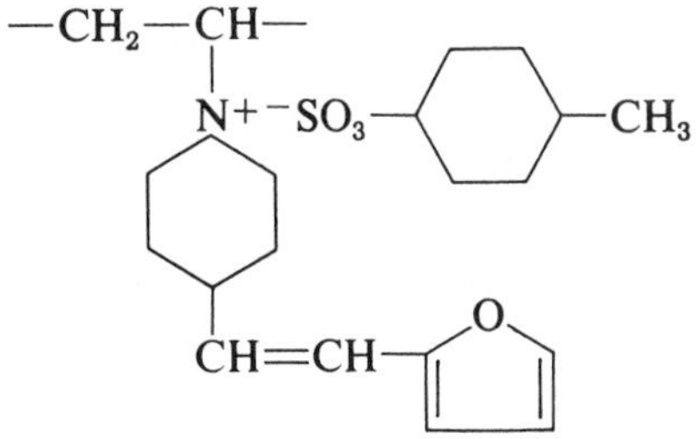

$$-CH_2-CH-$$

was obtained.

This polymer has a speed value of 14,000 compared to a sensitized polyvinyl cinnamate speed value of from 1000 to 2000. The exceptionally high speed value of this polymer is presumably due to the long chain of conjugation containing the 2-furyl substituents.

4.3 CHALCONE-TYPE COMPOUNDS

It is a well-known fact that benzalacetophenone, also known as chalcone, and its derivatives undergo a self-addition reaction at the styryl double bond with the formation of cyclic dimers:

$$2C_6H_5 \cdot CH{=}CH \cdot CO \cdot C_6H_5 \longrightarrow \begin{matrix} C_6H_5{-}CH{-}CH{-}CO{-}C_6H_5 \\ | \quad | \\ C_6H_5{-}CH{-}CH{-}CO{-}C_6H_5 \end{matrix} \quad (7)$$

Like the polymers containing cinnamic ester groups, polymers having, as a portion of their structure the chalcone group ($-C_6H_4CH{=}CH{-}CH{-}CO{-}C_6H_4{-}$), have the property of becoming insolubilized on exposure to ultraviolet light. Unruh (84,85) prepared a series of polyvinylaralacetophenones by condensing polyvinylacetophenone with benzaldehyde or other araldehydes (86,87). The sensitivity of these polymers to ultraviolet radiation was found to be much higher than that of polyvinyl cinnamate; this was apparently due to the absorption of considerably longer wavelengths.

Other polymers of this type are prepared by condensing 4′(β-hydroxyethoxy)-chalcone with a styrene/maleic-anhydride copolymer or other maleic anhydride copolymers (88). The process of preparation can be illustrated as follows:

4-(β-hydroxyethoxy) acetophenone reacts with 4-methoxybenzaldehyde to give 4-methoxy-4'-(β-hydroxy-ethoxy) chalcone:

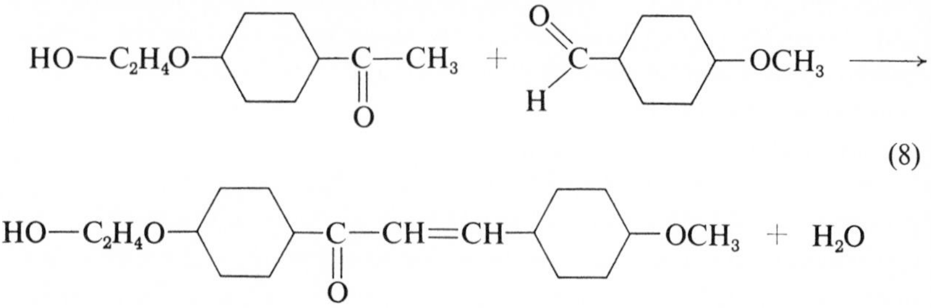

(8)

This process is followed by the reaction of the chalcone with a styrene/maleic-anhydride copolymer:

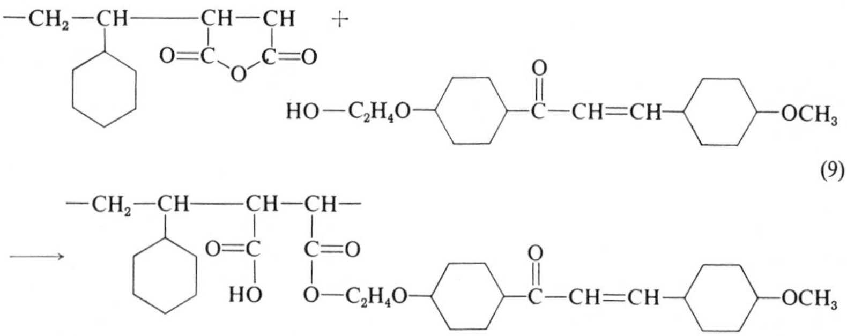

(9)

The styrene unit can be replaced with a vinyl-ester unit, such as vinyl acetate or vinyl propionate. Other copolymers of maleic anhydride are also usable, for example, alkylacrylate or methacrylate copolymers. Suitable ω-hydroxyalkoxyacetophenones include, in addition to the 4-(β-hydroxyethoxy) acetophenone, other derivatives, e.g., 4-(γ-hydroxy-propoxy) acetophenone.

Light-sensitive vinyl benzalacetophenone polymers, made by condensing vinyl acetophenone with benzaldehyde, were patented by Unruh and Allen (89). The light sensitivity of similar compounds, such as polyvinyl benzophenone, polyvinyl-p'-chlorobenzophenone, polyvinyl-p'-methoxy-benzophenone, polyvinyl-2-naphthophenone, etc., described by Merrill (90) can be increased by addition of 12-hydroxystearate, ethyl 12-hydroxy-stearate, p',p-dimethylaminobenzhydrol and borneol.

Suitable for the preparation of lithographic printing plates are the light-sensitive polyesters formed by condensing a polyhydric alcohol, such as polyvinyl alcohol, with a polybasic acid, e.g., cinnamic acid, chalcone compounds, or *p*-phenylene diacrylic acid (91). In another patent (92), it is claimed that printing plates, sensitized with the high-molecular-weight polymers obtained by reacting a copolymer of methyl methacrylate and *β*-isocyanatoethyl acrylate with a chalcone derivative, such as *p*-hydroxybenzal acetophenone, have very good storage properties. Equally suitable is the reaction product of polyvinyl alcohol or starch with *p*-isocyanatobenzal acetophenone.

The condensation product obtained from 2,2-(4,4'-dihydroxy-diphenyl) propane and 4,4'-dihydroxy-3-methoxychalcone is another example of a compound rendered insoluble on exposure to ultraviolet radiation because of crosslinking (93). The unexposed portions can be removed with methylene chloride. Thoma, Bayer, and Rinke (75), in addition to the above product, patented the production and use of soluble polyamides obtained, for instance, by reacting chalcone-4,4'-bis-hydroxy acetic acid ethyl ether with *γ,γ'*-diaminopropyl ether. The resin is soluble in dimethyl formamide and the solution can be cast on metal or glass plates; on exposure to light the film becomes insoluble, and the unexposed sections can be readily dissolved in dimethyl formamide and removed. To extend the sensitivity to light of longer wavelengths, cyanine, triphenylmethane, and anthraquinone dyes can be used.

4.4 STILBENE COMPOUNDS

Stilbene compounds have, as light-sensitive groups, the stilbene units $C_6H_5 \cdot CH{=}CH \cdot C_6H_5$, and show, with some exceptions, high sensitivity, not only to ultraviolet light but to practically the whole visible spectrum. Stilbene and its derivatives are converted photochemically to the corresponding phenanthrene derivatives (94,95) in the presence of oxidants such as molecular oxygen. The reaction is believed to proceed by way of the unorthodox dihydrophenanthrene which then undergoes hydrogen abstraction by the oxidant to give phenanthrene (96,97):

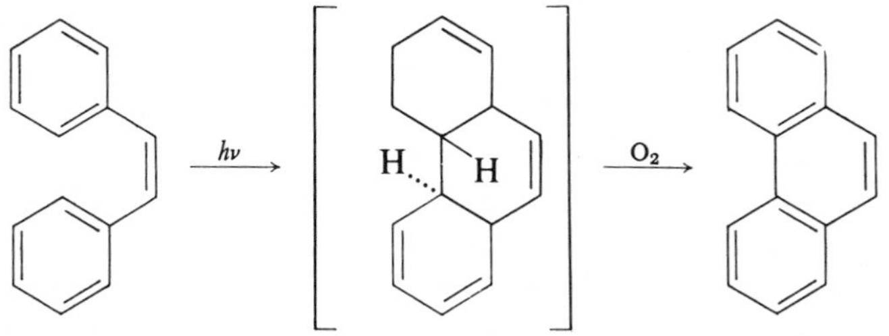

$$\xrightarrow{h\nu} \qquad \xrightarrow{O_2} \qquad (10)$$

| stilbene | dihydrophenanthrene | phenanthrene |

Light-sensitive stilbene compounds are suitable for the preparation of presensitized printing plates having excellent storage properties (98). When the exposed layer is treated with a suitable solvent, either the exposed areas or the unexposed areas can be removed, according to the compound used for sensitizing.   In the first case, a positive (in the second, a negative) printing plate is obtained from a positive master.   A number of compounds suitable for this application are listed in Table 4.2.

TABLE *4.2.* Presensitized Printing Plates

Stilbene Compound	Developer	Remarks
4,4′-dinitro-2,2′-disulfanilidostilbene		
	50% alcohol	positive plate from negative
2,2′-disulfanilidostilbene		
	3% Na_2CO_3 1% glycol monomethyl ether	positive plate from positive
4-nitro-2-sulfanilidostilbene		
	50% alcohol	positive plate from negative

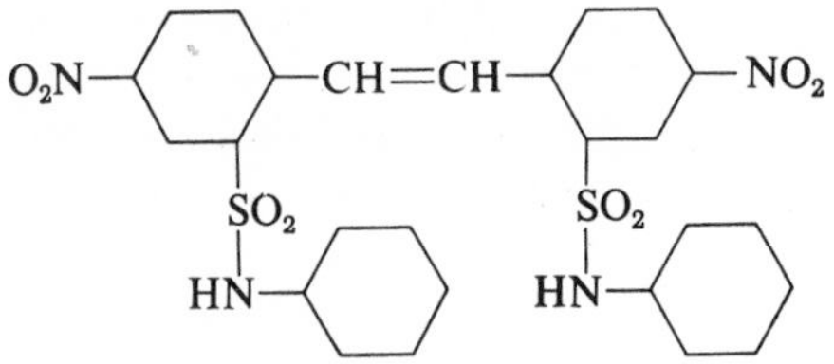

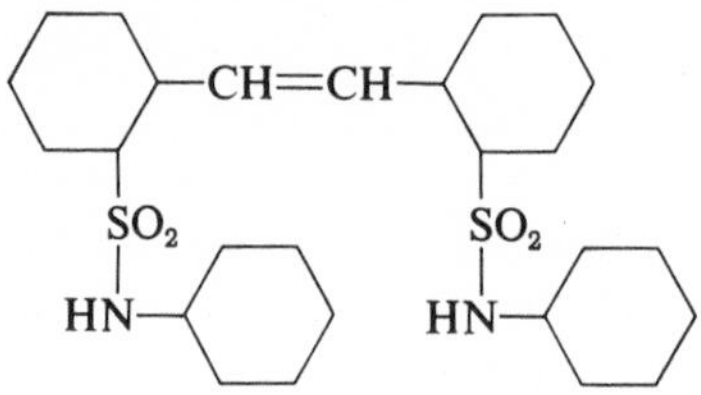

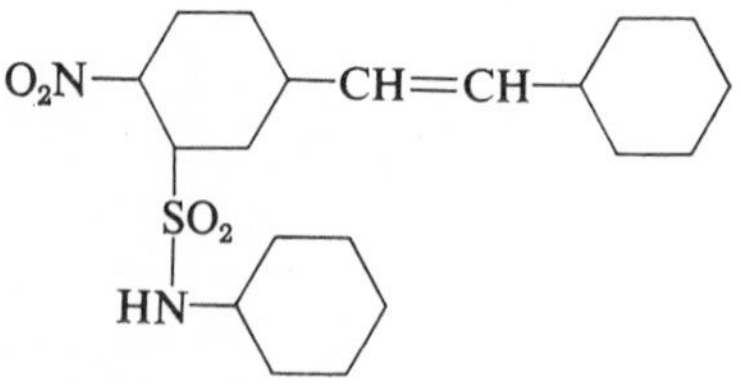

Stilbene Compound	Developer	Remarks

4-nitro-4′-methoxy-2-sulfanilido-
stilbene

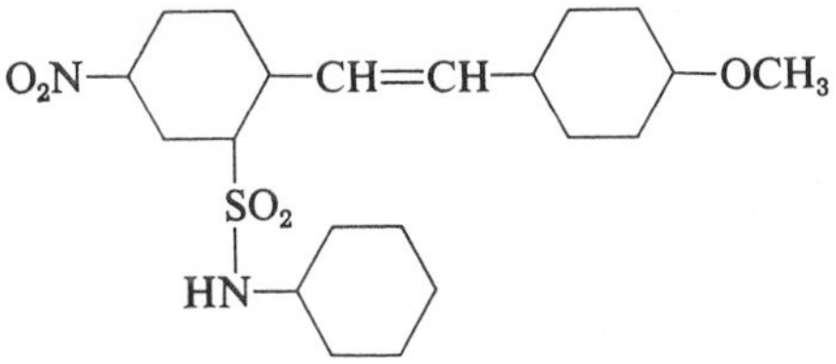

O_2N—⬡—CH=CH—⬡—OCH$_3$ 5% Na$_2$CO$_3$ positive plate
from negative

(with SO$_2$ / HN—⬡ substituent)

terephthalal-4,4′-dinitro-2,2′-
disulfanilidoditoluene

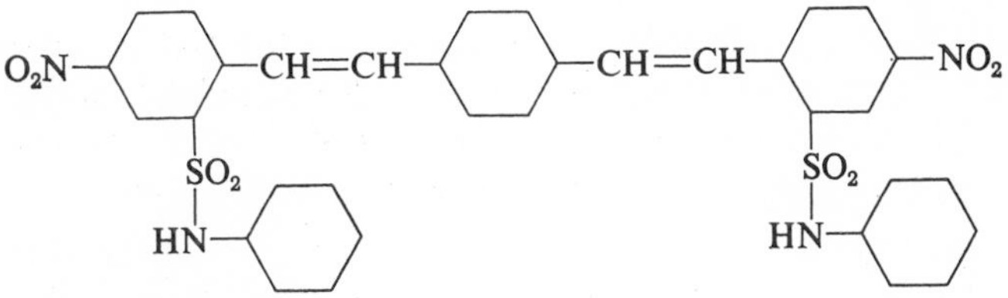

80% alcohol   positive plate
from negative

O_2N—⬡—CH=CH—⬡—CH=CH—⬡—NO$_2$

(with SO$_2$ / HN—⬡ substituents)

4,4′-diacetylamino-2,2′-
disulfanilidostilbene

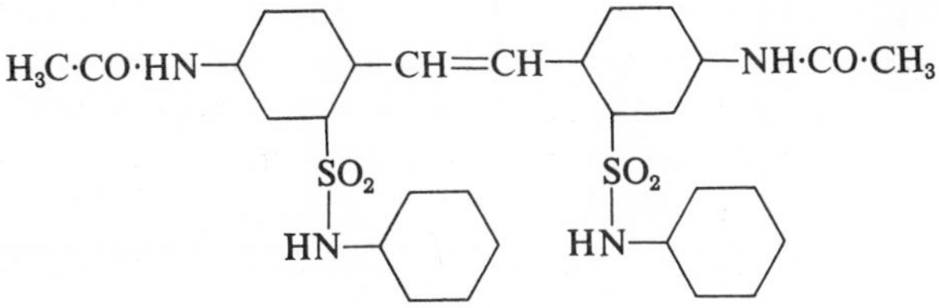

50% alcohol   positive plate
positive from

$H_3C\cdot CO\cdot HN$—⬡—CH=CH—⬡—NH·CO·CH$_3$

(with SO$_2$ / HN—⬡ substituents)

4,4′-dinitro,2,2′-bis-(sulfo-*m*-
chloro-anilido)stilbene

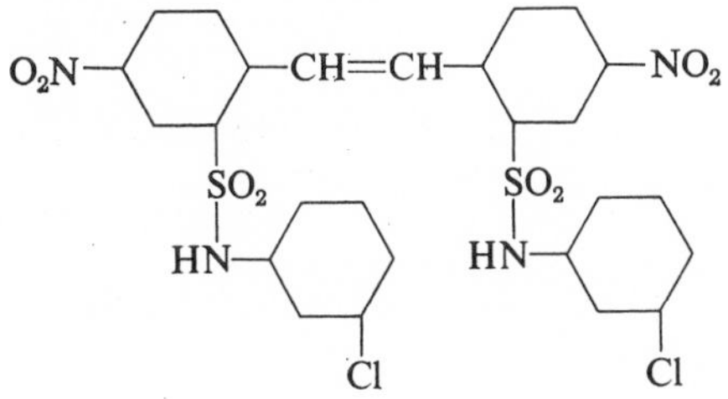

O_2N—⬡—CH=CH—⬡—NO$_2$ 10%   positive plate
Na$_2$HPO$_4$ from negative
1% Na$_3$PO$_4$

(with SO$_2$ / HN—⬡—Cl substituents)

Stilbene Compound	Developer	Remarks
2,2′-bis-(sulfo-*p*-methoxyanilido)-stilbene		
	50% alcohol	positive plate from negative

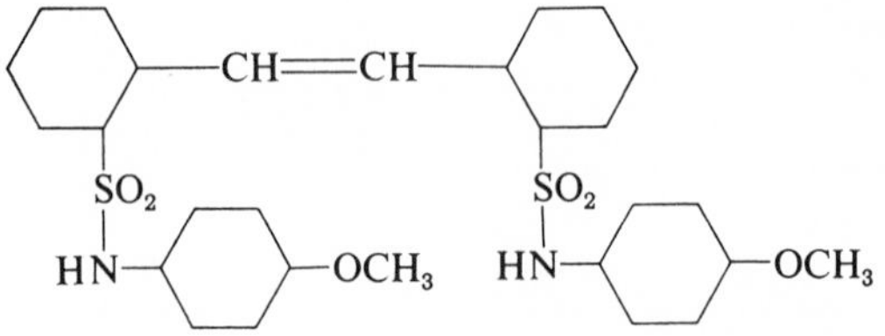

Tupis (99) describes a photographic process suitable for making color transparencies, in which the insolubilized polymer acts as a mordant for dyes. In this process, a mixture of a light-sensitive polymer and an aqueous dispersion of a water-insoluble acrylate resin coated on a support is exposed under a suitable negative. After dissolving the unreacted polymer from the unexposed parts, an image of insolubilized polymer distributed in the acrylate layer is left, which can be dyed with acidic or basic dyes to produce a visible image. In a similar way, two or more images are formed on top of each other so that a color reproduction in subtractive colors can be obtained.

Unsaturated linear polyamides (nylons) to which light-sensitive stilbene units are linked by a carbonyl or methylamino group, have been suggested for the preparation of gravure plates (100). The composition, which in some cases may require the addition of a small amount of photoinitiator and of polymerization inhibitor, is pressure-molded on curved aluminum backing and exposed through both a continuous-tone positive and a halftone screen positive. Ultraviolet light hardens exposed areas; other sections are washed away with alcohol, leaving a relief image. These printing plates, introduced by Time, Inc., are light, strong, and capable of press runs of more than 500,000 impressions.

REFERENCES

1. A. R. Olson and F. L. Hudson. *J. Am. Chem. Soc.*, **55**, 1410–1424 (1933).
2. J. Eggert, R. Schmidt, and B. Wendt. U.S. pat. 1,782,259/1930.
3. S. W. Pelletier and W. L. McLeish. *J. Am. Chem. Soc.*, **74**, 6292–6293 (1952).
4. A. H. Cook and D. G. Jones. *J. Chem. Soc.*, **1939**, 1309–1315.
5. W. R. Brode, J. H. Gould, and G. M. Wyman. *J. Am. Chem. Soc.*, **74**, 4641–4646 (1952); *ibid.*, 75, 1856–1859 (1953).

6. P. A. Leighton and F. A. Lucy. *J. Chem. Phys.*, **2**, 756–760 (1934).
7. L. W. Eberlin. U.S. pat. 1,878,684/1932.
8. M. C. Beebe, A. Murray, and H. V. Herlinger. U.S. pat. 1,574,356/1926; U.S. pat. 1,574,357/1926; U.S. pat. 1,574,358/1926; U.S. pat. 1,574,359/1926.
9. M. C. Beebe, A. Murray, and H. V. Herlinger. U.S. pat. 1,575,143/1926.
10. M. C. Beebe, A. Murray, and H. V. Herlinger. U.S. pat. 1,587,269/1926; U.S. pat. 1,587,270/1926; U.S. pat. 1,587,271/1926; U.S. pat. 1,587,272/1926; U.S. pat. 1,587,273/1926.
11. M. C. Beebe, A. Murray, and H. V. Herlinger. U.S. pat. 1,604,674/1926.
12. L. E. Clément. U.S. pat. 2,099,297/1937; Fr. pat. 793,614/1936.
13. C. J. Malm and C. R. Fordyce. U.S. pat. 1,973,493/1934.
14. M. C. Beebe and A. Murray. U.S. pat. 1,587,274/1926.
15. W. P. van Deusen. U.S. pat. 2,544,905/1951.
16. G. A. Schröter. U.S. pat. 2,980,535/1961; Ger. pat. 942,779.
17. G. A. Schröter and P. Rieger. *Kunstoffe*, **44**, 278–280 (1954).
18. M. Suzuki. *Bull. Chem. Soc. Japan*, **22**, 172–178 (1949).
19. A. P. Georges. Fr. pat. 1,229,883/1960.
20. A. Schönberg and A. Mustafa. *J. Am. Chem. Soc.*, **77**, 5755–5756 (1955).
21. G. Oster. Brit. pat. 848,414/1960.
22. Kalle A.G. Ger. pat. 955,379/1956.
23. J. J. Sagura and C. C. Unruh. U.S. pat. 2,824,087/1958.
24. A. Mustafa. *Chem. Rev.*, **51**, 1–23 (1952).
25. J. Bertram and R. Kürsten. *J. Prakt. Chem.*, **2**, 51, 325 (1895).
26. H. Stobbe. *Ber.*, **52B**, 670 (1919).
27. R. Stoermer and E. Laage. *Ber.*, **54B**, 77 (1921).
28. H. Stobbe. *Ber.*, **52B**, 666 (1919).
29. H. Stobbe and F. K. Steinberger. *Ber.*, **55B**, 2225 (1922).
30. H. Stobbe and A. Lehfeldt. *Ber.*, **58B**, 2415 (1925).
31. H. Stobbe and A. Hensel. *Ber.*, **59**, 2254 (1926).
32. H. Stobbe and K. Bremer. *J. Prakt. Chem.*, **2**, 123, 15, 28 (1929).
33. A. Murray. U.S. pat. 1,965,710/1934.
34. W. West. U.S. pat. 2,666,701/1954.
35. W. Neugebauer and M. Tomanek. U.S. pat. 2,768,077/1956.
36. W. Neugebauer and M. Tomanek. U.S. pat. 2,757,090/1956.
37. C. F. H. Allen and J. A. van Allan. U.S. pat. 2,566,302/1951.
38. L. M. Minsk, J. G. Smith, W. P. van Deusen, and J. F. Wright. *J. Appl. Polymer Sci.*, **2**, 302–307 (1959).
39. L. M. Minsk. U.S. pat. 2,725,372/1955.
40. L. M. Minsk and W. P. van Deusen. Brit. pat. 813,604/1959; Brit. pat. 813,605/1959; Ger. pat. 1,079,453/1960.
41. J. J. Murray and G. W. Leubner. U.S. pat. 2,739,892/1956.
42. A. Inami and K. Moritomo. *Kogyo Kagaku Zasshi*, **65**, 293 (1962).
43. E. M. Robertson, W. P. van Deusen, and L. M. Minsk. *J. Appl. Polymer Sci.*, **2**, 308–311 (1959).
44. L. M. Minsk, W. P. van Deusen, and E. M. Robertson. U.S. pat. 2,610,120/1952.
45. L. M. Minsk, W. P. van Deusen, and E. M. Robertson. U.S. pat. 2,751,296/1956.
46. L. M. Minsk, W. P. van Deusen, and E. M. Robertson. U.S. pat. 2,670,285/1954.

47. L. M. Minsk, W. P. van Deusen, and E. M. Robertson.   U.S. pat. 2,670,286/ 1954.
48. L. M. Minsk, W. P. van Deusen, and E. M. Robertson.   U.S. pat. 2,670,287/ 1954.
49. L. M. Minsk and W. P. van Deusen.   U.S. pat. 2,690,966/1954.
50. E. M. Robertson and W. West.   U.S. pat. 2,732,301/1956.
51. T. Tsunoda and S. Nozoki.   *Bull. Tech. Assoc. Graphic Arts Japan*, **5**, 1–4, (1962).
52. R. J. Rauner and J. J. Murray.   Belg. pat. 603,930/1963; Can. pat. 677,549/1964.
53. Eastman Kodak Company.   *Kodak Photosensitive Resists for Industry*, p. 4, 1962.
54. L. I. Martinson.   *Proceedings of Sixth Annual Meeting*, TAGA, pp. 33–38, (1954).
55. H. T. Lyman.   U.S. pat. 2,961,746/1960.
56. F. E. Kendall.   U.S. pat. 2,969,731/1961; Brit. pat. 888,935/1962.
57. L. M. Minsk and W. P. van Deusen.   U.S. pat. 2,732,297/1956; Brit. pat. 438,960/1935; Brit. pat. 517,914/1940.
58. J. G. Smith and L. M. Minsk.   U.S. pat. 2,691,584/1954.
59. L. E. Martinson.   U.S. pat. 2,697,039/1954.
60. R. A. C. Adams.   U.S. pat. 3,019,106/1962; Brit. pat. 921,529/1963.
61. A. Murray and E. M. Robertson.   U.S. pat. 2,787,543/1957.
62. C. C. Unruh, G. W. Leubner, and A. C. Smith, Jr.   U.S. pat. 2,861,058/1958; Brit. pat. 843,543/1960.
63. W. Schellenberg, O. Bayer, W. Siefken, and H. Rinke.   Fr. pat. 1,185,357/1959.
64. W. Thoma and H. Rinke.   U.S. pat. 3,066,117/1962; Brit. pat. 822,861/1959.
65. C. C. Unruh and D. A. Smith.   U.S. pat. 2,751,373/1956.
66. A. C. Smith and C. C. Unruh.   U.S. pat. 2,728,745/1955.
67. S. H. Merrill and D. A. Smith.   U.S. pat. 2,861,057/1956.
68. D. A. Smith, A. C. Smith, Jr., and C. C. Unruh.   U.S. pat. 2,811,509/1957.
69. L. M. Minsk and C. C. Unruh.   U.S. pat. 2,801,233/1957.
70. C. C. Unruh and D. A. Smith.   U.S. pat. 2,835,656/1955.
71. A. de Waile and J. H. Croker.   Brit. pat. 794,572/1958; Ger. pat. 1,104,339/1961.
72. R. A. C. Adams.   Ger. pat. 1,108,078/1961; Brit. pat. 921,530/1963.
73. R. A. C. Adams.   Brit. pat. 913,764/1962.
74. W. Thoma, O. Bayer, and H. Rinke.   U.S. pat. 3,023,100/1962.
75. M. J. S. Michiels, G. A. Philpot and R. P. J. G. Thiebaut.   Fr. pat. 1,351,542/ 1964.
76. A. Murray.   U.S. pat. 2,756,143/1956.
77. M. J. S. Michiels, R. P. J. G. Thiebaut, and G. A. Philpot.   U.S. pat. 2,956,878/ 1960; Brit. pat. 846,908/1960; Fr. pat. 1,137,056/1957.
78. A. C. Smith, Jr., D. A. Smith, and C. C. Unruh.   U.S. pat. 2,787,546/1957.
79. J. Vareine.   Fr. pat. 1,256,088/1961; Brit. pat. 951,928/1964.
80. W. Neugebauer and M. Tomanek.   U.S. pat. 2,759,820/1956; Ger. pat. 832,545/1952.
81. W. Schellenberg and O. Bayer.   U.S. pat. 3,030,208/1962.
82. G. A. Philpot.   Fr. pat. 1,316,465/1963.
83. J. L. R. Williams.   U.S. pat. 2,908,667/1959.
84. C. C. Unruh.   *J. Appl. Polymer Sci.*, **2**, 358–362 (1959).
85. C. C. Unruh.   *J. Appl. Polymer Sci.*, **3**, 310–315 (1960).
86. C. C. Unruh and C. F. N. Allen.   U.S. pat. 2,716,097/1955.

87. C. C. Unruh and C. F. N. Allen. U.S. pat. 2,716,102/1955.
88. A. C. Smith, J. L. R. Williams, and C. C. Unruh. U.S. pat. 2,816,091/1957; Brit. pat. 825,948/1959; Brit. pat. 820,173/1959.
89. C. C. Unruh and C. F. N. Allen. U.S. pat. 2,706,725/1955.
90. S. H. Merrill. U.S. pat. 2,831,768/1958.
91. Farbenfabriken Bayer, A-G. Brit. pat. 838,547/1960.
92. W. D. Schellenberg and H. Bartl. U.S. pat. 2,948,706/1960; Farbenfabriken Bayer, A-G. Brit. pat. 850,277/1960.
93. W. Thoma and H. Rinke. U.S. pat. 3,043,802/1962.
94. R. E. Buckles. *J. Am. Chem. Soc.*, **77**, 1040–1041 (1955).
95. W. M. Moore, D. D. Morgan, and F. R. Stermitz. *J. Am. Chem. Soc.*, **85**, 829–830 (1963).
96. F. B. Mallory, C. S. Wood, J. T. Gordon, L. C. Lindquist, and M. L. Savitz. *J. Am. Chem. Soc.*, **84**, 4361–4362 (1962).
97. F. B. Mallory, C. S. Wood, and J. T. Gordon. *J. Am. Chem. Soc.*, **86**, 3094–3102 (1964).
98. W. Neugebauer and M. Tomanek. U.S. pat. 3,070,443/1962; Brit. pat. 745,889/1956; Ger. pat. 937,569/1956; Fr. pat. 1,103,269/1955; Can. pat. 566,797/1958.
99. C. K. Tupis. U.S. pat. 2,887,376/1959.
100. M. H. Murray, R. H. Leekley. U.S. pat. 2,997,391/1961; Brit. pat. 875,377/1961; Brit. pat. 862,276/1961.

5

Photopolymerization Processes

5.1 INTRODUCTION

With the progress of polymer chemistry, polymerization processes and polymeric materials have started to take a definite part in the production of photographic materials and have found wide application in the preparation of film supports and as gelatin replacements or extenders in silver halide emulsions. From our point of view, however, the most important are light-activated image-forming polymerization systems which are, at the present time, moving closer to commercialization in a number of photographic and graphic-art processes.

According to the classical definition, a polymer is a large molecule built up by linear or branched repetition of small units, called monomers. Polymerization can proceed only when an initiator is present in the system. An initiator can be either a monomer molecule that has received enough energy to combine with another molecule or, in most instances, a different molecule, one more easily activated than the monomer, is added. The activation takes place through the absorption of energy, accompanied by the formation of short-lived intermediates. These intermediates have an odd number of electrons and are known as free radicals.

Free radicals can be generated in a number of ways, for example, by pyrolytic decomposition of the initiators; these include peroxides of several types, carbonyl compounds, sulfur compounds, various azo and diazo compounds, and metal alkyls. Radicals can also be produced by electron-transfer processes, giving single radicals. This is in contrast with dissociative processes, which form pairs of radicals. To obtain radicals by thermal dissociation, the molecule must have a sufficiently low dissociation energy, such as that between oxygen atoms in peroxides; for the majority of thermal initiators, the activation energy is roughly 30 kcal per mole.

Many substances which can be used as thermal initiators can dissociate also by the absorption of light quanta. The energy associated with a quantum of light, 95.5 kcal/mole at 3000 Å, 63 kcal/mole at 4550 Å, and 48.5 kcal/mole at 5900 Å, is of the same order of magnitude as that of most covalent bonds. The absorbed energy is then dissipated through bond rupture, with formation of free radicals:

$$CH_2{=}CHX \xrightarrow{h\nu} \cdot CH_2{-}CHX\cdot \qquad (1)$$

As illustrated in the foregoing reaction, polymerization can be, in many instances, initiated by light of sufficiently short wavelength, but this technique is seldom encountered. It is more convenient to add to the polymerizable composition, a photochemical initiator which decomposes into free radicals by absorption of light of lower energy per quantum. An impressive number of compounds useful as photoinitiators has been reported in the literature (1), and our attention will be given especially to those systems which can be applied to the formation of photographic images.

Free radicals, once formed, initiate polymerization by an addition reaction to the double bond of the monomer; this generates a new radical, which then undergoes further reaction:

$$R\cdot + CH_2{=}\!\!\overset{\displaystyle \overset{H}{|}}{\underset{\displaystyle \underset{X}{|}}{C}} \longrightarrow R{-}\!\!\overset{\displaystyle \overset{H}{|}}{\underset{\displaystyle \underset{X}{|}}{C}}\!\!{-}CH_2\cdot \xrightarrow{+\,n CH_2{=}CHX} R(CH_2{-}CHX)_n CH{-}\!\!\overset{\displaystyle \overset{H}{|}}{\underset{\displaystyle \underset{X}{|}}{C}}\cdot \qquad (2)$$

$$R(CH_2{-}CHX)_n CH{-}\!\!\overset{\displaystyle \overset{H}{|}}{\underset{\displaystyle \underset{X}{|}}{C}}\cdot \xrightarrow{+\,CH_2{=}CHX} R(CH_2{-}CHX)_{n+1} CH_2{-}\!\!\overset{\displaystyle \overset{H}{|}}{\underset{\displaystyle \underset{X}{|}}{C}}\cdot \qquad (3)$$

At each addition, the unpaired electron of the free radical pairs with one electron of the double bond, and the second electron generates a new free radical. The latter reacts with the next monomer molecule and the process goes on until long chains of covalently bonded atoms are produced. The chains do not grow indefinitely, however, and when the free-radical end of the growing chain reacts, for instance, with another free radical, the activity of the two radicals will be mutually annihilated and a "dead" molecule will be formed.

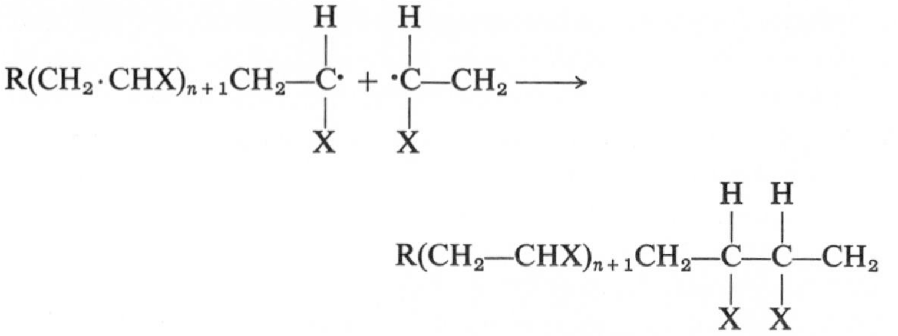

$$R(CH_2 \cdot CHX)_{n+1}CH_2 \overset{\overset{\displaystyle H}{|}}{\underset{\underset{\displaystyle X}{|}}{C}}\cdot + \cdot \overset{\overset{\displaystyle H}{|}}{\underset{\underset{\displaystyle X}{|}}{C}} CH_2 \longrightarrow$$

$$R(CH_2 - CHX)_{n+1}CH_2 \overset{\overset{\displaystyle H}{|}}{\underset{\underset{\displaystyle X}{|}}{C}} - \overset{\overset{\displaystyle H}{|}}{\underset{\underset{\displaystyle X}{|}}{C}} - CH_2 \quad (4)$$

It would be beyond the scope of this book to go into more detailed discussion of the mechanism of free-radical formation and the kinetics of photopolymerization. We must satisfy ourselves with the fact that through the absorption of actinic radiation free radicals are formed which initiate the growth of a polymeric chain. If we assume that one photon of absorbed light initiates the growth of one polymeric chain and that this chain continues to grow until it consists of, let us say, 20,000 monomer units, then we have an effective photomultiplication of 20,000. This photomultiplication effect can be considerably increased if crosslinking between two or more polymeric chains occurs. The possibility of obtaining polymeric substances of high molecular weight merely by absorption of a single photon makes photopolymerization processes very attractive for photographic applications, and, during the last ten years, many efforts have been made in this direction (2).

The formation of addition polymers, as described before, is usually connected with changes in the physical properties of the materials involved; these changes, in many instances, can be utilized for the formation of photographic images. The photographic processes described in the following pages are divided into several groups, according to the type of the photoinitiator employed.

5.2   PHOTOPOLYMERIZATION INITIATORS

5.2a   *Carbonyl Compounds*

A very important source of free radicals is carbonyl compounds. Lower aldehydes and ketones require near-ultraviolet radiation, and di- and polycarbonyl compounds absorb at longer wavelengths and are more suitable as polymerization initiators. Thus, diacetyl is dissociated by light in the neighborhood of 3600 Å and yields acetyl radicals:

$$CH_3 - (CO)_2 - CH_3 \xrightarrow{h\nu} 2CH_3\overset{\overset{\displaystyle O}{\|}}{C}\cdot \quad (5)$$

Another photoinitiator, which has found appreciable use in vinyl polymerization, is benzoin and its derivatives. Benzoin dissociates according to the following equation:

$$C_6H_5 \cdot CO \cdot CH(OH) \cdot C_6H_5 \longrightarrow C_6H_5 \cdot CO^{\cdot} + C_6H_5 \cdot CH(OH)^{\cdot} \quad (6)$$

The great diversity of carbonyl-type compounds listed in the literature as photopolymerization initiators can be seen in Table 5.1.

Benzoin and its derivatives in particular have been the center of intense research at the Du Pont Company, as indicated by the number of patents claiming the use of these compounds in photochemical printing processes. Plambeck (12) describes a light-sensitive layer for the preparation of letterpress printing plates containing (*a*) a photopolymerizable, ethylenically unsaturated compound, (*b*) a photoinitiator, such as benzoin or benzoin methyl ether, uniformly dispersed throughout the entire layer, and (*c*) a substantial amount of polyethylene glycol dimethacrylate, which acts as a crosslinking agent. This mixture, after being coated on a synthetic polymer, laminated paper, or a metal support, to a thickness of 3 to 250 mils, is exposed under a negative halftone transparency to a mercury-vapor lamp. After the unpolymerized compounds in the unexposed areas have been removed by washing with a suitable solvent, a relief image is obtained, which is, in many instances, superior to photoengraved reliefs.

The polymerizable composition can contain compatible polymers and finely divided transparent inorganic fillers in order to render the mixture nonflowable (13). To improve the hardening of the basic elements, the initiator in the lower portion of the layer is in higher concentration than in the surface portions; the closing of characters, such as "e" and "a," is eliminated (14). The effective rate of polymerization through the thickness of the polymerizable layer can be controlled also by altering the composition of the polymeric substances, and the proportions of other ingredients remain the same (15). By including progressively more initiator and less inhibitor (5) toward the bottom of the photopolymerizable layer, reliefs having sunken areas with tapered sides are produced as the result of differential polymerization in depth. Also, it has been found useful to include in the photopolymerizable printing-plate layer a crosslinking agent such as tris(ethyl acetoacetato)aluminum or a similar polymeric chelate of a polyvalent metal in order to enhance the difference in solubility between exposed and unexposed portions of the light-sensitive coating (16).

Photopolymerizable elements of this type usually have an anchorage layer between the light-sensitive layer and the support (17) and an antihalation backing layer (18). The photosensitive layers have the tendency

TABLE 5.1. Carbonyl Photoinitiators

General Formula	Compounds	Reference
Vicinal polyketaldonyl compounds	diacetyl	3
	benzil	
	phenylglyoxal	
	diphenyltriketone	
$R—(CO)_x—R'$	pentanedione-2,3	4
R and R′ = H or monovalent hydrocarbon	octanedione-2,3	
radical	1-phenylbutane dione-1,2	5
x = two or three		
α-Carbonyl alcohols	benzoin	
$R—CO—CHOH—R'$	butyroin	
R and R′ = H or monovalent hydrocarbon	tolyoin	6
radical	acetoin	7
Acyloin ethers	benzoin methyl ether	
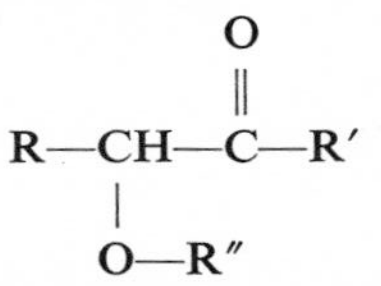	benzoin ethyl ether	
	benzoin propyl ether	8
	pivaloin ethyl ether	
	anisoin ethyl ether	
R, R′, and R″ = monovalent hydrocarbon radical		

$$R—CH—C—R'$$

with carbonyl group $\overset{O}{\underset{\parallel}{}}$ and $O—R''$ substituent.

General Formula	Compounds	Reference
α-Hydrocarbo-substituted Acyloins $$\begin{array}{c} R\quad O \\ | \ \ \| \\ Ar{-}C{-}C{-}Ar \\ | \\ OH \end{array}$$ Ar = monocyclic aromatic hydrocarbon R = monovalent hydrocarbon radical	α-alkylbenzoin α-methylbenzoin α-benzylbenzoin	9
Polynuclear quinones	9,10-anthraquinone 1-chloroanthraquinone 2-chloroanthraquinone 2-methylanthraquinone 2-*tert*-butylanthraquinone 1,4-naphthoquinone 9,10-phenanthrene quinone 2,3-diphenylanthraquinone 2,3-benzanthraquinone	10 11

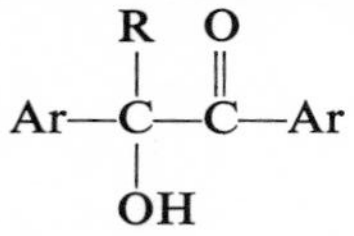

to become brittle and crack after aging, especially at low relative humidities and temperatures. After the washing-out operation, therefore, it is necessary to treat the plate with diluted hydrochloric acid for few minutes to restore flexibility to the polymer (19). Jennings (20) prepared a flexible layer free from the disadvantages just described, by adding polyethylene oxides and linear cellulose esters to ethylenically unsaturated compounds, e.g., acrylic acid diesters of a mixture of polyethylene glycols. Polyvinyl-pyridine and polyvinylpyrrolidone give an additional improvement (21). These plates, however, become less sensitive to light in storage; this deficiency can be explained by the diffusion of oxygen from the air into the photopolymerizable layer. Since the polymerization rate is lower at points deep in the layer than it is at the top surface, there is a tendency for the top layer to be overexposed before the optimum exposure of the lower surface is reached. The result is that the relief image is poorly anchored to the supporting base. It has been found by Notley (22) that red phosphorus, stannous chloride, or chromous chloride, if mixed with suitable binding agents and coated beneath the light-sensitive layer, overcomes these shortcomings. The same effect can be achieved when a layer containing phenanthrenequinone or uranyl nitrate as photoinitiator, situated underneath the image rendering layer, is pre-exposed to radiation actinic for the underlayer but to which the upper layer is relatively insensitive (23).

Photopolymerizable compositions useful for the preparation of relief images can contain a wide range of polymers, including polyvinyl acetate vinyl sorbate (24), polyvinyl ester acetal (25), cellulose-acetate hydrogenphthalate (26), cellulose alkyl ethers (27), polyalkylene ether glycol polyurethane (28), polyhexamethylene adipamide (29), β-diethyl-amino-ethyl-polymethacrylate (30), and polychlorophene (31). Thus, for example (32), alkali-soluble partially acylated cellulose acetate is mixed with triethylene glycol diacrylate, N,N'-methylene-bis-acrylamide, a small quantity of anthraquinone, p-methoxyphenol, and mucochloric acid; the mixture is milled at elevated temperature and moulded into sheets which are then laminated to a metal support.

On the processes described before, are based "Dycril" photopolymer plates, first publicly displayed in 1957 by the Du Pont Company (33,34,35). "Dycril" plates for wraparound and letterset printing are coated on thin steel and are produced in two thicknesses, 0.025 and 0.031 inches, which give relief heights of 0.010 and 0.016 inches, respectively. The plates must be conditioned for 24 hours in a carbon dioxide atmosphere prior to exposure in order to remove absorbed oxygen which retards photopolymerization and consequently gives rise to undercutting, poor adhesion, and poor quality of produced images (36,37). It is claimed that addition of stannous salts to the composition eliminates the storage of the plates in an inert, oxygen-free gas (38). After exposure to a high-intensity arc lamp under a high-contrast negative, the plate is developed with aqueous alkaline solution and washed in water. The result is a relief plate which can be run, stored, and reused in a conventional manner.

A similar material, based on the crosslinking of polyamides, was disclosed by Time, Inc. The light-sensitive layer consists of an alcohol-soluble nylon-type polyamide and *N,N*-methylenebisacrylamide. Benzil, benzoin, or benzophenone are the initiators (39). Polyamide plates can also be sensitized with ammonium dichromate (40) or with chromic acid (41). The unexposed areas are removed with either alcohol or a water-alcohol calcium chloride mixture, leaving a polymeric relief image which can be further hardened by heating at 200°F after exposure (42). The Time plates, designed for use on the rotary presses, are very strong and press runs of more than 500,000 impressions were reported. Patterns of more than 1000 lines/inch have been etched with a depth-to-width ratio of 1:1. Polyamide relief images are also suitable for microcircuitry (43).

Polyamide plates for printing were patented also by Freundorfer and Hörner (44,45,46). The light-sensitive component may be a polymer consisting of caprolactam, 4,4'-diaminodicyclohexylmethane and hexa-methylenediamine adipate. Unsaturated polyamides patented by Burg (47) are another variation of photopolymerizable compounds suitable, when laminated to an aluminum support, for printing plates; N-methoxy-methyl-polyhexamethylene-adipamide illustrates this invention. Water soluble composition suitable for printing relief images consist of a low polymeric linear polyamide and a difunctional monomer such as magnesium diacrylate, bis(2-methacrylamidoethyl)amine, or glycerol dimethacrylate (48).

Unsaturated polyamides are not the only polymers which can be made insoluble by exposure to light in the presence of a crosslinking agent. Rohm and Haas Co. (49) reports insolubilization of completely polymerized acrylic and/or methacrylic acid esters by exposure to ultraviolet radiation in the presence of benzaldehyde or benzoin. The unexposed sections can be removed with ethylene chloride. Besides the photographic application, this hardening effect prevents degradation of polymers in sunlight.

Another group of polymers capable of undergoing insolubilization upon exposure to actinic light are polyvinyl acetals; these compounds are pre-pared as in the patent of Martin (50) by condensing polyvinyl alcohol with an aldehyde having a conjugated terminal vinylidene group in the molecule. Among the examples mentioned are the following acetals:

p-vinylbenzaldehyde ethylene glycol acetal, *p*-vinylbenzene-sulfonamido-benzaldehyde ethylene glycol acetal, and methacryloylaminoacetaldehyde ethylene glycol acetal. Polyvinyl acetals containing a plurality of intra-linear vinyl alcohol (—CH₂CHOH—) groups and 4-formyl alkyl- or arylphenone acetal groups were patented by Burg (51); 4-formyl-benzo-phenone polyvinyl acetal, 4-formyl acetophénone polyvinyl acetal, and sulfobenzaldehyde/4-formylbenzophenone polyvinyl acetal are quoted as suitable for sensitizing printing plates.

In another application of photopolymerizable layers for printing purposes, advantage is taken of the adhesiveness of the unpolymerized layer for a dye or a pigment. In one such process (52) the photopoly-merizable layer consists of polyethylene terephthalate sebacate and a diacrylate of a polyethylene glycol. After exposure, the layer is heated to 40 to 170°C and is dusted with a coloring powder; adhering only to the unexposed parts of the plate, the powder can be transferred under light pressure and elevated temperature to a receiving sheet. The opera-tion can be repeated and used for multicolor prints. Instead of dusting with colored pigments, a suitable dye can be added directly to the poly-merizable composition (53). In another modification the exposed poly-meric surface is contacted with a layer of pigment loosely coated on a support and heated (54). As in the previous method, the pigment adheres only to the nonexposed areas giving a positive copy of the original. To shorten the exposure, it is recommended (55) that the surface of the foregoing or similar photopolymerizable composition be covered with a sheet of polyethylene terephthalate in order to exclude atmospheric oxygen during exposure. Photopolymerizable composition can also be coated on a moving belt of a copying apparatus. After imagewise exposure the composition is pressed against a receiving paper sheet to which the soft unexposed portions forming the positive image transfer (56).

Photopolymerization processes using carbonyl compounds as initiators were also suggested for the formation of colored relief images. Cohen and Firestine (57) use as active components amides of an aromatic amino-aldehyde with an acrylic or methacrylic acid dispersed in binding agents, such as polyvinyl alcohol. It is necessary that the monomer have in its molecule at least one dye-forming nucleus such as X—C≡CH or X—C≡C—C≡CH, in which X is an aldehyde, hydroxy, amino, or alkylamino group. After the exposure, the unhardened, unexposed portions are removed by washing and the polymerized portion of the layer is made to react with a dye-forming developer, usually *p*-aminodiethylaniline hydro-chloride. According to the monomer used, polymeric images of the following colors can be obtained:

Monomer	Color
m-methacrylamidobenzaldehyde	orange
m-methacrylamido-α-cinnamaldehyde	magenta
p-methacrylyloxybenzaldehyde	yellow
p-methacrylamidophenol	blue
o-methacrylamidophenol	green

Colored relief images can be obtained also by exposing to light a mixture of polyvinyl alcohol, benzoin methyl ether, and 6-methacrylamido-1-methylquinaldinium methosulfate, and by removing the unpolymerized portions by washing with alcohol or an alkali; a blue image results (58). Addition of 5,6-dimethoxy-1-methyl-2-methylthiobenzothiazolium methosulfate to the above composition makes the image red, and the methomethsulfate quaternary salt of 2-methylthiobenzothiazole produces an orange-red color.

5.2b *Organic Sulfur Compounds*

A wide variety of organic sulfur compounds are photopolymerization initiators for ethylenically unsaturated monomers. Examples of such sulfur-containing compounds include:

alkyl disulfides	di-*n*-butyl disulfide
	di-*n*-octyl disulfide
aralkyl disulfides	dibenzyl disulfide
aryl disulfides	diphenyl disulfide
	ditolyl disulfide
aroyl disulfides	dibenzoyl disulfide
acyl disulfides	diacetyl disulfide
	dilauroyl disulfide
cycloalkyl disulfides	dibornyl disulfide

Simple disulfides, such as dimethyl disulfide, have relatively strong S-S bonds, requiring 72 kcal to dissociate (59). More complicated substituents, e.g., diaryl disulfides, are less stable and produce free radicals upon irradiation with light of wavelengths in the range 2800 to 4000 Å (60). The cleavage of the S-S bond and the formation of free radicals can be expressed as follows (61):

$$C_4H_9S—SC_4H_9 \xrightarrow{h\nu} 2C_4H_9S \qquad (7)$$

In the case of diphenyl disulfide, cleavage at the S-S bond will produce radicals $C_6H_4S \cdot$. The mode of rupture in the disulfide linkage is of the greatest importance; asymmetric rupture of the C-S linkage provides inhibiting radicals $C_6H_5SS \cdot$ with a retarding effect on the process.

Other sulfur-containing photopolymerization initiators are:

mercaptans (62)

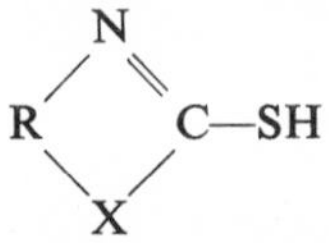

Example: 2-mercaptobenzothiazole
2-mercapto-4-phenylbenzothiazole
2-mercaptobenzoxazole
2-mercaptonaphthoxazole

$$\begin{array}{c} N \\ R\diagdown \ \diagdown \\ \quad C-SH \\ R\diagup \ \diagup \\ X \end{array}$$

R = ortho arylene radical
X = S, O, or NH

2-mercaptobenzimidazole
2-mercapto-4-tolylbenzimidazole
2-mercapto-5-chlorobenzoxazole

thiols (63)

R—SH

R = aryl or substituted aryl

Example: thiophenol, *p*-thiocresol, *o*-thio-
cresol, *o*-aminobenzene thiol,
o-tolylbenzene thiol, *p*-methoxy-
benzene thiol, α-naphthyl thiol,
β-naphthyl thiol, diisopropylbenzene thiol, phenylbenzene thiol

Photopolymerization initiators containing the S-H linkage form, through photolytic rupture, the radicals RS· and H·, which initiate the chain reaction.

metal mercaptides (64,65)
$(RS)_x M$
R = organic radical
M = Hg, Pb, Ag, Zn
Z = valency of M

Example: mercuric phenyl mercaptide, mercuric *tert*-butyl mercaptide, lead
tert-butyl mercaptide

dithiocarbamates (66)

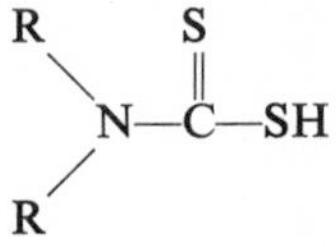

$$\begin{array}{c} R \diagdown \quad\ S \\ \quad\quad \| \\ \quad N-C-SH \\ R \diagup \end{array}$$

Example: carboxymethyl-N,N-dimethyl-
dithiocarbamate, carbethoxymethyl-N,N-pentamethyl-
enedithiocarbamate, bis-(carbethoxymethyl)ester of 1,4-piper-
azine-bis-(carbodithoic acid),
methyl-N,N-pentamethylene-
dithiocarbamate,
N,N′-dimethyldithiocarbamate

O-alkyl xanthene esters (65)

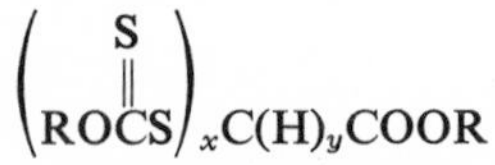

$$\left(\begin{array}{c} S \\ \| \\ ROCS \end{array} \right)_x C(H)_y COOR$$

Example: carbalkoxymethylene bis(*n*-propyl
xanthene), 2-oxopropylene bis-
(methyl xanthene)

R = alkyl radicals of 1 to 4 carbon atoms, inclusive, which may be the same or different;
x and *y* = positive integers from 1 to 2, inclusive, with the sum of $x + y$ being equal to 3.

thiuram derivatives (67,68,69,70)

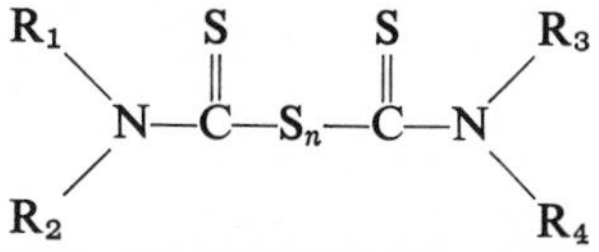

$$\overset{R_1}{\underset{R_2}{\diagdown}}N-\overset{\overset{\displaystyle S}{\|}}{C}-S_n-\overset{\overset{\displaystyle S}{\|}}{C}-N\overset{\diagup R_3}{\underset{\diagdown R_4}{}}$$

R = alkyl, phenyl or pentamethylene group
n = 1 for monosulfides
n = 2 for disulfides
n = 4 for tetrasulfides

Example: *N,N'*-dipentamethylenethiuram monosulfide
tetramethylthiuram monosulfide
tetraethylthiuram monosulfide
tetraisopropylthiuram monosulfide
bis-[di-(β-chloroethyl)thiocarbanyl]sulfide
bis-[*n*-(butylmethyl)thiocarbanyl]sulfide
tetramethylthiuram disulfide
dipentamethylenethiuram disulfide
tetramethylthiuram tetrasulfide
dipentamethylenethiuram tetrasulfide

According to Ferington and Tobolsky (71), the decomposition of tetramethylthiuram monosulfide is associated with the generation of free radicals, as shown below:

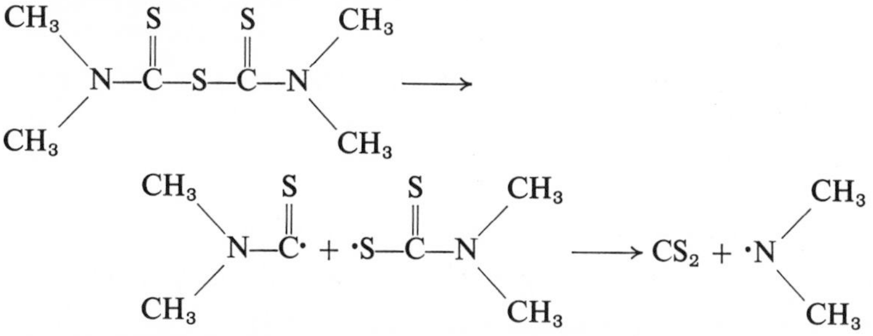

$$\overset{CH_3}{\underset{CH_3}{\diagdown}}N-\overset{\overset{\displaystyle S}{\|}}{C}-S-\overset{\overset{\displaystyle S}{\|}}{C}-N\overset{\diagup CH_3}{\underset{\diagdown CH_3}{}} \longrightarrow$$

$$\overset{CH_3}{\underset{CH_3}{\diagdown}}N-\overset{\overset{\displaystyle S}{\|}}{C}\cdot + \cdot S-\overset{\overset{\displaystyle S}{\|}}{C}-N\overset{\diagup CH_3}{\underset{\diagdown CH_3}{}} \longrightarrow CS_2 + \cdot N\overset{\diagup CH_3}{\underset{\diagdown CH_3}{}} \qquad (8)$$

Similarly, the photodissociation of tetramethylthiuram disulfides can be written as:

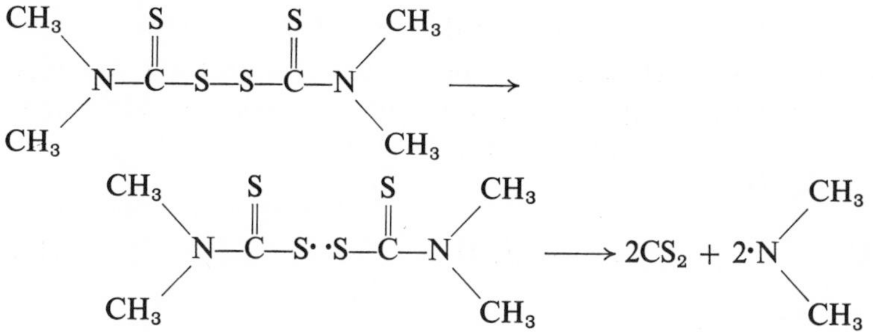

$$\overset{CH_3}{\underset{CH_3}{\diagdown}}N-\overset{\overset{\displaystyle S}{\|}}{C}-S-S-\overset{\overset{\displaystyle S}{\|}}{C}-N\overset{\diagup CH_3}{\underset{\diagdown CH_3}{}} \longrightarrow$$

$$\overset{CH_3}{\underset{CH_3}{\diagdown}}N-\overset{\overset{\displaystyle S}{\|}}{C}-S\cdot \; \cdot S-\overset{\overset{\displaystyle S}{\|}}{C}-N\overset{\diagup CH_3}{\underset{\diagdown CH_3}{}} \longrightarrow 2CS_2 + 2\cdot N\overset{\diagup CH_3}{\underset{\diagdown CH_3}{}} \qquad (9)$$

Sulfenates (72)

R—O—S—R'

R and R' = organic radicals

Example: *p*-chlorophenyl-*p*-chlorobenzene-
sulfenate,
ethyl-trichloromethanesulfenate,
allyl-trichloromethanesulfenate,
ethyl-2-benzothiazylsulfenate.

Sulfur chloride pentafluoride was used by Roberts (73) for photopoly-merization of tetrafluoroethylene. Because of the high energy required for the production of free radicals, sulfur-containing compounds are very seldom used in image-forming photopolymerization processes (74,75).

5.2c *Peroxides*

One very useful source of free radicals is peroxides, since the rupture of the peroxide linkage requires, on the average, only 34 kcal/mole. The simplest peroxide, hydrogen peroxide, has, however, only very limited use as a photopolymerization initiator and is known mainly as a component of redox systems, which will be discussed later. Hydrogen peroxide has been used by Dainton and Tordoff (76) in the photopolymerization of acrylamide, by Dainton and Sisley (77) in the photosensitized poly-merization of methacrylamide, and by Owens, Heerma, and Stanton (78) in the copolymerization of vinyl and vinylidene compounds in the presence of an ionizable salt. The same can be said about hydroperoxides, e.g., cumene hydroperoxide, which are very unstable and may decompose spontaneously without activation. Of greater importance are dialkyl peroxides, for instance di-*tert*-butyl peroxide, which dissociates as follows (79):

$$(CH_3)_3C—O—O—C(CH_3)_3 \longrightarrow 2(CH_3)_3C—O \cdot \qquad (10)$$

t-Butoxy radicals readily decompose into acetone and a methyl radical

$$(CH_3)_3C—O \cdot \longrightarrow (CH_3)_2CO + CH_3 \cdot \qquad (11)$$

According to Frey (80), the photodissociation of di-*tert*-butyl peroxide in the near ultraviolet may take a different course:

$$(CH_3)_3—C—O—O—C(CH_3)_3 \longrightarrow 2(CH_3)_3C \cdot + O_2 \qquad (12)$$

Diacyl peroxides, of which benzoyl peroxide is probably the best known and most widely studied, dissociate to aroyloxy radicals and, afterwards, into an aryl radical and carbon dioxide:

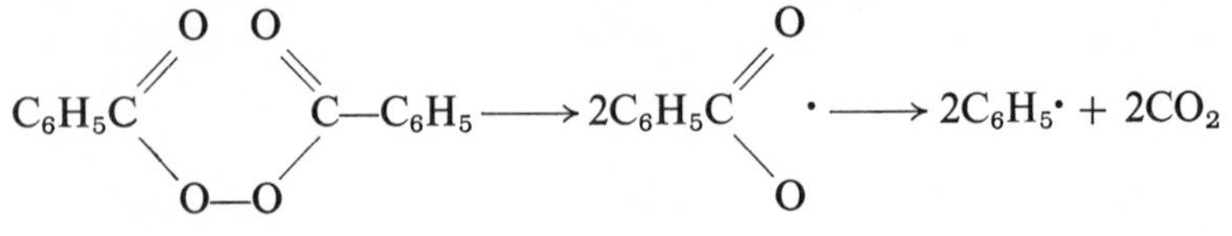

The behavior of other diaroyl peroxides is similar; however, the rate of dissociation is affected by the presence of substituents in the benzene ring, and it was shown by Swain, Stockmayer, and Clarke (81), that collected data follow Hammet's equation closely.

According to Smith (82), polymerizations involving the presence of "per" compounds exhibit an induction period which can be reduced or entirely eliminated by adding to the polymerizable composition a small amount of silver nitrate or silver acetate.

In spite of the fact that peroxides are a very useful source of free radicals, they are not very suitable initiators for photopolymerization systems applicable to photographic processes, and in the patent literature only a few such processes are reported.

Murray (83) found that benzoyl peroxide increases the light sensitivity of the carboxylic acid salt of certain nitrogen bases containing ethylenic linkages, for example, the reaction product of piperic acid with piperidine, called piperine:

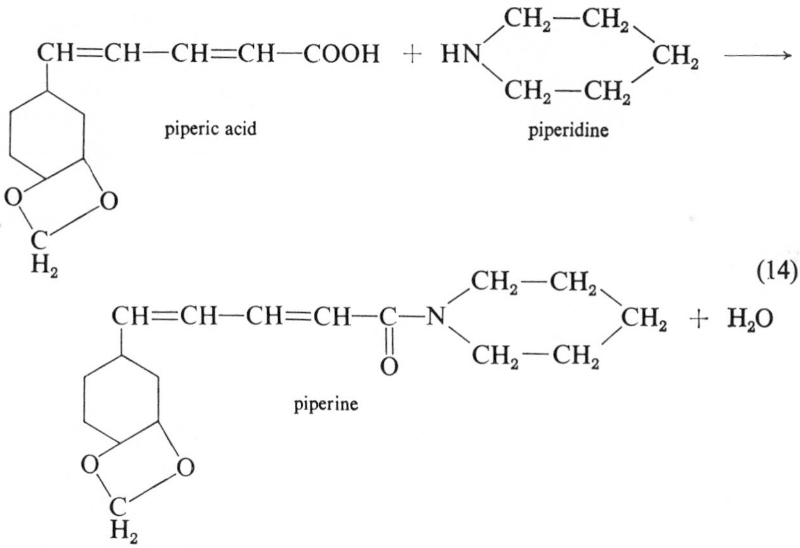

$$\tag{14}$$

Piperine can be polymerized under the influence of actinic radiation to a solid resinous material called by the inventor "piperite." The unreacted material is then removed with soap and water. The resulting relief image can serve as a photoresist in a number of photoengraving processes.

In another process utilizing benzoyl peroxide as photopolymerization initiator, three-dimensional images are produced by copolymerizing a styrene monomer with a liquid, ethylenically unsaturated, compound in the presence of gold chloride $AuCl_3 \cdot HCl \cdot 3H_2O$ (84). To obtain better stability in the polymerizable mixture, polymerization inhibitors, such as hydroquinone, can be added. Especially suitable is a composition of hydroquinone with copper naphthenate, giving not only good stability but also improved quality of the image. Instead of benzoyl peroxide, other peroxides initiating polymerization of unsaturated compounds may be used; methyl ethyl ketone peroxide is very effective. Prior to exposure, the above composition is allowed to polymerize until it reaches the state of incipient gelation; at this stage, the gel is exposed under a negative to radiation having wavelengths between about 3000 and 4000 Å; thereupon the image is developed and fixed by heating the composition to 60 to 70° C for 30 minutes, to produce a three-dimensional photograph distributed throughout the full thickness of the clear plastic material. The purpose of development is to form gold nuclei which will agglomerate to form a blue to bluish-red image. The color of the image can be changed into magenta by adding to the composition very small amounts of a palladium salt. Molybdenum carbonyl improves the light sensitivity. Images so produced appear as positives when viewed by transmitted light and as negatives when observed by reflected light. This phenomenon can be overcome by the addition of thiourea or hydrocarbon-substituted thioureas, e.g., N,N'-ethylene thiourea, to the liquid composition (85). A positive image is produced when viewed by either transmitted or reflected light. Encapsulated droplets containing a dye, lauryl methacrylate, α-chloromethylnaphthalene, and lauroyl peroxide, when coated on a support, can be used for a photographic transfer process (86). By an exposure to ultraviolet light, the fluid in the capsules polymerizes into a solid material and cannot be transferred, as the unexposed sections can, by pressure to a receiving sheet.

Amplification of silver images by peroxide catalyzed polymerization was suggested by Cohen (87). In this technique the silver image obtained by the standard photographic way is coated with a polymerizable layer containing carbon black and potassium persulfate; potassium persulfate diffuses to the image, oxidizes metallic silver to silver ions, which in turn diffuse to the polymerizable layer, where a redox reaction with persulfate initiates polymerization. As a result a silver image amplified with the pigmented polymer image is obtained.

Silver ions can also be furnished by the silver halides from unexposed areas of a developed, unfixed chlorobromide print (88). In such cases the polymerizable composition must contain a silver halide solvent, e.g., sodium thiosulfate.

5.2d *Redox Systems*

As photopolymerization initiators, organic peroxides suffer from the drawback that they show acceptable absorption only below 3200 Å. It has been found, however, that the presence of certain reducing agents appreciably accelerates their decomposition. An example of such a reducing agent which has received considerable attention is ferrous ion (89), which decomposes the peroxide with formation of an $HO\cdot$ free radical:

$$H_2O_2 + Fe^{2+} \longrightarrow HO\cdot + OH^- + Fe^{3+} \tag{15}$$

In the presence of a vinyl monomer, for instance acrylonitrile, methacrylic acid, acrylamide, or other compounds containing the $CH_2{=}CH{-}$ group, the $HO\cdot$ free radical initiates the polymerization (90); the reaction can be written as follows (91):

$$HO\cdot \; + \; M \longrightarrow HOM\cdot \quad M = \text{monomer} \tag{16}$$

$$HOM\cdot + M \longrightarrow HOM_2\cdot \tag{17}$$

$$HOM_2\cdot + nM \longrightarrow HO(M)_nM\cdot \tag{18}$$

The reaction of ferrous ions with substituted peroxides has also been observed to initiate polymerization. Of these, the most widely investigated is persulfate ion, which reacts with ferrous ion in the following manner (92):

$$S_2O_8^{2-} + Fe^{2+} \longrightarrow SO_4^{2-} + SO_4^{-}\cdot + Fe^{3+} \tag{19}$$

The $SO_4^{-}\cdot$ radical initiates the polymerization

$$CH_2{=}CH^- + SO_4^{-}\cdot \longrightarrow {-}SO_4{-}CH_2{-}\dot{C}H{-} \tag{20}$$

In 1944 Owens, Heerma, and Stanton (78) discovered that polymerization of vinyl or vinylidene compounds in the presence of a ferric compound and hydrogen peroxide can occur rapidly when this system is exposed to a 360-watt mercury-vapor arc lamp. During the exposure, the ferric ion is reduced to ferrous ion, which subsequently reacts with the peroxide and generates free radicals.

Despite the fact that the reduction of ferric compounds by light has been known for more than a hundred years, the potentialities of the vinyl polymerization, for photographic applications initiated by this redox system, have been realized only in the last decade. Complex salts of carboxylic acids, such as ferric ammonium citrate, tartrate, or oxalate have been used in a process for production of stencils (93), lithographic plates (94,95) and photoresists (96). In both processes, the light-sensitive composition consists of a water-soluble polymerizable material and the ferric salt, coated on a suitable base and allowed to dry. After being exposed to light of appropriate wavelength through a negative, the activated image areas are developed with an aqueous hydrogen peroxide solution or an ammonium persulfate solution, which renders the exposed region insoluble. The unreacted components are washed away with water, leaving a relief image the depth of which is proportional to the quantities of ferrous ions produced during the exposure. An apparent increase in speed can be achieved when development by peroxides is conducted in the presence of reducing agents, such as sodium sulfite, hydrazine, and gly-oxylic acid (97), which may be present either in the developing solution or in the light-sensitive composition. In order to produce colored images, the resulting relief is stained with a basic dye (98). Or, dyes such as nigrosine can be included in the photopolymerizable mixture; after expo-sure and development in a one per cent hydrogen peroxide solution, a negative image is obtained, which, when pressed onto a transfer sheet, produces a positive copy of the original (99,100). Evans (95) produced colored images in the same way.

From the photographic point of view, a more ingenious method for the preparation of polymer relief images was described by Dumers and Diener (101). The technique involves coating a suitable base with a silver halide gelatin emulsion mixed with a monomeric crosslinking agent, e.g., N,N'-methylene-bis-acrylamide, and acrylamide. After the exposure, the latent image is developed with a ferrous oxalate developer giving a silver image and ferric ions in the exposed areas, and the nonexposed areas contain only the unchanged ferrous ions of the developer. Treatment with hydro-gen peroxide or other peroxy compounds initiates the polymerization in these regions, which can be converted to a silver image by means of conventional photographic development. In the final step, the unpoly-merized material is removed by a water wash. This method is positive working; the areas of high exposure do not polymerize, whereas sections of low exposure containing unoxidized ferrous ions are subjected to polymerization.

The main advantage of this process compared to the one previously described lies in the amplification factor of highly sensitive silver-halide gelatin emulsion supplying the energy to initiate the polymerization. As a consequence, it is possible to prepare photopolymerizable material of greater sensitivity and wider spectral range than was possible with the before-mentioned methods. In another variation, a support containing a developed silver image is contacted with a layer containing an ethylenic-ally unsaturated compound and is subjected to the action of a peroxide and a catalyst capable of oxidizing metallic silver; free radicals which are formed initiate the polymerization in areas corresponding to the silver image (102).

Redox reactions also occur when a suspension of zinc oxide or titanium dioxide is irradiated with ultraviolet light in the presence of a vinyl monomer. It is assumed (103) that free radicals initiate the polymerization. The catalytic activity of the zinc oxide and titanium dioxide can be promoted, according to the above patent, with salts of heavy metals, for instance thallous nitrate, ferric chloride, mercuric sulfate, or with oxidizable organic compounds, for example, carboxylic acids, their salts, phenols, aromatic hydrocarbons, amides, or aldehydes. Zinc oxide or titanium dioxide coatings can also be optically sensitized with organic dyes (104); examples of such dyes are eosin, erythrosine, rose bengal, fluorescein, methylene blue, and rhodamine B. The mechanism of optical sensitization in this case is considered to be different from that described by Oster (182) and it was demonstrated that the sensitizing dyes are irreversibly photo-oxidized rather than photoreduced.

5.2e *Azo and Diazo Compounds*

Certain aliphatic and aromatic azo and diazo compounds have the ability to act as efficient photosensitizers for photopolymerization processes and have been the subject of many investigations during the last two decades. These compounds are light-sensitive and produce, upon photolysis, free radicals which subsequently act as polymerization initiators.

We will discuss, as an example of an azo compound, the decomposition of azomethane on illumination. Ramsperger (105) studied the photolysis of azomethane at wavelength 366 mμ and expressed the decomposition by the following reaction:

$$CH_3—N{=}N—CH_3 \longrightarrow C_2H_6 + N_2 \tag{21}$$

The quantum yield of the reaction was calculated to be about 2.0; this led to the assumption that each newly formed ethane molecule provides energy of activation for one new azomethane molecule.

Forbes, Heidt, and Sickman (106) found by employing six different wavelengths of monochromatic light that the quantum yield of the foregoing reaction approaches unity as its upper limit for initial decomposition at low pressure. In the region of 366 to 335 mμ, the quantum yield passes through a maximum, which is due to the maximum of absorption by the —N$=$N— bond. At lower wavelengths, the quantum yield decreases to a minimum and rises again when the N—C bond begins to absorb. Their calculations were based on the assumption that pressure changes were a measure of the percentage decomposition; this was later found by Burton, Davis, and Taylor (107) to be incorrect.

Experiments of Leermakers (108) and that of Rice and Evering (109) indicate that during the decomposition of azomethane, methyl radicals are formed according to the reaction

$$CH_3—N{=}N—CH_3 \longrightarrow N_2 + 2CH_3^{\cdot} \qquad (22)$$

Burton, Davis, Jahn, and Taylor (110) demonstrated that there is a secondary reaction between free methyl radicals, which combine with each other,

$$CH_3^{\cdot} + CH_3^{\cdot} \longrightarrow C_2H_6 \qquad (23)$$

or react with azomethane

$$CH_3—N{=}N—CH_3 + CH_3^{\cdot} \longrightarrow (CH_3)_2—N{=}N—CH_3 \qquad (24)$$

and that some of the azomethane may decompose with rearrangement to yield alkanes.

Patat (111) suggested following reaction for the photolytic decomposition of azomethane:

$$CH_3—N{=}N—CH_3 \xrightarrow{\; h\nu \;} CH_3 + N{=}N—CH_3 \qquad (25)$$

Later it was shown (112) that at higher temperatures the yield of ethane decreased considerably, and methane became the chief hydrocarbon product. These results suggest that ethane reacts with a methyl radical as follows:

$$CH_3^{\cdot} + C_2H_6 \longrightarrow CH_4 + C_2H_5^{\cdot} \qquad (26)$$

This reaction is much more complicated than has been assumed, and, at the present, there is not sufficient evidence for a valid conclusion as to the relative probabilities of reactions 21, 22, and 25. The work of Davis, Jahn, and Burton (113), however, indicates that azomethane decomposes almost exclusively by reaction 22 and that reaction 24 takes place quite readily.

While azomethane has never been used for polymerization initiation, another group of azo-compounds—the azo-nitriles—was recognized in the late nineteen forties as an effective source of free radicals (114,115). Unlike other polymerization initiators, such as the peroxide type, azo-nitriles decompose by a strictly unimolecular process, essentially independent of the nature of the solvent (116,117). Furthermore, the lack of induced chain decomposition leads to increased effectiveness and greater efficiency (118,119).

Because of their nonoxidizing nature, Burk (120) employed these compounds as polymerization initiators in a process for preparing polymers colored with organic dyes or pigments.

The best known and most widely studied azonitrile is α,α'-azobisisobutyronitrile (ABIN), (121), which undergoes photolysis at 3450 to 4000 Å in the following manner:

$$
\underset{\underset{CH_3}{|}}{\overset{\overset{CH_3}{|}}{NC-C}}-N{=}N-\underset{\underset{CH_3}{|}}{\overset{\overset{CH_3}{|}}{C}}-CN \longrightarrow 2\,\underset{\underset{CH_3}{|}}{\overset{\overset{CH_3}{|}}{NC-C\cdot}} + N_2 \tag{27}
$$

Talât-Erben and Bywater (122) assumed that in the thermal decomposition some of the radicals react as $(CH_3)_2C{=}C{=}N\cdot$, which, subsequently, can react under certain conditions with $(CH_3)_2C(CN)\cdot$ radicals to form dimethylketene-cyanoisopropylimine.

α,α'-Azobisisobutyronitrile and similar compounds such as 2-azo-bis-2-methylbutyronitrile (123) and 1-azo-bis-1-cyclohexane-carbonitrile (124), are, because of their absorption characteristics, very much suited for work employing a mercury-vapor lamp. Azonitriles are generally recognized as effective photoinitiators and as a very convenient source of free radicals, decomposing thermally at uniform rates in a variety of environments, as was shown by Lewis and Matheson (125). The same investigators studied the quantum yield in polymerization and showed that aliphatic azonitriles are superior in efficiency to a photosensitizer such as diacetyl (Table 5.2). 2-Azo-bis-propane (126) is a less efficient source of radicals. Among other azo-compounds, perfluoroazomethane was investigated by Prichard and Prichard (127).

Heterocylic azothioethers and a new series of azonitriles, are used together with suitable ethylenically unsaturated compounds, to form photopolymerizable compositions for use in the formation of images, especially by a heat-transfer process (128). Also, diazonium compounds were described in a few instances as generators of free radicals. Cooper (129) used *p*-nitrobenzenediazonium-*p*-chlorobenzenesulfonate as an initiator for the polymerization of methyl acrylate and acrylonitrile. Salts of an organic diazosulfonic acid, for instance, ammonium benzenediazosulfonate, in the presence of cupric sulfate or ferric chloride, were used by Howard (130) for the polymerization of vinyl or vinilidene compounds. Haward and Simpson (131) indicated that diazoaminobenzene can function not only as a polymerization initiator but also as retarder. The inhibiting effect of the phenolic decomposition products of certain diazo compounds was utilized by Schwerin and Millard (132,133) for a direct positive photographic process.

TABLE *5.2.*   Photopolymerization with Azo-Sensitizers at 3660° Å and 30°C (reference 125)

Azonitrile Sensitizer ($\sim$ 0.038 m/l) R—N=N—R	R—	Quantum Yield in Polymerization	
		Vinyl Acetate	Styrene
2-Azo-bis-isobutyronitrile	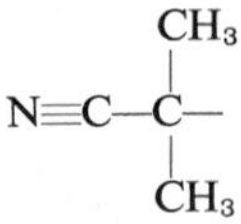 CH₃ — N≡C—C— — CH₃	360	55
2-Azo-bis-propionitrile	 CH₃ — HC— — CH₃		50
Dimethyl-2-azo-bis-isobutyrate	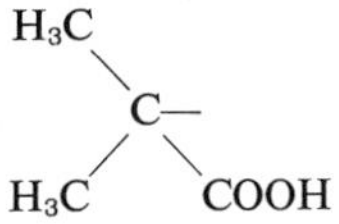 H₃C — C— — H₃C COOH	600	50
1-Azo-bis-1-cyclohexanecarbonitrile	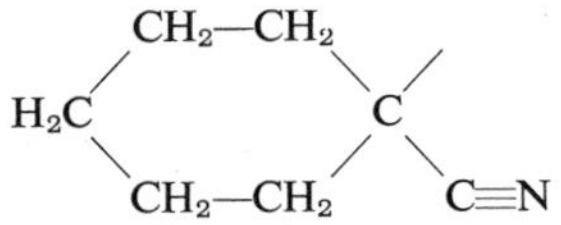 CH₂—CH₂ — H₂C C — CH₂—CH₂ C≡N	600	50
2-Azo-bis-2-methylheptonitrile	CH₃·CH·(CH₂)₄·C≡N	230	55
2-Azo-bis-2-methylbutyronitrile	CH₃·CH·CH₂·C≡N	255	60
4-Azo-bis-cyanopentanoic acid	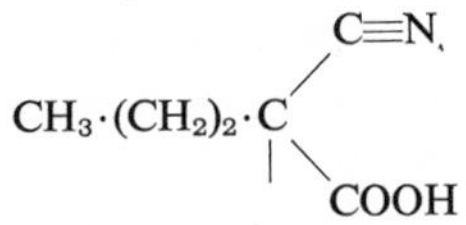 C≡N, — CH₃·(CH₂)₂·C — COOH	284	
2-Azo-bis-propane	CH₃·CH₂·CH₂—	80	2.8
Diacetyl		10.3	1.4

* Reprinted with the permission of the copyright owner, the American Chemical Society.

Irradiated layer containing an ethylenically unsaturated compound and a diazonium salt is treated with a solution of a ferrous compound followed by treatment with aqueous peroxide. Polymerization is effected in unexposed areas only and unpolymerized composition in exposed areas is removed to form a positive image. Diazonium fluoroborates were reported to be more efficient photopolymerization initiators than aryldiazonium chlorides (134), especially in the presence of hydroquinone or ferrous ammonium oxalate.

The preparation of photographic images obtained by means of the photopolymerization of vinyl compounds initiated by the photolytic decomposition products of light-sensitive diazonium salts was described by Oster and Oster (135). The light used for the exposure photolyzes the diazonium salt to give products, which, on subsequent heating, react with the undecomposed diazo compound remaining in the non-image areas, to give free radicals. The available free radicals initiate polymerization at areas exposed to actinic radiation. For photographic coatings, an aqueous solution of a vinyl monomer, a diazonium salt, and a suitable binder are coated on a support, such as paper or glass, and dried. After illumination through a transparency with a 500-watt tungsten lamp, the material is developed by heating to 75°C for one minute. The insoluble polymer produces light-scattering centers similar to the vesicular process. It is asserted that the quantum efficiency of the over-all process exceeds one million, whereas any process based on the light sensitivity of diazo compounds has never been greater than unity.

For polymerizing acrylic and methacrylic acid in the production of photoresists, the diazonium chloride of *p*-aminodiphenylamine has been recommended (136). Another application of diazo compounds in photopolymerization processes was patented by Levinos (137). In this process, which is suitable for the preparation of photographic prints, the light-sensitive layer contains, in addition to the monomers, cyanine or some other type of sensitizing dye and a diazonium compound. The process is attributed to a redox reaction involving the formation of free aryl radicals in which, according to this invention, the diazonium compound acts as an oxidizing agent (electron acceptor) and the dye, when excited by actinic radiation, as an electron donor. Later it was found (138) that more energetic photoinitiators are obtained when the diazonium compounds are treated with an excess of alkali; in such instances the diazotate ions are formed and react with the remaining diazonium salt to yield a diazoanhydride. Diazoanhydride decomposes into the aryl-free radicals which initiate the polymerization (139). The reaction mechanism is illustrated by the following equation:

$$R\overset{+}{-}N\!\!\equiv\!\!N \xrightarrow{\text{alkali}} R\!-\!N\!\!=\!\!N\!-\!OH \xrightarrow{\text{alkali}} R\!-\!N\!\!=\!\!N\!-\!O^- \xrightarrow{R\overset{+}{-}N\equiv N}$$

diazonium salt   diazonium hydroxide   diazotate ion

$$R\!-\!N\!\!=\!\!N\!-\!O\!-\!N\!\!=\!\!N\!-\!R \xrightarrow{h\nu} R\!\cdot\; +\; R\!-\!N\!\!=\!\!N\!-\!O\!\cdot\; +\; N_2 \quad (28)$$

diazoanhydride   diazoxy radical

The formation of free radicals by the decomposition of diazonium compounds and their utilization for vinyl polymerization led Richards (140) to the synthesis of diazonium derivatives of cellulose which acted as initiators of graft polymerization. For this purpose, cellulose *p*-aminophenacyl ether was prepared by the reaction of cotton with *p*-amino-phenacyl chloride, diazotized, and used to initiate the graft polymerization of acrylonitrile.

5.2f   *Halogen Compounds*

It is well known that organic halogen compounds may be readily affected by ultraviolet light. This is illustrated by the photodissociation of 2-chlorobutadiene by light of wavelength less than 2000 Å (141), by the photolysis of carbon tetrachloride (142), and by the photodecomposition of simple alkyl iodides (143,144,145). Lindsey and Ingraham (146) photolyzed 1-chlorocyclohexene with light of wavelength 2537 Å and assumed the formation of a cyclohexene free radical and a chlorine atom by the homolytic scission of the carbon-chlorine bond.

Free radicals formed during the photolysis can be utilized in a number of photopolymerization processes, such as in the photopolymerization of styrene, acrylate, and vinyl esters in the presence of 1-chloromethyl-naphthalene, phenacyl bromide, chloromethyl naphthyl chloride, and other halogen-containing compounds (147,148).

In Table 5.3 the polymerization of methyl methacrylate in the presence of different halogen initiators is shown; the indicated time represents the period required for the liquid monomer to be converted into a solid (about 60 per cent polymer). As a light source, a 250-watt mercury-vapor lamp was used, operating at a distance of $3\frac{1}{2}$ inches from the glass vessel containing the monomer.

TABLE *5.3*. Halogen Initiators (reference 148)

Sensitizer	Time, hr
None	Still fluid after 100-hr exposure
α-Chloromethylnaphthalene	7
Phenacyl bromide	$8\frac{1}{2}$
β-Toluenesulfonyl chloride	10
Chloroacetone	$10\frac{1}{2}$
Chloral hydrate	$11\frac{1}{2}$
Sulfuryl chloride	12
Acetyl chloride	17
Allyl chloroformate	19
Chloroacetyl chloride	20

Sachs and Bond (149) also used halosulfuryl compounds as initiators for the photopolymerization of ethylenically unsaturated monomers. Their effectiveness is illustrated in Table 5.4.

TABLE 5.4. Halosulfuryl Initiators (reference 149)

Sensitizer (1%)	Per Cent Polymer by Weight of Monomer Monomer Used: Methyl Methacrylate
None	0
Sulfuryl chloride	5.7
Benzene sulfonyl chloride	2.9
p-Toluene sulfonyl chloride	5.1
Xylene sulfonyl chloride	12.7
β-Naphthalene-sulfonyl chloride	31.9
Thionyl chloride	3.6

In another patent (150), certain mono-ketaldonyls are claimed as photopolymerization catalysts. As examples, desyl chloride and bromide and halogenated aldehydes, such as β-dichloropropionaldehyde or α,β-dibromopropionaldehyde, chloral and bromal, can be mentioned. Kharasch, Jensen, and Urry (151) investigated the decomposition of poly-halogen compounds with ultraviolet light and reported that carbon tetrachloride and carbon tetrabromide are split into free radicals which have the ability to initiate polymerization (152). Similar photopolymerization systems, in the presence of polyhalogen solvents, were investigated elsewhere (153). Chapiro and Hardy (154) described the spontaneous polymerization of N-vinylcarbazole when this monomer is mixed with a small amount of carbon tetrachloride; it is believed (155) that the polymerization is due to the presence of a trace of chlorine or other oxidants.

Dickinson and Silver (156) sensitized an ethylene oxide polymer and a phenol formaldehyde resin with iodoform; on exposure to light, iodine radicals are formed which react with the phenolic resin to give products of higher molecular weight, useful for the preparation of printing plates.

Probably the most distinctive feature of the halogen compounds used as initiators in the photopolymerizing systems, lies in the photosensitizing properties of silver halides. Levinos, Mueller, and Roth (157,158) have shown that the polymerization of vinyl monomers, on illumination, is promoted by silver-halide gelatin emulsions. Here, the type and nature of the gelatin used for the preparation of the emulsion affects the sensitivity of the final product to a remarkable degree, and, in this case, the initiation period of the polymerization. This reaction was suggested for rapid characterization of the photographic properties of gelatin.

Later, Levinos and Mueller (159) used the same combination for the production of relief images. By using silver-halide gelatin emulsions sensitized with optical sensitizers, they succeeded in extending the sensitivity of the system to longer wavelengths. The sensitizing dyes do not initiate photopolymerization by themselves; it can be assumed that the dyes act as optical sensitizers in the well-known manner, by transferring the absorbed energy to the silver halides.

According to these investigators, the absorbed radiation produces a bromine radical which reacts with the monomer to form a reactive radical:

$$AgBr + h\nu \longrightarrow Ag^+ + Br\cdot \qquad (29)$$

$$CH_2{=}CH{-}R + Br\cdot \longrightarrow Br{-}CH_2{-}\overset{\cdot}{C}H{-}R \qquad (30)$$

The polymerization is thus induced by bromine atoms at the silver halide surface. The activated monomer, now itself a free radical, adds another monomer unit in the well-known manner to produce a dimer free radical, which in turn reacts with a third unit to form a trimer free radical and so on, until a high molecular weight polymer is built. In the presence of a crosslinking agent for the polyvinyl chain, such as divinyl benzene or N,N'-methylene-bis-acrylamide, space network molecules will result.

Delzenne (160) interpreted the initiating action of silver halide emulsions on the photopolymerization of acrylamide as the primary release of electrons from halide anions $[Hal^-]_c$:

$$[Hal^-]_c \overset{h\nu}{\longrightarrow} [Hal\cdot]_c + e \qquad (31)$$

The halogen atom $[Hal\cdot]_c$ reacts, then, with water to form an hydroxyl radical

$$[Hal\cdot]_c + H_2O \longrightarrow [Hal^-]aq + H^+ + OH\cdot \qquad (32)$$

which acts as the initiator according to the free radical mechanism (see page 185):

$$M + OH\cdot \longrightarrow HO{-}M\cdot \qquad (33)$$

The rate of photopolymerization can be increased by adding to the polymerizable composition a small amount of sodium sulfite (161), which is an effective antioxidant and reduces the induction period. The rate at which vinyl monomers may be photopolymerized can also be greatly increased by employing, in addition to silver emulsions, water soluble silver compounds (162) or small amounts of metal oxides capable of forming amphoteric bases (163).

Instead of gelatin, other colloids may be used in the preparation of emulsions, and, as light-sensitive substances, silver citrate or benzenesulfinate can be employed (159).

Photopolymerization of olefinically unsaturated monomers involving silver halide emulsions was described earlier by Oster (164). He assumes that the developing agent, such as *p*-aminophenol hydrochloride, forms, during the development of exposed silver halide material, free radicals which initiate the polymerization of the vinyl monomer in corresponding areas. It is assumed that such polymer aggregation results in an increased optical density of the image and that an over-all increase in sensitivity of the photographic emulsion can be achieved in this way.

The processes described above can be used, in the form of dry-coated layers on suitable supports, for the preparation of relief images, printing plates (165), and photoresists. A reflex image-transfer copying process, based on the same principle was also suggested (166).

In order to make the printing surface prepared by the imagewise photopolymerization of an ethylenically unsaturated monomer containing hydroxyl groups, e.g., N-methylol acrylamide, hydrophobic, the plate is treated with an aromatic isocyanate such as phenyl isocyanate, benzyl isocyanate, or phenyl-*m*-diisocyanate, during which procedure an aryl ring is introduced into the polymer resist (167). The hydrophobic properties can be further increased by treatment with water which causes the crosslinking of the polycarbonate:

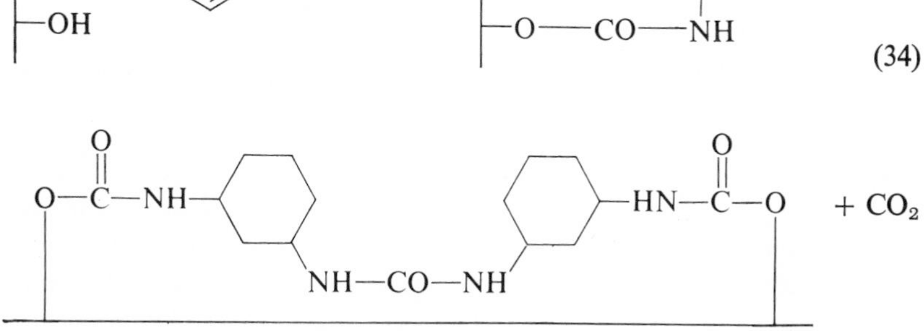

$$(34)$$

5.2g   *Photoreducible Dyes*

In previous pages we have seen that polymerization of vinyl compounds can be initiated with electromagnetic radiation when initiators such as organic peroxides, azonitriles, and diketone compounds are present. With the use of these sensitizers, visible light is usually not effective and higher energy radiation is required. Some of these shortcomings can be solved by photosensitization, so that more efficient use of available spectra, particularly of longer wavelengths, can be made (168).

It has been known for many years that certain dyes will, in the presence of electron donors, undergo reduction to their leuco form when illuminated by visible light (169,170,171,172,173,174,175,176,177). According to Oster and Adelman (178), the rate of the photoreduction R of the dye is proportional to the intensity I of the light absorbed and the concentration of the reducing agent (A); this relation is expressed with the following equation:

$$R = \frac{I(A)}{\alpha + \beta(A)} \tag{35}$$

where α and β are constants. The reduced dye can react with ambient oxygen to produce free radicals, which initiate the polymerization.

A number of photopolymerization processes were described on this principle (179,180,181). From our point of view, the Oster system (182) is the most interesting and will be handled here in detail.

According to this investigator (183) any polymerizable vinyl monomer, such as acrylonitrile, acrylic and methacrylic acid, acrylamide, vinyl acetate, or styrene, can be polymerized in this manner. Among the useful dyes which act as photosensitizers, are rose bengal, erythrosine, eosine, acriflavine, riboflavine, thionine, and others. The concentration of the dye is not essential, but to obtain best results the foregoing patent recommends an amount such that at least 95 per cent of the incident radiation is absorbed. The absorption spectrum of the dye determines, as can be expected, the spectral sensitivity of the system. For example, yellow dye such as riboflavine gives sensitivity to blue light only, whereas a red dye sensitizes the system to the green part of the visible spectrum. A blue dye, such as methylene blue, renders the system susceptible to the orange-red region. By proper selection of the dyes, sensitivity to the entire spectrum can be obtained.

Ethylenically unsaturated compounds can also be polymerized in the presence of a reducing compound and certain polyamines with a sensitizing dye attached through a chemical bond (184).

The reduction potential of the reducing agents recommended for Oster's process must be less than that necessary to reduce the particular dye in the absence of visible light; included are stannous chloride, ascorbic acid, allyl thiourea, etc. When the dye molecule contains a reducing group, as is in the case of riboflavine, the presence of an additional reductant is not required.

The mechanism of dye-sensitized photopolymerization can be represented in the following manner:

1. On illumination, the dye molecule absorbs light of the proper energy and is brought into the first excited singlet state:

$$D + h\nu \longrightarrow D^+ \tag{36}$$

2. The excited dye molecule can be reversed back to the ground state either by radiationless transition or by emission of fluorescence,

$$D^* \longrightarrow D \tag{37}$$

or a transition to the metastable state D' can take place (168):

$$D^* \longrightarrow D' \tag{38}$$

3. The metastable state then reacts with the reducing agent to form the leuco form of the dye (185):

$$D' + RH_2 \longrightarrow DH\cdot + RH\cdot \tag{39}$$

$$2DH\cdot \longrightarrow \underset{\text{(leuco dye)}}{DH_2} + D \tag{40}$$

4. On reaction with ambient oxygen, the semiquinone and hydroxyl radicals are produced which are able to initiate polymerization of the vinyl monomers (186):

$$DH_2 + \tfrac{1}{2}O_2 \longrightarrow \cdot OH + \cdot DH \tag{41}$$

5. The long-lived species can undergo reversion to the ground state with or without emission of a delayed fluorescence or phosphorescence:

$$D' \longrightarrow D \tag{42}$$

The deactivation can occur via reaction with unexcited dye or with some foreign molecule. On the assumption that the direct interaction between excited dye and monomer initiates the polymerization (187), and that some of the initiating radicals produced are rendered inactive by a unimolecular process, Oster, Oster, and Pratti (188) proposed a kinetic scheme as follows:

6. Free radicals formed by the redox reaction in step 4 react immediately with the vinyl monomer to create monomer free radicals:

$$\cdot OH + M \longrightarrow HOM\cdot \text{ (initiation step)} \qquad M = \text{monomer} \tag{43}$$

7. The monomer free radical, subsequently, reacts with another monomer to form a dimer free radical; the dimer free radical, in turn, reacts with another monomer to produce a trimer free radical, and the process goes on till a large polymeric free radical is formed:

$$
\left.\begin{aligned}
\text{HOM}^{\boldsymbol{\cdot}} + \text{M} &\longrightarrow \text{HOM}_2^{\boldsymbol{\cdot}} \\
\text{HOM}_2^{\boldsymbol{\cdot}} + \text{M} &\longrightarrow \text{HOM}_3^{\boldsymbol{\cdot}} \\
\vdots \qquad \vdots \qquad & \qquad \vdots \\
\text{HOM}_n^{\boldsymbol{\cdot}} + \text{M} &\longrightarrow \text{HOM}_{n+1}^{\boldsymbol{\cdot}}
\end{aligned}\right\} \quad \text{(propagation step)} \qquad (44)
$$

During this process one electron of the double bond of the monomer pairs with the odd electron of the free radical and forms a bond between the free radical and this carbon atom; the remaining electron of the double bond shifts to the other carbon atom which then becomes a free radical, and the active center is transferred to the newly added monomer.

8. When the two growing chain radicals collide, they combine to give a "dead" molecule and the continuing growth of the chain is stopped:

$$
\text{HOM}_{n+1}^{\boldsymbol{\cdot}} + \text{HOM}_{n+1}^{\boldsymbol{\cdot}} \longrightarrow \text{polymer (termination step)} \qquad (45)
$$

Because of the very low rate of termination between the growing polymer radicals, the rate of this type of polymerization far exceeds that of any other controllable polymerization initiated by free radicals and quantum yields exceeding 10^6 are possible. The quantum yield, which is inversely proportional to the square root of the intensity of light absorbed (I), can be derived from the rate of monomer consumption, given by the following equation:

$$
-\frac{d(M)}{dt} = k_3(M)\left(\frac{k_2}{k_4} \times \frac{k_1 I(M)^2}{k_2(M) + k_5}\right)^{1/2} \qquad (46)
$$

Keeping in mind the high quantum yield of this process, it is not surprising to learn that polymers of very high molecular weight can be obtained; a polyacrylamide of molecular weight exceeding ten million has been reported (188). By the use of acriflavine and allyl thiourea as a dye/reducing-agent combination (189), copolymers of acrylonitrile and vinyl acetate, and of acrylonitrile and allyl alcohol (190), with molecular weights far in excess of those produced by conventional catalysts, have been prepared. The photopolymerization of acrylamide, initiated by visible light in the presence of xanthene dyes and ascorbic acid or thiourea, was also investigated by Delzenne, Toppet, and Smets (191).

The fact that only a few free radicals produced by light initiate polymerization of many thousands of monomers renders the dye-sensitized photopolymerization suitable for the production of photographic materials (192) and for the preparation of relief images (186,193,194). The relatively long induction period, however, imposes a limitation on the over-all speed.

Natural or synthetic thiol polymers, e.g., thiolated gelatin, having at least two sulfhydryl side groups, also can be crosslinked by irradiation with visible light if a photoreducible dye is added to the polymer in order to oxidize the sulfhydryl groups to disulfide groups (195). Since the unexposed sections of such material can be removed with warm water, this process was suggested for producing plates for lithographic printing (196). Photoreducible dyes are also capable of initiating the polymerization of drying oils (197), so that printing inks containing such vehicles can be dried upon exposure to actinic light within a few seconds.

Photoreducible dyes can be used, also, for light-induced solubilization of many linear polymers, crosslinked by metallic ions. This is the case, for example, with acrylamide, crosslinked by mercuric chloride, or polyvinyl alcohol insolubilized by titanium lactate (198,199). On illumination with visible light, the photoreduced dye reduces the metallic ion to a lower valence; in this state, the ion no longer serves as a crosslinking agent; hence, the polymer becomes soluble and can be removed imagewise with a suitable solvent from the supporting base.

5.2h Other Initiators

Compounds of many other types can readily decompose into radicals photochemically. These include metal alkyls, such as tetraethyl lead (200), β-naphthol (201), and alkali metal salts of an anthraquinone sulfonic acid (202). Soluble salts of divalent tin, for instance, stannous chloride (203), or salts of iron, cobalt and nickel (204,205), are further examples of the variety of sources of free radicals. Sulfides, selenides, and tellurides of aluminum, mercury, zinc, chromium, cadmium, and metals of group VII were used by Levinos (75). The presence of water is required for the photopolymerization. Uranyl salts of mono- and dicarboxylic acids were also suggested as photopolymerization catalysts (206). These layers, which are developed after exposure by washing out unexposed material, contain N,N'-methylene-bis-acrylamide as the crosslinking agent. Mueller and Roth (207) found that photopolymerization of vinylidene compounds is accelerated by the presence of thallium nitrate, especially in combination with a sensitizing dye or a heavy metal salt. Also, silver salts are effective photoinitiators (208) and relief printing plates (209) can be made by polymerizing acrylamide in this way. This process is further accelerated when, in addition, a highly sensitive silver halide photographic emulsion (210) or a small amount of zinc oxide, titanium dioxide, etc. (163), is used. When such a layer is pressed after the exposure against a sheet coated with an amphoteric metal oxide such as zinc oxide, titanium dioxide, zirconium dioxide, or silicon dioxide, small amounts of the unreacted monomer and the initiator are transferred; after separating the two sheets, the receiving sheet is exposed to light to print out a dark silver image (211). The çatalytic effect of zinc oxide and titanium oxide is greatly promoted when used in combination with oxidizable organic compounds, e.g., monocarboxylic and dicaboxylic acids and their alkali-metal salts (112).

Sulfites and oxalates of zinc, strontium, silver, and cadmium and mercuric oxalate were suggested as photopolymerization initiators by Baxendale (213).

REFERENCES

1. G. Delzenne. *Ind. Chim. Belge*, **24**, 739–764 (1959).
2. D. W. Woodward, V. C. Chambers, and A. B. Cohen. *Phot. Sci. Eng.*, **7**, 360–368 (1963).
3. C. C. Agre. U.S. pat. 2,367,660/1945.
4. B. W. Howk and R. A. Jacobson. U.S. pat. 2,413,973/1947.
5. H. Crawford. U.S. pat. 2,993,789/1961; Brit. pat. 841,454/1960.
6. C. C. Agre. U.S. pat. 2,367,661/1945.
7. R. E. Christ. U.S. pat. 2,367,670/1945.
8. M. M. Renfrew. U.S. pat. 2,448,828/1948.
9. J. L. Crandal. U.S. pat. 2,722,512/1955.
10. N. T. Notley. U.S. pat. 2,951,758/1960; Brit. pat. 843,238/1960.
11. A. L. Barney, V. A. Engelhardt, and L. Plambeck, Jr. U.S. pat. 3,046,127/ 1962.
12. L. Plambeck, Jr. U.S. pat. 2,760,863/1956.
13. L. Plambeck, Jr. U.S. pat. 2,791,504/1957.
14. L. Plambeck, Jr. U.S. pat. 2,964,401/1960; Brit. pat. 834,733/1960.
15. E. I. du Pont. Brit. pat. 867,959/1961.
16. W. E. Mochel and L. Plambeck. U.S. pat. 3,016,297/1962; Brit. pat. 827,512/ 1960.
17. M. Burg. U.S. pat. 3,036,913/1962; Brit. pat. 864,041/1961; Ger. pat. 1,066,060/ 1959.
18. L. Plambeck. Brit. pat. 785,858/1957.
19. G. A. Thommes. Belg. pat. 627,820/1963.
20. A. B. Jennings. U.S. pat. 3,036,914/1962; Belg. pat. 599,193/1961; Brit. pat. 903,649/1962.
21. N. T. Notley. U.S. pat. 3,036,915/1962; Belg. pat. 599,102/1961; Brit. pat. 913,965/1962.
22. N. T. Notley. U.S. pat. 3,036,916/1962; Belg. pat. 579,710/1959.
23. E. I. du Pont. Brit. pat. 931,368/1963.
24. E. L. Martin. U.S. pat. 2,892,716/1959; Brit. pat. 815,277/1959.
25. E. L. Martin. U.S. pat. 2,902,365/1959; Belg. pat. 560,077/1957; Brit. pat. 825,795/1959.

26. E. L. Martin and A. L. Barney. U.S. pat. 2,927,022/1960; Brit. pat. 807,948/ 1959.
27. E. L. Martin. U.S. pat. 2,927,023/1960; Brit. pat. 834,337/1960; Fr. pat. 1,172,072/1959.
28. A. L. Barney. U.S. pat. 2,948,611/1960.
29. W. R. Saner and M. Burg. U.S. pat. 2,972,540/1961; Brit. pat. 854,980/1960.
30. A. L. Barney. Brit. pat. 802,853/1958.
31. W. J. McGraw. U.S. pat. 3,024,180/1962.
32. E. I. du Pont. Brit. pat. 883,558/1961.
33. F. Roblin. *Graphic Arts Progress*, pp. 53–54, 1960.
34. G. C. Compton and E. S. Koval. *Graphic Arts Progress*, p. 26, 1961.
35. Anon. *Graphic Technology* 1, **1**, 22–27 (1961).
36. H. E. Crawford. *TAGA Proceedings*, 193–193g (1960).
37. G. Geis and R. Geis. *Graphic Arts Monthly*, **33**, 18–20, 22 (1961).
38. E. I. du Pont de Nemours and Co. Brit. pat. 942,158/1963.
39. R. M. Leekley and R. L. Sorensen. U.S. pat. 3,081,168/1963; Brit. pat. 767,912/1957; Brit. pat. 875,378/1961; Ger. pat. 954,127/1956; Ger. pat. 1,103,019/1961.
40. Time, Inc. Brit. pat. 795,961/1958.
41. H. Hörner. U.S. pat. 3,102,030/1963; Brit. pat. 906,465/1962.
42. J. M. Lohse. *J. Appl. Phys.*, **33**, 2914–2915 (1962).
43. J. M. Lohse and P. F. Bruins. *Phot. Sci. Eng.*, **7**, 238–240 (1963).
44. R. Freundorfer and H. Hörner. U.S. pat. 3,060,027/1962.
45. Badische Anilin and Soda Fabrik A.G. Brit. pat. 881,273/1961.
46. H. Hörner. U.S. pat. 3,116,356/1963; Brit. pat. 927,217/1963; Ger. pat. 1,095,665/1960; Fr. pat. 1,224,836/1960.
47. M. Burg. U.S. pat. 3,043,805/1962.
48. E. I. du Pont. Brit. pat. 826,272/1959.
49. Rohm and Haas Co. Brit. pat. 899,943/1962.
50. E. L. Martin. U.S. pat. 2,929,710/1960.
51. M. Burg. U.S. pat. 3,068,202/1962; Belg. pat. 589,629/1960; Brit. pat. 893,616/ 1962; Fr. pat. 1,258,479/1961.
52. M. Burg and A. B. Cohen. U.S. pat. 3,060,023/1962; Fr. pat. 1,269,834/1961; Belg. pat. 593,834/1960.
53. M. Burg and A. B. Cohen. Belg. pat. 626,525/1963.
54. M. Burg and A. B. Cohen. U.S. pat. 3,060,024/1962; U.S. pat. 3,060,025/1962; Brit. pat. 945,807/1964; Fr. pat. 1,268,727/1961.
55. R. B. Heiart. U.S. pat. 3,060,026/1962; Belg. pat. 620,175/1963; Belg. pat. 625,606/1963.
56. R. B. Heiart. U.S. pat. 3,085,488/1963; Fr. pat. 1,333,983/1963.
57. A. B. Cohen and J. C. Firestine. U.S. pat. 3,070,442/1962; Belg. pat. 580,854/ 1959; Brit. pat. 875,248/1961; Fr. pat. 1,234,889/1960.
58. J. C. Firestine. U.S. pat. 3,073,699/1963; Belg. pat. 588,780/1960; Ger. pat. 1,112,403/1961.
59. J. L. Franklin and H. E. Lumpkin. *J. Am. Chem. Soc.*, **74**, 1023–1026 (1952).
60. L. M. Richards: U.S. pat. 2,460,105/1949.
61. K. E. Russel and A. V. Tobolsky. *J. Am. Chem. Soc.*, **76**, 395–399 (1954).
62. R. J. Kern. U.S. pat. 2,773,822/1956.
63. R. J. Kern. U.S. pat. 2,861,934/1958.
64. R. J. Kern. U.S. pat. 2,738,319/1956.

65. V. A. Engelhard and M. L. Peterson. U.S. pat. 2,716,633/1955.
66. L. M. Richards. U.S. pat. 2,423,520/1947.
67. R. J. Kern. U.S. pat. 2,861,933/1958.
68. H. L. Gerhart. U.S. pat. 2,673,151/1954.
69. R. J. Kern. *J. Am. Chem. Soc.*, **77**, 1382–1383 (1955).
70. T. E. Ferington and A. V. Tobolsky. *J. Am. Chem. Soc.*, **77**, 4510–4512 (1955).
71. T. E. Ferington and A. V. Tobolsky. *J. Am. Chem. Soc.*, **80**, 3215–3222 (1958).
72. G. H. Birum and R. J. Kern. U.S. pat. 2,769,777/1956.
73. H. L. Roberts. U.S. pat. 3,063,922/1962.
74. C. C. McDonald. U.S. pat. 3,055,758/1962; Can. pat. 637,655/1962.
75. S. Levinos. U.S. pat. 3,065,160/1962; Belg. pat. 594,285/1960; Brit. pat. 904,097/1962.
76. F. S. Dainton and M. Tordoff. *Trans. Faraday Soc.*, **53**, 499–511 (1957).
77. F. S. Dainton and W. D. Sisley. *Trans. Faraday Soc.*, **59**, 1369–1376 (1963).
78. J. Owens, J. Heerma, and G. W. Stanton. U.S. pat. 2,344,785/1944.
79. E. R. Bell, F. F. Rust, and W. E. Vaughan. *J. Am. Chem. Soc.*, **72**, 337–340 (1950).
80. H. M. Frey. *Proc. Chem. Soc. London*, **385** (1959).
81. C. G. Swain, W. H. Stockmayer, and J. T. Clarke. *J. Am. Chem. Soc.*, **72**, 5426–5434 (1950).
82. G. W. Smith. U.S. pat. 2,510,426/1950.
83. A. Murray. U.S. pat. 2,475,980/1949.
84. M. C. Agens. U.S. pat. 2,949,361/1960.
85. M. C. Agens. U.S. pat. 3,031,301/1962.
86. The National Cash Register Co. Brit. pat. 893,622/1962.
87. A. B. Cohen. Fr. pat. 1,320,131/1963.
88. A. B. Cohen and J. A. Sincius. Fr. pat. 1,319,116/1963.
89. F. Haber and J. Weiss. *Proc. Roy. Soc. (London)*, **A147**, 332–351 (1934).
90. J. H. Baxendale, M. G. Evans, and G. S. Park. *Trans. Faraday Soc.*, **42**, 155–169 (1946).
91. M. G. Evans, M. Santappa, and N. Uri. *J. Polymer Sci.*, **7**, 243–260 (1951).
92. I. M. Kolthoff, A. I. Medalia, and H. P. Raaen. *J. Am. Chem. Soc.*, **73**, 1733–1739 (1951).
93. A. K. Schwerin, W. F. Burrows, and H. D. Evans. U.S. pat. 3,136,638/1964; Can. pat. 679,353/1964.
94. J. L. Sorkin. U.S. pat. 2,927,021 (1960).
95. H. D. Evans and F. W. H. Mueller. U.S. pat. 3,101,270/1963; Brit. pat. 883,811/1961; Belg. pat. 590,192/1960; Can. pat. 642,882/1962; Fr. pat. 1,259,609/1961.
96. F. W. H. Mueller, H. Evans, and E. Cerwonka. *Phot. Sci. Eng.*, **6**, 227–230 (1962).
97. E. Cervonka and A. K. Schwerin. Fr. pat. 1,296,994/1962.
98. W. F. Burrows and A. K. Schwerin. Belg. pat. 605,776/1961; Can. pat. 672,777/1963.
99. A. K. Schwerin. U.S. pat. 3,130,050/1964; Can. pat. 683,328/1963; Belg. pat. 602,502/1961; Brit. pat. 905,182/1962; Belg. pat. 624,190/1962.
100. A. K. Schwerin and D. M. Dumers. Fr. pat. 1,289,257/1962.
101. D. M. Dumers and C. E. Diener. U.S. pat. 3,029,145/1962.
102. E. I. du Pont. Belg. pat. 642,477/1964.

103. H. D. Evans, F. W. H. Mueller, and S. Levinos. U.S. pat. 3,041,172/1962; Brit. pat. 879,892/1961; Belg. pat. 582,954/1959; Can. pat. 643,268/1962; Can. pat. 666,640/1963.

104. H. D. Evans, F. W. H. Mueller, and S. Levinos. U.S. pat. 3,147,119/1964.

105. H. C. Ramsperger. *J. Am. Chem. Soc.*, **50**, 123–132 (1928).

106. G. S. Forbes, L. J. Heidt, and D. V. Sickman. *J. Am. Chem. Soc.*, **57**, 1935–1938 (1935).

107. M. Burton, T. W. Davis, and H. A. Taylor. *J. Am. Chem. Soc.*, **59**, 1989–1993 (1937)

108. J. A. Leermakers. *J. Am. Chem. Soc.*, **55**, 3499–3500 (1933).

109. F. O. Rice and B. L. Evering. *J. Am. Chem. Soc.*, **55**, 3898–3899 (1933).

110. M. Burton, T. W. Davis, F. P. Jahn, and H. A. Taylor. *J. Am. Chem. Soc.*, **59**, 1038–1045 (1937).

111. F. Patat. *Naturwissenschaften*, **23**, 801 (1935).

112. M. Burton, T. W. Davis, and H. A. Taylor. *J. Am. Chem. Soc.*, **59**, 1989–1993 (1937).

113. T. W. Davis, F. P. Jahn, and M. Burton. *J. Am. Chem. Soc.*, **60**, 10–17 (1938).

114. M. Hunt. U.S. pat. 2,471,959/1949.

115. C. G. Overberger, M. T. O'Shaughnessy, and H. Shalit. *J. Am. Chem. Soc.*, **71**, 2661–2666 (1949).

116. L. M. Arnett. *J. Am. Chem. Soc.*, **74**, 2027–2031 (1952).

117. D. H. Johnson and A. V. Tobolsky. *J. Am. Chem. Soc.*, **74**, 938–943 (1952).

118. J. C. Bevington. *Trans. Faraday Soc.*, **51**, 1392–1397 (1955).

119. C. Walling. *J. Polymer Sci.*, **14**, 214–217 (1954).

120. R. F. Burg. U.S. pat. 2,500,023/1950.

121. G. S. Hammond, C. S. Wu, O. D. Trapp, J. Warkentin, and R. T. Keys. *J. Am. Chem. Soc.*, **82**, 5394–5499 (1960).

122. M. Talât-Erben and S. Bywater. *J. Am. Chem. Soc.*, **77**, 3710–3714 (1955).

123. Hajime Miyama. *Bull. Chem. Soc. Japan*, **30**, 10, 459 (1956).

124. Hajime Miyama. *Bull. Chem. Soc. Japan*, **29**, 715 (1956).

125. F. M. Lewis and M. S. Matheson. *J. Am. Chem. Soc.*, **71**, 747–748 (1949).

126. Hajime Miyama. *Bull. Chem. Soc. Japan*, **29**, 711 (1956).

127. G. O. Prichard and H. O. Prichard. *Chem. Ind.*, **20**, 564 (1955).

128. E. I. du Pont. Belg. pat. 625,541/1962; Belg. pat. 625,542/1962.

129. W. Cooper. *Chem. Ind.*, **17**, 407 (1953).

130. E. G. Howard. U.S. pat. 2,661,331/1953.

131. R. N. Haward and W. Simpson. *Trans. Faraday Soc.*, **47**, 212–225 (1951).

132. A. K. Schwerin and F. W. Millard. *Phot. Sci. Eng.*, **6**, 231–234 (1962).

133. A. K. Schwerin and H. D. Evans. U.S. pat. 3,110,592/1963; Belg. pat. 608,854/1961; Brit. pat. 926,583/1963; Fr. 1,329,590/1963; Jap. pat. 10244/1963.

134. C. S. Marvel, H. Z. Friedlander, S. Swann, Jr., and H. K. Inskip. *J. Am. Chem. Soc.*, **75**, 3846–3848 (1953).

135. G. K. Oster and G. Oster. U.S. pat. 2,996,381/1961; Fr. pat. 1,282,492/1961.

136. W. Neugebauer, S. Süs, and A. Rebenstock. Ger. pat. 1,072,478/1959.

137. S. Levinos. U.S. pat. 3,099,558/1963; Brit. pat. 893,063/1962; Belg. pat. 592,259/1960.

138. S. Levinos. U.S. pat. 3,138,460/1964; Belg. pat. 610,268/1961; Fr. pat. 1,324,234/1964.

139. Anon. *Chem. Eng. News*, **42** (31), 40–41 (1964).

140. G. N. Richards. *J. Appl. Polymer Sci.*, **5**, 553–557 (1961).

141. J. L. Bolland and H. W. Melville. *Proc. Rubber Tech. Conf. London*, Paper 90, p. 239 (1938).

142. M. S. Kharasch, L. V. Jensen, and W. H. Urry. *J. Am. Chem. Soc.*, **68**, 154–155 (1946); *J. Am. Chem. Soc.*, **69**, 1100–1105 (1947).

143. W. H. Hamill and R. H. Schuler. *J. Am. Chem. Soc.*, **73**, 3466–3470 (1951).

144. E. L. Cochran, W. H. Hamill, and R. R. Williams, Jr. *J. Am. Chem. Soc.*, **76**, 2145–2148 (1954).

145. C. E. McCavley, W. H. Hamill, and R. R. Williams, Jr. *J. Am. Chem. Soc.*, **76**, 6263–6266 (1954).

146. R. V. Lindsey and J. N. Ingraham. *J. Am. Chem. Soc.*, **75**, 5613–5614 (1953).

147. C. C. Sachs and J. Bond. U.S. pat. 2,505,067/1950; U.S. pat. 2,505,068/1950.

148. C. C. Sachs and J. Bond. U.S. pat. 2,548,685/1951.

149. C. C. Sachs and J. Bond. U.S. pat. 2,579,095/1951.

150. C. C. Sachs and J. Bond. U.S. pat. 2,641,576/1953.

151. M. S. Kharasch, E. V. Jensen, and W. H. Urry. *J. Am. Chem. Soc.*, **68**, 154–155 (1946).

152. M. S. Kharasch, E. V. Jensen, and W. H. Urry. *J. Am. Chem. Soc.*, **69**, 1100–1105 (1947).

153. K. W. Nagdasar'yan and R. I. Milyutinskaya. *Zh. Fiz. Khim.*, **28**, 498 (1954).

154. A. Chapiro and G. Hardy. *J. Chim. Phys.*, **59**, 993 (1962).

155. H. Scott and M. M. Labes. *Polymer Letters*, **1**, 413–414 (1963).

156. B. L. Dickinson and J. L. Silver. Fr. pat. 1,292,577/1962.

157. F. W. H. Mueller and C. B. Roth. *Sci. Phot., Proc. Intern. Coloq.*, pp. 327–333, Liege, 1959. (Publ. 1962.)

158. F. W. H. Mueller and C. B. Roth. *Phot. Sci. Eng.*, **4**, 151–154 (1960).

159. S. Levinos and F. W. H. Mueller. *Phot. Sci. Eng.*, **6**, 222–226 (1962); Brit. pat. 866,631/1961; Belg. pat. 577,894/1959; Can. pat. 647,912/1962.

160. G. A. Delzenne. *Phot. Sci. Eng.*, **7**, 335–339 (1963).

161. G. W. Luckey and W. West. U.S. pat. 3,038,800/1962.

162. S. Levinos. U.S. pat. 3,053,745/1962; Belg. pat. 580,584/1959; Brit. pat. 885,128/1961; Can. pat. 627,793/1961; Ger. pat. 1,103,586/1961.

163. S. Levinos and F. W. H. Mueller. U.S. pat. 3,050,390/1962; Belg. pat. 580,664/1958; Brit. pat. 867,980/1961; Can. pat. 661,384/1963.

164. G. Oster. *Nature*, **180**, 1275 (1957); U.S. pat. 3,019,104/1962; Ger. pat. 1,119,120/1961; Can. pat. 621,147/1961.

165. A. K. Schwerin. Belg. pat. 622,882/1963.

166. A. K. Schwerin, S. Levinos, and F. W. H. Mueller. Ger. pat. 1,085,423/1960; Brit. pat. 906,141/1962; Belg. pat. 582,913/1959; Can. pat. 641,963/1962.

167. C. B. Roth. U.S. pat. 3,147,116/1964.

168. G. O. Schenck. *Angew. Chem.*, **73**, 578 (1961).

169. M. Mudrovčič. *Z. Wiss. Phot.*, **26**, 171–192 (1928).

170. K. Weber. *Z. Phys. Chem.*, **B15**, 18–44 (1931).

171. G. M. Burnett and H. W. Melville. *Proc. Roy. Soc. (London)*, **A189**, 481–493 (1947).

172. M. G. Evans, M. Santuppa and N. Uri. *J. Polymer Sci.*, **7**, 243–260 (1951).

173. J. R. Merkel and W. J. Nickerson. *Biochem. Biophys. Acta*, **14**, 303–311 (1954).

174. G. Oster. *Nature*, **173**, 300–301 (1954).

175. W. J. Nickerson and J. R. Merkel. U.S. pat. 2,734,027/1956.

176. A. H. Adelman and G. Oster. *J. Am. Chem. Soc.*, **78**, 3977–3980 (1956).

177. G. Oster and N. Wotherspoon. *J. Am. Chem. Soc.*, **79**, 4836–4838 (1957).

178. G. Oster and A. H. Adelman. *J. Am. Chem. Soc.*, **78**, 913–916 (1956).
179. N. Uri. *J. Am. Chem. Soc.*, **74**, 5808–5809 (1952).
180. Hajime Miyama. *J. Chem. Soc. Japan*, **77**, 691–695 (1956); *J. Chem. Soc. Japan*, **77**, 1016–1018 (1956); *J. Chem. Soc. Japan*, **77**, 1361–1363 (1956).
181. A. Watanabe. *Bull. Chem. Soc. Japan*, **35**, 1562–1567 (1962).
182. G. Oster. *Photo. Eng.*, **4**, 173–178 (1953).
183. G. Oster: U.S. pat. 2,850,445/1958.
184. Gevaert Photo Producten, N.V. Belg. pat. 605,315/1961; Brit. pat. 924,238/1963.
185. J. Weiss. *J. Soc. Dyers and Col.*, **65**, 719 (1945).
186. C. J. Claus, I. T. Krohn, and P. C. Swanton. *Phot. Sci. Eng.*, **5**, 211–215 (1961).
187. I. M. Koizumi and A. Watanabe. *Bull. Chem. Soc. Japan*, **28**, 136–146 (1955).
188. G. K. Oster, G. Oster, and G. Pratti. *J. Am. Chem. Soc.*, **79**, 595–598 (1957).
189. M. Taniyama and G. Oster. *Bull. Chem. Soc. Japan*, **30**, 856–859 (1957).
190. G. Oster and Y. Mizutani. *J. Polymer Sci.*, **22**, 173–178 (1956).
191. G. Delzenne, S. Toppet, and G. Smets. *Bull. Soc. Chim. Belges*, **71**, 857–858 (1962).
192. G. Oster. U.S. pat. 2,875,047/1959.
193. G. Oster. U.S. pat. 3,097,096/1963.
194. G. K. Oster and G. Oster. U.S. pat. 3,145,104/1964; Brit. pat. 903,942/1963.
195. C. J. Claus and V. S. Mihajlov. *TAGA Proceedings*, **14**, 317–325 (1962).
196. Anon. *Reprod. Rev.*, **12**, No. 10, 54 (1962).
197. B. L. Sites and M. S. Agrus. U.S. pat. 3,047,422/1962.
198. G. K. Oster and G. Oster. U.S. pat. 3,097,097/1963; Can. pat. 664,566/1963.
199. G. K. Oster and G. Oster. *J. Am. Chem. Soc.*, **81**, 5543–5545/1959.
200. C. S. Marvel and R. G. Woolford. *J. Am. Chem. Soc.*, **80**, 830–831 (1958).
201. D. E. Adelson and H. Dannenberg. U.S. pat. 2,326,736/1943.
202. A. K. Schwerin. Brit. pat. 906,142/1962; Belg. pat. 590,978/1960.
203. A. A. Hiltz and E. G. Lendrat. U.S. pat. 2,880,152/1959.
204. P. Robinson. U.S. pat. 2,725,369/1955.
205. A. A. Hiltz and E. G. Lendrat. U.S. pat. 2,880,153/1959.
206. S. Levinos. U.S. pat. 3,061,431/1962; Belg. pat. 592,209/1960; Brit. pat. 906,143/1962; Can. pat. 663,951/1963.
207. F. W. H. Mueller and C. B. Roth. Brit. pat. 893,304/1962; Belg. pat. 594,253/1960; Fr. pat. 1,269,865/1961.
208. S. Levinos. U.S. pat. 3,075,907/1963; Brit. pat. 858,037/1960; Belg. pat. 573,717/1958; Can. pat. 627,748/1961.
209. A. K. Schwerin, H. D. Evans, and W. F. Barrows. Brit. pat. 891,898/1962; Belg. pat. 590,766/1960; Fr. pat. 1,270,017/1961.
210. General Aniline and Film Corp. Brit. pat. 868,631/1961.
211. H. H. Duerr. U.S. pat. 3,060,022/1962; Belg. pat. 592,841/1960; Brit. pat. 903,849/1962; Can. pat. 639,417/1962; Ger. pat. 1,106,172/1961.
212. H. D. Evans, F. W. H. Mueller, and S. Levinos. U.S. pat. 3,118,767/1964.
213. R. W. Baxendale. Can. pat. 675,792/1963.

6

Diazotype Processes

6.1 DIAZO COMPOUNDS

The discovery of the aromatic diazo and azo compounds goes back to the early days of organic chemistry. In 1834 Mitscherlich discovered azobenzene and in 1858 Griess began his classical research on the aromatic diazo compounds by synthesizing 4,6-dinitrobenzene-2,1-diazo oxide. Assuming that two hydrogen atoms in the benzene ring had been replaced by two atoms of nitrogen, Griess called this entirely new class of compounds the diazo compounds.

In general, aromatic diazo compounds are prepared by treating an aqueous solution of an aromatic amine salt, such as aniline hydrochloride, with sodium nitrite in the presence of hydrochloric or other mineral acid at temperatures of about 0°C. In order to prevent only partial diazotation and the formation of diazoamino compounds, the acid must be used in excess. The process of diazotization can be illustrated as follows:

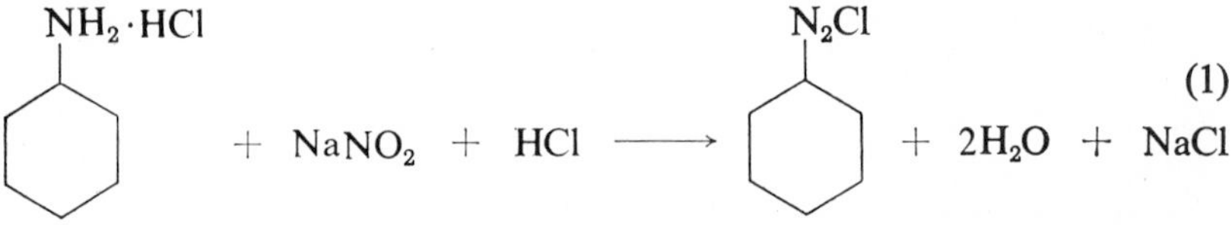

$$\text{NH}_2 \cdot \text{HCl} \qquad\qquad\qquad \text{N}_2\text{Cl}$$

$$\bigcirc + \text{NaNO}_2 + \text{HCl} \longrightarrow \bigcirc + 2\text{H}_2\text{O} + \text{NaCl} \qquad (1)$$

Instead of diazonium chlorides, oxalates or citrates can be prepared. These salts are claimed to have a higher sensitivity to light (1). Many other methods for the preparation of aromatic diazo compounds have been described and can be found in Saunders' and Zollinger's books (2,3).

Diazo compounds are very unstable, even to the point of explosive decomposition and, in the dry state, they have to be handled very carefully and only in small quantities. More stable diazo compounds are prepared from derivatives of *o*-aminophenols, *o*-aminonaphthols, *p*-amino-diphenyl-amines, *p*-aminodialkylanilines, and anhydroaldehyde-amino compounds (4).

The tendency to decompose spontaneously depends on the position and nature of the substituents on the aromatic nucleus, which gives the chemist some control at least.   Thus the hydroxyl group, for instance, attached to the molecule in the ortho position with respect to the diazo group has an excellent stabilizing effect.   On the other hand, the stability of phenyldiazonium chloride is decreased by *m*-hydroxy, *o*- or *m*-methyl, *m*-methoxy, and *o*- or *m*-phenyl substitution (5).

Comparatively stable diazo compounds can be obtained by forming a double salt with metal halides or nonmetallic fluorides.   Zinc chloride (6), cadmium chloride, stannic chloride, or fluoboric acid (7) are widely used. Fluosulfonates (8) and hydroborofluorides (9) also have been suggested. The double salts are usually prepared by adding chlorides of heavy metals to the solution of diazo compound, and consist of a metal halo-anion complex and a diazonium cation with the general formula

$$\left[\begin{array}{c} R{-}N \\ \mathrm{|||} \\ N \end{array} \right]_2^+ 2Cl^- \cdot ZnCl_2$$

With the complex acids such as fluoboric acid, the diazo compounds form complex salts corresponding to the formula

$$\left[\begin{array}{c} R{-}N \\ \mathrm{|||} \\ N \end{array} \right]^+ \left[\begin{array}{ccc} F & & F \\ & \searrow \ \nearrow & \\ & B & \\ & \nearrow \ \nwarrow & \\ F & & F \end{array} \right]^-$$

The role of the metal halo-anion in the stabilization of aromatic diazonium salts was studied by a number of Russian workers (10,11), by Aroney and co-workers (12), and more recently by Boudreaux (13); it is generally assumed that some covalent bonding exists between the complex metal anions and the diazonium group of the aromatic cations (14).   It is claimed that better stabilized diazonium compounds are obtained by first causing the diazotization product to react with an anionic surface agent containing at least one long-chain alkyl group, and then effecting the remainder of the stabilization with one of the usual stabilizers mentioned above (15,16).   By adding sulfonated resins (e.g., formaldehyde conden-sation products of *β*-naphthalene sulfonic acid, sulfonated cumarone-indene resin or sulfonated polybenzyl resin) to the diazotization solution, diazosulfonated resin complexes are formed which presumably have better stability than the corresponding metallic-halide double salts (17).

In this connection, it is of interest to note that the stability of diazo compounds does not always go hand in hand with their light sensitivity, in other words, there is no direct relationship between light sensitivity and thermal stability.

Like most other light-sensitive compounds, diazonium salts are affected by the action of light in the blue and near ultraviolet. The fundamental reaction taking place during the photolysis is:

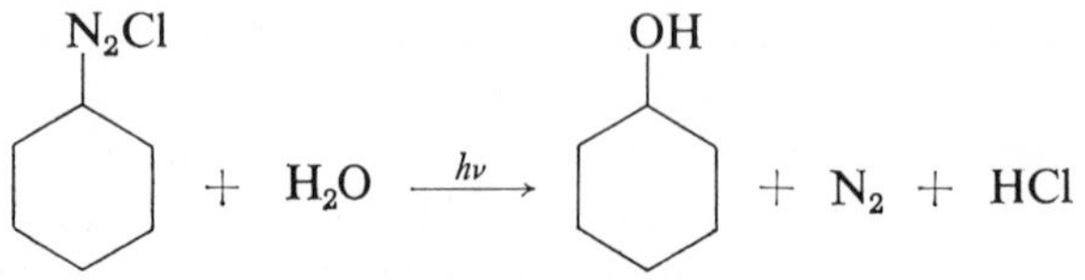

$$
\underset{N_2Cl}{\bigcirc} + H_2O \xrightarrow{h\nu} \underset{OH}{\bigcirc} + N_2 + HCl \tag{2}
$$

The mechanism of the photochemical decomposition of diazonium salts is, however, not completely understood; it appears (17,18,19), that the mode of decomposition is largely determined by the environment and the chemical species present.

The photochemical sensitivity of the diazo compounds generally used in diazotype papers is limited to a very narrow spectral region, having its maximum at about 375 mμ. This maximum varies to a certain degree with the particular diazo compounds, and Turner (20) and Schmidt (21) give a higher maximum, about 400 mμ. According to Nakagawa the maximum sensitivity lies at 410 to 420 mμ (22). The sensitivity spectrum corresponds closely to the absorption spectrum (23) when the absorption of short ultraviolet radiation by the base paper is taken into consideration (24).

Diazonium compounds derived from *o*-aminobenzenes have their absorption spectra shifted somewhat towards longer wavelengths and thus they can be exposed with incandescent light. Among these are: 2-diazo-3-dimethylaminotoluene, 1-diazo-2-dimethylamino-3-chlorobenzene, 1-diazo-2-dimethylamino-5-ethoxy-4-benzoylamine and 4-diazo-2,3′,6′-trimethoxy-2-dimethylaminobenzene.

The effect of substituents on the light sensitivity of diazo compounds was studied by many investigators (25,26), and it was found that the position of the substituents in the nucleus of the diazo compound is most important for the light sensitivity.

More recently, Brown (27) investigated the sensitivities of some 50 derivatives of aniline, and came to the conclusion that, in general, the orthoisomer is the most sensitive, followed by the meta and para. For papers of high sensitivity and stability, diazo compounds should be selected which have a positive polar substituent, such as dialkylamino, alkoxy, phenylamino, benzoylamino, or morpholino and piperidino groups. This is illustrated in Table 6.1, which is compiled from Brown's work.

TABLE *6.1.* Light Sensitivity of Substituted Diazobenzenes

Substituents in Aniline Molecule In Order of Polar Strength	Order of Decreasing Sensitivity to Ultraviolet Light
Most positive	
$-N(C_2H_5)_2$	*p,m,o,*
$-OCH_3$	*o,m,p,*
$-CH_3$	*o,m,p,*
$-Cl$	*o,m,p,*
$-Br$	*o,m,p,*
$-COOH$	*o,m,* = *p*
$-SO_3H$	*o,p,m,*
Most negative	

The light to which the diazotype material is exposed must supply sufficient energy to destroy all the diazo in the nonimage areas, and is thus completely responsible for the formation of the image. In silver halide layers, an average grain, consisting of roughly one and one half billion molecules, requires between one and two hundred quanta to become developable. Subsequent development reduces all the silver present in the grain and thus each absorbed quantum has affected millions of silver atoms. For this reason, in spite of the fact that the quantum efficiency in the diazotype process is of the same order as in silver halide photography (28), the energy required to form a "diazo image" is roughly a million times as great as that necessary to obtain an image in the silver halide process.

Because of these high energy requirements, powerful light sources rich in ultraviolet rays must be used for exposing material sensitized with diazonium compounds. The most suitable and most generally used are high-pressure mercury-vapor lamps. The light output of these lamps is limited to very narrow bands—mercury lines—having peaks at 3132, 3342, 3660, 4047, 4358, 5461, and 5770 Å. For standard diazotype papers, 3660 and 4047 Å are the most important, and have a destructive effect on the majority of benzene and naphthalene diazonium salts (29,30,31). 3132 and 3342 Å are of little, 5461 and 5770 Å of no, practical

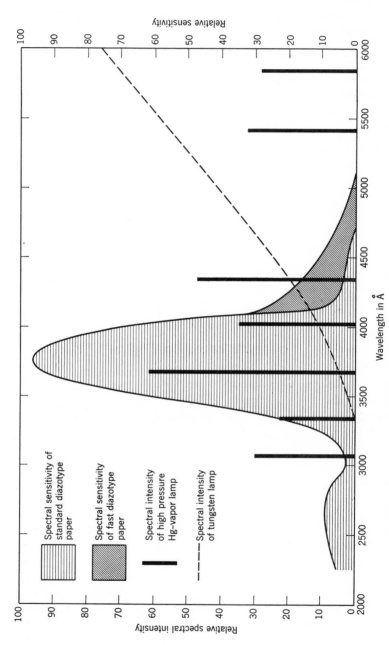

Figure 6.1. Spectral sensitivity of diazotype papers (reference 377). (Reprinted with the permission of Quartz Radiation Corp.)

value. The peak, at 4358 Å, also contributes to the decomposition of standard diazotype papers because of its high intensity, but is utilized more in papers sensitized with so-called "superfast" diazo compounds. The absorption spectrum of these compounds is shifted toward the visible region, as shown in Figure 6.1. They are morpholino derivatives of diazo-p-aminobenzenes, and were made available a few years ago. Super-fast diazotype papers can be exposed with tungsten or fluorescent lamps, which emit a low percentage of ultraviolet light but more violet and blue.

In the course of exposure to actinic radiation, the concentration of the diazo compound decreases in the following manner:

$$\frac{dC_{(t)}}{dt} = -\phi \, \Delta I \tag{3}$$

where $C_{(t)}$ = thickness of the diazo coating (mol/cm^2)
 ϕ = quantum yield
 ΔI = quantity of absorbed light (mol quanta/cm^2 sec)

If the amount of incident light is I_0 and the absorption coefficient $\epsilon\lambda$, then ΔI can also be written as (32)

$$\Delta I = I_0(1 - e^{-\varepsilon_{(\lambda)}C_{(t)}}) \tag{4}$$

By substituting this expression in equation 3, and integrating, we get (33)

$$\ln\left(\frac{1}{e^{\varepsilon_{(\lambda)}C_{(t)}} - 1}\right) = \epsilon_{(\lambda)}\phi t + \ln\left(\frac{1}{e^{\varepsilon_{(\lambda)}C_{(t=0)}} - 1}\right) \tag{5}$$

In other words, the quantum yield is independent of the concentration of the diazo compound (28,34), so that the decomposition under steady illumination proceeds at constant velocity (Figure 6.2). The quantum yield is, however, dependent on the frequency of the absorbed light, and, to a certain degree, on the temperature at which the photolysis takes place (35).

The quantum yields are poor compared to those with silver halide emulsions and vary between 0.2 and unity, depending on the product used, the pH, and the method of measurement. Eggert (36,37) gives for the photolysis of diazodiphenylamine the quantum yield, $\phi = 0.50$. Goodeve and Wood (25) investigated the influence of pH on the same reaction and found $\phi = 0.34$ for $\lambda = 365$ mμ at pH 4.2. The quantum yield increased to unity at pH 10. Schröter (28), by a bleaching method, found the quantum yield for the decomposition of 1-diazonium-2-hydroxynaphthalene-4-sulfonic acid to be $\phi = 0.40$; in methanol or ethanol solution, $\phi = 0.50$. Moraw and Munder (32) studied the photolysis of p-quinone-

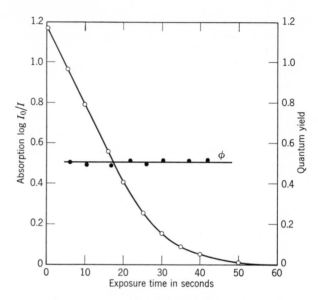

Figure 6.2. Photolysis of p-dimethylaminobenzene diazonium chloride *(reference 35).*

iminodiazides and calculated the quantum yield to be $\phi = 0.74$ in methanol solution and $\phi = 0.58$ in the solid state.

Solid anhydrous diazonium chlorides completely free of polar influences were observed to be photolyzed with a quantum efficiency of well over one (38). These results can be explained by considering the covalent diazo tautomer of the diazonium chloride, which decomposes symmetrically in the first step:

$$\text{R}\underset{}{\bigcirc}\text{N}{=}\text{N}{-}\text{Cl} \longrightarrow \text{R}\underset{}{\bigcirc}{\cdot} + \text{N}_2 + \cdot\text{Cl} \quad (6)$$

Free chlorine atoms and phenyl radicals so produced are highly reactive uncharged particles containing unpaired electrons, and are capable of continuing the original function of the utilized photon, for example:

$$\text{R}\underset{}{\bigcirc}\text{N}{=}\text{N}{-}\text{Cl} + \cdot\text{Cl} \longrightarrow \text{R}\underset{}{\bigcirc}{\cdot} + \text{N}_2 + \text{Cl}_2 \quad (7)$$

or

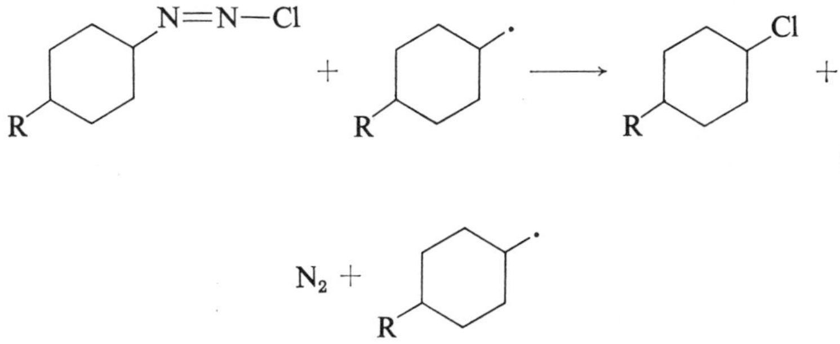

$$N=N-Cl \quad + \quad \cdot \quad \longrightarrow \quad Cl \quad +$$

(with R substituents on the rings) (8)

$$N_2 + \quad \cdot$$

(ring with R substituent)

The observed quantum yields were of the order of two. Such a free radical chain process is theoretically capable of continuing indefinitely under the proper conditions and thus exhibits the high quantum yields. The low thermal stability, however, prevents the practical use.

Diazo compounds are not sensitive to the green, yellow, or red portion of the visible spectrum, and no effective means of extending the sensitivity toward the red has yet been found. Thiazine, primuline, triphenyl-methane dyes, etc., were claimed to be sensitizing agents for colorless or light-colored diazo compounds; for example, 4-diazo-methoxy- or ethoxy-benzene sulfonic acid by Schmidt and von Poser (39). However, it seems to be possible to increase the quantum yield of these compounds by adding water-soluble keto-compounds, for example, disodium-2,7-anthraquinone disulfonate, to the diazotype coating (40). In another patent the low light sensitivity of diazophenols, diazophenol ethers, and diazophenol allyl ethers can be increased by the addition of polynuclear aromatic hydrocarbons, aliphatic ketones, etc., which have strong light absorption in the region of 330 to 440 mμ (41). Also, compounds such as ferric oxalate are claimed to accelerate the photolytic decomposition of diazonium compounds (42).

6.2 CLASSIFICATION OF DIAZO COMPOUNDS

Many thousands of diazo compounds have been prepared since the discovery of diazotization, but not all of them are suitable for the diazotype process and, as a matter of fact, only about a dozen are currently in use.

The diazonium compounds, to be useful in diazotype coatings, must meet certain requirements. First of all, they must have sufficient light sensitivity and stability to moderate temperature and mechanical shock so that they can be prepared, applied to the base, dried, stored, and exposed to give clear sharp prints. To be suitable for sensitizing solutions, diazonium compounds must be soluble in water or in some common solvent. Their photolysis product must be colorless to insure white background and prevent the darkening of the background areas; the photolysis product should not be affected by air or light.   And finally, diazo compounds must form in minimum time with suitable couplers, sufficiently dark and preferably water-insoluble and light-stable dyes.

The majority of diazonium compounds have been synthesized by chemists of Kalle A.G., and their formulas, preparation methods, and applications were published after the Second World War in *FIAT Report* 813.   This publication contributed much to the growth of the diazotype process and greatly furthered this industry in all countries.   The value of this report for research purposes was increased by Landau, who classified the available information in a logical and scientific order (43).   It is neither possible nor desirable to discuss in detail this mass of information which has been significantly enlarged since that time by the work done in the United States and abroad.   Chemists interested in more details and particulars can refer to the references cited and to *FIAT Report* 813.

Diazonium salts used in the diazotype process are unsaturated aromatic compounds bearing a diazo group attached to a carbon atom of an aromatic nucleus, the other valence being satisfied by an acid ion X (other than sulfo group).

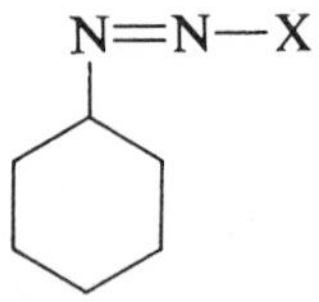

$$N{=}N{-}X$$

One can divide diazo compounds corresponding to the above formula as follows:

Substituted diazobenzenes.   In this group belong diazo compounds derived from diazobenzene excluding those having an amine, hydroxy, and mercapto group attached to the aromatic nucleus.   They correspond to the following general formula:

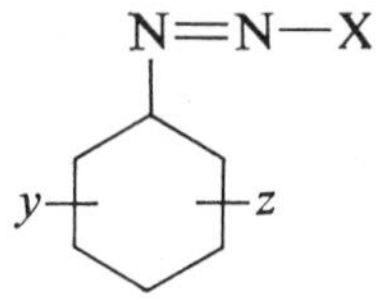

$$N{=}N{-}X$$

These compounds can be monosubstituted, as in 1-diazo-4-ethoxy-benzene(I) or di-substituted at 2 and 6 or 2 and 3, 2 and 4, 4 and 5, or 2 and 5.   The substituent is usually a methoxy or ethoxy radical; 1-diazo-2,5-dimethoxybenzene(II) and 1-diazo-2,5-diethoxybenzene(III) can serve as examples.

Trisubstituted derivatives have also been prepared; the substitution takes place at 2,4 and 5; 2,4 and 6; 2,3 and 4; 2,3 and 6 or 3,4 and 5. Those containing alkoxy groups at 2 and 5 and a halogen or an aryl group at 4, are the most important; 1-diazo-4-chloro-2,5-diethoxybenzene(IV) is an example.

In this category we can also include the diphenyl derivatives disclosed by Schmidt and Werner (44), for example, 4-diazo-2,5-dimethoxy-diphenyl(V) and 4-diazo-2,5,4′-triethoxydiphenyl(VI).

Diazo-p-aminobenzenes. These compounds, which can be unsubstituted, monosubstituted, in ortho or meta, or disubstituted, in the 2 and 6, 3 and 5, 2 and 3 or 2 and 5 positions, or polysubstituted, correspond to

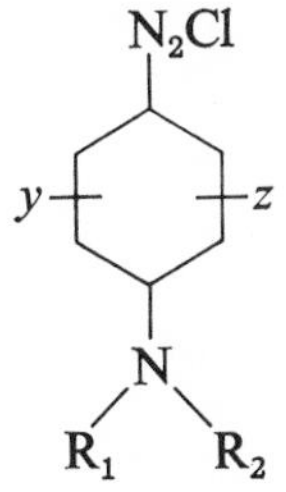

where z and y can be hydrogen, halogen, alkyl, carboxy, alkoxy, acetoxy, carbamyl, nitro group, etc. They can be derived from primary aromatic *p*-amines, where R_1 and R_2 are hydrocarbons, or from secondary and tertiary amines.

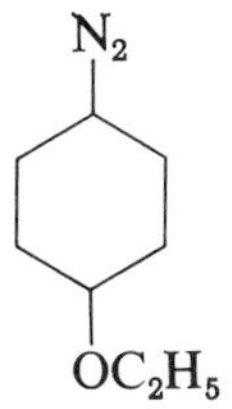

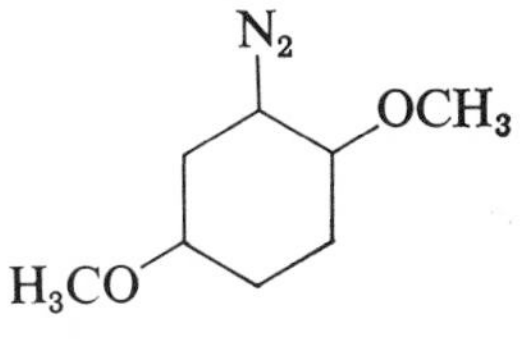

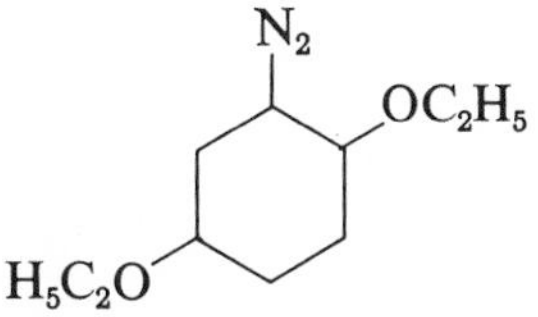

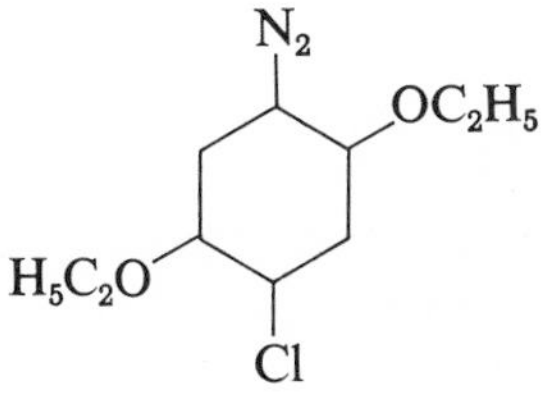

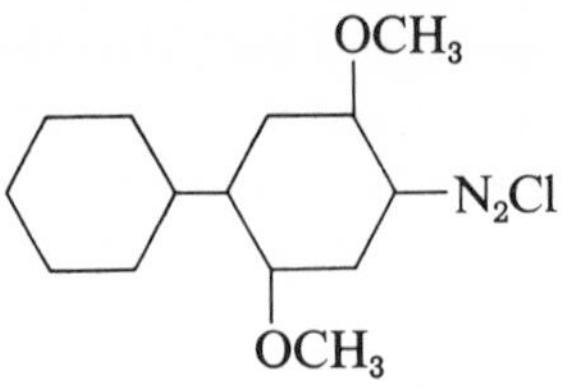

V 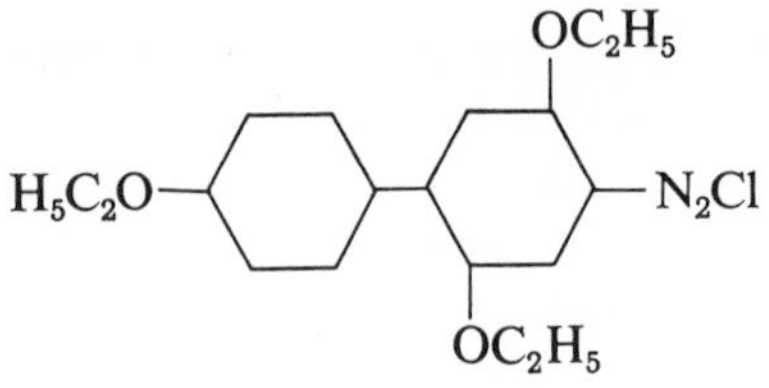   VI

Among the nonsubstituted derivatives are very important dialkyl-derivatives, such as *p*-dimethylaminobenzene diazonium chloride(VII) and *p*-diethylaminobenzene diazonium chloride(VIII) (45,46). Other members of this group are *p*-diethoxyaminobenzene diazonium chloride (IX) (47), *p*-dihydroxypropyl-aminobenzene diazonium chloride (X) (48), *p*-methylallyl-aminobenzene diazonium chloride(XI) (49), *p*-dibutyl-aminobenzene diazonium chloride(XII) (50), *p*-diamylaminobenzene diazonium chloride(XIII) (51).

Benzene diazonium salt containing, para to the diazo group, 1,3-oxazolidino or oxazino group, were disclosed by Cox and Moore (52). The diazonium salt from *p*-oxazolidinoaniline(XIV) is an example.

Comparatively little attention has been given to the tetrazo derivatives of diazotizable diamines. Slifkin (53) patented tetrazo compounds derived from the following diamines: *N,N'*-bis(4-aminophenyl) dimethylene-diamine(XV); *N,N'*-bis (4-aminophenyl) piperazine(XVI); *N,N'*-bis (4-aminophenyl) bis-trimethylenediamine(XVIII).

From the secondary *p*-amines are derived: *p*-cyclohexylaminobenzene diazonium chloride(XVII) (54), 9-(*p*-diazophenyl)carbazole(XIX) (55).

Monosubstituted derivatives can be represented by: 1-diazo-4-(di-hydroxyethyl)amino-3-methylbenzene(XX) (56), 1-diazo-3-methyl-4-monoethylaminobenzene(XXI), 1-diazo-3-methyl-4-dimethylaminobenzene(XXII), 1-diazo-2-methyl-4-(N-methyl, N-hydroxypropyl-amino-benzene(XXIII) (48), 1-diazo-4-dimethylamino-3-ethoxybenzene(XXIV) (57), 1-diazo-3-methoxy-4-(N-*n*-propyl-N-cyclohexyl)aminobenzene(XXV) (58), 1-diazo-4-diethylamino-3-chlorobenzene(XXVI), 1-diazo-2-ethoxy-4-diethylaminobenzene(XXVII), 1-diazo-2-carboxy-4-dimethylaminoben-zene(XXVII), 1-diazo-2-carboxy-2-diethylaminobenzene(XXIX), 1-diazo-3-oxyethoxy-4-pyrrolidone-aminobenzene(XXX) (59,60). Instead of 1-diazo-3-dialkylamino-3-chlorobenzenes, the corresponding -3-bromo- and -3-iodo- derivatives can be used; their coupling activity is greater and their absorption spectrum is shifted toward longer wavelengths (61).

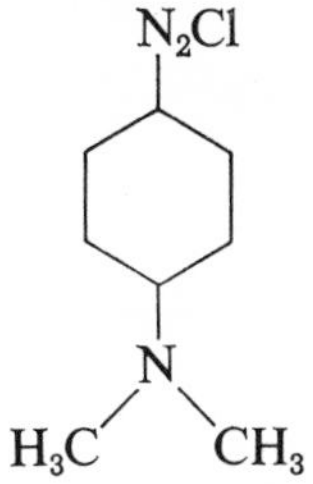

VII

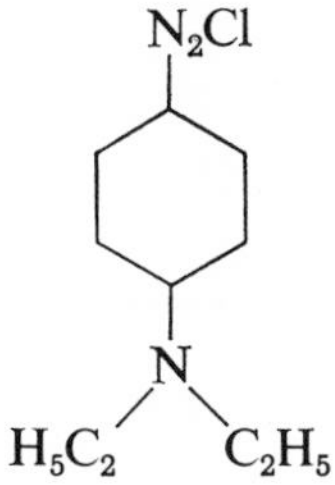

VIIII

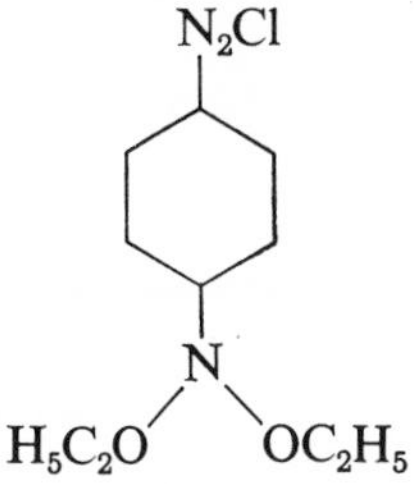

IX

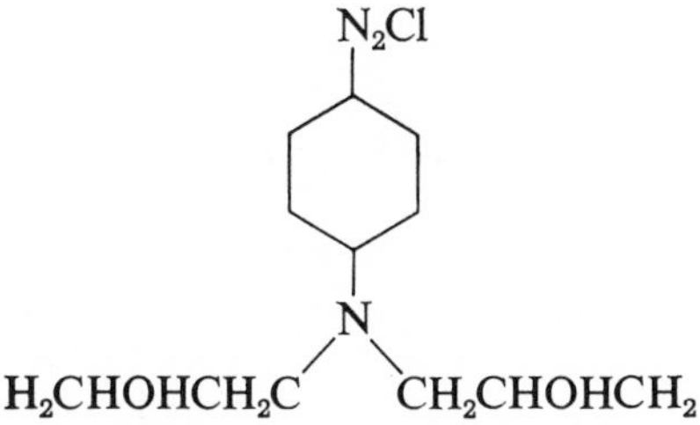

X

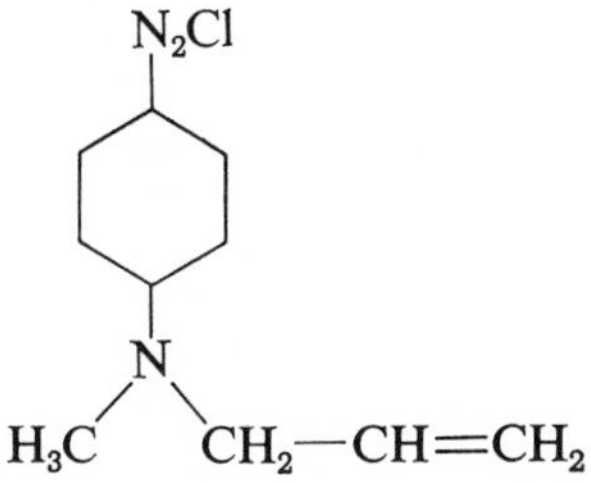

XI

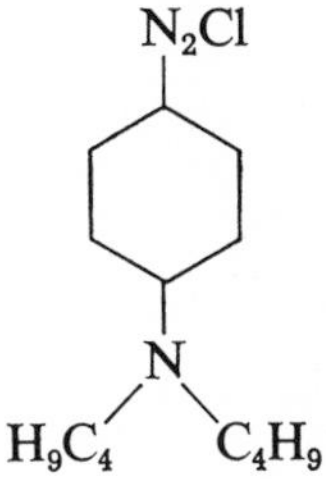

XII

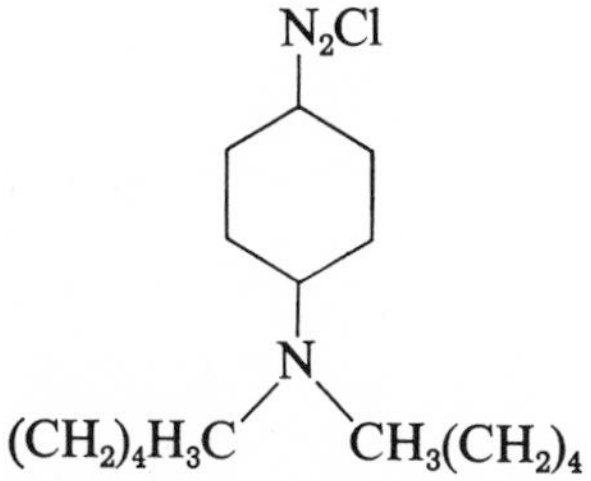

XIII

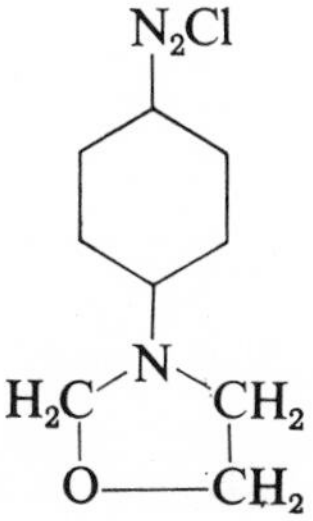

XIV

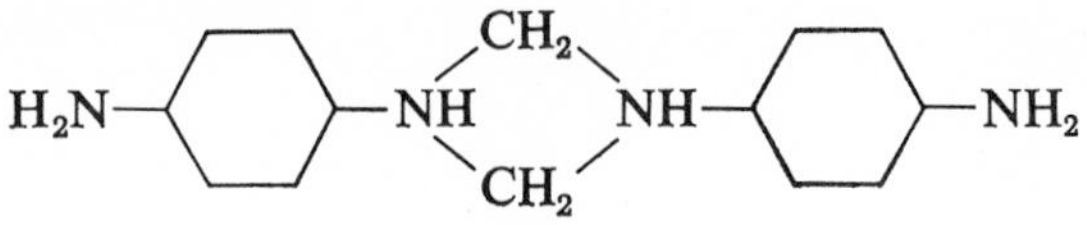

XV

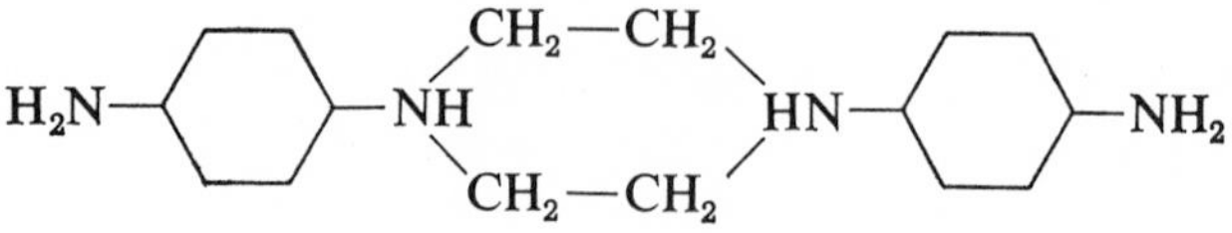

XVI

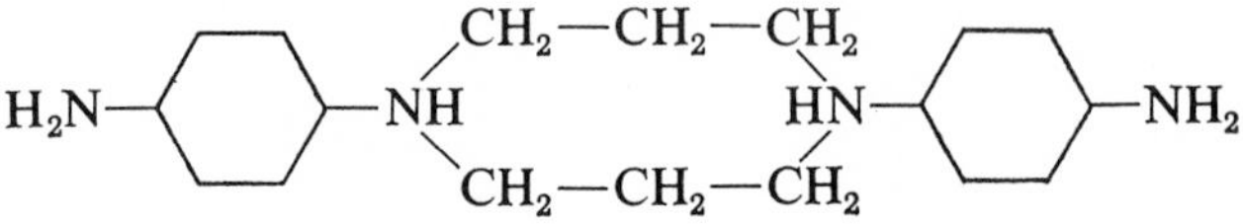

XVII

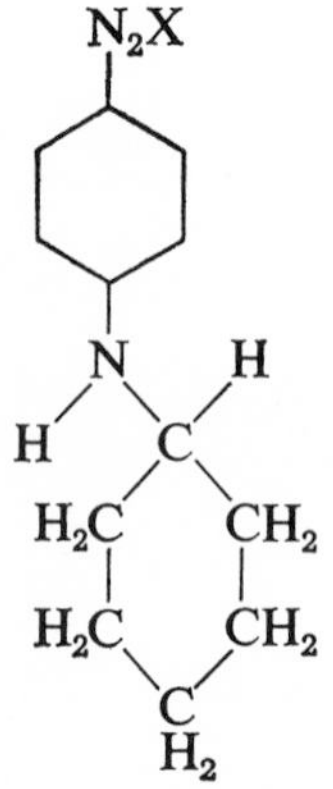

XVIII

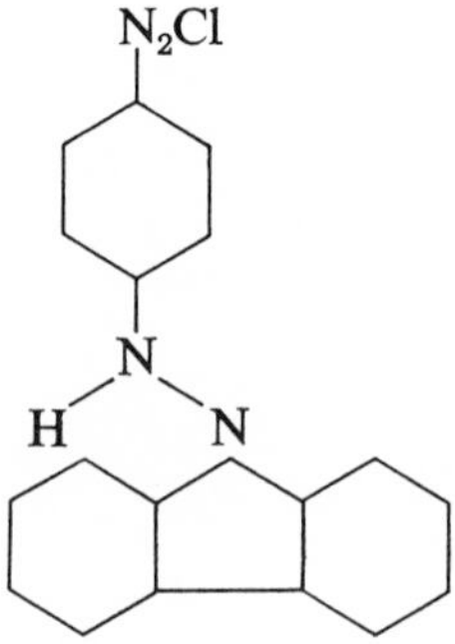

XIX

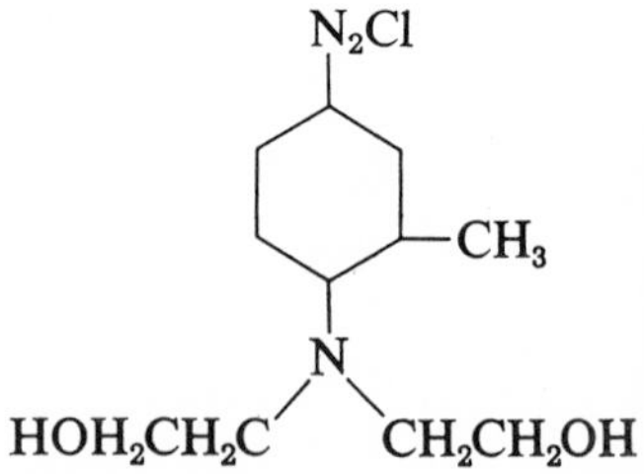

XX

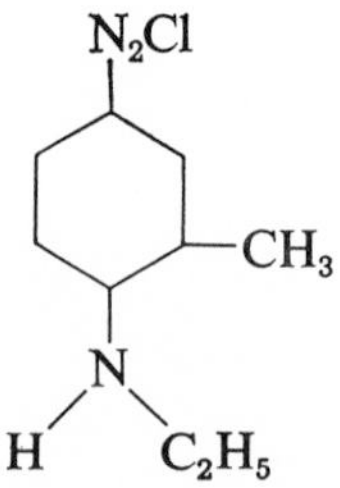

XXI

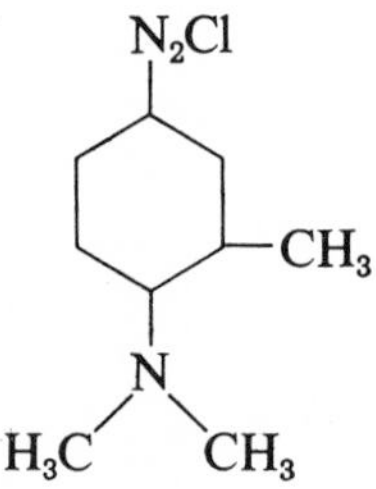

XXII

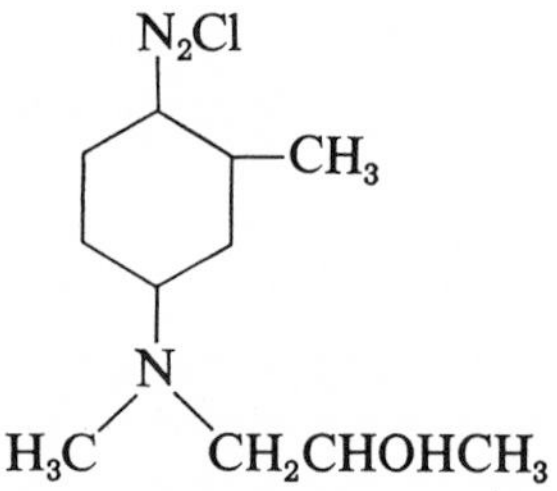

XXIII

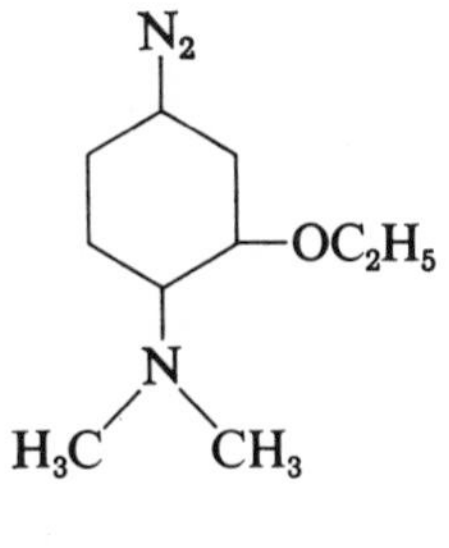

N_2

$-OC_2H_5$

N

H_3C CH_3

XXIV

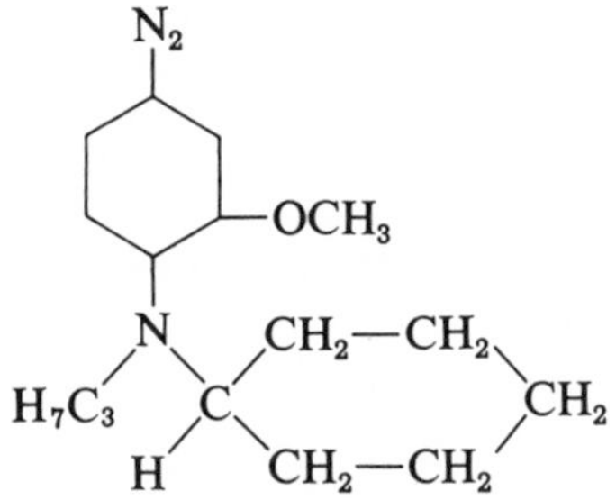

N_2

$-OCH_3$

N

H_7C_3 C CH_2-CH_2 CH_2

H CH_2-CH_2

XXV

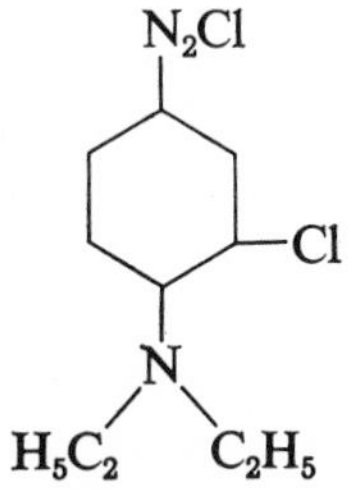

N_2Cl

$-Cl$

N

H_5C_2 C_2H_5

XXVI

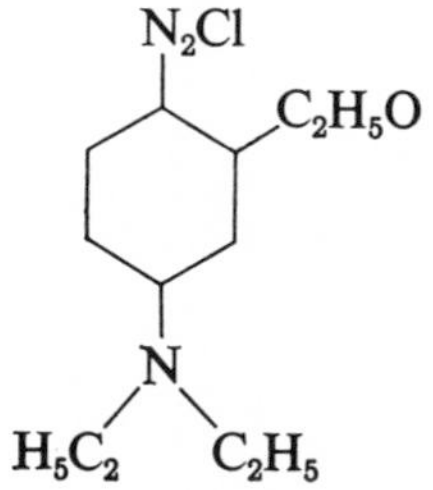

N_2Cl

C_2H_5O

N

H_5C_2 C_2H_5

XXVI

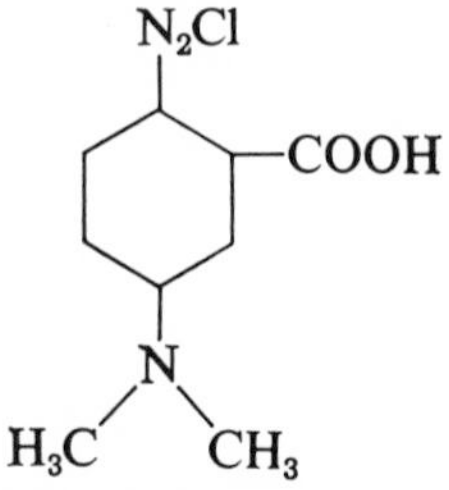

N_2Cl

$-COOH$

N

H_3C CH_3

XXVIII

N_2Cl

$-COOH$

N

H_5C_2 C_2H_5

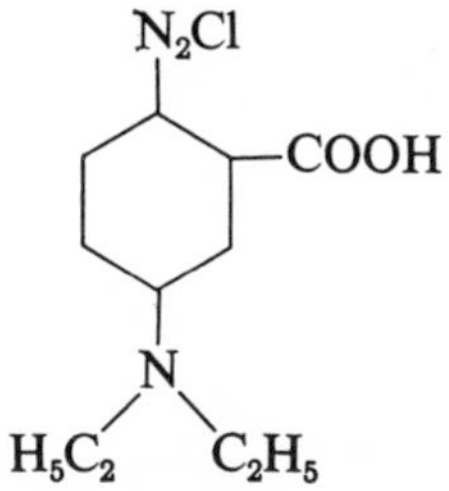

XXIX

From the disubstituted *p*-diazo amino-benzenes we can take, as an example, 1-diazo-2,5-diethoxy-4-acetoxyaminobenzene(XXXI), 1-diazo-4-methylamino-3-ethoxy-6-chlorobenzene(XXXII)(62), 1-diazo-2,5-dichloro-4-(N-methyl, N-cyclohexyl)-aminobenzene (XXXIII) (63), and 4'diazo-2',5'-diethoxy-5-phenyl-2-amino-4-imino-6-methyltriazine(XXXIV) (64).

To this group belong, also, compounds in which R_1 is benzyl or substituted benzyl and R_2 is hydrogen in the secondary and an alkyl, aryl, or similar group in tertiary diazo-*p*-aminobenzenes. They correspond to the general formula:

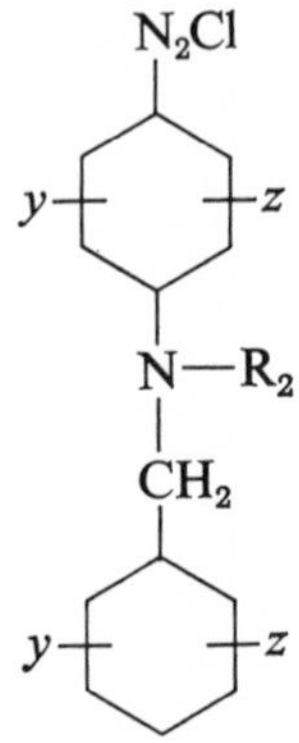

1-diazo-2,5-dichloro-4-benzylaminobenzene(XXXV) and similar compounds were prepared by Schmidt and Franke (65). 1-Diazo-4-ethyl-benzylaminobenzene(XXXVI) and 1-diazo-4-methylbenzylamino-3-ethoxybenzene(XXXVII) (66) are used as the sensitizer for one component diazotype papers.

Other examples are: 1-diazo-4-oxyethylbenzyl-3,6-diethoxyaminobenzene(XXXVIII), 1-diazo-4-methylbenzylamino-2,5-diethoxybenzene (XXXIX), and 1-diazo-4-ethylbenzyl-3-ethoxyaminobenzene(XL).

Another group of compounds belonging under the same heading are diazo-*p*-arylamines of the diphenylamine type, corresponding to the formula:

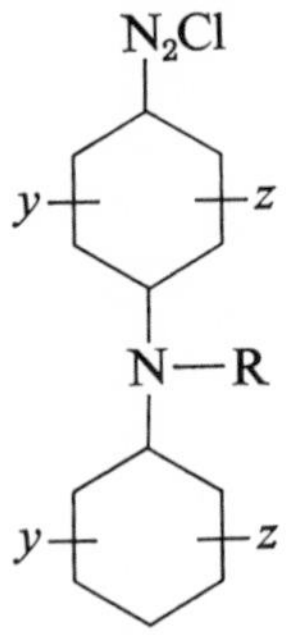

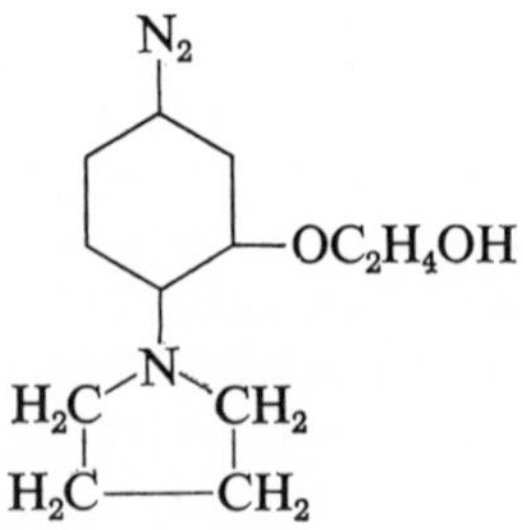

XXX

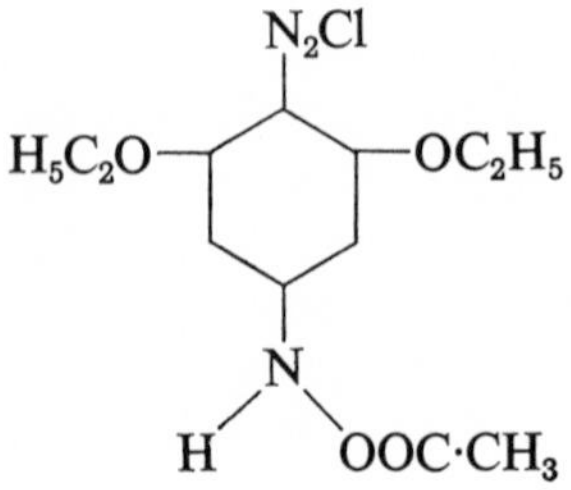

XXXI

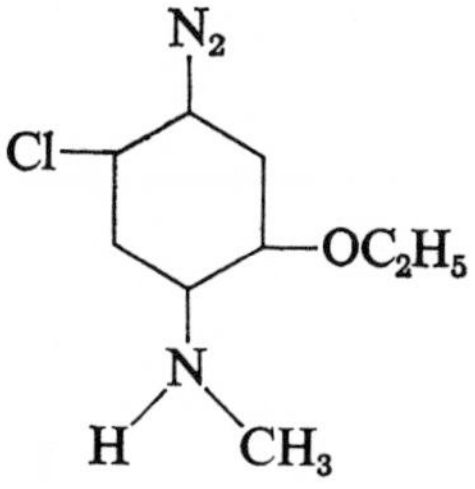

XXXII

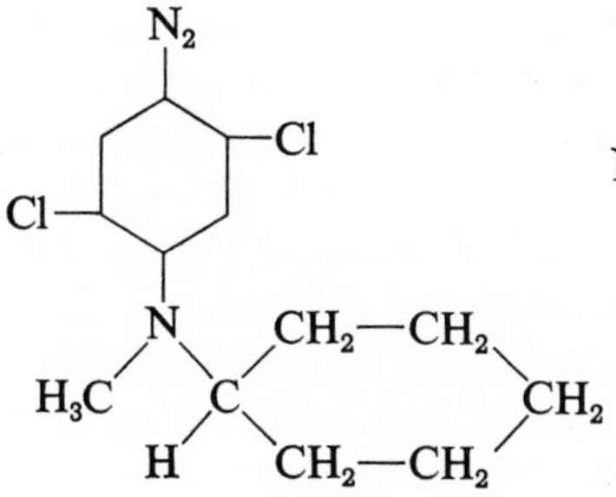

XXXIII

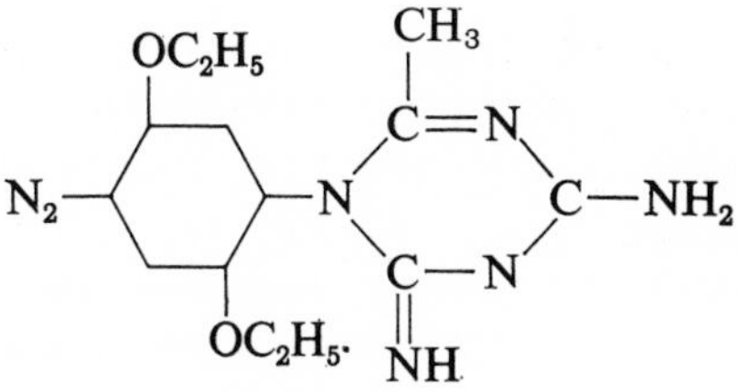

XXXIV

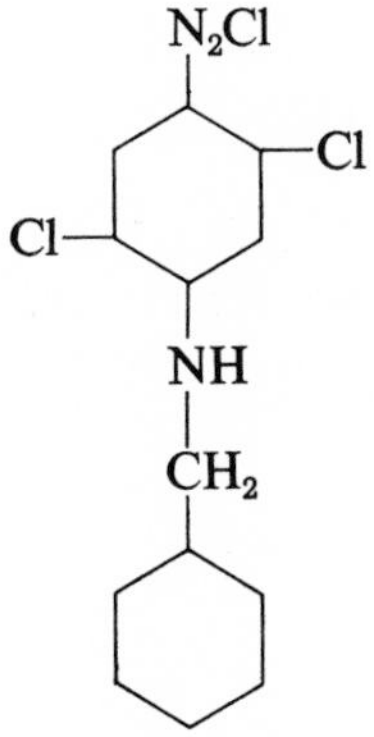

XXXV

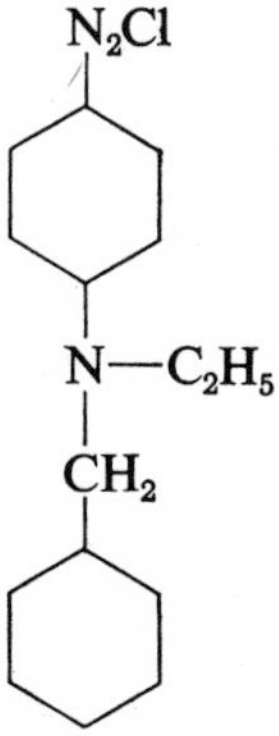

XXXVI

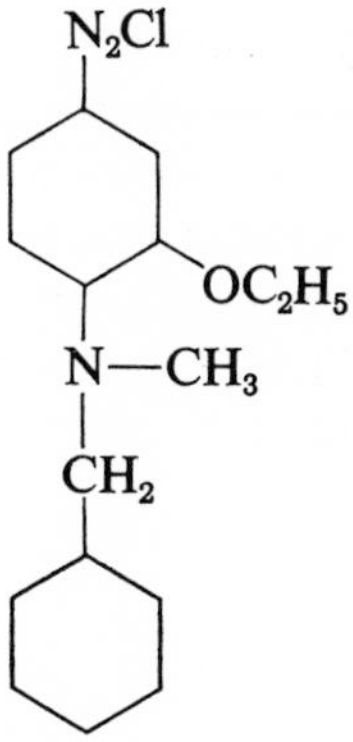

XXXVII

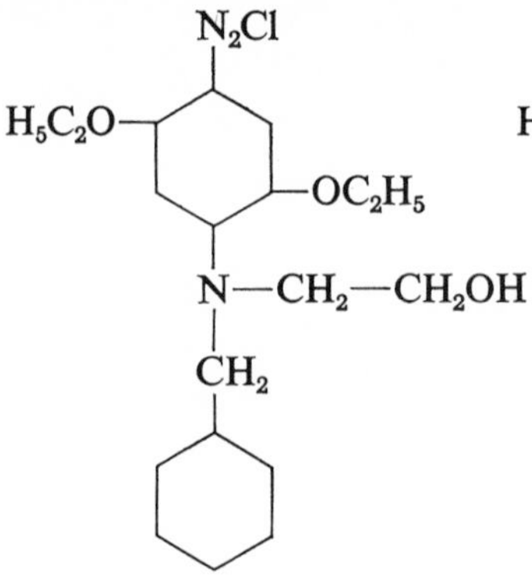

XXXVIII 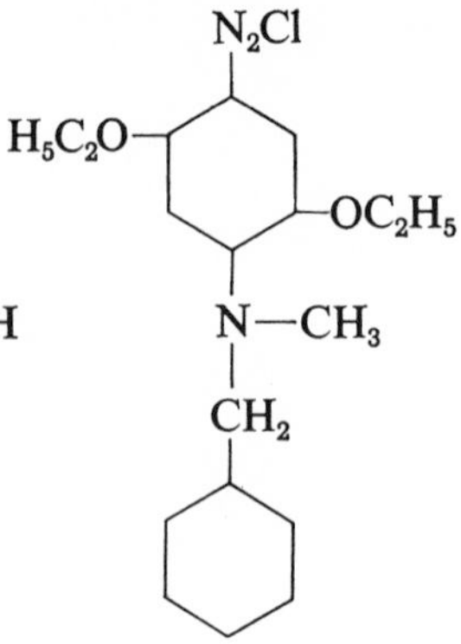   XXXIX 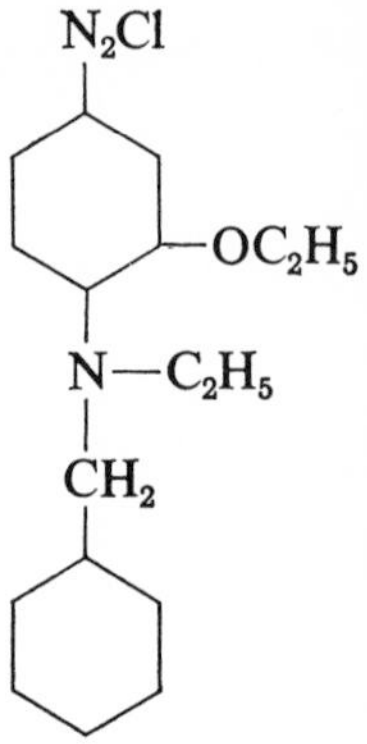   XL

The nucleus carrying the diazo group can, likewise, be substituted again in the ortho or para position. These compounds, of which diazotized *p*-aminodiphenylamine(XLI) is an example (67), are relatively resistant to precoupling and, for this reason, are mainly used as sensitizers of two-component papers. 4-Diazo-4'-ethoxydiphenylamine and other derivatives of *p*-aminodiphenylamine were patented by Lehmann (68).

A very important group of diazo compounds is the morpholino derivatives of diazo-*p*-aminobenzenes. Because of their extended light sensitivity to longer wavelengths, these compounds are very useful in sensitizing papers designed for copying letters typed on regular, semiopaque bond paper. The simplest is 1-diazo-3-morpholinoaminobenzene(XLII) (69). Other derivatives are (70): 1-diazo-4-morpholino-3-methoxyaminobenzene (XLIII), 1-diazo-4-morpholino-2,5-dimethoxyaminobenzene(XLIV), 1-diazo-4-morpholino-2,5-diethoxyaminobenzene(XLV), 1-diazo-4-morpholino-2-ethoxy-5-methoxy-aminobenzene(XLVI) (71), 1-diazo-4-morpholino-2,5-dipropoxyaminobenzene(XLVII), 1-diazo-4-morpholino-2,5-dibutoxyaminobenzene(XLVIII) (72).

Thiomorpholino compounds such as diazotized N-4'-amino-3'-ethoxyphenyl-(1')-thiomorpholine(XLIX), were disclosed in another patent (73).

Diazo-o-aminobenzenes. These compounds correspond to the general formula

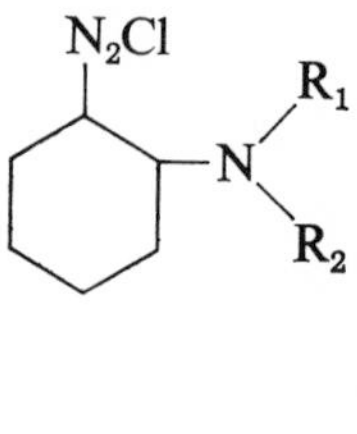

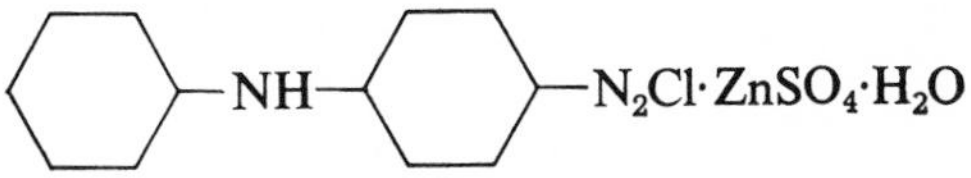

XLI

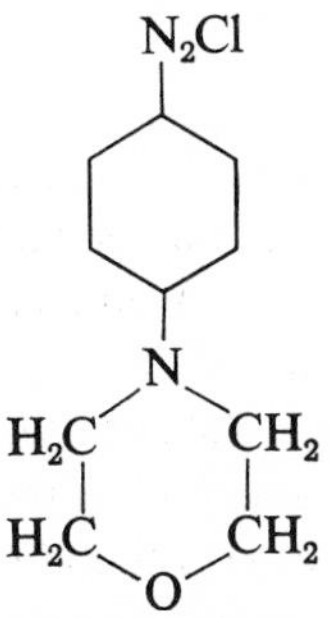

XLII

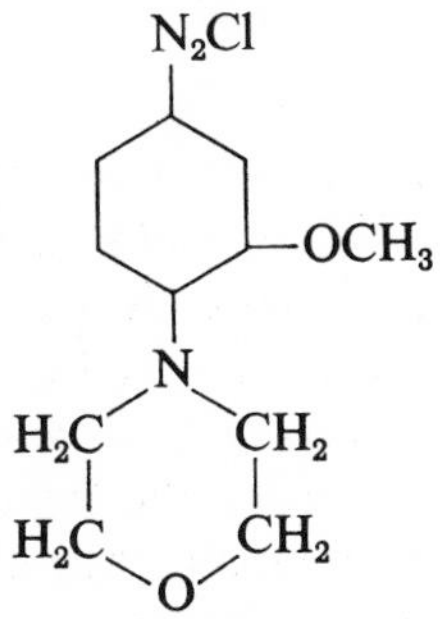

XLIII

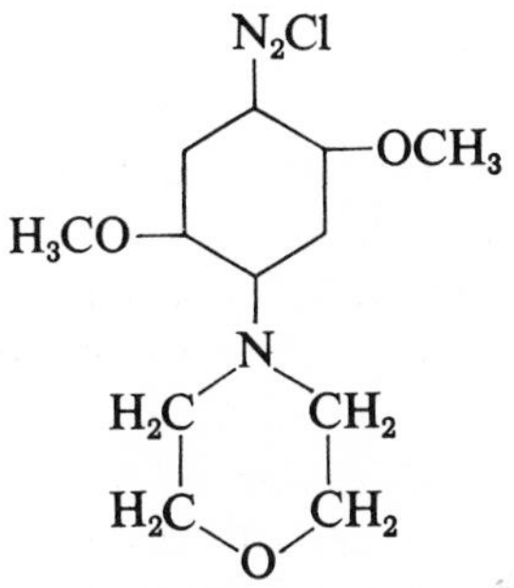

XLIV

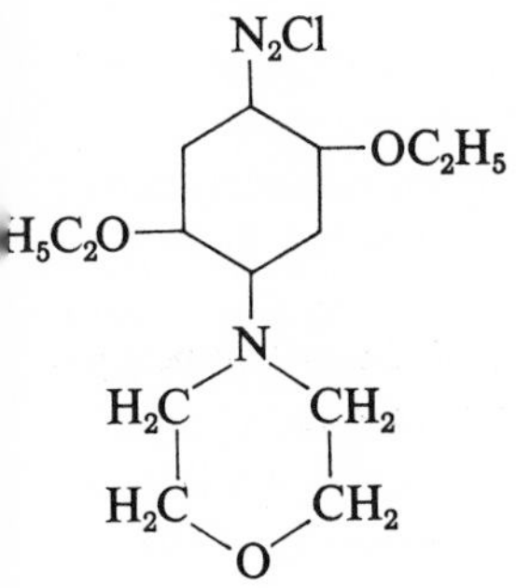

XLV

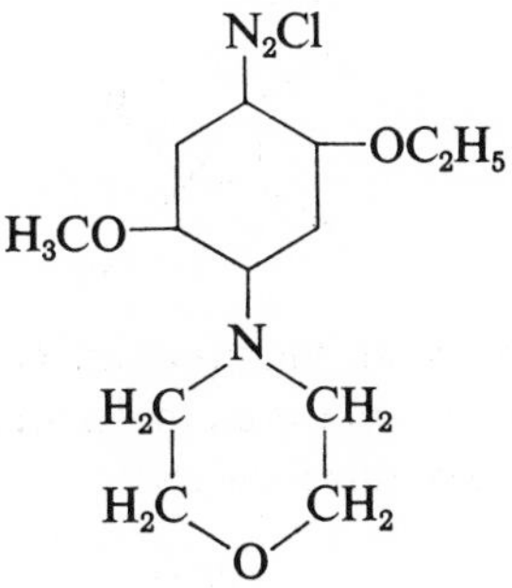

XLVI

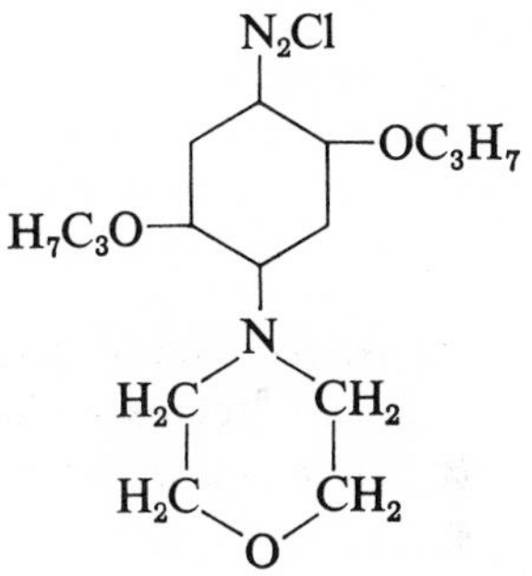

XLVII

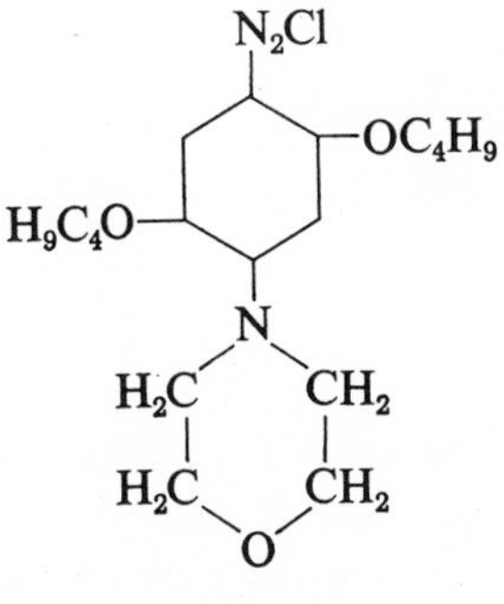

XLVIII

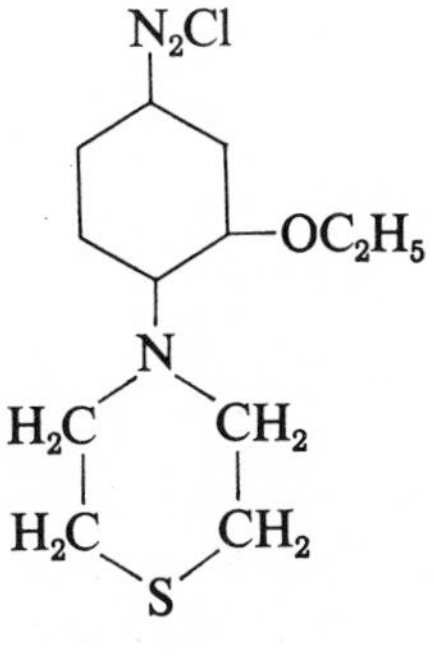

XLIX

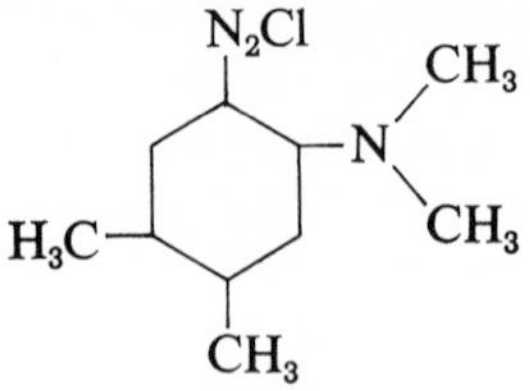

$$N_2Cl$$

(structure L: cyclohexene/benzene ring with N_2Cl, $N(CH_3)_2$, H_3C, and CH_3 substituents)

L

The aromatic nucleus can be substituted with alkyl, alkoxy, carboxy, acetoxy, aryl, and other groups. R_1 and R_2 can be a hydrogen, but usually are methyl or ethyl. These compounds are characterized by an intense color. Their absorption spectra are shifted towards the visible light, and thus they can be decomposed with incandescent light. Substitution meta to the diazo group increases the light sensitivity and lowers the stability. Because of their low stability their use is, however, very limited; 1-diazo-4,5-dimethyl-2-dimethylaminobenzene(L) may serve as an example.

Diazo-m-aminobenzenes. The general formula is:

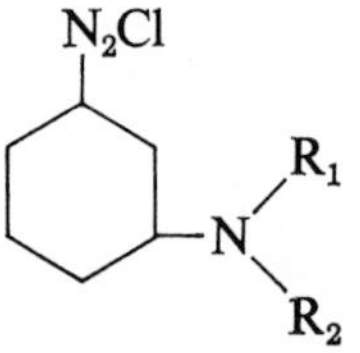

$$N_2Cl$$

(structure: benzene ring with N_2Cl and N with R_1 and R_2 substituents)

Diazo-*m*-aminobenzenes are an unimportant group of diazo compounds and, with few exceptions, are not used in diazotype processes.

Diazo o-amino esters have this formula:

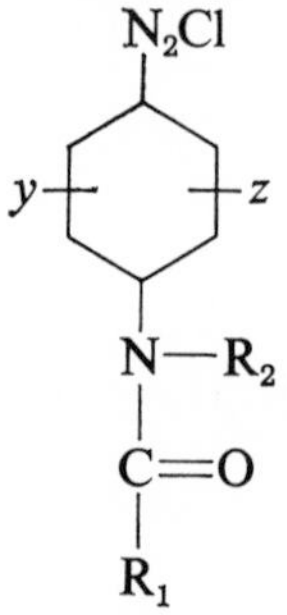

$$N_2Cl$$

(structure: benzene ring with N_2Cl, positions y and z, and $N-R_2$, $C=O$, R_1 substituents)

This general formula includes unsubstituted derivatives, monosubstituted (ortho or meta), disubstituted in positions 2 and 5, with alkoxy, halogen, or other groups; R_2 is usually a hydrogen and R_1 an alkyl, alkoxy, or aryl group (74). Here are included aminobenzoyl derivatives such as "blue salt" (75), which is a representative of this group; it is 1-diazo-2,5-

diethoxybenzoylaminobenzene(LI).   1-Diazo-2,5-dibutoxybenzoylamino-
benzene(LII) is of importance also.   They are used mainly in one-component papers.   Similar compounds were prepared by Werner (76), Leuch
(77), Jacobus and Bose (78), Johnston (79), and Mason and Norman (80).

One example of a compound in which R_1 is an alkoxy group is diazonium
sulfate of N-(4-amino-2,5-dibutoxyphenyl)ethylcarbamate(LIII), prepared
by Jacobus and Bose (81).

Related compounds are derivatives of diphenyl-(*a*) and naphthyl-(*b*)
p-amino esters:

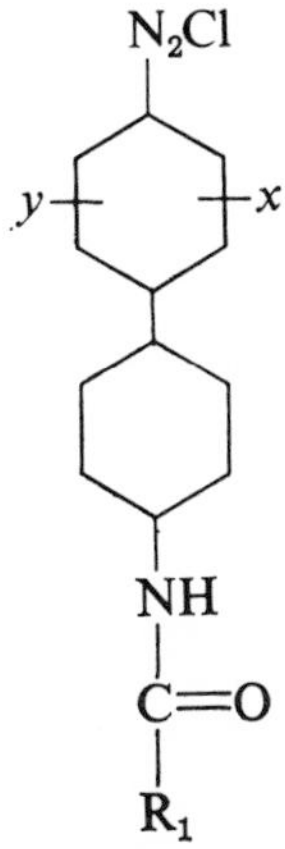

(*a*)

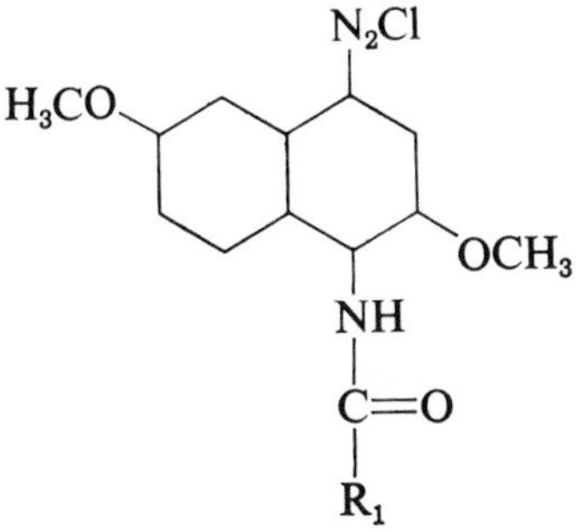

(*b*)

Diazo m-amino esters and Diazo o-amino esters.   Both groups are
unimportant for diazotype processes.

Diazo mercapto-benzenes.   These compounds have a mercapto group,
HS—, attached to the nucleus bearing the diazo group.   The mercapto
group can be in the ortho or meta position to the diazo group; however,
the para derivatives are more important; 1-diazo-4-ethylmercapto-2,5-
diethoxybenzene(LIV) was prepared by Werner (82).   1-Diazo-4-tolyl-
mercapto-2,5-diethoxybenzene(LV) is another example.   The ethoxy
group may be replaced with another alkoxy group; the tolyl radical may
be replaced with phenyl, benzyl, or an alkyl group (83).   Mason and
Norman (87) prepared a series of compounds corresponding to the general
formula

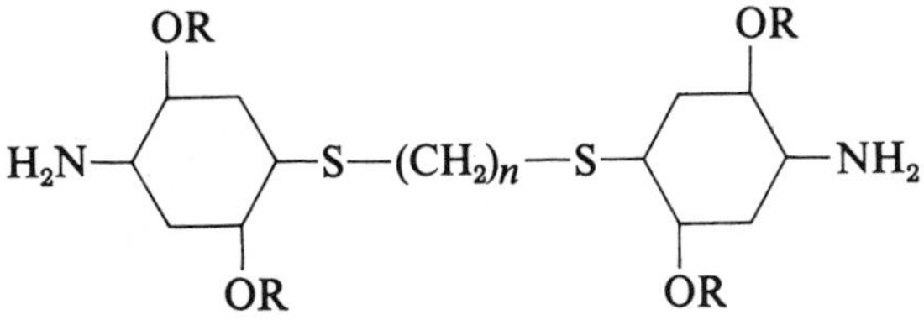

where R is a lower alkyl and *n* is 3 to 10; 1,5-bis-(2,5-diethoxy-4-amino-phenylthio)pentane is an example.

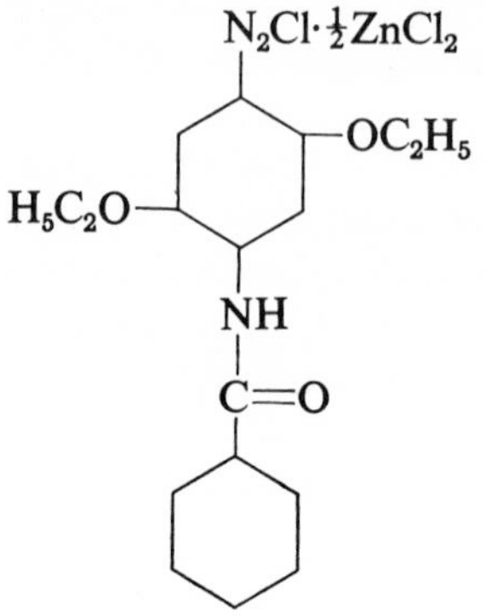

LI

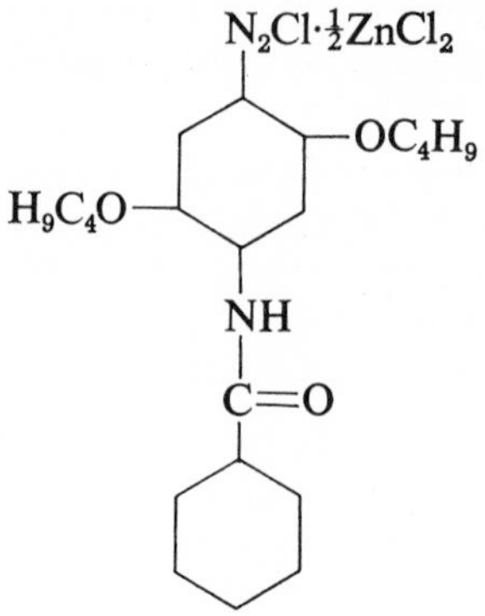

LII

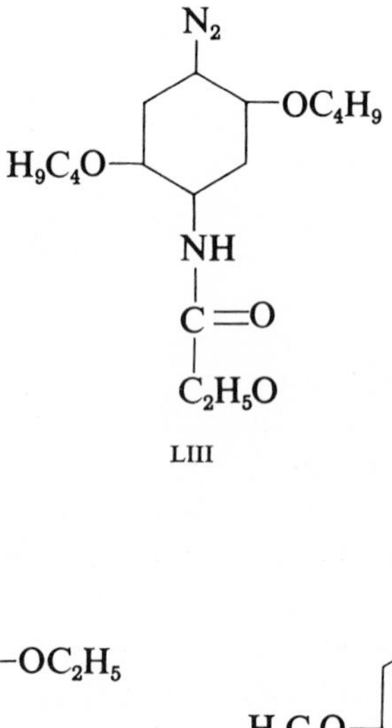

LIII

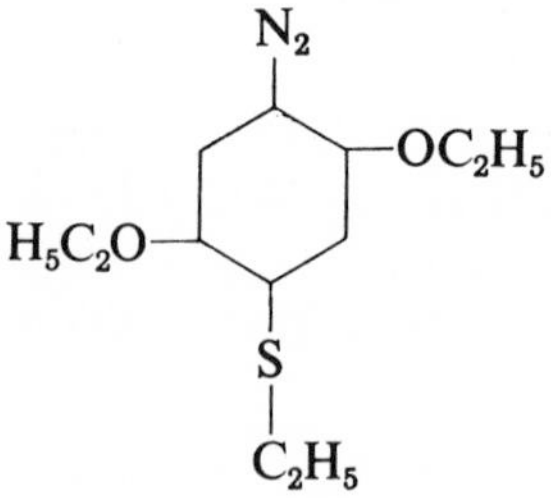

LIV

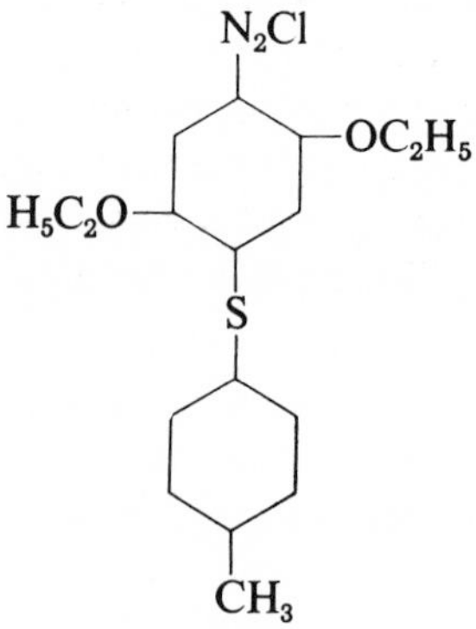

LV

6.3 COUPLING AND COUPLING COMPONENTS

A remarkable property of diazo compounds is their ability to combine with aromatic amines, phenols, phenol ethers, or aliphatic compounds containing active methylene groups to form colored oxyazo or aminoazo compounds known as azo dyes.

From the purely chemical view of color, the characteristic chromophore in azo dyes is the —N=N— link, which, in conjunction with auxochromes, is responsible for the light absorption and therefore for the color of the dyes. Auxochromes are, for example, the following groups: —OH, —OAlk, —NH$_2$, —NHAlk, —N(Alk)$_2$. The color is thus dependent on the constitution of the dye molecule. By making the molecule larger and more complex, the shade of the color is, in general, made deeper. An azo group conjugated with an ethylenic bond (—N=N—C=C—) produces yellow dyes, and conjugation with aromatic rings such as benzene and naphthalene causes progressive deepening of color. Thus, by coupling a diazonium salt with acetonitriles (85), yellow dyes are obtained and sepia and red dyes are produced with coupling components having a benzene ring. Similar naphthalene derivatives are maroon, violet, blue, and black. The nature, number, and position of the substituents influence the color of the azo dyes, and usually make the color deeper and more intense. The color of the azo dye is thus determined by the choice of both the diazo compound and the coupler. In many cases, fastness of the dyes to light, bleaching, and to acids, and their brightness can be improved by proper substitution, such as the introduction of one or more alkoxy groups into the molecule. By increasing the size of the alkyl or alkoxy group, not only can the color of the azo dye be darkened, but fastness to wet treatments is improved. This is of vital importance, especially in semiwet development methods. An exceptionally good example is dialkoxy derivatives of 1-diazo-4-morpholinoaminobenzenes. Although the 2,5-dimethoxy and diethoxy derivatives (70) are suitable only for dry diazotype process, the higher members of the series (72) are successfully used in semiwet process.

The mechanism of the coupling reaction is very important for an understanding of the azo dye formation, but since it has not yet been elucidated, there are differences in the interpretation of the known facts and the mechanism will be treated here only in outline (86).

The coupling between the diazo compound and the coupling component should be considered a reaction in which the azo group enters the nucleus of the azo component; the position which the azo group is taking depends mainly on the character of the substituents in the azo component, but the reactivity of the diazo compounds and the pH of the medium have their influence also.   As a rule, the azo group enters the para position in respect to the auxochromic group:

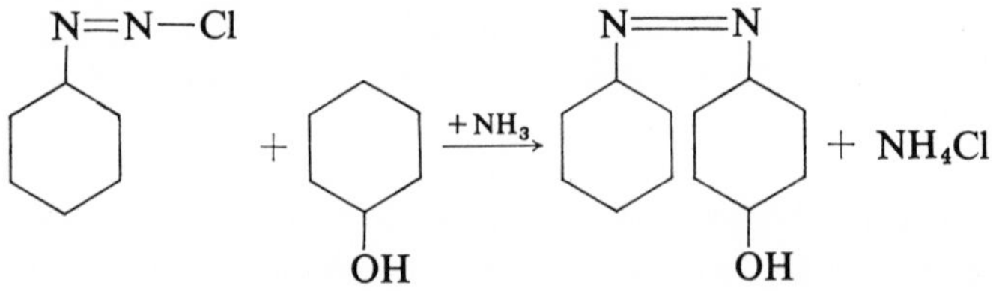

$$+ \text{NH}_4\text{Cl} \qquad (9)$$

when the para position is occupied, the azo group enters ortho position:

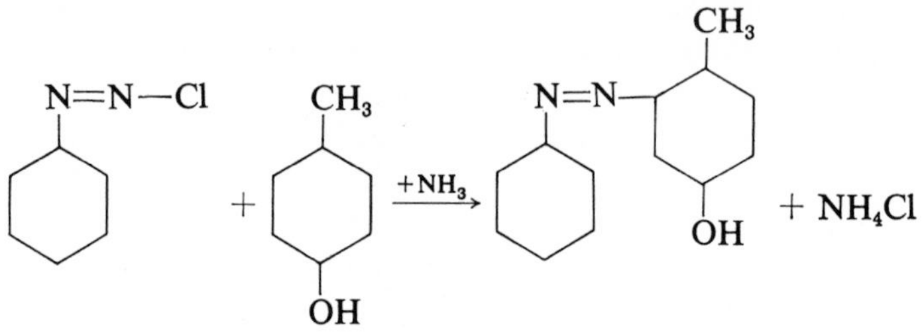

$$+ \text{NH}_4\text{Cl} \qquad (10)$$

Conant and Peterson (87), investigating the connection between acidity and rate of reaction, found the rate of coupling to be proportional to the hydroxyl-ion concentration in the range of pH of 4.5 to 9.15.   Thus, the rate of coupling is dependent on the pH of the system.   They also observed that in coupling with phenols and naphthols the rate increases by more than ten times when the pH is raised by one unit.   These results were confirmed twenty years later by Elofson and co-workers (88).

According to Conant and Peterson (87), the rate of coupling is governed by an acid-base equilibrium in one or the other of the reactants:

$$\text{ArN}_2{}^+ + \text{OH}^- \rightleftharpoons \text{ArN}_2\text{OH} \qquad (11)$$

$$\text{ArOH} \rightleftharpoons \text{ArO}^- + \text{H}^+ \qquad (12)$$

From this it would follow that the reaction is taking place between the undissociated diazo hydroxide and the undissociated phenol, and that the increase in alkalinity shifts the equilibrium of reaction (8) to the right.

In their kinetic study of the coupling of diazonium salts with aromatic amines, Wistar and Bartlett (89) concluded that the active components in the coupling reaction are the diazonium ion and the free amine or phenoxide ion; the positively charged diazonium ion is attracted to the negatively charged phenolate ion.

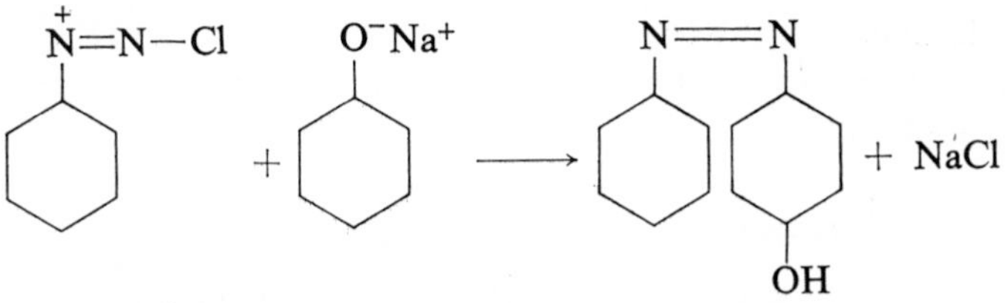

$$+ \; N\dot{a}Cl \quad (13)$$

The undissociated phenol is also capable of reacting, but the rate of coupling is extremely slow and practically undetectable (90).

Also, on the basis of electronic theories, it is expected that the positively charged diazonium ion is the active condensing agent rather than the diazo hydroxide. Hauser and Breslow (91) give an electronic mechanism for the azo-coupling between the diazonium cation and the arylamine as follows:

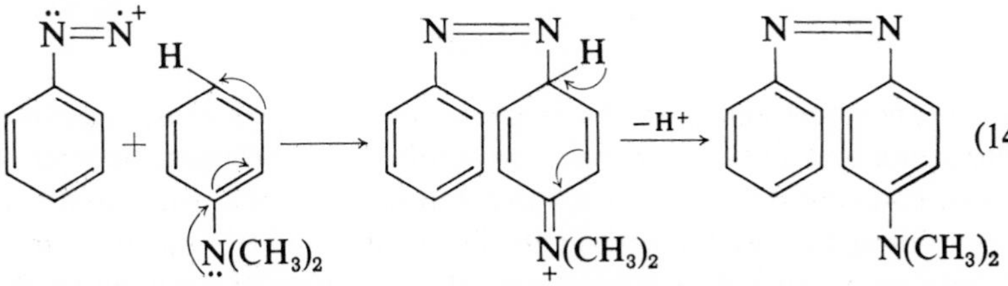

$$-H^+ \quad (14)$$

During the alkaline development, the dimethylanilinium ion is converted into the free amine, which is a stronger electron donating agent. Likewise, phenols are converted into phenoxide ions and naphthols into naphtholate ions (92). On the other hand, Hodgson (93), supported by the well-known fact that diazonium salts are converted in the presence of alkali into alkali diazotates, considers the diazo hydroxide as the reacting component.

The increasing alkalinity during the development also has an adverse effect on the azo dye formation. Diazonium compounds, in general, are very sensitive to the pH variations and undergo transformation as the alkalinity increases. First, diazonium hydroxide $(R—N\text{==}N)^+OH^-$ is formed, which later is transformed into syn-diazo hydroxide $R—N\text{==}N—OH$ and, at a still higher pH, into the diazotate ion $(R—N\text{==}N—O)^-$.

The reactions taking place between the diazonium salt and ammonia can be illustrated as follows:

1. Diazonium salts are strong electrolytes dissociated in solutions in ions $R—\overset{+}{N}\text{==}N$ and X^-; they are stable at acid pH, couple very slowly, and form diazonium hydroxide with alkalies:

$$\left[R—\overset{+}{\underset{N}{\overset{\|}{N}}} \right] X^- \xrightarrow{\text{alkali}} \left[R—\overset{+}{\underset{N}{\overset{\|}{N}}} \right] OH^- \quad (15)$$

2. Diazonium hydroxide is transformed almost immediately into slightly acid *syn*-diazohydroxide, which in the presence of alkalies forms salts—*syn*-diazotates:

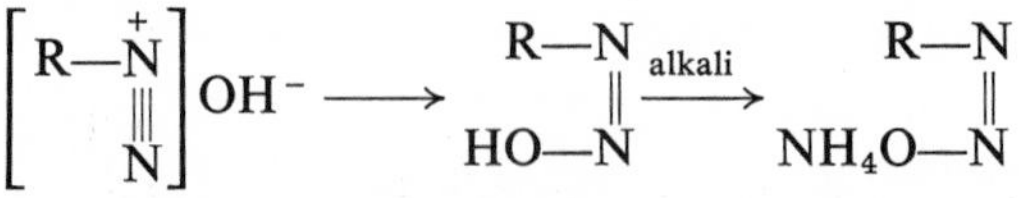

$$
\left[\begin{array}{c} R{-}\overset{+}{N} \\ \parallel\!\parallel \\ N \end{array} \right] OH^- \longrightarrow \begin{array}{c} R{-}N \\ \parallel \\ HO{-}N \end{array} \xrightarrow{\text{alkali}} \begin{array}{c} R{-}N \\ \parallel \\ NH_4O{-}N \end{array} \tag{16}
$$

Syn-diazotates are very unstable, couple very easily, and in water solutions again form *syn*-diazohydroxides.

3. At still higher pH, *syn*-diazotates form unreactive noncoupling anti-diazotates

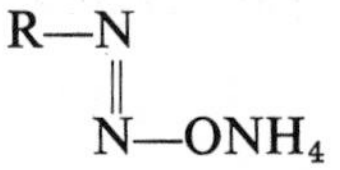

$$
\begin{array}{c} R{-}N \\ \parallel \\ N{-}ONH_4 \end{array}
$$

which are stable and have the character of very weak acids. Since the diazonium and diazo hydroxides are unstable, competition between the actual coupling reaction and the decomposition of the diazo compound exists during the development in alkaline media, and the maximum image density never reaches its theoretical value. A normal coupling reaction however, proceeds very rapidly and is completed before any noticeable decomposition of the diazonium salt takes place. The competition between the two reactions is more prominent and annoying in the thermal development of diazotype papers. For applications requiring a fast coupling reaction, a diazo compound having a diazonium ion concentration which decreases least with increasing pH, and a coupler which dissociates most into enolate ions at low pH conditions will be selected.

For the coupling reaction to proceed rapidly, the alkalinity of the system must be kept above a certain value, depending on the nature of the components. For every combination of a diazonium salt and a coupler there is an optimum pH range for coupling. The rate of coupling also depends on the electrochemical character of the diazonium group and on the electronegativity of the coupler. Introduction of electron-attracting groups in the diazonium ion favors the coupling and the relative rates for various substituents as given by Hammett (94) are:

Substituent	Relative Rate
p-NO$_2$	1300.0
p-SO$_3$	13.0
p-Br	13.0
None	1.0
p-CH$_3$	0.4
p-CH$_3$O	0.1

In general it can be said that diazo compounds having in their molecule negative substituents (—Cl,.—NO$_2$, =SO$_3$, etc.) are more reactive than those having positive groups (—CH$_3$, —NH$_2$, —N(CH$_3$)$_2$, etc.). The influence of negative and positive substituents is more pronounced when in ortho position in respect to diazo group, than in para or meta position.

The rate of coupling is also higher when the coupling components have many positive substituents; phloroglucinol, with three hydroxyl groups, reacts faster than resorcinol, with only two hydroxyl groups. Zollinger (95) correlated the reactivity of various combinations with the structure of the components and recognized that the effect of substituents upon the rate of the coupling reaction of differently substituted diazobenzenes follows Hammett's equation (96):

$$\log K = \log K^\circ + \delta\rho \tag{17}$$

where K = the rate constant for a substituted diazo compound;
  K° = the corresponding quantity for the unsubstituted diazo and the same coupling component;
  δ = a substituent constant depending upon the substituent;
  ρ = a reaction constant depending upon the temperature, the reaction, and the medium.

This correlation made it possible to calculate the reaction rates of more than 80 diazobenzenes, substituted differently in the meta or para position, with 2-naphtho-6-sulfonic acid and 2-naphthylamine-6-sulfonic acid.

The rate of coupling is also proportional to the water-vapor pressure in the vicinity of the reaction medium, and it was shown by Moraw and Munder (32) that, under certain conditions, no coupling takes place in the absence of moisture. Two-component diazotype papers, when thoroughly dry, cannot be developed with anhydrous ammonia.

The discovery of diazo compounds and their reactions had a tremendous impact on dye chemistry, and innumerable dyes have been prepared. Today, almost 2000 azo dyes, covering the whole spectrum, are recorded in the Color Index (97). Many hundreds of coupling components were synthesized in the last thirty years for diazotype papers but only a comparatively small number are used in the production of papers and films. This is because there are many requirements which the coupler has to meet besides forming a dye. First of all, a coupler suitable for diazotype papers must be white or colorless and remain colorless after printing. Any color change due to oxidation would result in discoloration of the print. Furthermore, the coupler must be soluble in water or another common solvent and not precipitate the diazo compound from the solution.

TABLE 6.2   Coupling Components for Diazotype Materials

Coupler	Formula	Soluble in	Color	Reference
Monohydric Phenols				
3-Acetamidophenol	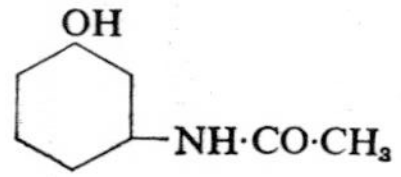	water	sepia	98
3-(N-3'-aminobenzoyl)aminophenol	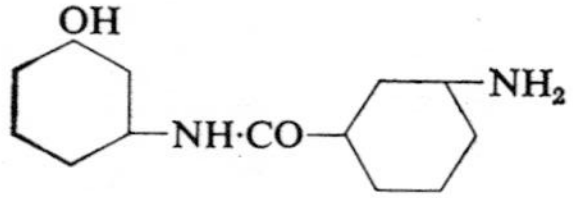	water	sepia	
3-(N-4'-aminobenzoyl)aminophenol	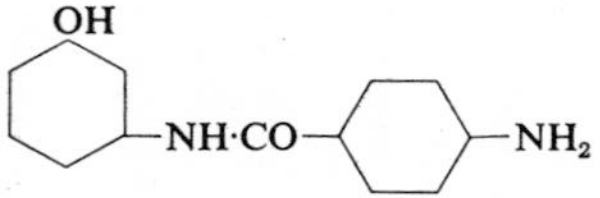	water	sepia	
3-Hydroxy-oxanilic acid	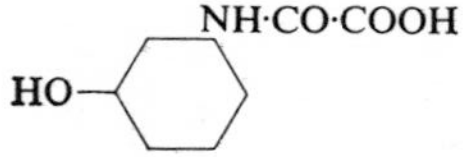	water	sepia	
3-(Aminophenylsulfonylamino)phenol	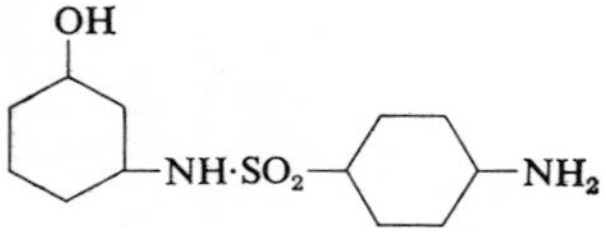	water	sepia	

Compound	Structure	Solvent	Colour	No.
Condensation product of *m*-Aminophenol and cyanuric chloride	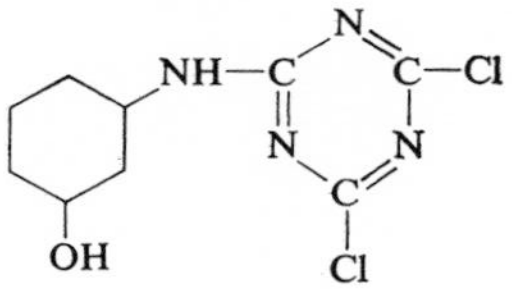	water	sepia	99
Urea of *m*-Aminophenol	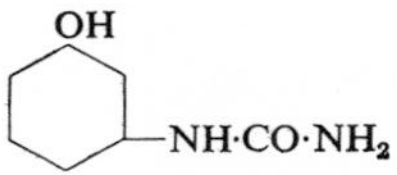		orange	
4-Hydroxyphenyl thiourea	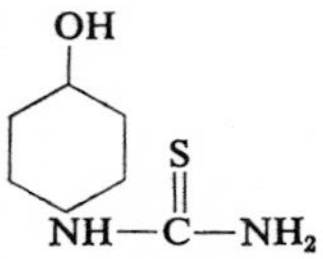	water	sepia	100
o-Hydroxyphenyl propionic acid	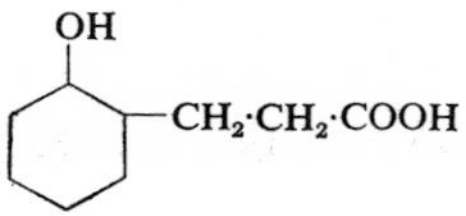		yellow	
1-Methyl-3-hydroxy-4-acetylamidobenzene	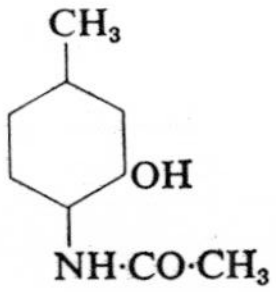			

Coupler	Formula	Soluble in	Color	Reference
m-Hydroxybenzyl alcohol	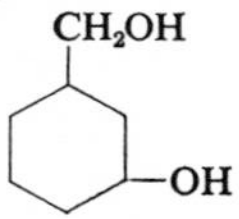 CH_2OH / OH (cyclohexene ring)	water	yellow	
2-Hydroxy-4-methylphenyl glutaric acid	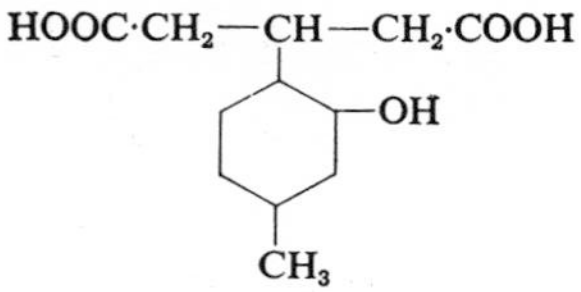 $HOOC \cdot CH_2 - CH - CH_2 COOH$, ring with OH and CH_3		yellow	
1-Dimethylaminomethyl-2-hydroxy-3,6-dimethylbenzene	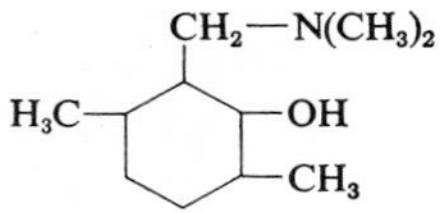 $CH_2 - N(CH_3)_2$, ring with OH, CH_3, H_3C		yellow-brown	
2,5-Dimethoxyphenol	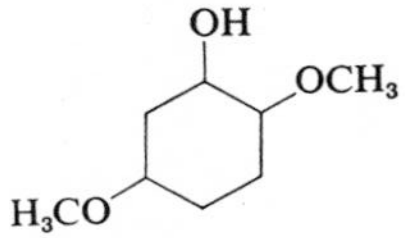 ring with OH, OCH_3, H_3CO	water	yellow-sepia	101
2,5-Diethoxyphenol	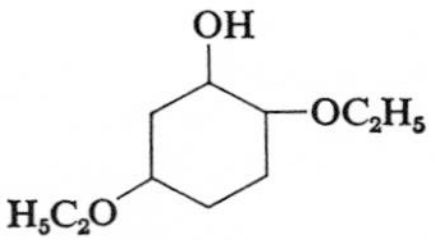 ring with OH, OC_2H_5, H_5C_2O	water	orange	

Compound	Structure	Solvent	Colour
3,5-Diethoxyphenol	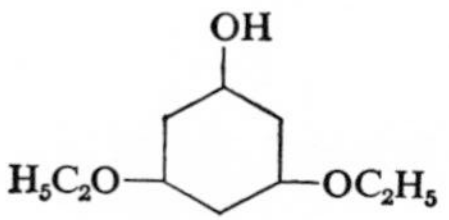		red
1-Methyl-3-hydroxy-4-acetyl-amidobenzene	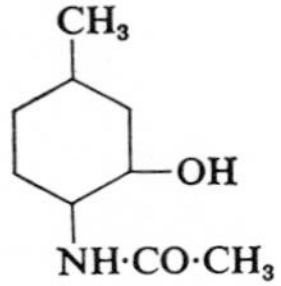		yellow
Catechol and its Derivatives			
1,2-Dihydroxybenzene	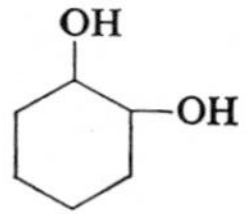	water	brown
Monohydroxyethylether of catechol	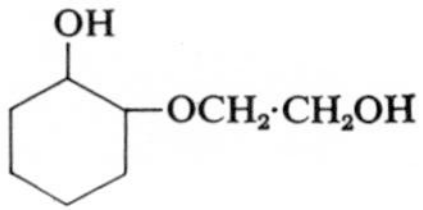	alcohol	yellow-brown
4,5-Dihydroxytoluene	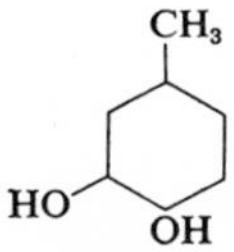		yellow-brown

Coupler	Formula	Soluble in	Color	Reference
Resorcinol and its Derivatives				
1,3-Dihydroxybenzene	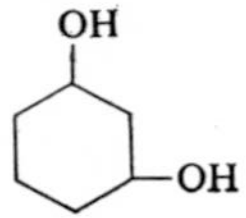	water	red-brown	
1,3-Dihydroxy-4-chlorobenzene	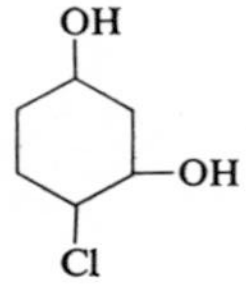	water	yellow-brown	
1,3-Dihydroxy-5-chlorobenzene	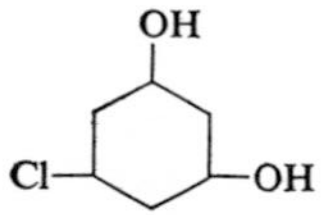		sepia	
4-Bromoresorcinol	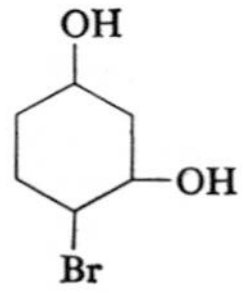	water	sepia	102
4-Iodoresorcinol	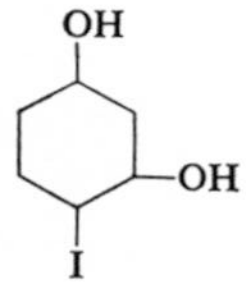	water	sepia	

Compound	Structure	Solvent	Colour	
4-Fluororesorcinol	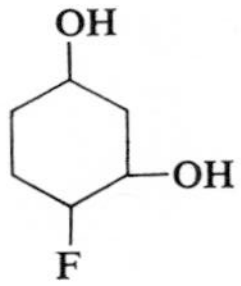	water	sepia	
2,4-Dichlororesorcinol	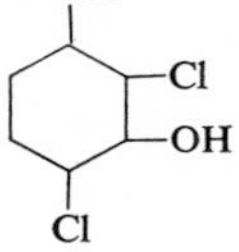		red-brown	
N-β-hydroxyethyl-α-resorcylamide	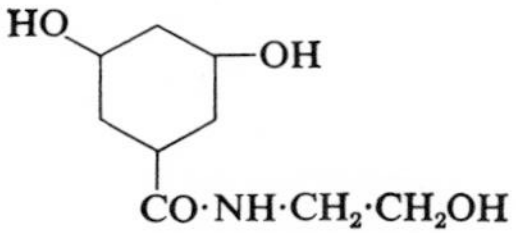	water	maroon	103
α-Resorcylamide	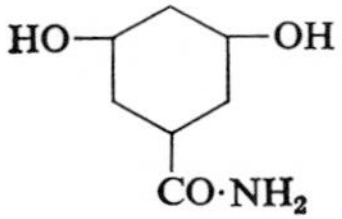	dimethyl-formamide	maroon	
N-phenyl-α-resorcylamide	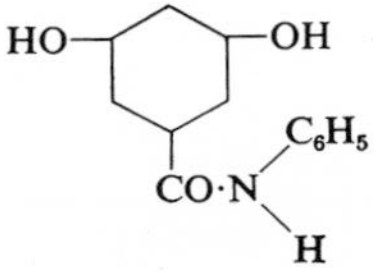	dimethyl-formamide	maroon	

Coupler	Formula	Soluble in	Color	Reference
Resorcinol monoacetate		water	sepia	104
Resorcinol monocarbazate		water	sepia	
Resorcinol monoethyl carbonate		water	sepia	
Resorcinol mono-N(β-aminoethyl) carbamate		water	sepia	
Resorcinol mono-N,N-diethyl carbamate		water	sepia	
Resorcinol-o-acetic acid	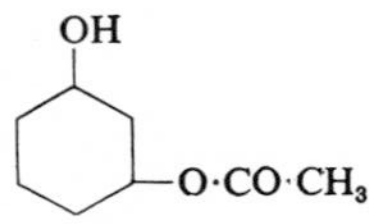 (structure: resorcinol with $O \cdot CO \cdot CH_3$ and OH)	water	yellow-brown	105
Resorcinol monomethylether	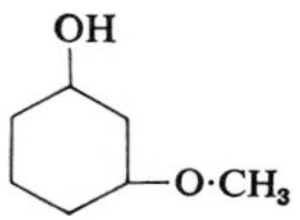 (structure: resorcinol with $O \cdot CH_3$ and OH)	water	sepia	
Diethylamidomonoethyl resorcinol ether	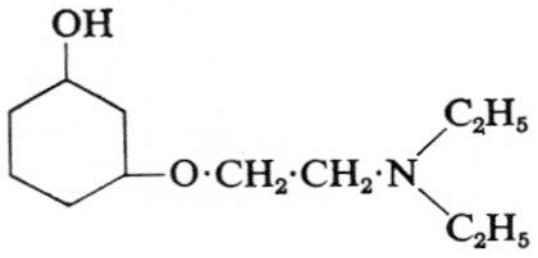 (structure: resorcinol with $O \cdot CH_2 \cdot CH_2 \cdot N(C_2H_5)(C_2H_5)$ and OH)			
1,3-Dihydroxybenzene-4,6-disulfonic acid	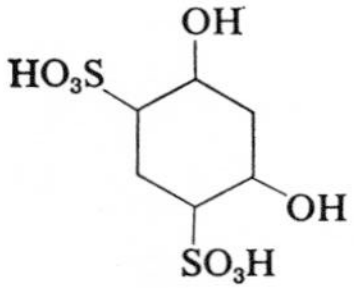 (structure: benzene with OH, OH, HO_3S, SO_3H)	water (Na-salt)	sepia	106

Compound	Structure	Solubility	Color
1,3-Dihydroxybenzene-6-chloro-4-sulfonic acid	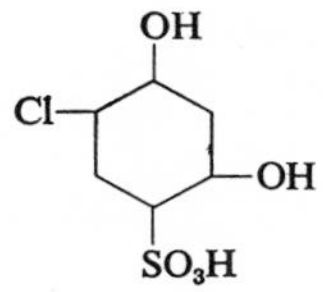	water (Na-salt)	
1,3-Dihydroxybenzene-6-methyl-4-sulfonic acid	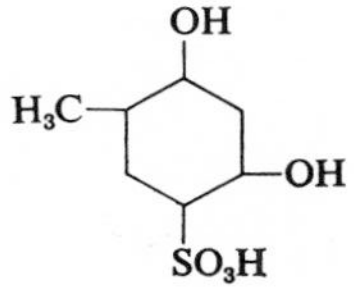	water (Na-salt)	
1,3-Dihydroxybenzene-5-sulfonic acid	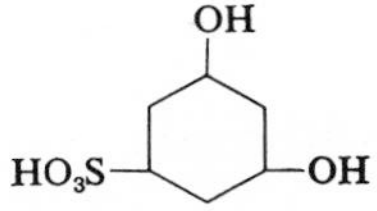	water (Na-salt)	sepia
3,5-Dihydroxytoluene	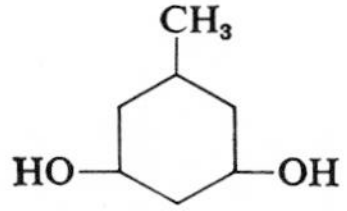		red-brown
2,6-Dihydroxytoluene	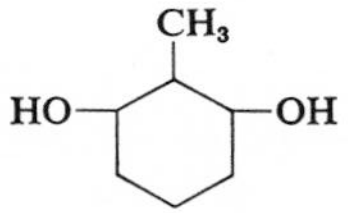		yellow-brown

Coupler	Formula	Soluble in	Color	Reference
1,2,4-Resorcylic acid methyl ester	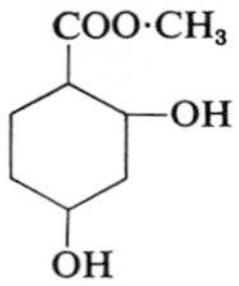 COO·CH₃, OH, OH (structure)		maroon	
1,3,5-Resorcylic acid ethanolamide	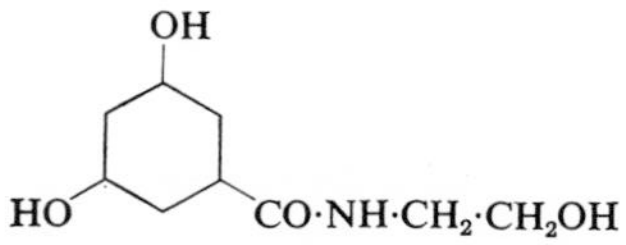 CO·NH·CH₂·CH₂OH, OH, HO (structure)	water	red-brown	
1,2,5-Resorcylic acid ethanolamide	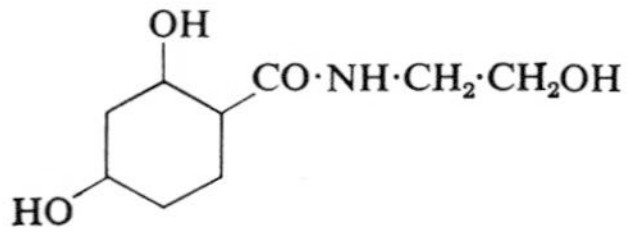 CO·NH·CH₂·CH₂OH, OH, HO (structure)		maroon	
1,3,5-Resorcylic acid anilide	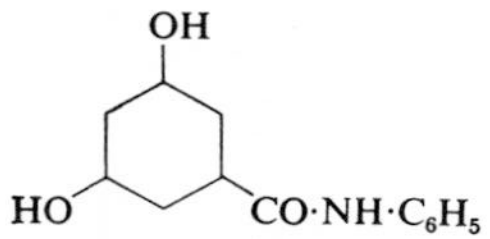 CO·NH·C₆H₅, OH, HO (structure)		red	
1,3,5-Resorcylic acid amide	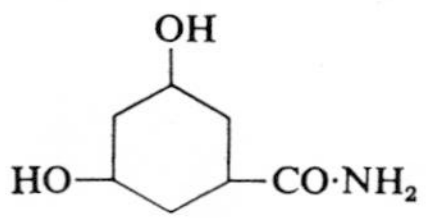 CO·NH₂, OH, HO (structure)		brown	

Name	Structure	Solvent	Colour	Ref.
4-Bromo-3,5-dihydroxybenzoic acid amide	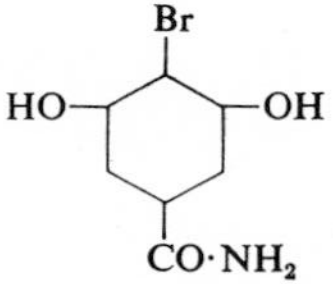 Br, OH, HO ring with CO·NH$_2$		maroon	
4-Chloro-3,5-dihydroxybenzoic acid amide	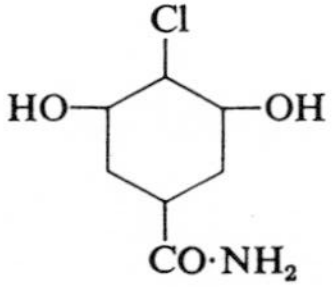 Cl, OH, HO ring with CO·NH$_2$		maroon	
3,5-Dihydroxybenzoic acid amide	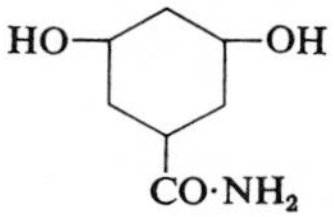 OH, HO ring with CO·NH$_2$			
m,m′-Trimethylene dioxydiphenol	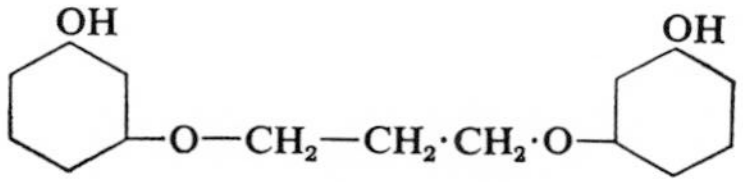 OH ring—O—CH$_2$·CH$_2$·CH$_2$·O—ring OH	water		
m,m′-1-Methyltrimethylene dioxydiphenol	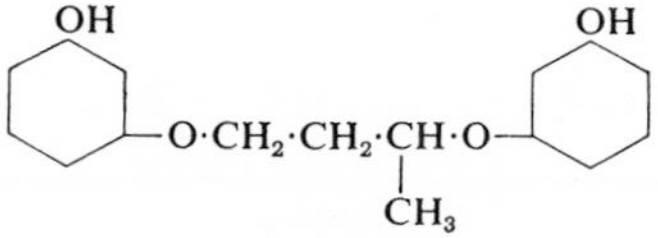 OH ring—O·CH$_2$·CH$_2$·CH·O—ring OH, CH$_3$			107

Coupler	Formula	Soluble in	Color	Reference
6,6'-Dimethyl-3,3'-trimethylene dioxydiphenol	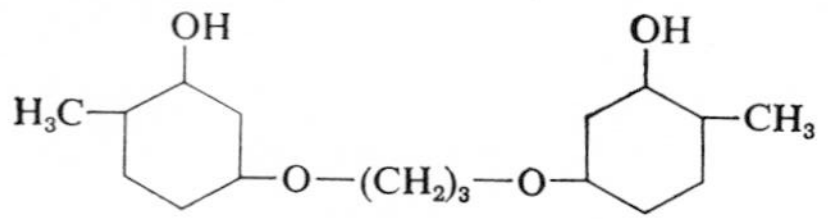			
m,m'-(p-Phenylene-dimethylenedioxy)-diphenol	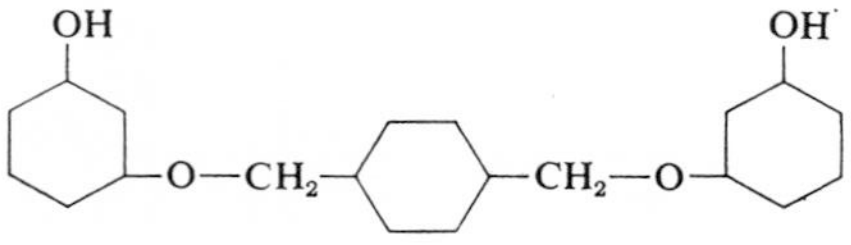			
6,6'-Dihexyl-3,3'-iso-propylidene dioxydiphenol	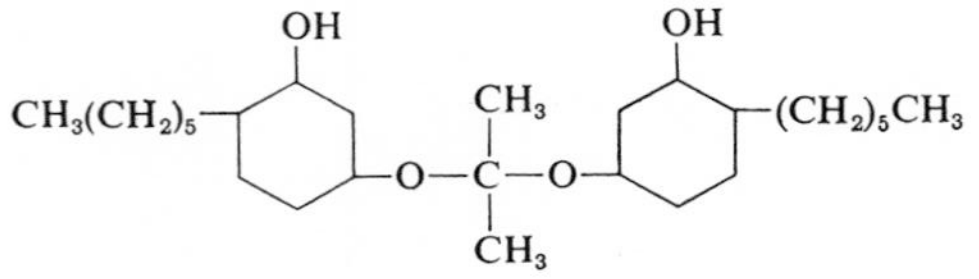			
Condensation Product of				
5-Aminoresorcinol and cyanuric chloride	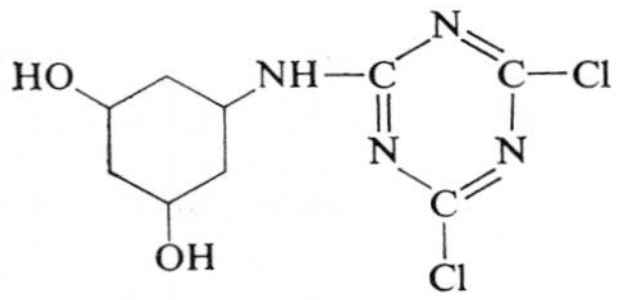		violet	99

Name	Structure	Solvent	Color	No.
Resorcinol and formaldehyde 4-Chlororesorcinol and acetaldehyde Resorcinol and arabinose	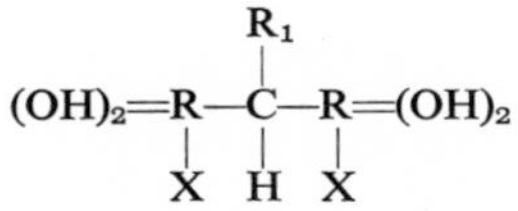 $(OH)_2=R-\underset{\underset{H}{\overset{\overset{R_1}{\mid}}{C}}}{}-R=(OH)_2$ $X \quad\quad X$ R = aryl R_1 = H or alkyl X = H, halogen, alkyl, etc.	water		108
Resorcinol and acetaldehyde	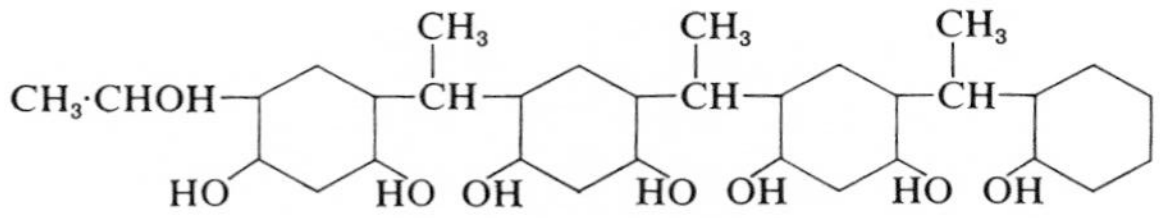 (structure)	water		109
Reaction Product of resorcinol and phosgen $n = 0, 1, 2, 3, \ldots$	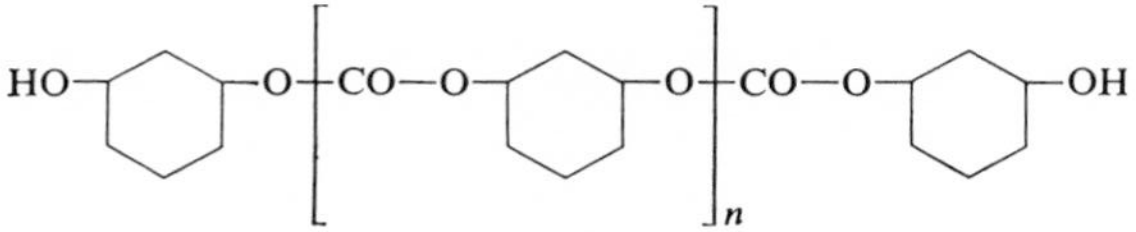 (structure)	water	sepia	110
Bis-(2,4-dihydroxyphenyl sulfide)	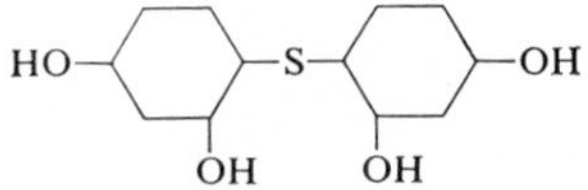 (structure)	water	yellow-brown	111
Bis-(2,4-dihydroxyphenyl sulfoxide)	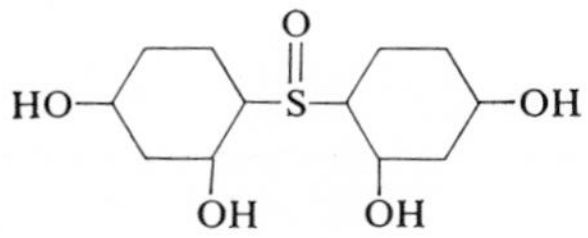 (structure)			

Coupler	Formula	Soluble in	Color	Reference
Hydroquinone Derivatives				
Hydroquinone monomethyl ether	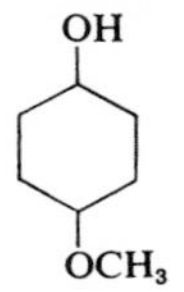 (structure)			
Trihydroxy-Benzenes				
Phloroglucinol	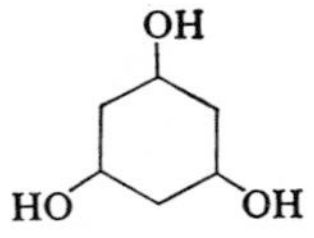 (structure)	water	brown-violet	112
Phloroglucinol monocarboxylic acid alkyl esters				
Condensation Product of Phloroglucinol and cyanuric chloride			blue	99
1,3,5-Trihydroxy-2-methylbenzene	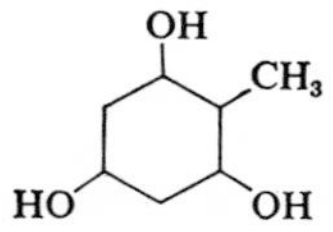 (structure)		red-brown	
Phloroglucinol monethyl ether	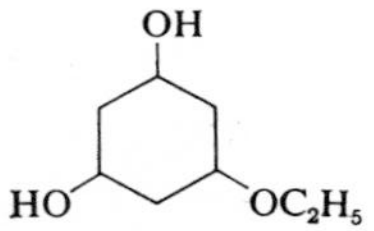 (structure)		red-violet	

Diphenyl Derivatives

Compound	Solvent	Color	No.
o-Hydroxydiphenyl	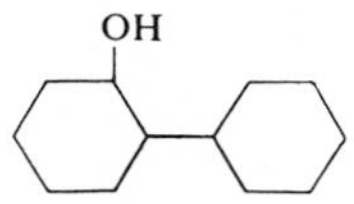	yellow-brown	113
3,3',5-Trihydroxydiphenyl	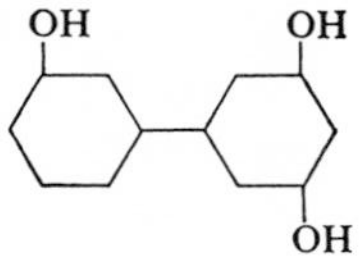 water	brown	
2,4,4'-Trihydroxydiphenyl	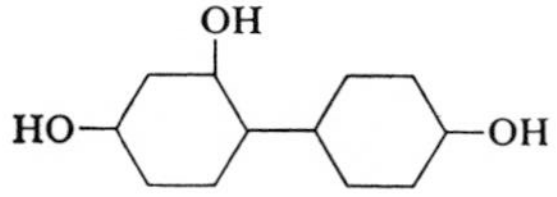	brown	
2,2',4,4'-Tetrahydroxydiphenyl	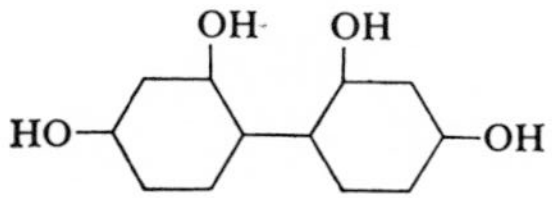 water	brown	114
3,3',5,5'-Tetrahydroxydiphenyl	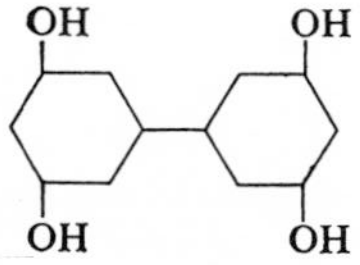 water	red-brown	115

Coupler	Formula	Soluble in	Color	Reference
4,4',6,6'-Tetrahydroxydiphenyl			brown	
Phloroglucide		ketones alcohols	violet-black	116
Naphthols				
1-Hydroxynaphthalene				
1-(3-Aminobenzamido)-7-naphthol		water	blue	117
2-(3-Aminobenzamido)-7-naphthol		water	sepia	
2-(4-Aminobenzamido)-7-naphthol		water	sepia	
2-(3-Aminobenzamido)-5-naphthol		water	sepia	
2-(4-Aminobenzamido)-5-naphthol		water	sepia	
1-(3-Aminobenzamido)-4-naphthol		water	blue	
1-Hydroxy-3-sulfanylnaphthalene			yellow	118

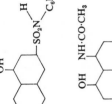

Compound	Structure	Solvent	Colour	
3-(N-phenylsulfanyl)-1-naphthol				
1-Acetylamido-2-naphthol-5-sulfonic acid				
2-Hydroxynaphthalene				
2-Hydroxynaphthalene-4-sulfonic acid		water (Na-salt)	red-brown	
2-Hydroxynaphthalene-6-sulfonic acid (Schaeffer salt)		water (Na-salt)	violet-brown	
2-Hydroxynaphthalene-3,6-disulfonic acid (**R**-salt)		water (Na-salt)	blue	122

Coupler	Formula	Soluble in	Color	Reference
2-Hydroxynaphthalene-6,8-disulfonic acid	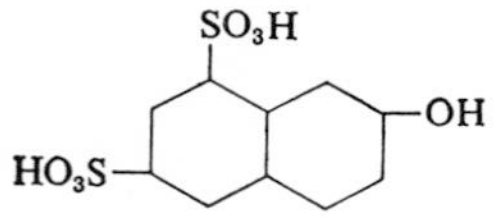 (structure: naphthalene with SO$_3$H, HO$_3$S, OH)	water (Na-salt)	red-brown	
2-Hydroxynaphthalene-7-sulfonic acid	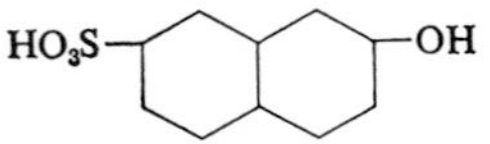 (structure: naphthalene with HO$_3$S, OH)		red-brown	
7-Hydroxynaphthalene-1-biguanidine-HCl	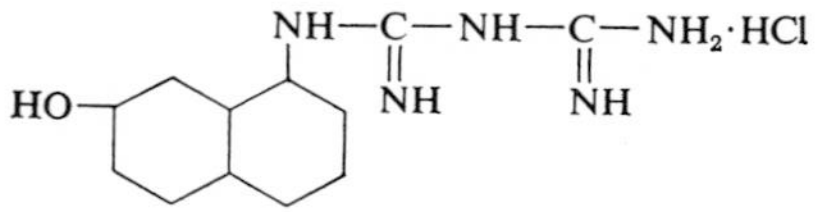 (structure: naphthalene with HO, NH–C(=NH)–NH–C(=NH)–NH$_2$·HCl)		violet	
2-Amino-5-hydroxynaphthalene-7-sulfonic acid monourea	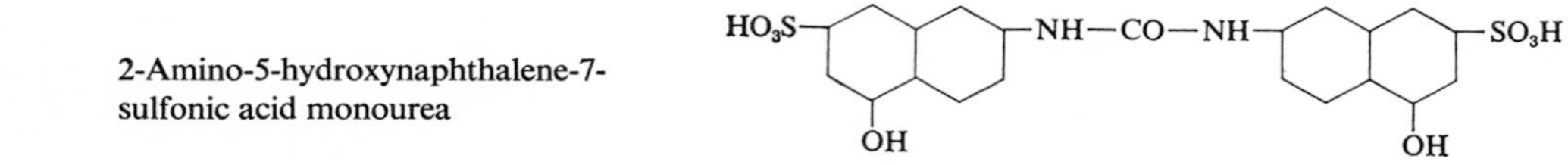 (structure: naphthalene with SO$_3$H, OH, HO$_3$S, NH–CO–NH)	water (Na-salt)	blue	
1-2',4'-Diamino-1'-2',3',4'-tetrahydro-1',3',5'-triazino-7-hydroxy-naphthalene	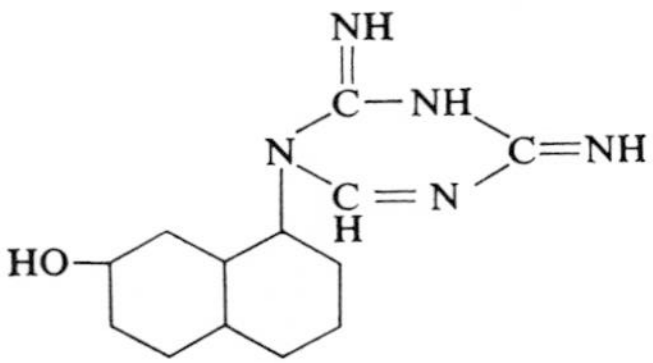 (structure: naphthalene with HO, triazine ring NH, C=NH, N=C(H)–N)		dark-violet	

Compound	Structure	Solvent	Color	Ref.
1-Methyl-ω-dimethylamino-2-hydroxynaphthalene	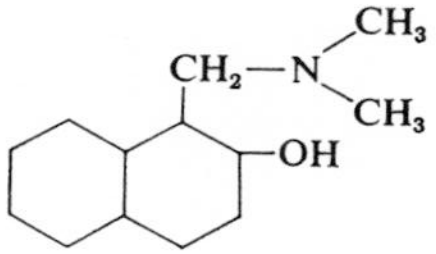	water		119
1-Methyl-ω-(methylmethylcarboxy-amino)-2-naphthol	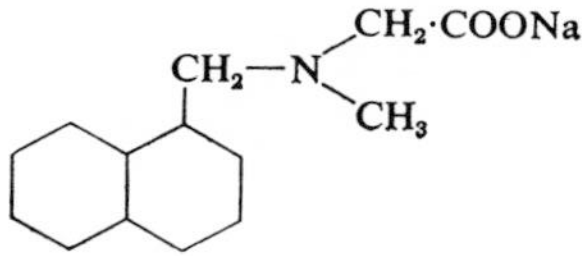	water		
Naphthoic Acid Derivatives				
2-Hydroxynaphthoic acid diethylene amide	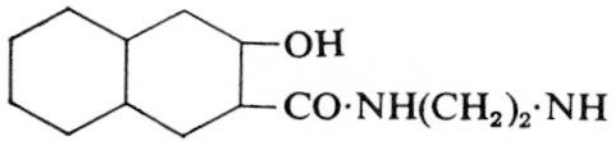		dark-violet	120
3-Hydroxy-2-naphthoic acid ethanolamide	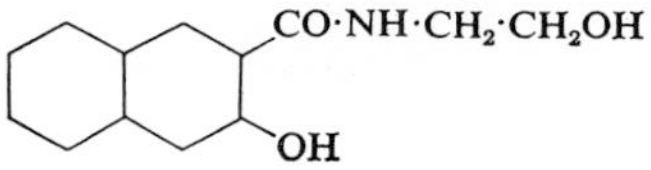		blue-violet	121
3-Hydroxy-2-naphthoic acid diethanolamide	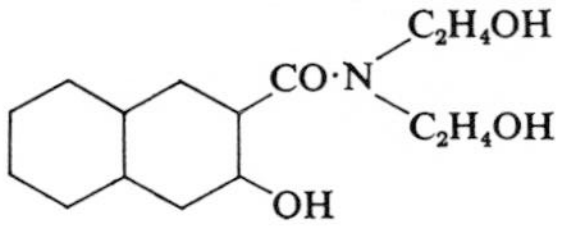	water	blue	
Dioxynaphthalene Derivatives				
2,3-Dihydroxynaphthalene	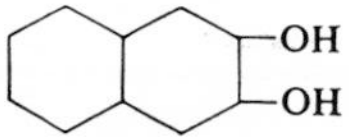		blue	122, 123

Coupler	Formula	Soluble in	Color	Reference
2,3-Dioxynaphthalene monooxyethyl ether	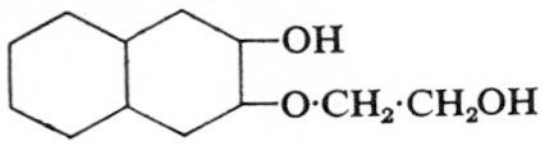 naphthalene with OH and $O{\cdot}CH_2{\cdot}CH_2OH$	water		
2,3-Dihydroxynaphthalene monoglycollic acid ether	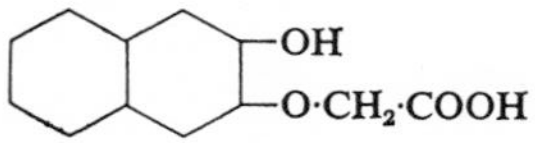 naphthalene with OH and $O{\cdot}CH_2{\cdot}COOH$		blue-black	
2,3-Dihydroxynaphthalene mono-N-dimethylamino(β)-ethyl ether	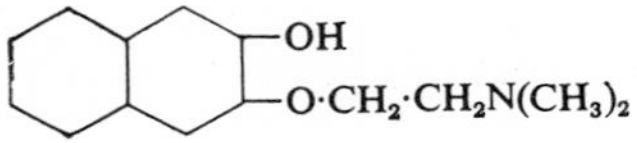 naphthalene with OH and $O{\cdot}CH_2{\cdot}CH_2N(CH_3)_2$	water	blue-black	
2,3-Dihydroxynaphthalene-6-sulfonic acid	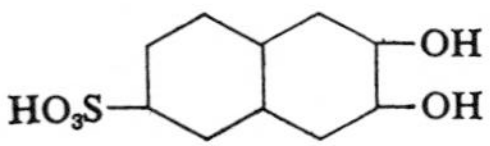 naphthalene with OH, OH and HO_3S	water (Na-salt)	blue	
2,7-Dihydroxynaphthalene	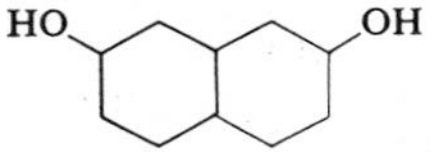 naphthalene with OH and HO		violet	124
2,8-Dihydroxynaphthalene-6-sulfonic acid	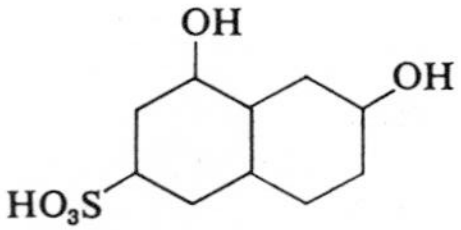 naphthalene with OH, OH and HO_3S	water (Na-salt)	blue	125

Compound	Solvent	Color	No.
2,8-Dihydroxynaphthalene-3,6-disulfonic acid	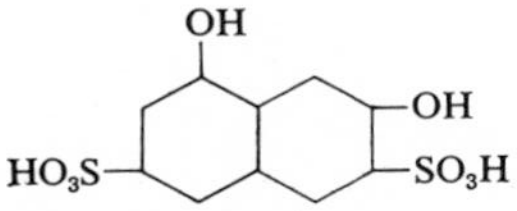 water (Na-salt)	blue	126
2,7-Dihydroxy-1-naphthalene-methane-sulfonic acid 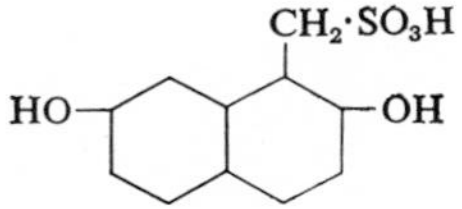		violet	
1,5-Dihydroxynaphthalene 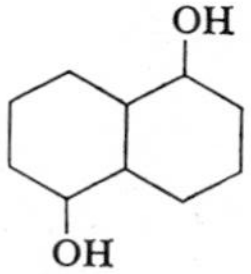			
1,6-Dihydroxynaphthalene-3-sulfonic acid	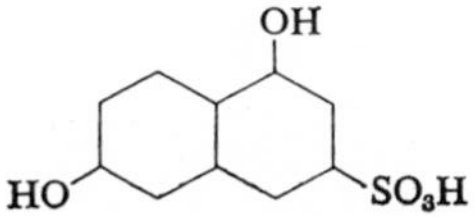 water (Na-salt)	blue-violet	127
2,7-Dihydroxynaphthalene-3,6-disulfonic acid	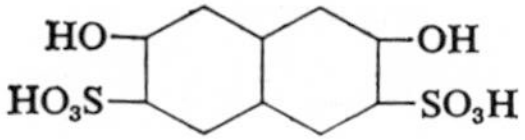 water (Na-salt)	blue	
2,7-Dihydroxynaphthalene-3-sulfonic acid	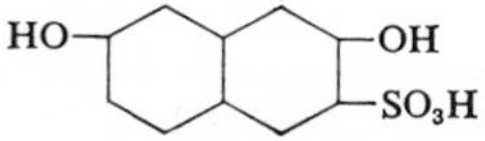 water (Na-salt)	maroon	

Coupler	Formula	Soluble in	Color	Reference
1,8-Dihydroxynaphthalene-3-sulfonic acid	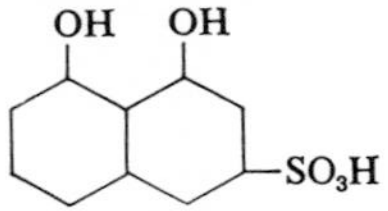	water (Na-salt)	blue	128
1-Hydroxy-8-aminonaphthalene-6-sulfonic acid	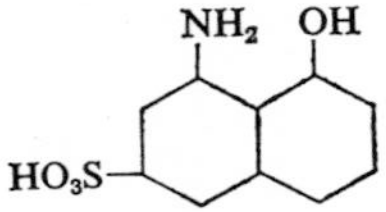	water (Na-salt)	blue	
Diketones				
5,5-Dimethyl-1,3-cyclohexanedione	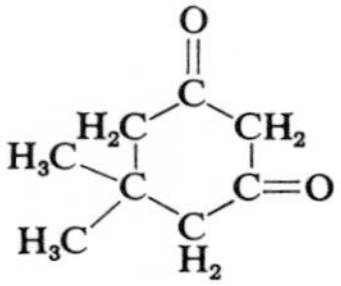	water acetone cellulose acetate	red	129
5-Methyl-5-ethyl-1,3-cyclohexanedione	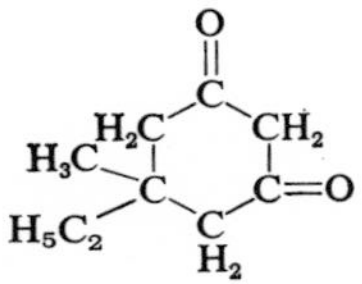	water acetone cellulose acetate	red	
2,2′-Butylidene-bis(5,5-dimethyl-1,3-cyclohexanedione)	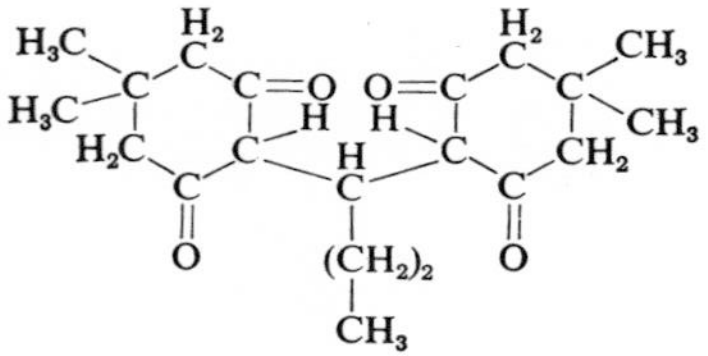	alcohol methyl cellulose acetate	red	130

Compound	Structure	Solvent	Colour	Ref
2,2'-Benzylidene-bis(5,5-dimethyl-1,3-cyclohexanedione)	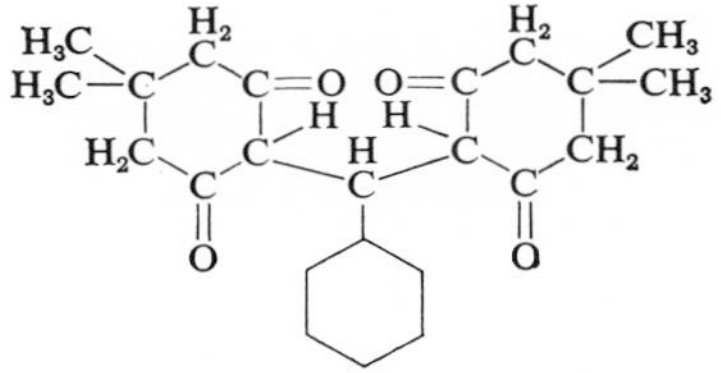 [structure]			
Acetonitriles				
Acetylacetonitrile	$CH_3 \cdot CO \cdot CH_2 \cdot CN$	water	yellow	85
Cyanoacetic acid	$HOOC \cdot CH_2 \cdot CN$	water / isopropanol	yellow	
p-Nitrobenzyl cyanide	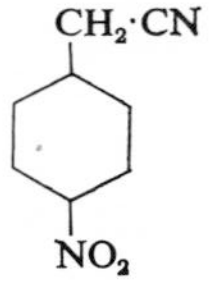 [structure] $CH_2 \cdot CN$, NO_2	water / isopropanol	yellow	
Cyanacetylamides				
Cyanacetanilide	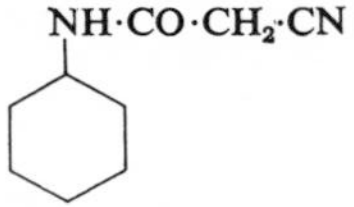 $NH \cdot CO \cdot CH_2 \cdot CN$ [structure]	water	sepia	131
Cyanacetylurea	$CN\!-\!CH_2 \cdot CO \cdot NH\!-\!\underset{\parallel O}{C}\!-\!NH_2$	water	sepia	
Cyanacetylbenzylamide	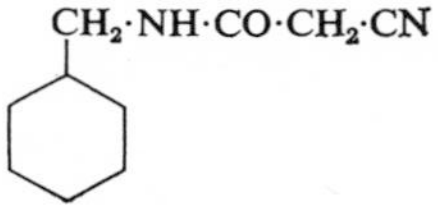 $CH_2 \cdot NH \cdot CO \cdot CH_2 \cdot CN$ [structure]	water	sepia	

Coupler	Formula	Soluble in	Color	Reference
Cyanacetamide	$CN \cdot CH_2 \cdot CO \cdot NH_2$	water	sepia	
Cyanacetylthiourea	$CN \cdot CH_2CO \cdot NH \cdot C \cdot NH_2$ $\parallel$ S	water	sepia	
Sulfonamides				
4-(Acetoacetamido)benzene sulfonamide	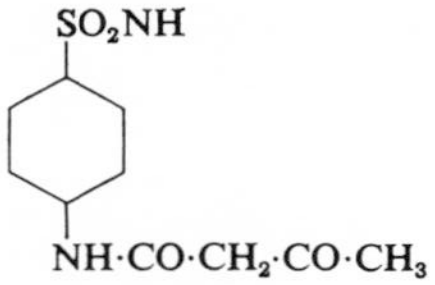 SO_2NH —⬡— $NH \cdot CO \cdot CH_2 \cdot CO \cdot CH_3$	water	orange	132
3-(3'Methyl-pyrazolone-5)benzene sulfonamide	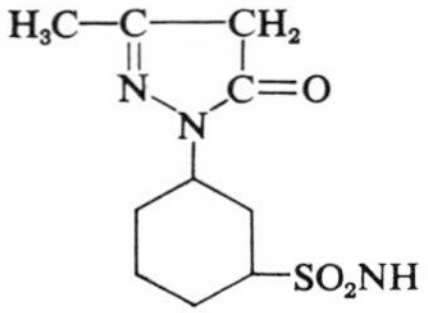 $H_3C-C \underset{N}{\overset{CH_2}{\diagdown}} C=O$, N—⬡—$SO_2NH$	water	red	
6,7-Dihydroxynaphthalene-2-(N-β-hydroxyethyl sulfonamide)	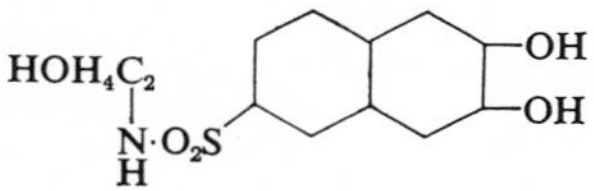 HOH_4C_2 $\underset{H}{N} \cdot O_2S$ — naphthalene — OH OH	water	blue	
Acetoacetic Acid Derivatives				
Acetoacetanilide	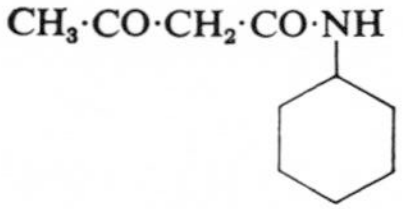 $CH_3 \cdot CO \cdot CH_2 \cdot CO \cdot NH$ —⬡	water	yellow	

Name	Structure	Solvent	Colour	Ref
Cyclohexylacetoacetic acid amide	NH·CO·CH₂·CO·CH₃ (cyclohexyl)	water	black (with phloroglucinol)	133
Acetoacetic acid benzylamide Acetoacetic acid-*o*-methylanilide Acetoacetic acid-α-aminopyridine 7-Hydroxynaphthalene-1-acetoacetic acid amide N-(β-acetoacetaminoethyl)acetoacetamide	CH₂·NH·CO·CH₂·CO·CH₃ CH₂·NH·CO·CH₂·CO·CH₃	water	orange-sepia	134
N,N'-(acetoacetyliminodiethylene)-diacetoacetamide	CH₂·CH₂·NH·CO·CH₂·CO·CH₃ N·CO·CH₂·CO·CH₃ CH₂·CH₂·NH·CO·CH₂·CO·CH₃	water	orange-sepia	
N,N-ethylene-bis-acetoacetamide	CH·NH·CO·CH₂·CO·CH₃ CH·NH·CO·CH₂·CO·CH₃			
2,4-Diacetoacetaminobenzene sulfonic acid	SO₃H / NH·CO·CH₂·CO·CH₃ / NH·CO·CH₂·CO·CH₃	water	sepia	135

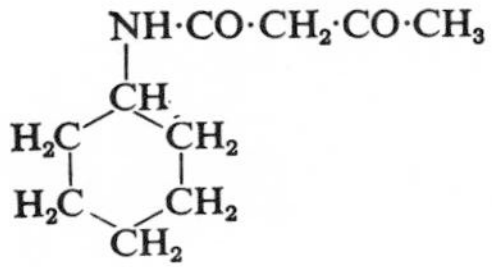

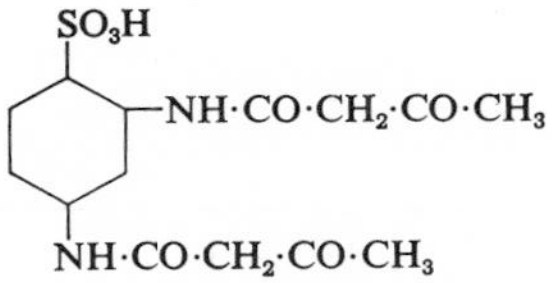

Coupler	Formula	Soluble in	Color	Reference
2,4-Diacetoacetaminotoluene	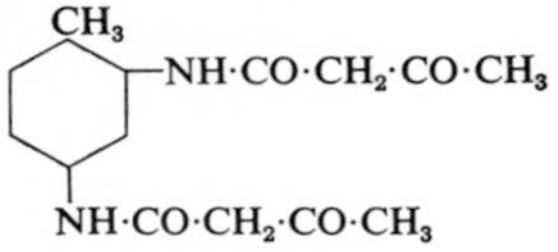	water	sepia	
Diacetoacetyl piperazine	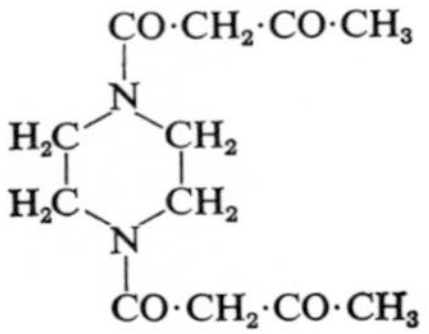	water	sepia	
Alkylmalonamates				136
Methyl malonamate	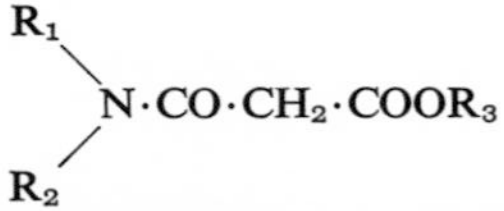 $R_1, R_2 = H$, alkyl, hydroxyalkyl, aralkyl $R_3 =$ alkyl or aryl	water	yellow	
Ethyl malonamate		water	yellow	
Pyronones				137
6-Ethylpyronone	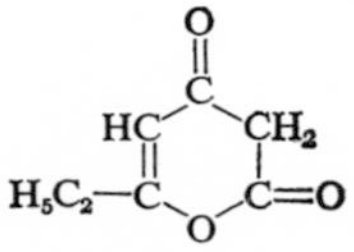	water	blue	
6-Methylpyronone		water	violet	
6-Propylpyronone		water	blue	
6-Phenylpyronone		water	blue	

Hydroxy Pyridones

Name		Solvent	Color	Ref
6-Methyl-4-hydroxy-2(1) pyridone	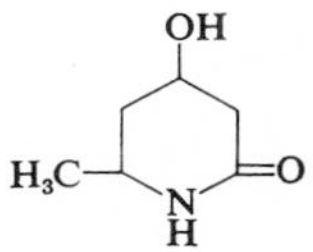	water	purple	138
6-Ethyl-4-hydroxy-1-methyl-2(1) pyridone	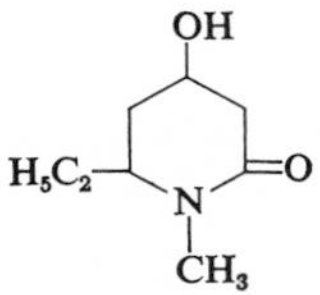	dimethyl formamide	purple	
6-Isobutyl-4-hydroxy-2(-1) pyridone	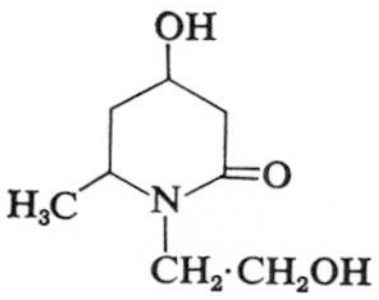	water		
6-Methyl-4-hydroxy-1-(β-hydroxy)-ethyl-2(1)-pyridone	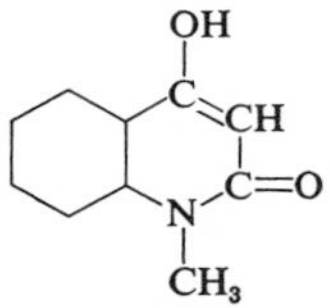	water		

4-Oxyquinolones

Name	Solvent	Color	Ref
N-methyl-4-oxyquinolone-2	water	violet	139
4-Oxyquinolone-2	water	blue	
N-methoxyphenyl-4-oxyquinolone-2	water	blue	
N-hydroxyethyl[4-oxyquinolone-2	water	maroon	

Coupler	Formula	Soluble in	Color	Reference
Pyrazolones				
3-Methyl-5-pyrazolone	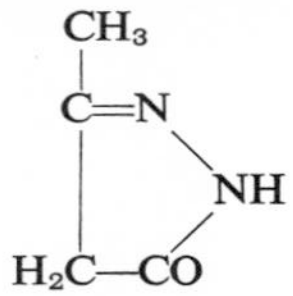			
1-Phenyl-3-methyl-5-pyrazolone	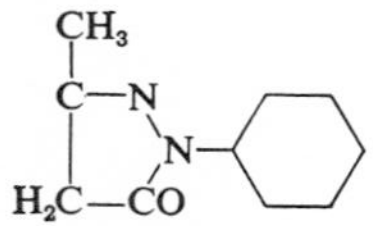		red	
1-*p*-Sulfophenyl-3-methyl-5-pyrazolone	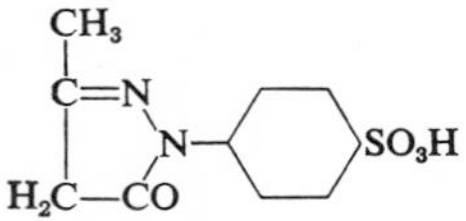		red	
Thiophene Derivatives				140
3-Hydroxythiophene-5-carboxylic acid		H_2O	blue	
3-Hydroxythiophene-5-carboxylic acid amide		H_2O	blue-violet	
3-Hydroxythiophene-5-carboxylic acid anilide		isopropanol	blue	
3-Hydroxythiophene-5-carboxylic acid methylester		H_2O	blue-violet	
2-Hydroxy-5-methylthiophene-4-carboxylic acid		H_2O	red	

Others

Compound	Structure	Solvent	Colour	No.
Thiobarbituric acid	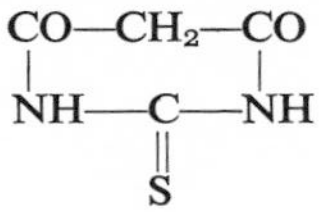 CO—CH$_2$—CO ; NH—C(=S)—NH	water	blue	141
Quaternary salts of 2-methyl-6-methoxybenzoselenazole		water	violet	142
Ethyl acetoacetate	CH$_3$—C(=O)—CH$_2$CO·OC$_2$H$_5$	water	sepia	143
Na-ethyl oxalacetate	NaO·OC—CO—CH$_2$CO·OC$_2$H$_5$	water	brown-black	
Ethyl cyanacetate	CN—CH$_2$CO·OC$_2$H$_5$	water	sepia	
N-acetonyl-pyridinium chloride		water	magenta	144
5-Oxo-1-phenyl-2-pyrazoline-3-carboxylic acid		water	red	145
6-Hydroxy-1,3-benzoxathiol-2-one		water	red-brown	
5-Chloro-6-hydroxy-1,3-benzoxathiol-2-one		water	red-brown	146
4-Hydroxy-2-methylbenzimidazole	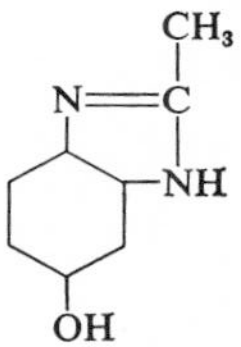	water	maroon	147
7-Hydroxynaphtho-1',2',4,5-imidazole	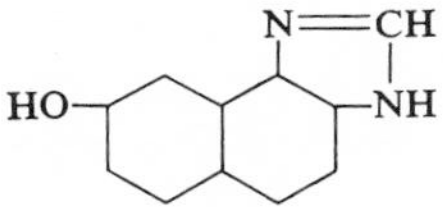		red-brown	148

Coupler	Formula	Soluble in	Color	Reference
2,5-Dimethyl-4-morpholinomethyl-phenol	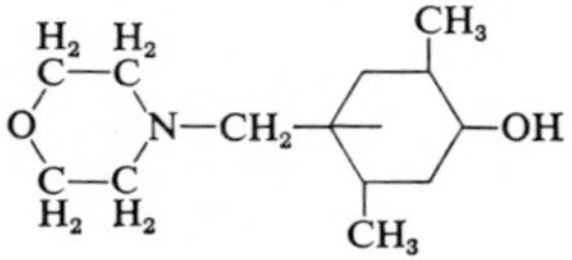		yellow-green	149
2-Methyl-5-isopropyl-4-morpholino-methylphenol				
3-Methyl-6-isopropyl-4-morpholino-methylphenol				
3-Methyl-6-ethyl-4-morpholinomethyl-phenol				
1-Morpholinoacetylamino-7-naphthol	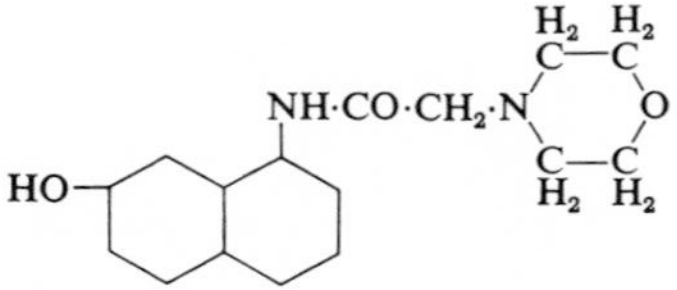	water	blue	150
7-Methyl-4-hydroxybenzotriazole	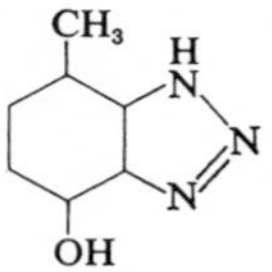	water	blue-violet	151

It should not interfere with the diazo decomposition by light and should not absorb actinic radiation. It is also required that the coupling energy be as high as possible and produce a dye of intense color.

After the Second World War, a wealth of information on the couplers synthesized by Kalle A.G. became available through *FIAT Report* 813. As mentioned already in connection with diazo compounds, this information was systematically tabulated by Landau (43).

In Table 6.2 the coupling components used in diazotype materials are divided into several groups according to their structures. Included are important couplers and representative couplers introduced after World War II. For more information, the reader is referred to the references cited here and to *FIAT Report* 813.

6.4 POSITIVE PROCESSES

6.4a *Principle*

All diazonium salts are, to a greater or lesser degree, affected by ultra-violet light and are decomposed under the formation of a nitrogen mole-cule, an acid, and a colorless phenolic compound (152,153,154):

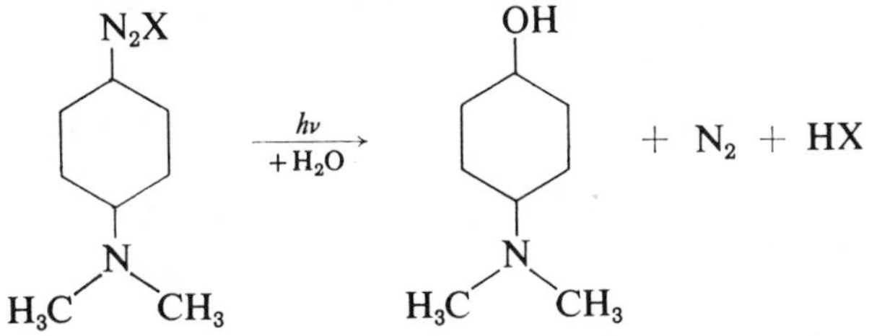

$$+ N_2 + HX \qquad (18)$$

In a dry state, where the possibility of the formation of an ionized diazonium salt is reduced, an aryl cation is formed which reacts with the chloride anion to form a halobenzene (155):

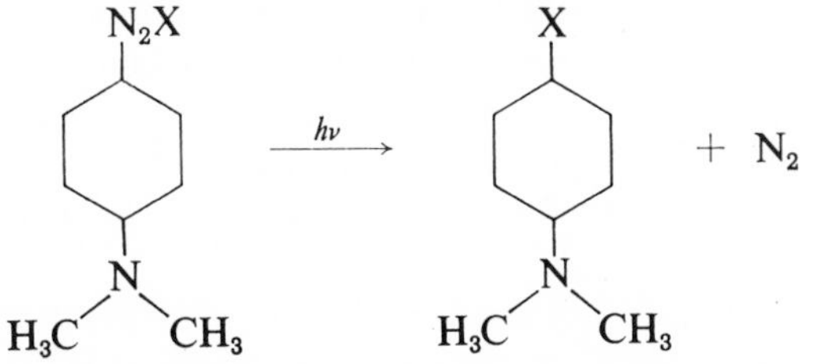

$$+ N_2 \qquad (19)$$

The formation of small quantities of more complex products, such as diphenyl, was reported by Crossley, Kienle, and Benbrook (5).

That part of the diazo coating which is unprotected from the ultraviolet radiation by the image of the original will become a colorless substance incapable of coupling to form a dye.   But the unaffected diazo compound which remains in those parts where the light has not acted is able to form an azo dyestuff with the coupling component when subjected to an alkaline medium.   Thus, wherever there was an opaque line on the original there is now a dye-line on the print.

If we take *p*-dimethylaminobenzene diazonium chloride as the diazo compound, and the sodium salt of 2,3-dihydroxynaphthalene-6-sulfonic acid as the coupling component, the following reaction takes place:

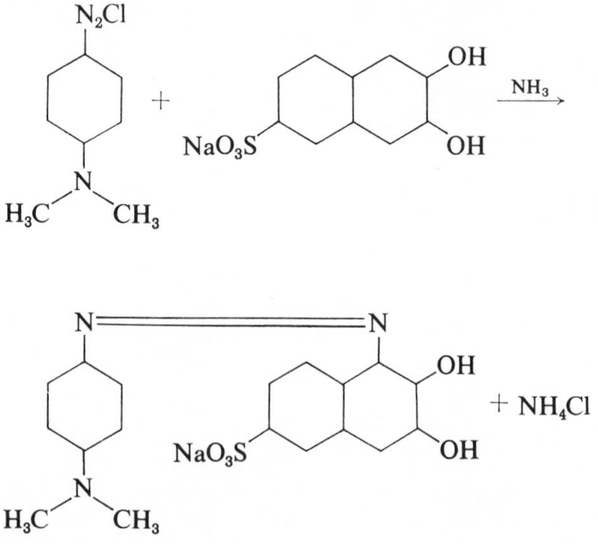

$$(20)$$

To prevent azo-dye formation prior to exposure and development an organic acid or a salt having an acid reaction is added to the diazo-coupler combination.   By immersing the paper in an alkaline medium after the exposure the acid is neutralized and coupling is brought about, producing the image.   The phenolic compound which remains after the light decomposition of the diazo compound in the exposed area is incapable of combining with the coupling component and, because it is colorless, it forms a white background for the reproduction.   The image obtained is, therefore, a positive copy of the original.

Although credit for producing the first positive print goes to Green, Cross, and Bevan (156), Andresen (157), Shoen (158), and Ruff and Stein (159), commercial application was made possible only after the introduction of diazo oxides, such as naphthalene-2,1-diazo-oxide-4-

sulfonic acid (*a*) and naphthalene-1,2-diazo-oxide-4-sulfonic acid (*b*) and their halogen or nitro derivatives by Kögel and Neuenhaus (160,161).

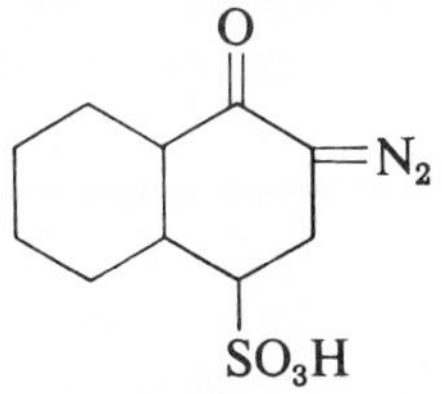

(*a*) 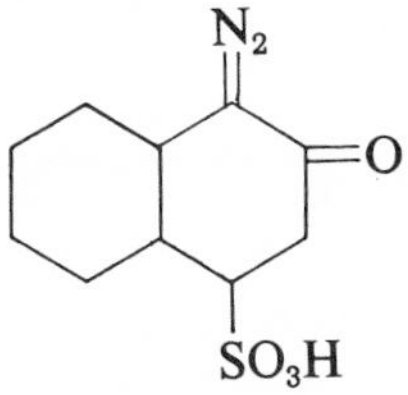   (*b*)

Diazo oxides are strongly yellow-colored compounds having the diazo group attached to one carbon atom and the oxygen attached to a neighboring carbon atom of the same six carbon ring. They are in an ortho position to each other. The diazo oxides, also called diazo phenols or quinone diazides, are formed by the action of nitrous acid on *o*- and *p*-aminophenols. They are sparingly soluble in water, are soluble in nonpolar solvents, are stable, and are slow coupling. In the course of photolysis, the hexagonal aromatic nucleus, to which the diazo nitrogen and the oxygen are attached, is transformed to cyclopentadiencarboxylic acid (162):

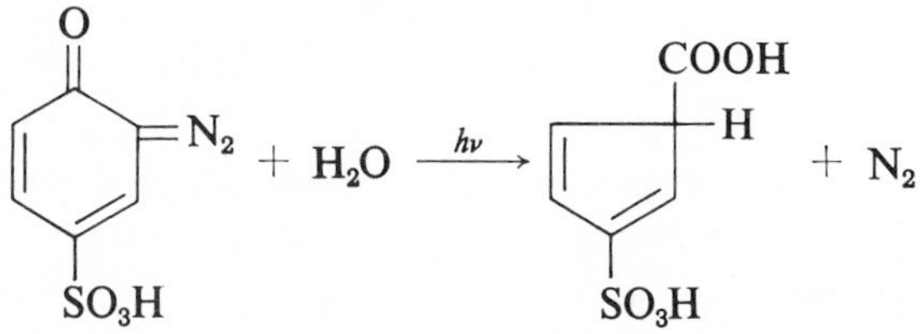

$$+ \ H_2O \ \xrightarrow{h\nu} \quad + \ N_2 \qquad (21)$$

Diazo oxides were used almost exclusively for sensitizing positive-working diazotype papers, but, because of the exceptionally long developing time required, they were soon replaced with dialkylaminobenzene diazonium salts. Another disadvantage of diazo-oxide sensitized papers was the background discoloration of the prints, which is due to the reaction with their photolysis products, forming a colored azo compound (*c*):

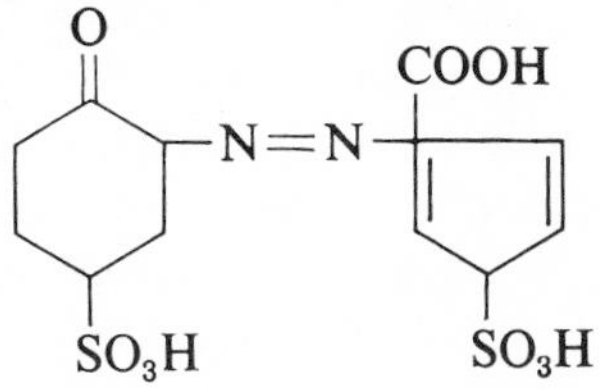

(*c*)

In the original "Ozalid" process introduced by Kalle A.G. in 1923, the diazo oxides were applied along with resorcinol, phloroglucinol, or methylphenylpyrazolone in near molecular proportions on a paper support and, after drying and exposure, the image was developed either by treating the layer with a solution of an alkali or by exposure to an atmosphere of ammonia 10 to 15 minutes. Since diazo oxides do not couple except when the ring has been opened by alkali, the stability of these papers was good. Later on the industry was forced to sell papers with poorer shelf life because of the demand for papers capable of being developed within a few seconds. In 1925 Schmidt and Krieger (163) disclosed the use of *o*- and *p*-aminodiazo compounds such as *p*-dimethylamino-benzene diazonium chloride (*d*) and *p*-diethylaminobenzene diazonium chloride (*e*).

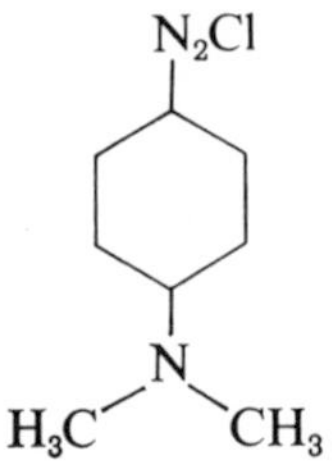

(*d*) 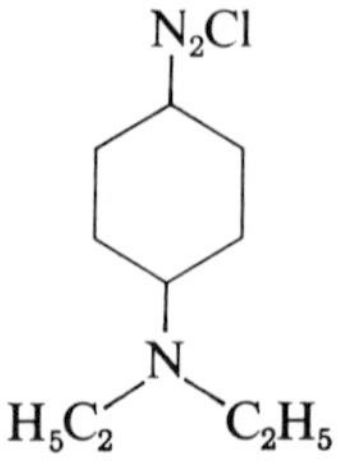   (*e*)

These compounds almost completely replaced diazo oxides recommended by Kögel, and they belong, up to the present time, among the few diazo compounds intensively used in positive two-component papers.

Positive diazotype prints from positive originals can also be obtained, as was shown by Schmidt and co-workers (164), by using diazo compounds which are stable in an acid solution, but which, in the presence of alkali, are capable of coupling directly with themselves without being subjected to the action of light. Thus, after exposure to light, which decomposes the nonimage areas, and development in ammonia, a positive copy is obtained. For this process, suitable diazo compounds contain at least one hydroxy or amino group situated in a nucleus other than that containing the diazo group. This substitution gives the molecule the property of an azo component. These diazo compounds are, for instance, produced from the aminohydroxynaphthalenes, such as 1-amino-8-hydroxynaphthalene-3,6-sulfonic acid (H-acid) (*f*); 2-amino-5-hydroxy-naphthalene-7-sulfonic acid (J-acid) (*g*); or 1'-amino-4'-piperidyl-3'-benzoyl-1-amino-8-hydroxynaphthalene-3,6-disulfonic acid (*h*).

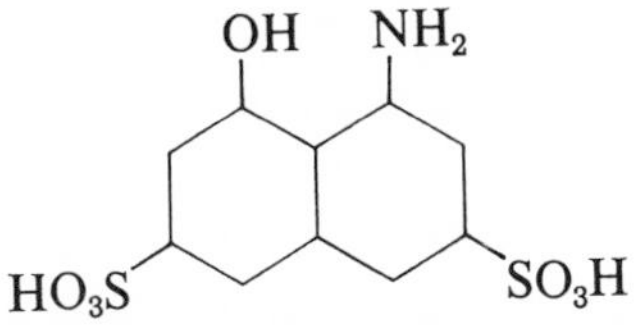

(f)

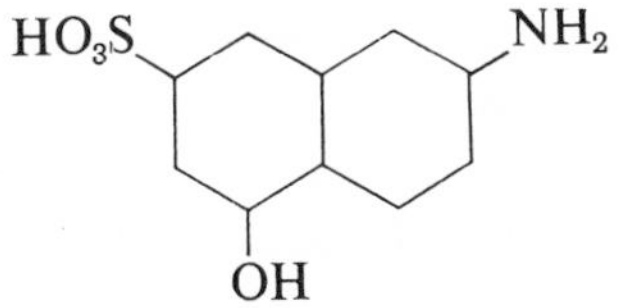

(g)

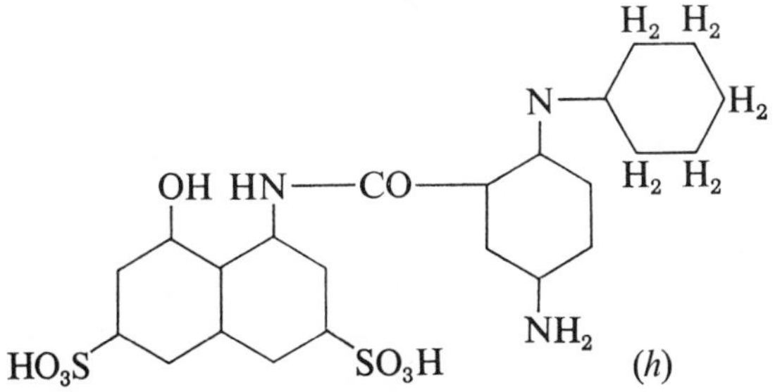

(h)

6.4b Dry Development

At the present time, positive-working diazotype papers are developed by two methods after being exposed. In the two-component system in which the coated paper contains both the aromatic diazo compound and the coupler necessary to produce the dye image, the image is developed by treating the exposed paper with ammonia plus water vapor in the developing section of an automatic printing and processing equipment. To stimulate the dissociation of ammonia so that more gas is liberated from diluted aqua ammonia, the addition of hydrogen peroxide was recommended (165). For improved developing efficiency, the ratio of water vapor and ammonia gas is kept constant by thermostatic control (166). The developing apparatus successively performs the two operations of exposure and development by transporting the original and the light-sensitive material in superposed relation, with the help of an endless belt conveyor (167), through separate exposure and development chambers. The conveyor belt has, preferably, a deep rib on its inside surface (168) which runs in grooves in the transport rollers. Modern machines are very easy to operate and are designed so that the only work required is the introduction of the transparent original and sensitized sheet into the machine at the feeding point; this pair is then carried around a revolving glass cylinder in the center of which is a high-pressure mercury-vapor lamp furnishing radiation of wavelength 360 to 420 mμ. Exposure of individual copies can be controlled by means of a photoelectric cell which measures the amount of light passing through the diazo coating as photolysis proceeds, in order to determine the completion of the process (169). In using the combination of an actinically fluorescent mercury-vapor lamp as the light source and diazotype material sensitized with a 1-diazo-4-alkylbenzylamino-3-alkoxybenzene, the progress of the bleaching of the yellow diazotype surface can easily be observed visually and the endpoint of the exposure determined (170). If the exposure is carried out in the light of a nonfluorescent mercury-vapor lamp, the sharp endpoint cannot be observed.

During the exposure, the translucent original and the sensitized sheet are in firm contact, which can be improved further by applying an electrostatic charge to the surface of the original (171).

The developed print is delivered either at the front or at the rear of the machine (172). In some more recent models, the feeding operation is made automatic by means of a suction device which lifts master sheets from a stack and feeds them, one by one, into the machine where they are paired with the sensitized paper (173,174). Machines designed for reproduction of large engineering drawings are able to handle continuous lengths of sensitized paper stored in a lightproof housing (175); the rolls are cut into appropriate size in a cutting station (176) and are fed with the originals into the exposure chamber.

After the exposure, the original is separated from the exposed sheet by a vacuum device (177,178) and discharged from the machine. The exposed paper is then carried on a moving blanket, belt, or banks of endless coiled springs (179) over a perforated metal surface of a developer tank containing ammonia fumes. The perforated surface through which developing vapor reaches the prints is covered in some copying machines by a perforated slip screen, which can be easily released and withdrawn to facilitate cleaning (180). To reduce the friction as the exposed sheet slides over the surface of the tank, the perforated top can be coated with a layer of polytetrafluorethylene, which has a very low coefficient of friction (181,182). Aqueous ammonia is pumped from a storage bottle and the flow is automatically controlled according to the processing speed of the machine. It can also be controlled manually to allow for other variables (183). A design of the plunger pump system is described in another patent (184).

Some machines are designed so that the prints pass across the ammonia vaporizing chamber on an endless flexible and perforated belt, which can run outside or, in order to avoid the heat and gas losses, inside the vapor chamber (185). In other designs, the exposed sheet is passed through the evaporating chamber by means of cylindrical guides (186) or by cylindrical tubes (187).

The ammonia vapor is produced by heating aqueous ammonia in the evaporating chamber by means of an electric heating element. To insure uniform distribution of the ammonia gas, the liquid ammonia is fed into the evaporating chamber through a valve and nozzle, and is ejected under pressure into the developing portion of the machine (188). Any surplus of ammonia is removed and recovered through a drain pipe located in the developing tray, so that the liquid cannot accumulate (189,190). The escape of ammonia vapor from the copying machine is avoided by a number of devices designed for this purpose (191,192,193). To prevent condensation of the ammonia vapor, which would cause wrinkling of the prints and smearing of the images, additional heating devices are provided within the upper part of the developing chamber, or, the perforated surface through which the developing gas acts on the sensitized layer is heated (194). In order to speed up development, the sensitized sheet can be preheated before it enters the developing chamber (195,196); this arrangement is especially useful for development of diazotype papers containing several couplers. Another heater arrangement which uniformly heats the surface of the light-sensitive material during its entire travel across the perforated plate, and which evaporates just the right amount of ammonia for proper development, was suggested by von Meister (197,198).

During the entire image-reproduction process the copy sheet is kept dry, which is a great advantage. Because of this advantage, ammonia development is used, almost exclusively, for the reproduction of engineering drawings, and, more recently, has also found application in the growing field of office documentation.

6.4c Semiwet Development

In the one-component system promoted by L. van der Grinten (199,200), the exposure of sensitized material is the same as that described for two-component systems. The sensitized sheet contains only the aromatic diazo compound and some other substances, and the coupling component is applied to the surface of the exposed print in a developing solution. The developing solution is usually made slightly alkaline with sodium carbonate, phosphate, or acetate, in order to neutralize the acid present in the light-sensitive layer and enable the formation of the azo dye. In order to lower the tendency of the developed prints to discolor, it was recommended that borax be added to the developing solution (201); the solubility of borax can be enhanced by the addition of sorbitol, glucose, or gluconic acid (202).

In some cases, for example, when 2,5,4'-triethoxydiphenyl-4-diazonium oxalate is used as a sensitizer (203,204), the developing solution can be acidic (pH 4.5 to 7) (205,206,207,208,209). Compounds like this one have higher coupling energy than diazos used for the alkali-type process.

The alkaline-type diazo papers have a better shelf life, but when developed the prints discolor more quickly and to a greater extent than do acid-developed prints. In solution the alkaline-type developer darkens much faster, as the result of the oxidation of the coupling component, and it is necessary to replace the developer about every other week. However, alkaline-developed prints maintain tear and fold resistance for a longer time and do not lose strength, as was observed on acid-developed copies.

In both acid- and alkali-type development, the developing solution must be able to form the image in a very short time, before the thin layer of the liquid dries on the surface of the print, or before the diazo compound has a chance to dissolve. For this last reason, the coupling activity of the diazo compounds and couplers used in semiwet processes is of vital importance. The fastness of the azo-dye images to washing can be further improved by including into the sensitizing solution substituted 1',2',4,5-naphthimidazoles (210).

The most important diazo compounds used for sensitizing one-component papers are: 1-diazo-2,5-diethoxybenzoylaminobenzene(I), 1-diazo-2,5-dibutoxybenzoylaminobenzene(II),   4-diazo-2,5,4'-triethoxydiphenyl-(III), 1-diazo-4-tolylmercapto-2,5-diethoxybenzene(IV) and 1-diazo-2,5-dimethoxy-1-*p*-toluylmercaptobenzene(V).

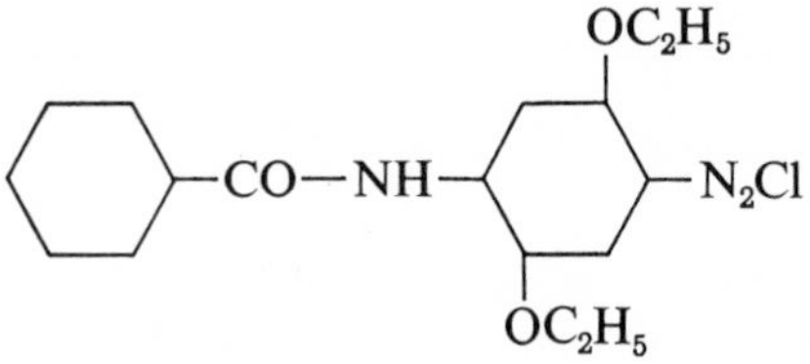

I

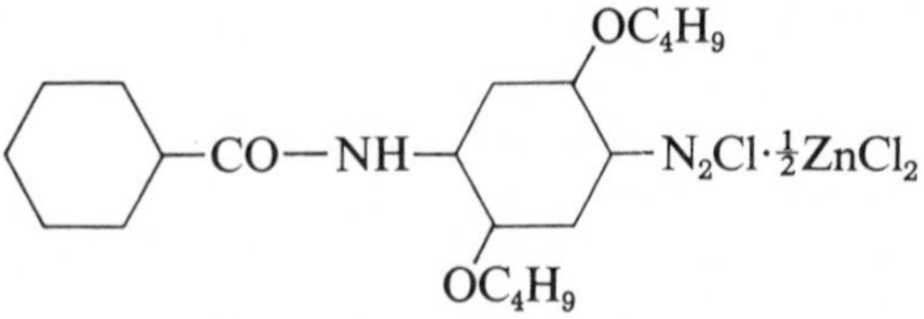

II

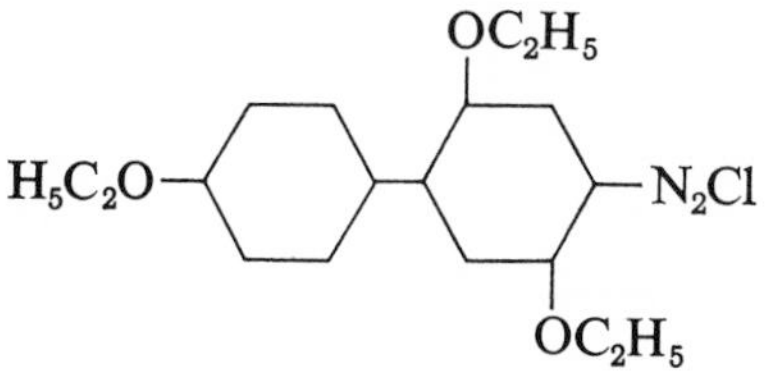

III: H_5C_2O-(ring)$-$(ring with OC_2H_5 top, OC_2H_5 bottom)$-N_2Cl$

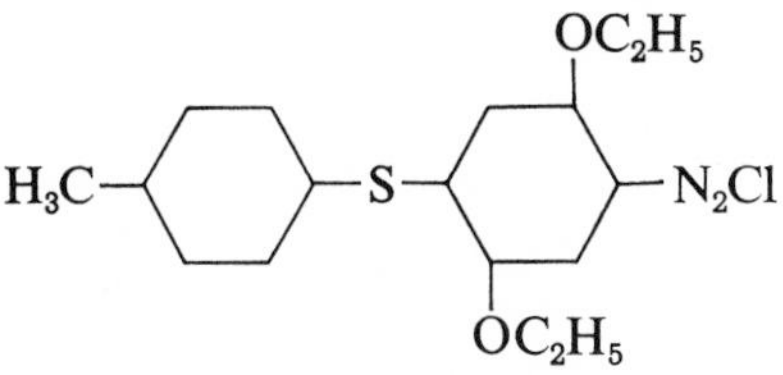

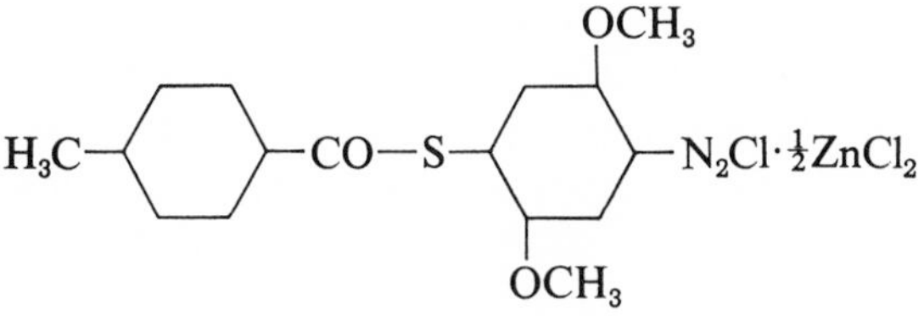

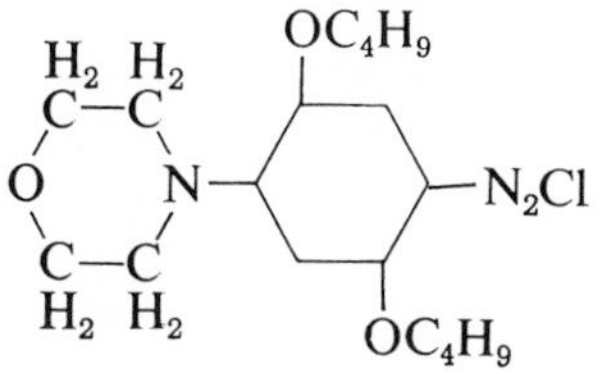

IV: H_3C-(ring)$-S-$(ring with OC_2H_5 top, OC_2H_5 bottom)$-N_2Cl$

V: H_3C-(ring)$-CO-S-$(ring with OCH_3 top, OCH_3 bottom)$-N_2Cl \cdot \frac{1}{2}ZnCl_2$

VI: morpholine ring (O, H_2C-CH_2, H_2C-CH_2, N) $-$(ring with OC_4H_9 top, OC_4H_9 bottom)$-N_2Cl$

Diazo compounds derived from 3,5-dialkoxy-*p*-phenylenediamine, in which one amino group is substituted with two alkyl groups or forms part of a morpholine, piperidine, or piperazine ring, are especially suitable for their high coupling capacity and light sensitivity; 2,5-dibutoxy-4-morpholino-1-benzene diazonium chloride (72) is one of these compounds (VI).

The one-component sensitizing solution contains, besides the diazo compound, a stabilizing acid. Succinic and glutaric acids were suggested by Sanders and Roncken (83), especially in combination with a dialkyl or alkyl aralkyl aniline compound having a *p*-diazo group and an *o*-alkoxy group, for example, 4-diazo-2,5-dialkoxy acylanilides, mercaptobenzenes, or diphenyls. To improve the blackness of the image, the developer contains, in addition to phloroglucinol, a xanthine such as caffeine.

As coupling components, compounds of high coupling energy are used, for instance, resorcinol, phloroglucinol, β-naphthol, and others. The stability of their alkaline solution can be improved by the addition of a small quantity of a tin compound (211). The solution is made alkaline with an alkaline salt of an alkali metal or a mixture of such salts. Volatile amines have also been employed (212,213). Developers containing organic polyhydroxy compounds (mannitol, sorbitol, dextrose, glycerol, dextrin, etc.) (214) or potassium borates (215) all claimed not to cause background discoloration of the prints. A small addition of sodium sulfite or, better yet, hydrosulfite, considerably diminishes the oxidation of alkaline developer. The appearance of diazotype copies can be further improved by the presence of optical bleaching agents, such as a blue fluorescent salt of a 4,4'-diaminostilbene-2,2'-disulfonic acid with one or more 1,3,5-triazine rings attached to the amino groups (216).

It would be expected that the keeping properties of papers for the semiwet process would be better compared with those for the dry process. This is not the case, since for the sensitizing of semiwet papers diazo compounds of high coupling speed have to be used and these are in themselves less stable. Material which can be safely stored for a prolonged period of time, it is claimed, can be prepared by sensitizing the paper with an aqueous solution of p-diazodiphenylamine sulfate containing a large amount of tartaric acid (217).

The developing solution is, in general, applied to the exposed sheet by means of a roller which rotates in the liquid and transfers a definite quantity of the developer to the material to be developed, or the developing solution is applied in an apparatus in which the exposed prints pass through a meniscus of developer picked up from troughs by a grooved plastic roller (218) and are squeezed, to remove excess, by wringer rollers (219). In another design, the excessive and uneven application of the liquid developer is avoided with two sets of nip rollers through which the paper passes during development. One of the pairs is an applicator roller and the other a wringer roller (220). The print emerges dry to the touch. Some machines are equipped with a pumping system which dispenses the liquid in a discrete amount at recurrent intervals (221), or are equipped with other devices which apply the minimum effective quantity of the developer to the exposed sheet (222,223,224,225,226,227). After development the print is carried, in most instances, around a heated roller which touches the rear surface of the sheets where it is dried without washing or other means of removing unreacted chemicals. In addition, especially when the developer is incapable of fully developing the print, the elevated temperature promotes the development (228). The individual prints are then delivered from the machine in substantially flat, smooth, and dry condition. Both dry and semiwet diazo machines range in size from desk-top printers to big reproduction machines capable of reproducing the largest size drawings.

6.5 THERMAL DEVELOPMENT

A disadvantage of the diazotype process has been that the chemical development requires either ammonia vapors or a liquid developer. In the first instance an installation of exhaust equipment to remove the ammonia fumes is necessary, and even with this precaution the ammonia odor cannot be completely eliminated. Attempts to mask the odor by addition of some substances were disappointing (229). The semiwet developing method does not require the use of ammonia, but other inconveniences characteristic of this type of processing are introduced. The instability of the developing solution, resulting in the discoloration of the prints, and the necessity of drying the developed copy are examples. It is not surprising to note that many efforts have been made in the past to find some way to avoid these objections (230,231,232).

In recent years installation of an anhydrous ammonia system has been recommended to eliminate handling of liquid ammonia. It is, however, necessary to have a small amount of water in the developing tank of the machine to which the anhydrous ammonia is supplied through plastic tubing (233). The ammonia supply and external components may be conveniently placed as far as one thousand feet from the printing equipment. The ammonia flow is metered with a regulator. Since there is no high temperature required in the developing chamber, it is claimed that this system prolongs the life of belts and other components of the equipment in addition to simpler operating procedures.

Another approach, also to eliminate liquid ammonia handling, was taken by General Aniline and Film Corp.; the ammonia is generated by heating a 40 per cent aqueous ammonium carbonate solution (234). Dieterle (235) developed diazotype prints by subjecting them to ammonia given off by heat decomposition of ammonium compounds, such as ammonium carbonate, bicarbonate, acetate, and formate. These compounds can be impregnated either in a permeable woven textile material in the form of an endless belt passing continuously over a rotating heated roller against which is placed the diazotype sheet conveyed from the exposure unit (236), or introduced in the form of pellets into an electrically heated cup (237). On this principle was built the developing unit introduced by Filmsort, a subsidiary of Minnesota Mining and Manufacturing Co., for development of diazotype microfilm. This device contains means for metering out sufficient ammonium carbonate crystals to provide enough ammonia gas, on heating, to develop a single print (238).   Similar ideas came from Ellsworth and Johnson (239,240), who constructed a diazotype printing apparatus in which one side of the sensitized paper is exposed through an original to a light source, and the other side is pressed by a foam-rubber pad impregnated with ammonium carbonate.   When heated this compound again decomposes to give ammonia so that it is possible to expose and develop the print simultaneously.

In another patent (241) the idea of replacing ammonia with a solution of hexamethylene tetramine or triethanolamine in water was brought up.

More recently, Frantz (242) obtained a patent on an apparatus in which the exposed sheet is placed in contact with an endless belt made from an absorbent material and previously wetted with an alkaline solution of ammonia, ammonium carbonate, or ammonium formate.   Any liquid remaining on the developed sheet is evaporated by means of heating elements.   It was also suggested (243) that two-component diazotype papers be developed by applying an aqueous solution containing an organic amine and then heating the coated paper for a short time.

In another method the alkaline solution is applied to the other side of the sensitized sheet (244), the coupling being effected by the penetration of the solution through the sheet.   If the sheet is sensitized with a diazo compound and overcoated with a polystyrene and dammar solution containing phloroglucinol and an alkali, it can be developed, after exposure, by simply applying a thin film of water (245).

Similar efforts have also been made in semiwet developing methods. Even in the early days of diazotype processes, the problems connected with the oxidation of coupling components in an alkaline solution were realized, and many suggestions were made.   In one, the exposed one-component paper was subjected to vapors of an aromatic amine capable of coupling with the diazo compound. α-Naphthylamine or m-amino-phenol were proposed (246).   Another proposal (247) suggested pressing the exposed sheet against a jelly-like mass containing the developing agent.

All these proposals were largely unsuccessful, for they introduced many other serious disadvantages, and it was only logical to question whether the accelerating effect of heat on the coupling reaction could not be utilized for the development of diazotype papers.   In principle, the answer would be positive but, even here, the practice seems to be more complicated. First of all it must be understood that in the two-component systems the diazo and the coupler are mixed very intimately in the same layer and a careful selection of these two components has to be made to prevent immediate coupling.   It is known that not all diazo compounds and couplers available to the industry interact at the same rate.   There are slow-coupling diazo compounds and slow-reacting couplers; this combination offers a comparatively stable system. This combination is, however, unsuitable for heat development because of the destructive action of heat on the diazo compounds which are decomposed before the coupling can take place. Besides, slow-reacting diazo compounds are very often less light sensitive, which hinders their application in the office-copying field, even in combination with a coupler of high-coupling energy. A fast diazo and a slow coupler give a material of sufficient sensitivity, but the coupling reaction is too slow to give us a print of adequate contrast. In another extreme, combination of a fast diazo and a fast coupler, the shelf-life problem is predominant. Coating containing conventional diazonium salt, acid stabilizer, thiourea, and one of the ketomethylene couplers (248) can serve as an example of the simple formulations. Premature coupling, as previously explained, can be delayed by lowering the pH of the sensitizing solution; the presence of acids has, however, an adverse effect on the developing speed. Greig (249) tried to overcome that by using trichloroacetic acid, which decomposes at the developing temperature and consequently does not hinder the coupling reaction. Even in this case, the results were far from satisfactory for commercial application.

Another possibility arises with the consideration of the use of compounds decomposing at elevated temperatures with the formation of an alkali which would trigger the coupling reaction. There is a long list of substances having this property, starting with inorganic and organic ammonium salts and organic amines and ending with ureas and thioureas and their derivatives.

In one such effort (250) a solution of a slow-coupling diazo compound and an azo component was coated, together with a salt of a strong base and a weak volatile acid (sodium acetate, potassium malonate, etc.), on paper and cautiously dried to avoid coloring of the background. After the exposure, during the heat development, the salt is decomposed into an alkali, which starts the coupling, and the acid volatilizes. Schmidt and Süs (251) achieved the development of two-component papers containing zinc, cadmium, or lead formates or acetates, by means of steam; during this procedure oxides or basic salts are formed and the acid evaporated so that the coupling process can take place.

In another attempt urea was added to the sensitizing solution (252, 253,254,255,256). Urea seems to be very suitable for this application; it is very soluble in water, decomposes in a favorable temperature range, and, being almost neutral, it does not markedly change the pH of the sensitizing solution.

Other compounds that have been investigated include substituted ureas and thioureas and their derivatives, such as guanidine and biuret (257).

In such formulations stabilizing agents are used, including a hydroxy-carboxylic acid, an oxamide, a malonamide, a cyanocarboxylic acid, or an oxaluric acid.　As a source of alkali, crystalline adducts of a bisphenol and a volatile organic amine can also serve; these are added to the sensitizing solution (258), and, on heating, liberate an amine.　For example, a latent developer is formed by dissolving bisphenol A and iso-propylamine in toluene and recrystallizing after chilling at $-30°$F.　Also, combinations of urea with di-*n*-butylamine are suitable as latent developers, liberating a base by thermal dissociation rather than by decomposition.　The following can also be mentioned as alkali-releasing agents: dicyandiamide (259), quaternary ammonium compounds such as trimethyl phenyl ammonium chloride or tetramethyl ammonium chloride (260), acrylamide (261), and hexamethylene tetramine (262).　Although such methods can be made to work, the impossibility of controlling the decomposition in such a way as to allow decomposition to occur only at the higher temperature was mainly responsible for the limited success of this material.

In heat development of diazotype papers, the time necessary for the generation of all the alkali required for the reaction is of vital importance (263); this is illustrated in Figure 6.3.　Curve *A* is a decomposition curve of the particular diazo compound obtained by heating to 300°F the diazo-coupler coated paper for the indicated time and by plotting the optical densities measured after ammonia development.　From the steepness of the line, the high decomposition rate of diazo at elevated temperature can be seen.　Curve *B* was obtained in a similar way, with paper containing urea in addition to diazo and coupler, and, instead of

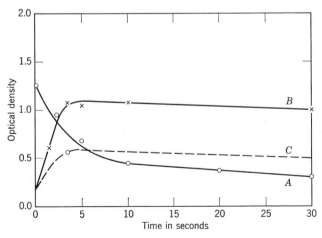

Figure 6.3.　Decomposition of diazonium compounds at 300°F (reference 263).

ammonia, heat development for the indicated time was used. It is obvious from these two curves that to solve the problem of heat development of diazotype papers it is necessary to employ a diazo compound of high thermal stability, azo components of high coupling energy, and alkali-generating agents which are stable at normal temperatures but which decompose rapidly and completely at the developing temperature.

To make such a selection is not a simple task. The thermal stability of diazo compounds varies slightly according to their structure, and they start to decompose around 120°C. By using a diazo compound with a lower decomposition point, the maximum density of the developed image will be lower, as is shown by the curve *C*. The slight slope of curves *B* and *C* after they reach maximum density can be attributed to the heat decomposition of the dye by prolonged development.

The rate of coupling increases slightly at higher temperatures, however, not to such a degree as the diazo decomposition rate. Based on the work of Crossley, Kienle, and Benbrook (5), who investigated the energy of activation of several diazo compounds, and that of Conant and Peterson (87), who determined the energy of several azo coupling reactions, Zollinger (264) concluded that for every 10°C rise in temperature the rate of coupling increases 2.0 to 2.4 times, and the rate of diazo decomposition rises 3.1 to 5.3 times.

Figure 6.4, the decomposition curves of several compounds, indicates the amount of ammonia released by heating them at 150°C for a specified time. It is very clear that ammonium carbonate releases its ammonia at a high rate and would be an excellent supply of alkali for the thermal diazotype papers if no decomposition took place at room temperature. The same can be said about ammonium benzoate and other ammonium salts. By selecting a compound of a higher stability at room temperature, the decomposition rate is too slow at developing temperature and consequently not enough ammonia is made available. Ethyl urea is an example. Urea is approximately in the middle of these two extremes; its developing power is adequate, and papers containing urea, if properly packaged, can be stored for a few months.

Among many attempts in the past to prevent premature coupling was one in which the coupler and/or an alkaline salt was dusted on the sensitized paper (265,266,267,268). The sensitized material was developed, after being exposed, merely by the application of moisture or steam. A device for this operation was patented by Alink and Aninga (269). These results were disappointing because of nonuniform dye intensity and poor shelf life. Neugebauer and Süs (270) suggested producing the alkali at the moment of development by the chemical conversion of properly selected neutral or acid components, for instance, a mixture of sodium

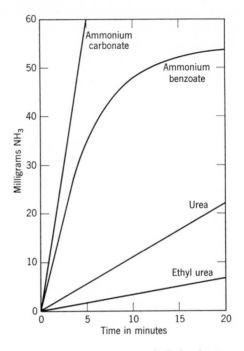

Figure 6.4.   Decomposition curves of alkali-releasing agents.

fluoride and aluminum acetate.   In another formulation, the alkali required for developing diazo prints was produced by the reaction of secondary sodium phosphate with ammonium molybdate (271).   Improved
shelf life of heat-developable diazotype papers is claimed to be obtained
by using a thermolobile pyrrole compound which, on being heated to
120 to 130°C, decomposes to form a coupler (272); 2,4-dimethyl-3-
ethoxycarbonyl-5-*t*-butoxycarbonyl-pyrrole can serve as an example.

Efforts have also been made to separate the active ingredients by
coating the coupler solution on the opposite side of the paper.   In a recent
patent specification (273) a vapor-permeable base, such as paper or cloth,
was sensitized on one side with a diazo-coupler combination, whereas the
other side contained an alkali-generating layer.   Since the components
diffuse and migrate through the supporting base, prevention of precoupling
to a satisfactory degree cannot be expected.   A developing apparatus for
these or similar papers was designed by Thomiszer (274,275); it consists,
in principle, of a thin-walled aluminum drum heated by an infrared lamp,
over which is passed the exposed sheet by means of a fiberglass belt
impregnated with Teflon (polytetrafluoroethylene).

In the next logical step, the active components were separated by an intermediate layer which, when heated to a certain temperature, melts and allows the chemicals to react (276). For example, the paper is first coated with a diazonium salt and, when dry, overcoated with a solution of polyethylene glycol and dried again. Next, a coupling component is applied, one such as resorcinol with stearylamine, which assists the coupling reactions (277). This last formulation has the advantage that, if coated on a suitable support and placed in contact with an original carrying an image in printer's ink, either black or an inorganic pigment, and subjected to infrared radiation, the fusible interlayer melts in areas corresponding to image areas. In this manner the components come into intimate contact, and a positive image of the original is obtained. The diazo compound present in the nonimage areas can be more readily decomposed by light, so that the resulting copy is light- and heat-stable. A similar process, using infrared radiation, was patented by Dietzgen and Thomiszer (278). In another patent, the two-component diazotype paper is separated from the alkali-releasing agent with a layer of polyvinyl acetate (279), or the sensitized paper is overcoated with a layer of an organic binder containing a fine dispersion of developing agent (280).

Separation of the active chemicals can also be achieved by encapsulating extremely minute particles of one of the components in a continuous nonpermeable shell (281). After the exposure the capsules are ruptured by pressure and release their contents for reaction with the basic coating. In one such example, finely powdered barium hydroxide was encapsulated in paraffin wax and used for producing alkali by heating (282). In another example, the coupling component is encapsulated in a water-insoluble organic substance, which isolates the coupler from the diazo compound and which melts when heated to about 150°C. Land (283) encapsulated the source of ammonia in gas-tight capsules which are ruptured by pressure to develop the exposed sheet.

Both these methods of separating the components from each other are characterized by the fact that, when the separating layer is made heavy enough or made from a material which will completely prevent contact, the development of the exposed sheet is either incomplete or does not take place at all. On the other hand, when the protective coating is made thinner or from a more permeable material, the protection is not sufficient and results in poor keeping qualities for the sensitized papers.

It is certainly clear from the foregoing description that the formulation of diazotype papers developable by heat is extremely difficult if they are to have a satisfactory shelf life. However, the problem can be solved by using separate developing sheets which are brought into contact with the sensitized side of exposed two-component diazo paper and heated. The developing sheets are impregnated with one or more compounds, that, when heated, liberate ammonia or another alkali. Urea (284), and a chromium hexamino compound (285) were used in the past. A salt of an amine and a weak acid was proposed in another patent (286). One side of the developing sheet can be sealed with a gas-impermeable resin, or covered with a metal foil (287). Instead of an alkali-releasing agent, the developing sheet can be impregnated with a coupler capable of thermal diffusion (288).

The useful coupler may be selected from the group consisting of phenols, naphthols, and compounds containing a reactive methylene group which are free of primary amino groups, for example, phloroglucinol, 2,3-dihydroxynaphthalene, resorcinol, acetoacetanilide, and 3-methylpyrazolone.

The two-sheet process has many advantages compared with the ammonia and semiwet process or with the developing methods just described, but in spite of this the handling of two sheets seems to be objectionable from the commercial point of view.

Up to this point, only diazonium compounds capable of reacting with the azo components were considered. There are diazo compounds, however, which are indifferent toward couplers at room temperature but can be activated by heat. Such compounds include, for instance, diazosulfonates. In one such process, paper treated with a solution of diazosulfonate and a coupling component is first exposed to ultraviolet light for a time sufficient to decompose the diazonium salt completely. Next, the print is developed by heating it sufficiently to form a dye in the areas which were not exposed to light. Suitable for this process are diazosulfonates, which have only a moderate velocity of coupling and do not react with the photolysis product. p-Amino-benzene diazosulfonates were used by Süs (289).

The shelf life of this material is comparatively good and can be improved further by addition of sodium bisulfite, along with ketones, ketonic acids, or aromatic aldehydes (290). This is, of course, at the cost of lower light sensitivity. More suitable for the same purpose are water-soluble salts of substituted aromatic sulfonic acids of the benzene and naphthalene series, such as 1-ethoxybenzene-4-sulfonic acid or 1-methoxynaphthalene-4-sulfonic acid (291).

Images on diazosulfonate papers can also be formed by selective heating of predetermined areas and subsequent exposure to strong actinic radiation to bleach out the remaining diazosulfonate (292). Aromatic diazo-N-sulfonate of an N,N-dialkyl-p-phenylenediamine substituted by an alkoxy group in the ortho position to the diazo group is suitable. Sulfonates of the diazo compound of 1-N,N-diethylamino-4-amino-3-ethoxybenzene (*a*) and that of 1-N,N-dipropylamino-4-amino-3-ethoxybenzene (*b*) are claimed. An azo coupling component of great coupling energy is recommended.

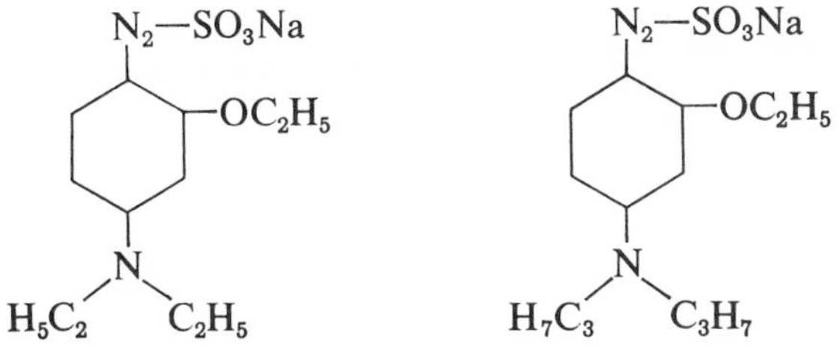

$$N_2-SO_3Na \qquad\qquad N_2-SO_3Na$$
$$-OC_2H_5 \qquad\qquad -OC_2H_5$$

$$H_5C_2 \quad C_2H_5 \qquad\qquad H_7C_3 \quad C_3H_7$$

(*a*) \qquad\qquad (*b*)

Another class of compounds having similar properties are aryl diazo sulfones, such as 2-methyl-4-diethylaminobenzene diazophenylsulfone, which on heating rearranges to an aryl disulfinate of higher coupling power (293). Low light sensitivity of the above compounds hinders their commercial application.

Mention should also be made of diazo compounds of phenylene diamine derivatives, in which one amino group is substituted with an alkyl, aryl, or acyl group, or forms a nitrogen-ring compound such as morpholine, for example, 4-morpholinobenzene diazonium chloride $ZnCl_2$ complex. Papers sensitized with such compounds, and having citric acid and thiourea as the only additional components, produce dark-violet prints upon heating for a short time at 130°C (294).

6.6 NEGATIVE PROCESS

6.6a *Autocoupling*

The diazotype process is basically a positive printing process in the sense that the nonimage areas of the original transmit actinic radiation to the light-sensitive coating, and, in these areas, the diazo compound is decomposed and its capacity for coupling destroyed. The decomposition product is of phenolic nature and, if its coupling energy is low enough, it does not react with the parental diazo compound during the exposure. The low coupling energy of the photolysis product is the principal requirement for a positive diazotype printing process. If the photolysis product is reactive enough, it can react under favorable conditions with the nondecomposed diazo compound and a dye is formed in the exposed areas but not in the areas protected from light. Thus, a negative print of the original results.

The reactions taking place can be expressed as follows:

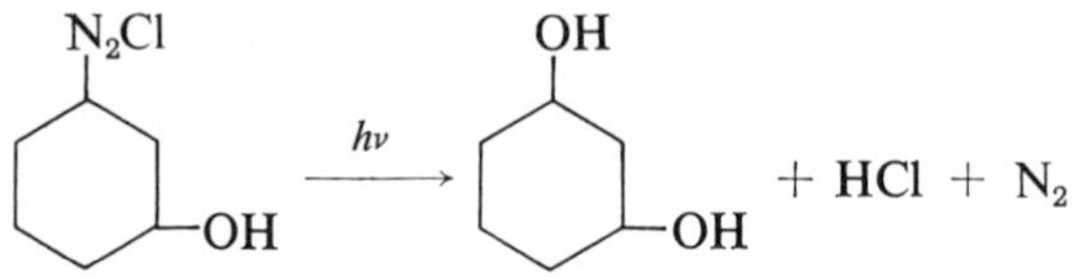

$$\text{(22)}$$

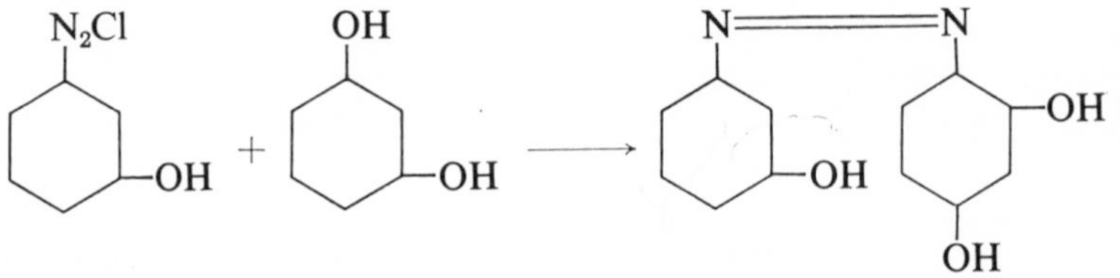

$$\text{(23)}$$

A negative working process was first proposed by West (295) and further explored by Feer (296), Andressen (297), and others. In these processes, the sensitized paper is exposed to ultraviolet radiation under a transparency long enough to decompose about 50 per cent of the diazo compound. By increasing the pH of the paper with a weak solution of ammonia, the coupling reaction is started and a negative print of the positive transparency is obtained. The remaining diazo is removed by washing in water or is decomposed by a second exposure. To improve the stability, Schmidt and Krieger (298) proposed the employment of two or more diazo compounds of approximately equal sensitiveness to light in different molecular proportions with the addition of a stabilizing agent. One of these diazo compounds must have a great coupling capacity. It was suggested by Frangialli (299) that this autocoupling reaction be used for a positive-working process. For exposure, a strong actinic radiation is used, destroying all diazo compound in the unprotected areas. With the tracing withdrawn, the undecomposed sections are exposed to light of lower intensity. The outline of the original becomes colored. A similar process, using a diazonium compound produced from methylamino-naphthimidazole, was proposed by Barde (300). Landau (301), in an analogous method, used two diazo compounds of different spectral sensitivity. During the exposure to ultraviolet light, one of the diazo compounds is decomposed in all except the image areas; the second exposure, this time to visible or infrared radiation with the original removed, causes breakdown of the second diazo compound to a coupler. As in the previous examples, the azo component reacts instantly with the undecomposed diazo in the image areas to form the final reproduction without further processing.

Neither the negative nor the positive diazotype processes based on autocoupling properties have been commercialized, since the proper ratio of the photolysis product to the residual diazo is very difficult to control.

6.6b   *Diazosulfonates*

All diazotype processes so far described employ diazo compounds which have the ability to couple with azo components under favorable conditions.   If the diazo compounds are, however, treated with sodium sulfite at a low temperature and at controlled pH (302,303), *syn*-diazosulfonates are formed which are unstable and rearrange rapidly into the more stable anticompounds (304).

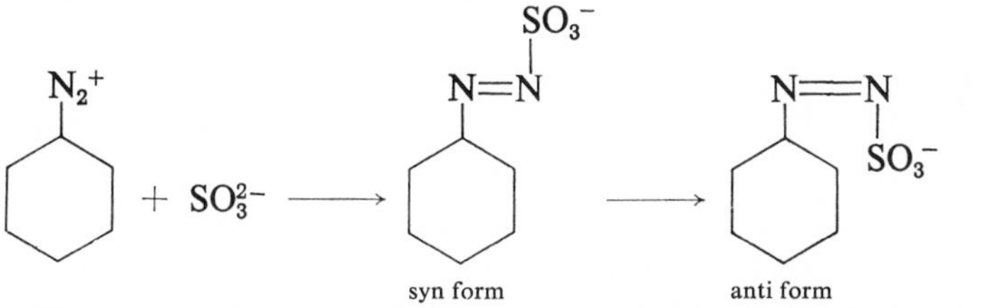

(24)

syn form   anti form

Anti-diazosulfonates do not have the ability to couple, even after long periods of storage, until heat or light restores the active form.   When exposed to light or heat, the primary product is the *syn*-diazosulfonate which dissociates rapidly into diazonium ion and sulfite ion (305):

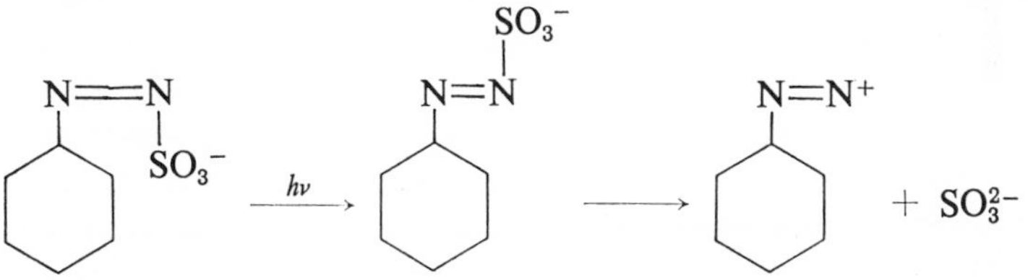

(25)

At more energetic action, diazosulfonates decompose under the liberation of nitrogen gas.   Instead of sodium sulfite, sulfonated polymers, such as polymerized formaldehyde naphthalenesulfonic acid can be used in the preparation of diazosulfonates (306).

Based on these properties, diazosulfonates were suggested for a number of negative diazotype processes (307,308,309).   In one such process, paper coated with diazosulfonate solution is exposed under a negative transparency and developed in an alkaline solution of a coupler.   On the exposed parts, where the diazonium compound has been "re-activated," an azo dye is formed, and the unexposed section remains unchanged and is washed out during the fixing operation. A positive copy of the negative transparency is thus obtained. For this process, a fast-coupling diazosulfonate, such as the diazosulfonate of *p*-anisidine, must be selected.

Another suitable diazosulfonate contains, in the nucleus carrying the diazo group, two esterified oxy groups, but no amino group or substituted amino group (310). 2,5-Diethoxy-4-chlorobenzene diazosulfonate is an example. In some instances, as in preparation of diazosulfonate films, it may be advantageous to use, as a carrier for the light-sensitive coating, a mixture of a hydrophobic resin with a copolymer of maleic anhydride and polyvinyl methyl ether (311). In this patent, sodium *p*-ethoxybenzene diazosulfonate with a polyhydric phenol was used for sensitizing. In another modification (312), cellulose acetate and vinyl methyl-ether/ maleic-anhydride copolymer, coated on cellulose acetate film, is sensitized with a solution containing an ester amide of 2-diazo-1-naphthol-5-sulfonic acid. The sensitized sheet is exposed imagewise to a halftone color separation negative and the positive image is removed with an alkaline solution. The print is then redeveloped with an alkaline solution of a basic dye. The residual diazo coating is removed with solvent and the entire process can be repeated for other colors. A similar color process was suggested by Tranchant (313).

A negative-working diazotype material can be prepared also by using a combination of one or more coupling diazo compounds and a diazo-sulfonate which, in a free state, has a strong coupling power. During the exposure, the diazo compound is decomposed and an azo component is formed. Simultaneously the light "activates" the diazosulfonate which reacts with the photolysis product yielding a dye image. The copy can be fixed by washing out with water the unreacted diazo components. The sodium salt of naphthalene-β-diazo-N-sulfonic acid, together with 1-ethylamino-4-diazonaphthalene or 1-benzoylamino-2,5-diethoxy-4-diazo benzene-N-sulfonic acid in combination with 4-diethylamino-2-hydroxy-1-diazobenzene, is recommended (314).

6.6c   *Diazobiguanides*

Diazobiguanides are prepared by reaction of a diazonium salt with biguanide or its derivative (315). Diazobiguanides are, like diazo-sulfonates, more stable than the diazonium salts, but are also less light sensitive. They do not have the ability to couple with the azo-components; this ability can be restored upon treatment with heat or exposure to light (316). A suitable diazobiguanide, made from diazotized 4-benzoylamino-2,5-diethoxyaniline and the biguanine of metanilic acid, has the following formula:

$$\text{C}_6\text{H}_{10}\!-\!\text{CO·NH}\!-\!\underset{\underset{\text{OC}_2\text{H}_5}{|}}{\overset{\overset{\text{OC}_2\text{H}_5}{|}}{\text{C}_6\text{H}_8}}\!-\!\text{N}\!=\!\text{N}\!-\!\overset{\text{H}}{\text{N}}\!-\!\underset{\text{NH}}{\overset{\|}{\text{C}}}\!-\!\text{NH}\!-\!\underset{\text{NH}}{\overset{\|}{\text{C}}}\!-\!\text{NH}\!-\!\text{C}_6\text{H}_4\!-\!\text{SO}_3\text{H}$$

Another example in the above patent is made from diazotized 4-amino-2-methylsulfonamido-4'-dimethylaminoazobenzene and biguanide. The product has following formula:

$$\underset{\text{H}_3\text{C}}{\overset{\text{H}_3\text{C}}{>}}\text{N}\!-\!\text{C}_6\text{H}_4\!-\!\text{N}\!=\!\text{N}\!-\!\underset{\overset{|}{\text{SO}_2\text{NH·CH}_3}}{\text{C}_6\text{H}_3}\!-\!\text{N}\!=\!\text{N}\!-\!\overset{\text{H}}{\text{N}}\!-\!\underset{\text{NH}}{\overset{\|}{\text{C}}}\!-\!\text{NH}\!-\!\underset{\text{NH}}{\overset{\|}{\text{C}}}\!-\!\text{NH}_2$$

6.6d   *Auto-oxidation*

Positive copies from a negative can also be obtained by treating papers sensitized with diazo compounds of *p*-aminodiphenylamines, after exposure to light, with an oxidizing agent, for example, potassium dichromate or hydrogen peroxide. Better colors result when the copying material contains, in addition to the diazo compound, one or more aromatic phenols or amines capable of yielding dyestuffs with the light decomposition products of the diazo compounds present (317).

Another negative working diazotype process was patented by De Boer, Dippel, and Alink (318,319). This process does not utilize the coupling properties, but is based on the oxidizing properties of certain diazonium compounds. Again, the first exposure is chosen so that only about half of the diazo compound is decomposed into a phenol, which is almost simultaneously oxidized by the nondecomposed diazo or by some other diazonium compound provided to form a colored oxidation product. A second exposure, with the original removed, destroys the remaining diazo.

The reaction is accelerated by dampening the paper or by incorporating hygroscopic agents in the light-sensitive coating and by moderate heating of the copy after the exposure. The contrast can also be promoted by the addition of copper salts.

For this process, suitable diazo compounds are those which yield, after the exposure, polyphenols such as *p*-hydroxybenzene diazonium chloride or diazo compounds, having in the benzene nucleus at least one hydroxyl or amino group in ortho or para position to the diazo group (320,321,322). 1-Hydroxy-2-diazo-4-benzene sulfonic acid or 2-diazonium-1-hydroxy-5-

methyl-4-benzene sulfonic acid are examples. Naphthalene diazonium compounds, such as 1-diazonium-2-hydroxynaphthalene-4-sulfonic acid, have greater stability than benzene derivatives (323). In general, diazonium compounds used in this process must be decomposed by light into phenols which are oxidized by nondecomposed diazonium compound into a colored product at a faster rate than the coupling of the diazo compound with the phenol. To obtain a satisfactory shelf life of the unexposed material, it is necessary to remove moisture from the coated paper to a greater extent than is done in drying regular diazotype papers, and to store it in an extremely dry atmosphere in hermetically sealed containers (324).

6.6e *The Metal-Diazonium Process*

In general, diazo compounds, when exposed to light, yield decomposition products having reducing properties. When a reducible water soluble metallic salt, such as silver nitrate, is included in light-sensitive coating containing diazo compounds, this material yields after exposure and after treatment with an alkali (borax, sodium acetate, ammonia, etc.), a negative silver image of the original (325). In order to remove the unreacted substances, the image is washed and fixed in solution of sodium thiosulfate.

In an attempt to bypass solution treatments, Reichel (326) suggested making the unreacted diazo compound innocuous by incorporating into the light-sensitive coating a suitable coupler which will form, in the unexposed parts, with the diazo an azo compound with high ultraviolet transmission properties.

The most suitable couplers are aliphatic or aromatic primary or secondary amines, which form with the diazo compounds colorless diazo, amino, or diazo imino compounds. Among these, the following were specified in the patent just mentioned: cyanamide, methylamino ethane sulfonic acid, diethanolamine, morpholine, sarcosine, etc.

A process developed by Philips Co. is based on the same principle (327,328,329,330,331). Light-sensitive material of this type is obtained by applying a suitable diazo compound plus a mercurous salt to a support such as cellophane or paper. In its simplest form, this process can be illustrated in the following way: regenerated cellulose is sensitized with a solution of hydroxy-1-diazonium-2-methyl-6-benzene-4-sulfonic acid, mercurous nitrate and a small amount of nitric acid; after drying, the film is exposed, in contact with a photographic negative, to a high-pressure mercury-vapor lamp and developed in a physical developer containing silver nitrate, tartaric acid, and metol.

In a system like that, where mercurous ions are present, chemical equilibrium also requires the presence of mercuric ions and mercury atoms:

$$Hg_2^{2+} \rightleftharpoons Hg^{2+} + Hg \tag{26}$$

During the exposure, when the diazo compound is decomposed, the photolysis product—cyclopentadiene carbonic acid—reacts with the mercuric ions and removes them from the system. The excess of mercury atoms is then deposited, in the form of very fine droplets, imagewise in the exposed areas (332). Some metallic complexes, by reacting with mercuric ions, increase the formation of metallic mercury (333). The visibility of the "latent" image immediately after exposure will increase with the moisture present at the time of exposure, and will fade out after some time because of oxidation of mercurous and mercuric compounds. Addition of a salt of a metal which lies higher in the electromotive potential series of metals than does mercury will prevent the fade-out effect. Platinum, gold, and silver salts are suitable (334).

In another modification of this process, only diazonium salts are included in the light-sensitive layer. The latent image is formed by reaction of the exposed diazo with mercurous ions. If this reaction does not take place immediately after the exposure, the sensitivity decreases and can disappear completely. This decrease in sensitivity is called "regression" and can be reduced by the addition of cations of heavy metals, for instance, lead, cadmium, zinc, or cobalt, to the diazo sulfonic acid (335,336). Another method of preventing regression, as mentioned in this patent, is addition of either coupling components of high energy, such as resorcinol or β-naphthol, or a salt such as ammonium tungstate or ammonium molybdate. At least in this last method the effect is explained by formation of less soluble diazonium compounds. Water-soluble organic acids, such as lactic and citric acid and their alkali-metal salts, or soluble benzene and naphthalenesulfonic acids, for example, naphthalenetrisulfonic acid, are also suitable.

To eliminate the fading of the "latent" image and to increase its visibility, a process of physical development is used to deposit metallic silver on the specks of mercury. As a developer, an aqueous solution of silver nitrate and a reducing agent is used. During the process of development, a reaction between the locally formed metallic mercury and silver nitrate takes place; the mercury droplets act as nuclei upon which more and more silver is deposited. The rate at which silver is deposited in the image areas can be regulated and controlled by the acidity of the developing solution. The physical developers are unstable systems and deteriorate rapidly with the separation of metallic silver, which can be deposited during the developing process even on the unexposed areas of the print.   This can be avoided either by using a fresh developer for each print or by developing all the exposed prints at the same time (337).

After development is complete, the image can be fixed by simple rinsing with water.   Since the image is composed of silver, its permanence is as good as that of normal photographic material.

According to the foregoing patents, diazo compounds having an hydroxyl group in the *p*- or *m*-position are suitable.   1-Hydroxy-benzene-4-diazonium borofluoride and 1-hydroxybenzene-5-diazonium-4-sulfonic acid-6-carboxylic acid are examples.   Better results are claimed with diazo compounds having the hydroxyl group in the *o*-position, as in 1-hydroxybenzene-2-diazonium fluorosulfonate.

In another patent (338), the use of stable aromatic diazo cyanides is described.   Examples of suitable compounds of this class are *p*-toluene diazocyanide, *o*- and *p*-chlorobenzene diazocyanide and *p*-methoxybenzene diazocyanide.

The latent metal image can also be formed in a layer containing a diazo-sulfonate; during the exposure to ultraviolet light, diazosulfonate is decomposed into diazonium salt and a sulfite.   The regression of the

$$
\underset{\text{dark}}{\overset{h\nu}{\rightleftarrows}}
$$

$$
N{=}N{-}SO_3^{-} \quad \underset{\text{dark}}{\overset{h\nu}{\rightleftarrows}} \quad N{=}N^{+} + SO_3^{2-} \tag{27}
$$

diazosulfonates can be repressed by adjusting the pH, by proper choice of diazosulfonates, and by addition of regression salts as mentioned before. When the exposed material is moistened with a dilute $HgNO_3$-$AgNO_3$ solution, the sulfite reduces the mercurous salt to mercury nuclei, which is developable with a physical developer.

$$
Hg_2(NO_3)_2 + SO_3^{2-} \longrightarrow Hg_2SO_3 + 2NO_3^{-}
$$
$$
Hg_2SO_3 \longrightarrow HgSO_3 + Hg \tag{28}
$$

The spectral sensitivity of the metal-diazonium process lies, as in all diazotype processes, in the near ultraviolet region with a maximum in the vicinity of 3800 Å.

Theoretically, every two quanta of absorbed light produce one atom of elementary mercury, each of which could be enlarged by a deposit of silver, with consequent density increase in the image areas.   In other words, the effect of light would be greatly multiplied with physical development.   Unfortunately this is not the case.   The mercury atoms do not remain separated but condense, first into minute droplets of mercury, and later into relatively large conglomerates, so that the development can have only a limited intensification effect. Thus, the ultimate density of the final image is very closely related to the number of developable mercury specks. The number of developable mercury specks can be increased by including in the sensitizing solution, anions, such as lactates, acetates, and citrates (339), which are capable of reducing the activity of mercurous ions through the formation of compounds that are only slightly dissociated.

In spite of all these efforts, the metal-diazonium process did not show the multiplication effect of silver halide photography, and the effective sensitivity is not more than 5 to 30 times that of the normal diazotype process, depending not only upon the choice of the ingredients but also on the nature of the supporting material.

The gamma value of the metal-diazonium system can be controlled, to a great extent, by changing the intensity and duration of the exposure (340) and the moisture content of the film (341). High light intensity and low moisture content give a maximum gamma value of at least 6, and can be reduced to a gamma as low as 1.0 if the moisture content is increased to 25 or 30 per cent by weight. One of the advantages of this process is the possibility of varying the contrast side by side within the same film by controlling the exposure and moisture content of the respective areas.

The gradation can also be lessened by using a transparent lyophilic film containing a colloidally dispersed pigment that is insoluble in the developing solution. Basic bismuth nitrate is suitable (342). Its action is explained as causing local variations in the concentration of the diazo compound in the light-sensitive layer. The metal-diazonium system possesses a very high resolving power (1000 lines per millimeter). This is most probably due to the fact that a homogeneous solution used for sensitizing produces a grainless material.

The remarkable properties of the system suggested applications in the copying of picture-sound film and in micro and macro documentation but, for some reasons, in spite of very low cost, the metal-diazonium system did not prove to be so successful as was originally expected.

The formation of images by physical development of Hg nuclei is not limited to the application with diazonium salts; as light-sensitive substances the following were also used: the cyanohydrins or alkali-metal bisulfite addition-products of *o*- or *p*-nitrobenzaldehyde (343), *o*- and *p*-nitromandelic acid (344), and light-sensitive ferric salts (345). For example, saponified cellulose acetate film is sensitized with an aqueous solution containing mercuric chloride, ferric ammonium oxalate, and ammonium oxalate; after exposure under a negative, the film is washed in water for a few minutes and then treated with an aqueous solution of silver nitrate, ammonia, and thioindoxyl. A latent metallic image is formed, together with a dye image.   The developed film is washed again and the metallic image is removed with Farmer's reducer, giving a red positive image.   The use of indoxyl instead of thioindoxyl gives a blue dye image.

6.6f   *Vesicular Process*

Diazotype processes described so far are based on the formation of a dye as a result of the reaction of a diazo compound with its decomposition product or with a coupling component.   In the vesicular process, advantage is taken of the nitrogen released during the photolysis of the diazo compound which, serving as a sensitizer, is dispersed in a suitable vehicle and coated on a transparent backing material.   On subsequent heating, the gas expands to form microscopic vesicules which, as a result of a different refraction index, scatter the light falling on them and constitute the image.   Thus vesicular prints are based on the phenomenon of incident light scattering as opposed to previously described diazotype processes which rely on light absorption.   When vesicular prints are viewed from the direction of incidence of the light, the image appears white, and, when used as a transparency for projection, the light-scattering elements appear dark and can be used as standard black and white slides or motion picture film (346).

Vesicular images can be prepared from a light-sensitive layer consisting of a hydrophilic material such as gelatin (347), glue, or polyvinyl alcohol and a diazo compound.   After the exposure, during which the nitrogen is liberated, the material is softened with steam or water so that the gas can expand and form minute vesicles.   Gelatin or similar colloids, which are subject to the effects of ambient moisture, proved to be, in spite of efforts to reduce the sensitivity to high humidity with Werner-type chromium carboxylic acid complexes (348), not the best choice, and thermoplastic hydrophobic resins such as cellulose acetate, polyvinyl acetate, vinyl ether-maleic acid copolymer, and others were suggested (349).   Satisfactory results were also obtained with a mixture of gelatin and polystyrene (350) with the advantage that, by varying the ratio of the colloid to the resin, the sensitometric characteristics of the material could be changed according to the requirements.   Higher concentration of gelatin in the light-sensitive layer gives a material of very soft gradation, suitable for reproduction of continuous tone.   Coatings containing a higher ratio of the resin, because of increased contrast, could be used for reproduction of black and white line work.

To assure proper formation of the image, the binder must have certain physical properties which determine their usefulness in this process.

The binder must have proper diffusivity for the nitrogen formed within the layer, correct permeability in order to make possible the escape of the gas to the atmosphere, and a correct degree of rigidity, which is instrumental in determining the bubble expansion. The diffusion of the gas within the binder determines the photographic characteristics of the recording medium, such as density and contrast. The permeability constant of the vehicle (351), which can be defined as the number of cubic centimeters of gas transmitted by an area of one square centimeter in one second at 30°C, when the pressure gradient is one centimeter of mercury per centimeter of thickness, should not be greater than

$$P_{max} = 8 \times 10^{-10}[cm^3 \ cm^{-2} \ sec^{-1}(cm \ Hg/cm)^{-1}] \qquad (29)$$

and not lower than

$$P_{min} = 8.6 \times 10^{-16}[cm^3 \ cm^{-2} \ sec^{-1}(cm \ Hg/cm)^{-1}] \qquad (30)$$

The permeation characteristics are important mainly in the fixation of the developed image and determine the rate and completeness of the removal of nitrogen from the layer to prevent later background formation.

Within the foregoing permeability limits, in addition to polyvinyl chloride, polyvinylidene chloride, and polysterene, are copolymers of acrylonitrile and vinyl chloride, styrene, vinylidene chlorofluoride and 1,1-difluoroethylene, and copolymers of vinyl chloride and methyl acrylate, acrylic acid, diethyl maleate, and vinyl acetate. Another group of suitable binders comprises copolymers of vinylidene chloride and vinyl chloride, vinyl acetate, vinyl alcohol, and ethyl acrylate. The rigidity, gas diffusibility, and permeability of the thermoplastic material can be controlled by incorporation of a modifier (352); for example, vinylidene chloride/acrylonitrile copolymer (Saran F-120) can be modified with methyl polymethacrylate (acryloid A-101), to obtain the desired properties.

Because the light-sensitive component is enclosed in the hydrophobic, thermoplastic resin, which makes it highly resistant to moisture, the shelf life of unexposed material is exceptionally good.

Diazo compounds of benzene and naphthalene series are used for sensitizing. Especially valuable are *p*-diazodimethyl- and diethylaniline zinc chloride; *p*-diazodiphenylamine sulfate, *p*-diazoethylhydroxyethyl-aniline zinc chloride, 1-diazo-2-oxynaphthalene-4-sulfonate, 4-benzoyl-amino-2-5-diethoxybenzene diazonium chloride, and *p*-chlorobenzene-sulfonate of 4-diazo-2-methoxy-1-cyclohexylaminobenzene are also suitable. 7-Dimethylamino-8-methoxy-3-oxo-dihydro-1,4-thiazine-6-diazonium chloride and similar compounds were claimed by Baril and Klein (353). Bruni and Morgan (354) recommended 1-dimethylamino-4-naphthalene diazonium fluoroborate because of its sensitivity to the visible region of the spectrum. Higher light sensitivity is also claimed when 3-oxo-7-dialkylaminobenzothiazine diazonium borofluorides are used (355).

Among other compounds which can be employed for the formation of vesicular images by exposure to light and thermal development are 1-carbazido-2:5-dihydroxybenzene, 2-amino-1-carbazidobenzene, 2-carbazido-1-naphthol, and 1,4-dicarbazido-2,3-dihydroxyfurane (356). In another patent (357) 3- or 4-azidophthalic anhydride was used. All these compounds have in their molecule an azido group —N_3, which, on exposure to light, decomposes into nitrogen gas. Diazo oxides, diazosulfonates, diazo quinonyl-sulfonamide, azides and quinone diazides, particularly sodium 1:2-naphthoquinone-2-diazide-5-sulfonate were used by Herrick and Halperin (358).

Vesicular images can also be formed by the photolytic decomposition products of ferric ammonium citrate (359) or photodepolymerization of polyketones such as the polymer of 2,4-dimethyl-1-penten-3-one (360); it is claimed that films sensitized with the latter compounds differ from diazo-sensitized films in that one quantum of light forms many monomers which can be utilized to form vesicles, whereas in processes utilizing diazo compounds many quanta of light are required per vesicle. Another material suggested for use in the vesicular process consists of a layer containing a compound, which, when exposed to actinic radiation, splits off a hydrogen halide (361); suitable compounds are polyvinyl chloride, polyvinylidene chloride, chlorinated paraffin, or rubber, N-bromosuccinimide, etc. The second component of the light-sensitive layer is an alkali or alkaline earth carbonate, bicarbonate, oxalate, or tartrate, which forms a gas with the hydrogen halide. Recording material of this type is heated after the exposure at 130°C for 30 sec to form a visible image.

The diazo compound is dissolved or dispersed in the solution of the vehicle and coated on any suitable support such as opaque black paper, glass, polyethylene terephthalate (362), or polyethylene (363). Cellulose acetate is unsuitable because of the presence of wandering plasticizers; the tendency of plasticizers to wander into layers on the support, however, can be eliminated by interposing a barrier layer. In some cases it might be necessary to improve the adhesion of the light-sensitive layer by pre-treatment of the surface of the base. For example, it was recommended that the film of linear polethylene be treated with flame or bombarded with an electron beam. In other instances, chemical treatment with chlorine is preferred.

In general, any transparent material is satisfactory for the production of vesicular material, provided it withstands the operational temperature. For records to be viewed with reflected light, an opaque supporting base, such as paper of any desired color, can be used. The most suitable is black; then the print appears white on a black background.

Vesicular material, as well as all systems sensitized with diazo compounds, is primarily sensitive to near ultraviolet light, with the maximum at 3850 Å. The amount of radiation required to produce maximum density at this wavelength is about 200 mw-sec/cm^2 (384). As light sources, high- and low-pressure mercury-vapor lamps, carbon-arc lamps, and black-light fluorescent tubes are most suitable. This material is resistant to nuclear radiation.

Vesicular material is slow compared with silver halides but because, during the development, small capture cross sections are blown up to large scattering cross sections, the sensitivity is about three to five times higher than in conventional diazo processes. Increased sensitivity is claimed in material containing, in the sensitive layer, finely divided pigment having an index of refraction substantially the same as the vehicle (365). Lower contrast and increased threshold speed can be achieved by immersing the vesicular material, before exposure, in a bath containing hydroxyethyl-2-heptadecenyl glyoxalidine and acetic acid (366), at 140 to 212°F, for a period of 10 to 300 sec, according to the reduction in gamma and increase in speed required. Similar results can be achieved by overall pre-exposure to ultraviolet radiation and short development. The coating is left for about 16 hours to allow the gas pressure in the bubbles to equilibrate to atmospheric pressure. The minute bubbles act as traps for the gas liberated by the image-forming exposure. It is claimed that this prenucleation treatment gives films with more accurate reproduction (367). Furthermore, the sensitivity of vesicular material to light can be increased by including in the sensitive layer a thermolytic agent capable of releasing a gas at an elevated temperature (368), for example, *m*-methoxybenzene diazonium fluoroborate, phenylazo-*n*-butyl sulfone or a mixture of sulfamic acid and triethylamine. On heating, the thermolytic agent generates a gas which combines with the photolytically released nitrogen and increases the size of the vesicle. In this way the density of the image and contrast are increased.

During the exposure, which can be made in an apparatus designed (369) for this purpose, the temperature of the film should not be allowed to rise above 110°F in order to prevent premature vesicle formation and the diffusion of the gas out of the layer. Exposures longer than three minutes are not recommended unless precautions are taken to keep the temperature down. The reciprocity law is valid over a wide range of exposure times from 0.05 to 60 seconds.

Development of the exposed material can be accomplished by any convenient heat source. Heated rollers are suitable for larger sheets, and for small areas an electric plateau is satisfactory. A stream of hot air or a heated liquid heat-transfer medium, for instance glycerin or water, are also adequate. A device for developing vesicular material was patented by Nieset (370). Both the time and temperature of development are not exact and can be varied within wide limits. Satisfactory development can be obtained at temperatures ranging from 180 to 300°F, in a time ranging from fractions of a second to about 5 seconds. The calculated energy required to develop the image is approximately 1,13 cal/cm²/mil or 0635 watt-sec/cm²/mil (total thickness).

During the development, under the influence of the increased pressure of the molecular nitrogen, the softened binder is pushed out to form a minute vesicle. In the time of cooling the polymer forms dense crystalline shells around the vesicles which serve to scatter the light falling on them and form the image. The size of these scattering centers is much greater than the sum of the cross-sectional areas of the molecules which produced them and, depending on the composition of the layer, can be about $\frac{1}{4}$ to 2 microns.

The vesicular latent image is, as we have seen, composed of gas bubbles which have a tendency to escape from the layer. Obviously it is of the greatest importance to develop the film within a short time after its exposure has been completed. Noticeable density loss may occur if more than one minute elapses between exposure and development.

The sensitizer which remains after the exposure within the vehicle can be rendered ineffective by uniformly exposing the developed film and permitting the gas to diffuse at a temperature below 110°F. This operation, which may require several hours, is not necessary when the film can be protected either from exposure to elevated temperature or from exposure to actinic radiation.

The vesicular process is also suitable for making reversal images (371). The technique consists of letting the nitrogen gas diffuse from the exposed areas and re-exposing the entire film. During the heating, the released gas forms bubbles in the previously unexposed areas, giving the positive image of the original transparency. The procedure can be accelerated by making the film less rigid and more plastic, hence more permeable to the gas.

A properly developed and fixed vesicular image is stable in light and heat up to about 160°F; it is not affected by moisture, and, under normal storage conditions, it can be considered as one of the most permanent photographic images (372). Another advantage results from the low infrared absorption which causes silver transparencies to buckle and warp when the illuminating source has a high percentage of this radiation.

As a consequence of the remarkable characteristics of vesicular film and in contrast to conventional photographic material the effective density

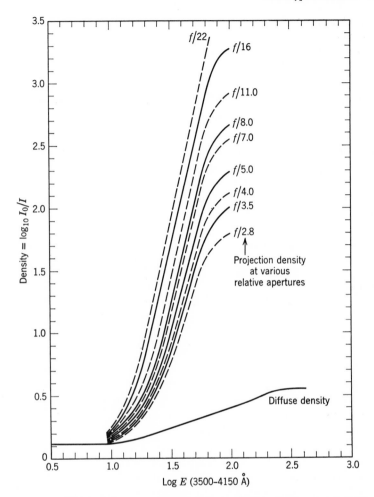

Figure 6.5. Characteristic curve—projection and diffuse density vs log exposure. Film type, Kalvar 7BTC.   Exposure, 40 sec at 350 to 415 mμ (reference 373).

of the projected image depends upon the aperture of the projecting lens (373,374).   This is shown in Figure 6.5 where the projection density for various apertures is plotted against the logarithm of the exposure.   It follows that the contrast can be varied merely by adjusting the light in the projector.

Vesicular material of the type just described was developed to the present stage of perfection by Kalvar Corp. and marketed under the same name.   The first commercial application of this film was in the field of microfilming for copying silver originals.   The high resolution of Kalvar microfilm (up to 500 lines/mm) makes it very suitable for this application. The sharpness of the image and the resolution, are however, influenced by the wavelength of the radiation used for exposure and by the developing conditions. In general, exposure to radiation of shorter wavelength and shorter development at lower temperature produce images of better resolution and sharpness. These precautions are not necessary when resolution of about 150 lines/mm is adequate.

Vesicular process was also suggested for the preparation of printing plates or Braille records (375). In such applications the exposed vesicular material is placed in contact with a receptor sheet coated with a thermoplastic resin and subjected to heat and pressure; expansion of gas within the exposed areas forms a relief image corresponding to the original light image.

6.7 REFLEX COPYING*

The first dry-developing diazotype paper was produced in the early twenties and since that time application of the light sensitivity of diazo compounds has become a distinct part of photographic technology. Over the past years numerous refinements have contributed to the wide use of the diazotype process. This process is, however, limited to the copying of transparent originals, and has found its widest usage in the reproduction of plans and tracings. In office copying the use of diazotype paper is handicapped primarily by the inability of diazo paper to produce reflex prints from opaque documents, or those printed on both sides.

For copying an image that is on an opaque support, or one that is printed on both sides, a reflex method is necessary (376). This copying method makes use of a radiation-sensitive layer, coated on a base that transmits the type of radiant energy capable of activating the sensitive layer. The image to be copied is placed in contact with the sensitive layer, and suitable radiation is sent through the base which is transparent to this radiation. A portion of this radiation (Figure 6.6) then passes through the sensitive layer and strikes the image; light image-areas reflect most of this radiation back to the sensitive layer, and dark image-areas, relatively little. The sensitive layer transmits part of this reflected radiation back to the support. A part of this transmitted radiation, in turn, is then reflected from the surface of the support, and repeats the path of the original incident radiant energy. This cycle—the back-and-forth travel of radiation between the back surface of the copying material and the image—is repeated until all the incident radiant energy has been absorbed.

---

* Reprinted from *Reprographie*, O. Helwich, Darmstadt, 1964, pp. 217–220.

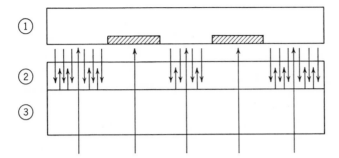

Figure 6.6. 1 *Original,* 2 *radiation-sensitive layer,* 3 *support.*

For negative-working systems a laterally reversed negative is obtained on the exposed and developed copying paper. This negative can be viewed by transmitted light, or, like any photographic negative, it can be used to make a positive copy.

Silver halide emulsions are used for most commercial reflex copying. In the past, other light-sensitive systems, such as dichromated-colloid layers or diazotype papers, were suggested. Such substances, however, suffer from inherent defects when applied to reflex copying. The lack of success in using these systems was primarily due to the failure in understanding the conditions which must be fulfilled if perfection is to be approached. The quality of the reflex print depends on many factors:

1. The quality of the original.
2. The properties of the radiation-sensitive layer.
3. The properties of the supporting base material.
4. The spectral characteristics of the radiation energy used for exposure.

The expected quality of the reflex copy can be expressed by calculating the reflex exposure ratio (RER), which can be defined as the fraction of the incident illumination absorbed in portions of the radiation-sensitive layer situated opposite nonimage areas as compared with the fraction absorbed in those parts of the emulsion that face image areas. The higher the ratio the better the quality of the reflex print.

Calculation of this ratio reveals that in order to obtain a satisfactory reflex copy both the radiation-sensitive layer and the supporting base material must be relatively transparent to the light used for exposure. For example, consider a diazotype paper with a supporting base (Figure 6.7) that transmits 20 per cent of the radiation striking its back surface ($Ts = 20$) to a radiation-sensitive top layer that, in turn, transmits 10 per cent of the light it receives ($Te = 10$) to the image being copied and absorbs the remaining part ($A = 100 - Te = 90$).

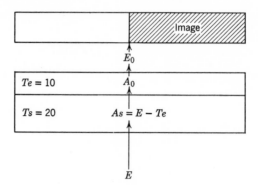

Figure 6.7

Thus, of the total incident illumination E ($E = 100$) striking the back surface of the copying paper, the percentage (E_0) that reaches the image being copied is $(Ts \times Te)/E$, or $20 \times 10/100$, which equals 2. The remaining part, (A_0), is absorbed by the sensitive layer ($A_0 = (Ts \times A)/E = 20 \times 90/100 = 18$).

Assume that the white or nonimage section of the document reflects 75 per cent of the radiation falling on it ($Rw = 75$), and the dark image section 10 per cent ($Rb = 10$). Thus, of the total illumination (E) originally falling on the back surface of the copying paper (Figure 6.8), the percentage re-entering the emulsion by reflection from the white section of the original (Ew_1) equals

$$Ew_1 = \frac{E_0 \times Rw}{E} = \frac{2 \times 75}{100} = 1.5 \tag{31}$$

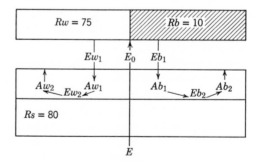

Figure 6.8

Similarly, the percentage from the black areas (Eb_1) equals

$$Eb_1 = \frac{E_0 \times Rb}{E} = \frac{2 \times 10}{100} = 0.2 \tag{32}$$

Since the radiation-sensitive layer absorbs 90 per cent of the illumination it receives, the percentage of E (the original illumination striking the reflex paper) absorbed in the radiation-sensitive layer after reflection from the white and dark areas, respectively, of the print being copied (Aw_1 and Ab_1), can be calculated as follows:

$$Aw_1 = \frac{(A_0 \times Ew_1)}{E} = \frac{18.0 \times 1.5}{100} = 0.27 \tag{33}$$

$$Ab_1 = \frac{(A_0 \times Eb_1)}{E} = \frac{18.0 \times 0.2}{100} = 0.036 \tag{34}$$

The unabsorbed radiation is transmitted through the light-sensitive layer to the supporting base, which, in turn, reflects a percentage (Rs) back to the photographic layer. Of the base-reflected illumination that re-enters the photographic layer (Ew_2 or Eb_2, according to whether the previous path has included reflection from white-image areas or from dark areas), the percentage A is then absorbed in the emulsion layer.

For example, if Rs is 80 per cent, the respective percentage of E absorbed by the sensitive coating after the first reflection from the base (Aw_2 and Ab_2) can be calculated as follows:

$$Ew_2 = \frac{(Ew_1 - Aw_1)Rs}{E} = \frac{(1.5 - 0.27) \times 80}{100} = 0.984 \tag{35}$$

$$Eb_2 = \frac{(Eb_1 - Ab_1)Rs}{E} = \frac{(0.2 - 0.036) \times 80}{100} = 0.131 \tag{36}$$

$$Aw_2 = \frac{A_0 \times Ew_2}{E} = \frac{18 \times 0.984}{100} = 0.177 \tag{37}$$

$$Ab_2 = \frac{A_0 \times Eb_2}{E} = \frac{18 \times 0.131}{100} = 0.023 \tag{38}$$

In a similar manner unabsorbed residual illumination continues until completely absorbed, to be reflected back and forth through the radiation-sensitive layer.

In our example the effect of subsequent reflections on the reflex exposure ratio is negligible, so that we obtain the following value for RER:

$$RER = \frac{18 + 0.27 + 0.177}{18 + 0.036 + 0.023} = \frac{18.447}{18.059} = 1.02 \tag{39}$$

The formula for calculating the reflex exposure ratio is then

$$\text{RER} = \frac{A_0 + Aw_1 + Aw_2 + \cdots + Aw_n}{A_0 + Ab_1 + Ab_2 + \cdots + Ab_n} \tag{40}$$

The initial light reflection from the side of support facing the radiation source and the light scattering within the emulsion layer are not taken into consideration.

A reflex exposure ratio of 1.02 is too small to allow proper registration of the image and nonimage areas of the original on the copy paper, for the nonimage areas receive only 1.02 times more light than the image areas.

To get acceptable reflex copy it is necessary that the areas on the copy sheet facing the nonimage section receive about 1.5 times more light than those facing the printed matter.

Higher values of RER can be obtained by using originals of high contrast and having the light-sensitive layer coated on highly reflecting base material to make possible multiple light reflections between the paper base of the copy sheet and the white background of the original.

Figure 6.9 shows the effect of (*A*) reflection from white areas in the original and the effect of (*B*) light absorption by the black areas on the reflex exposure ratio.   The steeper course of curve *A* indicates the higher importance of background reflectance for the quality of the reflex copy.

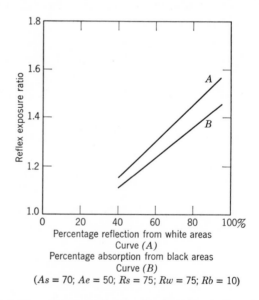

Figure 6.9.   The reflex exposure ratio as a function (A) of reflection from the background of the original, and (B) of light absorption by printed matter in the original.

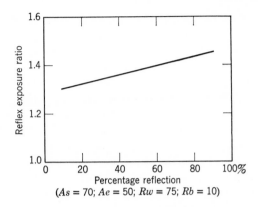

Figure 6.10. The reflex exposure ratio as a function of reflectance of the paper base.

Figure 6.10 shows that in reflex copying paper a highly reflecting base increases the RER, making multiple reflections between paper base and white image areas possible.

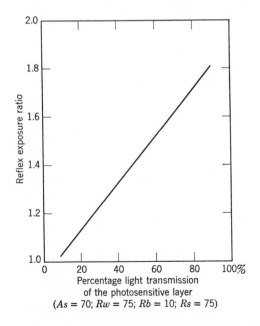

Figure 6.11. The reflex exposure ratio as a function of the transparency of the photo-sensitive layer.

It is also evident that increasing the transparency (*Te*) of the light-sensitive layer, thereby decreasing A_0, will raise the RER, and thus improve the quality of the reflex negative.   Multiple reflections intensify this effect.   In Figure 6.11 the calculated RER has been plotted against the percentage transmission, *Te*.

In diazotype coatings the only means of decreasing the light absorption is to use a lower concentration of diazonium compounds.   Lower amounts of these compounds per unit area, however, will definitely result in lower image density with consequent poorer contrast of the copy.

Spectral absorption characteristics together with spectral sensitivity of diazonium compounds are responsible for the incapability of diazotype papers to produce reflex copies.   This is demonstrated in Figure 6.12. A diazotype layer exposed to light in the spectral region to which it is most sensitive, around 4000 Å (377,12), transmits about 10 per cent of that radiation, and only after incident light has decomposed the bulk of the diazonium compound in the coating can the layer transmit sufficient light to the original so that it can be reflected back to the sensitive coatings. At this time, however, very little of the diazonium compound would be left to give an acceptable image after development.

To overcome excessive absorption of actinic light by the diazotype coating, Lumiere (378) suggested the use of a fine screen to divide the

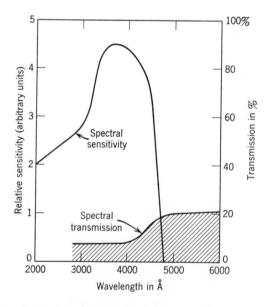

Figure 6.12.   *Spectral sensitivity and transmission curves of diazotype paper.*

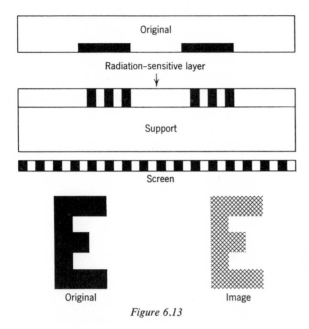

Figure 6.13

incident radiation into areas of high and low photochemical activity. Van der Grinten (379,380,381,382,383,384,385) exposed a diazo-sensitized sheet through such a screen and obtained, after development, a positive copy having a corresponding screen pattern in the image area (Figure 6.13). In this procedure the fraction of the incident light that passes through the interstices of the screen into the light-sensitive layer decomposes the bulk of the diazonium compound it intercepts, leaving relatively transparent areas which transmit light to the original (Figure 6.14). The light that is then diffusely reflected from the original re-enters not only these cleared areas, but also the opaque areas previously protected by the screen, where it decomposes part of the diazo material present. In commercial application, the fine mesh screen (having 250,000 openings per square inch), is actually part of the light-sensitive material and is removed from the transparent film base after the exposure by means of a stripper. The image is developed by the semiwet method giving a positive copy of the original from which an unlimited number of prints can be made.

Von Poser (386) avoided filters or screens by using colorless diazo compounds, for example, 1-diazo-2,4-dimethoxybenzene, 1-diazo-2,4-dimethoxybenzene-5-sulfonic acid, or 1-diazo-4-methoxy-3-methylbenzene. The reflex prints he obtained, however, rarely possessed sufficient contrasts

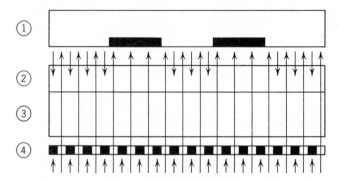

Figure 6.14.   1 *Original,* 2 *radiation-sensitive layer,* 3 *support,* 4 *screen.*

or clean backgrounds.   Derivatives of 1,2-naphthoquinonesulfonic acid for sensitizing reflection-copying layers were suggested by Polgar and Halmos (387).

In another effort to make diazo-sensitized material that is suitable for reflex copying, Herrick (388) sensitized polyvinyl alcohol film with 4-aminodiphenyl-4'-diazonium chloride and stretched the coated material, still wet, about five times its original length with gentle heating.   After drying, when the stretch becomes permanent, the film is placed over an original and exposed to plane-polarized light whose transmission axis is parallel to the transmission axis of the diazo compound.   The transmitted light is then reflected from the surface of the original to be copied, depolarized, and exposes the sensitive material.

Diazotype paper suitable for reflex exposure can also be made by coating a translucent support either with an ultraviolet absorbing agent (389) or with a fluorescent substance (390) which alters the wavelength of light to which the diazo compound is not, or is only slightly, sensitive. Such a treated paper is then overcoated, or coated on the opposite side, with a diazotype sensitizing solution.

Another way to overcome the excessive absorption of light by diazonium salts is to use radiation of longer wavelength, which these salts do not absorb.

While long wavelength or infrared radiation has not previously been used for exposing diazotype papers, the method of producing diazotype images by heat is not new, and many efforts have been made and a number of different methods have been suggested for preparing heat-developable diazotype papers (230).

From the formula for the reflex exposure ratio, it is obvious that the first requirement for copying with infrared radiation is to have the sensitizing solution coated on a support which freely transmits this radiation. The second requirement is that the support must be sensitized with a composition that forms a dye at elevated temperature. This can be achieved, for instance, by selecting a diazo-coupler combination that has such a property. Another possibility is the use of a diazonium salt, a coupler, and an alkali-releasing agent, for example, urea (278). Instead of an alkali-releasing agent, a distillable or sublimable coupling component coated on a separate sheet can be used (391). Especially suitable for this process are aryl diazosulfonates in combination with a coupling component containing a tautomeric keto-enol group (392). In making a copy, the heat-sensitive diazo sheet is placed in contact with the graphic original and subjected to infrared radiation, as in the familiar Thermo-Fax process. This procedure is graphically illustrated in Figure 6.15. After passing through the sensitive layer and the supporting base, the infrared radiation is absorbed in the image areas where it is converted to heat and re-radiated back to the copying sheet; here it triggers a reaction and thereby produces a visible copy of the original. At this stage the copy is still sensitive to heat. This sensitivity is easily destroyed by decomposing the remaining diazonium salt, either by exposing it to daylight, or when faster action is required, to a more intense ultraviolet light.

This procedure yields right-reading positive copies of transparent or opaque originals printed on one or both sides, copies which are, contrary to the majority of thermographic reproductions, light- and heat-stable.

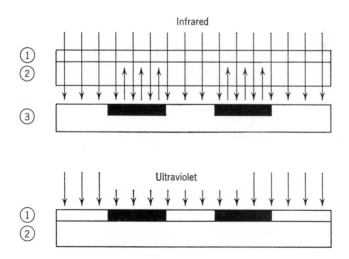

Figure 6.15. Reflex printing with infrared radiation. 1 Radiation-sensitive layer, 2 support, 3 original.

6.8   MANUFACTURE OF DIAZOTYPE MATERIAL

The manufacture of diazotype material consists of three operations: (1) formulation of the sensitizing solution; (2) preparation of the base material; (3) the coating and converting operation.

6.8a   *Formulation of the Sensitizing Solution*

The formulation of diazotype sensitizing solution, though simple in theory, is much more complicated in actual practice.   Light-sensitive layers, containing only the coupling component and the diazo compound, would be subject to excessive deterioration; heat and humidity play a vital role in this respect.   This deterioration is caused, in principle, by two reactions: the decomposition of the diazo compound and the premature coupling of the diazo compound, either with the product of its own decomposition or with the coupling component which is already present. This action leads not only to a loss of contrast resulting from the background discoloration, but it also affects the density of the image and the printing speed.   The decomposition of the diazo compound is not of great importance so long as the decomposition product has a low coupling energy and does not form a dye with the diazo compound during storage. The tendency to deteriorate during storage can be decreased by mixing the stabilized diazonium salt and powdered glucose (393) with the additional advantage of obtaining a dust-free product of improved water solubility.

A number of stabilizers are added to the sensitizing solution to prevent premature coupling.   Most frequently used are inorganic or organic acids such as oxalic, citric, or tartaric; boric acid prevents the premature formation of the azo dye to a greater extent than organic acid alone (394). Phosphoric acid is also effective (395).   Alpha-beta unsaturated acrylic acids, for example, crotonic acid, pentennic acid, sulfocinnamic acid, $\beta(\alpha\text{-pyridyl})$-acrylic acid, and β-2-methyl-quinolyl-(5)-acrylic acid, were suggested by Reichel (396).   The tendency for diazotype material to decompose or couple prematurely is reduced by adding to the sensitizing solution sulfonated o-hydroxycarboxylic acids of the benzene or naphthalene series, such as 5-sulfosalicylic acid or 6-sulfo-2-hydroxy-3-naphthalenecarboxylic acid (397), or 5-sulfo-N-methylanthranilic acid (398).   As solubilizer and stabilizer, the sodium salt of naphthalene-1,3,6-trisulfonic acid is used.   Sodium 1,5-naphthalene disulfonate was also used successfully.   Their solubilizing effect is attributed to highly soluble sulfonic acid groups, which combine with the unstable portion of diazo solution products.   These acids can cause background discoloration of the prints if used in excess.   Welch (399) found that naphthalene mono- or disulfonic acids or their alkali-metal salts also function as stabilizers and give cleaner backgrounds and show reduced print yellowing than when 1,3,6-naphthalenesulfonic acid is used. Examples of compounds which were found to be particularly effective are: 2,7-naphthalenedisulfonic acid, 2,6-naphthalenedisulfonic acid, 1,5-naphthalenedisulfonic acid and their sodium salts, sodium 1-naphthalene-sulfonate and sodium 2-naphthalene-sulfonate. Itaconic acid and α-methyleneglutaric acid are other examples of stabilizing acids (400). For the same purpose, addition of a saturated or unsaturated γ-lactone (401) or a wax or waxlike material (402) was claimed. In the last example, stearyl triethanolamine esters of long chained fatty acids were used as a dispersing agent.

Another method of improving the storage quality of diazotype papers is to mix the diazonium compound with a finely divided water-insoluble cation-exchange resin, such as a sulfonated phenolic resin, which insolubilizes the diazo compound and makes the light-sensitive layer more stable (403).

These corrective measures can be used only to a limited extent since the use of any stabilizer tends to slow the developing speed of the paper. It is practically impossible to stabilize the coating completely for long periods, and, in practice, commercial firms limit their guarantees from three to six months. In an atmosphere of controlled temperature and humidity, diazotype papers last longer.

After development of diazotype paper, an excess of alkali and of the coupling component remains on the surface of the paper, and after a certain time, depending upon the particular compounds used, the backgrounds of such prints discolor because of slow oxidation of the coupler and of the photolysis products of the diazo compounds in the presence of alkali. The reason for this is that coupling components, usually of polyphenolic or aminophenolic nature, give, in a basic medium, colored oxidation products. Similar products are obtained by the photolysis of diazo compounds; 1-diethyl-aminobenzene-4-diazonium chloride is decomposed by light into 1-diethylamino-4-oxybenzene

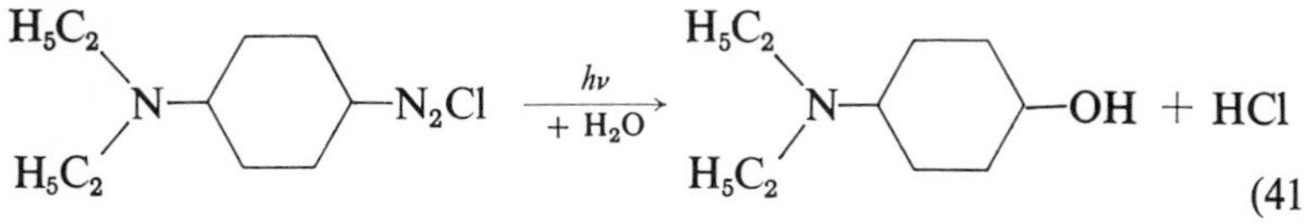

$$\text{(41)}$$

and 4-diazo-diphenylamine gives 4-oxydiphenylamine

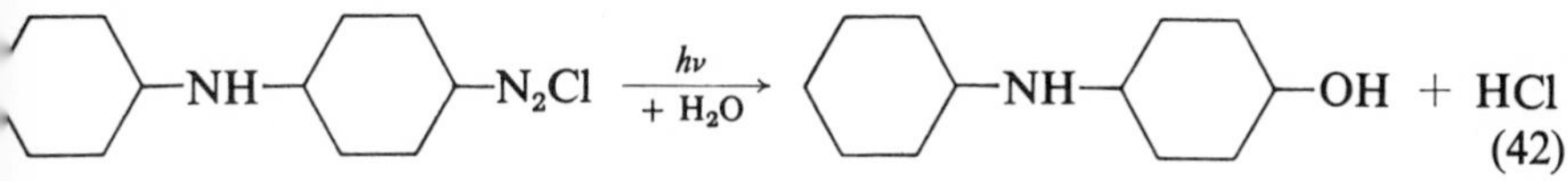

$$\text{(42)}$$

It is possible, of course, to remove these harmful compounds from the surface of the paper by washing the prints in water after development, as was done in the primuline process, or treating the developed prints with an aqueous solution of secondary sodium phosphate (404). By this action, however, the advantage of a dry process would be lost. Indeed, progress of the diazotype process has been checked for many years by the unsuccessful attempts to prevent background areas of prints from becoming yellow and finally brown.

It was proposed in the past to treat the prints with an inorganic reducing agent after development (405), but the problem of background discoloration was not solved until Krieger and Zahn (406) suggested the use of derivatives of thiocarbonic acids, for example, thiourea, thiosinamine, thiocarbamic, and thioglycolic acid. Thiourea especially proved to be very effective, and practically all diazotype materials have thiourea incorporated in the light-sensitive layers. Since it is a mild reducing agent under acidic conditions, thiourea counteracts discoloration of the background areas by oxidation. However, diazotypes which are to be interfiled with iron-silver brownprints should not contain sulfur stabilizers since gradual bleaching of the silver images may take place (407). *o*-Morpholinobenzene diazonium chloride and resorcinol-3-sulfonic acid, a combination which does not exhibit background discoloration even without the addition of thiourea, is recommended for manufacture of diazotypes which can be stored with silver Van Dyke prints (408).

Another series of reducing agents, for instance, aldehydes, glucose, and aliphatic hydroxy acids, was suggested by van der Grinten (409). A mixture of nickel sulfate and lactose or other saccharride was recommended as a further improvement (410).

Various attempts to mask the discoloration of the background have been made by employing as base material a paper made from dyed stock, taking advantage of the power of a light-blue color to mask a yellow or tan color on white (411). Aluminum or bronze powder incorporated into the light-sensitive layer was used for the same purpose (412).

The presence of the foregoing reducing agents also has a beneficial influence on the light stability of the azo-dye image (413). Moureu, Du Fraisse, and Badoche (414) have verified that certain dyes, particularly methylene blue and dyes of the triphenylmethane group—malachite green, crystal violet, etc.—also produce an antioxidizing effect. Zinc chloride complexes of methylene blue and of urea were reported to be effective in this respect (415). Besides the stabilizing effect of zinc chloride on diazonium salts, already mentioned earlier, it promotes faster coupling and chelates with the dye to form a brighter image. The mechanism by which zinc chloride performs all these functions is obscure.

Also generally included in the sensitizing solution are numerous humectants, used to promote the desired reaction and to control the flatness of the finished prints. Glycerin or ethylene glycols are most often used. Yet, under unfavorable conditions, the maximum amount of humectant that can be used without deleterious effect is not sufficient to assure full development. Thus, acetamide, urea, or other carboxamides (416) are mixed in a sensitizing solution. 1-Allyl-3-β-hydroxyethyl-2-thiourea (417) or tetrahydrofurfuryl alcohol (418) were also proposed. The tendency of the coated material to curl can be prevented by coating the reverse side of the paper base with plain water. In other instances it might be necessary to employ gelatin, polyvinyl alcohol, or some other water-soluble film-forming material before sensitizing the front side (419). Other additions and modifications may be necessary to avoid tackiness and brittleness of the coated material.

In the sensitizing solution for one-component papers, practically all of the ingredients just mentioned are used, except, of course, the coupling component which forms the essential part of the developer. Also zinc chloride is excluded because in this case it inhibits rather than aids the coupling reaction. As mentioned earlier, in the preparation of one-component papers the selection of diazo compounds is restricted to those which form a dye immediately upon application of the liquid developer. Among others, tetrazo-N,N'-bis (4-aminophenyl)alkylene-diamines were recommended as suitable for one-component papers (420). If the reaction is slow, a portion of the diazo compound dissolves and spreads sidewise, causing poor contrast and fuzzy lines. This effect is called "bleeding." As an additional action to prevent the bleeding of the image, it may be necessary to incorporate morpholine citrate or cyclohexylamine (421), or a condensation product of dicyandiamide, formaldehyde, and an ammonium salt (422). 2-Hydroxymethyl-1',2',4,5-naphthimidazole also improves the water fastness of the azo-dye images (423) in copies made on two-component diazotype paper containing a diazo compound and an azo component with a group enhancing the solubility in water. By replacing with a magnesium salt a part of the zinc chloride usually used in the formulation, it is claimed that brighter and better azo-dye images with less tendency to bleed are produced (424). It has been found previously by Kögel and Neuenhaus (161) that the bleeding of images, when in contact with water, can be prevented with copper, nickel, mercury, and other metallic salts. These salts apparently form a metal complex with the diazo compound. Depending on the metal, the shades or tones of the images can be varied to a certain degree.

For color improvement, nickel or copper sulfate was recommended (402). Later Schmidt and Krieger (426,427) used complex salts of titanium with an organic hydroxy acid, for example, titanium potassium oxalate, titanium sodium citrate or tartrate, for the same purpose.   In order to increase the visual density of diazotype images, inorganic bromides (428) or water-soluble chromium salts (429) are added to the sensitizing solutions.   The brightness of the developed dye image can be considerably improved with phenylphosphinic acid, phenylphosphonic acid, borophosphoric acid, phenylsulfinic acid, etc., or their soluble salt.   The dye-brightening agent can be included in the sensitizing solution or can be a part of a precoat, and is especially noted in formulations which produce blue, black, maroon, or sepia prints (430,431).   Additional benefits derived from using the dye-brightening agents include increased stability of the dye images against atmospheric gases and improvement in the shelf life of the sensitized material.   In some instances, a hypsochromatic shift was observed as in material in which the dye is formed by 2,3-dihydroxy-naphthalene-6-sulfonic acid; the purplish hue of the blue dye loses its red character.   Incorporation of aryl derivatives of guanidine, such as phenylbiguanidine, improves the water resistance (432), and a xanthine, for example, caffeine or theophylline, improves the general quality of diazotype reproductions (123).   Many other chemicals contribute to the finer quality of diazotype prints and their use is by no means standard with all diazotype coaters.   They must be very carefully selected so that they perform the particular function expected of them and do not have adverse effects on other properties.   It requires, obviously, much experimentation and painstaking mutual adaptation of all factors—base material, coating technique, and final use, if a satisfactory product is to be produced.

In preparing the sensitizing solution the order in which the components are dissolved is, in most instances, unimportant.   Generally the acid is dissolved first.   The solution is prepared at about 40 to 50°C, and is allowed to cool to 20 to 25°C before coating.   Prior to coating a small quantity of saponin or other wetting agent is added.

6.8b   *Preparation of the Base Material*

Various base materials, such as opaque or transparent paper, cloth, and films, can be sensitized with diazotype solution.   Also metals such as aluminum have been suggested for some applications (433,434).   Paper is, however, the most generally used base material.   Most popular is standard-weight (20 lb for 500 17 × 22 inch sheets), which is tough and durable enough for most uses.   Where prints are not handled a great deal, lightweight paper (17 lb) can be used, whereas heavyweight paper (32 lb) is recommended for hard usage over a long period.   In order to obtain high spectral transmittance in the ultraviolet region, pulp of low lignin content and a proper kind of filler is used in the manufacture of the base paper. Also, the extent of beating strongly influences the ultraviolet transmittance (435). A special grade of hydrogenated resin is used for sizing to insure high "wet-strength," good fold- and tear-strength, both of which are required. Aftersizing with starch and its derivatives is often necessary. Sodium alginate, with or instead of starch sizing, was used by Slifkin (436). All the chemicals which are used in the preparation of paper for diazotype must be iron- and copper-free, to prevent the formation of highly colored products, with the phenolic components of the sensitizing solution (437). Copper, iron, lead, and their salts also catalytically accelerate the decomposition of diazonium compounds. For this reason, all parts of the paper-making machine, such as drying rollers, which come into contact with the paper, must be plated. Many times, blue or green dyes, in very small amounts, are added to the paper pulp to improve the appearance of the final product. Additional brightness can be achieved by adding optical brighteners and fluorescent dyes which absorb ultraviolet light normally present in daylight and fluorescent light, and emit it as visible light.

Care must be given to the selection of the dye, since many, either alone or in combination with phenols, exhibit undesirable color characteristics. In order to obtain smoother paper, a small amount of hardwood fiber is added. The receptivity of the sensitizing solution is controlled by calendering, which must be performed to a definite degree.

Today many diazotype papers are precoated prior to sensitizing in order to prevent diffusion of the solution into the paper, so that all diazonium salts will remain on the surface. If a nonprecoated sheet is used, much of the salts will soak into the paper and will be hidden behind paper fibers where the light cannot penetrate. The precoating can be applied as a separate procedure or the paper can be precoated prior to the application of the sensitizing solution.

Several materials can be used for precoating. Alumina pigment with a particle-size range of 0.02 to 0.04 micron, together with sodium caseinate, which serves as a film-forming binder, was recommended by Frederick (438). In a similar formulation an aqueous colloidal dispersion of silica and polysterene (439) or silica and styrene/maleic-acid copolymer (440) was employed. In another patent, a suspension of silica in an aqueous solution of a condensation product of dicyandiamide, ammonium chloride, and formaldehyde, was recommended in order to obtain a material with increased image density and better resistance to storage (441,442). All the advantages of the silica-precoated material plus prevention of feathering and running of subsequently applied ink are achieved by precoating the paper with silicates of a metal of the second and third groups of the periodic system (443). Aluminum silicate, also, is recommended by Ozalid Co. Ltd. (444). Jahoda (445) prefers a discontinuous layer of discrete, brittle, water-impervious resin particles obtained on the paper surface by evaporating polystyrene resin or similar material. The discontinuous precoat layer presents an enlarged surface with a high degree of orderliness. With colloidal polystyrene precoat the prints do not show the fibrous structure of the base paper (446). Increased dye-line density and improved smoothness can be obtained with an aqueous dispersion of rice starch (447) or with a suspension of unburst maize-starch grains in a low-viscosity solubilized starch (448). Combination of colloidal silica, starch, and barium sulfate with a binder such as polyvinyl alcohol is also claimed to improve the density and contrast of diazotype prints (449). The purpose of the barium sulfate is to increase smoothness and whiteness of the paper. The starch, on the other hand, is claimed to improve the water and ink fastness and the fingerprint resistance of the prints. Metal fluorides, substantially insoluble in water, were proposed by Landau (450). Precoating with noncolloidal silica in conjunction with binding material is the subject of another patent (451). The claims are restricted to a weight ratio of silica/binder of $1:1$ to $3:1$. Addition of finely divided silica or alumina to an aqueous dispersion of polyvinyl acetate gives diazotype material of improved printing speed and yields prints of high densities (452,453). Polyvinyl acetate can be replaced with polyvinyl alcohol or starch (454). Carboxymethylcellulose and other water-soluble cellulose ethers were employed by Slifkin (455). Duerr (456) prevented mottled effect in sensitized baryta-coated papers by interposing between the diazo and the base a gelatin layer containing a guanide or a biguanide base, for example, heptylguanide, benzoylguanide, and heptylbiguanide. An intermediate layer of polymethacrylic acid ester improves over-all quality of the printed sheet (457).

To eliminate the separate coating operation Franke (458) suggested the application of a suspension of silica with or without starch to the paper at a given point in the drying section of the paper machine. Or finely divided silica in the dry state is brushed into the paper surface (459).

Attempts have been made to supersede precoating by the inclusion of colloidal silica in one solution together with the sensitizing chemicals (460). High density lines and uniform surface are obtained when modified corn starch and polyvinyl acetate emulsion is added to the sensitizing solution (461). Alumina having a particle size ranging from 5 microns down was used in a similar manner (462), reducing the penetration of the sensitized solution into the base without producing a tendency in the finished print to curl.   Colloidal titanium dioxide improves, in addition, the whiteness of the prints (463).   The "one-pot" solution yields, under certain conditions, very intense images but by precoating a further increase in contrast can be achieved.

Dyes can be added to the precoat solution in order to make tinted diazotype papers useful for office reproduction where the color is an important mark of identification.   These dyes, of course, must be stable in acid and alkaline medium, water-insoluble, and lightfast.

In recent years the diazotype process has become increasingly more important in the preparation of intermediate prints on a translucent or transparent base material.   Transparentized paper (464), cellulose ester (465), glass-filled polyester base (466), saponified cellulose acetate (467, 468), vinyl polymers (469,470), polycarbonates (471), etc., are used for this purpose.   Glassine paper was employed by Peterson (464).   These products must satisfy quite different requirements than do products for regular diazotype papers.   The most important is the opaqueness of the azo-dye images to ultraviolet light (472).   Other flexible supports, such as cellophane (473) or cellulose acetate, are impregnated with an alcoholic solution of diazonium compounds (474).   The purpose of the solvent is to swell the surface of the material to be sensitized so that the sensitizer can penetrate through part of its thickness. γ-Lactones were recommended as swelling agents for cellulose ethers (475).   Water-repellent vinyl polymers and copolymers are sensitized by applying a solution of diazotype sensitizing components in a mixture of low-boiling ketones and γ-lactones, for example, γ-valerolactone (476).   Solutions containing inflammable solvents have to be handled in rooms properly ventilated and coated in fireproof machines.   Paper-plastic laminate such as thin cellulose acetate films coated with polyvinyl acetate adhesive and cemented to a smooth surface of high-tear strength paper was suggested as the support for diazotype layers by Parry and Torday (477).   Woven cloth intended for diazotype coatings must first be pretreated by coating with a water-resistant resin such as polyvinyl butyral (478,479), polyamide copolymers (480), and others.   The adhesion of the resins can be improved by addition of urea-formaldehyde resins (481).

In many instances, the base material must first be provided with a subbing layer, to take and hold the sensitizing solution (482) which usually contains a polymeric binder or film former.   The nature of the polymeric substance depends mainly on the characteristics of the supporting base, on the required properties of the film, and on the solubility.   Nitrocellulose (483), cellulose acetate butyrate (484), vinylidene copolymers (485), and polyvinyl acetate (486) are often used.   Linear superpolyamide (487) or copolymers of styrene and maleic acid or vinyl acetate and maleic acid (488) were likewise applied.   Straw (489) dispersed diazo compound and coupler in a water- and acid-insoluble copolymer, such as vinyl-acetate/crotonic-acid or styrene/maleic-anhydride.   Vinyl-acetate/ crotonic-acid copolymer (490) and butadiene acrylonitrile or butadiene styrene copolymer (491) were also employed as an intermediate layer for polyethylene terephthalate films.   Finely divided pigments can be added to obtain opaque films or to adapt the surface for writing.   Sometimes it it is necessary to increase the surface of the film by roughening the film in order to improve the adhesion of diazotype coatings as is the case with terephthalate films (492,493).

A water emulsion of polyvinyl acetate was recommended by Krieger (484) and by Franke and Murray (495).   The elimination of inflammable solvents in the foregoing patents is of great advantage in the preparation of waterproof light-sensitive lacquer coatings.

6.8c   *Coating*

In the manufacture of diazotype material the sensitizing solution is applied on paper or other material on a specially designed coating machine, consisting essentially of an unwind arbor, coating applicator, drying channel, and rewind arbor.   The coating is done so that the material to be coated is threaded from a supply roll, which can be several thousand yards long, through a series of metal rollers, and is led to the applicator. The applicator, a rubber-covered metal roller about six inches in diameter, is partially immersed in sensitizing solution, and, by rotating opposite the direction the material is traveling, applies the sensitizing solution to the underside of the moving web.   The excess solution is wiped off with a glass bar at a point three to four feet beyond the point of application. More modern machines, designed for coating at high speeds, are equipped with an air knife to remove the excess of diazo coating solution by an air stream emerging from a pressure chamber through an adjustable slot. The air knife must be lined up at a certain distance from the moving web, depending on the slot opening.   The air pressure must also be controlled accurately to insure even and smooth coating.   During the coating it is necessary to keep the density of the sensitizing solution constant; other-wise, the density of the developed paper would change from the start to the end of the coating operation.   This is due to the evaporation of the solvent and to the accumulation of lint.   It is advisable, therefore, to frequently filter the solution and replace the lost liquid.   Continuous feeding by a circulating system is necessary for long runs.   The liquid level in the coating tray and the temperature of the solution are other factors which must be kept constant to insure uniform quality.   Most coating machines are equipped with rotating rollers with a bow pointing in the direction of the web movement. These rollers are located after the coating station, and their purpose is to prevent moisture wrinkles by minimizing internal stresses.

The solution is not laid upon the surface in the form of a layer, as in gelatin coating for example, but it penetrates slightly into the surface of the paper. The penetration can be controlled by the tension and temperature of the paper. After the solution has been applied and the excess removed by a rigid scraper bar or by means of an air doctor, the coated paper enters a drying channel where it is dried with hot air or infrared radiation. When entering the drying channel the temperature of the paper rises very quickly and after reaching the maximum stays constant until the moisture is reduced to about 30 per cent. After reaching this point it is important to avoid overheating; otherwise the paper can become brittle. It is recommended that the coated paper be dried to a moisture content of about 3.5 per cent, based on the dry weight of the paper, in order to obtain the best possible keeping quality. For fast-coupling combinations it is recommended that the paper be dried slightly more than 3.5 per cent (496). Higher moisture content has an adverse effect on keeping quality, whereas more complete drying increases brittleness. Paper which is too dry develops slowly and has a reduced printing speed. For this reason routine determination of the moisture content is a must. This measurement is based on the electric conductivity and is done with moisture meters, either on tear-outs of the coated paper or on the moving web immediately before the wind-up of the dried paper. A moisture meter can be permanently attached to the coating machine and by connecting it with a recording instrument permanent records can be obtained.

After passing the drying section of the coating machine the paper is cooled by contact with a chilled roller and is wound up, then re-rolled in the converting department into small rolls or cut into sheets. Folded paper is a relatively recent development. Next it is packaged with waxed and wrapping papers in order to protect it from moisture and light. In special cases small bags containing water-absorbing agents, such as silica gel, are placed in a metal container with the paper. As soon as the package or the roll is opened, however, the sensitized paper starts to absorb moisture; this can result in as much as a 20 per cent increase in printing speed in a humid atmosphere. When the paper is stored at high humidity for several days the diazonium salts will migrate deeper into the paper and longer exposures will be necessary to decompose the coating. This effect is often accompanied by a loss in color and density.

6.9 APPLICATIONS

The diazotype process gets its name from diazo compounds, which are, as we have seen, the light-sensitive substances used for sensitizing. The diazotype process is also called "whiteprinting," since a positive dye image of the original is formed on a white background. This is in contrast to blueprints, which provide a blue-colored negative copy from a positive master. The diazotype process is an economical and convenient method for making direct reproductions of written, drawn, or typed material, and is primarily used in the drafting, engineering, and architectural professions.

Diazotype material usually has high contrast, and is especially suitable for the foregoing applications. The contrast depends on the maximum dye density which the layer can develop, and thus the gamma of the material is in direct relation to the concentration of diazo compound in the layer. For monochromatic actinic illumination Herrick (497) derived a theoretical equation relating monochromatic dye density to exposure. It was shown that the initial actinic optical density of the diazo compound is of the greatest importance in determining the general sensitometric behavior of the diazotype layer; in other words, the contrast is directly proportional to the actinic light absorption of the diazo component.

The characteristic curve of diazotype material has no, or a very short, straight-line portion. In general, the toe is short, turns quickly into a convex curve, and flattens off at higher densities. As the density of the print is lowered by exposure, the contrast increases continuously and reaches a moderately high value in the low-density region. This is almost an ideal situation for reproduction of line work. Unlike silver halide photographic layers, the sensitometric characteristics can be affected only very slightly by the formulation of the sensitizing solution, the exposure, and development. According to one patent (498), the addition of ascorbic acid to the sensitizing solution gives lower contrast and greater printing latitude. In another (451) the contrast can be increased up to 30 per cent by precoating the paper base with a noncolloidal silica suspended in an aqueous solution of resin. Very soft gradation can be obtained by employing two types of light-sensitive diazo compounds having different extinction coefficients (499).

Diazotype papers are manufactured to give images in a range of colors. The oldest commercial prints were red-line positives which are still preferred in some countries. In the United States the blue line is most popular, and since World War II there has been a growing demand for black-line prints. Red and blue diazotype papers can be produced by the use of a single coupler, whereas diazotype material producing neutral black shades contains a mixture of two (500) or more coupling components, for instance, a combination of acetoacetanilide, 2,3-dihydroxynaphthalene-6-sulfonic acid and diresorcyl sulfide or sulfoxide (111), or a combination of acetoacetanilide, 2,3-dihydroxynaphthalene and 2,3-dihydroxynaphthalene-6-sulfonic acid (501). Black images are also obtained from material sensitized with diazotized *p*-phenylenediamine derivative and containing a *m,m*-dioxydiphenol as yellow coupler and a dihydroxy-2-naphthanilide as blue coupler (502). In some instances a shift toward a purer black is accomplished by including into the sensitizer a colorless noncoupling benzimidazole hydrochloride (503). Diazonium salts derived from 4-morpholino-2,5-dialkoxyanilines may be coupled with a mixture of dihydroxynaphthalenes and acetoacetamides, yielding blue and yellow dyes to give a good black color (504). By using the semiwet process reasonably good black lines are obtained with phloroglucinol in the developing solution. Black color becomes especially significant in the production of intermediate diazotype prints where a dye line of the high ultraviolet absorption is of vital importance. The most suitable image color for a diazotype intermediate is yellow, such as that obtained when using a monoether of resorcinol and 1-diazo-3-methyl-4-diethylanilide, but, because of poor visibility in ordinary light, most intermediates are compromises, giving brown or sepia images. The demand for this material has increased considerably in the last few years and the intermediates have become an indispensable part of engineering reproduction systems. Because diazotype is a positive working process the intermediate does not function as a reversal means, as does the negative in conventional photography. In many instances the intermediates, or, as they are sometimes called, the "second originals," yield, on recopying, better copies than can be made from the original tracings. For the purpose of making changes or additions to the original drawings more visible, diazotype intermediate papers with semireproducible characteristics have been introduced. When a corrected intermediate of this type is reproduced the original lines appear weak and faded whereas the changes stand out very clearly and sharply (505). Diazotype images can be erased by the means of chemical eradicators consisting of an oxidizing agent, such as potassium permanganate in acid solution or a reducing agent, for example, stannous chloride in hydrochloric acid. The chemical removal of the image is followed by a secondary step involving neutralizing and bleaching with sodium metabisulfite in the first case and potassium bicarbonate in the second.

The simplicity, economy, and convenience of diazotype printing has resulted in its increasing use for different applications. One comparatively recent development is the utilization of diazotype papers in office systems and office "convenience copying." For this purpose papers of different weights are used. The bulk of the production is on 20.5 lb paper, but thinner papers are also used. Diazotype paper sensitized on both sides can be produced by impregnating the paper support first with an ultra-violet absorbing agent, for example, benzophenone derivatives or derivatives of 4,4'-diaminostilbene-2,2'-disulfonic acid (506); such paper can be exposed on both sides. Obviously this treatment prevents the use of the copy for further copying (507). The demand for different colored supports, for color coding, soon became evident and, at the present time, diazotypes on yellow, green, blue, or red-tinted base paper can be made. To match various printing machines diazotype papers of different sensitivities must be made available and are manufactured in as many as five printing speeds, often labeled "very slow, slow, medium, fast, and ultra-fast," or as "standard, rapid, extra rapid, and super rapid." This sensitivity designation merely reflects differences in the diazo concentration in the sensitized layer, since, for a heavier coating, a longer time is needed for exposure. Obviously the higher printing speed of fast papers is obtained at the expense of the line density. It is quite difficult to control the printing speeds of diazotype papers to a margin close enough so the user will not notice variations, since the moisture content of the paper and heat of the printer contact glass also have an effect upon the printing speed. Thus, a sheet removed from a sealed box and exposed immediately, will, most likely, be slower than one which has been out of the package for 30 minutes.

In spite of many advantages the use of diazotype papers in the office is handicapped by the long exposure time required when semiopaque originals are used. To improve this situation the National Association of Blueprint and Diazotype Coaters (NABDC), in cooperation with several paper manufacturers, introduced a new type of paper called "General Purpose Bond" for preparing originals. This paper is opaque in appearance but sufficiently transparent for diazo reproduction. The recent appearance of diazo compounds with an increased light-sensitivity range, however, is a substantial improvement and the only serious factor limiting the use of diazotype papers in office copying is their inability to produce, in one single step, prints from opaque originals or documents printed on both sides.

Attempts to use diazotype material for the reproduction of continuous tones were unsuccessful, mainly because of the high contrast in the low densities and low contrast in the higher densities; no portion of the sensitometric curve is linear to a degree sufficient to be useful for continuous tone work. To obtain moderately satisfactory results it was recommended that an original positive transparency be used, with the maximum density not more than 1.3 and the minimum density not less than 0.20 (508). The structure of the base paper and the color of the image also contribute to the quality of continuous tone reproduction.

Certain improvements were achieved by interposing an ultraviolet absorbing layer between two diazo layers (509,510). During the exposure the upper layer receives the shadow image of the continuous tone original, and the protected lower layer receives only the highlights. Another effort to control the halftone effect of reproduction was made by Sanders and Wilders (511) by adding an azo-coupling component to the copy during alkaline intermediate treatment. Better rendition of continuous tone diapositives was reported from the use of two diazo compounds of different sensitivities (512). The more light-sensitive diazo is destroyed more rapidly so that the high-density contrast is increased, whereas the slower diazo contributes to the production of a lower highlight contrast. The two-diazo system was also suggested for the copying of drawings having lines of different densities (513).

Diazotype material coated on a photographic base and having a softer gradation was introduced by Ozalid under the name "Drytone," a process which yields quite satisfactory continuous tone prints.

The latitude of diazotype papers can be further increased by using screened halftone masters obtained from continuous tone negatives (514). The continuous tone is transformed into discontinuous dots which vary in size, and only the high densities of the sensitive paper are used for image formation. A simplified screening method employing high contrast positive films was described by Landau (515). As in previous methods the contrast of the print cannot be controlled by the type of sensitive layer and developing methods as in conventional photography, but is controlled by the contrast of the master.

The copying of drawings and plans on diazotype papers accounts for the bulk of current consumption, and other base materials have been used for sensitizing. Specially treated cloth is used where durability of the copy is important. In the last few years there has been a noticeable trend to diazotype material coated on films, such as cellulose acetate or polyethylene terephthalate, where transparency and dimensional stability are particularly important (516). The great variety of modern polymeric film formers has stimulated these developments, and these have almost entirely replaced the ordinary transparent diazo papers. Since the sensitive layer is located on the top of the support and is completely independent of the characteristics of the base material, it produces sharper images of higher contrast.

This new technology opened an entirely new area for the reproduction engineer. The first diazo films were made on cellophane and were introduced in 1932 by Kalle A.G. under the name "Ozaphane." Films of this nature were very moisture sensitive and for this reason it was recommended that they be overcoated with moisture-proof film formers (517). Soon after diazo films were first made on cellophane, cellulose nitrate and cellulose acetate (518), saponified or not saponified, were introduced as a supporting base material. Further research and new developments made the production of brilliant-colored dye images on clear, transparent films possible; these find application in the preparation of cartoons and educational materials. Their main advantage lies in their economy, easy processing, and the choice of color. By overlaying cyan, magenta, and yellow and black diazotype images made from appropriate color separation positives, full color rendition can be obtained. This technique, together with the possibility of easy retouching, is valuable in the field of photomechanical reproduction. A negative diazotype color-proofing process was described by Straw and Herrick (519).

Diazotype film, or foils as they are sometimes called, are often used for the preparation of large slides for overhead projectors; for this method of visual communication, which is rapidly winning recognition (520), foils in blue, red, orange, green, and violet are manufactured in addition to the foregoing colors. By superimposing one color over another impressive color effects can be achieved, giving life and increased interest to the projected subject. To secure perfect registration, a special printing unit was made available (521). Attempts have also been made to produce a multicolored print on a single sheet of diazotype film. In principle the technique for obtaining two- or three-color prints is simple: a one-component diazo foil is treated after the exposure with different coupling components in selected areas and is developed by passing the print through an ammonia developer. Another method, patented by Slifkin (522,523), employs in the sensitive layer a combination of couplers: a slow acting coupler which produces blue tones in the high density areas and a fast coupler which forms contrasting yellow tones in the low density areas. Two-colored prints can also be made from material sensitized with two types of diazo compounds of different spectral sensitivity, each being destroyed by different electromagnetic radiation (524,525). The simplest solution is, however, to coat the front and back surfaces of a transparent support containing an ultraviolet absorber with a diazo sensitizing solution. On development, this gives two different colors (526).

Diazotype films are also playing an important role in the field of microfilm reproduction and are used for copying 35 and 16 mm silver negatives (527,528). Since the diazo process is a direct-positive process, any number of negatives can be made from the original negative roll or from the diazotype duplicate. In this way the original can be used only once. The loss of definition from copy to copy is very small, only about 4 per cent, as opposed to 20 per cent loss of definition when silver halide films are used. The azo-dye image is, for all practical purposes, grainless, and for this reason the enlargements made from diazotype films are sharper and cleaner than those obtained from conventional photographic micro-films. Characteristics of the diazo-film duplicates and their suitability for further printing were studied by Benbrook (529) and by Smith (530). The unusual combination of high resolution at approximately unit gamma in diazotype films is of considerable advantage in high-acuity reproduction, where the image detail must be preserved through several generations (531). The image-definition capabilities of diazo and silver halide materials were compared by Alfaya (532); it was shown that the resolving power of commercially available diazo film is exceeded only by that of the highest resolution spectrographic emulsions. Diazotype images are capable of high resolution because of the essentially grainless structure of the dye molecules which compose the image. A silver image is composed of inorganic particles approximately 3000 Å in diameter, and a diazo image is an organic dye only about 15 Å in size. Because of a tougher surface diazotype films are more resistant to scratching and abrasion than gelatino/silver halide films and thus stand up better under constant handling. Another advantage, which is very significant in microfilming, is the possibility of mounting the diazotype film in aperture cards prior to exposure. The diazotype image, when properly processed and stored, is, contrary to general opinion, quite stable and will last for at least 50 years, which is longer than is required by most applications.

While the foregoing applications of diazo compounds account for the volume of the present usage, other uses have been patented. A method of forming relief Braille records was suggested by Peterson and Fabian (375), and is based, like the Kalvar system, on the evolution of nitrogen from diazo compounds on exposure to light. Among other applications, multicolor printing of textiles might be worth mentioning. These processes, among others (533,534,535), were described by Slifkin (536, 537) and by Ravich (538,539).

REFERENCES

1. L. Starotin. Fr. pat. 689,318/1930.
2. K. H. Saunders. *The Aromatic Diazo Compounds*, E. Arnold and Co., London, 1949.
3. H. Zollinger. *Diazo and Azo Compounds*, Interscience Publishers, New York, 1961.

4. W. E. Kemmerlich.   U.S. pat. 1,973,148/1934.

5. M. L. Crossley, R. H. Kienle, and C. H. Benbrook.   *J. Am. Chem. Soc.*, **62**, 1400–1404 (1940).

6. M. Lucius and Brüning.   Ger. pat. 89,437/1896; A. Feer.   *Bull. Soc. Mulhause*, **61**, 220 (1891).

7. I. G. Farben.   Brit. pat. 296,008/1928; Fr. pat. 657,695/1927; Fr. pat. 672,466/ 1929.

8. The British Thomson-Houston Co. and E. D. Regis.   Brit. pat. 303,427/1929.

9. E. C. Marks.   Brit. pat. 317,335/1929.

10. A. N. Nesmeyanov, K. A. Kockeshkov, V. A. Klimova, and N. K. Gipp. *Ber.*, **68B**, 1877 (1935).

11. S. S. Nametkin and N. W. Melnikov.   *Compt. Rendu. Acad. Sci. USSR*, **1**, 228 (1935).

12. M. Aroney, R. J. W. Le Fevre, and R. L. Werner.   *J. Chem. Soc.*, **1955**, 276.

13. E. A. Boudreaux.   *Dissertation*, Tulane University, 1962.

14. L. A. Kazitsyna, O. A. Reutov, and Z. F. Buchkovskii.   *Russ. J. Phys. Chem.*, **34**, 404 (1960).

15. K. Yamatani.   Japan. pat. 39–4273/1964.

16. W. H. Von Glahn and H. A. Bergstrom.   U.S. pat. 2,612,494/1952.

17. J. M. Straley.   U.S. pat. 2,498,722/1950.

18. D. F. DeTar and T. Kosuge.   *J. Am. Chem. Soc.*, **80**, 6072–6077 (1958).

19. P. J. Zandstra and E. M. Evleth.   *J. Am. Chem. Soc.*, **86**, 2664–2666 (1964).

20. J. L. F. Turner.   *Brit. J. Phot.*, **100**, 420–421 (1953).

21. M. P. Schmidt in E. Stenger.   *Fortschritte der Photographie*, Vol. I, pp. 374–395, Leipzig, 1938.

22. Y. Nakagawa.   *Nippon Shashin Gakkai Kaishi* 26, **4**, 179–188 (1963).

23. Y. Nakagawa and Y. Kunitomo.   *Nippon Shashin Gakkai Kaishi* 25, 175–182 (1962); *ibid.*, 26, 15–22 (1963).

24. K. Hoffmann and L. Fisher.   *Angew. Chem.*, **66**, 593–595 (1954).

25. K. J. P. Orton and J. E. Coates.   *J. Chem. Soc.*, **1907**, **91**, 35–36.

26. A. Seyewitz and D. Mounier.   *Bull. Soc. Chim.*, **43**, 648–654 (1928).

27. D. J. Brown.   *Chem. Ind.*, **22**, 146–148 (1944).

28. W. Schröter.   *Z. Wiss. Phot.*, **28**, 1–29/1930.

29. M. Horio.   *J.S.C.I. Japan*, **37**, 322–326 B, 1934.

30. H. Yamamoto.   *J.S.C.I. Japan*, **38**, 275–280 B, 1935.

31. M. Horio and S. Yamashita.   *Z. Wiss. Phot.*, **33**, 273–280, 1935.

32. R. Moraw and J. Munder.   *Kolloquium Über Wiss. Photographie*, Section IV/II, Zürich, 1961; *Photographic Science*, edited by W. F. Berg, Focal Press, London, 1963, pp. 390–399.

33. C. F. Goodeve and L. J. Wood.   *Proc. Roy. Soc. (London)*, **166A**, 342–343 (1938).

34. N. Fukushimo and M. Horio.   *J.S.C.I. Japan*, **34**, 367–377 B (1931).

35. R. Moraw.   *Reprographie*, **4**, 19–21 (1964).

36. J. Eggert.   *Z. Electrochem.*, **34**, 602 (1928).

37. J. Eggert.   *Photo. J.*, **76**, 17–26 (1936).

38. G. Gavlin.   *Government Report PB 101*, 866, April 1950.

39. M. P. Schmidt and G. von Poser.   Ger. pat. 763,388/1952.

40. G. von Poser.   U.S. pat. 2,322,982/1943.

41. M. P. Schmidt and G. von Poser.   U.S. pat. 2,378,583/1945.

42. W. M. Hinman.   U.S. pat. 2,027,226/1936.

43. This study, written in French, can be obtained from Andrews Paper and Chemical Co., Inc., Port Washington, New York.
44. M. P. Schmidt and G. Werner. U.S. pat. 2,158,836/1939; Dutch pat. 47,899/1938.
45. M. P. Schmidt and W. Krieger. U.S. pat. 1,628,279/1927.
46. W. Neugebauer, M. Tomanek, and H. Böttger. U.S. pat. 2,672,418/1954.
47. W. H. von Glahn, L. N. Stanley, and G. T. Parker. U.S. pat. 2,528,460/1950.
48. W. H. von Glahn and L. N. Stanley. U.S. pat. 2,552,354/1951.
49. W. G. von Glahn and L. N. Stanley. U.S. pat. 2,597,412/1952.
50. L. van der Grinten. Brit. pat. 281,604/1926.
51. T. P. W. Sanders and J. H. A. Widers. U.S. pat. 2,773,768/1956.
52. R. J. Cox and R. G. D. Moore. U.S. pat. 2,948,613/1960.
53. S. C. Slifkin. U.S. pat. 2,632,703/1953.
54. E. W. Sproengerts and R. Franke. U.S. pat. 1,870,930/1932.
55. W. D. Peterson. U.S. pat. 2,605,182/1952.
56. W. H. von Glahn and L. N. Stanley. U.S. pat. 2,529,464/1950.
57. Chem. Fabriek L. van der Grinten. Brit. pat. 867,629/1961.
58. Chem. Fabriek L. van der Grinten. Ger. pat. 1,155,331/1963.
59. Kalle A.G. Belg. pat. 629,326/1963.
60. W. Vanselow, A. Weissberger, and D. B. Glass. U.S. pat. 2,350,843/1944.
61. Chem. Fabriek L. van der Grinten. Dutch pat. 70,612/1952.
62. Chem. Fabriek L. van der Grinten. Brit. pat. 867,630/1961.
63. Chem. Fabriek L. van der Grinten. Belg. pat. 629,466/1963.
64. O. Süs. U.S. pat. 2,665,985/1954.
65. M. P. Schmidt and R. Franke. U.S. pat. 2,037,542/1936.
66. A. van Loon and K. M. Hutgens. Ger. pat. 1,092,767/1960.
67. S. Sakurai. U.S. pat. 1,983,005/1934.
68. E. Lehman. U.S. pat. 1,753,708/1930; Ger. pat. 487,247/1926; Ger. pat. 515,205/1928.
69. A. Weissberger and W. Vanselov. U.S. pat. 2,298,444/1942.
70. H. D. Murray and A. Tyrrell. Brit. pat. 538,869/1941.
71. Chem. Fabriek L. van der Grinten. Brit. pat. 937,510/1963; Fr. pat. 1,269,874/ 1961; Fr. pat. 1,269,875/1961; Fr. pat. 1,269,876/1961.
72. G. Werner and G. von Poser. U.S. pat. 3,028,240/1962; Belg. pat. 594,327/ 1960; Brit. pat. 853,020/1960; Brit. pat. 941,838/1963; Ger. pat. 1,086,126/1960; Fr. pat. 1,269,905/1961; Japan. pat. 39–10163/1964.
73. O. Süs, G. Werner, and W. Wettlauffer. U.S. pat. 2,840,472/1958.
74. W. P. Leuch. U.S. pat. 2,198,827/1940.
75. M. P. Schmidt, W. Neugebauer, and R. Franke. U.S. pat. 1,816,989/1931.
76. G. Werner. U.S. pat. 2,063,832/1963.
77. W. P. Leuch. U.S. pat. 2,215,739/1940.
78. D. D. Jacobus and J. R. Bose. U.S. pat. 2,375,366/1945.
79. D. Johnston. U.S. pat. 2,456,514/1948.
80. E. N. Mason and D. J. Norman. Brit. pat. 539,031/1941.
81. D. D. Jacobus and J. R. Bose. U.S. pat. 2,326,782/1943.
82. G. Werner. U.S. pat. 2,286,701/1942.
83. T. P. W. Sanders and H. W. H. M. Rocken. U.S. pat. 3,016,298/1962; Brit. pat. 895,250/1962.
84. E. N. Mason and D. J. Norman. Brit. pat. 740,565/1955.
85. S. C. Slifkin. U.S. pat. 2,531,004/1950.

86. For more information, see K. Venkataraman. *The Chemistry of Synthetic Dyes*, Academic Press, New York, 1952.

87. J. B. Conant and W. D. Peterson. *J. Am. Chem. Soc.*, **52**, 1220–1232 (1930).

88. R. M. Elofson, R. L. Edsberg, and P. A. Mecherly. *J. Electrochem. Soc.*, **97**, 166 (1950).

89. R. Wistar and P. D. Bartlett. *J. Am. Chem. Soc.*, **63**, 413–417 (1941).

90. Z. J. Allan. *Collection Czech. Chem. Commun.*, **16–17**, 620 (1952).

91. C. R. Hauser and D. S. Breslow. *J. Am. Chem. Soc.*, **63**, 418–420 (1941).

92. R. Pütter. *Angew. Chem.*, **63**, 188–192 (1951).

93. H. H. Hodgson. *J. Soc. Dyers Col.*, **58**, 228–231 (1942).

94. L. P. Hammett. *Physical Organic Chemistry*, p. 314, McGraw-Hill Book Co., Inc., New York, 1940.

95. H. Zollinger. *Helv. Chim. Acta*, **34**, 591 (1951); **36**, 1723 (1953); **36**, 1730 (1953); **36**, 1732 (1953); **39**, 1600 (1956).

96. L. P. Hammett. *J. Am. Chem. Soc.*, **59**, 96–103 (1937).

97. Color Index, edited by Soc. Dyers Col. and Am. Assoc. Tex. Chem. Col., 2nd edition, Bradford and Lowell, 1956–1958, 4 volumes.

98. W. H. von Glahn and L. N. Stanley. U.S. pat. 2,485,122/1949.

99. H. G. J. de Boer and E. D. G. Frahm. U.S. pat. 3,039,872/1962.

100. W. H. von Glahn and L. N. Stanley. U.S. pat. 2,432,549/1947.

101. W. H. von Glahn and L. N. Stanley. U.S. pat. 2,523,889/1950.

102. W. H. von Glahn and L. N. Stanley. U.S. pat. 2,490,605/1949.

103. F. W. Neumann. U.S. pat. 2,467,358/1949.

104. W. H. von Glahn and L. N. Stanley. U.S. pat. 2,437,868/1948.

105. W. H. von Glahn and L. N. Stanley. U.S. pat. 2,516,931/1950.

106. W. H. von Glahn and L. N. Stanley. U.S. pat. 2,545,057/1951.

107. C. E. Herrick and C. S. Slimowicz. U.S. pat. 2,940,852/1960; Brit. pat. 840,945/1960; Can. pat. 597,079/1960; Ger. pat. 1,068,556/1959.

108. W. H. von Glahn and L. N. Stanley. U.S. pat. 2,541,727/1951.

109. S. R. Buck. U.S. pat. 2,593,839/1952.

110. W. H. von Glahn and L. N. Stanley. U.S. pat. 2,536,989/1951.

111. J. Sulich. U.S. pat. 2,717,832/1956; Brit. pat. 786,981/1955.

112. O. Süs. U.S. pat. 2,286,656/1942.

113. M. Tomanek. U.S. pat. 2,829,976/1958; Brit. pat. 804,501/1958; Ger. pat. 1,014,432/1957.

114. G. W. Pedlow and F. W. Neumann. U.S. pat. 2,542,566/1951.

115. F. W. Neumann. U.S. pat. 2,542,560/1951.

116. J. M. Straley. U.S. pat. 2,432,593/1947.

117. W. H. von Glahn and L. N. Stanley. U.S. pat. 2,551,570/1951.

118. C. E. Slimowicz. U.S. pat. 2,970,909/1961; Ger. pat. 1,068,555/1959.

119. M. P. Schmidt and O. Süs. U.S. pat. 2,150,565/1939.

120. O. Süs. U.S. pat. 2,233,038/1941.

121. T. P. W. Sanders and J. H. A. Wilders. U.S. pat. 2,792,303/1957.

122. R. Zahn, O. Süs, and R. Franke. U.S. pat. 2,196,950/1940; Brit. pat. 496,090/1938; Dutch pat. 47,840/1940.

123. F. A. H. Kessels. U.S. pat. 2,617,726/1956; Dutch pat. 68,034/1951.

124. M. P. Schmidt and W. Krieger. U.S. pat. 1,758,676/1930.

125. W. H. von Glahn and L. N. Stanley. U.S. pat. 2,487,034/1949; Brit. pat. 624,472/1949.

126. S. C. Slifkin. Brit. pat. 634,341/1950.

127. S. C. Slifkin. U.S. pat. 2,560,137/1951.
128. S. C. Slifkin and T. J. Trojan. U.S. pat. 2,494,906/1950.
129. J. M. Straley. U.S. pat. 2,500,099/1950.
130. D. Straw. U.S. pat. 2,915,396/1957.
131. W. H. von Glahn and L. N. Stanley. U.S. pat. 2,537,001/1951.
132. S. C. Slifkin and T. D. Trojan. U.S. pat. 2,537,098/1951.
133. M. P. Schmidt and O. Süs. U.S. pat. 1,989,065/1935.
134. W. H. von Glahn and L. N. Stanley. U.S. pat. 2,537,106/1951.
135. W. H. von Glahn and L. N. Stanley. U.S. pat. 2,688,543/1954.
136. H. C. Unkauf. U.S. pat. 2,533,185/1950.
137. W. H. von Glahn and L. N. Stanley. U.S. pat. 2,542,849/1951.
138. J. F. Morgan. U.S. pat. 2,431,190/1947.
139. W. H. von Glahn and L. N. Stanley. U.S. pat. 2,542,850/1951.
140. O. Süs and M. Glos. U.S. pat. 2,974,042/1961; Brit. pat. 814,581/1959; Ger. pat. 1,025,265/1958.
141. W. H. von Glahn and L. N. Stanley. U.S. pat. 2,542,848/1951.
142. J. M. Straley. U.S. pat. 2,532,744/1940.
143. W. H. von Glahn and L. N. Stanley. U.S. pat. 2,552,355/1951.
144. A. van Dormael. U.S. pat. 2,531,091/1950.
145. S. C. Slifkin. U.S. pat. 2,536,398/1951.
146. W. H. von Glahn and L. N. Stanley. U.S. pat. 2,547,843/1951.
147. F. W. Neumann. U.S. pat. 2,548,845/1951.
148. M. P. Schmidt and O. Süs. U.S. pat. 2,212,959/1940; Ger. pat. 697,051/1940.
149. O. Süs and H. Schlesinger. U.S. pat. 2,946,684/1960; Ger. pat. 1,086,124/1960.
150. O. Süs. Ger. pat. 1,134,588/1962; Belg. pat. 615,223/1962.
151. O. Süs and G. Werner. Ger. pat. 838,692/1952.
152. J. De Jonge, R. J. H. Alink, and R. Dijkstra. Rec. Trav. Chim., **69**, 1448 (1950).
153. J. Schmidt and W. Maier. *Ber.*, **64**, 767 (1936).
154. J. de Jong and R. Dijkstra. *Rec. Trav. Chim.*, **68**, 426 (1949).
155. W. Hückel. *Theoretical Principles of Organic Chemistry*, Vol. I., p. 803, Elsevier Publishing Co., New York, 1955.
156. A. G. Green, C. F. Cross, and E. J. Bevan. *Brit. J. Phot.*, **37**, 657 (1890); *J. Soc. Chem. Ind.*, **9**, 1001 (1890); *Ber. Deut. Chem. Ges.*, **23**, 3131 (1890); Ger. pat. 56,606 (1890).
157. M. Andresen. *Phot. Korr.*, **32**, 284 (1895).
158. M. Schoen. Ger. pat. 111,416 (1899).
159. O. Ruff and V. Stein. *Ber. Deut. Chem. Ges.*, **34**, 1668 (1901).
160. G. Kögel and H. Neuenhaus. *Z. Wiss. Phot.*, **24**, 171 (1926).
161. G. Kögel and H. Neuenhaus. U.S. pat. 1,444,469/1923; Brit. pat. 210,862/ 1923; Brit. pat. 234,818/1924; Ger. pat. 376,385/1917; Ger. pat. 381,551/1920; Ger. pat. 386,433/1921; Ger. pat. 419,987/1923; Ger. pat. 422,972/1924.
162. O. Süs. *Ann.*, **556**, 65–84, 85–90 (1944); *ibid.*, 557, 237 (1947).
163. M. P. Schmidt and W. Krieger. U.S. pat. 1,628,279/1927.
164. M. P. Schmidt, W. Krieger and E. Spröngerts. U.S. pat. 1,936,957/1933.
165. B. W. Colman. U.S. pat. 2,671,728/1954.
166. Ozalid Co., Ltd. Fr. pat. 1,301,579/1962.
167. J. G. B. Halden. Brit. pat. 900,816/1962.
168. J. G. B. Halden. Brit. pat. 919,125/1963.
169. Chem. Fabriek L. van der Grinten. U.S. pat. 3,077,401/1963; Brit. pat. 842,243/1960; Brit. pat. 871,315/1961; Ger. pat. 1,126,734/1962.

170. A. van Loon and K. M. Hutgens. U.S. pat. 3,081,166/1963.
171. C. E. Herrick, Jr. U.S. pat. 3,087,403/1963.
172. J. G. B. Halden. Brit. pat. 911,915/1962.
173. J. G. B. Halden. Brit. pat. 853,859/1960.
174. J. G. B. Halden. Brit. pat. 895,946/1962.
175. C. A. Ackermann. U.S. pat. 3,060,828/1962.
176. J. G. B. Halden. Brit. pat. 895,945/1962.
177. J. G. B. Halden. Brit. pat. 902,562/1962.
178. H. Stegonwalner. Brit. pat. 865,031/1961.
179. R. C. Goodman and E. G. Mastroianni. Brit. pat. 872,771/1961; Belg. pat. 588,980/1960.
180. L. J. Bagnelle. Brit. pat. 873,424/1961.
181. F. O. Trump. U.S. pat. 2,839,978/1954.
182. F. O. Trump. U.S. pat. 2,878,742/1956.
183. General Aniline and Film Corp. Brit. pat. 807,486/1959.
184. F. G. Wilde. Brit. pat. 821,904/1957.
185. F. H. Frantz. U.S. pat. 2,887,942/1955.
186. H. H. Sullivan, W. L. Sullivan, and F. G. Wilde. U.S. pat. 2,475,809/1949.
187. F. G. Wilde. U.S. pat. 2,909,980/1955.
188. G. K. Hurlbut. U.S. pat. 2,895,397/1957.
189. F. H. Frantz. U.S. pat. 2,735,346/1956.
190. F. H. Frantz. U.S. pat. 2,895,824/1954.
191. G. L. Hassler. U.S. pat. 2,431,041/1944.
192. J. G. B. Halden. U.S. pat. 3,020,818/1962.
193. J. A. Bungay. U.S. pat. 2,812,699/1957; Brit. pat. 782,353/1957.
194. J. R. Reed. U.S. pat. 2,200,996/1940.
195. Ozalid Co., Ltd. Brit. pat. 925,871/1963.
196. G. R. Lambert. U.S. pat. 3,144,334/1964; Brit. pat. 923,883/1963.
197. F. W. von Meister. U.S. pat. 2,302,277/1942.
198. F. W. von Meister and F. W. Andrew. U.S. pat. 2,308,130/1943.
199. L. van der Grinten. U.S. pat. 1,841,653/1932.
200. J. M. Eder. *Z. Wiss. Phot.*, **33**, 1–12 (1934).
201. M. P. Schmidt and K. Hessert. U.S. pat. 1,837,679/1931.
202. Chem. Fabriek L. van der Grinten. Dutch pat. 65,605/1950.
203. Kalle A.G. Ger. pat. 684,334/1939.
204. W. P. Leuch. U.S. pat. 2,113,944/1938.
205. Chem. Fabriek L. van der Grinten. Brit. pat. 957,838/1964; Belg. pat. 629,466/1963; Fr. pat. 1,227,310/1961.
206. Chem. Fabriek L. van der Grinten. Brit. pat. 961,515/1964.
207. Chem. Fabriek L. van der Grinten. Brit. pat. 957,837/1964; Japan. pat. 39–8147/1964.
208. Chem. Fabriek L. van der Grinten. Brit. pat. 957,836/1964.
209. J. H. A. Wilders and B. H. M. Leonen. Brit. pat. 961,515/1964.
210. Chem. Fabriek L. van der Grinten. Belg. pat. 606,539/1961; Brit. pat. 953,908/1964.
211. T. P. W. Sanders and J. van Rensen. U.S. pat. 2,199,925/1940; Brit. pat. 510,407/1939; Dutch pat. 47,625/1940.
212. C. A. Crowley and J. B. Mullen. U.S. pat. 2,308,058/1943.
213. Kalle A.G. Belg. pat. 448,643/1943.
214. F. A. H. Kessels. U.S. pat. 2,657,137/1953.

215. F. A. H. Kessels. U.S. pat. 2,657,141/1953.

216. F. A. H. Kessels. U.S. pat. 2,657,140/1953; Dutch pat. 74,109/1954.

217. G. Pop. U.S. pat. 2,776,888/1957.

218. F. van der Grinten. Dutch pat. 53,196/1942.

219. J. Hruby, P. B. Streigh, and J. L. Tregay. U.S. pat. 2,981,171/1961.

220. C. Bruning. Brit. pat. 818,017/1959.

221. F. H. Frantz. U.S. pat. 2,836,110/1958.

222. W. Longdon and K. P. Farrell. Brit. pat. 890,530/1962.

223. Chem. Fabriek L. van der Grinten. Brit. pat. 784,898/1957.

224. W. Longdon and K. P. Farrell. Brit. pat. 908,812/1962.

225. F. H. Frantz. Brit. pat. 910,779/1962.

226. J. A. Bungay. Brit. pat. 788,939/1958.

227. D. J. Norman, A. L. Newman, E. Woodham, and E. H. Goodchild. 926,951/ 1963 and 926,952/1963.

228. W. P. Leuch. Brit. pat. 570,027/1945.

229. S. C. Slifkin and J. Sulich. U.S. pat. 2,546,791/1951.

230. J. Kosar. *Phot. Sci. Eng.*, **5**, 239–243 (1961).

231. J. E. Dietzgen. *Reprod. Rev.*, February 1962, 14, 15, 22, 26.

232. B. Friedland. *J. Phot. Sci.*, **10**, 174–177 (1962).

233. H. Denstman. *Ind. Phot.* 12, **6**, 76–77 (1963).

234. C. E. Herrick. U.S. pat. 2,923,625/1956; Brit. pat. 810,081/1959.

235. P. Dieterle. U.S. pat. 2,228,562/1941.

236. P. Dieterle. U.S. pat. 2,918,858/1959.

237. C. E. Herrick. U.S. pat. 2,948,208/1960.

238. Minnesota Mining and Manufacturing Co. Brit. pat. 853,406/1960.

239. I. W. Ellsworth and K. S. Johnson. U.S. pat. 2,817,279/1957.

240. I. W. Ellsworth and K. S. Johnson. U.S. pat. 2,979,404/1961.

241. Salvadori & Leperche, and Frangialli & Cie. Fr. pat. 1,010,585/1952.

242. F. H. Frantz. U.S. pat. 3,027,822/1962.

243. K. Yamamoto. Japan. pat. 39–8141/1964.

244. H. J. Brunk and M. Dickason. U.S. pat. 2,141,103/1938.

245. J. H. de Boer and R. J. H. Alink. U.S. pat. 2,239,704/1941; Ger. pat. 714,560/ 1941.

246. G. D'Hauterive. U.S. pat. 1,966,755/1934.

247. Neulipa G.m.B. H. Ger. pat. 506,412/1930.

248. J. J. Dorel, L. R. Dorel, G. Laplace, and R. Nicole. Fr. pat. 1,301,867/1961.

249. H. G. Greig. U.S. pat. 2,653,091/1953.

250. F. van der Grinten. Dutch pat. 30,636/1933.

251. M. P. Schmidt and O. Süs. U.S. pat. 2,216,137/1940.

252. M. Morrison. U.S. pat. 2,732,299/1956.

253. R. J. Klimkowski, G. E. Beauchamp, and W. D. Bauer. Belg. pat. 609,912/1961.

254. R. J. Klimkowski, L. Amariti, and A. Janda. Belg. pat. 625,554/1962.

255. H. Goto. Japan. pat. 37–17,734/1962.

256. H. D. Murray, A. Tanenbaum, and R. P. Royer. Brit. pat. 818,912/1954.

257. Bauchet & Cie. Brit. pat. 909,491/1962; Fr. pat. 1,249,913/1960; Belg. pat. 597,307/1960.

258. W. R. Lawton and E. F. Lopez. U.S. pat. 3,076,707/1963; Belg. pat. 612,963/ 1962; Fr. pat. 1,294,386/1962.

259. C. M. Aebi and F. W. Haining. U.S. pat. 3,154,417/1964; Belg. pat. 641,904/ 1963; Fr. pat. 1,352,900/1964.

260. H. C. Hills. U.S. pat. 3,135,607/1964.
261. J. Kosar. Belg. pat. 645,321/1964.
262. J. Kosar. U.S. pat. 3,157,503/1964; Belg. pat. 645,320/1964.
263. T. T. Kashiwabara. Unpublished results.
264. H. Zollinger. *Diazo and Azo Compounds*, p. 250, Interscience Publishers, Inc., New York, 1961.
265. J. H. de Boer. U.S. pat. 2,113,193/1938; Ger. pat. 704,070/1941.
266. R. J. H. Alink and J. H. de Boer. U.S. pat. 2,178,771/1939.
267. R. J. H. Alink, J. H. de Boer, K. H. Klaassens, and C. F. Veenemans. U.S. pat. 2,311,016/1943; Austral. pat. 20,573/1943.
268. M. P. Leuch and S. C. and P. Harding, Ltd. Brit. pat. 438,805/1935; Brit. pat. 427,962/1935.
269. R. J. H. Alink and J. Aninga. U.S. pat. 2,172,783/1939.
270. W. Neugebauer and O. Süs. U.S. pat. 2,205,991/1940; Brit. pat. 476,122/1937; Ger. pat. 674,144/1939.
271. W. Neugebauer and O. Süs. Ger. pat. 680,268/1939.
272. G. Fritz. U.S. pat. 3,140,180/1964; Brit. pat. 937,160/1963; Fr. pat. 1,360,701/ 1963.
273. R. J. Klimkowski and J. W. Krueger. U.S. pat. 3,046,128/1962; Brit. pat. 953,254/1964.
274. H. J. Thomiszer. U.S. pat. 3,012,141/1961; Brit. pat. 912,890/1962; Belg. pat. 607,276/1961.
275. E. Dietzgen Co. Brit. pat. 915,337/1962.
276. A. Schaeffer. Fr. pat. 1,255,950/1959.
277. J. D. Kendall and K. Reynolds. Brit. pat. 815,005/1959.
278. J. E. Dietzgen and H. J. Thomiszer. Belg. pat. 605,810/1960; Brit. pat. 907,724/ 1962; Brit. pat. 932,589/1963.
279. Chem. Fabriek L. van der Grinten. Dutch pat. 626,167/1962.
280. Bauchet & Cie. Fr. pat. 1,336,307/1963; Fr. pat. 1,325,692/1962.
281. R. M. Lindquist and Z. Reyes. U.S. pat. 3,111,407/1963.
282. Kalle A.G. South Afr. pat. 63/301.
283. E. Land. U.S. pat. 2,600,996/1952.
284. H. G. Greig. U.S. pat. 2,691,587/1954.
285. T. U. Marron and C. J. Shoemaker. U.S. pat. 2,774,669/1956.
286. A. Tanenbaum and R. P. Royer. Brit. pat. 816,601/1959.
287. K. Kubo. Japan. pat. 38–12096/1963.
288. C. H. Benbrook and C. E. Herrick. U.S. pat. 2,789,904/1957; Can. pat. 575,744/ 1959.
289. O. Süs. U.S. pat. 2,217,189/1940; Brit. pat. 544,702/1942; Ger. pat. 734,302/ 1943.
290. W. H. von Glahn and M. K. Reichel. U.S. pat. 2,429,249/1947.
291. O. Süs. U.S. pat. 2,694,009/1954.
292. O. Süs. U.S. pat. 2,680,062/1954.
293. J. J. Sagura and J. A. van Allan. U.S. pat. 3,113,865/1963; Belg. pat. 603,419/ 1960; Brit. pat. 931,746/1963.
294. H. Behmenburg and M. Glos. Ger. pat. 1,117,387/1961; Brit. pat. 948,661/1964.
295. R. B. West. *Anthony's Phot. Bull.* 15, 335 (1884).
296. A. Feer. Ger. pat. 53,455/1889.
297. M. Andressen. *Ber. Deut. Chem. Ges.*, **28**, 327 (1886); Ger. pat. 82,239/1894.
298. M. P. Schmidt and W. Krieger. U.S. pat. 1,760,780/1930.

299. P. Frangialli. Can. pat. 468,451/1950.
300. E. Barde. U.S. pat. 2,313,288/1943.
301. R. Landau. Brit. pat. 864,011/1961.
302. A. Hantzsch. *Ber.*, **27**, 1715 (1894).
303. H. H. Hodgson and E. Marsden. *J. Chem. Soc.*, 470 (1943).
304. E. S. Lewis and H. Suhr. *Ber.*, **92**, 3031 (1959).
305. R. Dijkstra and J. de Jorg. *Rec. Trav. Chim.*, **77**, 538 (1958).
306. General Aniline and Film Corp. Brit. pat. 615,685/1949.
307. A. Feer. Ger. pat. 53,455/1889.
308. A. and L. Lumiere and A. Seyewetz. *Bull. Soc. Franc. Photogr.*, February 1896.
309. M. P. Schmidt and H. Neuroth. Fr. pat. 729,841/1932; Ger. pat. 597,450/1934.
310. G. von Poser, M. P. Schmidt, and G. Werner. U.S. pat. 2,197,456/1940; Brit. pat. 518,129/1940; Brit. pat. 518,162/1940.
311. C. E. Herrick and A. H. Balk. U.S. pat. 2,854,338/1958; Brit. pat. 786,403/1957.
312. General Aniline and Film Corp. Brit. pat. 865,507/1961.
313. J. F. P. Tranchant. Fr. pat. 1,336,808/1963.
314. M. P. Schmidt and H. Neuroth. U.S. pat. 1,934,011/1933.
315. H. Z. Lecher. U.S. pat. 2,125,509/1938.
316. J. J. Chechak. U.S. pat. 2,418,623/1947.
317. M. P. Schmidt and G. von Poser. U.S. pat. 1,967,371/1934.
318. J. H. de Boer, C. J. Dippel, and R. J. H. Alink. U.S. pat. 2,034,508/1936.
319. J. H. de Boer and R. J. H. Alink. U.S. pat. 2,095,408/1937.
320. J. H. de Boer, C. J. Dippel, and R. J. H Alink. Austral. pat. 7303/1932.
321. R. J. H. Alink. U.S. pat. 2,083,285/1937.
322. J. H. de Boer. Austral. pat. 8224/1932.
323. J. H. de Boer and K. H. Klaassens. U.S. pat. 2,106,868/1938.
324. R. J. H. Alink and J. H. de Boer. U.S. pat. 1,973,788/1934.
325. G. von Poser and R. Franke. U.S. pat. 2,066,918/1937.
326. M. K. Reichel. U.S. pat. 2,618,555/1952.
327. R. J. H. Alink, C. J. Dippel, and K. J. Keuning. *Philips Technical Review*, Vol. 9, 289–300 (1947–1948).
328. R. J. H. Alink, C. J. Dippel, and K. J. Keuning. *J. Soc. Motion Picture Television Engrs.*, **54**, 345 (1950).
329. C. J. Dippel. *Phot. J.*, **90B**, 34–41 (1950).
330. Philips. N.V. Belg. pat. 637,058/1963; Brit. pat. 953,431/1964.
331. Philips. N.V. Belg. pat. 637,400/1963; Brit. pat. 960,695/1964.
332. J. G. Bos, R. J. H. Alink, and C. J. Dippel. *Rec. Trav. Chim.*, **71**, 945–953 (1952).
333. J. de Jong, J. Jonker, K. J. Keuning, and C. J. Dippel. U.S. pat. 2,764,484/1956.
334. R. J. Alink, K. H. Klaassens, and H. J. Houtman. U.S. pat. 2,067,690/1937; Dutch pat. 72,259/1953; Ger. pat. 707,461/1941.
335. C. J. Dippel and J. J. Houtman. U.S. pat. 2,838,398/1958.
336. C. J. Dippel and J. J. Houtman. U.S. pat. 2,735,773/1956; Dutch pat. 77,917/1955; Ger. pat. 921,245/1954.
337. R. J. H. Alink, C. J. Dippel, and H. J. Houtman. U.S. pat. 2,609,295/1952.
338. J. de Jong, H. Jonker, K. J. Keuning, and C. J. Dippel. U.S. pat. 2,923,626/1960.
339. T. W. van Rijssel, H. J. Houtman, and H. Jonker. U.S. pat. 2,733,144/1956.

340. J. G. Bos.   U.S. pat. 2,571,670/1951.
341. J. G. Bos, N. H. Haack, C. J. Dippel, and K. J. Keuning.   U.S. pat. 2,571,671/1951.
342. C. J. Dippel, R. J. H. Alink, and K. J. Keuning.   U.S. pat. 2,183,447/1939; Dutch pat. 53,832/1942; Brit. pat. 511,816/1939.
343. J. de Jonge, H. Jonker, K. J. Keuning, and C. J. Dippel.   U.S. pat. 2,868,643/1959.
344. Philips. N.V.   Dutch pat. 81,921/1956.
345. C. J. Dippel and H. Jonker.   U.S. pat. 2,750,292/1956.
346. N. R. Bacon and R. B. Lindemeyer.   *J. SMPTE*, **73**, 213–215 (1964).
347. A. Baril, I. H. De Barbieris, and R. T. Nieset.   U.S. pat. 2,911,299/1952.
348. R. Parker Jr. and P. Reimann.   U.S. pat. 3,081,169/1963; Brit. pat. 877,842/1961; Can. pat. 667,235/1963; Ger. pat. 1,129,825/1962.
349. C. E. Herrick Jr. and A. K. Balk.   U.S. pat. 2,699,392/1955.
350. C. E. Herrick Jr. and A. K. Balk.   U.S. pat. 2,703,756/1955.
351. R. W. James and R. B. Parker.   U.S. pat. 3,032,414/1962; Brit. pat. 861,250/1961; Fr. pat. 1,285,563/1962.
352. R. W. James.   Ger. pat. 1,155,329/1963.
353. A. Baril and E. Klein.   U.S. pat. 2,976,145/1961; Brit. pat. 925,992/1963; Can. pat. 639,043/1962.
354. R. J. Bruni and C. R. Morgan.   U.S. pat. 2,923,703/1960.
355. U. Vahtra and R. M. Lindquist.   Fr. pat. 1,308,936/1962.
356. Kodak-Pathé.   U.S. pat. 3,143,418/1964; Brit. pat. 956,336/1964; Fr. pat. 1,327,315/1963.
357. Kodak Ltd.   Brit. pat. 962,557/1964.
358. C. E. Herrick and B. I. Halperin.   Ger. pat. 1,081,757/1960; Brit. pat. 850,954/1960.
359. W. Zindler.   Brit. pat. 935,428/1963; Ger. pat. 1,175,987/1964.
360. J. D. Michaelsen.   U.S. pat. 3,091,532/1963.
361. Int. Business Machine Corp.   Ger. pat. 1,178,298/1964.
362. R. E. Glavin.   U.S. pat. 2,950,194/1960.
363. F. T. Neth.   U.S. pat. 3,037,862/1962.
364. W. A. Seifert and W. F. Elbrecht.   *Phot. Sci. Eng.*, **5**, 235–238 (1961).
365. A. Schoen.   U.S. pat. 2,908,572/1959.
366. Kalvar Corp.   Brit. pat. 874,698/1961.
367. L. E. Contois and R. J. Rotondo.   Brit. pat. 956,337/1964; Fr. pat. 1,335,058/1963.
368. H. O. McMahon.   U.S. pat. 3,108,872/1963.
369. R. H. Kay.   U.S. pat. 2,993,805/1961.
370. R. T. Nieset.   U.S. pat. 2,916,622/1959.
371. R. M. Lindquist.   U.S. pat. 3,120,437/1964.
372. The Kalvar Handbook, Kalvar Corp., *Technical Bull.* 102 (1963).
373. R. T. Nieset.   *J. Phot. Sci.*, **10**, 188–195 (1962).
374. R. T. Nieset.   *Proceedings National Microfilm Assoc.*, 177–191, 10th Annual Convention 1961.
375. W. D. Peterson and R. W. Fabian.   U.S. pat. 3,093,478/1963; Brit. pat. 814,299/1955.
376. J. Kosar.   *Reprographie. 1. Internationaler Kongress für Reprographie*, Köln 1963. O. Helwich, Darmstadt, 1964, pp. 217–220.
377. Louis Rampp.   *Intern. Blue Printer*, **35**, pp. 15–16 (1962).

378. L. Lumière. Fr. pat. 693,635/1930.
379. L. P. F. van der Grinten. U.S. pat. 2,022,014/1935.
380. L. P. F. van der Grinten. U.S. pat. 2,026,292/1935.
381. L. P. F. van der Grinten. U.S. pat. 2,051,582/1936; 2,051,583/1936; 2,051,584/1936; 2,051,585/1936; 2,051,586/1936.
382. L. P. F. van der Grinten. U.S. pat. 2,602,740/1952; 2,602,741/1952.
383. L. P. F. van der Grinten. Dutch pat. 48,339/1940; 65,185/1950; 65,879/1950; 65,967/1950.
384. W. M. Buskes, T. P. W. Sanders, M. M. P. Vallen, and K. M. Hutgens. U.S. pat. 2,602,742/1952.
385. W. M. Buskes, M. M. van Rhijn, and T. P. W. Sanders. U.S. pat. 3,010,391/1961.
386. G. von Poser. U.S. pat. 2,246,425/1941; U.S. pat. 2,245,628/1941; Brit. pat. 513,560/1939; Brit. pat. 503,996/1939.
387. A. Polgar and C. Halmos. Fr. pat. 854,354/1940.
388. C. E. Herrick Jr. U.S. pat. 2,660,526/1953.
389. T. Aizawa. Jap. pat. 38–12085/1963.
390. Oriental Photo Industr. Co. Jap. pat. 38–26136/1963.
391. Ozalid Ltd. Fr. pat. 1,321,669/1963.
392. Kalle A.G. Belg. pat. 635,248/1963; Fr. pat. 1,364,896/1964.
393. C. Streck. U.S. pat. 3,086,033/1963.
394. M. P. Schmidt and W. Krieger. U.S. pat. 1,758,676/1930.
395. S. C. Slifkin. U.S. pat. 2,442,061/1948.
396. M. K. Reichel. U.S. pat. 2,354,088/1944.
397. M. K. Reichel. U.S. pat. 2,416,773/1947.
398. W. H. von Glahn and L. N. Stanley. U.S. pat. 2,496,240/1950.
399. W. J. Welch. U.S. pat. 3,102,812/1963; Brit. pat. 935,922/1963; Fr. pat. 1,305,116/1962.
400. S. C. Slifkin. U.S. pat. 2,495,827/1950.
401. M. K. Reichel. U.S. pat. 2,374,563/1945.
402. J. E. Frederick. U.S. pat. 2,807,545/1957; Brit. pat. 796,117/1956.
403. H. D. Murray, A. Tanenbaum, and R. P. Royer. Brit. pat. 818,911/1958; Ger. pat. 1,079,454/1960.
404. S. C. Slifkin. U.S. pat. 2,489,728/1949.
405. H. D. Murray. U.S. pat. 1,753,059/1930.
406. W. Krieger and R. Zahn. U.S. pat. 1,803,906/1931; Brit. pat. 306,408/1929; Ger. pat. 526,370/1931; Fr. pat. 687,956/1930.
407. R. P. Weegar. *Intern. Blue Printer*, **36**, 7, 24 (1963).
408. C. E. Slimowicz. Brit. pat. 867,432/1961; Ger. pat. 1,160,732/1964.
409. K. van der Grinten and L. van der Grinten. U.S. pat. 1,821,281/1931; U.S. pat. 1,841,653/1931; Dutch pat. 20,192/1929.
410. R. H. Franke. Brit. pat. 849,739/1960.
411. W. M. Hinman. U.S. pat. 2,157,206/1939.
412. T. J. Trojan. U.S. pat. 2,606,117/1952.
413. A. Seyewetz and D. Mouniere. *Chemie et Industrie*, **21**, 513 (1929).
414. C. Moureu, C. Du Fraisse, and M. Badoche. *C.R. Ac. Sc.*, **183**, 823–826 (1926).
415. L. Mester. *Science Ind. Phot.* (2), 23, 337–341 (1952).
416. C. Botkin and J. Sulich. U.S. pat. 2,727,820/1955.
417. J. Sulich and C. E. Herrick. U.S. pat. 2,755,185/1956.
418. R. J. Klimkowski and E. A. Kahn. U.S. pat. 3,027,256/1962.

419. J. Sulich and C. Botkin.   U.S. pat. 2,993,803/1961.

420. S. C. Slifkin.   U.S. pat. 2,661,291/1962.

421. W. H. von Glahn and L. Stanley.   U.S. pat. 2,531,485/1950.

422. F. W. Neumann.   U.S. pat. 2,593,911/1952.

423. J. H. A. Wilders and W. J. van Rhijn.   U.S. pat. 3,140,181/1964; Belg. pat. 606,539/1961; Brit. pat. 953,908/1964; Fr. pat. 1,296,409/1963.

424. C. Botkin and J. Sulich.   U.S. pat. 2,694,010/1954; Fr. pat. 1,074,641/1954.

425. M. P. Schmidt, W. Krieger, and W. Spietschka.   U.S. pat. 1,906,240/1933.

426. M. P. Schmidt and W. Krieger.   U.S. pat. 1,964,358/1934.

427. W. Krieger.   U.S. pat. 1,853,462/1932.

428. M. K. Reichel.   U.S. pat. 2,381,984/1945.

429. S. C. Slifkin.   U.S. pat. 2,523,882/1950.

430. E. C. Bialczak.   U.S. pat. 3,078,162/1963; Ger. pat. 1,161,480/1964.

431. E. C. Bialczak and W. J. Welch.   Brit. pat. 917,250/1962.

432. E. Spröngerts.   U.S. pat. 1,807,761/1931.

433. R. J. Alink.   U.S. pat. 2,318,352/1943; Dutch pat. 56,197/1946.

434. R. P. Weegar and H. C. Unkauf.   U.S. pat. 2,871,119/1959.

435. Y. Nakagawa and Y. Kunimoto.   *Oyo Butsuri*, **32**, 164–169 (1963).

436. S. C. Slifkin.   U.S. pat. 2,617,723/1952.

437. D. C. Poudrier.   *Tappi*, **46**, 147 A–150 A (1963).

438. J. E. Frederick.   U.S. pat. 2,709,655/1955.

439. H. C. Unkauf.   U.S. pat. 2,805,159/1957.

440. General Aniline and Film Corp.   Brit. pat. 815,956/1959.

441. General Aniline and Film Corp.   Ger. pat. 1,002,623/1957.

442. K. Röhrich.   Ger. pat. 936,006/1955.

443. O. Süs, W. Neugebauer, H. Böttger, F. Endermann, and W. Schäfer.   U.S. pat. 2,813,792/1957.

444. B. Benjamin and H. D. Murray.   Brit. pat. 826,005/1959.

445. E. Jahoda.   U.S. pat. 2,726,956/1955.

446. F. W. von Meister.   U.S. pat. 2,781,265/1957.

447. A. J. Ferzola and C. Botkin.   U.S. pat. 2,780,547/1957; Brit. pat. 808,527/1959.

448. H. D. Murray.   Brit. pat. 825,361/1959.

449. Andrews Paper & Chem. Co.   Brit. pat. 943,113/1963.

450. R. Landau.   U.S. pat. 2,953,471/1960; Brit. pat. 828,386/1960; Ger. pat. 1,081,760/1960; Fr. pat. 1,163,200/1958.

451. J. Sulich and J. E. Frederick.   U.S. pat. 2,662,013/1953.

452. J. F. Kosalek and J. Sulich.   U.S. pat. 2,746,863/1956.

453. J. F. Kosalek and J. Sulich.   U.S. 2,822,272/1957.

454. J. F. Kosalek and J. Sulich.   U.S. pat. 2,772,974/1956.

455. S. C. Slifkin.   U.S. pat. 2,474,700/1949.

456. H. H. Duerr.   U.S. pat. 2,545,423/1951.

457. Chem. Fabriek L. van der Grinten.   Brit. pat. 732,424/1955.

458. R. H. Franke.   Ger. pat. 1,118,605/1961.

459. R. H. Franke.   Ger. pat. 1,112,890/1961.

460. W. H. von Glahn and L. N. Stanley.   U.S. pat. 2,566,709/1951.

461. J. E. Frederick.   U.S. pat. 2,807,544/1957; Ger. pat. 958,984/1957.

462. W. J. Welch.   Belg. pat. 634,557/1963.

463. E. H. Gay.   Fr. pat. 1,115,684/1956.

464. W. D. Peterson.   U.S. pat. 2,501,874/1950.

465. S. C. Slifkin and W. Beese.   U.S. pat. 2,591,309/1953.

466. R. P. Weegar and H. C. Unkauf. U.S. pat. 2,873,207/1959.
467. J. E. Brandenberger. U.S. pat. 2,276,151/1942.
468. K. Kubo and Y. Nagamine. Japan. pat. 38–11078/1963.
469. W. Krieger and R. Mittag. Ger. pat. 700,252/1940.
470. J. L. Sorrin. U.S. pat. 3,002,851/1961.
471. H. Kosche and H. Winzer. Brit. pat. 931,668/1963; Ger. pat. 1,112,892/1961.
472. General Aniline and Film Corp. Brit. pat. 828,390/1960.
473. Chem. Fabriek L. van der Grinten. Dutch pat. 47,670/1940.
474. British Ozaphan, Ltd. Brit. pat. 536,714/1941.
475. S. C. Slifkin. U.S. pat. 2,593,928/1952.
476. H. C. Unkauf. U.S. pat. 2,613,149/1952.
477. E. Parry and J. Torday. Brit. pat. 867,200/1961.
478. C. Dunbar and J. Hawksworth. Brit. pat. 873,325/1961.
479. C. Dunbar, J. Hawksworth, H. Hempling, and D. J. Norman. Brit. pat. 886,652/1962.
480. H. Schmitz. *Ger. P. Appl.* R-16376, March 31, 1955.
481. J. Torday and J. L. Bull. Brit. pat. 892,882/1962.
482. Entwistle, Thorpe and Co. Brit. pat. 563,547/1944.
483. M. P. Schmidt and W. Krieger. U.S. pat. 1,756,400/1930.
484. W. J. Maxcy. U.S. pat. 2,603,564/1952.
485. J. P. Printy and E. W. Wagner. U.S. pat. 2,990,281/1961.
486. V. B. Sease and D. W. Woodward. U.S. pat. 2,405,523/1946.
487. W. Kühne. U.S. pat. 2,365,416/1944.
488. H. D. Murray and E. Parry. Brit. pat. 832,910/1960.
489. D. Straw. Ger. pat. 1,065,724/1959.
490. A. M. Barba. Ger. pat. 1,062,111/1959.
491. Chem. Fabriek L. van der Grinten. Belg. pat. 632,667/1963.
492. E. Parry. Brit. pat. 847,241/1960; Ger. pat. 1,093,207/1960.
493. J. Torday and E. Parry. Brit. pat. 849,820/1960.
494. W. A. Krieger. U.S. pat. 2,822,271/1957.
495. R. H. Franke and H. D. Murray. U.S. pat. 2,720,467/1955; Brit. pat. 841,131/1960.
496. L. P. F. van der Grinten and K. J. J. van der Grinten. U.S. pat. 1,861,330/1932.
497. C. E. Herrick Jr. *J. Opt. Soc. Am.*, **42**, 904–910 (1952).
498. C. Botkin and S. C. Slifkin. U.S. pat. 2,465,424/1949.
499. Chem. Fabriek L. van der Grinten. Dutch pat. 80,603/1956.
500. R. J. Cox. U.S. pat. 3,064,049/1962; Brit. pat. 904,484/1962.
501. S. C. Slifkin. U.S. pat. 2,537,919/1951.
502. E. C. Bialczak. U.S. pat. 3,113,025/1963. Brit. pat. 908,548/1962.
503. W. J. van Rhijn. Belg. pat. 625,148/1963.
504. Chem. Fabriek L. van der Grinten. Brit. pat. 937,510/1963; Fr. pat. 1,282,622/1963.
505. R. J. Maguire. *Ind. Photo.* 8, No. 10, p. 29 (1959).
506. K. Kubo and S. Amagasaki. Japan. pat. 38–12084/1963.
507. W. Krieger and H. Buchner. U.S. pat. 2,162,456/1939.
508. J. Wolfe. *Photo. Tech.* 1, No. 7, 14, 44 (1939).
509. C. E. Herrick, Jr. U.S. pat. 3,069,268/1962; Can. pat. 638,203/1962.
510. General Aniline and Film Corp. Belg. pat. 579,138/1959; Brit. pat. 871,216/1961.
511. T. P. W. Sanders and J. H. A. Wilders. U.S. pat. 2,739,061/1956.

512. T. P. W. Sanders and K. M. Hutgens.   U.S. pat. 2,793,118/1957.
513. de Atlas.   Dutch pat. 83,936/1957.
514. G. W. Smith.   *Brit. J. Phot.*, **105**, 164–165 (1958).
515. R. Landau.   *J. Phot. Sci.*, **10**, 32–35 (1962).
516. A. R. A. Beeber and D. S. Spechler.   U.S. pat. 2,999,016/1961.
517. V. M. Fridman.   *Kinofotokhim. Prom.*, No. 2, 38–40 (1938).
518. I. I. Levkoev and V. P. Petrov.   *Kinofotokhim. Prom.*, No. 12, 52–57 (1938).
519. D. Straw and C. E. Herrick, Jr.   U.S. pat. 2,993,788/1961.
520. J. Kosar.   *Intern. Blue Printer*, **36**, No. 6, 20–21 (1963).
521. J. W. Coffman.   U.S. pat. 3,067,666/1962; Technifax Corp.   Brit. pat. 881,029/1961.
522. S. C. Slifkin.   U.S. pat. 2,542,715/1951.
523. S. C. Slifkin.   U.S. pat. 2,542,716/1951.
524. R. Landau.   Fr. pat. 1,169,732/1959.
525. W. P. Leuch.   U.S. pat. 2,659,672/1953.
526. Richo Co. Ltd.   Japan. pat. 39–10164/1964.
527. H. G. Hunt.   *Reprod. Rev.*, **12**, No. 4, 26–34 (1962).
528. A. D. Even.   *Reprod. Methods*, **1**, No. 5, 14, 22, 23, 49 (1961).
529. C. H. Benbrook.   *Phot. Eng.*, **7**, 7–11 (1956).
530. G. W. Smith.   *J. Phot. Sci.*, **10**, 83–91 (1962).
531. A. Tyrrell.   *J. Phot. Sci.*, **12**, 96–101 (1964).
532. R. Alfaya.   *Phot. Sci. Eng.*, **6**, 258–264 (1962).
533. D. A. Shiraeff and F. Jacobs.   U.S. pat. 1,972,323/1934.
534. V. C. Akintievsky.   U.S. 1,997,507/1935.
535. K. Bene and S. Novak.   Brit. pat. 914,159/1962.
536. S. C. Slifkin.   U.S. pat. 2,537,097/1951.
537. S. C. Slifkin.   U.S. pat. 2,541,178/1951.
538. L. E. Ravich.   U.S. pat. 2,616,803/1952.
539. L. E. Ravich.   U.S. pat. 2,756,144/1956.

7

Presensitized Printing Plates

Some of the chief drawbacks of dichromated-colloid systems are low sensitivity to light, poor shelf life of the coated layers, and variable sensitivity owing to the age and atmospheric conditions. These characteristics have long been recognized as undesirable and many attempts have been made in the past to replace dichromates with other substances which

1. would have, on exposure to light, the same or better hardening action on colloids;
2. would be less affected by atmospheric conditions;
3. would make it possible before exposure and development to store sensitized material for a prolonged period of time at room temperature;
4. would have fewer skin-irritating properties.

7.1 DIAZO SENSITIZERS

Considerable effort has been made to use aromatic diazo compounds as substitutes for dichromates. In one such attempt advantage was taken of the reducing properties of decomposition products of (*o*- or *p*-) hydroxy- or amino-diazo compounds, which, when allowed to react with chromates or dichromates, were capable of producing a tanning reaction (1). Among the diazo compounds mentioned as suitable for this process, are: 1-diazo-4-dimethylaminobenzene hydrofluoroborate, 4-diazo-3-methyl-4-dimethyl-aniline sulfate, 1-diazo-3-monoethylnaphthylamine, and diazotized *p*-aminodiphenylamine. 1-Hydroxy-2-diazoniumbenzene-4-sulfonic acid is claimed in another patent (2).

Instead of diazo compounds, light-sensitive dyestuffs such as 2,7-anthraquinone disulfonate were used by Kögel (3). As in the previous method, it was necessary to soak the exposed layers in a 2 per cent solution of a dichromate to get the tanning effect. All these suggestions were based on the fact that the photolytic products reduce dichromates into a trivalent chromium compound, which subsequently acts as a tanning agent.

Kögel (4,5) later introduced various aromatic nitro-compounds which rendered organic-colloid layers light sensitive. These compounds, when exposed to ultraviolet radiation, yield products capable of tanning the colloid substances of the layer. Nitro-derivatives introduced in the foregoing patent are 1-nitro-naphthalene compounds, substituted by a carboxylic or a sulfonic group in *o*- or *p*- position. We will mention, for example, 1-nitronaphthalene-8-sulfonic acid, 1-nitronaphthalene-2-sulfonic acid, 1-nitronapthalene-3-8-disulfonic acid, and 1-nitro-8-methylnaphthalene-4-sulfonic acid. All these compounds are water soluble, whereas 1-methyl-8-nitronaphthalene and 1-nitronaphthalene-8-carboxylic acid are soluble in alcohols and hydrocarbons. Acetals of aromatic nitroaldehydes and aliphatic polyhydric alcohols, for example, *o*-nitrobenzylidenedulcitol and *o*-nitrobenzylindeneglycerin also render gelatin light sensitive and were the subject of a dusting-on process (6). Condensation products of polyvinyl alcohol with aromatic or heterocyclic *o*-nitroaldehydes were suggested as sensitizers for offset plates (7). 4-Nitro-3-aldehyde phenyl carbonate is decomposed by the action of light to 4-nitroso-3-carboxyphenyl carbonate which, owing to its solubility in diluted sodium triphosfate solution, was suggested for positive-working printing plates (8).

Gelatin can be hardened in the presence of color couplers such as 1-lauryl-2-(2'-(1'-hydroxy)-naphthyl) benzimidazole-5-sulfonic acid; after exposure to the ultraviolet light the coating is immersed in a *p*-N,N-dialkylaminoaniline type color developing solution for a few minutes and then contacted with a solution of an oxidizing agent. During this treatment color coupling reaction between the oxidation products of *p*-phenylene-diamine and the color coupling component is taking place. The image is then developed by removing the unhardened gelatin and the dye from the unexposed areas, leaving a dyed hardened gelatin image (9). In the above patent the color developer can be substituted with diazonium salts, sulfohydrazides and similar compounds which react with the color couplers to produce a colored dye. Since the latter compounds react directly with the color couplers, no oxidizing agents are required.

Zahn (10) introduced diazo compounds whose light-decomposition products possess direct tanning action on the colloids; they generally have a fairly large molecule, for instance, the diazo compounds of

4-amino-1(N-methyl-6-naphthalene-tetrahydride-1,2,3,4)-aminobenzene,

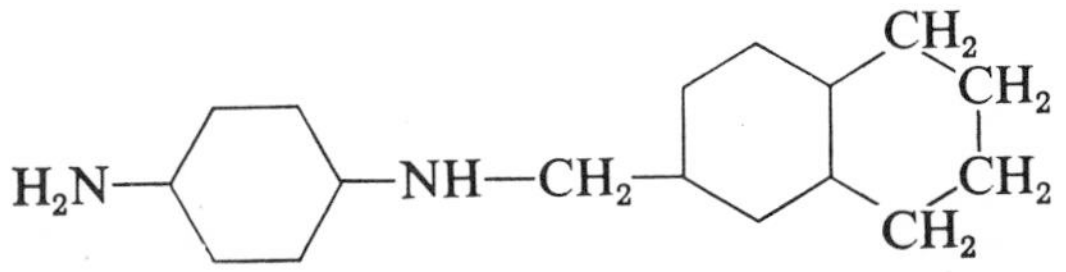

$$H_2N-\langle\rangle-NH-CH_2-$$

4″,4‴-diamino-2″,2‴-disulfo-1″,1‴-N,N-diphenyl-4,4′-
diamino-1,1′-diphenyl,

$$H_2N-\langle\rangle-NH-\langle\rangle\langle\rangle-NH-\langle\rangle-NH_2$$

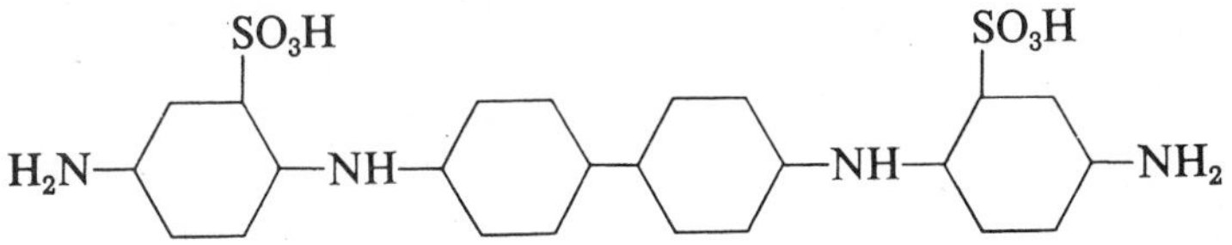

4″-amino-2″-carboxy-1″-N-phenyl-4,4′-diamino-1,1′-diphenyl-methane,

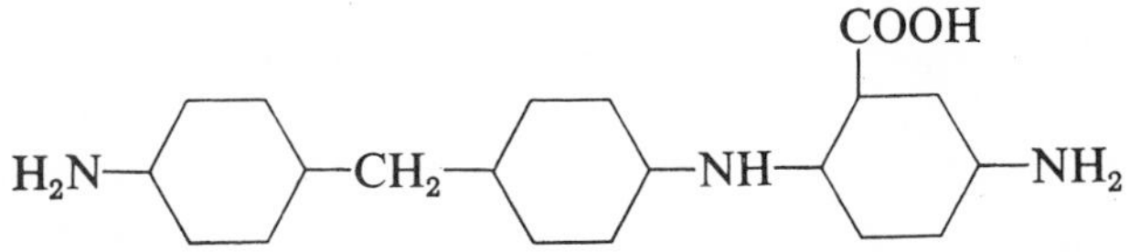

$$H_2N-\langle\rangle-CH_2-\langle\rangle-NH-\langle\rangle-NH_2$$

The foregoing compounds were utilized as sensitizers for polyvinyl butyral by Boersma (11).

Another method of sensitizing organic colloids to light involves condensation products of an active carbonyl compound, such as formaldehyde or paraformaldehyde, with a diazo compound such as 4-diazo-1,1′-diphenylamine (12,13,14,15,16). The condensation preferably takes place in the presence of phosphoric (17) or sulfuric acid (18). These condensates are high-molecular-weight diazonium salts in which the single molecules of diazodiphenylamine are connected by a methylene bridge (Figure 7.1).

In spite of having a large structure, these complex compounds remain water soluble owing to the presence of the ionic diazo groups; when these are destroyed by exposure to light, an insoluble resin is formed (19). More recently, amorphous precipitation products obtained from *p*-aminobenzenediazonium salts and sulfonated phenol-formaldehyde resins were suggested for light-sensitive printing plate coatings (20); Schmidt and Süs (21) suggested the condensation products of a sulfonic acid halide of a quinone-1,2-diazide and a phenol-formaldehyde resin.

According to de Boer (22), high-molecular-weight diazonium compounds can be prepared by linking, with cyanuric chloride, an amino-diazonium compound, for example, 4-amino-2,5-diethoxy benzenediazonium chloride to a macromolecular compound such as cellulose, casein, or polyvinyl alcohol. Compared with previously mentioned compounds these are

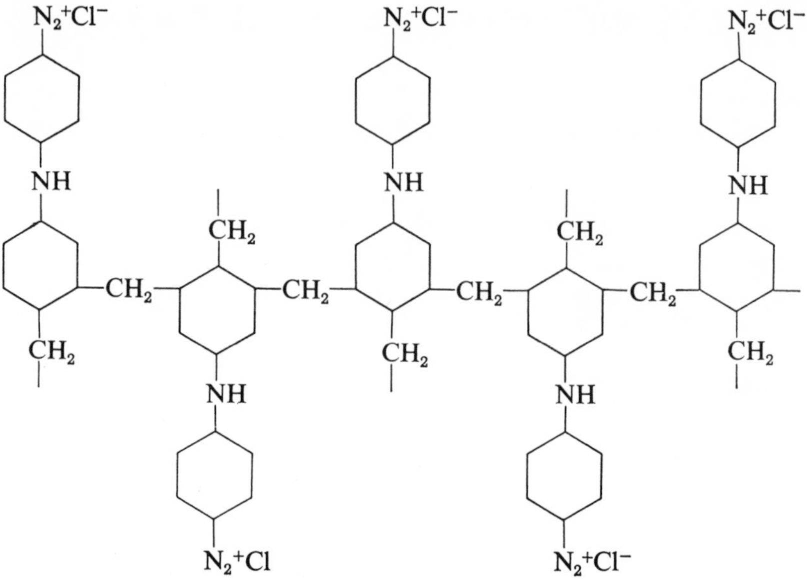

Figure 7.1

supposed to be superior in shelf life and mechanical strength. Exposure to light converts the condensation products into an insoluble resin resembling bakelite. The chemical reaction taking place is somewhat obscure; it is difficult to accept that the formation of an insoluble compound is responsible for the hardening of the colloid layer. Most probably the diazo resin reacts with some specific groups of the colloid and produces crosslinks between the linear chains of the polymeric binder.

Diazo-formaldehyde condensates can be used in combination with organic colloids, for example, gelatin, dextrin, and gum arabic; or with synthetic materials, for example, polyvinyl alcohol (23), methyl cellulose, or polyamides (24,25). Sensitized layers are yellow, which is bleached during the exposure to grey. The light sensitivity increases with higher concentrations of the sensitizer and because of the much darker color which absorbs actinic radiation to a higher degree, the maximum sensitivity is reached at much lower concentrations than with dichromates.

An advantage of this type of sensitizer is that its dark reaction rate is relatively low at normal temperature so that presensitized material can be stored for several weeks or months. The storage life of the sensitizing solution is also quite good provided it is protected from light.

In view of the fact that images obtained by this means were capable of retaining greasy ink, this method has been used for the production of photomechanical printing plates. To insure the hydrophilic properties of the nonimage areas, it was, however, necessary to anodize the surface of the aluminum support or to treat it with sodium silicate. After the exposure the plate was lacquered with a mixture of furfuryl alcohol and an epoxy-resin condensate to give a harder surface. The unexposed areas were removed by development with a gum-arabic phosphoric acid solution containing octyl alcohol and *p*-chlorophenol (26).

Another method for improving the ink receptivity and wear resistance of the printing areas involves top-coating with a polyvinyl formal or other hydrophobic resin, which becomes solvent insoluble above the exposed sections of the plate (27).

By coating an aluminum plate with a photolytic product of a diazonium compound and overcoating this surface with a hydroxy-ethyl cellulose solution containing a diazonium compound, a printing plate, which can be made directly from a positive, is obtained (28). Hydroxy-ethyl cellulose can be substituted by a similar material which hardens on exposure to light but remains hydrophilic. A positive-working lithographic printing plate based on the same principle was patented by Case (29). The silicate-treated aluminum sheet is coated with *p*-diazo-diphenyl amine-formaldehyde condensate, the entire surface is exposed to light, and diazo-sensitizing solution is applied. This solution contains, in addition to the diazo resin, a water-soluble vinyl polymer, for instance, polyacrylamide. On exposure to light through a positive transparency, the unreacted sensitizer is removed from unexposed sections with water; because the underlying surface is hydrophobic, it accepts printing ink, whereas the exposed areas, in spite of being insolubilized, remain hydrophilic. Positive lithographic printing plates can also be made by using hydrophilic light-sensitive material which has been overcoated with a diazo sensitizer having the property of becoming oleophilic on exposure to light. After exposure to a positive original, the plate is washed and completely re-exposed; a positive, ink-receptive surface is left (30). On the other hand, a negative working offset plate is made by coating the base with a vinyl alkyl ether/maleic-anhydride copolymer and overcoating with a layer of a suitable diazonium compound; the nonimage areas can be removed and made water-receptive with a solution of an alkanolamine and a fatty acid in glycerin or glycol (31).

Diazotype printing plates which have as the light-sensitive layer an acrylic or methacrylic acid polymer containing diphenylamine-4-diazonium chloride, for example, 4'-bromodiphenylamine-4-diazonium chloride, were suggested by Neugebauer, Süs, and Rebenstock (32). In a similar patent, the diazonium chloride or bromide, of 3-aminocarbazoles, for example, 2-methoxycarbazole-3-diazonium bromide, were proposed for sensitizing polyacrylic acid (33). Tsunoda and Fujiishi (8) found that for image-hardening polyvinyl alcohol, the diazonium metal double salts of *o*-methoxy-*p*-aminodiphenylamine and the tetrazonium metal double salts of 1,1'-diethylbenzidine, *o,o'*-dimethylbenzidine, and dianisidine, can be used.

Diazotype printing plates can also be made by an indirect process. In one such method a transparent original is exposed to a diazo-sensitized sheet, which is, after the exposure, brought into contact with a wetted offset plate coated with a vinyl methylether/maleic anhydride copolymer (34). The diazo compound, which remains unchanged in the unexposed areas, is still water soluble and migrates, in a sufficient amount, to the polymer layer. On subsequent exposure without the positive, areas containing the diazo compound are insolubilized.

Another transfer process was described by Buskes (35); exposed pigmented sheet is pressed against a specially prepared and wetted surface so that unexposed and unhardened areas can be transferred from the first sheet to the second, forming a positive image of the original. The following diazo compounds were used: *p*-diazonium borofluoride, bis (4-diazophenyl)amine, *p*-diazomonoethylaniline, *p*-diazo-N-ethyl-N-(2-hydroxyethyl)aniline, etc. After conventional processing the plates are ready for use.

All the foregoing processes utilize a combination of a diazonium compound with an organic colloid or a synthetic resin. It was found, however, that photolytic products of some diazonium compounds, especially of diazotized *p*-phenylene diamine condensate with formaldehyde or a phenol-formaldehyde resin, were, in themselves, capable of retaining greasy ink (36). Soon after this discovery was made a number of presensitized printing plates were introduced by American and European companies. In 1951 Keuffel and Esser Co. introduced presensitized plates consisting of hydrolyzed cellulose ester laminated to a high-strength paper. An orange-dyed adhesive employed for lamination also served as an antihalation layer. The fragility of the hydrolyzed cellulose acetate has led to their abandonment and aluminum plates took their place. 3M-brand sensitized aluminum photo-offset plates of Minnesota Mining and Manufacturing Co. and Tri-Ply plates of Sunset Plates Inc. were among the first ones. The nature of the sensitizers used has not been revealed; however, we can safely assume that it was one of the foregoing types.

Light-sensitive diazo resins coated on a metal support would deteriorate very rapidly; to avoid reaction of the diazonium salt with the metal, aluminum plates are coated prior to sensitizing with hydrolyzed cellulose ester or an aqueous solution containing sodium phosphate glass, alkali-metal silicate, and sodium metaborate, phosphomolybdate, or silicomolybdate; this layer will give the metal a permanently hydrophilic siliceous surface (37,38). The sodium silicate treatment consists of dipping cleaned aluminum foil in the sodium silicate solution maintained at temperatures of 180 to 212°F and washing away the excess of soluble silicate. Alkali-metal silicate coatings can be hardened with calcium nitrate or with an organic acid which will not attack the metal (39). Citric and tartaric acids are suitable. This treatment neutralizes any alkali which may be present in the silicate undercoating without affecting the hydrophilic properties. A slightly different method was described by Cohn (40). When necessary, halation in the exposed halftone printing can be substantially reduced by graining the aluminum plate prior to silicate treatment (41). Better protection against reaction between the aluminum surface and the diazonium salt is achieved with water-soluble alkylated methylol melamine-formaldehyde or polyalkylene-polyamine-melamine-formaldehyde resins, which are, after being coated, cured to an insoluble state (42). The same effect is provided with urea-formaldehyde resin modified with a polyamide (43). A hydrophilic surface can be also achieved by dipping degreased aluminum plate in a 1 per cent aqueous solution of polyacrylic acid, polymethacrylic acid, or sodium salt of carboxymethylcellulose or carboxymethyl(hydroxyethyl)cellulose (44). Magnesium plates are treated with a 1 per cent aqueous solution of a methylvinyl-ether/maleic-anhydride copolymer. Other suitable acidic polymers include lignosulfonic acid, sulfomethylcellulose, or a styrene/maleic-anhydride copolymer. Mellan and Gumbinner (45) suggested zirconium hexafluoride for the same purpose.

Processing of diazo-sensitized plates is an extremely simple operation, and requires only one or two minutes. After being taken from the package and exposed under a line or halftone negative, the plate is developed with a specially formulated solution to dissolve the unexposed diazo coating. In many cases an acidified gum-arabic solution serves as the developer. Or, the exposed plate can be lacquered to cover the exposed areas with a film of a resin and pigment (46). The plates are then ready for ink application.

Often it is advantageous to treat the printing plate with an "image developer" in order to make the printing areas visible. Printer's developing ink or pigmented water-in-oil emulsions can be used (47). An emulsion like this contains, in the aqueous phase, gum arabic, and, in the solvent phase, a soft epoxy resin (epichlorohydrin-bisphenol resin) and pigment (toluidine toner). Ethylene dichloride and cyclohexanone are the solvents (48). This emulsion has a high viscosity and is applied on the still wet plate and wiped over the image area with a cotton wad. This action removes any resin which may adhere to nonimage areas, and the epoxy resin adheres firmly to the image portions of the plate and provides an oleophilic surface. The pigment or toner is taken up by the resin coating on the printing areas and produces a colored image.

To simplify the development of presensitized diazo plates containing no colloid, Adams (49) recommended an oil-in-water emulsion. The oil phase contains boiled oil, aluminum stearate, and a vinyl resin dissolved in cyclohexanone; the water phase contains sodium carboxymethyl-cellulose and polyethylene glycol. The emulsion is poured on the exposed plate and rubbed with a soft pad to remove the water-soluble diazo compound from the nonprinting areas by means of the water phase while depositing a thin film of sodium carboxymethyl cellulose. This deposit increases the hydrophilic properties of the nonprinting areas. The oil phase of the emulsion, which is separated from the water phase during the rubbing, deposits aluminum stearate on the printing areas and increases the ink receptivity. Addition of gum arabic enables the plate to be gummed simultaneously. Another oil-in-water emulsion contains a water-insoluble dye dissolved in a water-immiscible organic solvent, which dissolves the nonimage areas of the coating (50). For increased resistance to wear, lithographic plates having a diazo-sensitized layer are developed with an emulsion containing in the aqueous phase a gum, wetting agent, and phosphoric acid; the solvent phase consists of phenolic resin dissolved in a mixture of solvents (51).

A planographic printing plate sensitized with negative working diazo resin can be converted into a positive acting plate by treating the sensitive layer with a solution of potassium ferrocyanide which inhibits the insolubilization of the resin by exposure to light (52); thus the exposed portions can be removed by washing in water and treatment with β-naphthol makes the unexposed sections ink receptive.

During the years many other diazo compounds were introduced as sensitizers for lithographic printing plates, e.g., diazotized 3-nitro-anthranilic acid (53), diazosulfonates of aromatic or heterocyclic amines (54,55), reaction products of aromatic or heterocyclic diazosulfonates with diazonium salts (56), or diazo compounds prepared by reacting an aryl carboxylic acid chloride with diazo methane (57); these compounds correspond to the general formula $R-CO-CH=N_2$ where R is an aryl radical. Diazo compound obtained from 1-amino-2,5-dipropyl-1,4'-methyldiphenyl sulfide was used by Neugebauer (58). Exposure and coupling with an azo coupler carrying a hydrophilic group, e.g., phenyl-methylpyrazolene sulfonic acid, causes the nonimage areas to become hydrophilic; a second exposure decomposes the residual diazo compound to an oleophilic product (59,60). Or, the sensitized plate can be coated with a hydrophilic colloid such as polyvinylpyrrolidone which, after the exposure, forms hydrophilic areas (61).   In other patents (62,63), a paper base sensitized with a diazo compound of N-(2,3,4,6-tetrachlorobenzyl)-*p*-phenylenediamine is exposed under a negative and subsequently treated with dextrin solution and re-exposed with the negative removed.   Previously unexposed areas are no longer light sensitive, but still repel fatty inks, whereas areas where the diazo was previously decomposed are still ink receptive.

The use of azo dyes as the ink-receptive images for positive working offset plates has been suggested by Woitach and Herrick (64).   Since the oleophilic properties of the dye images improve with increasing molecular weight, coupling components capable of coupling with more than one diazo molecule are preferred.   Ethylene dioxy-5,5'-resorcinol is the representative coupler of the foregoing patent; it consists of two phloroglycinol nuclei linked together with a CH_2—CH_2— linkage:

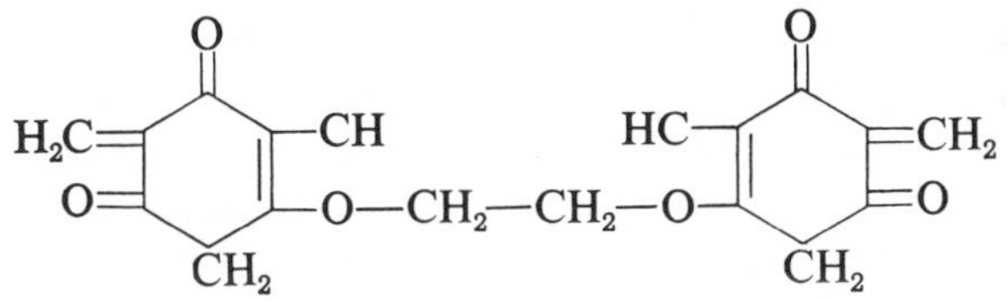

The linkage takes place through oxygen atoms, and, thus, the coupling activity of this type of compound is not appreciably decreased.   Ethylenic-dioxy-5,5'-diresorcinols are water insoluble and highly hydrophobic; this property is, however, reversed during the development with moist ammonia fumes.

Another means of obtaining hydrophobic and hydrophilic surfaces was described first by Marron and Diedrich (65) and later by Marron, White, and Rosenberger (66); a plate carrying a hydrophobic siloxane layer is sensitized with a diazonium fluoroborate.   On exposure to light, hydrofluoric acid is set free and decomposes the silicon to a hydrophilic compound.   The plate does not need processing and is ready for use.

Diazo derivatives of 5-membered carbon-nitrogen rings, for instance, pyrrolenines, isoimidazoles, isopyrazoles, triazoles, and diazo-indiazoles are also suitable for preparation of printing plates (67).   These compounds are water insoluble and must be removed after the exposure by washing with phosphoric acid solution.   Some diazo-nitrogen heterocycles become water soluble on exposure to light, and can be washed off from the nonimage areas (68); 3-diazo-2,4-diphenyl-3H-pyrrolenine and 3-diazo-5,7-dibromoindiazole are examples.

Diazo-sensitized plates have a limited shelf life and can be stored only for about six months without deterioration (69).   For this reason, careful attention has been given to other organic compounds with similar light-sensitive properties. These include certain aromatic azides, quinone-diazide derivatives, nitrothiophenes, etc.

7.2   AROMATIC AZIDO COMPOUNDS

Aromatic azides are compounds having in their molecule at least one —N_3 (azido) group.   Whether azido compounds possess ring structure (*a*), as suggested by Curtius (70), or linear structure (*b*), as proposed by Thiele (71), has long been the subject of discussion.

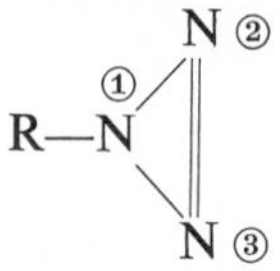

$$R-N \overset{①}{\underset{N \; ③}{\overset{N \; ②}{|||}}}$$

$$R-N \overset{①}{=} N \overset{②}{=} N \overset{③}{}$$

(*a*)   (*b*)

As can be seen from formulas *a* and *b*, nitrogen atoms 2 and 3 in the ring structure are equivalent; this is not the case in the linear arrangement. By means of N^{15}, Clusius and Weisser (72) proved that the structure of aromatic azido compounds is in accord with formula *b*.

Organic azides decompose photolytically into nitrogen and a free radical:

$$-R-N_3 \overset{h\nu}{\longrightarrow} -RN\cdot + N_2 \tag{1}$$

The imine radical can couple with another imine or it can react with some other molecule.   In many instances crosslinking is involved with consequent insolubilization.   Thus, by imagewise exposure to light, insolubilization will occur according to the light pattern, and the unexposed areas remain soluble and can be removed with a suitable solvent.

Among the aromatic azido compounds which have been proposed as light-sensitive hardening agents for organic colloid layers, we can mention aryl azides, such as *p*-azidodiphenylamine carboxylic acid, diazidodiphenylamine carboxylic acid, etc. (73), and azidostyrylketones and azidostyrylarylazides (74); these compounds can be represented by the following general formula

$$N_3-R-CH=CH-R_1$$

where *R* is a phenylene group and R_1 is an acyl group or an azidoaryl group.   Included are the following compounds:

4,4′-diazidostilbene-2,2′-disulfonic acid

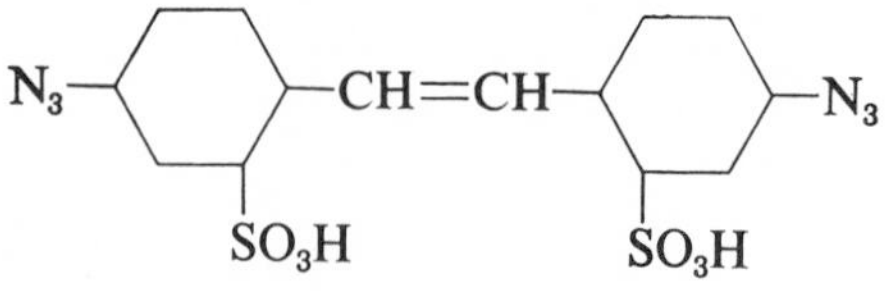

4'-azido-4-azidobenzalacetophenone-2-sulfonic acid

$$N_3-\bigcirc-CH=CH-\overset{\overset{\displaystyle O}{\|}}{C}-\bigcirc-N_3$$

$$SO_3H$$

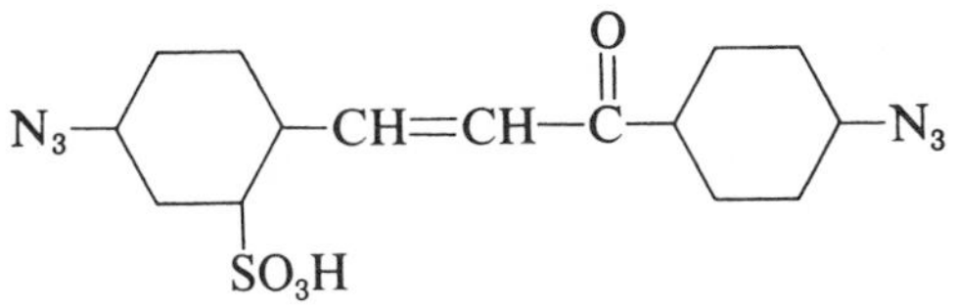

4,4'-diazidostilbene-α-carboxylic acid

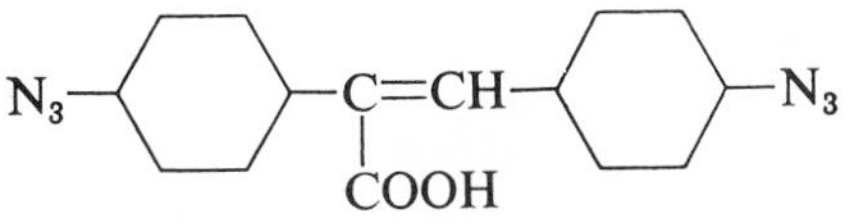

$$N_3-\bigcirc-\underset{\underset{\displaystyle COOH}{|}}{C}=CH-\bigcirc-N_3$$

di-(4-azido-2'-hydroxybenzal) acetone-2-sulfonic acid

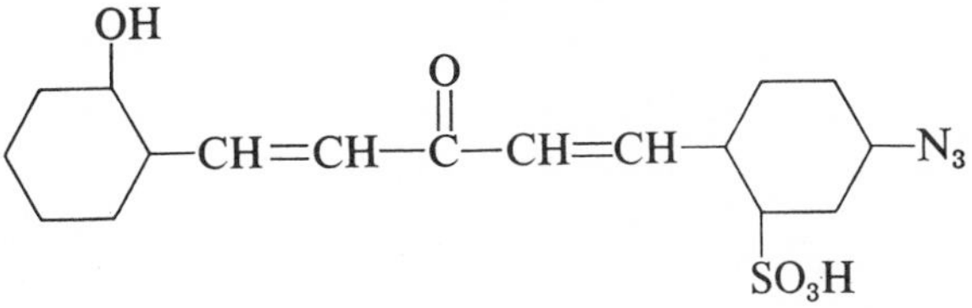

$$OH$$

$$\bigcirc-CH=CH-\overset{\overset{\displaystyle O}{\|}}{C}-CH=CH-\bigcirc-N_3$$

$$SO_3H$$

4-azidobenzalacetophenone-2-sulfonic acid

$$N_3-\bigcirc-CH=CH-\overset{\overset{\displaystyle O}{\|}}{C}-\bigcirc$$

$$SO_3H$$

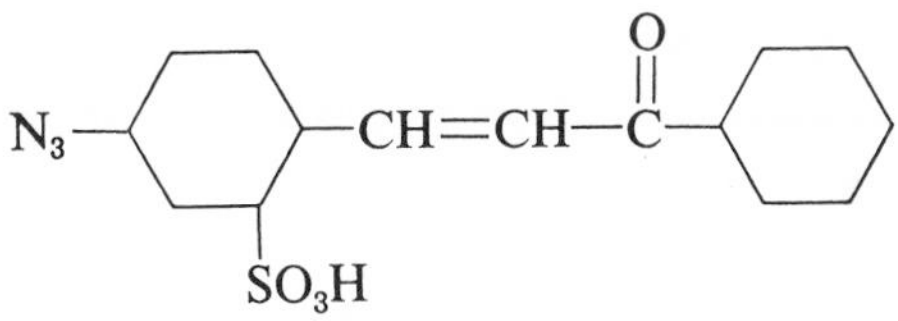

Sodium salts of these acids are water soluble and, when used for sensitizing organic colloids, they form very stable layers which can be stored for a long time without being subject to any alteration. Dark reaction is practically nonexistent. In combination with gelatin, glue, gum arabic (75), etc., aromatic azido compounds were suggested for about the same processes as previously described dichromates and diazo compounds.

Synthetic polymers, for instance, polyacrylamide and its derivatives (76), copolymers of acrylic acid, and acrylonitrile (77), or superpolyamides (24) also can be sensitized with aromatic azido compounds. Superpolyamides, when coated on terephthalate polyester film, form hardenable layers, the unexposed areas of which can be removed with alcohols. Coatings like this were also recommended for preparation of screen-printing stencils (78) and for sensitizing offset plates. In order to increase the ink acceptance of the image areas, however, addition of rubber latex to the colloidal material may be necessary (79), or the hardened printing areas may have to be treated with a hydrosol of silicic acid at pH 1 to 2 (80).

A light-sensitive coating suitable for a deep-etch resist on aluminum or zinc plates is made from a combination of polyacrylic acid and polyvinyl-pyrrolidone together with sodium 4,4′diazidostilbene-2,2′-disulfonate, which is converted to the tetrazo form by the addition of sodium azide NaN_3 (81).

Aqueous dispersions of water-insoluble butadiene copolymer can also be sensitized with water-soluble aryl azido compounds (82). Organic solvent soluble colloidal materials containing no polar groups, for example, natural and synthetic rubbers, must be sensitized with aryl azido compounds which are soluble in the same solvents. Hepher and Wagner recommended, for this purpose, compounds with a —CO— group, such as *p*-azidobenzophenone and 4,4′-diazidobenzophenone (83) or compounds having in their molecule two aryl azido nuclei linked by a chain of three or more carbon atoms, including the —CO—CH= grouping (84). Specific examples of these compounds are: 4,4′-diazidodibenzal-acetone, 1,3-di-(4-azidophenyl)-2:3-propane-1-one, and 1,2-di(4-azido-cinnamoyloxy)-ethane. In one process which utilizes the light sensitivity of these compounds, the exposed layer of sensitized polymeric colloid is moistened with an organic solvent and pressed against a receiving support. The unexposed and nonhardened areas are transferred to the reception sheet and if pigments, dyes, or color formers were included in the coating, colored positives of the original are obtained (85).

Synthetic rubber or other organic solvent soluble colloids can be rendered light sensitive with heteroxyclic bis-azido compounds, for example, 6-azido-2-(4-azidostyryl) benzimidazole (86). Three-component polymers, consisting of ε-caprolactam, adipic acid, and hexamethylene diamine, can be sensitized with aromatic azido compounds of the type N_3—C_6H_3X—CH=CR—Y, where R is an aliphatic or aromatic nucleus or a nitro group, Y is hydrogen, an acyl or a carboxylic group, and X is hydrogen, sulfonamide, or a group which forms a water-soluble alkali metal salt (87). Compounds, such as 4,4-diazido-stilbene-2,2′-disulfonic acid anilide (*a*) and 2-azido-1,4-naphthalenedibenzenesulfonamide (*b*), in which the

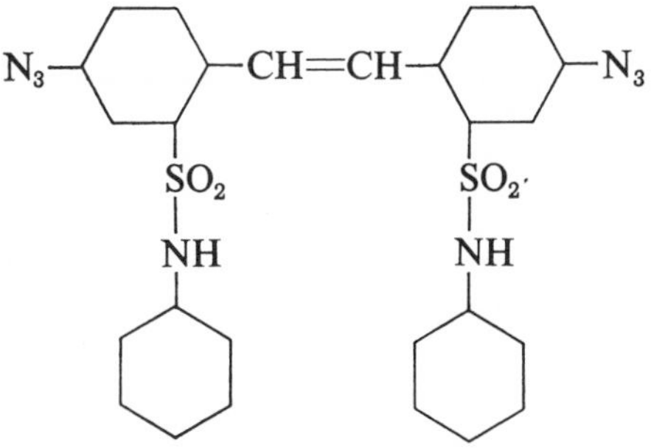

(*a*) 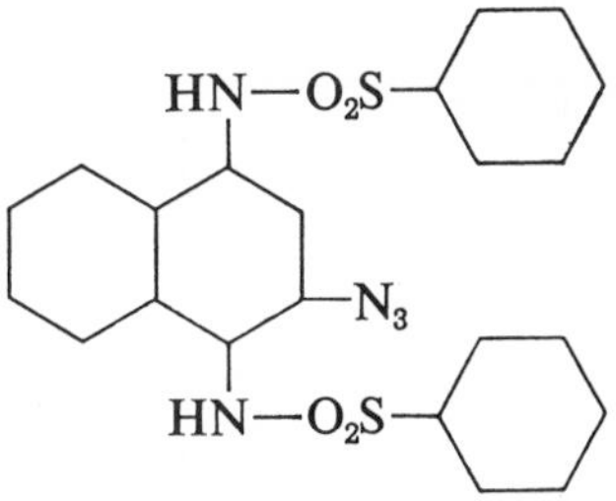   (*b*)

azido-bearing nuclei is modified by a sulfo group amidated with a primary aromatic amine or by a primary amino group substituted with the sulfonyl residue of an aromatic sulfo acid, are eleophilic, and, when coated on a metal base, can be used as sensitizers for planographic printing plates. The image is developed by treating the exposed plate with a dilute alkaline solution which removes either the unexposed parts of the layer or the light-decomposition products from those areas affected by light, depending on the compound used. For example, azido compounds containing an alkoxy group give light-decomposition products which are more soluble in diluted alkalies than the original compounds and, for this reason, can be used for positive-working printing plates (88).

A negative-working lithographic plate is obtained by coating on an aluminum support a colloid-free solution of an azido-substituted aromatic imidazole (89), for example:

2-(4′-azidophenyl)-5 (or 6)-methylbenzimidazole

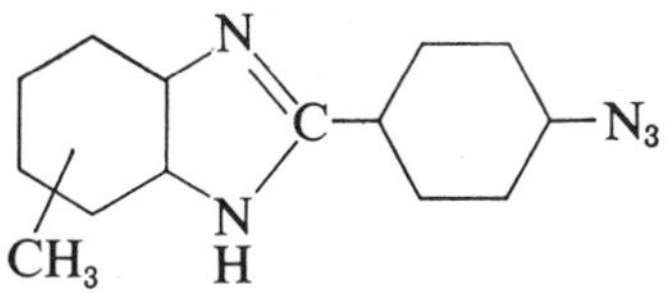

2-(4′-azidophenyl)-6-phenylbenzimidazole

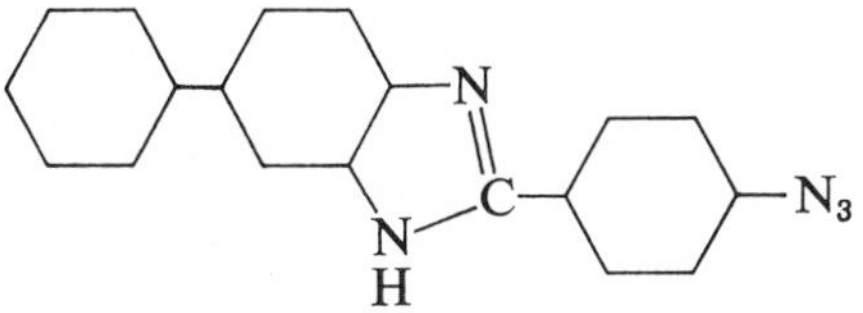

2-(4″-azidophenyl)-naphtho-1′,2′:4,5-imidazole

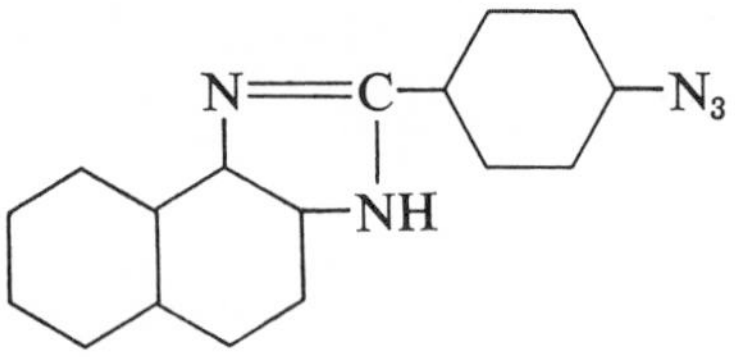

2-(4′-azidophenyl)-acenaphthimidazole

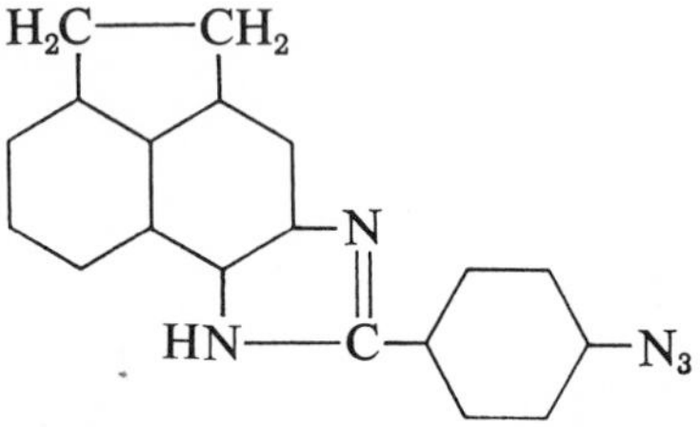

After the exposure to light under a master, the azido compound in areas which were not struck by light are removed with dilute alkaline solution. The image areas are washed with water and treated with dilute phosphoric acid.   After inking with greasy ink, a positive printing plate is obtained from a negative.

Sagura and Van Allan (90) introduced another group of azido compounds for sensitizing organic solvent soluble colloidal material.   These are

4,4′-diazidochalcone

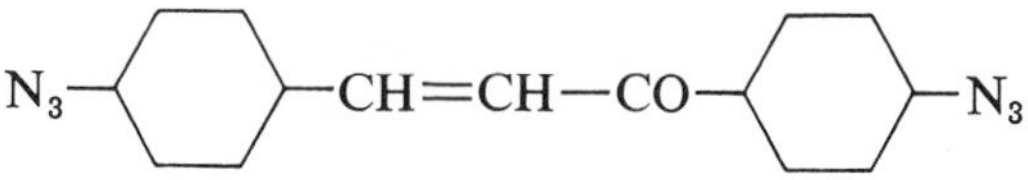

2,6-di-(4′-azidobenzal)-cyclohexanone

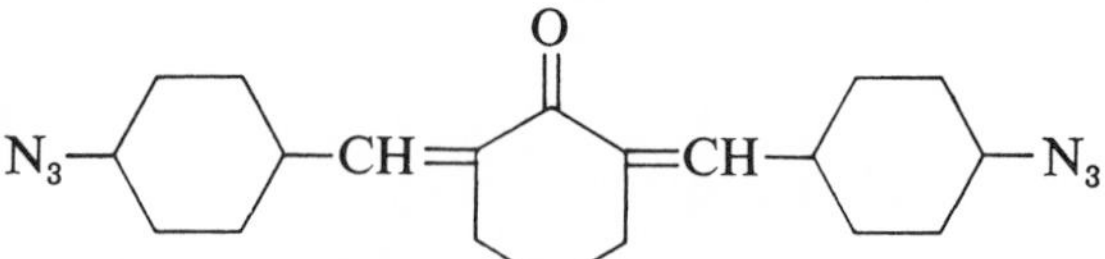

and 2,6-di-(4'-azidobenzal)-4-methylcyclohexanone

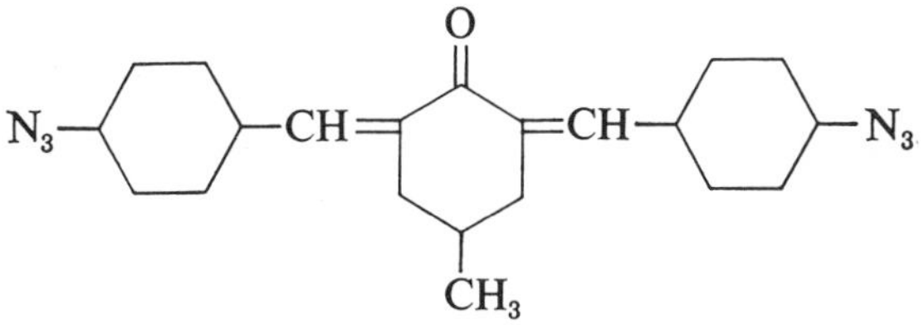

The azido group can be attached by various linkages to the recurring units of a polymer chain; in such a case, light-sensitive substances with properties similar to those of the foregoing mixtures are obtained (91); then the polymer performs the functions of both the vehicle and the sensitizer. By exposure to light through a negative, the polymer will be selectively crosslinked, and only those areas which were protected from the action of light can be removed with a solvent. Of particular interest are vinyl polymers containing azidostyrene or vinyl azidophthalate units (92). One such example is a polyvinyl acetate-3-4-azidophthalate copolymer. The sensitivity to ultraviolet radiation can be increased up to thirtyfold by sensitizers such as 2-(3-sulfobenzoylmethylene)-1-methyl-β-naphthothiazoline and 2-benzoylmethylene-1-methyl-β-naphthothiazoline, which extend the absorption range from 260–400 mμ to 270–460 mμ.

Light-sensitive azido polymers can be prepared by the reaction of either fully or partially acylated polyvinyl alcohol with azidophthalic or azidobenzoic acid anhydride (93,94). Other suitable polymers can be made by esterification of styrene maleic anhydride with a nuclear substituted azidophenyl alkanol, for example, β-(4-azidophenoxy) ethanol.

The light sensitivity of these polymers can be greatly increased by addition of certain sensitizing agents, for instance, 1-ethyl-2-(β-styryl) quinolinium iodide, 1-ethyl-2(p-hydroxyethoxystyryl) quinolinium iodide, and 1-methyl-4'-hydroxyethoxystilbazolium methosulfate. The preparation of these sensitizers is described in the foregoing patent specification. Certain dibenzothiophene-5,5-dioxide sulfonic acid salts and stilbene compounds were disclosed by Robertson and Van Allan (95). Later, the same investigators disclosed 4-oxo-1,4-diazanaphthalenes, 4a-azanaphthalenes, 4-oxo-1-thia-3a,7-diazaindenes and acridones and thioacridones as optical sensitizers for polymers containing recurring aromatic azide (96). These compounds extend the absorption range into the region of longer wavelengths; wavelengths as high as 530 mμ can be used for exposure.

Azido polymers are useful in photomechanical processes. Polymer layers coated on an aluminum plate are exposed to actinic radiation under a negative transparency and, when the exposure is completed, the un-exposed polymer is removed with a solvent, which can be water, an alkaline solution, or an organic solvent, depending on the nature of the polymer. The insolubilized sections remain on the plate and form a resist image suitable for further use. The unexposed areas of light-sensitive polymers containing an azido group can also be heat transferred to a receiving sheet to provide duplicating masters for use in a lithographic or hecto-graphic copying process (97).

Light-sensitive layers formed from aromatic azido compounds have a remarkably long shelf life. Another advantage lies in the production of colored images formed by the light-decomposition products; as the exposure progresses, the intensity of the color increases. This effect can be used for establishing proper exposure time. The use of aryl azido compounds and, equally, of diazo compounds, appears, however, to possess the disadvantage that these compounds, on exposure to light, evolve nitrogen which is trapped in the dry colloid. If such a sheet is immersed in water immediately after the exposure, bubbles or blisters can form as a result of the swollen conditions of the colloid layer; such a sheet is obviously unsuitable for further use. Mally (98) described a method which aims at the elimination of this effect by treatment of the exposed colloid layers with methyl or ethyl alcohol prior to development in water, and Powers (99) recommends subjecting the exposed material to a relatively high degree of suction for a short period of time prior to the wetting.

When light-sensitive colloid layers of these types are used for the prep-aration of printing plates, the unexposed areas are washed off and the metallic surface of the base material, thereby laid bare, is coated with a lacquer. Subsequently the tanned colloid is removed and a positive printing plate is obtained. Neugebauer and his co-workers (100) found that images with a good affinity for greasy inks can be obtained immedi-ately from negative-working colloid layers, if, after the exposure and the removal of the unhardened portions, the remaining tanned colloid image is subjected to the influence of high temperature. The optimum heating temperature depends, of course, on the specific composition of the layer, and usually varies between 200 and 400°C.

7.3   *p*-QUINONE DIAZIDES

In more recent times, Schmidt and Süs synthetized a series of *p*-quinone-(1,4)-diazides, which in combination with organic colloids, or without, can be used in the production of light-sensitive layers. Colloids suitable for this process can be either natural materials, such as gelatin (101), synthetic resins, for example, a vinyl/maleic acid copolymer, or carboxy-methyl-ethers of phenol-aldehyde condensate; for etherification of the latter, (mono) chloroacetic acid is used, which reacts with the hydroxyl groups of the phenol-aldehyde resin forming the carboxymethylether groups. Depending on the degree of etherification, the solubility of the reaction product in alkaline solutions can be varied (102).

Combinations like these were suggested mainly for the sensitizing of printing plates; after the exposure, the areas protected from light are removed with water or any other suitable solvent or with a specially prepared dispersion of a water-immiscible organic solvent, for example, 1,2,3,4-tetrahydronaphthalene, in aqueous gum-arabic solution containing 2 to 6 per cent of phosphoric acid (103). It is recommended that plates sensitized with *p*-naphthoquinonediazide sulfonic ester or amide be developed in aqueous alkaline solution containing the sodium salt of hexafluotitanic acid, hexafluosilicic acid, hexafluoboric acid, etc. (104).

Suitable are *p*-diazoquinones corresponding to the general formula (105):

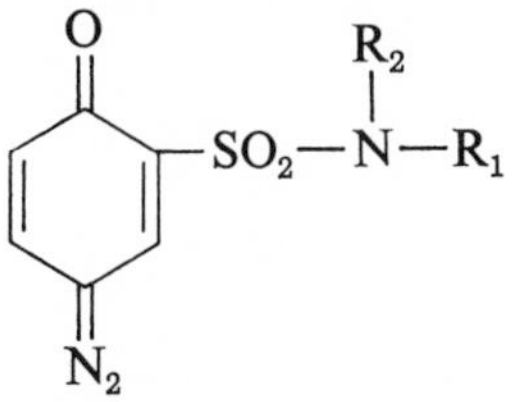

R_1 = H, alkyl, aralkyl
R_2 = aryl

such as benzoquinone-(1,4)-diazide-(4)-2-sulfonic acid-β-naphthylamide:

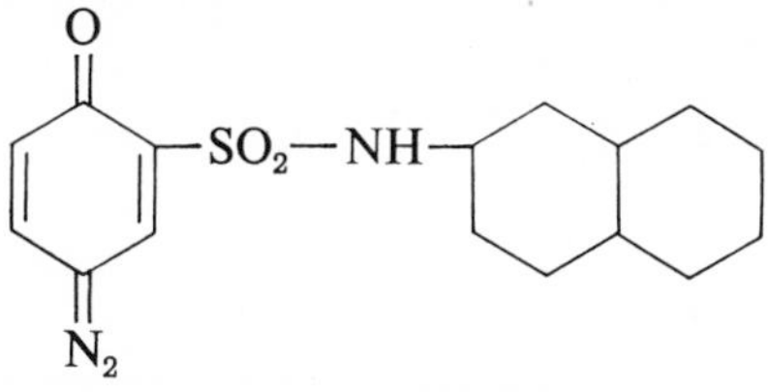

(2)

which decomposes by the action of light as follows:

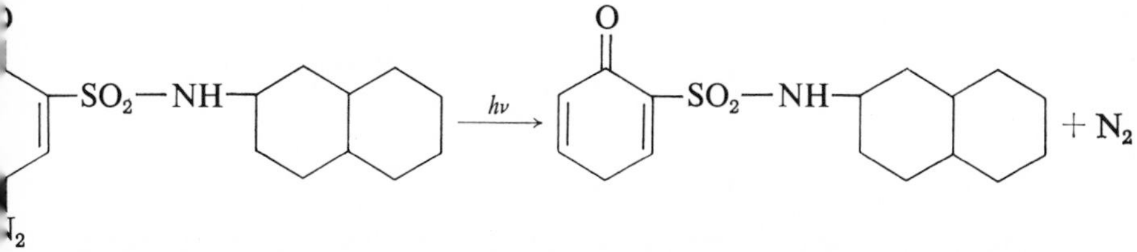

Because of the strong positive charge of the sulfonamide group, the thermal stability of these compounds is very good, but their light sensitivity is too low for practical purposes (106).

On the other hand, *p*-iminoquinone-diazides derived from N-aryl-sulfonyl-*p*-phenylene-diamines have good light sensitivity, but decompose quite easily at higher temperature. These compounds can be represented by the general formula

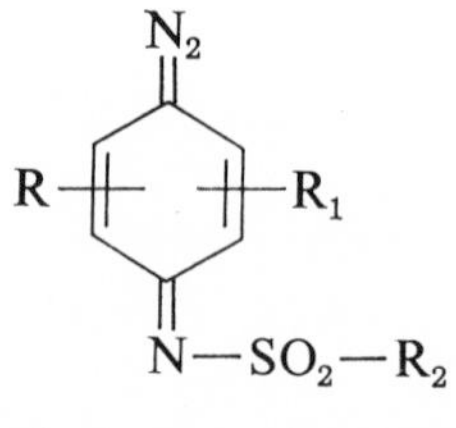

$$
\begin{array}{c}
\text{N}_2 \\
\| \\
\text{R}\text{—}\!\!\boxed{}\!\!\text{—R}_1 \\
\| \\
\text{N}\text{—SO}_2\text{—R}_2
\end{array}
$$

where R and R_1 stands for hydrogen, alkyl, alkoxy, or halide groups and R_2 is an aryl radical (107). As examples we can mention N-(4'-methyl-benzenesulfonyl)-imino-2,5-diethoxybenzoquinone-(1,4)-diazide-4:

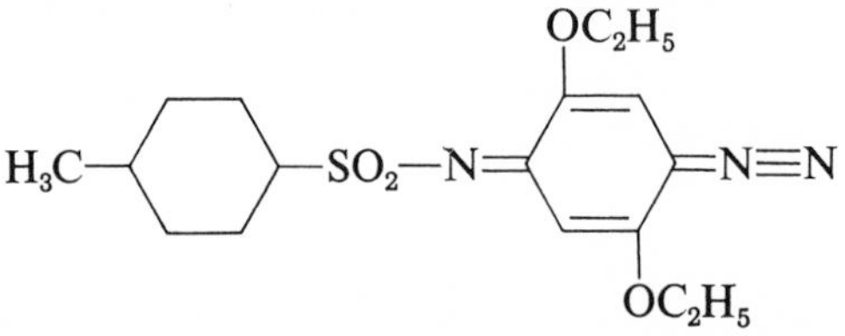

$$
\text{H}_3\text{C}\!-\!\!\bigcirc\!\!-\!\text{SO}_2\text{—N}\!\!=\!\!\overset{\displaystyle \text{OC}_2\text{H}_5}{\underset{\displaystyle \text{OC}_2\text{H}_5}{\bigcirc}}\!\!=\!\text{N}\!\equiv\!\text{N}
$$

Iminoquinone diazides are used preferably in combination with a poly-acrylic or polymethacrylic acid, or their copolymers (108). Exposed to light, they are transformed into oleophilic products insoluble in dilute alkalies, acids, and organic solvents. Plates sensitized with iminoquinone-diazides are developed with water without any need for subsequent treatment.

The reaction taking place during the exposure can be illustrated by the following equation:

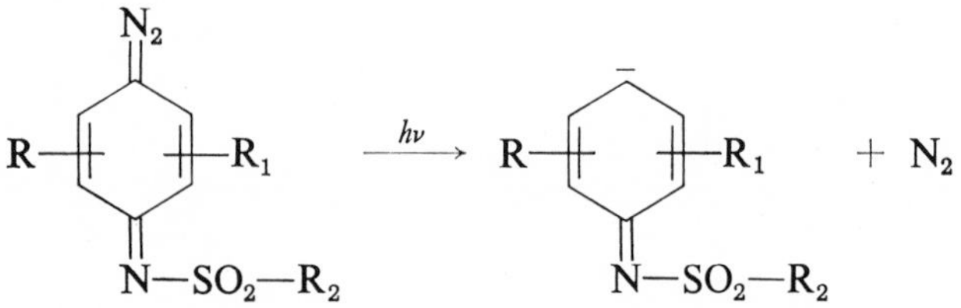

$$
\begin{array}{c}
\text{N}_2 \\
\| \\
\text{R}\text{—}\!\!\boxed{}\!\!\text{—R}_1 \\
\| \\
\text{N}\text{—SO}_2\text{—R}_2
\end{array}
\xrightarrow{h\nu}
\begin{array}{c}
\overset{-}{} \\
\text{R}\text{—}\!\!\boxed{}\!\!\text{—R}_1 \\
\| \\
\text{N}\text{—SO}_2\text{—R}_2
\end{array}
+ \text{N}_2
\qquad (3)
$$

The thermal stability of *p*-aminoquinone-diazides can be considerably improved by introduction of the sulfonamido group into the molecule, which, as we have just seen, lowers the light sensitivity. This undesirable effect can be made less pronounced by the introduction of negative groups, such as halogens, alkyl groups, and alkoxy groups. The resulting group of compounds (109) can be characterized by the general formula:

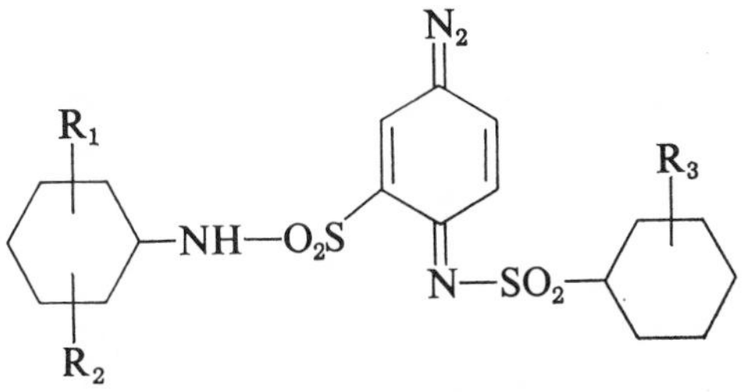

R_1, R_2, and R_3 = alkyl, alkoxy, or a halogen

Very suitable are methyl-substituted compounds, which not only have acceptable light sensitivity but are also good film formers, and adhere well to the aluminum support. During the exposure, the sulfimino group is changed into a sulfamido group; when developed with a developing solution containing alkaline-earth cations, the metal ion replaces the hydrogen; this rearrangement increases the difference between the exposed and unexposed sections.

In some instances it may be advantageous to use the iminoquinone-1,4-diazides in mixtures with diazonium salts, particularly when the diazo compound has a tendency to crystallize on the surface of the coated material.

Additional examples of *p*-quinone-diazides are listed in Table 7.1.

7.4 *o*-QUINONE DIAZIDES

In the last few years work has been directed toward the use of diazoquinones, without the addition of a colloid material. They can be used alone (114), or in combination with a solid, primary, aromatic amine (115), which, on exposure to light, reacts to form an acid amide of a relatively high molecular weight and a low degree of solubility in a developing solution. The use of these compounds is based on the difference in solubility between the diazoquinone compounds and their photolyzed products; depending on the type of the sensitizer and the type of developer employed, presensitized printing plates can be either negative working or positive working. In negative-working plates, the organic solvent soluble sensitizer becomes insoluble in the same solvent on the exposed areas, whereas, in the positive-working plates, the exposed sections can be removed with aqueous solutions of alkalies.

A number of compounds undergoing the differential change in solubility during the action of actinic radiation is listed in Table 7.2. These compounds are usually intensely yellow substances, having the diazo

TABLE 7.1   *p*-Quinone-Diazides

General Formula	Example	Reference
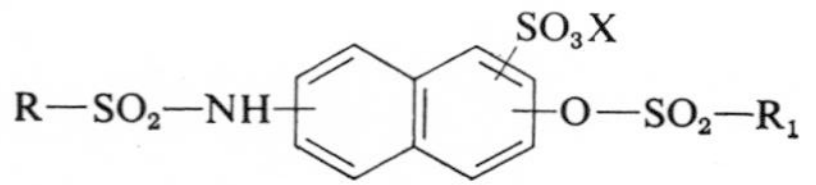 Quinone-diazide sulfo ester and sulfamide derivatives	condensation product of 2-amino-5-hydroxynaphthalene-7-sulfonic acid with naphthoquinone-(1,4)-diazide-(4)-2-sulfochloride: 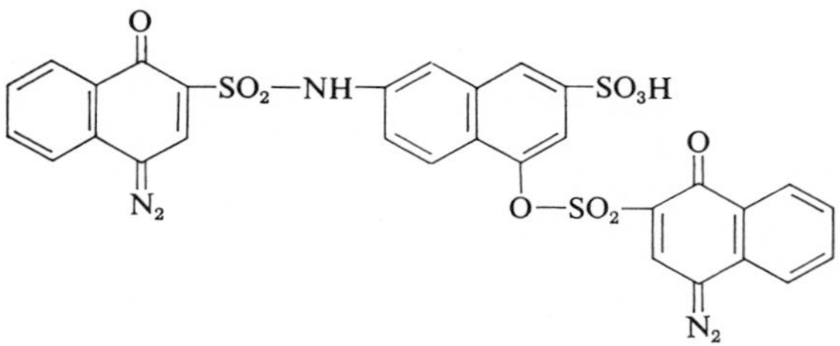	(110)
R and R$_1$ = quinone-(1,4)-diazide group X = H or a metal cation		
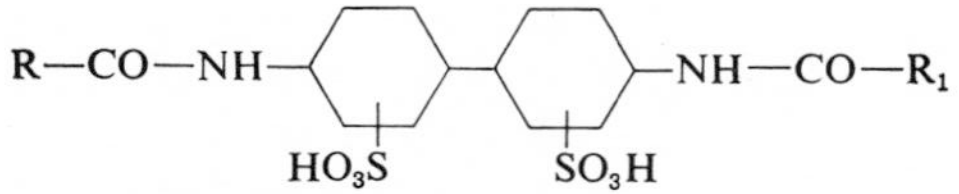 Sulfonic or carboxylic acid of *p*-quinone-diazide carboxylic acid amides	condensation product of bis-amide of benzoquinone-(1,4)-diazide-(4)-2-carboxylic acid and 4,4′-diamino-diphenyl-2,2′-disulfonic acid: 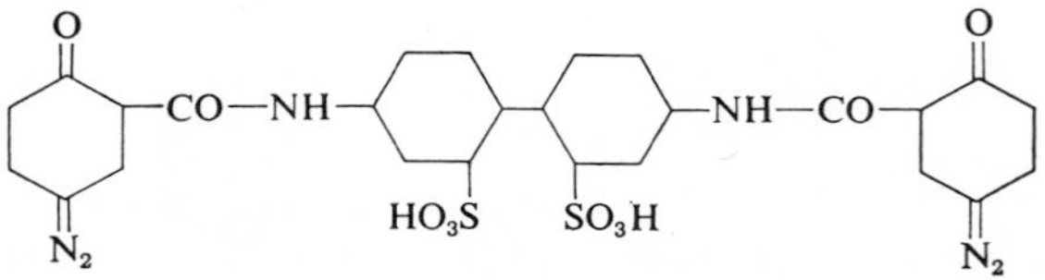	(111)
R and R$_1$ = quinone-(1,4)-diazide group		

(112)

4,4′-bis-(naphthoquinone-(1″,4″)-diazide-(4″)-2″-(sulfonyl-amino)-diphenyl-2,2′-disulfonic acid

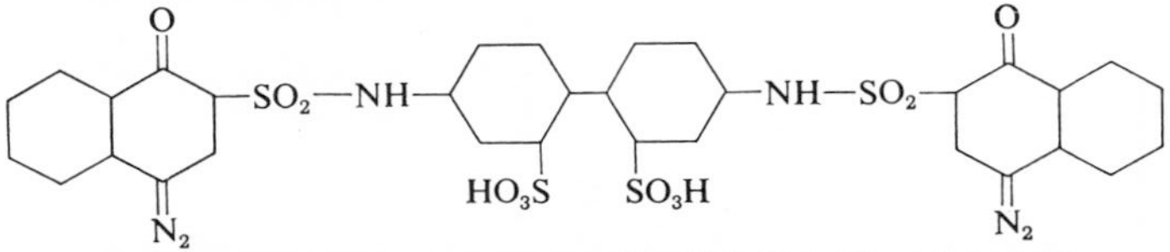

2,2′-bis-(naphthoquinone-(1″,4″)-diazide-(4″)-2″-(sulfonyl-amino)-diphenyl-4,4′-disulfonic acid

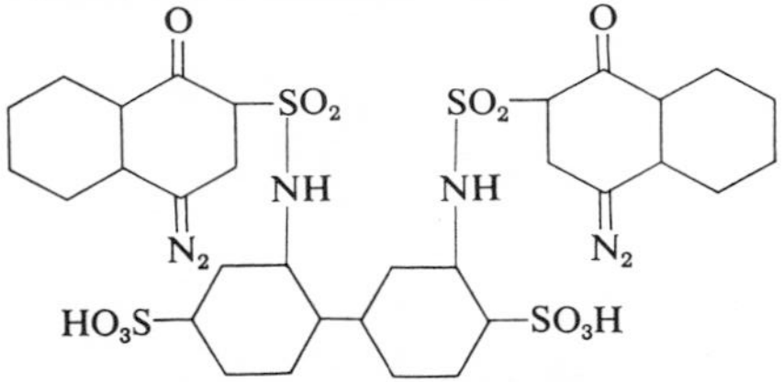

(113)

condensation product of N,N′-bis-(5-hydroxy-7-sulfonic acid naphthyl-(2))-urea with naphthoquinone-(1,4)-diazide-(4)-2-sulfonic acid

Sulfonic or carboxylic acids of *p*-quinone-diazide sulfamides

$R-SO_2-NH-R_1-R_2-R_3-NH-SO_2-R_4$
R and R_4 = quinone-(1,4)-diazide group
R_3 = arylene group

$R_2 = -N=N-$

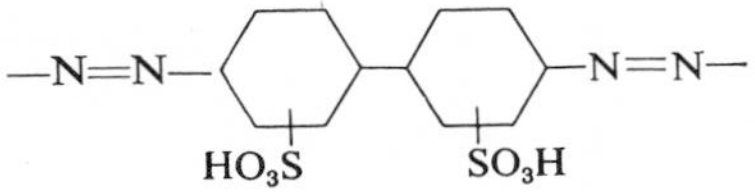

or $-NH-$

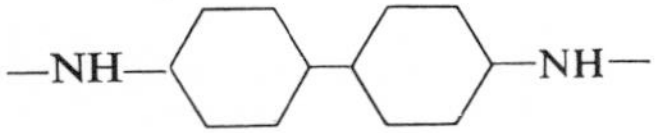

Sulfonic or carboxylic acids of *p*-quinone-diazide sulfonic acid esters

$R-SO_2-O-R_2-O-SO_2-R_1$
R and R_1 = quinone or naphthoquinone-(1,4)-diazide group
R_2 = a linking group in which the sulfonic acid ester groups are linked directly to an arylene group substituted by at least one radical, e.g., $-SO_3H$ or $-COOH$

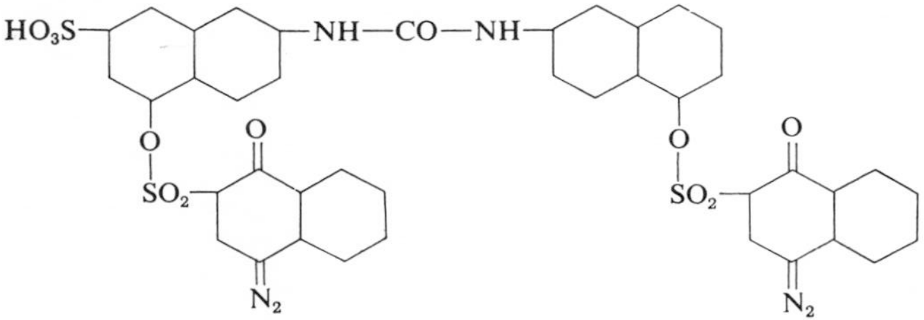

group attached to one carbon atom and the oxygen to another carbon atom of the same six carbon ring. They are in ortho position to each other. *o*-Diazoquinones of the naphthalene series are the most important; they are initially more or less ink receptive, and, after the exposure, can be dissolved out of the light-exposed areas by aqueous alkaline solution. The unexposed parts retain their oleophilic properties. The chemical changes taking place during the exposure were expressed by Süs (116) as follows:

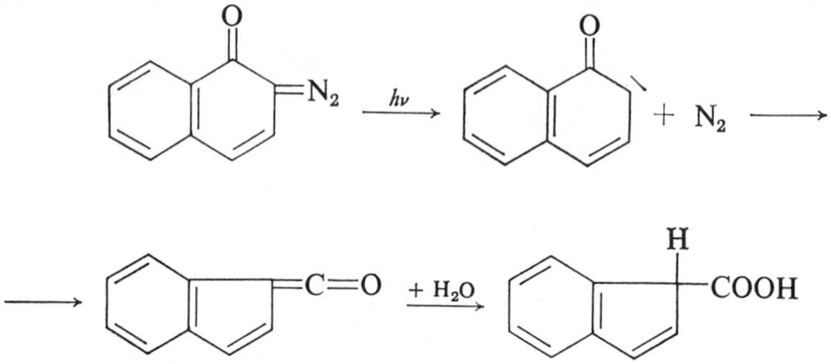

$$\text{(4)}$$

The light induced decomposition of *o*-quinone-diazides may be accompanied by dimer formation (117):

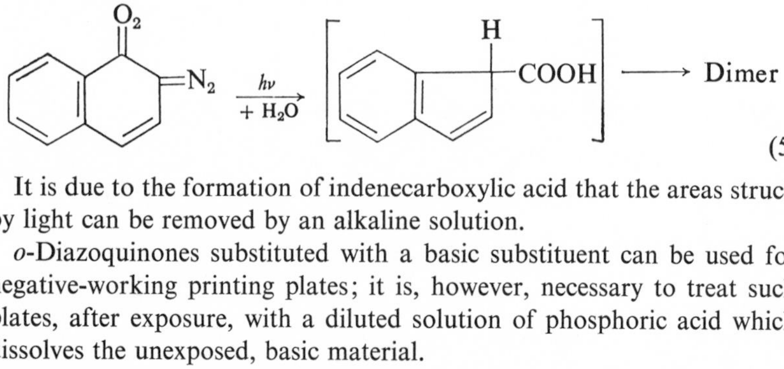

$$\text{(5)}$$

It is due to the formation of indenecarboxylic acid that the areas struck by light can be removed by an alkaline solution.

o-Diazoquinones substituted with a basic substituent can be used for negative-working printing plates; it is, however, necessary to treat such plates, after exposure, with a diluted solution of phosphoric acid which dissolves the unexposed, basic material.

By proper selection of sensitizer, presensitized printing plates can be made either negative or positive working, depending on the composition of the developer. Neugebauer (118) describes hydroxy-(1,2,1′,2′)-pyridobenzimidazole esters of *o*-quinone-diazide sulfonic acid or of a naphthoquinone-1(2)-diazide sulfonic acid as suitable sensitizers, which can be processed either with an organic solvent to give a negative plate, or with a trisodium phosphate solution to obtain a positive plate.

Positive lithographic printing plates can also be made by protecting a layer of water-insoluble *o*-quinone-diazides with a coating of an aqueous

TABLE 7.2 *o*-Quinone-Diazides

General Formula	Example	Reference
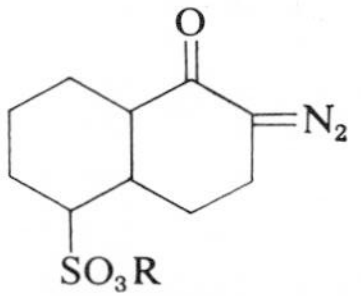 R = alkoxy, aryloxy, amino, arylamino, aralkylamino, carbalkoxyalkyl group	2-diazo-1-naphthol-5-sulfonic acid ethyl ether 2-diazo-1-naphthol-5-sulfonic acid methyl ether 2-diazo-1-naphthol-5-sulfonic acid naphthyl ether 2-diazo-1-naphthol-5-sulfonamide	(120) (121)
Esters of quinone-(1,2)-diazide-sulfo acids and cyclic alcohols	Naphthoquinone-(1,2)-diazide-(2)-5-sulfo acid-cyclohexyl ester 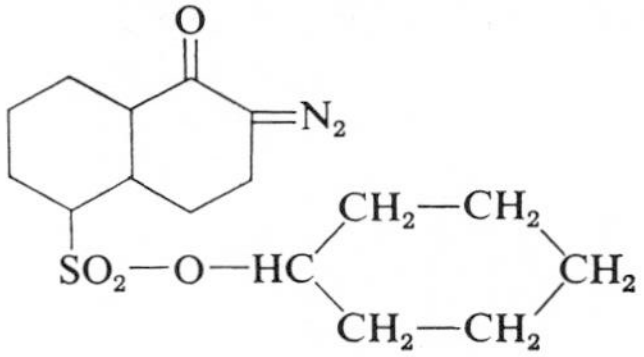	(122)
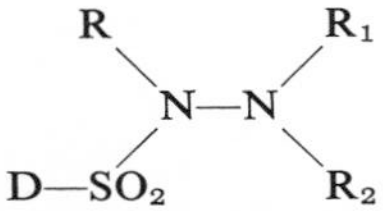 D = *o*-quinone-diazide group R and R_1 = H or a hydrocarbon R_2 = an acyl group or a hydrocarbon group or	N-benzoyl-N′-[naphthoquinone-(1,2)-diazide-(2)-5-sulfonyl]-hydrazine 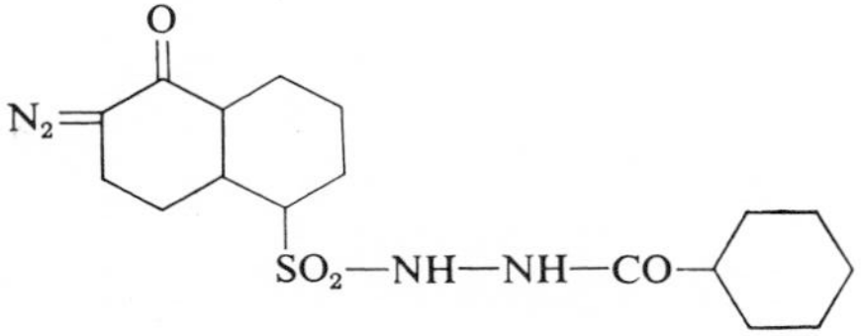	(123)

General Formula	Example	Reference
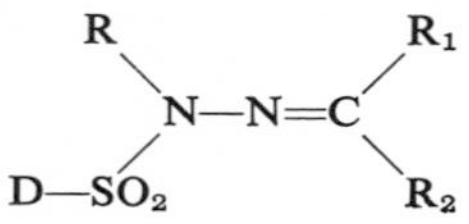	Benzophenone-N-[naphthoquinone-(1,2)-diazide-(2)-4-sulfonyl]-hydrazine 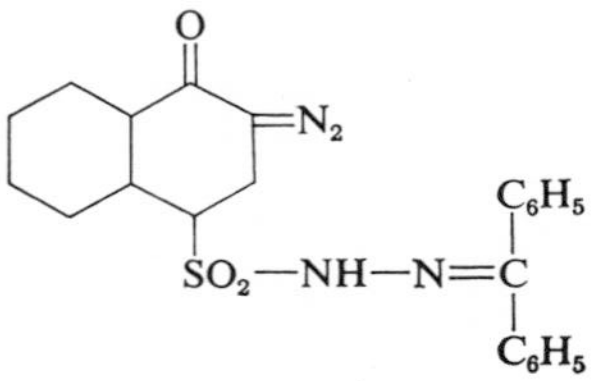	(124)
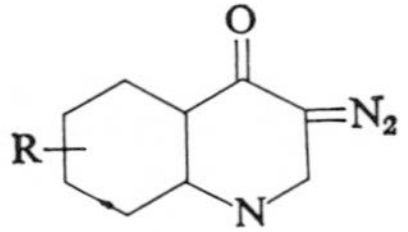	Quinoline-quinone-(3,4)-diazide-(3) 6-chloro-quinoline-quinone-(3,4)-diazide-(3) 6,8-dimethoxy-quinoline-quinone-(3,4)-diazide-(3) 7-phenyl-quinoline-quinone-(3,4)-diazide-(3) quinoline-quinone (3,4)-diazide-(3)-6-sulfonic acid phenyl ester	
 R = esterified sulfo group or a halide or alkoxy $D-SO_2-N$⎯⎯⎯Z D = o-quinone-diazide group N = a ring member in a heterocyclic system supplemented by Z so as to form a ring, in which N is directly linked to at least one further ring-nitrogen atom	1-[Naphthoquinone-(1',2')-diazide-(2')-5'-sulfonyl]-3,5-dimethyl pyrazole 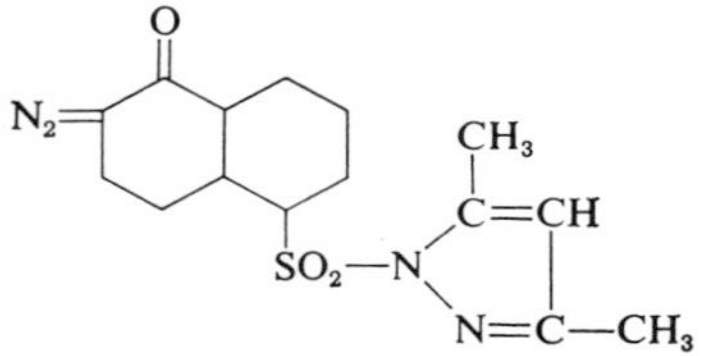	(125)

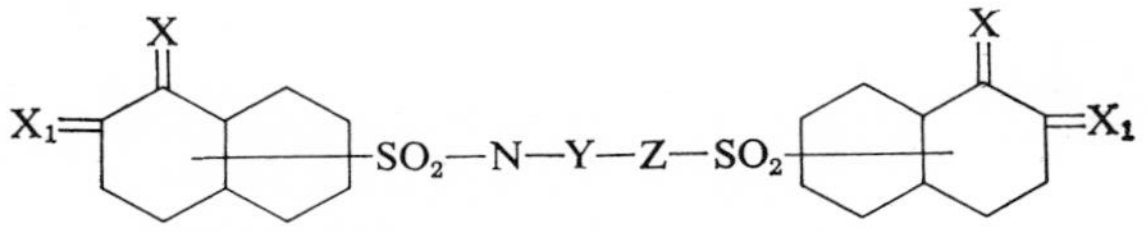

Condensation product of 2 moles of 2-diazo-naphthol-(1)-5-sulfonic acid chloride and 1 mole of 4,4'-diaminobenzophenone

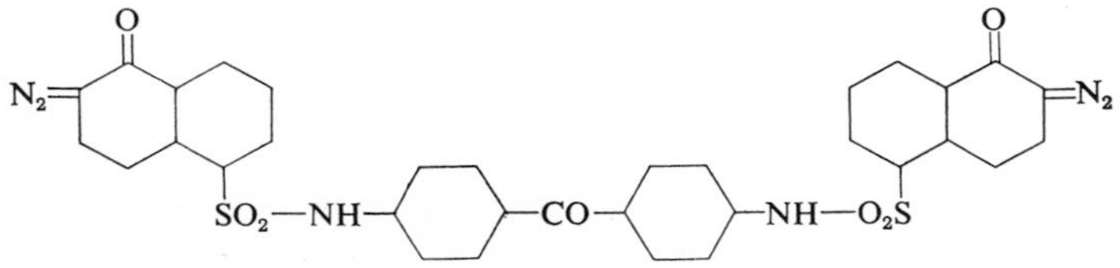

(126)

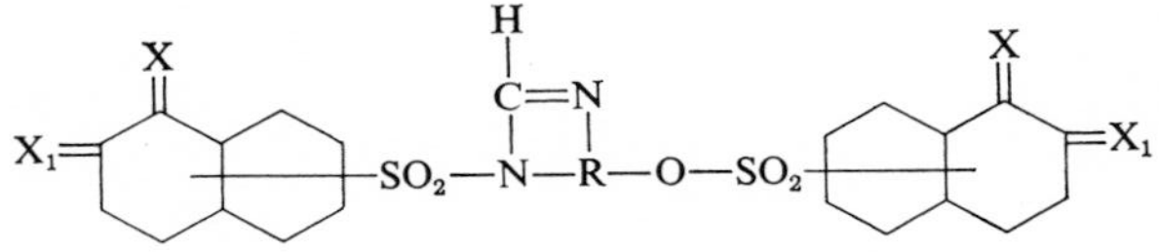

X and X_1 = N_2 or O
Y = organic linkage (arylene or alkylene groups)
Z = O or a —NR_1 group
R and R_1 = H, alkyl or aryl

Condensation product of 1 mole of 7'-hydroxy (naphtho-1'-2':4,5-imidazole) and 2 moles of 2-diazonaphthol-(1)-5-sulfochloride

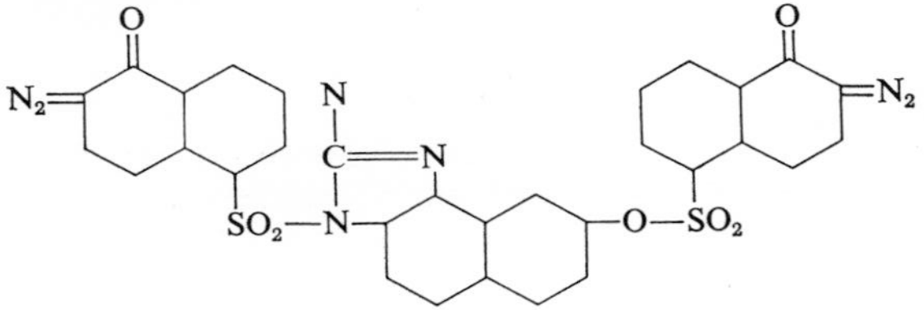

(127)

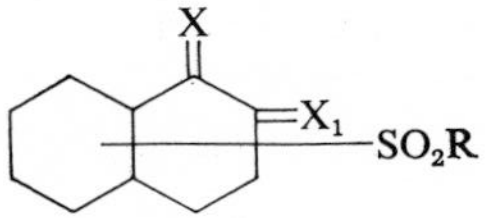

X and X_1 = N_2 or O
R = an arylene group

Naphthoquinone-1,2-diazide-(2)-phenyl sulfone-(4)

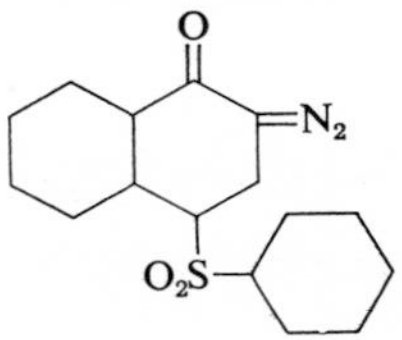

(128)

X and X_1 = N_2 or O
R = an aryl or substituted aryl group

General Formula	Example	Reference
$\begin{array}{c} R \\ \mid \\ D-SO_2-N-R_1 \end{array}$ D = a phenanthraquinone (*o*-diazophenanthrol)-radical R = H or an alkyl group R₁ = an aryl	*o*-Quinone-diazide of 1-amino-2-phenanthrol	(129)
X and X₁ = N₂ or O R and R₁ = alkyl	1-*n*-butyl-2-*n*-propylnaphtho-[1,2-α]-imidazole-7-yl-naphthoquinone-1,2-diazide-(1)-carboxylic acid ester	(130)
D—A—B—R—N=N—R₁ D = an ortho-quinone-diazide group A = —SO₂— or —CO— B = —O— or —NX—, wherein X is selected from the group consisting of H and groups which, taken together with R, form an imidazole ring R = arylene group R₁ = aryl group	Naphthoquinone-(1,2)-diazide-(2)-5-sulfonic acid ester of 4'-hydroxydiphenyl-4-azo-β-naphthol	(131)

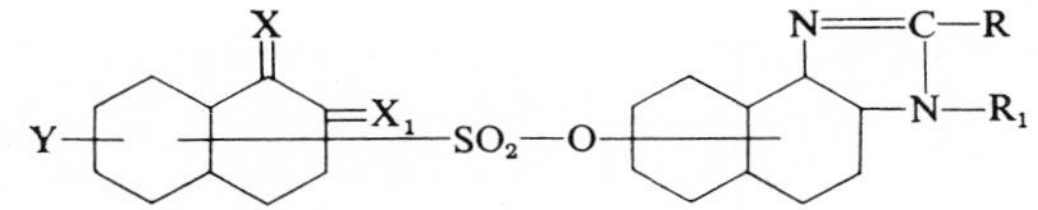

Naphthoquinone-(1,2)-diazide-(2)-4-sulfonic acid ester of 7'-hydroxy-2-ethyl-N-(n-propyl)-naphtho-1',2':4,5-imidazole

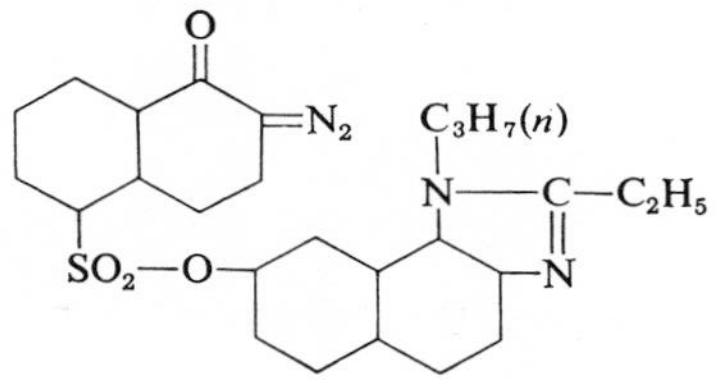

(132)

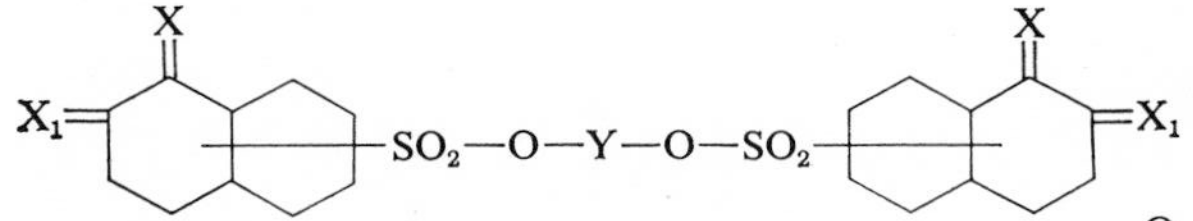

X and X_1 = N_2 or O
Y = H or halogen
R = H or an alkyl
R_1 = an alkyl group

Condensation product of 2 moles of naphthoquinone-1,2-diazide-(2)-5-sulfochloride and 1 mole of 4,4'-dihydroxy-1,1'-diphenyl sulfone

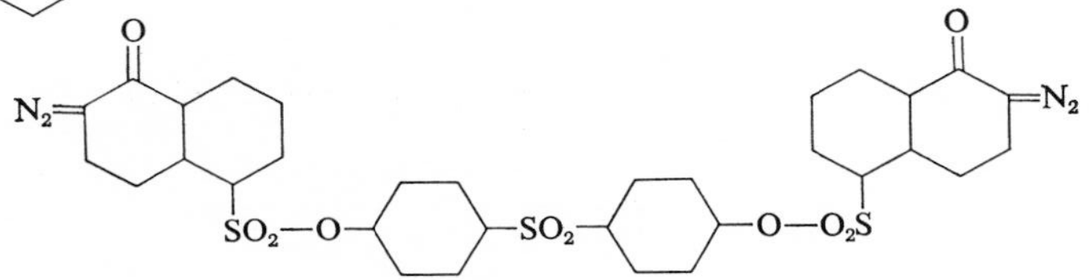

(133)

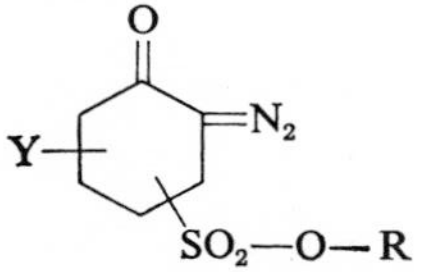

X and X_1 = N_2 or O
Y = an arylene or heterocyclic group

Benzoquinone-(1,2)-diazide-(2)-4-sulfonic acid phenyl ester

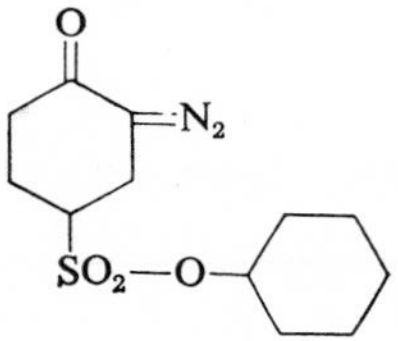

(134)

R = an aryl or heterocyclic radical
Y = H or an alkyl

General Formula	Example	Reference
X and X_1 = N_2 or O Y = H or halogen R = an aryl or heterocyclic radical	*o,o′*-di-[benzoquinone-(1″,2″)-diazide-(2″),-4″-sulfonyl]-4,4′-dihydroxydiphenyl 	
	Naphthoquinone-1,2-diazide-(2)-4-sulfonic acid-*p*-tolylester: 	(135)
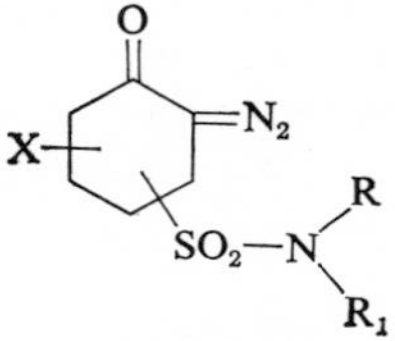 R = H, alkyl or aryl R_1 = aryl or aralkyl	Benzoquinone-(1,2)-diazide-(2)-4-(N-ethyl-N-β-naphthyl)-sulfonamide 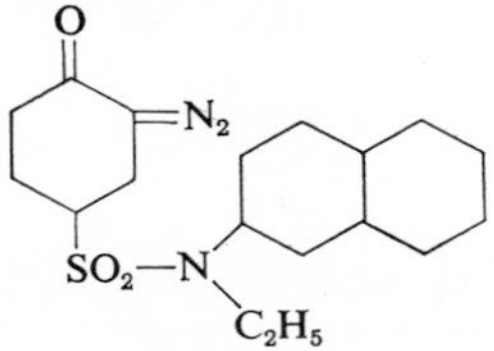 	

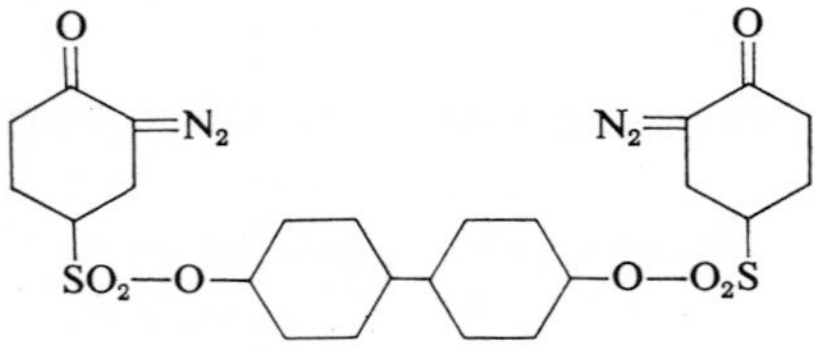

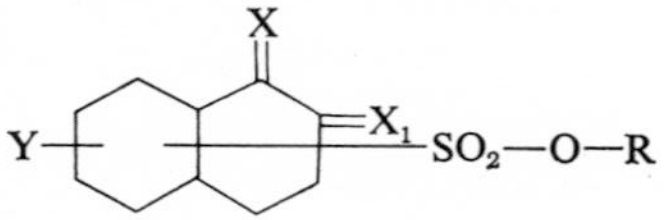

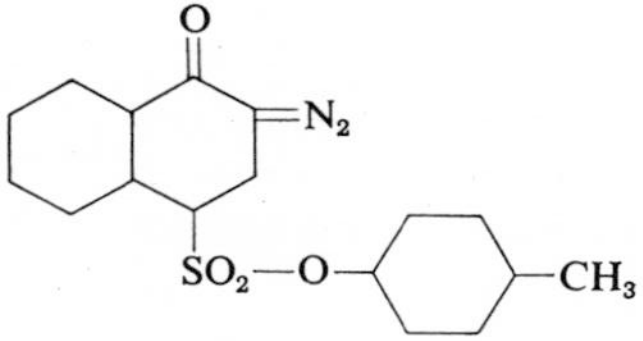

(136)

Benzoquinone-(1,2)-diazide-(2)-4-chlor-6-(N-β-naphthyl)-sulfonamide

R and R$_1$ are forming together a heterocyclic ring

X = H, halogen or alkyl

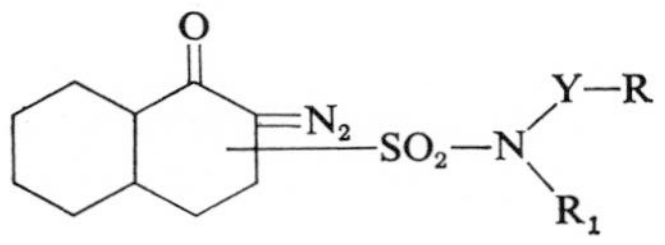

(137)

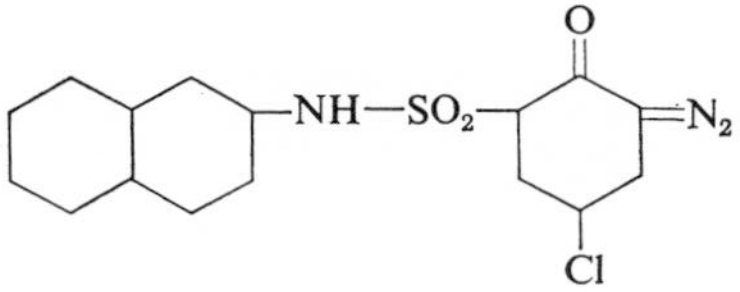

N,N-di-[naphthoquinone-(1,2)-diazide-(2)-5-sulfonyl]-aniline

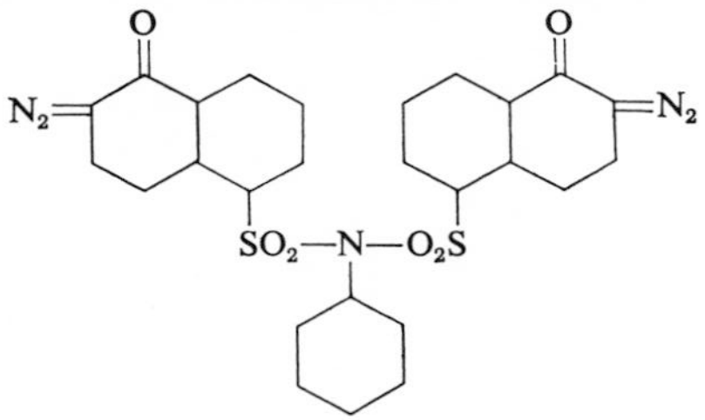

Y = —SO$_2$ or —CO—
R = an aryl or amido group
R$_1$ = an alkyl or an aryl radical
N, Y, R and R$_1$ taken together may form a heterocyclic ring

(138)

Reaction product of 7'-hydroxy-1'-2',4,5-naphthimidazole and naphthoquinone-(1,2)-diazide-(2)-4-sulfochloride

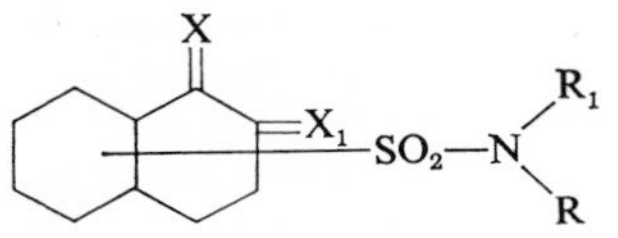

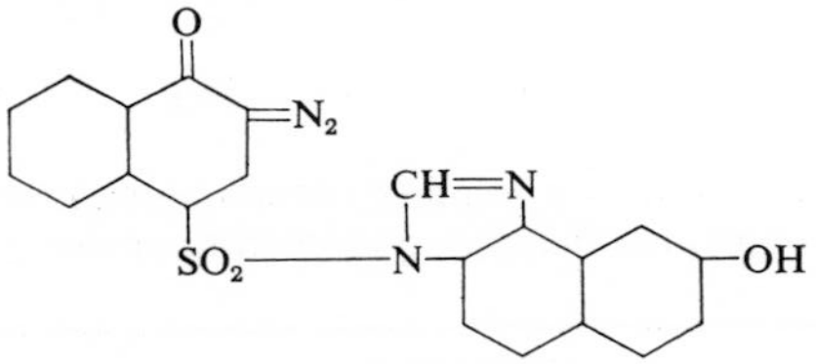

X and X$_1$ = N$_2$ or O
R and R$_1$ = H, alkyl, substituted alkyl, aryl or heterocyclic group
R and R$_1$ taken together may form a heterocyclic ring

General Formula	Example	Reference
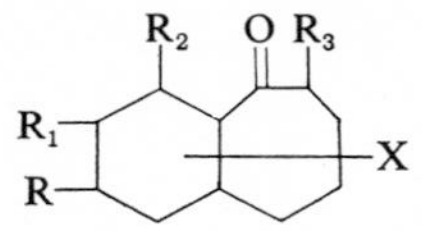 R, R_1 and R_2 and R_3 = hydroxyl-naphthoquinone, quinone-diazide sulfonyloxy group X = H or halogen	Reaction product of 1 mole purpurogallin and 1 mole of naphthoquinone-(1,2)-diazide-(2)-sulfonic acid chloride-(5) 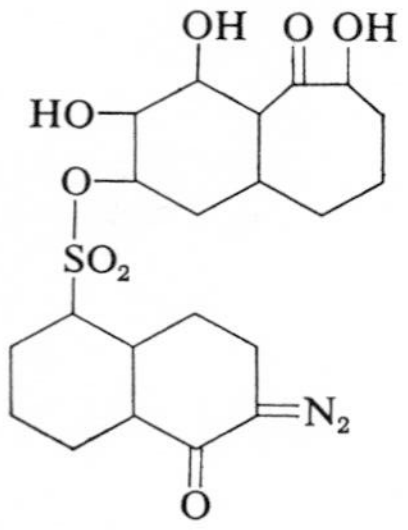 	(139)
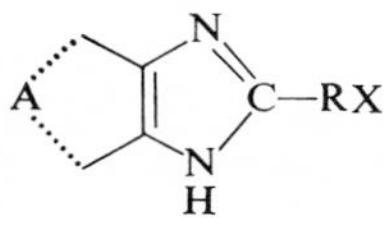 A = atoms necessary to complete an aromatic ring system which can have an N_3-group R = aliphatic, arylaliphatic, aromatic, or heterocyclic group X = H or N_3	2-(4'-azido-phenyl)-5-methyl-benzimidazole (*a*) 2-(4''-azidophenyl)-naphtho-[1',2',4,5] imidazole (*b*) 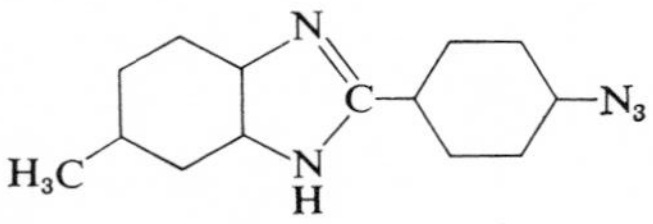 (*a*) 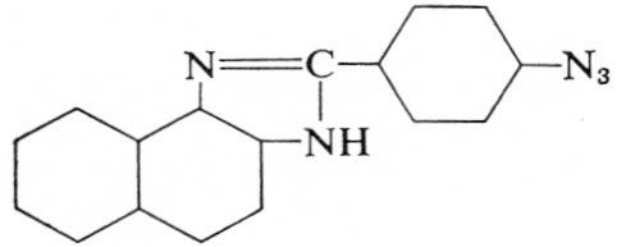 (*b*)	(89)

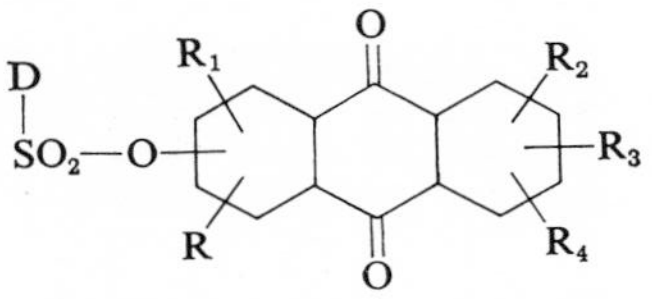

2-(naphthoquinone-(1,2)-diazide-(2)-sulfonyloxy-5-monohydroxy-
(1)-anthraquinone

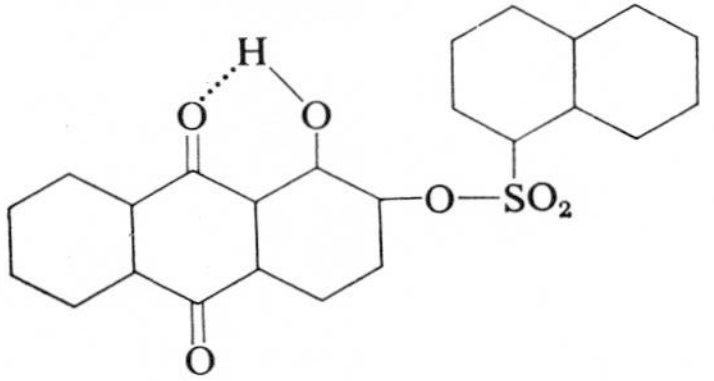

(140)

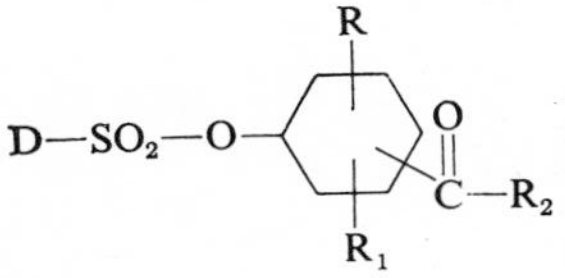

D = naphthoquinone-1,2-diazide group
R, R_1, R_2, R_3, R_4 = H, OH, NO_2, halogen alkyl,
alkoxy or naphthoquinone-
1,2-diazide sulfonyloxy
group

2,3,4-trihydroxy-benzophenone-naphthoquinone-(1,2)-diazide-
(2)-5-sulfonic acid ester

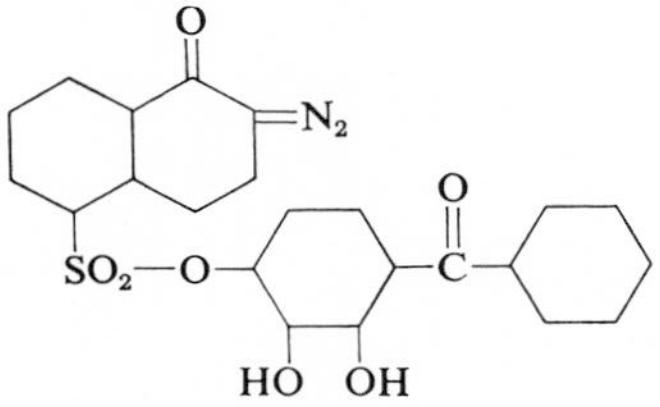

(141)

D = naphthoquinone-1,2-diazide group
R and R_1 = H or OH
R_2 = H, alkyl, aryl, alkoxy or amino group

solution of gum arabic, dextrin, or some other water-soluble colloid (119); after exposure, the plates are developed with an alkaline solution to produce a positive image from a positive original or a negative image from a negative master.

7.5   OTHER SENSITIZERS

The acceptance of presensitized printing plates soon after their introduction induced a search for other compounds which could be used as sensitizers. Tomanek and Neugebauer (142) claimed as sensitizing materials, producing either positive- or negative-working plates, acenaphthenes of the general formula:

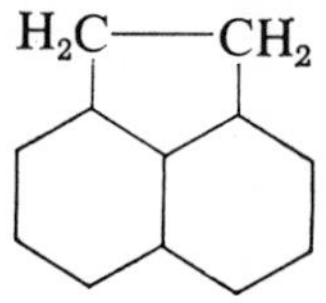

$$H_2C\text{——}CH_2$$

substituted in the 5 or 5 and 6 positions with halogens, nitro, alkoxy, acelated-amino, or acylated-hydroxyl or acyl groups. An alcoholic or glycol-monomethyl-ether solution of 5-nitroacenaphthene or 6-nitro-5-benzoylacenaphthene might be mentioned as a sensitizing medium. The same investigators introduced negative-working unsaturated sulfones:

$$R\text{—}SO_2\text{—}CH\text{=}CH\cdot CH\text{=}CH\text{—}R'$$

where R and R' can be aromatic or substituted aromatic radical (143); 1-(phenylsulfonyl)-2-styrylethylene and 1-(p-tolylsulfonyl)-2-(2-methoxy-styryl) ethylene are examples. Coatings containing sulfones are developed with a 1 per cent solution of phosphoric acid.

Among other compounds usable in planographic and offset printing processes are 2-sulfanilido-9-methylene-fluorenes in which one of the hydrogen atoms of the methylene is replaced by an aromatic or heterocyclic group (144). Compounds like these are coated from organic solvent solutions, and are removed after the exposure with a trisodium phosphate or sodium carbonate solution.

Presensitized printing plates stable for a long time can also be prepared, by coating a suitable support with S-alkylthiodiarylamine perchlorates (145), for example, S-ethylthiodiphenylamine sulfonium perchlorate (*a*) or S-methylthio-di-α-naphthylamine sulfonium perchlorate (*b*):

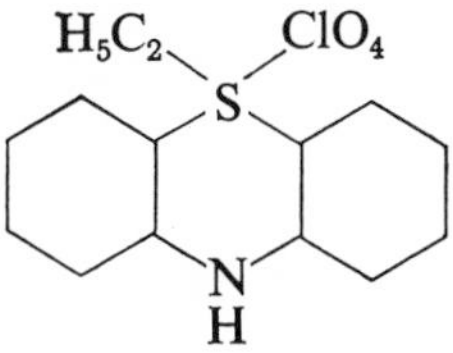

(a) 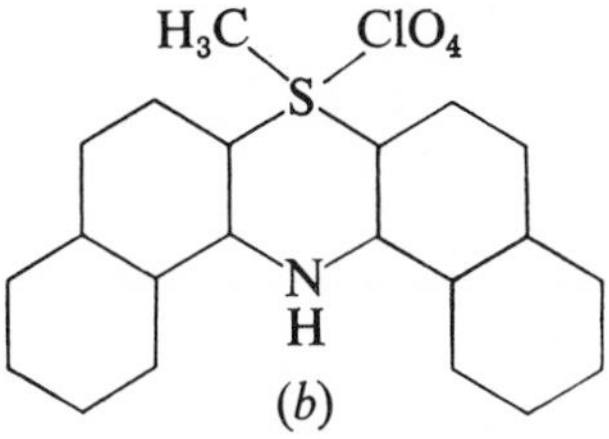   (b)

Decomposition products are removed from the exposed portions with a 5 per cent solution of sodium acetate; the plates are thus positive working.

Another patent claims the use of nitrothiophene derivatives, for example, 2-iodo-5-nitrothiophene, 5-nitro-2-thienyl-*o*-carboxyphenyl sulfide in combination with an organic colloid. After exposure to light, the plate may be developed in diluted acid to give a negative relief image (146).

7.6 WIPE-ON PLATES

The performance of this new type of plate is similar to that of presensitized plates. As the name implies, these plates are prepared in the plateroom by wiping the sensitizing solution on a metal plate. In general, the metal used for wipe-on plates is some type of grained aluminum especially treated to prevent oxidation of the metal. Under the auspices of the American Zinc Institute, the Lithographic Technical Foundation has produced a zinc wipe-on process (147).

For sensitizing both aluminum and zinc plates, a basic solution and diazotype sensitizer are used, similar to those described previously; they are supplied in separate containers to improve the shelf life. When mixed, the solution must be stored in a cool place, well protected from light. The storage life is approximately two to three weeks. Once coated and dried, the plate must be exposed and processed within eight hours. Processing chemicals and techniques are like those for presensitized printing plates; the manufacturer's instructions should be followed carefully.

The main advantage of wipe-on plates seems to be their relatively low cost, ease of preparation, greater exposure latitude, and flexibility on the press. Solids and halftones are reproduced more accurately, and it is claimed that longer runs are possible than with presensitized plates under similar conditions of printing.

Wipe-on plates, along with presensitized plates, are being used for all types of printing, including multicolor work, and are almost completely replacing albumin and casein surface plates.

REFERENCES

1. M. P. Schmidt, R. Zahn, and W. Krieger.   U.S. pat. 1,762,033/1930.
2. Philips Lamps, Ltd.   Brit. pat. 534,341/1941.
3. G. Kögel.   U.S. pat. 1,843,822/1932.
4. G. Kögel.   U.S. pat. 2,099,404/1937.
5. G. Kögel and R. Zahn.   Ger. pat. 615,958/1935.
6. G. Kögel.   U.S. pat. 2,090,450/1937.
7. Z. Bukač and B. Obereigner.   Czech. pat. 95,637/1960.
8. T. Tsunoda and M. Fujiishi.   *Bull. Tech. Assoc. Graphic Arts Japan*, **4**, 58–62 (1961).
9. R. F. Coles.   U.S. pat. 3,099,559/1963.
10. R. Zahn.   U.S. pat. 2,100,063/1937.
11. T. T. Boersma.   U.S. pat. 2,819,164/1958.
12. M. P. Schmidt and R. Zahn.   Ger. pat. 596,731/1934.
13. R. Zahn.   Ger. pat. 581,697/1931.
14. R. P. Seven and J. J. Miyashiro.   U.S. pat. 2,679,498/1954.
15. I. Mellan.   U.S. pat. 3,050,502/1962.
16. Kalle A.G.   Belg. pat. 608,789/1962.
17. Kalle A.G.   Belg. pat. 630,565/1963.
18. Kalle A.G.   Belg. pat. 630,566/1963.
19. M. Hepher.   *J. Phot. Sci.*, **12**, 181–190 (1964).
20. O. Süs and E. Lind.   Ger. pat. 1,134,887/1962; Brit. pat. 941,835/1963.
21. M. P. Schmidt and O. Süs.   U.S. pat. 3,046,120/1962.
22. H. G. J. de Boer.   Belg. pat. 605,395/1962; Brit. pat. 948,637/1964; Fr. pat. 1,306,635/1962.
23. Kalle A.G.   Belg. pat. 615,056/1962.
24. G. R. Hodgins.   U.S. pat. 2,826,501/1958.
25. Kalle A.G.   Brit. pat. 833,586/1956; Ger. pat. 954,308/1956.
26. G. R. Hodgins.   U.S. pat. 3,091,533/1963; Litho Chem. and Supply Co.: Brit. pat. 851,819/1958.
27. G. W. Larson.   Ger. pat. 1,133,243/1962.
28. R. P. Seven and J. J. Miyashiro.   U.S. pat. 2,937,085/1960.
29. J. M. Case.   U.S. pat. 3,085,008/1963; Brit. pat. 885,086/1961; Belg. pat. 563,723/1958; Fr. pat. 1,200,135/1959; Can. pat. 631,184/1961.
30. W. Neugebauer and J. Barthenbeier.   U.S. pat. 2,667,415/1954.
31. C. E. Herrick and P. Chebiniac.   U.S. pat. 3,130,051/1964; Brit. pat. 880,051/1961.
32. W. Neugebauer, O. Süs, and A. Rebenstock.   U.S. pat. 3,061,429/1962; Brit. pat. 824,148/1959; Ger. pat. 1,055,957/1959.
33. W. Neugebauer, O. Süs, and A. Rebenstock.   U.S. pat. 3,062,644/1962; Ger. pat. 1,067,307/1959.
34. C. E. Herrick and P. T. Woitach.   U.S. pat. 2,982,648/1961; Brit. pat. 867,264/1961.
35. W. M. Buskes.   Ger. pat. 1,024,355/1960; U.S. pat. 3,010,389/1961; Ger. pat. 1,024,356/1960; U.S. pat. 3,010,390/1961; U.S. pat. 3,091,528/1963; U.S. pat. 3,091,529/1963.
36. M. P. Schmidt.   Ger. pat. 876,951/1953.
37. C. L. Jewett and J. M. Case.   U.S. pat. 2,714,066/1955; Brit. pat. 718,525/1954.
38. P. Chebiniak.   U.S. pat. 3,030,210/1962.

39. R. Gumbinner. U.S. pat. 2,922,715/1960.
40. B. Cohn. U.S. pat. 2,882,153/1959.
41. B. Cohn. U.S. pat. 2,882,154/1959.
42. Lithoplate, Inc. Brit. pat. 907,289/1962.
43. E. F. Deal and I. M. Richlin. U.S. pat. 3,136,639/1964; Lithoplate, Inc. Brit. pat. 907,718/1962.
44. C. L. Jewett, J. M. Case, and J. F. Dowdall. U.S. pat. 3,136,636/1964; Brit. pat. 815,471/1959; Ger. pat. 1,091,433/1955.
45. I. Mellan and R. Gumbinner. U.S. pat. 2,946,683/1960.
46. G. R. Hodgins and R. F. Leonard. U.S. pat. 2,865,873/1958.
47. C. Gramlich. Belg. pat. 619,369/1962; Fr. pat. 1,326,241/1963.
48. M. W. Hall. U.S. pat. 2,754,279/1956; Brit. pat. 799,102/1958.
49. D. N. Adams. U.S. pat. 3,019,105/1962.
50. R. A. C. Adams. U.S. pat. 3,019,106/1962.
51. Kalle A.G. Belg. pat. 620,344/1963.
52. I. Mellan. U.S. pat. 3,113,024/1964.
53. R. R. Zemp. U.S. pat. 2,729,562/1956.
54. O. Süs and G. Werner. Ger. pat. 949,383/1956; Brit. pat. 772,650/1957.
55. O. Süs. Ger. pat. 955,928/1957.
56. O. Süs and G. Werner. U.S. pat. 2,890,115/1959.
57. W. Neugebauer, O. Süs, and F. Endermann. U.S. pat. 2,959,482/1960.
58. W. Neugebauer. U.S. pat. 2,649,373/1953.
59. W. Neugebauer and J. Barthenbeier. U.S. pat. 2,702,242/1955.
60. W. Neugebauer and J. Barthenbeier. U.S. pat. 2,810,341/1957.
61. W. Neugebauer and J. Barthenbeier. U.S. pat. 2,810,342/1957.
62. W. Neugebauer and J. Barthenbeier. U.S. pat. 2,626,866/1953.
63. W. Neugebauer and J. Barthenbeier. U.S. pat. 2,739,889/1956.
64. P. T. Woitach and C. E. Herrick. U.S. pat. 3,086,861/1963.
65. T. U. Marron and J. L. Diedrich. U.S. pat. 2,804,388/1957.
66. T. U. Marron, K. F. White, and H. M. Rosenberger. U.S. pat. 2,875,046/1959.
67. R. G. D. Moore and P. T. Woitach. Brit. pat. 816,382/1959.
68. R. J. Cox, R. G. D. Moore, and M. L. Moskowitz. U.S. pat. 2,997,467/1961.
69. J. F. Dowdall. *Proceedings of Seventh Annual Meeting*, TAGA, p. 77, 1955.
70. T. Curtius. *Ber.*, **23**, 3023 (1890).
71. J. Thiele. *Ber.*, **44**, 2522 (1911).
72. K. Clusius and H. R. Weisser. *Helv. Chim. Acta*, **35**, 1548 (1952).
73. M. P. Schmidt and R. Zahn. U.S. pat. 1,845,989/1932.
74. M. K. Reichel and W. Neugebauer. U.S. pat. 2,663,640/1953; Belg. pat. 447,449/1943; Ger. pat. 514,057/1930.
75. Kalle. A.G. Fr. pat. 886,716/1942.
76. W. Neugebauer. U.S. pat. 2,687,958/1954.
77. Kodak, Ltd. Brit. pat. 824,282/1959; Fr. pat. 1,153,617/1958.
78. M. K. Reichel and W. Neugebauer. Ger. pat. 1,123,204/1959.
79. M. Hepher. U.S. pat. 2,848,328/1958; Brit. pat. 763,288/1956.
80. A. M. Vincent. Brit. pat. 824,317/1959.
81. R. F. Leonard and M. Beckett. U.S. 3,118,765/1964.
82. M. Hepher. Brit. pat. 901,735/1962.
83. M. Hepher and H. M. Wagner. U.S. pat. 2,852,379/1958; Brit. pat. 767,985/1957.
84. M. Hepher and H. M. Wagner. Brit. pat. 892,811/1962.

85. M. Hepher. Brit. pat. 892,812/1962; Ger. pat. 1,064,808/1959.
86. H. M. Wagner and M. Hepher. Brit. pat. 886,100/1961; Belg. pat. 570,732/ 1958.
87. Kalle. A.G. Brit. pat. 790,131/1958.
88. O. Süs and W. Schäfer. U.S. pat. 3,092,494/1963; Ger. pat. 929,460/1955.
89. M. Tomanek and W. Neugebauer. U.S. pat. 3,061,435/1962; Ger. pat. 950,618/ 1956.
90. J. J. Sagura and J. A. van Allan. U.S. pat. 2,940,853/1960.
91. O. Süs and K. Reiss. Brit. pat. 942,199/1963; Ger. pat. 1,114,704/1961; Fr. pat. 1,249,176/1961.
92. S. H. Merrill, E. M. Robertson, and H. C. Staehle. U.S. pat. 2,948,610/1960; Brit. pat. 843,541/1960.
93. S. H. Merrill and C. C. Unruh. U.S. pat. 3,002,003/1961; Brit. pat. 962,557/ 1964; *J. Appl. Polymer Sci.*, **7**, 273–279 (1963).
94. S. H. Merrill and C. C. Unruh. U.S. pat. 3,096,311/1963.
95. E. M. Robertson and J. A. van Allan. U.S. pat. 2,870,011/1959.
96. G. A. Reynolds, E. M. Robertson, and J. A. van Allan. U.S. pat. 3,072,485/ 1963.
97. F. J. Rauner, I. F. Rosati, and E. M. Robertson. U.S. pat. 3,100,702/1963.
98. J. P. Mally. U.S. pat. 2,695,846/1954.
99. A. J. Powers. U.S. pat. 2,690,968/1954.
100. W. Neugebauer, A. Rebenstock, and T. Scherer. U.S. pat. 2,692,826/1954.
101. E. Rouse, F. W. Sharp, and C. C. Hunt. Brit. pat. 859,781/1961.
102. W. Neugebauer, O. Süs, and H. R. Stumpf. U.S. pat. 3,050,387/1962.
103. M. A. Landau. U.S. pat. 2,994,609/1961; Belg. pat. 560,264/1957; Brit. pat. 860,386/1961; Ger. pat. 1,086,555/1960.
104. H. Heiss and D. Osswald. U.S. pat. 3,110,596/1963; Brit. pat. 881,593/1961.
105. M. P. Schmidt and O. Süs. U.S. pat. 2,754,209/1956; Fr. pat. 1,058,067/1954.
106. O. Süs, J. Munder, and H. Steppan. *Angew. Chem.*, **74**, 985–988 (1962).
107. M. P. Schmidt and O. Süs. U.S. pat. 2,759,817/1956; Belg. pat. 513,394/1952; Fr. pat. 1,069,931/1954.
108. W. Neugebauer, O. Süs, and A. Rebenstock. U.S. pat. 3,050,388/1962; Brit. pat. 852,496/1960; Ger. pat. 1,075,950/1960; Fr. pat. 1,209,323/1961.
109. O. Süs, J. Munder, and H. Steppan. Ger. pat. 1,104,824/1961; Belg. pat. 594,514/1960; Brit. pat. 942,404/1963; Fr. pat. 1,269,881/1961.
110. M. P. Schmidt and O. Süs. U.S. pat. 2,975,053/1961.
111. M. P. Schmidt and O. Süs. U.S. pat. 2,994,608/1961.
112. M. P. Schmidt and O. Süs. U.S. pat. 2,995,442/1961.
113. M. P. Schmidt and O. Süs. U.S. pat. 3,029,146/1962; Brit. pat. 788,975/1958.
114. Kalle. A.G. U.S. pat. 3,050,389/1962; Belg. pat. 569,884/1958; Brit. pat. 837,368/1960; Fr. pat. 1,209,341/1960; Ger. pat. 1,047,622/1959.
115. O. Süs and K. Möller. U.S. pat. 3,126,281/1964; Brit. pat. 937,159/1963; Belg. pat. 587,146/1960; Ger. pat. 1,097,273/1961.
116. O. Süs. *Liebigs Ann. Chem.*, **556**, 65–84, 84–90 (1944).
117. O. Süs. *Liebigs Ann. Chem.*, **557**, 237 (1947).
118. W. Neugebauer. Brit. pat. 844,039/1960; Ger. pat. 1,058,845/1958.
119. M. P. Schmidt, W. Neugebauer, and A. Rebenstock. U.S. pat. 3,046,131/1962.
120. C. E. Herrick Jr., P. T. Woitach, and E. J. Trojan. U.S. pat. 2,772,972/1956; Brit. pat. 784,001/1957; Fr. pat. 904,255/1945; Ger. pat. 1,108,079/1961.
121. C. E. Herrick Jr. and B. I. Halperin. Brit. pat. 889,363/1961.

122. M. P. Schmidt. U.S. pat. 2,767,092/1956.
123. O. Süs and M. P. Schmidt. U.S. pat. 2,766,118/1956.
124. O. Süs and M. Glos. U.S. pat. 2,859,112/1958.
125. M. P. Schmidt and O. Süs. U.S. pat. 2,907,655/1959.
126. M. P. Schmidt. U.S. pat. 3,046,110/1962.
127. M. P. Schmidt. U.S. pat. 3,046,111/1962.
128. M. P. Schmidt and O. Süs. U.S. pat. 3,046,112/1962.
129. M. P. Schmidt and O. Süs. U.S. pat. 3,046,113/1962.
130. O. Süs. U.S. pat. 3,046,114/1962.
131. M. P. Schmidt and O. Süs. U.S. pat. 3,046,115/1962.
132. M. P. Schmidt and O. Süs. U.S. pat. 3,046,116/1962; Ger. pat. 1,047,627/1958.
133. M. P. Schmidt. U.S. pat. 3,046,118/1962.
134. O. Süs. U.S. pat. 3,046,119/1962.
135. M. P. Schmidt. U.S. pat. 3,046,121/1962.
136. O. Süs. U.S. pat. 3,046,122/1962.
137. O. Süs, W. Neugebauer, and M. P. Schmidt. U.S. pat. 3,046,123/1962.
138. M. P. Schmidt. U.S. pat. 3,046,124/1962.
139. F. Uhlig, F. Endermann, and W. Neugebauer. U.S. pat. 3,061,430/1962.
140. F. Endermann, F. Uhlig, and P. Stahlhofen. U.S. pat. 3,102,809/1963.
141. W. Neugebauer and F. Endermann. U.S. pat. 3,106,465/1963; Brit. pat. 941,837/1963; Fr. pat. 1,269,894/1961.
142. M. Tomanek and W. Neugebauer. U.S. pat. 2,773,767/1956; Ger. pat. 885,198/1953.
143. W. Neugebauer and M. Tomanek. U.S. pat. 2,696,435/1954.
144. W. Neugebauer and M. Tomanek. U.S. pat. 3,028,239/1962; Brit. pat. 768,065/1957; Ger. pat. 945,673/1956.
145. G. Werner. U.S. pat. 2,859,111/1958; Brit. pat. 765,020/1957; Ger. pat. 947,852/1956.
146. O. Süs and M. Glos. U.S. pat. 3,046,126/1962; Brit. pat. 784,569/1957; Ger. pat. 955,379/1956.
147. A. S. Porter. *Litho-Printer*, **5**, 561, 563 (1962).

8

Photochemical Formation and Destruction of Dyes

It was recognized even in the early days of photography that addition of color would increase the appearance and authenticity of a photograph. Many systems have been suggested for producing color images, the most successful of which use silver halide emulsions and color couplers. The present chapter describes dye processes which, probably, will never offer a solution to the problems of color photography, but which do suggest a possible extension of useful light-sensitive systems. Included are processes based on the photochemical formation and destruction of dyes.

8.1 PHOTOCHEMICAL FORMATION OF DYE IMAGES

Many processes have been suggested for the production of dye images. According to whether the images are formed in the unexposed or in the exposed areas of the light-sensitive material, these processes can be divided into two general groups: the first type, direct positive processes, produce positive images from positive originals, and the second type, negative processes, give negative images of the originals.

The most widely known direct positive process is based upon the light sensitivity of aromatic diazo compounds, which, because of its importance, was discussed at length in Chapter 6. Other such processes of less importance include: a process based upon the light sensitivity of N-nitroso-N-arylamides, for example, N-nitroso-N-(p-diethylaminophenyl)-urea and N-nitroso-N-phenyl stearamide, which form, with a suitable azo coupling component, an azo dye (1); a process based on the light sensitivity of potassium 1,2-naphthoquinone-4-sulfonate, producing, on exposure and development with an aqueous solution of 1-methyl-2,4-diaminobenzene, a positive image (2).

358

Also diazo sulfones, prepared by the reaction of a diazo compound with a sulfinic acid, can be used. The undecomposed diazo sulfone reacts with the coupler in alkaline medium and forms the image (3). It is believed that an active methylene group of the coupling component adds to the polarized azo linkage in the diazo sulfone and that the sulfinic acid is subsequently split to give the azo dye. Dye bleach-out processes form a class by themselves, and will be treated at the end of this chapter.

The negative processes employ light-sensitive compounds, which, on exposure to light of the proper wavelength, decompose into smaller fragments which may be colored or which may react with a second component to form a colored product. Examples of compounds which can be used in this manner are the ammonium salt of 2,2'-dinitrobenzidine-di-oxamic acid and the silver salt of 6,6'-dinitro-*o*-tolidine-dioxamic acid (4), which produce respectively, on exposure to light, yellow and red dyes.

Various organic azido compounds are capable of producing colored print-out images. The chemistry of this process is based on the discovery of Sagura and van Allan (5) that indoaniline and azomethine dyes are formed when certain aromatic or heterocyclic azides are exposed to actinic radiation in the presence of a *p*-phenylene diamine-type color-developing agents and color-forming couplers containing reactive methylene or methine groups. This oxidative condensation is illustrated by the following reaction:

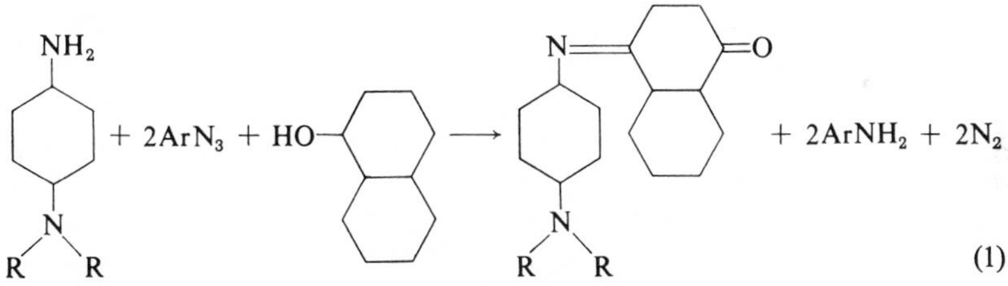

$$\tag{1}$$

In the preferred form, derivatives of *p*-phenylene diamine are used, in which the primary amino group is replaced with the azido group. The reaction takes place according to equation 2.

Colored images can also be obtained by exposing to ultraviolet light layers containing N-monoaryl-hydroxylamines, such as N-phenylhydroxyl-amine and N-α-naphthylhydroxylamine or their condensation products with aldehydes and ketones (6). These condensation products are called nitrones and correspond to the general formula

$$R_1R_2C{=}\overset{\uparrow}{\underset{}{N}}{-}Ar,$$

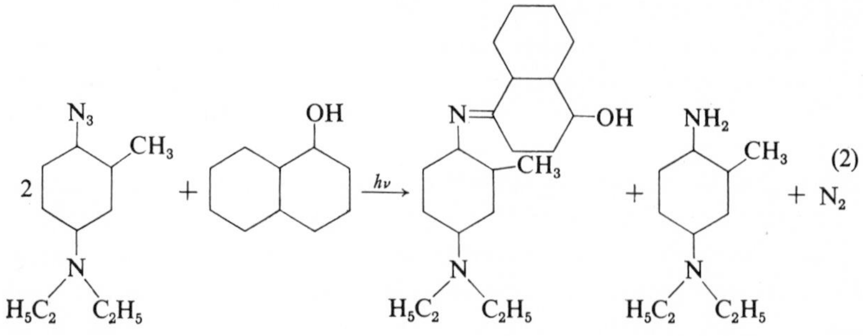

$$(2)$$

where R_1 and R_2 are hydrogen or an aliphatic, aromatic or heterocyclic hydrocarbon radical and Ar is an aryl group. These compounds are characterized by greater stability than the N-monoarylhydroxylamines. Light-sensitive elements are prepared by coating a suitable base with a solution of a N-monoarylhydroxylamine (reaction 3) or nitrone (reaction 4), or with their dispersion in various hydrophilic colloids. During the exposure, a symmetrical azo dye is formed as shown in the following equations:

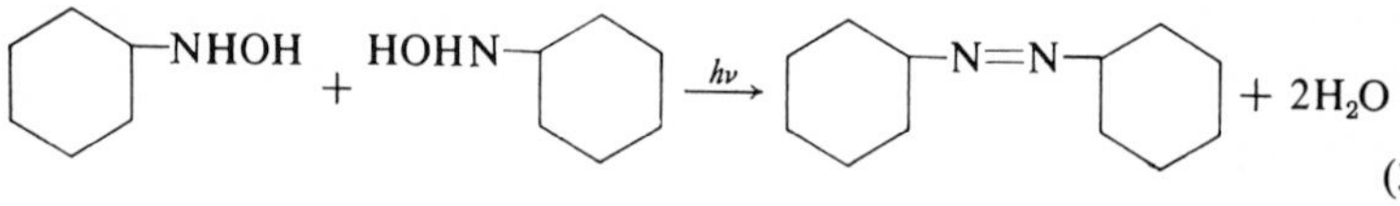

$$(3)$$

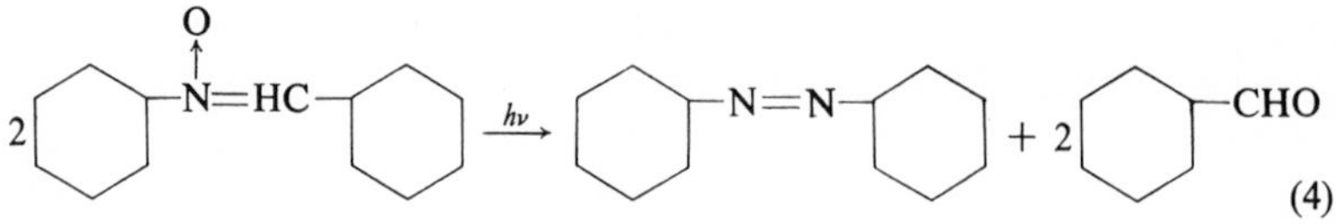

$$(4)$$

By proper selection of the components, it is possible, at least theoretically, to produce dyes of any desired spectral characteristics. Fixing is accomplished by washing the print in warm water to remove the unexposed and colorless material. Another process of interest is based on the discovery (7) that the arylsulfonyl compounds of aminonaphthol sulfonic acid, on exposure to light, acquire the ability to reduce silver or mercury salts or to couple with diazo compounds. The noncoupling light-decomposable compounds are aminonaphthol sulfonic acids having the hydroxy group esterified by an arylsulfonyl group and the amino group acylated by an arylsulfonyl group, so that they may be considered as arylsulfonyl esters of arylsulfonamidonaphthol sulfonic acids. It is believed that during the exposure to actinic radiation the ester grouping and in some cases also the amide linkage is hydrolyzed, resulting in the restoration of the coupling capacity of the aminonaphthol sulfonic acid.

A somewhat different method of producing visible images upon exposure to light employs halogenated resins capable of degradation with the formation of sufficient conjugated double bonds to form visible color bodies. Suitable are vinyl chloride and vinylidene chloride polymers. Nonhalogenated resins, such as polyvinyl acetate, can also be used; however, in such cases it is necessary to add a halogenated paraffin or some other halogenated compound which readily releases its halogens when exposed to light (8). During the exposure, the liberated halogen ion is sequestered by aluminum oxide, zinc acetate, or any organic or inorganic salt, which, in the presence of halide ions, will form a Friedel-Crafts type catalyst (9). Thus, this catalyst is formed only in the light-struck areas; exposed areas, on subsequent heating, undergo very rapid degradation to form very dark polyene images (10). The depth of the color depends on the number of conjugated double bonds present, and varies from brown to blue-black. In order to promote the dehydrohalogenation of the resin, silver salts of organic acids, phenols, and mercaptans are included in the system (11,12). In other formulations, unsaturated cyclic diketones such as anthraquinone, 2-ethyl-anthraquinone, and 1,4-naphthoquinone are used. For the purpose of stabilizing the nonimage areas against further action of light, resorcinol monobenzoate is added, which is converted, during the exposure, to ultraviolet-absorbing hydroxylbenzophenone (13). Cerous fluoride can replace (14), or be used in combination with (15), resorcinol monobenzoate. This light-sensitive system is given greater photosensitivity by the addition of a small amount of a vinyl chloride telomer (16,17).

In discussing photopolymerization processes initiated with halogen compounds, we have seen that halogenated hydrocarbons, such as iodoform, bromoform, or more complex derivatives, decompose when exposed to actinic radiation. During this reaction, the halogen is set free and can react with a number of compounds to produce a change in color in the exposed areas. In one such process, a layer containing starch, agar-agar, polyvinyl acetate, polyvinyl alcohol, or divinyl formal gives, with iodine, intense colors ranging from red-brown to blue and almost black, according to the compounds employed (18). The reaction can be sensitized with periodic acid or quinine hydrochloride. Directly visible colored images are also obtained by exposing to actinic radiation layers consisting of a linear polymer of cyclopentadiene or cyclohexadiene and a halogenated sensitizer (19).

Reaction of free radicals generated from organic polyhalogen compounds by ultraviolet or visible light with arylamines was utilized for a negative-working print-out process by Sprague, Fichter, and Wainer (20,21). In this process, a mixture of diphenylamine and carbon tetrabromide in a solution of polystyrene or similar film former is coated on a suitable substrate. After drying, the film is exposed through a negative transparency to ultraviolet radiation between 5 and 60 seconds. A blue positive image is obtained. The image can be stabilized against

TABLE *8.1.* Color Producing Properties of Aryl Amines (reference 21)

Aryl Amine	CCl₄	CBr₄	CHJ₃
4,4′,4″-Methylidenetris (N,N-dimethylaniline)	violet	blue	green
p,p′-Benzylidenebis (N,N-dimethylaniline)	blue-green	green	green
p,p′-Iminylidenebis (N,N-dimethylaniline)	yellow	yellow	red
p,p′,p″-Triamino-o-methyl-triphenylmethane	violet	red	red
p,p′,p″-Triaminotriphenyl carbinol	pink	red	red
p,p′-Tetramethyldiamino diphenyl-4-anilinonaphthyl methane	violet	blue	blue-black
p,p′,p″-Triaminotriphenyl methane	pink	red	red
1,2-Dianilinoethylene	yellow-green	yellow	yellow
N,N-Dimethyl-p-phenylene diamine	green	green	yellow-green
p,p′-Tetramethyldiamino-diphenylmethane	green	green	green-brown
Aniline	yellow	brown	brown
Diphenylamine	black	black	purple
N,N-Diethyl aniline	purple	purple	purple
N,N-Dimethyl aniline	purple	black	black
o-Toluidine	yellow		
N-Methyldiphenylamine	black	green	green-yellow
2,5-Dichloroaniline	purple	black	black
Diaminodiphenylmethane	yellow	yellow	green-yellow
Naphthylamine	green	green	green
Triphenylamine	green		
1,2,3-Triphenylguanidine	green		
o-Bromo-N,N-dimethylaniline	green	green-yellow	yellow
4-Chloro-o-phenylene diamine	green	green-yellow	yellow
o-Bromoaniline	green	green-yellow	yellow
o-Chloroaniline	green	green-yellow	yellow
4,4′-Biphenyl diamine	blue	green	dark green

background discoloration by removing the unreacted halogenated compound either by heating the material at a temperature of 60 to 100°C for about two minutes or by extracting with an appropriate solvent. The extraction method is preferable when film or glass is used as the supporting base. After such treatment, the unexposed portions are insensitive to light for practical periods of time. The removal of the residual amount of photolytically active organic halogen-containing compounds from the exposed films is easier when the diphenylamine coated paper is activated with the halogenated hydrocarbon just prior to exposure (22). The stability of the image can be improved by converting it to a more stable salt with phosphotungstic acid.

According to Sprague (23), who suggested the above method for preparation of triphenylmethane dyes, the reaction proceeds through a chain reaction.

The color of the image can be changed by substituting another aryl amine for diphenylamine, as illustrated in Table 8.1. Some of the arylamines, especially those of complex structure with numerous side chains attached to the aryl nucleus, yield black or very dark colors. Black is also obtainable by using a properly adjusted mixture of amines producing violet, blue, green, yellow, and red colors. In this way, complete light absorption can be achieved.

The color of the image is especially important when the film is used for subsequent printing on orthochromatic material. Most useful for this purpose is indole /CBr$_4$/ indole carboxaldehyde system which reacts on exposure according to the following equation and gives a yellow-orange colored image (24):

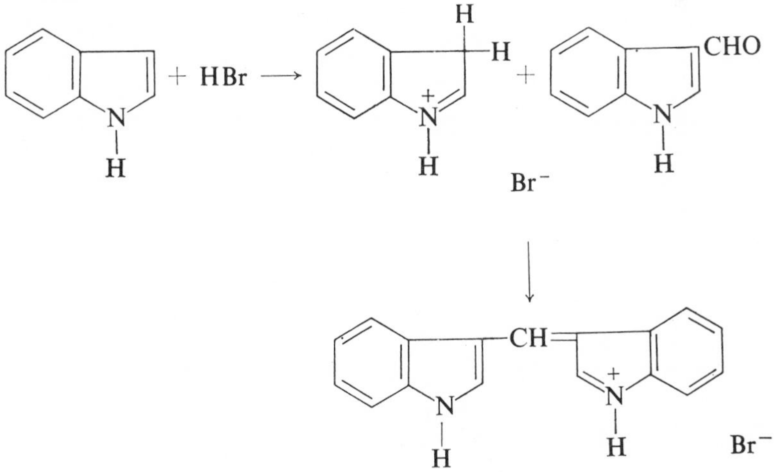

3-Methylindole gives an intense black image of lower contrast. The printing speed is in the diazo range.

In general primary arylamines are slow in forming the dye images; tertiary amines are faster. The most suitable amines are claimed to be secondary arylamines, but some combinations of primary amines, such as a mixture of aniline, *p*-toluidine, and *o*-toluidine, are comparable in sensitivity to secondary amines.

The nature of the halogenated compound also has some effect on the color of the image formed during the exposure. For example, carbon tetrachloride used as the photohalogenator for 4,4',4"-methylidenetris-(N,N-dimethylaniline) produces a violet image, carbon tetrabromide a blue, and carbon tetraiodide a green. In other cases, as in combinations with naphthylamine or N,N-diethylaniline, the color is the same or only slightly different.

Halogenated compounds used in this process are usually alkyl derivatives halogenated to the maximum extent possible; the degree of halogenation has a marked influence on the reactivity. Carbon tetrachloride is a very effective agent whereas chloroform is practically useless. Also, aromatic compounds having more than one halogen attached directly to the aryl ring are preferred. If another substituent is present, for instance an alkyl, aryl, or a nitro group, these compounds are effective even if a single halogen atom is involved.

The effectiveness of radical formation from halogenated compounds is given by the dissociation energy of the particular compound. The energy required to produce the first halogen-free radical from a number of halogenating compounds is listed in Table 8.2. From this table it is obvious that carbon tetrabromide will be a more effective halogenating agent than carbon tetrachloride. It is also claimed (25) that by including several halogenated compounds, such as a mixture of CJ_4—CBr_4—C_2Cl_6, the light sensitivity is twice that of a composition which uses only one halogenated compound.

Theoretically the amount of the halogenating agent that should be used in combination with an arylamine is that necessary to produce one free radical for each amine side chain available in the aryl amine; in practice, however, it has been found that much less is required to produce the full depth of color.

The speed with which the color is formed seems to be an indicating factor for the stability of the system. Systems containing chlorine compounds are generally more stable than compositions with corresponding bromine or iodine compounds; thus, by a proper choice of the halogenating agent, the stability of the system can be controlled to a certain degree. This is, of course, at the cost of the sensitivity. For-

TABLE *8.2.* Dissociation Energy of Halogenated Compounds (reference 21)

Halogenating Compounds	Bond dissociation energy (energy to produce first halogen-free radical) kcal per mole
Iodoform	44
n-Bromosuccinimide	46
Carbon tetrabromide	49
2-Chloroanthraquinone	52
Tetrabromo-*o*-cresol	54
Brominated polystyrene	54
Tetrabromphenolphthalein	56
n-Chlorosuccinimide	56
1,2,3,4-Tetrabrombutane	59
1,2,3,5-Tetrachlorobenzene	66
1,2,3,4-Tetrachlorobenzene	68
Carbon tetrachloride	68
2,4-Dichlorophenol	69
Tetrachlortetrahydronaphthalene	69
1-Chloro-4-nitrobenzene	70
Hexachlorobenzene	70
p-Bromacetanilide	71
4-Brombiphenyl	71
Hexachloroethane	71
p-Dichlorobenzene	74

tunately, other means of stabilization are available. Premature dye formation prior to exposure is effectively prevented by relatively small additions of alkyl amines or zinc oxide. Fogging of the unexposed sections of the image after fixing is reduced or completely eliminated by addition of aromatic reducing agents having at least one hydroxyl group attached to the benzene ring and another hydroxyl or amino group attached to the same ring in another position. Hydroquinone, phloroglucinol, and aminophenols are examples. As a rule more active systems require a higher amount of stabilizers.

To eliminate this comparatively complicated stabilization, Wainer (26) suggested the use of inorganic or organic sulfur compounds, such as metallic sulfides, thioureas, thioacetamides, or thiols. After exposure to ultraviolet light, the image is fixed by exposure to moist air for several hours; the heat fixing is no longer required. Stabilization of the unexposed image areas can also be accomplished by acylation of the unchanged amine by heating it for one minute at 95 to 100°C in the presence of maleic or other carboxylic acid anhydride that is solid at room temperature (27); for this purpose the anhydride can be included in the light-sensitive layer.

As a film former, polyvinylidene chloride, polyethylene, polymethylmethacrylate, polystyrene, polyvinyl chloride, cellulose acetate, cellulose nitrate, etc., can be used. There is apparently not too much difference among the various types, but the oxygen-free binders are preferred, since they form systems of somewhat higher light sensitivity.

The diphenylamine/carbon tetrabromide system has a peak sensitivity in the range from 3730 to 4076 Å. There the beginning of the absorption continuum of carbon tetrabromide approaches the violet and visible spectrum (3500 Å) (28) and the sensitivity of the system to these relatively long wavelengths is attributed to the complex formation between the carbon tetrabromide and diphenylamine. By suitable choice of the organic halogen compound the spectral sensitivity can be properly controlled so that it is possible to adjust the sensitivity to the energy available from a given light source (25). For instance halogenated methane compounds in which at least one hydrogen has been replaced by iodine are sensitive in spectral range from 5100 to 5500 Å. Spectral range of brominated compounds is 3900 to 4000 Å, and chlorinated derivatives are sensitive to radiation of 3000 Å.

The choice of amine does not influence the spectral sensitivity to a marked degree. However, amines which form yellow and red dyes can be used as sensitizers for visible light. For this purpose p,p'-amino (N,N-dimethylaniline) is of particular value. Systems containing these components are first given a very short exposure to ultraviolet radiation to induce the formation of the sensitizer, and subsequently are exposed to visible light. Polyphenylmethane carbinols as sensitizers were subjects of another patent specification (39).

In order to extend the sensitivity to light of longer wavelength, the addition of yellow azo compounds, such as N,N'-dimethylphenylazoaniline or 4-phenylazodiphenylamine (26), or saturated straight-chain or branched-chain hydrocarbons of the normal and iso-paraffin type in combination with a N-vinyl compound (29) was suggested. Since the last composition becomes, in the exposed areas, insoluble in hydrocarbons, this system was recommended for photoresists (30).

Hydrophilic-hydrophobic differentiation is also available when, in place of the aromatic amines, styryl dye bases and their higher vinylene homologues are used in combination with suitable organic halogen-containing compounds and a film-forming binder (31). As a consequence, these systems are useful for producing photoresists, lithographic plates, and for formation of colored images (32).

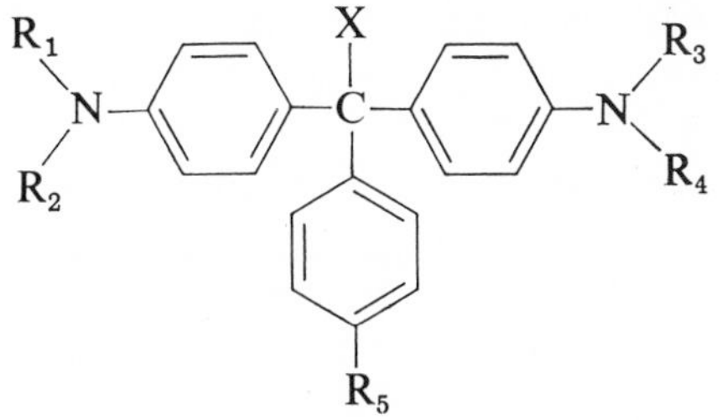

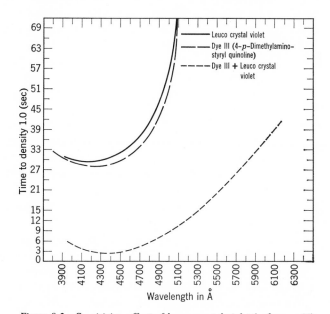

R_1, R_2, R_3 and R_4 = H, alkyl, aralkyl or aryl group;

$$R_5 = H \text{ or } -N\begin{array}{c} R_1 \\ \\ R_2 \end{array}$$

X = H for leuco base and —OH for the carbinol base

Figure 8.1.

By the addition of a leuco base or a carbinol base of a triphenyl-methane dye (Figure 8.1) to the styryl-base /CBr_4 photosystem, the light sensitivity is greatly improved (33,34). Another effect of the addition of a leuco base to the system is improved contrast, extension of sensitivity

Figure 8.2 Sensitizing effect of leuco crystal violet (reference 33).

to slightly longer wavelength, and an increased response to post exposure red light intensification.

This effect is illustrated in Figure 8.2, where the printing speed of leuco-crystal violet, and that of 4-*p*-dimethylaminostyrylquinoline, are compared to the printing speed of the combination of both.

In the foregoing system carbon tetrabromide or similar activators can be advantageously substituted with tribromoacetophenone compounds, for example, α,α,α-tribromoacetophenone and its substitutes (35), which enhance the sensitivity of the leuco base to both the visible and ultraviolet radiation. In addition, the resulting images can be intensified by brief exposure to heat.

Styryl dye bases can be prepared either by an aldehyde-condensation reaction on heterocyclic bases, such as 2-methylbenzothiazole, or by condensation of such bases with cinnamal-type compounds; 4-*p*-dimethyl-aminostyrylquinoline

$$CH=\!\!=\!\!=CH$$

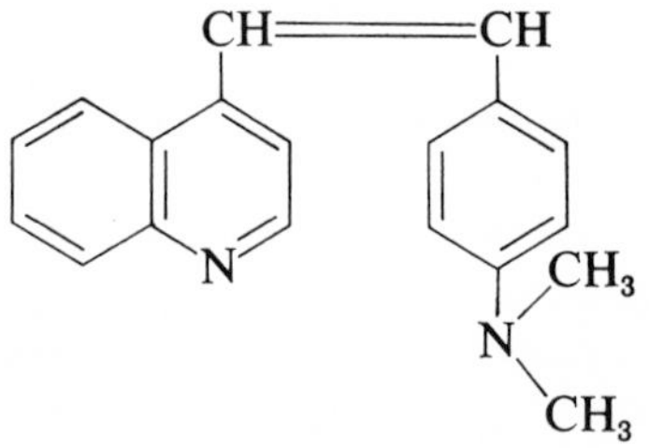

and 4-[4-(*p*-dimethylaminophenyl)-1,3-butadienyl] quinoline

$$CH=CH-CH=CH$$

can be quoted as representatives.

Styryl dye bases are available in a large variety and can be selected so as to give a full range of sensitivity to visible light. It is thus possible to obtain, as the result of exposure to light, dyes with narrow spectral ranges of absorption: blue-sensitive styryl dye bases produce a yellow color, green-sensitive give a magenta color, and red-sensitive yield a cyan color. By employing multilayer coatings, each containing a dye base of appropriate absorption, full-color prints can be obtained. Color formation can be enhanced by brief heating the exposed print to about 100°C.

In a similar way, cyanine dye bases, known to impart increased sensitizing action to cyanine dyes used as optical sensitizers in silver halide emulsions, may be used (36). When mixed with an organic halogen-containing compound they produce, on exposure to light, intense colors of high brilliance. Contrary to the above mentioned systems utilizing various aromatic amines, the great variety of the cyanine- as well as styryl-base type compounds makes a full range of sensitivity to the visible light available. Aromatic amines can be also substituted with merocyanine dyes (37).

Weakly colored dye progenitors also belonging to the class of merocyanine dyes are capable, in the presence of an organic halogen-containing compound, of producing intense colors on exposure to light (38). These systems are also characterized by an enhanced speed due to a synergistic effect obtained by the inclusion of leuco bases or carbinol bases of polyphenylmethane dyes. The exposed and unexposed sections create, in addition to the colored images, hydrophylic-hydrophobic differentation which can be utilized not only for the fixing of the printed images but also for producing lithographic printing plates.

All the foregoing systems are relatively slow print-out processes requiring exposures in the range of 1 to 60 seconds. A much faster system requiring only few milliseconds of exposure to visible light was also patented by Wainer (40). In principle, this material contains, in addition to the halogenated compound and arylamine, a N-vinyl compound in which the vinyl grouping is directly attached to the nitrogen atom as is the case, for instance, in N-vinylimide, N-vinylamine or N-vinylamide, N-vinylcarbazole, N-vinylphthalimide or N-vinylpyrrole. During a very short exposure, a substantially nonvisible latent image is formed, which is capable of being developed to high image density by heating it in a specified temperature range for periods varying from 5 to 60 seconds. Addition of alkali and alkaline-earth iodides, iodates and periodates (41), radically increases the sensitivity of the system, mainly in combination with citric or other weak organic acids. This system is a negative-positive process, and by pre-exposure of the film to ultraviolet light, and subsequent exposure to infrared radiation through a black image, a positive copy of the original can be obtained. The N-vinylcarbazole-carbon tetrabromide systems show high sensitivity to electron beams and medium sensitivity to X-rays.

Also, films containing an acid-base indicator can produce print-out dye images (42). The dye formation is based, as in the previous process, on the generation of free radicals from carbon tetrabromide or some other light-sensitive halogenated hydrocarbon, which in turn reacts with an organic binder such as polyvinyl acetate. During this reaction, an acid is liberated that changes the pH of the layer and causes the color change of the indicator dye.

Carbon tetrabromide also acts as photosensitive acid precursor in a process based on acid catalysis of the aldol condensation of polymethyl isopropenyl ketone (43).   By exposing and heating a film of polymethyl isopropenyl ketone containing carbon tetrabromide, color changes from blue-green to deep red-brown take place in the irradiated areas.   The development temperature as well as the development time is critical when images of high density and clear background have to be obtained.   Also, the resolution limit of the developed image has been found to be a function of the development temperature.   The sensitivity of this composition is considerably increased by the addition of a hydrogen donor, e.g., triphenylmethane, and the spectral sensitivity can be extended from 300 up to 400 mμ with diphenylamine.   The initial quantum efficiency of HBr formation in the polymethyl isopropenyl ketone-CBr$_4$ films is approximately 0.1 and increases to 0.5 by the addition of triphenylmethane. The over-all quantum yield for the dye formation depends, however, on the absorption at which the optical density of the dye is measured, and was estimated to be 4.5 at 490 mμ.   This means that there is an amplification factor of about 10.

An analogous process for producing images by photolysis of trihalomethyl compounds in the presence of an aromatic or heterocyclic compound containing a nuclear CH-group activated by suitable substituents was described by Lässig, Ulrich, and Steinert (44).   In this process, which is also completely dry, monomethine dyes or their colored salts are produced; for example, a red image is obtained with 1-methyl-2-phenylindone, blue with N,N-dimethyl-aniline, and N,N-dimethyl-α-naphthylamine chlorohydrate gives a green image, and 2-ethylaminonaphthalene a yellow image.   The images can be fixed, as in Wainer's process, by evaporating the halogenated compound from the coating.

8.2   LIGHT-SENSITIVE LEUCO DYES

The leucocyanides of certain triphenylmethane dyes are colorless or nearly colorless compounds, which, when coated on a suitable support, such as paper, film, or cloth, in conjunction with an activator, are photosensitive.   When exposed to actinic radiation, these dye cyanides are converted into the associated dyes; this property makes them of value, and some attempts to employ them in photographic systems have been made (45,46,47,48).   Aside from the photographic applications, light-sensitive leucocyanides are useful for detecting, measuring, and recording short wave ultraviolet light (49,50).

The conversion of triarylmethyl leuco nitriles in alcoholic solution into colored bodies has been known since 1919 (51), and has formed the basis of a number of actinometers for ultraviolet radiation (52,53,54). The dye-forming photoreaction can be represented by the following equation:

$$Ar_3C\text{---}CN \longrightarrow Ar_3C^+ + CN^- \qquad (6)$$
$$\text{colorless} \qquad\qquad \text{colored}$$

The end effect is the ionization of the dye cyanide, which can take place only in solvents of dielectric constant higher than 4.5 (55). In a solvent of low dielectric constant, the triarylmethyl radical is formed:

$$Ar_3C\text{---}CN \longrightarrow Ar_3C^\cdot + CN \qquad (7)$$

Sporer (56) pointed out that the dielectric constant and dipole moment of the solvent are not the sole criteria for the photoionization reaction. Kinetic studies of the photochromic reaction of methyl violet with potassium cyanide in several solvent media were made by Brown, Adisesh, and Taylor (57).

The triphenylmethane dyes are highly colored compounds having at least one auxochromic group, such as an amino or hydroxyl group in the para position to the methane carbon atom. Examples of aminotriphenylmethane dyes corresponding to the formula are:

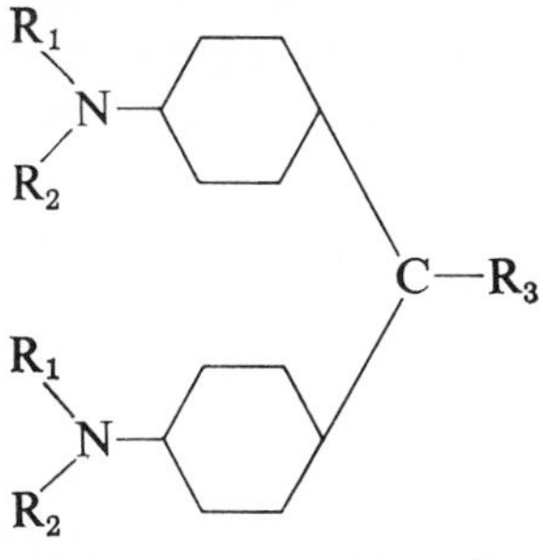

Malachite green, where $R_1 = R_2 = CH_3$; $R_3 = C_6H_5$;
Brilliant green, where $R_1 = R_2 = C_2H_5$; $R_3 = C_6H_5$;
Crystal violet, where $R_1 = R_2 = CH_3$; $R_3 = C_6H_4N(CH_3)_2$;

Victoria blue, where $R_1 = R_2 = CH_3$; $R_3 =$

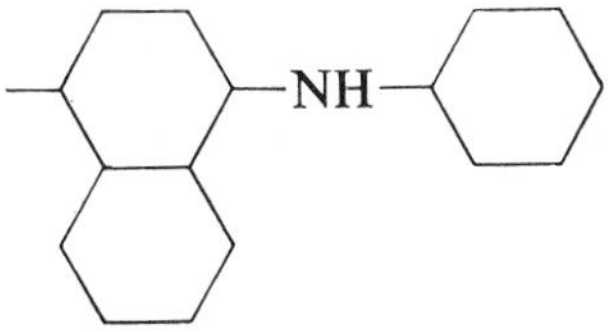

Cyanides of these dyes, investigated mainly by Chalkley, are prepared by treatment of their aqueous solutions with a soluble ionized cyanide at room temperature or by heating in a sealed vessel (58,59,60,61). The dye cyanides prepared by these methods are usually contaminated with the original dye, and in order to secure good photographic properties it is necessary to separate the two components by recrystallization from a suitable solvent (62).

In general, cyanides of the amino-triphenylmethane dyes are water insoluble, and in order to produce light-sensitive coatings on cellulose it is necessary to use solvents which have the ability to penetrate into the cellulose micelles (63). Examples of such swelling agents are aliphatic amines, lower aliphatic acids, carboxylic acid amides, and dimethyl sulfoxide. By the addition of a hydrophilic group, such as a hydroxyl group, a sulfonic acid or a quaternary ammonium group (64) to the molecule, the hydrophobic dye cyanides are made water soluble without having their sensitivity to light affected. The solubilizing group may be associated with one of the amino nitrogen atoms, or it may be attached directly to a carbon atom of one of the benzene rings. Higher water solubility can be achieved when the sulfonic acid group is a substituent in a benzyl group attached to one of the amino nitrogen atoms (65) or when a hydroxyalkyl group is added to the amino radicals (66). Acid fuchsine cyanide and acid violet 6B cyanide are very soluble, while hydroxyalkyl rosaniline cyanides are more soluble than their alkyl analogues. The advantage of water solubility is in the possibility of forming light-sensitive combinations with hydrocolloids, for instance, gelatin, animal glues, albumins, vegetable gums, polyvinyl alcohol, dextrine, and methylcellulose so as to form compositions capable of forming films (67). A number of the triarylmethane-dye cyanides are listed in Table 8.3.

TABLE *8.3.* Light-Sensitive Triarylmethane-Dye Cyanides

4,4′,4″-Triaminotriphenylacetonitrile

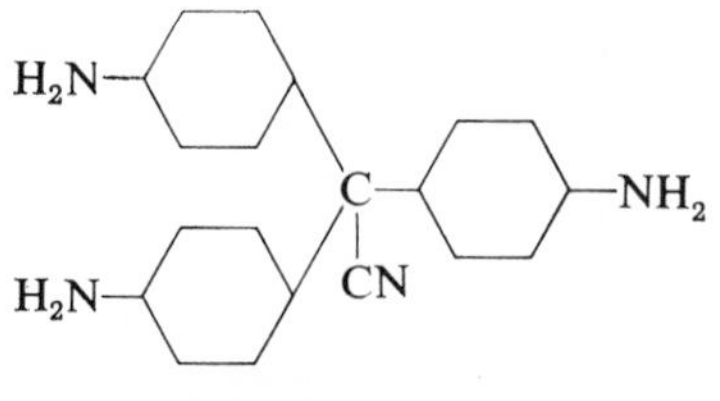

4,4′,4″-Triamino-3-methyltriphenylacetonitrile (45,76)

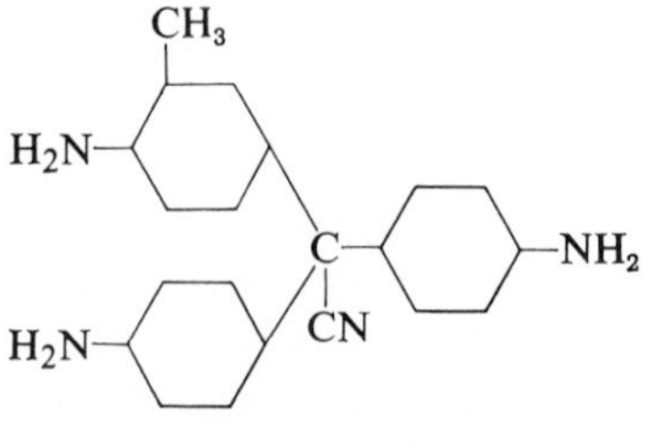

4,4′,4″-Triamino-3,3′,3″-trimethyltriphenylacetonitrile (102)

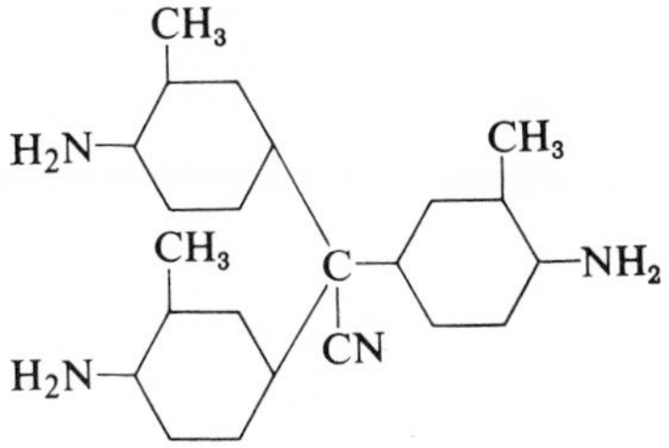

Aurin cyanide (103)

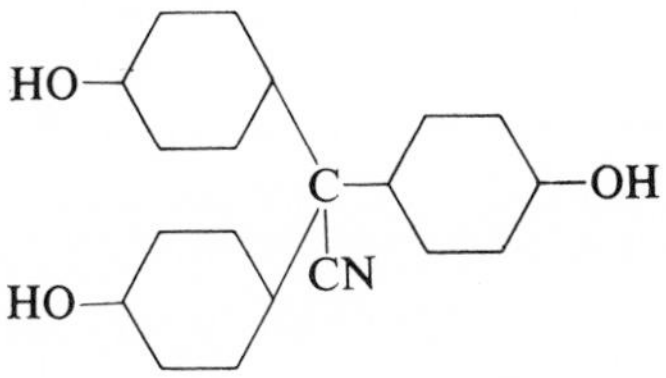

Ethyl green cyanide (104)

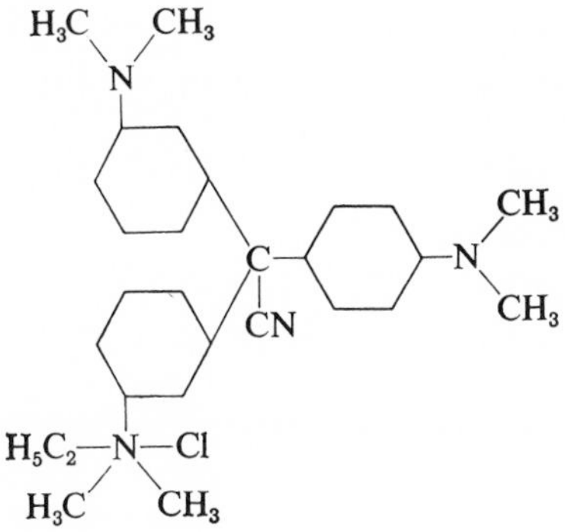

Xylene blue VS cyanide (60,105)

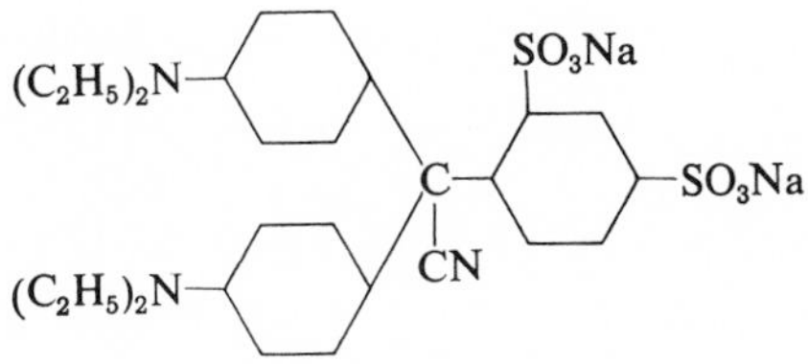

Light green SF cyanide (60)

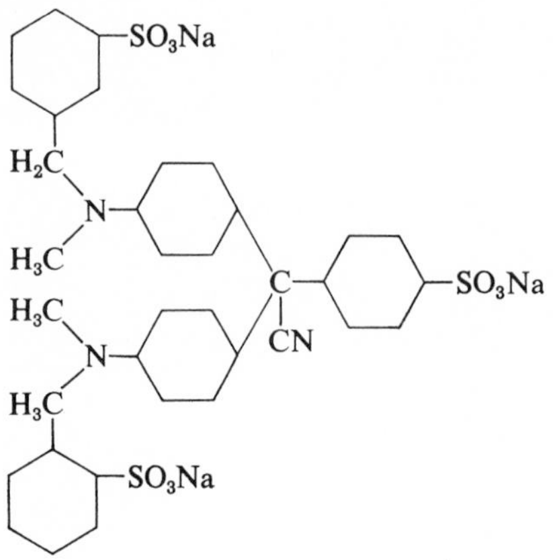

Acid violet 6B cyanide (65)

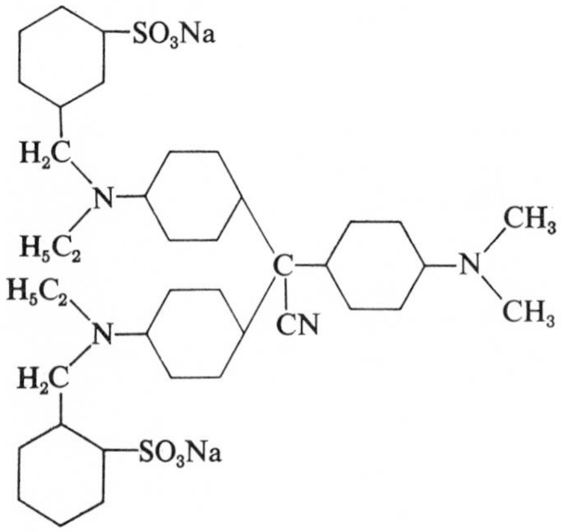

Soluble blue cyanide (106)

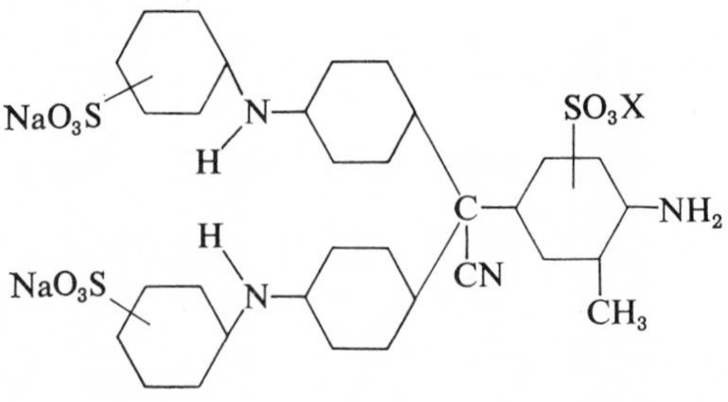

4,4′-Bis-dimethylamino-2″-chloro-triphenylacetonitrile (107)

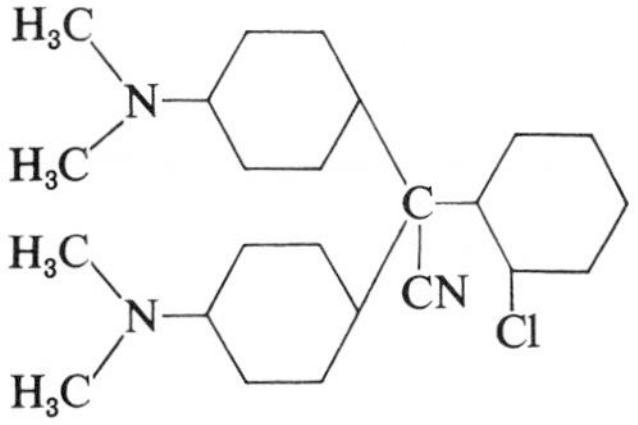

Helvetia green cyanide (108)

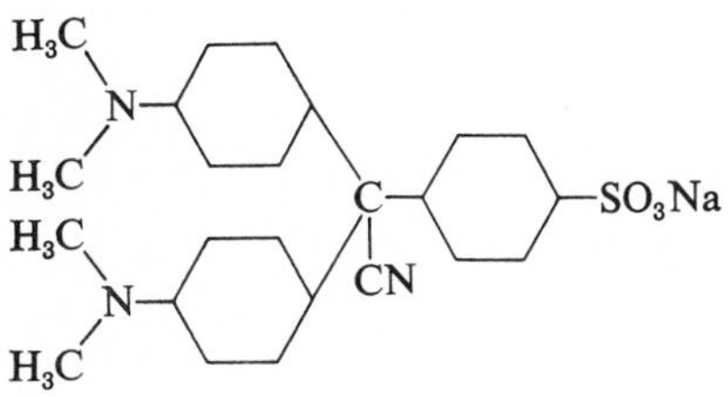

Acid fuchsine cyanide (109)

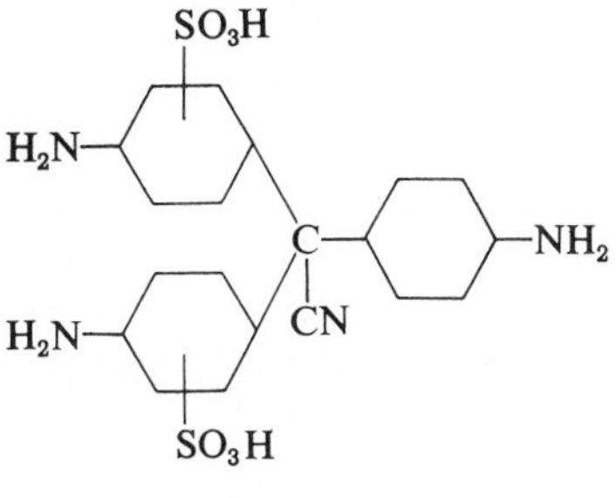

Hexa-β-hydroxyethyl-*p*-rosaniline cyanide (62)

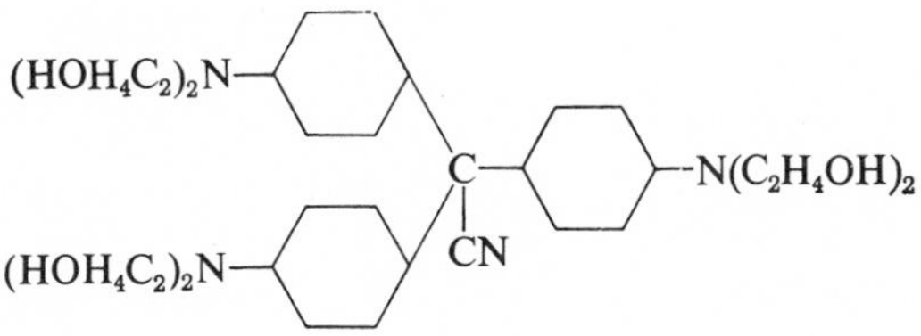

Acid green 16-cyanide (103)

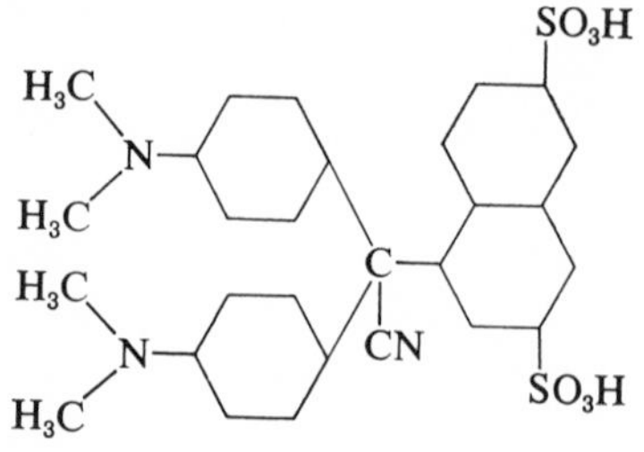

Naphthalene green V-cyanide (77)

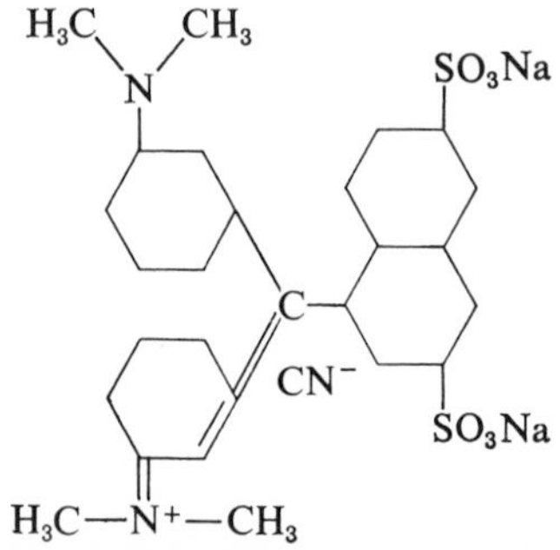

In order to make dye cyanides light sensitive, it is necessary to activate them by the addition of a suitable substance. Water-soluble dye cyanides can be activated with water (68), and the insoluble ones will require an alcohol, for instance, ethyl alcohol, benzyl alcohol, or β-(*p-tert* butyl-phenoxy) ethyl alcohol. Among other compounds, the following are suitable: carboxylic acids, e.g., acetic, propionic, caprylic, and valeric (69), as well as other carboxylic acids and their esters, certain nitriles, and primary and secondary aromatic amines (70), aromatic carbinols, phosphoric acid esters, e.g., triethyl and tributyl phosphate, polyoxy-compounds, carboxylic acid amides (71), and a number of other compounds (72). For the purpose of desensitizing the background areas of the image made by exposing the material to ultraviolet radiation under a negative, these activators can be removed after the exposure, either by solution in a suitable solvent or, when the activator is volatile, by evaporation.

Titanium esters derived from tetrahydroxy-alkylene, e.g., tetrakis (2-hydroxypropyl) ethylene diamine-iso-propyl titanate and titanium ester of N,N,N′,N′-tetrakis (2-hydroxypropyl) ethylene diamine can also be used as activators (73). The darkening of the background of the exposed papers is reduced with mononuclear aryl esters of hydroxy-benzoic acid or salicylic acid and certain substituted benzophenones.

As examples one can note phenyl para-hydroxybenzoate, benzyl salicylate, butyl phenyl salicylate, and 2-hydroxy-4-methoxy benzophenone.
These compounds can be either incorporated into the sensitizing composition or can be applied at a later stage.

Triarylmethane dyes regenerated from leucocyanides tend to fade in a
relatively short period of time. Harris, Kaminsky, and Simard (79) have
offered the following mechanism for the photolysis of malachite green
cyanide and for the dark reaction:

$$(CH_3)_2N\text{-}\underset{\substack{|\\CN}}{C}\text{-} \xrightarrow{h\nu} (CH_3)_2N\text{-}C^+ + CN^- \xrightarrow{\text{hydrolysis}} (CH_3)_2N\text{-}C\text{-}OH \quad (8)$$

colorless   colored   colorless

The final product of the dark reaction is not the original leucocyanide,
but the colorless carbinol. Attempts have been made to meet the
problem of the dark reaction by proper selection of the leucocyanide-
activator combination, by the addition of a mercuric or silver compound
(75), or a nonvolatile organic acid, such as stearic acid (76), to the system,
and by treatment with a polyacid of tungsten or molybdenum (77).
Phosphotungstic acid, phosphomolybdic acid, silicomolybdic acid, phosphotungstomolybdic acid, silicotungstic acid, and their salts are suitable.
The ion of the polyacid converts the regenerated dyestuff into an insoluble
pigment and reacts with the unchanged leucocyanide to give a complex
which is no longer sensitive to light. By this treatment, a dual action is
performed: the image is prevented from fading, and the background from
discoloring.

Light-sensitive coatings of this type are slow and require long exposure
times. The quantum yield for the photochemical dye formation has been
found to be essentially unity throughout the spectral absorption region
of the leucocyanide from 2480 to 3340 Å (78,79). However, the printing
speed of the coated papers can be increased by addition of sodium or
potassium cyanide, which has the disadvantage of promoting the dark
reaction. Agruss (80) found that the tendency to promote the dark
reaction can be practically eliminated by using, instead of cyanides,

compounds of cyanuric acid, such as cyanuric chloride or triethylbenzyl-cyanurate; such coatings are claimed to be extremely sensitive to ultra-violet radiation. When utilizing printing-out materials that have a high temperature coefficient of photochemical reaction, such as that composed of naphthalene green V cyanide, the printing time can be reduced ten times by heating the sheet, during the exposure, to 70 to 160°C (81). After the exposure, when the print is cooled again to room temperature, the original low sensitivity is regained and the unexposed portion will not fog in general use.

The leucocyanides of triphenylmethane dyes are not sensitive to light in the visible range. Their absorption spectrum corresponds essentially to the sum of the absorption spectra of the individual aryl groups and ranges from very short ultraviolet to about 3200 Å. The prints can be examined in daylight for a limited time, unless a filter material, for example, 2-methyl-4,5,6,7-tetrachlorobenzotriazole (82), is included in the coating. This compound absorbs that portion of the solar spectrum (2800 to 3400 Å), to which the system responds. Also, the normal and mono-acid salts of the para-amino dye cyanides show little or no sensitivity to sunlight, where the upper limits of sensitivity are, in general, shifted to a shorter region of the spectrum (83). The maximum sensitivity of such systems is at about 2500 Å. Fixing is thus not required; this fact presents the opportunity for printing additional information on the same sheet at a later date.

The property of being affected by ultraviolet light does not pertain only to leucocyanides of triphenylmethane dyes. Certain types of quaternary ammonium triphenylmethane carbinol compounds will develop good color upon exposure to electromagnetic radiation of less than 4000 Å (84); as activators, phenylphosphorodichloridate, chloromethylphosphorodichloridate, and corresponding bromine and iodine derivatives are used. Suitable activators are also alkoxiboroxines, such as trimethoxyboroxine and tripropoxyboroxine (85). These compounds may be represented by the formula

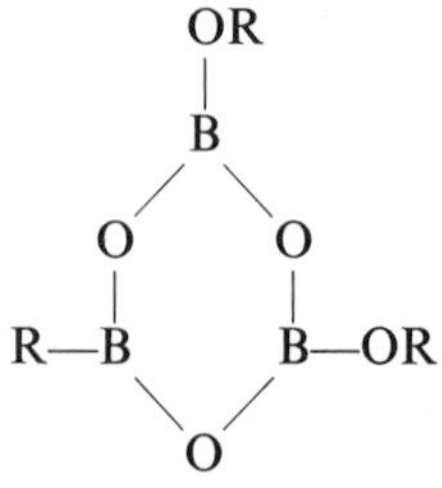

$$
\begin{array}{ccc}
 & OR & \\
 & | & \\
 & B & \\
 & \diagup \ \diagdown & \\
O & & O \\
| & & | \\
R{-}B & & B{-}OR \\
 & \diagdown \ \diagup & \\
 & O &
\end{array}
$$

where R is an alkyl or halogen-substituted alkyl group. Other compounds which are likewise useful as activators for the above mentioned carbinols are ortho-nitrobenzaldehyde and hydroxyl ammonium chloride. Under the influence of ultraviolet rays, these substances are converted to chemical compounds of sufficient acidity to enhance the development of coloration of the triphenylmethane dye. Audet (86,87) photo-oxidized leuco-compounds of Capri blue, rhodamine B, and auramine O, in the presence of hydrogen peroxide and/or a nitro compound, such as nitromannitol. Also, leuco uranine can be photo-oxidized by exposure to ultraviolet radiation; this reaction can be sensitized by acridine (88,89).

Abbott and Yackel (90) obtained negative images by oxidizing a leuco base of a triphenylmethane dye with photolytic halogen liberated from a silver halide emulsion by exposure to light. The light-sensitive element consists of a hydrophilic organic colloid containing silver halide, the leuco base of a dye, a polyalkylene oxide, and a soft acrylate polymer. After the exposure, the light-sensitive layer is heated in contact with a receiving sheet, so that the oxidized dye-image dissolved in the poly-alkylene oxide can be transferred to give a negative reproduction of the original. The leuco base of malachite green, pararosaniline, and auramine are mentioned as examples of the dyes.

Another photosensitive material (91) consists of a sheet impregnated, for example, with a colorless derivative of a triphenylmethane dye and carbon tetrabromide; when exposed to light under a negative, a blue image is formed, which may be fixed against further coloration by heat. The change in color produced in the leuco bases of crystal violet and malachite green by its reaction with the oxidizing decomposition products of halogenated hydrocarbons was suggested for determining the quantities of γ-radiation and X-radiation (92).

Likewise, photosystems based on leuco bases of triphenylmethane dyes, such as leuco opal blue, possess an enhanced sensitivity to visible light when a suitable activator selected from the group consisting of sulfonyl halides and sulfenyl halides, is present (93). As examples of this type of activators the following can be noted: *p*-nitrobenzenesulfonyl chloride, 1,3-benzene-disulfonyl chloride, benzenesulfonyl bromide, 2,4-dinitro-benzenesulfenyl chloride, and *o*-nitrobenzenesulfenyl chloride. These systems can also be readily fixed by heat alone.

The sensitivity of leuco bases of triphenyl-methane dyes to the ultraviolet radiation can be enhanced by including into the composition alkyl, aryl, or alkyl aryl ketones, such as α,α,α-tribromoacetophenone (94,35).

Images obtained from photosensitive compositions based on leuco bases of triphenylmethane dyes activated with aliphatic and aromatic acids and acid anhydrides such as benzoic, acetic, or substituted phenoxy-acetic acid, can be stabilized with ammonia or alkyl amines (95,96).

In a similar process, the photo-oxidation of di- or tri-arylmethane leuco dyes with photolytic halogen, Pfoertner (97) was able to increase the sensitivity by the presence of a plasticizer, namely, heavy metal salts or chelates of benzoyl benzoate and of anthracene. Exposure to X-rays or other ionizing radiation liberates chlorine ions, for example from hexa-chloroethane, and regenerates the dye. This material is insensitive to visible light.

Phthalocyanines can be regenerated from their leuco forms by exposing them to actinic radiation in the presence of diazonium compounds, which on exposure to light produce a reducing agent of redox potential between -0.877 and $+0.50$ volt (98). For this purpose, the most suitable one was found to be copper phthalocyanine (99). Diazo compounds correspond-ing to the above specification include diazotized 1,2- or 1,4-aminohydroxy- and dihydroxybenzenes and naphthalenes, *p*-aminodialkylanilines or *p*-aminodiphenylamines. Gelatin, polyvinyl alcohol, or polyvinyl acetals can be used as carriers for the light-sensitive composition. When exposed to actinic light (3000 to 4800 Å) under a negative, a blue positive print-out image, composed of copper phthalocyanine pigment, is formed. The undecomposed leuco-phthalocyanine and remaining diazonium salt are subsequently removed with alcohol and water. In a similar process (100) a blue image was formed by exposing copper phthalocyanine pro-pigment (101) in the presence of oxalic acid to ultraviolet radiation.

8.3   PHOTOCHROMISM

Photochromism is the phenomenon involving the change of color of a substance on exposure to light; in a stricter sense, photochromism is defined as the reversible coloring of compounds under suitable radiation, associated with an alteration in their molecular structure. Substances which undergo photoinduced reversible color transformation are also called tenebrescent substances or scotophores. They are usually colorless in one state and colored in the other state, but compounds with two colored forms are known also.

Photochromism is a photochemical phenomenon and, as such, follows the Grothus-Draper law; only the light absorbed by the photochromic substance is active. As the exposure to light proceeds, the intensity of the color increases till an equilibrium is reached beyond which the further action of light is without effect.

Photochromism is a reversible phenomenon; when the light source is removed, the system is restored to its original state:

$$\text{colorless form} \underset{\text{dark}}{\overset{\text{light}}{\rightleftharpoons}} \text{colored form} \tag{9}$$

In general, the process is not as simple as indicated in the foregoing equation and, ordinarily, the two opposing reactions take place simultaneously.

The wavelength of the light which is effective in bringing about the photochromic change, and the rate at which the changes take place, depend on the nature of the substance and on the temperature. As a rule, an increase in temperature causes the absorption bands to shift toward longer wavelengths. Higher temperature also accelerates the "dark" reaction which takes place simultaneously with the color-forming reaction and which destroys the color induced by light, but, because the light reaction proceeds at a much greater rate, the retarding effect is usually of no importance. The rate at which the photoinduced color changes take place is dependent also on the solvent.

A considerable number of inorganic and organic compounds show the photochromic change either in the solid state or in solution (111). Among inorganic compounds, we can mention compounds of mercury (112,113, 114,115,116), copper (117), zinc (118), and metal hexacarbonyls of chromium, molybdenum, and tungsten (119). Of some importance also is sodalite, a sodium aluminum silicate $Na_6Al_6O_{24} \cdot 2NaCl$, which occurs in nature as a crystal of cubic lattice structure with a definite blue color. It may be bleached to a colorless state by heating it to 450°C; exposure to X-rays restores the original blue color. Medved (120) prepared synthetic sodalite by heating a mixture of sodium hydroxide, aluminum oxide, silica, and sodium chloride in a reducing atmosphere afforded by hydrogen or by use of a graphite crucible, to 1050°C for 24 to 72 hours. The resulting material darkens to a magenta color when exposed to short ultraviolet radiation and reverts to a colorless substance under visible light radiation.

Among organic compounds are the following:

Benzaldehyde phenylhydrazone (121,122)

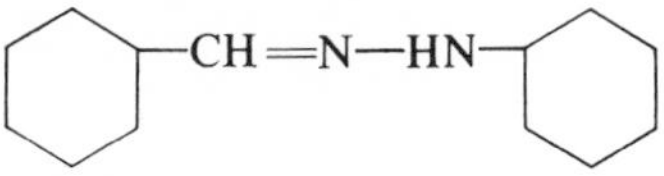

Benzyl phenyl osazone (123)

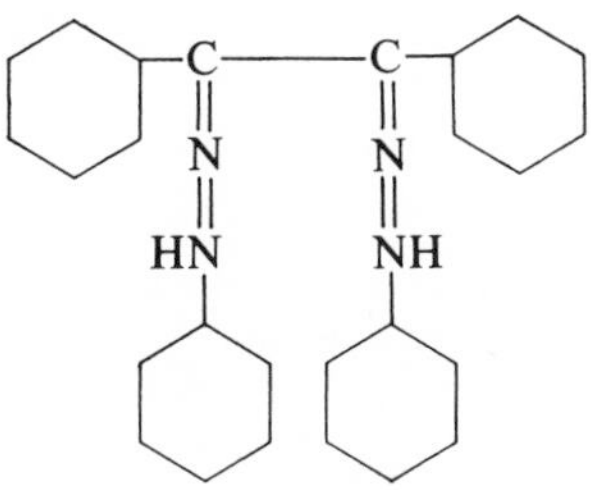

Anils (= condensation products of aldehydes and primary amines), for example, salicylidene aniline (124,125,126,127,128)

Fulgides, for example, diphenyl-dimethyl fulgide (129,130,131,132,133, 134)

Stilbene derivatives, for example, diformyl-*p,p'*-diamino-dibenzoyl-4,4'-diaminostilbene-2,2'-disulfonic acid (135)

Disulfoxides, for example, acetanilide-*p*-disulfoxide (136,137)

Aromatic nitro compounds, for example, 2-(2',4'-dinitrobenzyl)-pyridine (138,139,140,141,142,143)

Aromatic aci-nitro compounds, for example, phenylnitromethane (144)

$$CH_2 \cdot NO_2$$

Sydnones, for example, N-3-pyridylsydnone (145)

Anhydrous quinoquinoline hydrochloride (146)

HCl

Tetrachloroketodihydronaphthalene (147,148)

Tetraphenyl-dihydrotriazine (149)

Camphor derivatives, for example, α-naphthylamino camphor (150,151)

Dithizone derivatives, for example, (*a*) mono-dithizone mercuric chloride and (*b*) mercuric bis-dithizonate (152)

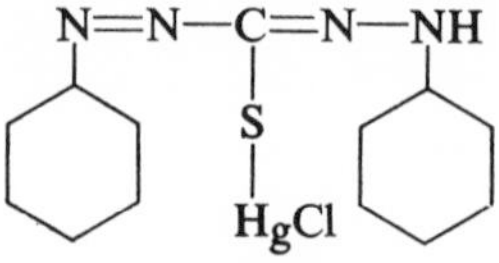

(*a*)

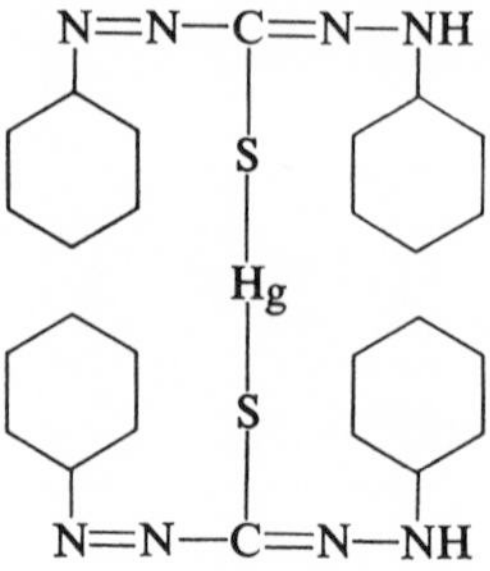

(*b*)

Formazanes, for example, triphenylformazane (153)

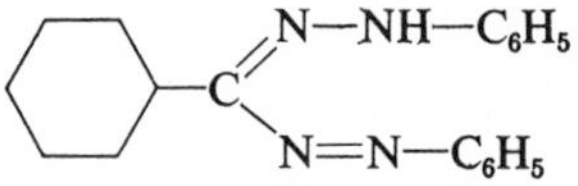

The photochromism of some compounds takes place in the solid state, and the color changes are, in general, more pronounced when the photochromic substances are dissolved in an appropriate solvent. In image-forming applications, the solution of the photochromic substance is applied on a suitable support just before it arrives at the printing station, or the photochromic material, coated in solid form on a support, is wetted with the solvent prior to exposure. The handling of the liquid can be eliminated, in some instances, by incorporating the photochromic substance into a binder (132,154), or, better, by coating the supporting base with an emulsion prepared by emulsifying the light-sensitive component (dissolved in diethylbenzene) in a hot aqueous solution of gelatin (155,156). When the emulsion cools and sets on the support, the internal phase is trapped in a pressure-rupturable film as microscopic droplets (157). The image is formed by exposing the coated surface to light in selected pattern. By applying pressure on the material and rupturing the film, the solvent is allowed to evaporate; this operation leaves both the colored and uncolored areas insensitive to light. The liquid medium will, in time, however, leak to the surface and make the material unusable. An improvement in this respect is achieved by an encapsulation technique (158), enclosing the volatile solvent in microscopic pressure-rupturable capsules which are, together with the photochromic substance, coated on the supporting base. These capsules are ruptured by pressure just before the exposure, making the solvent available for dissolving the photochromic compound (159,160).

For this application, the most suitable photochromic substances are derivatives of xanthylidene-anthrone and indolino-benzopyrylospiran. As examples of these compounds, we can cite 3-methyl-10-(9′-xanthylidene)-anthrone and 1,3,3-trimethylindolino-6′-nitro-8′-methoxybenzo-pyrylospi-ran (161). The first compound is light yellow and turns red when exposed to light of wavelength shorter than 4000 Å. The second compound is colorless and changes to a deep blue. Both compounds, whether colored or not, are insensitive to light when dry. Besides the foregoing compounds, the following were found to possess photochromic properties: derivatives of 3-alkyl-3′-methyl-spiro-[benzothiazole-2:2′-(2′H-1)-benzo-pyran)] (162,163) and their benzoxazole analogues (164), which darken on exposure to blue or ultraviolet light and revert to the colorless state on exposure to infrared light; derivatives of 1:3:3-trimethyl-spiro-2′(H-1′-benzopyran-2′:2′-indoline) (165,166,167,168), which have photochromic properties between −20 and +20°C; they turn dark blue under ultraviolet light and become colorless under visible or infrared; derivatives of 3′-methyl-spiro (2H-1-β-naphthopyran-2:2′[2′H-1′-benzopyran]) (169); derivatives of 3-phenyl-spiro (2H,1-benzopyran-2,2′-[2′H,1′-benzopyran]) (170).

The molecules of these compounds contain a ring having a carbon-oxygen bond which is broken by the action of ultraviolet radiation and reformed by visible light. The normal compound is transparent, the open ring version is colored.

For their capabilities and the ease of being switched at will from one stable state to another by means of electromagnetic radiation of two different wavelengths in a fraction of a second, and for their capacity for storing a large number of bits of information per square inch, the obvious application for photochromic substances is in the memory devices for high density storage of computer data (171). With such photosensitive systems impressive 48.400:1 area reduction is possible so that a microfilmed book of 1250 pages will occupy a film chip no larger than 2 square inches (172). Photochromic films are also suitable for forming masking images during contact or projection printing, as they reduce large density differences of the negatives (173). Freedom from fatigue with repeated light and dark cycling is a basic requirement for most of the applications and only a few known photochromic substances fulfill this requirement.

It may be of interest to note that the ability of photochromic substances to be restored to their original state after they have been kept in the dark for a period of time can be utilized for other than photoimaging purposes.

Tamblyn and Armstrong (174) found that photochromic dyes, such as *p*-phenylazodiphenylamine, *p*-[*p*-(dimethylamino) phenylazo] acetanilide, *p*-[*o*-chlorophenylazo]-N,N-dimethylaniline, and 2,5-dimethoxy-4-phenyl-azoaniline, when mixed with a cellulose ester, protect the polymer from degradation by radiation. The absorbed light energy causes the dye molecule to undergo a reversible internal rearrangement, which later in the dark reverts to its original form with a release of the energy in small vibrational packets which are not harmful to the plastic.

Other potential uses of photochromic materials include sunglasses, windshields, window panes, eye-protecting devices for military purposes, and other objects where dynamic control of sunlight is desired. High reversibility, which is required for these applications, is made possible by the use of glasses containing salts of cerium or europium (175) or glasses sensitized by precipitation of microscopic silver halide crystals in alkali metal borosilicate glass matrix (176,177). In the latter glasses the photo-lytic dissociation taking place during the light exposure is basically the same as in the photographic process. Because of the fact that there is no loss of reaction products from the reacting zone, the silver and halogen can return to their original state. The process can be illustrated by the following reaction:

$$\underset{\text{clear}}{Ag^+} + Cl^- \underset{\text{light off}}{\overset{\text{light on}}{\rightleftharpoons}} \underset{\text{dark}}{Ag^\circ + Cl^\circ} \tag{10}$$

This darkening and clearing cycle can be repeated indefinitely. The wavelengths that induce darkening range from near ultraviolet through the visible spectrum to about 6500 Å, depending on the chemical composition and prior heat treatment. The color is generally a neutral grey and absorbs all the radiations from near ultraviolet to near infrared. The time required to regain original transmittance ranges from minutes to hours, depending again on the composition, temperature, and thermal history of the glass. Ultraviolet sensitive glasses, as those containing silver chloride, fade more rapidly in visible light than in the dark. The sensitivity of photochromic glasses to light can be considerably increased by including polyvalent oxides of arsenic, antimony, tin, and copper; the photochemical reaction can be expressed as follows:

$$Ag^+ + Cu^+ \underset{\text{light or heat}}{\overset{\text{light}}{\rightleftharpoons}} Ag^\circ + Cu^{2+} \tag{11}$$

Silver halide photochromic glasses are believed to be truly reversible and immune to fatigue.

8.4 BLEACH-OUT PROCESS

Attempts to produce photographic color images by bleaching of dyes date from the early days of the dye industry when many dyes were found to bleach out or change their color so rapidly that they were useless for commercial purposes. Based on the discovery that dyes are bleached in proportion to the exposure, this deficiency was suggested as the basis for a direct-positive printing process (178). Since dyes transmit their own color and absorb the remainder of the visible spectrum, dyes sensitive to the action of light are affected by light of the same wavelength which they absorb (complementary color). A yellow dye will fade when exposed to ultraviolet or blue light, whereas magenta and cyan will be sensitive mainly to green and red light, respectively.

When dyes of different colors, preferably magenta, cyan, and yellow, are distributed over the paper in such a ratio as to give an approximately greyish mixture and are exposed to white light under a color transparency, the dyes will be bleached wherever the light of the corresponding color reaches the dye mixture. Thus, where a patch of blue light falls on the paper, yellow dye will absorb it and fade rapidly (Figure 8.3). Light of other wavelengths will produce a similar effect: green light will bleach the magenta dye and the red light will affect the cyan dyestuff to an extent dependent upon the length and intensity of exposure. Where no light falls on the paper, the dyes will remain unaffected and will form a positive image of the transparency in the true color.

The bleach-out process is the most fascinating method of color reproduction and it seems to be a simple and elegant theoretical solution to the problems of color photography. In the past at least two attempts have been made to produce commercial paper, namely Utopaper and Utocolor,

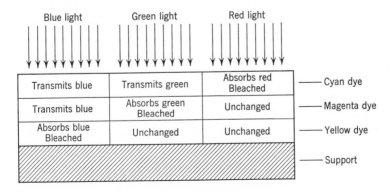

Figure 8.3. Dye-bleach-out process.

TABLE 8.4 Bleaching-Out Dyes

Type	Chromophore	Dye	Color	Solubility	Reference
Diphenylmethane ($\diagup\!\diagdown C=NH$)		Auramine O	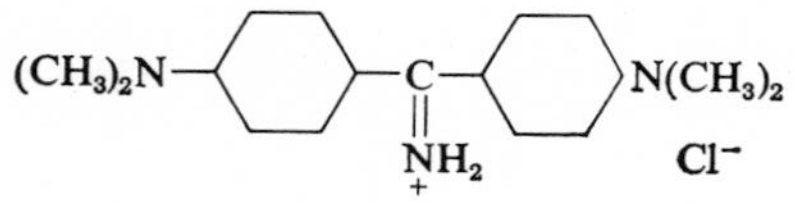 yellow	H_2O	C.I.41000
		Auramine G	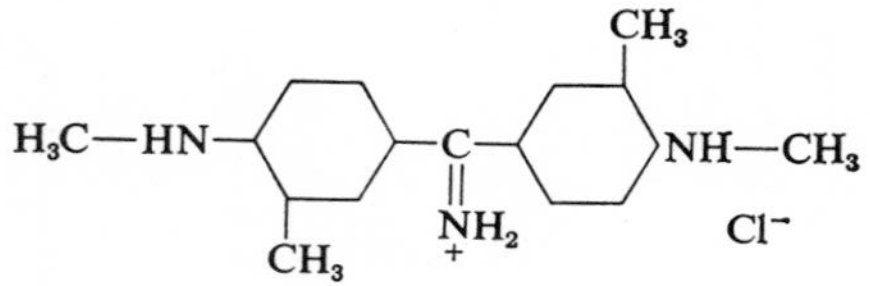 yellow	H_2O	C.I.41005
Triphenylmethane ($\diagup\!\diagdown C=Ar=NH$, Ar = aryl)		Victoria blue	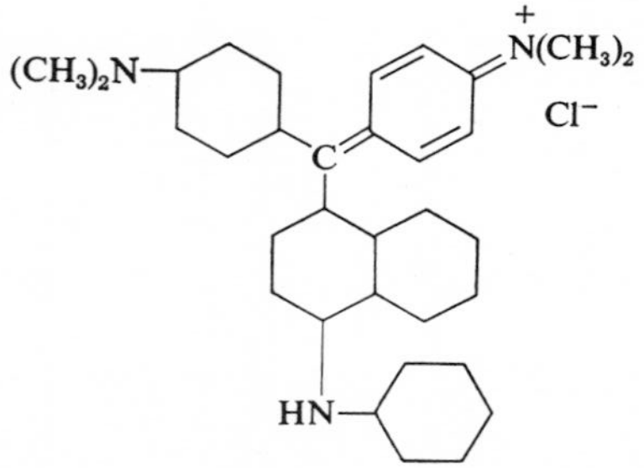 blue	H_2O	C.I.44045

Azines

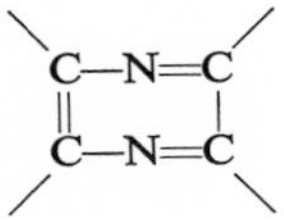

Oxazines

Thiazines

flavinduline O   yellow H_2O C.I.50000

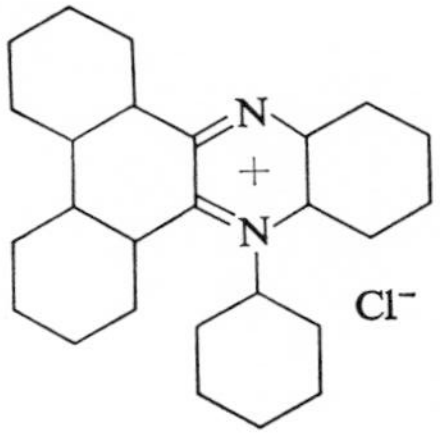

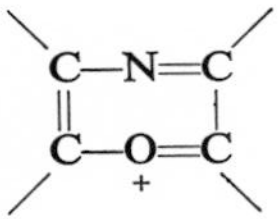

Mendola's blue   blue H_2O C.I.51175

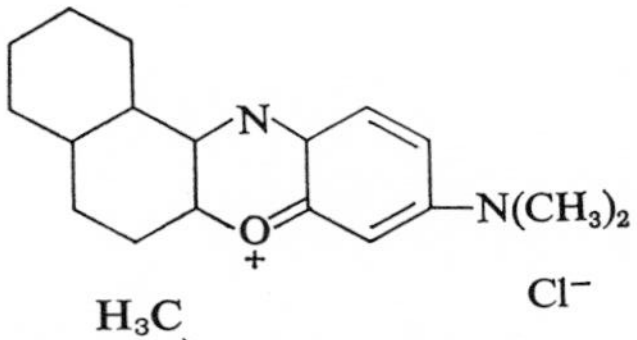

Capri blue   blue H_2O C.I.51015

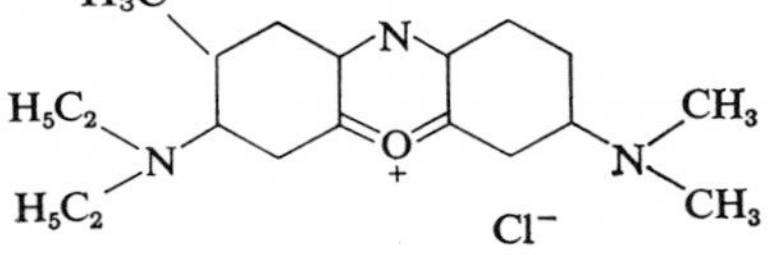

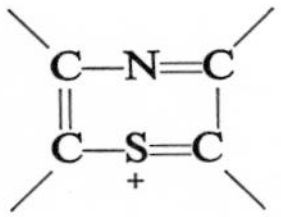

methylene blue   blue H_2O C.I.52015

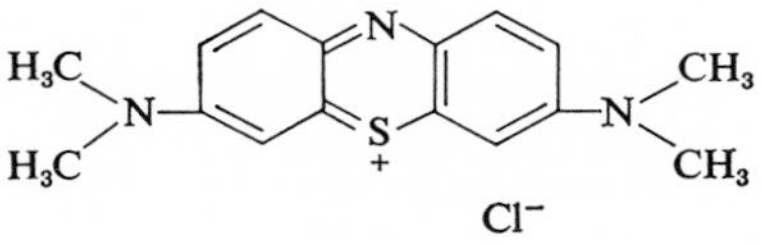

$N(CH_3)_2$

Cl^-

CH_3

CH_3

H_3C

H_5C_2

H_5C_2

Cl^-

H_3C

H_3C

CH_3

CH_3

Cl^-

Chromophore	Dye	Color	Solubility	Reference
Thiazoles	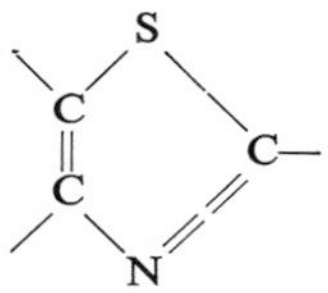 thioflavine TCN	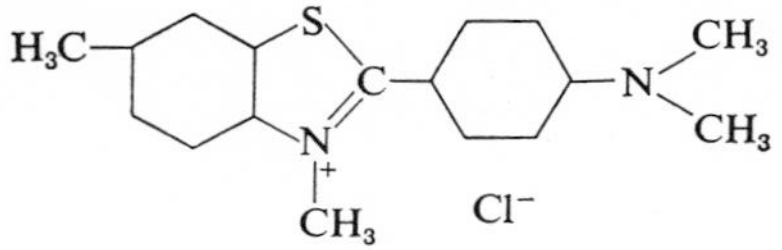 yellow	H_2O	C.I.49005
Xanthenes	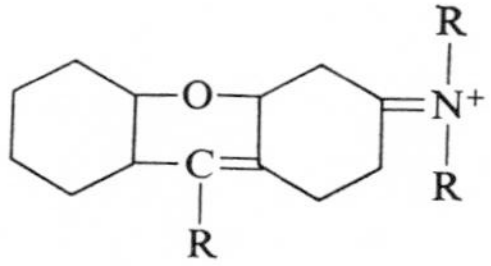 rhodamine B	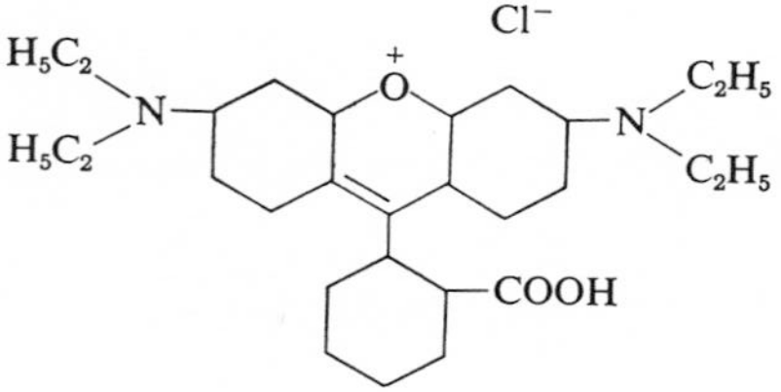 magenta	H_2O	C.I.45170
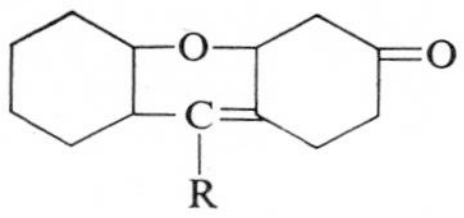 Xanthenes	fluorescein	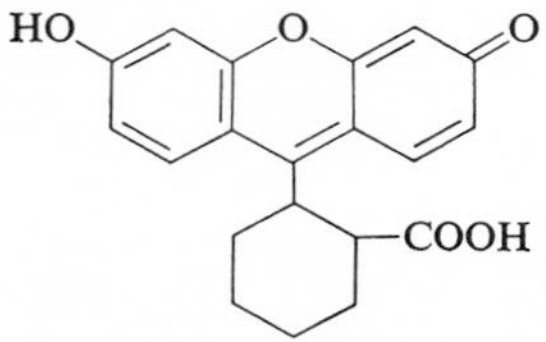 yellow	H_2O	C.I.45350

Xanthenes

erythrosine   magenta H_2O C.I.45430

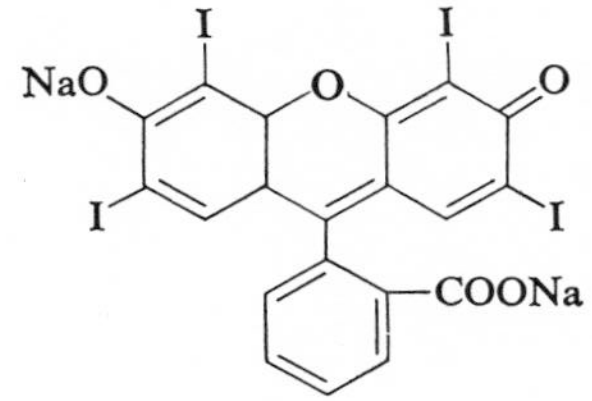

Thioxanthenes

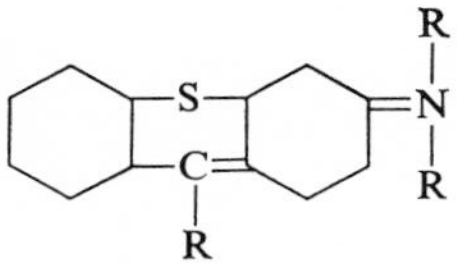

3,6-tetramethyldiamino-9-cyano-thioxanthonium chloride   blue H_2O (188)

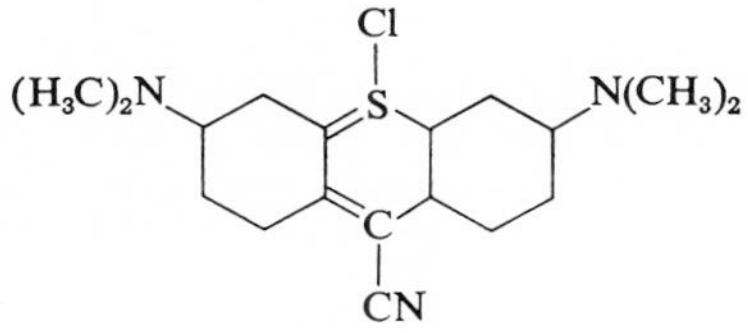

3,6-diamino-thioxanthonium chloride   yellow H_2O

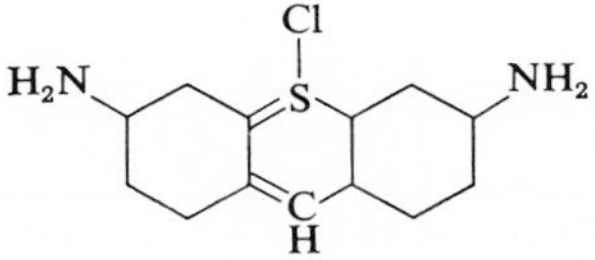

Chromophore	Dye	Color	Solubility	Reference
Selenoxanthenes	2,7-dimethyl-3,6-tetraethyldiamino-9-cyanoselenoxanthonium chloride	blue	H_2O	(188)
	1,4,5,8-tetramethyl-3,6-diamino-selenoxanthonium chloride 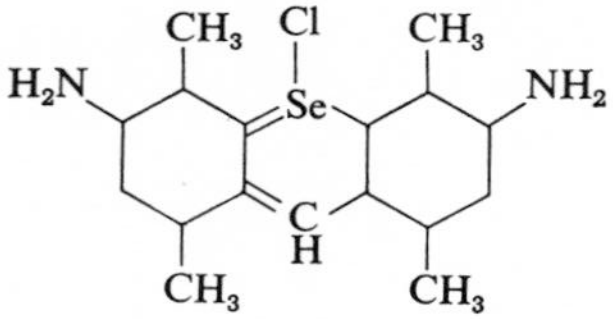	magenta	H_2O	

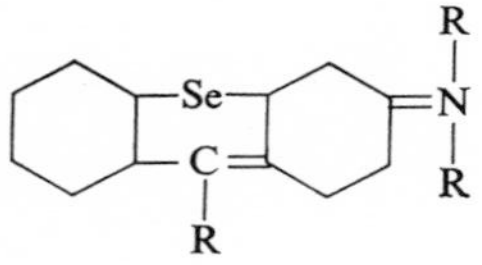

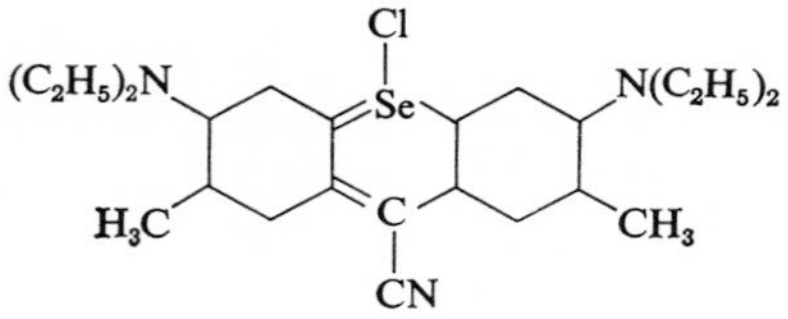

introduced before the First World War by Smith (179). In spite of many efforts to make these products successful, a number of problems remain unsolved; the bleach-out processes are still, more or less, laboratory curiosities and, at the present time, of no practical value. Because of the obvious simplicity of the system, however, hopes for achieving its practical realization have not been completely abandoned, and occasional references in the current literature (180,181,182,183,184,185,186,187) give evidence of, at least, some activity in this field.

Among the serious obstacles which have to be overcome in a successful bleach-out process is the difficulty of obtaining clean whites in the bleached areas and insufficient sensitivity of the dyes to light, resulting in extremely long exposures. Another factor which has to be kept in mind is the unequal rate at which the different dyes bleach when exposed to the entire spectrum range. The failure to obtain equal bleaching for all the dyes involved affects the neutrality of the grey areas.

Of the large number of dyes which are affected by light, for example, dyes of diphenylmethane, triphenylmethane, oxazine, azine, thiazine, phthalein, and xanthonium types (Table 8.4) and basic dyes of the xanthene family are claimed to be the most suitable. Wendt and Fröhlich (188) recommended thioxanthonium and selenoxanthonium dyes, in which the oxygen-bridging atom in the xanthoxonium dyes has been exchanged for sulfur or selenium. These dyes have the advantage of higher sensitivity and of giving comparatively pure whites in the exposed sections. Some oxonium dyes (189) and xanthoxolium dyes (190) also bleach very clearly and yield pictures of high contrast, especially when coated on baryta paper, which absorbs very little of the sensitizing solution and gives a good white foundation for the print.

The sensitivity of dyes to the bleaching action of light varies widely with different dyes. In most instances, various sensitizers or accelerators have to be added to increase their light sensitivity (191). The most effective sensitizers are 1-methoxy-4-propenylbenzene (anethole), CH_3O—C_6H_4—CH=CH—CH_3, and thiourea, NH_2—CS—NH_2. The hydrogens of thiourea can be replaced by alkyl or aryl groups, but most of the derivatives, with the exception of the alkylthioureas, have about the same sensitizing action as the parent compound (192). Thiosinamine, another name for allylthiourea, was used for the first time in Utocolor. When the two hydrogens of the amino group opposing the allyl group are substituted by alkyl groups, such as in N,N-diethyl-N'-allylthiourea (C_2H_5)$_2$N—CS—NH—CH_2—CH=CH_2, the sensitizing effect is further increased. Unfortunately, the increase in sensitizing activity of the substituted thiourea derivatives runs parallel to the reduction of solubility in water, so that the most active sensitizers are water insoluble and unsuitable for gelatin systems.　By introducing one or more organic groups containing at least one hydroxyl group into the molecule, Polgar and Halmos (193) succeeded in restoring the solubility of these compounds in water without any effect on their sensitizing properties.　N-Hydroxyethyl-N'-allylthiourea, $OH—C_2H_4—NH—CS—NH—CH_2—CH{=}CH_2$, is an example.

Bleaching of the acid-type dyes, which are comparatively very stable, is considerably accelerated if, in addition to the foregoing sensitizers, a suitable activator for such sensitizers is introduced into the coating composition (194).　Such an activating substance can be a phenol, sodium formaldehyde-sulfo-oxalate, or a salt of vanadium or titanium.　Addition of an inorganic or an organic acid to the bleaching-out dye composition increases its sensitivity to light also and makes the dyes bleach out without leaving any disturbing residues (195).　Wheatley and Wheatley (196) introduced as bleaching accelerators compounds of chromium, molybdenum, tungsten, or uranium in combination with oxalic acid.　A specific example which has given good results is oxalo-molybdic acid.　Kögel (197) described the preparation of a bleach-out material consisting of methylene blue and accelerators, such as cystine and cysteine.　The bleaching of dyes such as methylene blue is accelerated in the presence of zinc oxide, and the effect can be further increased with traces of manganese and cadmium salts.

The concentration of sensitizers added to the dye mixture must be chosen so that all the dyes present will bleach out practically to the same extent in a given time; otherwise, the reproduction of colors will be incorrect (198).

The bleaching rates of dyes can be adjusted, also, by the introduction of certain substituents into the aromatic residues linked directly or indirectly to the chromogen (199).　Hydrogenation of the dye molecule or the introduction of a halogen or of a cyano, thiocyano, nitro, carbonyl, or carbalkoxy group enhances the bleaching-out rates, whereas the introduction of an alkyl, aryl, hydroxy, etc., decreases the rate at which the dye bleaches.　It is claimed that these substituents have the same effect on all classes of dyestuffs.　The positions of the substituents in the aryl group also has an influence on the reactivity; an ortho- and meta-substitution will have a greater effect than a para position.

Various binding agents have been suggested as carriers for the dyes. For water-soluble dyes, gelatin or polyvinyl alcohol (200) are suitable binders; for others, collodion or incompletely acylated or etherified cellulose, containing enough free OH— groups to permit swelling of the layer in water, is preferable (201).　In light-sensitive elements where the three dyes are coated on top of each other, the diffusion of the dyes from one layer to another can be prevented by employing binders of different characteristics for each particular dye. The property, swelling in water, of the binder is of primary importance in the fixing step because in order to stabilize the finished print against further action of light, the sensitizing component has to be removed from the system by washing in water or some other suitable solvent in which the dyes composing the image do not dissolve. Another method of deactivating the sensitizer is by complex formation with mercuric chloride (202) or by destruction with sulfurous acid (203). A mixture of two or more binders, one of which dissolves the dye while the others are capable of swelling in the fixing agent, was recommended by Wendt and Bincer (204). To insure the durability of the image, the prints can be washed in a water solution of a mordanting agent, for example, tannic acid or a copper salt. It is recommended that images composed of basic triphenylmethane dyes be treated with complex metallic salts, for instance, salts of phosphotungstic acid. Thioxantho-nium—and selenoxanthonium-dye images are fixed, preferably with a solution of an alkali-metal borofluoride (205) which forms, with the dyes, compounds insoluble in the solvents used for the removal of the sensitizer.

In order to secure neutral tones in the grey areas of the print, it is neces-sary to select a combination of dyes which require approximately the same length of exposure to bleach to the same extent. This is a very difficult task, and to obtain neutral black or grey shades it may be necessary to add to the sensitive composition substances which have the property of becoming black after proper treatment. In one patent (198), ferric chloride is used as an example; in the exposed areas it is reduced to ferrous chloride while in the unexposed sections of the print it reacts with tannin to form black pigment.

Sensitized bleach-out dye papers are not very stable, and, in a more or less short period of time, a colored background is formed which does not change on exposure to light. Thus, material like this can be kept only for a very limited time prior to being exposed to light. The stability can, however, be considerably improved by incorporation of the sensitizing agent in the finished dye layer just before use (206), or by including in the sensitive layer compounds like acylamides, carbamides, amidines, guanidines, and hydrazides (207).

A study of the reactions involved in the photochemical decomposition of dyes indicates that during the bleaching process the dyes can be reduced or oxidized, depending on the nature of the dye. Dyes like methylene blue, which can be sensitized with mild reducing agents such as thiosin-amine, undergo photoreduction and form colorless leuco-forms, whereas dyes such as polymethine dyes are oxidized. Thiourea-type sensitizers retard the effect of light and have a more or less desensitizing effect on the system (208,209,210). Dyes which are bleached by oxidation are frequently destroyed by exposure to atmospheric oxygen, and reducing agents (for instance, ferrous salts or thiosulfates) have to be added for stabilizing purposes. As sensitizers, hydrogen peroxide, solid organic peroxides (211) or other per-compounds are effective. Also, anthraquinone and benzanthrone and their derivatives are suitable, particularly for azo-dyes (212). Among the dyes which are bleached by oxidation are cyanine and merocyanine dyes, well known as optical sensitizers of silver halide emulsions. These dyes, when coated on a support in a suitable binder, provide a direct positive dye-bleach system capable of producing full-color prints. Carbon tetrabromide or hexachloroethane is used as an accelerating agent, and seems to form with the dye component a complex which requires less energy to be raised to an excited state and thus permit the desired photolytic reaction than when such complexes do not form (213,214,215). To destroy the residual activator in the unexposed areas the print is given an infrared exposure; this step prevents further bleaching on exposure to light.

REFERENCES

1. D. E. Sargent. U.S. pat. 2,411,811/1946.
2. M. Raek. U.S. pat. 1,830,854/1931.
3. J. A. Sprung and W. A. Schmidt. U.S. pat. 2,465,760/1949.
4. H. J. C. Tendeloo. U.S. pat. 2,193,574/1940.
5. J. J. Sagura and J. A. van Allan. U.S. pat. 3,062,650/1962.
6. D. M. McQueen. U.S. pat. 2,426,894/1947.
7. A. Schoen. U.S. pat. 2,416,021/1947.
8. S. B. Elliott. U.S. pat. 2,789,052/1957.
9. S. B. Elliott. U.S. pat. 2,772,158/1956.
10. S. B. Elliott. *Phot. Eng.*, **4**, 133–141 (1953).
11. S. B. Elliott. U.S. pat. 2,712,996/1955.
12. S. B. Elliott. U.S. pat. 2,772,159/1956.
13. C. H. Fuchsman, L. I. Charnas, and S. B. Elliott. U.S. pat. 2,905,554/1959.
14. C. H. Fuchsman, L. I. Charnas, and S. B. Elliott. U.S. pat. 2,905,555/1959.
15. C. H. Fuchsman, L. I. Charnas, and S. B. Elliott. U.S. pat. 2,905,556/1959.
16. F. F. Ogden. U.S. pat. 3,046,136/1962.
17. F. F. Ogden. U.S. pat. 3,046,137/1962.
18. L. E. Clement. U.S. pat. 2,099,297/1937; Kodak A.G. Ger. pat. 737,289/1943.
19. Kodak-Pathé. Fr. pat. 1,639,723/1963.
20. R. H. Sprague, H. L. Fichter, Jr., and E. Wainer. *Phot. Sci. Eng.*, **5**, 98–103 (1961).
21. E. Wainer. U.S. pat. 3,042,515/1962; Belg. pat. 600,757/1961; Fr. pat. 1,289,654/1961.
22. G. Fidelman. U.S. pat. 3,114,635/1963.
23. R. H. Sprague. U.S. pat. 3,046,209/1962.
24. R. H. Sprague and M. Roscow. *Phot. Sci. Eng.*, **8**, 91–95 (1964); Horizons, Inc. Belg. pat. 641,329/1963.

25. Horizons, Inc. Fr. pat. 1,313,761/1963; E. Wainer. U.S. pat. 3,056,673/1962.
26. E. Wainer. U.S. pat. 3,042,516/1962; Horizons, Inc. Fr. pat. 1,302,610/1962; Ger. pat. 1,172,115/1964.
27. R. H. Sprague. U.S. pat. 3,082,086/1963; Japan. pat. 39–17701/1964.
28. A. Henrici. *Z. Physik.*, **77**, 35–51 (1932).
29. E. Wainer. U.S. pat. 3,042,519/1962; Brit. pat. 959,035/1964.
30. E. Wainer. U.S. pat. 3,046,125/1962; Horizons, Inc. Fr. pat. 1,314,392/1963.
31. R. H. Sprague, H. L. Fichter, Jr., and W. P. Hamilton. U.S. pat. 3,095,303/1963; Brit. pat. 959,037/1964.
32. R. H. Sprague and H. L. Fichter. *Phot. Sci. Eng.*, **8**, 95–103 (1964).
33. R. H. Sprague, H. L. Fichter, Jr., and W. P. Hamilton. U.S. pat. 3,102,810/1963.
34. H. L. Fichter, Jr., and W. P. Hamilton. U.S. pat. 3,102,029/1963.
35. R. H. Sprague and P. W. Sprague. U.S. pat. 3,121,633/1964; Fr. pat. 1,364,896/1964.
36. R. H. Sprague, H. L. Fichter, Jr., and W. P. Hamilton. U.S. pat. 3,100,703/1963.
37. R. H. Sprague and H. L. Fichter, Jr. U.S. pat. 3,106,466/1963; Horizons, Inc. Fr. pat. 1,329,800/1963.
38. R. H. Sprague and J. J. Urbancik. U.S. pat. 3,109,736/1963.
39. H. L. Fichter, Jr. and W. P. Hamilton. U.S. pat. 3,102,029/1963; Horizons, Inc. Fr. pat. 1,329,807/1963.
40. E. Wainer. U.S. pat. 3,042,517/1962; Brit. pat. 959,034/1964; Horizons, Inc. Fr. pat. 1,303,075/1962; Ger. pat. 1,175,986/1964.
41. E. Wainer. U.S. pat. 3,042,518/1962; Brit. pat. 959,036/1964; Horizons, Inc. Fr. pat. 1,313,083/1962.
42. E. Wainer. U.S. pat. 3,112,200/1963; Horizons, Inc. Brit. pat. 959,033/1964; Fr. pat. 1,302,010/1962.
43. A. H. Sporer. *Phot. Sci. Eng.*, **8**, 35–43 (1963).
44. W. Lässig, H. Ulrich, and H. Steiner. Belg. pat. 596,094/1960; Brit. pat. 957,192/1964.
45. L. Chalkley. U.S. pat. 2,829,052/1958.
46. L. Chalkley. *J. Phot. Sci.*, **11**, 42–45 (1963).
47. L. Chalkley. *Phot. Sci. Eng.*, **3**, 174–177 (1959).
48. W. and G. Ritzerfeld. Brit. pat. 860,218/1961.
49. L. Chalkley. *J. Opt. Soc. Am.*, **42**, 387–392 (1952).
50. G. A. Mikhalchenko and I. K. Karpov. *Opt. Spectry. (USSR)*, **13**, 391–393 (1962).
51. I. Lifschitz. *Ber.*, **52B**, 1919–1926 (1919).
52. W. Frankenburger, R. Robl, and W. Zimmermann. U.S. pat. 1,845,835/1932.
53. L. Harris and J. Kaminsky. *J. Am. Chem. Soc.*, **57**, 1154–1159 (1935).
54. J. G. Calvert and H. J. L. Rechen. *J. Am. Chem. Soc.*, **74**, 2101–2103 (1952).
55. E. O. Holmes, Jr. *J. Phys. Chem.*, **61**, 434–441 (1957).
56. A. H. Sporer. *Trans. Faraday Soc.*, **57**, 983–991 (1961).
57. G. H. Brown, S. R. Adisesh, and J. E. Taylor. *J. Phys. Chem.*, **66**, 2426–2430 (1962).
58. L. Chalkley. U.S. pat. 2,325,038/1943.
59. L. Chalkley. U.S. pat. 2,366,179/1945.
60. L. Chalkley. U.S. pat. 2,839,543/1958.
61. L. Chalkley. *J. Org. Chem.*, **26**, 408–412 (1961).

62. L. Chalkley.   U.S. pat. 2,829,148/1958.
63. L. Chalkley.   U.S. pat. 3,122,438/1964.
64. L. Chalkley.   *J. Am. Chem. Soc.*, **77**, 1848–1850 (1955).
65. L. Chalkley.   U.S. pat. 2,864,751/1958.
66. L. Chalkley.   U.S. pat. 2,877,169/1959.
67. L. Chalkley.   U.S. pat. 2,855,303/1958.
68. I. Lifschitz.   *Ber.*, **58B**, 2434 (1925).
69. L. Chalkley.   U.S. pat. 2,528,496/1950.
70. L. Chalkley.   U.S. pat. 2,844,465/1958.
71. L. Chalkley.   U.S. pat. 2,936,235/1960.
72. L. Chalkley.   U.S. pat. 2,676,887/1954.
73. M. S. Agruss.   U.S. pat. 3,131,062/1964.
74. L. Harris, J. Kaminsky, and R. G. Simard.   *J. Am. Chem. Soc.*, **57**, 1151–1154 (1935).
75. L. Chalkley.   *J. Am. Chem. Soc.*, **63**, 982–987 (1941).
76. L. Chalkley.   U.S. pat. 2,441,561/1948.
77. L. Chalkley.   U.S. pat. 2,855,300/1958.
78. L. Harris and J. Kaminsky.   *J. Am. Chem. Soc.*, **57**, 1154–1159 (1935).
79. J. G. Calvert and H. J. L. Rechen.   *J. Am. Chem. Soc.*, **74**, 2101–2103 (1952).
80. M. S. Agruss.   U.S. pat. 3,079,258/1963.
81. L. Chalkley.   U.S. pat. 3,071,464/1963.
82. E. E. Ryskiewicz.   U.S. pat. 2,927,025/1960; Brit. pat. 862,291/1961; Fr. pat. 1,196,884/1959; Ger. pat. 1,081,758/1960.
83. L. Chalkley.   U.S. pat. 2,936,276/1960.
84. M. S. Agruss.   U.S. pat. 3,121,012/1964.
85. M. S. Agruss.   U.S. pat. 3,123,473/1964.
86. J. P. Audet.   Fr. pat. 1,300,214/1961.
87. J. P. Audet.   Fr. pat. 1,300,215/1961.
88. K. Uchida, S. Kato, and M. Koizumi.   *Bull. Chem. Soc. Japan*, **35**, 16–22 (1962).
89. K. Uchida and M. Koizumi.   *Bull. Chem. Soc. Japan*, **35**, 1871–1881 (1962).
90. T. I. Abbott and E. C. Yackel.   U.S. pat. 3,033,677/1962.
91. P. L. Foris.   U.S. pat. 3,140,947/1964; Belg. pat. 612,013/1961; Brit. pat. 917,919/1963.
92. J. W. Schulte and J. F. Suttle.   U.S. pat. 2,957,080/1960.
93. R. H. Sprague, J. A. Stewart, and J. M. Lewis.   U.S. pat. 3,113,024/1963; Brit. pat. 967,945/1964.
94. R. H. Sprague and J. A. Stewart.   U.S. pat. 3,121,632/1964; Brit. pat. 955,029/1964.
95. J. A. Stewart and R. H. Sprague.   U.S. pat. 3,140,948/1964; Fr. pat. 1,336,543/1963; Japan. pat. 39–14404/1964.
96. R. H. Sprague and J. A. Stewart.   U.S. pat. 3,140,949/1964.
97. K. Pfoertner.   Ger. pat. 1,135,755/1962.
98. R. R. Zemp.   U.S. pat. 2,884,326/1959; Brit. pat. 798,200/1958.
99. G. Barnhart and B. F. Skiles.   U.S. pat. 2,772,284/1956; Brit. pat. 745,359/1956.
100. C. J. Pedersen.   U.S. pat. 2,915,392/1959.
101. C. J. Pedersen.   U.S. pat. 2,662,895/1953.
102. L. Chalkley.   U.S. pat. 2,829,149/1958.
103. L. Chalkley.   U.S. pat. 2,855,304/1958.
104. L. Chalkley.   U.S. pat. 2,839,542/1958.

105. L. Chalkley. U.S. pat. 2,864,752/1958.
106. L. Chalkley. U.S. pat. 2,864,753/1958.
107. L. Chalkley. U.S. pat. 2,877,166/1959.
108. L. Chalkley. U.S. pat. 2,877/167/1959.
109. L. Chalkley. U.S. pat. 2,877,168/1959.
110. L. Chalkley. U.S. pat. 2,951,855/1960.
111. L. Chalkley. *Chem. Rev.*, **6**, 217–280 (1929).
112. G. H. Brown and W. G. Shaw. *Rev. Pure Appl. Chem.*, **11**, 2 (1961).
113. P. C. Ray. *J. Chem. Soc.*, **1917**, 111, 101–109.
114. E. L. Rao, K. Varahalu, and M. V. Narasimhaswami. *Nature*, **124**, 303 (1929).
115. B. S. V. R. Rao and H. E. Watson. *J. Phys. Chem.*, **32**, 1354–1365 (1928).
116. L. Suchow. U.S. pat. 2,723,914/1955.
117. G. Singh. *J. Chem. Soc.*, **1922**, 121, 782–785.
118. H. B. Weiser and A. D. Garrison. *J. Phys. Chem.*, **31**, 1237–1245 (1927).
119. M. A. Ei-Sayed. *J. Phys. Chem.*, **68**, 433–434 (1964).
120. D. B. Medved. U.S. pat. 2,761,846/1956.
121. H. Biltz. *Ann.*, **305**, 170 (1899).
122. F. D. Chattaway. *J. Chem. Soc.*, **1906**, 89, 462–467.
123. H. Biltz. *Z. Physik. Chem.*, **30**, 527–528 (1899).
124. A. Senier and F. G. J. Shepheard. *J. Chem. Soc.*, **1909**, 95, 441–445.
125. M. D. Cohen and G. M. J. Schmidt. *J. Phys. Chem.*, **66**, 2442–2446 (1962).
126. A. Senier and R. B. Forster. *J. Chem. Soc.*, **1914**, 105, 2462–2471.
127. A. Aharoni, H. Ditkovski, E. H. Frei, and A. Tzalmova. *J. Phys. Chem. Solids*, **24**, 927–931 (1963).
128. G. Wettermark and L. Dogliotti. *J. Chem. Phys.*, **40**, 1486–1487 (1964).
129. H. Stobbe. *Ber.*, **37**, 2236–2240 (1904).
130. H. Stobbe. *Ber.*, **40**, 3372 (1907).
131. O. Vierling. U.S. pat. 2,186,942/1940.
132. O. Vierling. U.S. pat. 2,305,799/1942.
133. L. Hanel. U.S. pat. 2,305,693/1942.
134. O. Vierling. U.S. pat. 2,335,465/1943.
135. H. Stobbe and H. Mallison. *Ber.*, **46**, 1226–1238 (1913).
136. C. M. Bere and S. Smiles. *J. Chem. Soc.*, **1924**, 125, 2359–2363.
137. R. Child and S. Smiles. *J. Chem. Soc.*, **1926**, 130, 2696–2702.
138. A. E. Chichibabin, B. Kundshi, and S. V. Benewalenskaja. *Ber.*, **58**, 1580 (1925).
139. W. C. Clark and G. F. Lothian. *Trans. Faraday Soc.*, **54**, 1790–1796 (1958).
140. R. Hardwick, H. S. Mosher, and P. Passailaigue. *Trans. Faraday Soc.*, **56**, 44–50 (1960).
141. H. S. Mosher, C. Souers, and R. Hardwick. *J. Chem. Phys.*, **32**, 1888–1889 (1960).
142. J. D. Margerum, L. J. Miller, E. Saito, M. S. Brown, H. S. Mosher, and R. Hardwick. *J. Phys. Chem.*, **66**, 2434–2438 (1962).
143. G. Kortum, M. Kortum-Seiler, and S. D. Bailey. *J. Phys. Chem.*, **66**, 2439–2442 (1962).
144. G. H. Dorion and K. O. Loeffer. U.S. pat. 3,127,335/1964.
145. F. I. Metz, W. C. Servoss, and F. E. Welsh. *J. Phys. Chem.*, **66**, 2446 (1962).
146. W. Marckwald. *Z. Physik. Chem.*, **30**, 140–145 (1899).
147. G. Scheibe and F. Feichtmayr. *J. Phys. Chem.*, **66**, 2449–2455 (1962).
148. I. I. Ostromislensky. U.S. pat. 2,233,429/1941.

149. R. J. Walther. *J. Prakt. Chem.*, **67**, 445–472 (1903).
150. B. K. Singh. *J. Am. Chem. Soc.*, **43**, 333–334 (1921).
151. B. K. Singh. *Quart. J. Indian Chem. Soc.*, **1**, 45 (1924).
152. C. A. Wagner and H. B. Wagner. U.S. pat. 2,921,407/1960.
153. J. Hauser, D. Jerchel, and R. Kuhn. *Ber.*, **82**, 515 (1949).
154. H. B. Wagner. Fr. pat. 1,329,892/1963.
155. B. K. Green. U.S. pat. 2,299,693/1942.
156. B. K. Green. U.S. pat. 2,299,694/1942.
157. E. Berman and H. Schwab. U.S. pat. 3,072,481/1963; Austral. pat. 40,624/ 1958; Brit. pat. 872,005/1961; Ger. pat. 1,086,556/1960.
158. B. K. Green and L. Schleicher. U.S. pat. 2,730,456/1956.
159. E. Berman. U.S. pat. 3,090,687/1963; Can. pat. 661,744/1963.
160. R. E. Miller. U.S. pat. 3,116,148/1963; Can. pat. 672,914/1963; Fr. pat. 1,283,893/1961.
161. E. Berman, R. E. Fox, and F. D. Thomson. *J. Am. Chem. Soc.*, **81**, 5605–5608 (1959).
162. The National Cash Register Company. Belg. pat. 592,982/1960; Brit. pat. 887,902/1961; Fr. pat. 1,262,398/1960.
163. Y. Hirshberg. *J. Am. Chem. Soc.*, **78**, 2304–2312 (1956).
164. The National Cash Register Company. Brit. pat. 889,186/1961.
165. Y. Hirschberg and E. Fisher. *J. Chem. Soc.*, **1954**, 297–303.
166. Y. Hirschberg and E. Fisher. *J. Chem. Soc.*, **1954**, 3129–3137.
167. R. Heiligman-Rim, Y. Hirschberg, and E. Fisher. *J. Chem. Soc.*, **1961**, 156–163; *J. Chem. Soc.*, **1962**, 2465–2470; *J. Chem. Soc.*, **1962**, 2470–2477.
168. E. Berman. U.S. pat. 3,100,778/1963; Brit. pat. 887,958/1961.
169. E. Berman and D. B. McQuain. U.S. pat. 2,978,462/1961; Brit. pat. 889,586/ 1962.
170. E. Berman and D. B. McQuain. U.S. pat. 3,022,318/1962.
171. E. Berman. U.S. pat. 2,953,454/1960.
172. Anon. *Product Engineering*, **35** (20), 46–47 (1964).
173. Logetronics, Inc. Brit. pat. 891,992/1962.
174. J. W. Tamblyn and G. M. Armstrong. U.S. pat. 2,735,783/1956.
175. A. J. Cohen and H. L. Smith. *Science*, **137**, 981 (1962).
176. W. H. Armstead and S. D. Stookey. *Science*, **144**, 150–154 (1964).
177. S. D. Stookey. *Ceram. Ind.*, **82** (4), 97–101 (1964).
178. F. Limmer. *Das Ausbleichverfahren*, W. Knapp, Halle, 1911.
179. H. J. Smith. *Phot. J.*, **50**, 141 (1910).
180. F. Millich and G. Oster. *J. Am. Chem. Soc.*, **81**, 1357–1363 (1959).
181. G. Oster. *Phot. Eng.*, **4**, 173–178 (1953).
182. G. Oster. *J. Polymer Sci.*, **16**, 235–244 (1955).
183. G. Oster and J. S. Bellin. *J. Am. Chem. Soc.*, **79**, 294–298 (1957).
184. C. A. Parker. *J. Phys. Chem.*, **63**, 26–30 (1959).
185. R. Havemann and H. Pietsch. *Z. Physik. Chem.*, **211**, 257–273 (1959).
186. H. Pietsch and co-workers. *Z. Wiss. Phot.*, **54**, 91–117, 185–197, 208–220 (1960).
187. S. Matsumoto. *Bull. Chem. Soc. Japan*, **35**, 1860–1869 (1962).
188. B. Wendt and A. Fröhlich. U.S. pat. 1,850,220/1932.
189. B. Wendt and H. Bincer. U.S. pat. 1,880,573/1932.
190. J. Eggert, B. Wendt, and A. Fröhlich. U.S. pat. 2,097,119/1937.
191. J. S. Friedman. *Am. Phot.*, **32**, 821–825 (1938).

192. M. Mudrovčič. *Z. Wiss. Phot.*, **26**, 171–192 (1928).
193. A. Polgar and C. Halmos. U.S. pat. 2,268,324/1941.
194. B. Gaspar. U.S. pat. 2,049,005/1936.
195. B. Wendt, H. Bincer, and A. Fröhlich. U.S. pat. 1,916,350/1933.
196. C. W. C. Wheatley and C. C. H. Wheatley. U.S. pat. 2,145,960/1939; Brit. pat. 486,006/1938.
197. G. Kögel. *Phot. Ind.*, **29**, 1296 (1931).
198. E. Rüst and A. Polgar. U.S. pat. 2,054,390/1936.
199. B. Wendt and H. Bincer. U.S. pat. 1,880,572/1932; Brit. pat. 348,232/1931.
200. A. Polgar and C. Halmos. Fr. pat. 847,596/1939.
201. B. Wendt. U.S. pat. 2,130,572/1938.
202. A. Polgar and C. Halmos. U.S. pat. 2,319,344/1943.
203. B. Wendt and H. Bincer. U.S. pat. 1,850,162/1932; Brit. pat. 341,371/1931; Ger. pat. 506,100/1930.
204. B. Wendt and H. Bincer. U.S. pat. 1,916,779/1933; Brit. pat. 341,151/1931.
205. B. Wendt and H. Bincer. U.S. pat. 1,871,830/1932; Brit. pat. 348,102/1931.
206. B. Wendt and A. Fröhlich. U.S. pat. 1,955,898/1934.
207. A. Polgar and C. Halmos. U.S. pat. 2,328,166/1943.
208. M. Mudrovčič. *Photo. Ind.*, **27**, 1318–1320 (1929).
209. P. Lasareff. *Trans. Faraday Soc.*, **21**, 475–476 (1925).
210. P. Lasareff. *Z. Physik. Chem.*, **78**, 657–660 (1912).
211. H. C. Staehle. U.S. pat. 2,346,090/1944.
212. G. von Poser and M. P. Schmidt. U.S. pat. 2,281,895/1942.
213. R. H. Sprague, H. L. Fichter, Jr., and W. P. Hamilton. U.S. pat. 3,104,973/1963; Japan. pat. 38–17236/1963; Ger. pat. 1,152,608/1963.
214. R. H. Sprague, H. L. Fichter, Jr., and J. G. Fidelman. U.S. pat. 3,102,027/1963; Japan. pat. 38–17237/1963.
215. J. G. Fidelman. Fr. pat. 1,318,555/1963.

9

Thermography

9.1 RECORDING PAPERS

For the graphic presentation of measured values, continuous recording devices are used in which a heated stylus in place of an ink-fed marking pen is brought into contact with temperature-sensitive paper (1). These papers react under the influence of localized heating by a change in color so that data supplied by the measuring instrument may be read immediately as they are being recorded. Papers of this type are usually impregnated with one (or more) chemical(s), which, after being heated by the stylus to a predetermined temperature, will react and produce a change in color (2,3,4,5,6,7,8,9,10).

Heat-sensitive recording papers can be prepared, also, by overcoating black-colored paper with a light-colored covering layer. On contact with the heated stylus, the top layer will melt and reveal the undercoating; in other words, the contrast arises because of the local uncovering of the contrasting color of the underlying paper. Typical coatings of this type are made by coating a solution of some polymeric material over black paper and rapidly evaporating the solvent by conducting a strong current of cold air over the liquid layer on the paper so that microscopic water droplets are deposited in the layer and cause it to appear white (11,12,13).

Another method of producing "blushed" coatings consists of using a solution of polystyrene or some other polymeric material in a low-boiling solvent mixed with another liquid of a higher boiling point in which the resin is insoluble (14). When this composition is coated on the black surface of carrying paper and dried, the low-boiling solvent evaporates more quickly, disturbing the solvent balance and causing the particles of the resin to precipitate out. The resulting film appears as a white, opaque layer hiding the dark background of supporting base.

402

The "blushed" resin coatings are, in general, difficult to control, since the humidity conditions during the coating operation affect the opacity and whiteness of the obscuring film. This situation is, presumably, improved by preparing films which contain microscopic voids dispersed throughout a continuous phase of a thermoplastic resin (15), or by employing so-called "molecular compounds" (16); these compounds dissociate under the influence of heat to yield the original materials which composed them. An example of a molecular compound is tetrachlorobisphenol A/diethanolamine which, when dispersed in a transparent thermoplastic resin and coated on a black-surfaced paper, forms, because of the light-scattering effect of the dispersed finely divided particles, an opaque layer producing legible markings under the heated stylus. Thermographic layers responding to a heated stylus can also be prepared by coating a dark paper support with monoperoxyphthalic acid and *m*-aminophenol in a solution of cellulose acetate butyrate (17). The contact with the stylus initiates an exothermic reaction between the peroxy acid and the amine, the heat of which causes fusion of the layer down to the black support.

By varying the composition of the thermosensitive layer, recording papers of different sensitivity and response can be made. They are usually not transparent to infrared radiation and, when exposed to such radiation, the entire sheet will discolor. By proper formulation, it is, however, possible to obtain heat-sensitive layers which do not absorb short infrared rays and are thus suitable for preparing copies of printed originals.

9.2 THERMOGRAPHIC COPYING PAPERS

9.2a *Single Component Papers*

In the earlier systems, thermographic papers were prepared in the same way as the recording papers, by overcoating black-surfaced paper bases with a fusible material. This gave the paper an opaque, whitish cover which was caused to melt in areas corresponding to printed areas of the original to be copied and allowed the black backing to show through. The fusible material can consist of waxy particles dispersed in a resinous film-forming binder (18), or of a mixture of cadmium stearate and siliceous particles in ethyl cellulose (19), or of cadmium stearate in rubber latex (20). Calcium stearate, magnesium stearate, and zinc behenate dispersed in a cellulose ester or ether was the subject of Dalton's patent (21). Titanium dioxide dispersed in a polymeric binder and coated in sufficient thickness to mask the black color was suggested by Owens (22). Miller (23) recommended, as a heat-sensitive layer, a coating consisting of methylene blue and mercuric stearate dispersed in ethyl cellulose. A dye, finely dispersed in a spongy blushed coating of ethyl cellulose, was used by Neuman and Schlotzhauer (24). When exposed to concentrated heat, the coating melts and exhibits a higher dye density. Another thermographic material suitable for document copying is prepared by coating the paper base with a colored waxy layer and overcoating it with a blushed resin layer (25). On exposure to infrared radiation in contact with a graphic original, the blushed resin layer melts and exposes the colored layer in areas corresponding to image areas.

In the copying process utilizing thermographic papers and commercialized by Minnesota Mining and Mfg. Co., the original to be copied is placed in heat-conductive contact with the heat-sensitive paper with the treated side face up over the side to be copied, and briefly irradiated with infrared radiation. The intense illumination produces a pronounced heating effect at the printed image areas, which are selectively warmer than the white areas by virtue of the selective absorption of the infrared radiation. Localized heat is transmitted to the adjacent copy paper where it triggers a reaction thereby producing a positive duplicate of the original. In some instances the generated heat can be of such magnitude as to burn out silver areas of a negative or positive image leaving a relief suitable for letterpress printing (26). In order to prevent the fibers of the paper base from burning at the temperature of the thermal reaction, Schoemaker and Igler (27) included in the thermosensitive composition a small amount of an organosilicon compound, for example, dimethyl-polysiloxane.

9.2b   *Chemical Papers*

Chemical thermographic papers consist of two or more reactants which, at normal temperatures, do not come into physical contact with each other; but, on application of heat at least one of them melts and a reaction that produces a colored product takes place. One such copy sheet, which has attained considerable commercial success, has a heat-sensitive layer containing, as reactants, a salt or soap of some heavy metal, such as iron or nickel, and another component with which a dark-colored product can be formed (28,29,30,31,7,32); for instance, a complex of hexamethylene tetramine and gallic acid reacts with low-melting ferric stearate to form black ferric gallate. Ferric stearate in combination with 3,4-dihydroxy-tetraphenylmethane was suggested by Glos (33), whereas Grieshaber (34) preferred to use ferric stearate and spiroindone. Ferric stearate in combination with an aromatic polyhydroxy compound, such as pyrocatechol, and an aliphatic hydroxy polycarboxylic acid was employed by Kalle A.G.

(35). Rubeanic acid or its polymeric derivatives in conjunction with nickel salts form colored products suitable for thermographic images (36). Multivalent ionizable metallic salts, such as nickel oxalate or cadmium nitrate, are also suitable, together with amines or amides which have been cocrystallized with tetrachlorobisphenol A (37).

Other thermographic compositions involve reduction of certain metallic ions and precipitation of the metal in a pattern corresponding to the heat pattern generated by the copying procedure (38).

The foregoing materials require that the heat-sensitive components be prevented from reacting at room temperature, but it is not always necessary to separate them from one another. A typical copy paper of this type includes in the heat-sensitive layer a water-insoluble silver salt (Ag-behenate) and an appropriate organic reducing agent, of which proto-catechuic acid is representative (39). This sheet can be stabilized against the loss of legibility resulting from discoloration by sunlight, by including up to 1 per cent of a difunctional alkylene imine, for example, N,N′-bis-1,2-ethyleneisophthalimide (40), which is believed to act as electron acceptor. It is claimed that due to this stabilization such paper will withstand exposure to sunlight 1 to 4 weeks, depending on the amount of imine added. Resistance to finger smudging and to discoloration by light can be, in this particular instance, improved by including in the heat-sensitive layer a thermoplastic terpene resin (41). Heat-sensitive papers containing silver behenate also have the disadvantage of darkening when stored at room temperature for prolonged periods of time. The darkening can be retarded without any effect on the image formation by adding to the coating mixture a small amount of a perhalogenated phthalic acid compound (42). Darker colors and increased contrast can be obtained by incorporating into the thermographic composition either an organic carboxylic acid, for example, gluconic, malic, oxalic, 2-hydroxy-1-naphthoic acid (43), or a heterocyclic toning agent containing at least two hetero-atoms in the heterocyclic ring, for instance, phthalazinone, barbituric acid, and saccharin (44). An oxidation-reduction type of reaction yielding a colored product is also taking place when a layer consisting of an organo-metallic salt, such as ceric behenate or stearate, is heated in the presence of a cyclic organic reducing agent, for example 4-methoxy-1-dihydro-naphthalene (45).

Another example of a thermographic composition requiring no physical separation of the components is that involving an indole derivative and a phenolic compound (46) or an organometallic compound of the Grignard type and thiourea (47) dispersed in a film former.

Thermographic images can also be composed of an organic dye formed by reacting colorless diazoamino dye bases (48) or the triazine type of dye bases (49) with a naphthol coupling component. The reaction takes place preferably in an acid milieu (50). Azo-dye images can also be obtained by using the condensation product of a heterocyclic hydrazone and an azo component in the presence of an oxidizing agent having a positive chlorine atom attached to a nitrogen atom (51). This process can be exemplified by the cleavage and oxidation of 3-methyl-2-benzo-thiazolinone-1'-hydroxy-2'-naphthoylhydrazone in the presence of N,N'-dichloro-N,N'-bis(m-nitrobenzene-sulfonyl)-ethylenediamine, yielding a diazo fragment and a coupling component, which immediately react together to give a deep purple product:

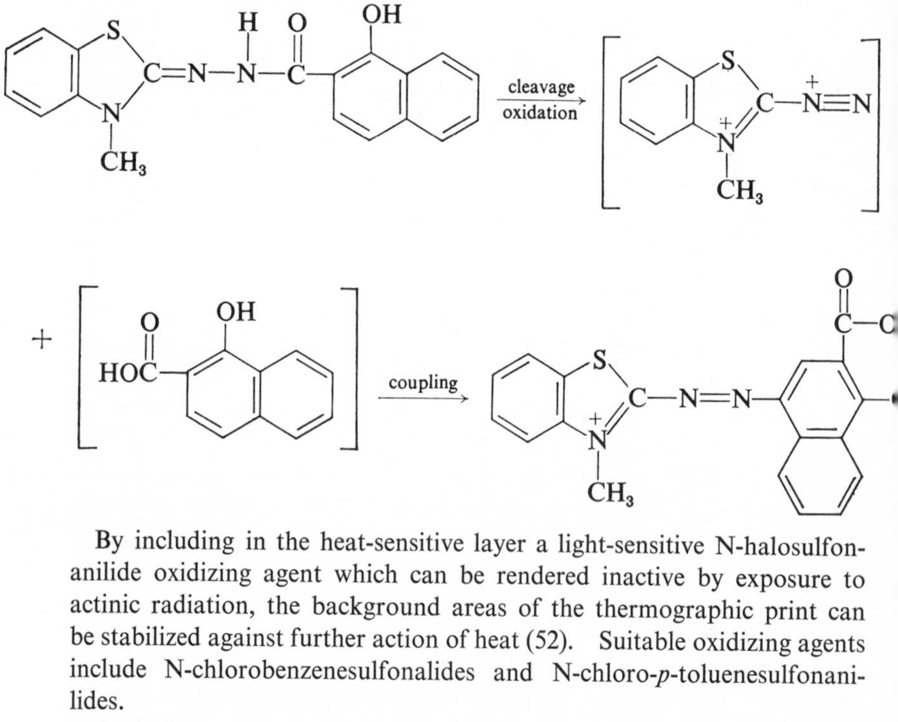

By including in the heat-sensitive layer a light-sensitive N-halosulfon-anilide oxidizing agent which can be rendered inactive by exposure to actinic radiation, the background areas of the thermographic print can be stabilized against further action of heat (52). Suitable oxidizing agents include N-chlorobenzenesulfonalides and N-chloro-*p*-toluenesulfonani-lides.

A similar system is provided by including in the heat-sensitive layer as the essential color-producing reactants a colorless 2-aminothiazole, for example 2-amino-6-methylbenzothiazole, and an organic oxidizing agent having a positive chlorine atom attached to a nitrogen atom, such as N,N'-bis-(m-nitrobenzenesulfonyl)-N,N'-dichloroethylenediamine (53).

Photochromic substances were employed by National Cash Register Co.; in one such application (54), 1,3,3-trimethylspirobenzopyranindoline and a leuco malachite blue are used as color formers. Thiocarbanilide can be added as a color intensifier, and urea as a color fixer. When heated this composition produces a dark-blue color which can be stabilized by the presence of a chelating metal salt, such as a mixture of calcium resinate and cobalt naphthenate (55). By proper selection of the metal and the indoline substituents, various colors can be formed. The photochromic components can be encapsulated in gelatin gum-arabic capsules which can be broken in the heat-absorbing areas; the image is developed by an ultraviolet exposure and fixed mechanically by breaking residual capsules (56).

The colorless carbinol base of a triphenylmethane or styryl dye and an acid former, for example, chloroacetamide, which on exposure to elevated temperature neutralizes the alkali, was recommended by Sprague (57).

Some salts, such as piperidinium or guanidinium trichloroacetate and 1-methyl-2(2,4-dinitrobenzyl)-pyridinium *p*-toluene-sulfonate, are decarboxylated by heat, leaving an organic base capable of forming a distinctive color (58). Copying sheets with improved stability to humidity and greater heat sensitivity are claimed to be prepared by coating the paper support with a composition containing an indicator dye and a latent developer, as, for example, a crystalline addition product of an organic amine and a hydroxyphenyl-substituted chroman (59). This complex dissociates at higher temperature in free amine which causes the color change. Sahler (60) prepared heat-sensitive copy material by coating transparent paper with a mixture of an aromatic amine salt or metal-halide double salts with diphenylnitrosamine or related compounds; as an example, the combination of phenyl-2-naphthylnitrosamine and *o*-aminophenol hydrochloride can be mentioned. The two components couple under the action of heat and produce a highly colored dye. The amine component may be a salt of 1-benzoylamino-4-amino-2,5-diethylbenzene, or the salt of aminohydroquinone diethyl ether. As a binder, cyclized rubber dissolved in petroleum ether is used. Heat-sensitive copying material is also prepared by coating a thin supporting base with a water-insoluble triazene dyestuff, a coupling agent, such as resorcinol or phloroglucinol, and a solid amide dispersed in a thin, translucent plastic vehicle (61).

Among other thermographic compositions described in patents we should mention mono-substituted aminothiatriazole and its acid salts (62), the combination of a *p*-quinone and a dihydroxybenzene compound (63), and mixtures of a polyketohydrindene (1:2:3: triketohydrindene) and an amino carboxylic acid or a salt formed by reaction of a primary amine with a carboxylic or sulfonic acid (4-amino-1-ethoxybenzene chloroacetate). These compounds react under the influence of heat to form a dye (64). 2-Methylamino-4-phenyl-5-bromothiazole is the active component of thermographic papers producing violet images (65). Heat-responsive materials that produce a color change also include the reaction product of ammonia or lower alkyl monohydroxy alcohols with succino-nitrile (66).

The ability of thermographic papers to resolve fine details is much less than that of photographic papers, and thus thermographic copies are usually not as sharp as is desirable. The reason for this is because as the image areas of the graphic original start to heat up, they are also losing heat by lateral conduction to the background. If the conditions are such that short exposures are possible, the tendency for heat diffusion is smaller and consequently the resolution is better. As one increases the exposure time to build up image density, resolution suffers owing to heat and image spread. Enhanced definition particularly of fine print is achieved by placing a thin clear plastic film between the original and the copy sheet (67). The plastic film absorbs only small amounts of the incident infrared radiation, permitting the black print on the original to heat up more freely than the background. Holland and Wayrynen (68) claimed to have obtained papers of good resolving power by using as heat-sensitive components a 5-hydroxy-3-pyrrolin-2-one in combination with a metal salt of a mono- or di-basic carboxylic acid.

In general, thermographic substances are uniformly distributed throughout a film-forming binder, which is required for maintaining the heat-sensitive reactants in position. The resin used as binder should have a sufficiently high melting point so that it will not cause the paper to stick to the original at the image-producing temperature. Some compositions, such as those consisting of a phosphomolybdate and related compounds (69), or 3-substituted 5-hydroxy-2 (5H)-pyrrolone (70), or an organic amine molybdate (71) and a reducing agent, can be coated on the base material directly, without employing any polymeric binder.

Supporting base material is usually thin paper, for example, cellophane or glassine paper or some other flexible material of low thermal conductivity. For most applications, it is required that the base transmit infrared radiation freely in order to permit the formation of the image through the entire thermographic layer. In such instances, it is also necessary to use papers transparent to white light; here the image is formed on the reverse surface. In order to increase the opacity of the sheet and to provide stronger contrast between the image and background areas in the finished copy, a white opaque protective coating transmitting infrared rays is frequently placed over the heat-sensitive layer (72).

Until now, two types of thermographic papers have been described. One is the copy paper which is white on one side and black on the other; the other type is composed of one or more layers containing the heat-sensitive composition. Copies on both types remain heat sensitive, and are thus only of temporary nature. To overcome this disadvantage, thermographic intermediate transfer sheets coated with a waxy layer containing some coloring matter were suggested (73,74,75,76,77,78,79,80,81,82,83, 84). The dye can be transferred from the transfer sheet to a transparent receptor sheet, in which case a full-size transparency of the original suitable for use in overhead projector is obtained (85). As heat-absorbing and color-forming components, carbon black (86,87) or dyes (88), for example, sudan blue (89) and 1,4-ditoluido-anthraquinone blue (90), are suitable. Dyes which sublime in the proper temperature range were suggested by Haydn, Weyde, and Mueller (91) and by Miller and Cheng (92). Some alcohol- or fat-soluble dyes, when coated on a thermoplastic film such as polyethylene, nylons, or polyvinyl chloride, and exposed to infrared radiation in contact with a graphic original, fuse into the support, and the remainder can be wiped off in clear areas (93). These dyes can be incorporated in a silver halide emulsion; when the exposed and developed coating is placed in contact with a thermoplastic film and heated, the dye migrates into the film and forms an image (94). In another process, the thermographic layer, consisting of polyethylene glycol (Carbowax 4000), polyvinyl-acetate-3-azido-phthalate, and Durol black, is hardened in the exposed areas and transferred from the unexposed areas to a receiving sheet (95).

In copying, the receiving sheet, such as standard typewriter paper, or a sheet impregnated with a thermoplastic resin (96), is sandwiched between the heat-sensitive transfer sheet and the original to be copied. During exposure to infrared radiation, conduction of heat in the image areas causes transfer of the dyed waxy layer to the copy sheet, giving a right-reading positive copy insensitive to the further action of heat. A printing apparatus for this process was designed by Groak (97) and by Kalle A.G. (98). A slightly different method for obtaining transfer images was described by Agfa (99); here, in the image areas the thermographic paper is exposed imagewise from the back with simultaneous action of a high-frequency electric field.

Another variation of producing right-reading reproduction on opaque receiving sheets was described by Meissner (100). In this method the original is contacted with a sheet containing catechol. When heat is applied, catechol vaporizes and condenses on the printed image areas of the original. Then the treated original is placed in contact with the transfer image forming sheet coated with a mixture of ferric stearate, lecithin, and a binder, and heated to form a visible image. Other combinations include 8-hydroxyquinoline with ferric stearate, dimethylglyoxime or thiourea with a nickel salt, ammonium thiocyanate with a cobalt salt, and protocatechuic acid and silver behenate. Graphic originals can also be copied on an untreated receptor surface; the method consists of first producing an intermediate, the image of which is physically transferred at a later stage to a plain receiving sheet (101). The heat-sensitive intermediate sheet is coated with a suitable composition including, for example, ferric stearate, spiroindone, ethyl cellulose, triphenyl phosphate, and acetone.

Some heat-sensitive copying papers can be desensitized to heat by later exposure to actinic light or by treatment with hydrochloric or acetic acid (102). In the latter example, the heat-sensitive component is the lead salt of benzyldithiocarbamic acid, which can be made sensitive to a lower temperature by addition of a heat-sensitive amine or ammonium salt. Thermographic images obtained by reacting 3-cyano-4,5-dimethyl-5-hydroxy-3-pyrrolin-2-one with copper acetate can be fixed by a brief water wash (103). Heat-sensitive papers sensitized with silver behenate or an equivalent noble metal salt and a reducing agent can be rendered incapable of undergoing thermographic reaction by exposure to near ultraviolet radiation, or by including in the thermographic layer certain substituted alpha-naphthols, for example, 4-methoxy-1-naphthol (104). Thermographic composition containing nickel stearate becomes insensitive to heat after being exposed to near ultraviolet radiation if the second component is, instead of dithiooxamide, a substituted dithiooxamide, as, for example N,N'-bis-furfuryl dithiooxamide (105).

Heat generated in image areas can also be utilized for evaporating liquids from these sections. Originally designed by Herschel and later by Czerny (106) for recording infrared spectral lines, this principle was used by Games (107) for document copying. The document to be copied is fed into an apparatus where a thin "oil" film is applied to it, and is exposed to infrared rays while in contact with a sheet of writing paper. As the result of selective heating, the fluid evaporates from the image areas and condenses on the cool copy sheet. By dusting the latent image with a resin containing carbon black or some other coloring matter and fusing the resin, a copy of the original is obtained. In this case, also, the duplicate is heat stable, and will not darken upon accidental exposure to elevated temperatures. The "oils" which can be used include vegetable or mineral oils, glycerols and glycols with a boiling point of 275 to 390°C, and hydrogenated terphenyls, chlorinated polyphenyls, and kerosene for faster evaporation (108,109,110). It is said that the original document suffers no damage even after repeated application of a thin film of oil. The foregoing patents also claim image development by chemical reaction in which case one reagent is mixed with the distillable oil and the other is applied to the copy sheet.

To eliminate the application of an oil to the original, it was suggested that an intermediate oil-covered sheet which is sandwiched to the copy sheet (111) be used. This 2-ply assembly is placed in heat-conductive association with the original and is irradiated, distilling the oil from the intermediate sheet to the copy sheet in the image areas. These areas are dusted with appropriate powder and fused. In another variation, the original is covered with a colored fusible powder (112) or with a powdered ink (213). Irradiated with infrared, the powder or the ink is transferred to the receiving sheet.

The dusting operation is not required in the process employing two sheets, one coated with a distillable or sublimable coupler, for instance, 2,3-dihydroxynaphthalene or phloroglucinol, and the second with a diazonium compound. When exposed to infrared radiation in conjunction with a graphic original, the coupler sublimes from the first sheet to the superposed diazo sheet, to form, after development in ammonia vapors, a positive azo-dye image of the original (114). All processes employing single transfer of chemicals or toners from the original to the receiving sheet produce mirror images and the copies have to be read right side up by looking at them through the opposite side of the sheet.

During the rapid and intense heating that occurs during the exposure of printed matter to infrared radiation, many plastic films, for example, polyethylene, nylon, and cellulose acetate, undergo some sort of physical or chemical changes. By making use of the altered properties in the heated areas, it is possible to develop the latent image in a number of ways. A polyamide surface, when exposed to infrared radiation, accepts resinous pigmented powder so that, by imagewise exposure, photographic copies of the master can be obtained (115,116). The adhering pigment can be transferred to another sheet of paper so that one or more copies can be made from one exposure of the original (117). Instead of polyamides, polyesters of aliphatic dicarboxylic acids having a narrow melting range can be employed (118). The latent image consisting of heat-softened areas is developed with a powder made up of colophony, carbon black, and nigrosine, and is fixed by warming in trichloroethylene vapor. Thermoplastic layers of polyethylene, polystyrene, polyacrylic esters, and so forth, act in similar way (119).

The Ektafax process introduced by the Recordak Division of Eastman Kodak Co. is also based on physical changes which take place during the exposure to intense heat. This process utilizes a matrix sheet consisting of a noninfrared-absorbing dye dissolved in a thermoplastic binder. The heat generated during the exposure softens the thermoplastic resin in the areas corresponding to the printed matter on the original and offsets it on the receiving sheet by passing the composite between heated rollers of the transfer machine. For this process two matrixes have been made available. One matrix, after a single thermographic exposure, is capable of producing up to ten copies, whereas the second matrix is intended for single copy use. The advantage of this matrix lies in the fact that the latent heat image disappears in a few minutes after heat exposure so that it can be reused to copy ten to twenty originals.

Another thermographic copying method is based on an imagewise dissipation of electrostatic charge by heat. It is known that the conductivity of an electrically insulating layer varies with temperature. Thus, if an electrostatically charged layer of a dielectric material such as polyethylene or cellulose acetate is placed in contact with the document to be reproduced, and exposed to infrared, the charge will be conducted away more rapidly in the heated areas. The graphic information of the original is then represented by a charge pattern which can be made visible by any of the standard electroscopic developing techniques, for example, with toner particles charged to the same polarity; these will stick only to image areas where heat has dissipated the charge, and will be repelled from the charged background areas. A positive copy of the original will result (120). Cassiers (121) indicated that the success of this technique is due to a critical point in the resistivity versus temperature curve of many inorganic and organic materials which makes them suitable for this process. Mention should also be made of the thermoxerographic process patented by Curme (122), which is based on the fact that electrical resistivity of some material increases on being heated and does not revert to the original value on lowering the temperature. Thus, after a thermographic exposure the copy sheet is corona charged and xerographically developed. If one employs an electroscopic toner with the same charge as the electrostatic charge on the dielectric, this process would yield a negative copy of the original, whereas the Cassiers technique yields a positive copy. Similar systems were disclosed by Dulmage and Light (123), McNaney (124), and Lind and Munder (125).

Having considered electrostatic techniques for development of latent heat images, we may also mention analogous magnetic methods. Sims and Norton (126) disclose the technique of preparing a latent magnetic image by uniformly magnetizing a surface and projecting a heat image onto the surface to demagnetize the image areas. Use is made of the Curie point, the temperature above which the magnetic properties of a material are suppressed, of the magnetic material. This transition is sharp, and, of course, in the absence of any new magnetic fields the materials will remain demagnetized. The heat latent image, which has been converted to a magnetic image, may be developed with paramagnetic particles of iron, nickel, and cobalt; such particles adhere only to the magnetized areas. This powder image may be transferred to a receiving sheet.

Swoboda (127) creates a magnetic latent image by the use of chromium-manganese antimonides. These materials are nonmagnetic up to a critical temperature, at which point they exhibit a first-order thermodynamic change and undergo a sharp transition to a magnetic state. Heat rays projected upon a layer of the antimonide will result in a pattern which is magnetic and which may be toned up with a magnetic powder such as Fe_3O_4.

9.2c *Copying of Colored Originals*

In order to obtain a thermographic reproduction it is required that the ink on the original absorbs infrared radiation. In general, any ink of any color containing metallic or carbon constituents is suitable; thus, black printing of any kind (typing, printing, pencil writing, india-ink drawings, etc.), can be copied. Colored inks, such as those based on synthetic dyes and used in many ballpoint pens, do not convert radiant energy to heat to a sufficient degree, and are not practical for thermal reproductions unless infrared absorbers are added for this purpose to the coloring matter. Suitable infrared absorbers include graphite (128), metal powders, finely divided antimony (129), metal oxides and sulfides (130), or manganous complexes of certain diazo compounds (131), for example, 4-hydroxy-5-(2,4-diamino-phenylazo) benzenesulfonic acid. Salts of a substituted 9-phenylfluorene-9-ols have been suggested as an addition to the dyes used in inks so that the characters written with them can be successfully copied.

To obtain thermographic copies of dye images not suitable for direct heat copying Yutzy and Yackel (132,133,134) suggested the employment of the heat-sensitive composition with a silver halide emulsion containing a developing agent. In one such application the silver image is developed, after exposure through the original to white light, by fuming with moist ammonia vapor and is subsequently exposed to infrared rays to give an image in the heat-sensitive layer. Residual emulsion is then removed by rinsing in warm water.

An ingenious solution to the problem of thermographic copying of colored originals was described by Workman (135). In this method, transparent film base coated with a solution of 4-methoxy-1-naphthol and erythrosine, or some other photoreducible dye that is able to reduce silver salt, is placed in contact with the colored original to be copied and irradiated from the film side by reflex with tungsten light of high intensity. A pattern of undecomposed material corresponding to the image is left on the film. The exposed film is then placed with its coated surface in contact with a sheet of paper sensitized with silver behenate; then the sandwich is covered with a thin black foil, placed in a jacket consisting of a sheet of stiff paper and transparent silk screen fastened together along their upper edges (136), and run through a thermographic copying machine. A blue-black image is formed on the paper sheet and is clearly visible through the colored film, which is then removed and discarded together with the thin black sheet. In the "Dual Spectrum" machine introduced by the Minnesota Mining and Manufacturing Company, the black foil can be eliminated.

9.2d   *Applications*

Thermographic papers may be used for copying originals printed on both sides or on one side only. In the first case, the heat-sensitive layer is placed against the page to be copied, and radiant heat is applied through the copying paper. Originals with only one side printed may be copied by the same method, or by radiating the heat first through the original which has been placed in contact with the copy sheet. This method of back-printing is most satisfactory for originals printed on a thin paper or for typewriting or letterpress printing having printed characters deeply embossed as from high pressure.

In most commercially available copying machines, the radiant energy is supplied by an incandescent filament lamp, such as GE "T-J"; the voltage employed heats the lamp to about 2800° Kelvin. The lamp is mounted in an elliptical reflector which focuses the radiation in a narrow beam, across which the assembled original and the superposed copy sheet is moved by means of an endless transparent heat-resistant belt. The purpose of the belt, which can be made from polytetrafluorothylene (137), is to hold the copy sheet in contact with a metal roller during heat exposure. The design and construction of thermographic copying machines is protected by a number of patents (138,139,140,141,142,143, 144,145,146,147). In some machines the lamp travels from one side to the other, and the original and copy paper are stationary. The exposure time is controlled by the speed at which the lamp travels. Especially suitable for printing on infrared opaque sheets is a method consisting of a brief and direct application of intense radiant energy to the original and a rapid contraction of the irradiated surface with the heat-sensitive copy sheet. The heat pattern imparted to the differentially radiation absorbing original is of sufficient intensity and duration to cause a visible change in the heat-sensitive layer (148,149). Apparatus especially designed for recording library transactions (150) or for transcribing information from a series of coded cards (151) has also been patented. In order to assure uniform transfer of heat from the image areas to the thermosensitive layer, the original and the copy sheet must be in good contact. For this purpose Wartman and O'Mara (152) plasticized the heat-sensitive layer sufficiently to render the coating moderately tacky at a temperature slightly below the temperature at which the reaction occurs. The temperatures at which, and the time for which, thermographic papers must be held in order to obtain satisfactory images vary with the composition of the heat-sensitive layer and with the nature and characteristics of the supporting base. To avoid deterioration of the thermographic paper due to the exceedingly high-intensity radiant energy, the exposure must be very short. In thermographic material now on the market the color-generating reaction is brought about by heating to above 80°C; copying of a conventional letter-size original requires about 1 to 6 seconds.

One of the most important factors involved in the use of thermographic papers is the exposure latitude. The exposure range is generally quite short and can be controlled to a certain degree by the formulation of the heat-sensitive coating. If the temperature at which the color change starts to show is only about 5°C lower than that at which the maximum visible change occurs, it is difficult to reproduce fine lines without blurring the heavy lines. If the temperature difference is greater than 20°C, then the nonimage background areas will be darkened with consequent low contrast of the final copy. It should be kept in mind that in continued use the copying unit heats up appreciably so that both the original and the copy sheet receive considerable nonimage heating. To compensate for this increase in temperature, the rate of advance of the graphic original and copy paper through the apparatus has to be increased. A temperature recording dial has been designed for this purpose (153).

Because of its simplicity and rapidity for obtaining satisfactory direct positive copies, this completely dry process became an important reproduction process employed mainly in copying of business correspondence. For obtaining multiple copies, thermographic methods have also been adapted for spirit-duplicating (154), hectographic processes (155,156,157), for production of ink-receptive areas on the offset plates (158), and for manufacturing of stencils (159,160). In one such process (110), a cellulose acetate sheet coated with leuco malachite green is placed in contact with a second sheet impregnated with a polymethacrylic acid ester and an oxidizing agent, for example, tetrachloroquinone, 2,4-dichlorobenzoyl peroxide, or quinone. When exposed to infrared radiation the dye is regenerated in the image areas and forms the basis of the spirit duplicator. Thermographic images can also be obtained by projection printing, when enlarged or reduced images are desired (162). Wolf (163) achieved this by projecting an image to be reproduced on the heat-sensitive layer and by irradiating its back surface with an infrared lamp. It is assumed that infrared radiation will penetrate the light areas of the projected image and be absorbed in the shadow areas where the color-forming thermal reaction will take place.

REFERENCES

1. E. A. Boyan. U.S. pat. 2,922,688/1960.
2. K. C. D. Hickman and L. A. Staib, Jr. U.S. pat. 1,880,449/1932.
3. K. C. D. Hickman and L. A. Staib, Jr. U.S. pat. 1,897,843/1933.
4. J. Russell. U.S. pat. 2,336,299/1943.
5. M. Morrison. U.S. pat. 2,681,277/1954.
6. M. Morrison. U.S. pat. 2,732,299/1956.
7. W. Gordon and S. E. Eaton. U.S. pat. 2,813,042/1957.
8. R. W. James. U.S. pat. 2,855,266/1958.
9. R. E. Miller and L. Schleicher. U.S. pat. 2,929,736/1960.
10. M. Morrison. U.S. pat. 2,625,494/1953.
11. R. W. James. U.S. pat. 2,519,660/1950.
12. W. F. Kallock. U.S. pat. 2,299,991/1942.
13. W. H. Vander Weel. U.S. pat. 2,927,039/1960.
14. D. F. A. Mohnhaupt. U.S. pat. 3,020,172/1962.
15. F. Rosenthal. U.S. pat. 2,739,909/1956.
16. W. R. Lawton, J. N. Copley, and H. A. Smith. U.S. pat. 3,090,697/1963.
17. D. Mohnhaupt. Ger. pat. 1,153,612/1963.
18. B. L. Clark and C. S. Miller. U.S. pat. 2,859,351/1958; Brit. pat. 810,863/1959.
19. N. W. Taylor and B. L. Clark. U.S. pat. 2,668,126/1954.
20. B. L. Clark and C. S. Miller. U.S. pat. 2,710,263/1955; Reissue 24,554/1958.
21. H. R. Dalton. Brit. pat. 922,999/1963.
22. R. Owen. U.S. pat. 2,916,395/1959; Brit. pat. 934,177/1963.
23. C. S. Miller. U.S. pat. 2,880,110/1959.
24. D. A. Neuman and A. T. Schlotzhauer. U.S. pat. 3,057,999/1962.
25. W. H. Vander Weel. Brit. pat. 943,681/1963.
26. H. E. Crawford. U.S. pat. 2,868,124/1959.
27. C. J. Schoemaker and E. J. Igler. U.S. pat. 2,749,253/1956.
28. C. S. Miller. U.S. pat. 2,663,654/1953.
29. C. S. Miller. U.S. pat. 2,663,657/1953.
30. C. S. Miller and B. L. Clark. U.S. pat. 2,663,655/1953.
31. C. S. Miller and B. L. Clark. U.S. pat. 2,663,656/1953.
32. C. S. Miller and C. A. Kuhrmayer. Ger. pat. 1,086,719/1957.
33. M. Glos. Ger. pat. 1,104,535/1961.
34. E. W. Grieshaber. Ger. pat. 1,145,643/1963.
35. Kalle A.G. Brit. pat. 943,996/1963.
36. D. A. Ostlie. U.S. pat. 3,111,423/1963.
37. M. F. Baumann and W. R. Lawton. Belg. pat. 627,029/1963.
38. M. van Dam. U.S. pat. 2,897,090/1959.
39. R. Owen. U.S. pat. 2,910,377/1959.
40. E. A. Grant, Jr. U.S. pat. 3,028,254/1962; Brit. pat. 967,440/1964; Fr. pat. 1,269,464/1961.
41. T. G. Wartmann. U.S. pat. 3,107,174/1963; Brit. pat. 943,993/1963; Ger. pat. 1,146,078/1963.

42. L. E. Wingert. U.S. pat. 3,031,329/1962.
43. R. Owen. U.S. pat. 3,074,809/1963.
44. E. A. Grant, Jr. U.S. pat. 3,080,254/1963.
45. R. Owen. U.S. pat. 3,108,896/1963.
46. F. D. Allen, J. A. Van Allan, and J. J. Sagura. U.S. pat. 2,967,785/1961; Belg. pat. 593,980/1960.
47. H. A. Wark. Belg. pat. 631,000/1963; Fr. pat. 1,360,416/1964.
48. D. A. Newman, A. T. Schlotzhauer, A. M. Vogel, D. B. Albert, and J. J. Quattrone. U.S. pat. 2,967,784/1961.
49. G. T. Richey. U.S. pat. 2,995,465/1961; Brit. pat. 962,545/1964; Brit. pat. 963,981/1964.
50. D. P. Sorensen. U.S. pat. 2,995,466/1959.
51. R. F. Coles, V. Tulagin, and R. A. Miller. U.S. pat. 3,076,721/1962; Japan. pat. 37–18,992/1962.
52. W. R. Workman. U.S. pat. 3,129,101/1964.
53. W. R. Workman. U.S. pat. 3,129,109/1964.
54. National Cash Register Company. Brit. pat. 951,507/1964.
55. National Cash Register Company. Brit. pat. 953,150/1964; Fr. pat. 1,373,659/1964.
56. National Cash Register Company. Fr. pat. 1,283,893/1963.
57. R. H. Sprague. U.S. pat. 2,940,866/1960.
58. J. F. Tinker and J. J. Sagura. Fr. pat. 1,333,723/1963.
59. W. R. Lawton. Belg. pat. 632,833/1963; Fr. pat. 1,363,501/1963.
60. W. Sahler. U.S. pat. 3,097,297/1963; Brit. pat. 893,511/1962; Ger. pat. 1,100,655/1961; Fr. pat. 1,231,931/1960.
61. Ilford, Ltd. Belg. pat. 633,059/1963.
62. J. D. Kendall and K. Reynolds. Brit. pat. 877,334/1961.
63. T. V. Creuling, D. J. Haag, and T. I. Abbott. U.S. pat. 2,899,334/1959; Brit. pat. 927,895/1963.
64. O. Süs and M. Glos. U.S. pat. 3,024,362/1962; Fr. pat. 1,240,124/1960; Ger. pat. 1,109,712/1961.
65. AGFA A.G. Belg. pat. 628,346/1963.
66. B. S. Wildi. U.S. pat. 3,132,039/1964.
67. R. B. Russell. U.S. pat. 3,121,791/1964.
68. R. S. Holland and R. E. Wayrynen. U.S. pat. 3,063,863/1962; Brit. pat. 905,699/1963.
69. D. L. Thomsen. U.S. pat. 2,980,551/1961; Brit. pat. 947,633/1964.
70. E. G. Howard. U.S. pat. 2,950,987/1960.
71. R. Owen. U.S. pat. 3,028,255/1962.
72. B. L. Clark. U.S. pat. 2,813,043/1957; Brit. pat. 829,001/1960; Ger. pat. 1,149,730/1963.
73. Eastman Kodak Company. Brit. pat. 928,039/1963.
74. D. A. Newman. U.S. pat. 3,119,014/1964.
75. W. A. Raczynski and R. N. Quoss. U.S. pat. 3,122,997/1964.
76. D. A. Newman. U.S. pat. 3,129,661/1964.
77. R. B. Russell. U.S. pat. 3,131,080/1964.
78. E. Lind. U.S. pat. 3,120,611/1964.
79. P. A. Roman and M. E. Pfaff. U.S. pat. 3,121,162/1964; Fr. pat. 1,262,059/1960.
80. A. B. Dick Company. Fr. pat. 1,371,136/1963.

81. E. Lind and F. Schloffer. Ger. pat. 1,162,389/1964.
82. W. H. Vander Weel. Brit. pat. 943,682/1963.
83. Ditto Inc. Brit. pat. 844,695/1960.
84. Eastman Kodak Company. Brit. pat. 928,039/1960.
85. D. J. Newman. U.S. pat. 3,147,377/1964.
86. W. Ritzerfeld and G. Ritzerfeld. Brit. pat. 922,682/1963.
87. E. Lind. Brit. pat. 944,871/1963; Ger. pat. 1,100,656/1961.
88. S. D. Warren Company. Brit. pat. 894,527/1962.
89. W. Neugebauer and E. Lind. Brit. pat. 941,827/1963; Ger. pat. 1,113,947/1961.
90. J. M. Tien. U.S. pat. 2,939,009/1960.
91. H. Haydn, E. Weyde, and R. Müller. Fr. pat. 1,306,830/1962.
92. R. E. Miller and J. K. Cheng. Belg. pat. 625,049/1963.
93. H. Haydn and E. Weyde. Ger. pat. 1,149,023/1963.
94. H. Haydn and E. Weyde. Ger. pat. 1,152,711/1963.
95. F. J. Rauner, I. F. Rosati, and E. M. Robertson. U.S. pat. 3,100,702/1963.
96. W. Ritzerfeld and G. Ritzerfeld. Brit. pat. 922,666/1963; Brit. pat. 922,682/1963.
97. J. Groak. U.S. pat. 2,616,961/1952.
98. Kalle A.G. Fr. pat. 1,334,804/1963.
99. G. Mache. Brit. pat. 860,590/1961; Ger. pat. 1,047,013/1958.
100. W. L. Meissner. U.S. pat. 3,121,650/1964.
101. E. W. Grieshaber. U.S. pat. 3,103,881/1963; Brit. pat. 943,992/1963; Can. pat. 662,653/1963; Ger. pat. 1,145,643/1963.
102. W. Sahler. U.S. pat. 2,999,035/1961; Brit. pat. 910,511/1962; Ger. pat. 1,100,464/1961.
103. A. B. Cohen. U.S. pat. 3,070,428/1962; Belg. pat. 590,572/1960.
104. E. A. Grant, Jr. U.S. pat. 3,094,619/1963.
105. J. L. Reitter. U.S. pat. 3,094,620/1963; Belg. pat. 612,242/1962.
106. M. Czerny. *Z. Physik*, **53**, 1 (1929).
107. A. Games. *J. Phot. Sci.*, **10**, 100–103 (1962); Anon. *Reproduction Methods*, July 1961.
108. A. Games. Brit. pat. 943,401/1963.
109. A. Games. Brit. pat. 943,402/1963.
110. A. Games. Brit. pat. 943,403/1963.
111. Philips N.V. Belg. pat. 639,795/1963.
112. A. Murray. U.S. pat. 2,503,758/1950.
113. A. Murray. U.S. pat. 2,503,759/1950.
114. Ozalid Company Ltd. Belg. pat. 615,436/1962.
115. E. Lind. Ger. pat. 1,125,453/1962.
116. E. Lind. Ger. pat. 1,140,953/1962.
117. A. G. Gulko. U.S. pat. 3,081,699/1953.
118. Gevaert Photo-Producten, N.V. Belg. pat. 628,105/1963.
119. E. Lind. Ger. pat. 1,166,795/1964.
120. Kodak S.A. Belg. pat. 602,975/1961.
121. P. M. Cassiers. *Phot. Sci. Eng.*, **4**, 199–202/1960.
122. H. G. Curme. Fr. pat. 1,318,118/1963.
123. W. J. Dulmage and W. A. Light. U.S. pat. 3,128,198/1964.
124. J. T. McNaney. U.S. pat. 3,106,692/1963.
125. E. Lind and J. Munder. U.S. pat. 3,089,953/1963.

126. J. C. Sims, Jr., and C. A. Norton. U.S. pat. 2,793,135/1957.
127. T. J. Swoboda. U.S. pat. 3,126,492/1964.
128. F. G. Francis and J. A. Seaward. U.S. pat. 2,936,247/1960.
129. F. G. Francis and J. A. Seaward. U.S. pat. 2,992,121/1960.
130. Gevaert Photo-Producten N.V. Belg. pat. 615,804/1962.
131. R. A. Coleman and J. L. Rodgers. U.S. pat. 3,042,624/1962.
132. H. C. Yutzy and E. C. Yackel. Belg. pat. 591,479/1960.
133. H. C. Yutzy and E. C. Yackel. Brit. pat. 958,962/1964.
134. H. C. Yutzy and E. C. Yackel. Brit. pat. 958,963/1964.
135. W. R. Workman. U.S. pat. 3,094,417/1963; Belg. pat. 612,241/1962.
136. D. R. Hurley and J. F. McHugh. U.S. pat. 3,066,679/1962.
137. 3 M. Brit. pat. 829,002/1960.
138. C. S. Miller. U.S. pat. 2,740,895/1956.
139. C. S. Miller. U.S. pat. 2,740,896/1956.
140. C. A. Kuhrmeyer. U.S. pat. 2,891,165/1959.
141. C. S. Miller and C. A. Kuhrmeyer. U.S. pat. 2,844,733/1958.
142. C. A. Kuhrmeyer, D. G. Kimble, and C. S. Miller. U.S. pat. 2,919,349/1959.
143. C. A. Kuhrmeyer. U.S. pat. 2,976,415/1961.
144. O. R. Urbach. U.S. pat. 3,053,175/1962.
145. E. A. O'Mara. U.S. pat. 2,927,210/1960.
146. A. R. Kotz, R. H. Appeldorn, E. W. Grieshaber, E. J. Peterson, and N. L. Giorgini. U.S. pat. 3,056,904/1964.
147. E. Wedel. U.S. pat. 3,129,328/1964.
148. D. G. Kimble. U.S. pat. 3,131,302/1964.
149. Itek Corp. Brit. pat. 959,402/1964.
150. A. Brody. Brit. pat. 883,107/1961.
151. H. H. Nelson and A. R. Kotz. U.S. pat. 3,038,994/1962.
152. T. G. Wartman and E. A. O'Mara. U.S. pat. 3,089,952/1963; Fr. pat. 1,277,840/1960.
153. R. M. Cisek, P. A. Enblom, and R. J. Kline. U.S. pat. 3,128,379/1964.
154. A. I. Rishkind. U.S. pat. 2,769,391/1956.
155. T. U. Marron. U.S. pat. 2,970,534/1961.
156. D. A. Newman and A. T. Schlotzhauer. U.S. pat. 3,054,692/1962.
157. D. A. Newman. U.S. pat. 3,088,028/1963.
158. A. I. Roshkind. U.S. pat. 2,808,777/1957; A. B. Dick Company: Belg. pat. 615,531/1962.
159. K. S. Hoover. U.S. pat. 2,699,113/1955.
160. K. Wolfson, L. C. Austin, and O. Baturay. U.S. pat. 3,131,628/1964.
161. W. Ritzerfeld and G. Ritzerfeld. Brit. pat. 921,673/1963.
162. A. B. Cohen and R. Sedgwick. U.S. pat. 3,073,953/1963.
163. H. Wolf. Ger. pat. 1,077,977/1960.

AUTHOR INDEX

Abbott, T. I., 379, 417
Abney, W. de W., 68, 100
Ackermann, C. A., 312
Adams, D. N., 122, 134, 328, 355
Adams, R. A. C., 84, 100, 101, 133, 134, 135, 147, 156, 355
Adamson, A. W., 43
Adressograph-Multigraph Corp., 136
Adelman, A. H., 184, 192, 193
Adelson, D. E., 193
Adisesh, S. R., 371, 397
Aebi, C. M., 313
Agens, M. C., 190
AGFA A. G., 409, 417
Agre, C. C., 188
Agruss, M. S., 193, 377, 398
Aharoni, A., 399
Aisaka, K., 71, 101
Aizawa, T., 317
Akintievsky, V. C., 320
Albert, D. B., 417
Albert, J., 51
Albrecht, J., 124, 125, 134
Alfaya, R., 307, 320
Algraphy, Ltd., 133
Alink, R. J. H., 45, 263, 271, 311, 313, 314, 315, 316, 318
Allan, Z. J., 310
Allen, C. F. H., 141, 150, 155, 156, 157
Allen, F. D., 417
Alles, F. P., 132

Allmand, A. J., 26, 43
Amagasaki, S., 319
Amariti, L., 313
American Zinc Institute, 353
Amering, C. F., 135
Ammann, H., 68, 100
Andresen, M., 250, 311, 314
Andrew, F. W., 312
Andrews Paper and Chemical Co., 309, 318
Anfinsen, C. B., Jr., 99
Aninga, J., 263, 314
Anson, M. L., 99
Appeldorn, R. H., 419
Armistead, W. H., 42, 400
Armstrong, G. M., 386, 400
Army Map Service, 121
Arnett, L. M., 191
Aroney, M., 195, 308
Artigue, V., 49
Asperger, S., 69, 101
Astbury, W. T., 99
Audet, J. P., 379, 398
Austin, L. C., 419
Autotype Company, Ltd., The, 102

Babcock, C. S., 45
Bacon, N. R., 316
Badische Anilin and Soda Fabrik A.G., 189
Badoche, M., 294, 317
Bagnelle, L. J., 312

Bailey, S. D., 99, 399
Baker, A. R., 133
Baker, T. T., 133
Baker, W. N., 133
Baldwin, G. S., 132
Balk, A. K., 315, 316
Barba, A. M., 319
Barde, E., 268, 315
Baril, A., 277, 316
Barnes, R. B., 43, 44, 45
Barney, A. L., 188, 189
Barnhart, G., 398
Barrow, G. M., 40
Barrows, W. F., 193
Barthenbeier, J., 354, 355
Bartl, H., 157
Bartlett, P. D., 216, 310
Bassist, E., 100, 129, 134, 135
Bath, J. D., 99
Baturay, O., 419
Bauchet & Cie, 313, 314
Bauer, W. D., 313
Baumann, M. F., 416
Baxendale, J. H., 190
Baxendale, R. W., 188, 193
Bayer, O., 148, 151, 156
Bayer, P., 132
Beauchamp, G. E., 313
Beckett, M., 355
Becquerel, E., 47
Beebe, M. C., 138, 155
Beeber, A. R. A., 36, 45, 320
Beekman, S. M., 43
Beese, W., 318
Behemburg, H., 314
Bekk, J., 87, 101
Bell, E. R., 190
Bellin, J. S., 400
Benbrook, C. H., 249, 263, 307, 308, 314, 320
Bene, K., 320
Benewalenskaja, S. V., 399
Benjamin, B., 318
Bennett, C. N., 45
Berczeli, H., 54, 99
Bere, C. M., 399
Berezyuk, Y. N., 135
Berger, D., 130, 136
Bergstrom, H. A., 308

Berman, E., 400
Bertram, J., 155
Bertsch, E., 44
Bevan, E. J., 250, 311
Bevington, J. C., 191
Bialczak, E. C., 318, 319
Biltz, H., 399
Biltz, M., 68, 69, 70, 72, 100
Bincer, H., 395, 401
Birum, G. H., 190
Black, O. D., 132
Blandhoel, B. E., 132
Blum, F., 99
Blumann, S., 45
Boersma, T. T., 100, 323, 354
Boettner, J., 43
Bolland, J. L., 192
Bond, J., 181, 192
Borchers, H. H., 134
Borgman, V. A., 42
Borth, P. F., 132
Bos, J. G., 315, 316
Bosch, W. C., 42
Bose, J. R., 213, 309
Botkin, C., 317, 318, 319
Böttger, H., 43, 309, 318
Bouček, J., 72, 96, 101, 102
Boudreaux, E. A., 195, 308
Bowen, E. J., 101
Boyan, E. A., 416
Boyer, M. R., 132
Bradley, J. W., 132
Brandenberger, J. E., 319
Brandstreet, S. W., 134
Braver, E., 41
Bremer, K., 155
Breslow, D. S., 217, 310
Brill, R. H., 41
Brinnick, F. E., 130, 134, 136
Brintzinger, H., 70, 99, 101
British Ozaphan, Ltd., 319
British Thomson-Houston Co., 308
Britton, H. T. S., 102
Brode, W. R., 154
Brody, A., 419
Brown, C. A., 100, 132, 135
Brown, D. J., 196, 197, 308
Brown, E., 45
Brown, G. H., 371, 397, 399

Brown, M. S., 399
Bruins, P. F., 189
Bruni, R. J., 277, 316
Bruning, C., 313
Brunk, H. J., 44, 313
Bruno, M. H., 100, 101, 102, 121
Bryce, R. S., 133
Buchkovskii, Z. F., 308
Buchner, H., 319
Buck, A. W., 134
Buck, S. R., 310
Buckles, R. E., 157
Bucklin, G. W., 136
Bukač, Z., 354
Bull, J. L., 319
Bungay, J. A., 312, 313
Burg, M., 165, 166, 188, 189
Burg, R. F., 191
Burley, G., 41
Burnett, G. M., 192
Burrows, W. F., 134, 190
Burrows, W. H., 132
Burton, M., 176, 191
Buskes, W. M., 317, 326, 354
Butler, C. L., 63, 100
Buxton, G. V., 43
Byer, M., 42
Byers, D. J., 73, 77, 80, 101
Bywater, S., 177, 191

Calvert, J. G., 397, 398
Cannon, R. V., 132
Cartledge, G. H., 43
Cartwright, H. M., 132, 133
Cartwright, M., 73, 97, 101, 111, 133
Case, J. M., 325, 354, 355
Cassie, A. B. D., 60, 99
Cassiers, P. M., 412, 418
Cathcart, J. A., 135
Caton, T. R., 99, 129, 134, 135
Cavanaugh, E. F., 99
Cazares, J. L., 31, 44
Cerwonka, E., 190
Chalkley, L., 21, 22, 42, 371, 397, 398, 399
Chambers, V. C., 188
Chapiro, A., 181, 192
Charlton, A. E., 131
Charnas, L. I., 396

Chattaway, F. D., 399
Chebiniak, P., 133, 354
Chechak, J. J., 315
Cheng, J. K., 409, 418
Cherney, I., 91, 102
Chichibabin, A. E., 399
Child, R., 399
Chismar, A. B., 133
Chistoserdov, V. G., 42
Christ, R. E., 188
Christie, G. S., 135
Cipriand, J. F., 43
Cisek, R. M., 419
Claffy, E. W., 43
Clark, B. L., 416, 417
Clark, W., 135
Clark, W. C., 399
Clarke, J. T., 171, 190
Claus, C. J., 193
Clément, L. E., 138, 155, 396
Clerc, L. P., 45
Clusius, K., 330, 355
Coates, J. E., 308
Cochran, E. L., 192
Cochran, T. R., 21, 42
Coffman, J. W., 320
Cohen, A. B., 166, 172, 188, 189, 190, 418, 419
Cohen, A. J., 400
Cohen, M. D., 399
Cohn, B., 133, 327, 355
Colberg, K. H., 128, 135
Coleman, R. A., 419
Coles, R. F., 354, 417
Colman, B. W., 311
Colt, R. S., 100, 135
Compton, G. C., 189
Conant, J. B., 216, 263, 310
Contois, L. E., 316
Cook, A. H., 154
Cooper, W., 191
Copestake, T. B., 43
Copley, J. N., 416
Corning Glass Works, 24, 43
Cotton, L. J., 92, 102
Countryman, R. C., 41
Cowan, P. M., 99
Cox, F. C., 101
Cox, R. J., 99, 204, 309, 319, 355

Cox, R. S., 53, 132
Crandal, J. L., 188
Crawford, H. E., 188, 189, 416
Crawford, J., 99
Cretcher, L. W., 63, 100
Creuling, T. V., 417
Crick, F. H. C., 99
Croker, J. H., 148, 156
Cross, C. F., 250, 311
Crossley, M. L., 249, 263, 308
Crowley, C. A., 29, 36, 43, 44, 45, 312
Curme, H. G., 412, 418
Curtius, T., 330, 355
Cuttler, L. H., 132
Czerny, M., 410, 418

Daguerre, L. J. M., 47
Dainton, F. S., 170, 190
Dalton, H. R., 403, 416
Dalton, R. H., 42
Danehy, J. P., 63, 99
Dagelmajer, C., 134
Dannenberg, H., 193
Daugherty, P. M., 132
Davis, A. B., 132
Davis, T. W., 176, 191
Dawood, R. I., 17, 41
Deal, E. F., 134, 355
de Atlas, 320
De Barbieris, I. H., 316
de Boer, H. G. J., 310, 323, 354
de Boer, J. H., 41, 271, 313, 314, 315
Deeks, H. C. J., 99
de Jong, J., 311, 315
De Jonge, J., 311, 315, 316
De Lesseps, F., 102
Dell, E. F., 99, 134
Delzenne, G. A., 182, 186, 188, 192, 193
Denstman, H., 45, 313
de Chezeaulx-Meyer, T., 101
DeTar, D. F., 308
Deusen van, C. H., 62, 99, 136
Deusen van, W. P., 131, 138, 141, 155, 156
Devores, E., 45
de Waile, A., 148, 156
Dhar, N. D., 40

D'Hauterive, G., 313
Dick Co., A. B., 136, 417, 419
Dickason, M., 44, 313
Dicke, T., 43
Dickerson, M. H., 39, 43, 45
Dickinson, B. L., 181, 192
Diedrich, J. L., 329, 355
Diener, C. E., 174, 190
Dieterle, P., 259, 313
Dietz, H. J., 18, 41
Dietzgen Co., E., 314
Dietzgen, J. E., 265, 313, 314
Dijkstra, R., 311, 315
Dippel, C. J., 41, 271, 315, 316
Ditkovski, H., 399
Ditto, Inc., 136, 418
Doering, J. G. W., 43
Dogliotti, L., 399
Dolder van den, J. M. H., 36, 45
Dorel, J. J., 313
Dorel, L. R., 313
Dorion, G. H., 399
Dorst, P. W., 73, 86, 101, 134
Douglas, C., 134
Dowdall, J. F., 355
Doyle, W. T., 13, 40
Drey, N., 132
Dubois, M., 92, 102
Duerr, H. H., 193, 298, 318
Du Fraisse, C., 294, 317
Dugan, J. M., 110, 133
Dulik, K., 100
Dulmage, W. J., 412, 418
Dumers, D. M., 174, 190
Dunbar, C., 319
du Pont E. I. de Nemours and Co., 108, 113, 133, 161, 164, 188, 189, 190, 191

Easley, J. A., 132
Eastman Kodak Co., 113, 129, 141, 156, 411, 417, 418
Eaton, S. E., 416
Eberlin, L. W., 21, 42, 155
Eckardt, C., 100
Eden, W. E., 132
Eder, J. M., 40, 67, 68, 70, 91, 100, 102, 312
Edsall, J. T., 99

Edsberg, R. L., 310
Eggert, J., 21, 42, 68, 69, 70, 72, 100, 154, 199, 308
Ehrenthalier, A., 135
Eichorn, A., 43
Einstein, A., 2, 5
Ei-Sayed, M. A., 399
Eisler, P., 132
Elbrecht, W. F., 316
Elliott, S. B., 396
Ellis, C., 40
Ellis, J. W., 99
Ellsworth, I. W., 260, 313
Elöd, E., 54, 99, 101
Elofson, R. M., 216, 310
Elston, L. W., 132
Enblom, P. A., 419
Endermann, F., 43, 318, 355, 357
Engelhardt, V. A., 188, 190
Ensink, A., 130, 134, 136
Entwistle, Thorpe & Co., 319
Ericks, W. P., 43
Etablissement Tiflex, 133
Evans, H. D., 134, 174, 190, 191, 193
Evans, L. W., 42
Evans, M. G., 190, 192
Even, A. D., 320
Evering, B. L., 176, 191
Evleth, E. M., 308

Fabian, R. W., 307, 316
Fairbrother, F., 99
Farben, I. G., 308
Farbenfabriken Bayer, A. G., 157
Farmer, E. H., 50
Farrell, K. P., 313
Farrer, W. J. G., 18, 41
Feer, A., 268, 314, 315
Feichtmayr, F., 399
Feldmann, W., 73, 101
Ferington, T. E., 169, 190
Ferzola, A. J., 318
Fichter, H. L., 39, 45, 362, 396, 397, 401
Fidelman, J. G., 396, 401
Fiedler, F., 99
Firestine, J. C., 166, 189
Fishaber, M. H., 132
Fisheden, R. B., 133

Fisher, E., 400
Fisher, J. R., 44
Fisher, L., 308
Fletcher, A. E., 45
Forbes, G. S., 175, 191
Fordyce, C. R., 138, 155
Foris, P. L., 398
Formstecher, F., 16, 41
Forster, R. B., 399
Forty, A. J., 17, 41
Fowler, W. F., 133
Fox, R. E., 400
Frahm, E. D. G., 310
Francis, F. G., 419
Frangialli & Cie., 313
Frangialli, P., 268, 315
Frankenburger, F., 41, 397
Franke, R., 208, 309, 310, 315
Franke, R. H., 298, 300, 317, 318, 319
Franklin, J. L., 189
Frantz, F. H., 260, 312, 313
Frederick, J. E., 297, 317, 318
Frei, E. H., 399
Freundorfer, R., 66, 100, 132, 165, 189
Freundorfer, T., 132
Frey, H. M., 170, 190
Fridman, V. M., 320
Friedland, B., 313
Friedlander, H. Z., 191
Friedman, J. S., 400
Fritsche, R., 45
Fritz, G., 314
Frölich, A., 393, 400, 401
Frost, A. V., 101
Frost, F. F., 100
Frost, F. H., 134, 136
Fruth, H. F., 131
Fuchs, W., 40, 45
Fuchsman, C. H., 396
Fujiishi, M., 325, 354
Fujiyama, C., 35, 44
Fukushimo, N., 308

Galashin, E. A., 101
Galinsky, A., 70, 101
Games, A., 410, 418
Garrison, A. D., 399
Gaspar, B., 401

Gavlin, G., 308
Gay, E. H., 318
Gees, C. F., 127, 135
Geis, G., 189
Geis, R., 189
General Aniline & Film Corp., 193, 259, 312, 315, 318, 319
Georges, A. P., 155
Gerhart, H. L., 190
Gevaert Photo Producten, N. V., 108, 193, 418, 419
Gibson, J. H., 132
Giebel, J., 41
Gilman, P. B., 16, 40, 41
Ginther, R. J., 42, 43
Giorgini, N. L., 419
Gipp, N. K., 308
Glass, D. B., 309
Glavin, R. E., 316
Glos, M., 311, 314, 357, 404, 416, 417
Glushko, V. D., 135
Goeij, H. J. A. de, 108, 132
Gold, R. M., 36, 45
Goodchild, E. H., 313
Goodeve, C. F., 199, 308
Goodman, R. C., 312
Goodyear, G. H., 29, 36, 43, 44, 45
Gordon, J. T., 157
Gordon, W., 416
Gorodnitzky, M. A., 93, 102
Goto, H., 313
Gottfried, C., 42
Gould, J. H., 154
Gramlich, C., 355
Grant Jr., E. A., 416, 417, 418
Green, A. G., 250, 311
Green, B. K., 400
Green, L. P., 89, 102
Gregory, V. L., 134
Greig, H. G., 261, 313, 314
Greiner, A. F., 100
Gresham, D. C., 131
Gretener, E., 45
Griess, P., 194
Grieshaber, E. W., 404, 416, 418, 419
Griffith, J. S., 134
Griggs, W. H., 116, 133
Groak, J., 409, 418
Grumbine, A. W., 132

Gulko, A. G., 418
Gumbinner, R., 133, 327, 355

Haack, N. H., 316
Haag, D. J., 417
Haber, F., 190
Haehnel, W., 100
Haigh, A., 134
Haining, F. W., 313
Halden, J. G. B., 311, 312
Hall, M. W., 355
Hall, W. P., 43
Hallam, C. D., 134
Halmos, C., 290, 317, 394, 401
Halperin, B. I., 278, 316, 356
Ham, G. P., 43, 44, 45
Hamill, W. H., 192
Hamilton, M. H., 135
Hamilton, W. P., 397, 401
Hammett, L. P., 218, 310
Hammond, G. S., 191
Hanel, L., 399
Hannay, N. B., 40
Hansman, J. F., 133
Hanson, H. H., 43
Hantzsch, A., 315
Harding, S. C. & P., Ltd., 45, 314
Hardwick, R., 399
Hardy, A. C., 68, 96, 100, 102
Hardy, G., 181, 192
Harper, L. R., 44
Harris-Intertype Corp., 100
Harris, L., 377, 397, 398
Harrison, A. P., 64, 100
Hartsuch, P. J., 121
Hassler, G. L., 312
Hatchard, C. J., 26, 43
Hauberrisser, G., 92, 102
Hauser, C. R., 217, 310
Hauser, J., 400
Hausmann, E. A., 134
Havemann, R., 400
Haward, R. N., 191
Hawksworth, J., 319
Haydn, H., 409, 418
Hecht, G. H., 40
Heerma, J., 170, 173, 190
Heiart, R. B., 189
Heidt, L. J., 175, 191

Heigl, A., 101
Heiligman-Rim, R., 400
Heiss, H., 356
Helfrich, J., 132
Hempling, H., 319
Henrici, A., 397
Henrici, F., 101
Hensel, A., 155
Hepher, M., 332, 354, 355, 356
Herberts, K. & Co., 101
Herch, S. L., 41
Herlinger, H. V., 138, 155
Herrick, C. E., 278, 290, 302, 306, 310, 312, 313, 314, 315, 316, 317, 319, 320, 329, 354, 355, 356
Herrmann, W. O., 100
Herschel, Sir John, 28, 410
Hessert, K., 312
Hickman, K. C. D., 43, 416
Hills, H. C., 314
Hiltz, A. A., 193
Hinkel, G. A., 36, 45
Hinman, W. M., 44, 133, 308, 317
Hirshberg, Y., 400
Hislop, W. B., 99, 132
Hislop, W. J. C., 132
Hnatek, A., 27, 31, 43, 44
Hodgins, G. R., 354, 355
Hodgkins, G. R., 134
Hodgson, H. H., 217, 310, 315
Hoffmann, K., 308
Hofmester, F., 99
Holden, J., 43, 44
Holland, R. S., 408, 417
Hollmann, W. G., 133
Holmes, Jr., E. O., 397
Holsapple, H. T., 135
Hooff, G. O't., 94, 102
Hoover, K. S., 419
Hoover, S. R., 59, 99, 101
Hopkins, C. W., 132
Horio, M., 308
Horizons, Inc., 396, 397
Hörner, H., 66, 100, 165, 189
Horning, H., 134
Houck, R. C., 60, 70, 99
Houtman, H. J., 315
Howard, E. G., 177, 191, 417
Howard, H. L., 53, 89, 99, 102

Howe, G. T., 109, 132
Howk, B. W., 188
Hruby, J., 313
Hückel, W., 311
Hudson, F. L., 154
Hudson, H., 117, 133
Hudson, J. H., 40, 154
Huebner, W. C., 134
Hughes, L., 132
Hunt, C. C., 356
Hunt, H. G., 320
Hunt, M., 191
Hurlbut, G. K., 312
Hurley, D. R., 419
Hutgens, K. M., 309, 312, 317, 320
Husch, H. P., 45

Igler, E. J., 404, 416
Ilford, Ltd., 417
Inami, A., 141, 155
Ingraham, J. N., 180, 192
Inskip, H. K., 191
International Business Machine Corp., 316
Itek Corp., 419
Iversen, K. M., 132
Ives, F. E., 101

Jacobs, F., 320
Jacobson, K., 94, 102
Jacobson, R. A., 188
Jacobus, D. D., 213, 309
Jahn, F. P., 176, 191
Jahoda, E., 31, 43, 44, 298, 318
James, R. W., 316, 416
Janda, A., 313
Janet, D. J., Jr., 133
Jankowski, F. P., 133
Jaspert, W. P., 132
Jennings, A. B., 164, 188
Jensen, E. V., 181, 192
Jerchel, D., 400
Jewett, C. L., 354, 355
John, R., 92, 102
Johnson, D. H., 191
Johnson, K. S., 260, 313
Johnston, D., 213, 309
Jones, D. G., 154
Jones, R. W., 132

Jonker, H., 45, 315, 316
Jorgensen, G. W., 74, 100, 101, 102
Jurisch, M. J., 133

Kahn, E. A., 317
Kalle, A. G., 133, 134, 139, 155, 202, 249, 252, 306, 309, 312, 314, 317, 354, 355, 356, 404, 409, 416, 418
Kallock, W. F., 416
Kalvar Corp., 281, 316
Kaminsky, J., 377, 397, 398
Karanka, S., 43
Karpov, I. K., 397
Kashiwabara, T. T., 314
Kato, S., 398
Kaulen, R., 132
Kaupp, W. O., 134
Kawasaki, M., 20, 31, 41, 44
Kay, R. H., 316
Kazimin, S. D., 135
Kazitsyna, L. A., 308
Keel, G. I., 113, 133
Keil, H. L., 99
Keilich, K. H., 96, 102
Keller, A., 135
Kemmerlich, W. E., 308
Kendall, F. E., 156
Kendall, J. D., 314, 417
Kenyon, W. O., 135
Kern, R. J., 189, 190
Kerr, R. W., 64, 100
Kerutskite, M. K., 94, 102
Kessels, F. A. H., 310, 312, 313
Keuffel & Esser Co., 326
Keuning, K. J., 315, 316
Keys, R. T., 191
Kharasch, M. S., 181, 192
Kidd, N. A., 41
Kienast, J. F., 31, 38, 44, 45
Kienle, R. H., 249, 263, 308
Kikuchi, Y., 43
Kimble, D. G., 419
Klaassens, K. H., 315
Klein, E., 277, 316
Klič, K. V., 47
Klick, C. C., 43
Klimkowski, R. J., 313, 314, 317
Klimova, V. A., 308
Kline, R. J., 419

Kmetz, E. W., 133
Knaggs, J., 99
Koch Processes, Ltd., 136
Koch, R. W., 73, 77, 80, 101
Kockeshkov, K. A., 308
Kodak A. G., 396
Kodak, Ltd., 316, 355
Kodak-Pathé, 41, 316, 396
Kögel, G., 28, 43, 251, 252, 295, 311, 321, 322, 354, 394, 401
Köhler, T., 135
Koizumi, I. M., 193
Koizumi, M., 398
Kolthoff, I. M., 190
Korn, A. H., 59, 99, 101
Kortum, G., 399
Kortum-Seiler, M., 399
Kosalek, J. F., 318
Kosar, J., 39, 45, 313, 314, 316, 320
Kosche, H., 319
Kosuge, T., 308
Kotz, A. R., 419
Kreidl, N. J., 42
Krell, O. E., 135
Krieger, W., 252, 268, 294, 295, 300, 309, 310, 311, 314, 317, 318, 319, 354
Krohe, W., 100, 134
Krohn, I. T., 193
Krueger, J. W., 314
Kubo, K., 314, 319
Kuhn, R., 400
Kühne, W., 319
Kuhrmayer, C. A., 416, 419
Kundshi, B., 399
Kunimoto, Y., 308, 318
Küntzel, A., 101
Kürsten, R., 25, 155
Kuwayama, S., 42
Kwech, R. E., 45
Kyte, D. J., 132

Laage, E., 140, 155
Labes, M. M., 192
Lambert, G. R., 312
Lambert, J. L., 125
Land, E., 265, 314
Landau, M. A., 356

Landau, R., 202, 249, 268, 298, 305, 315, 318, 320
Lantz, O. D., 44
Lappala, L. L., 103, 131
Laplace, G., 313
Larson, G. W., 354
Lasareff, P., 401
Lässig, W., 370, 397
Lawton, W. R., 313, 416, 417
Lazar, N., 42
Lebedenko, N., 101
Lecher, H. Z., 315
Lee, J., 43
Leeds, W. A., 133
Leekley, R. M., 128, 135, 157, 189
Leermakers, J. A., 16, 40, 176, 191
Le Fevre, R. J. W., 308
Lehfeldt, A., 155
Lehmann, E., 68, 309
Leighton, G. W., 45
Leighton, P. A., 155
Lendrat, E. G., 193
Leonard, R. F., 355
Leonen, B. H. M., 312
Lerner, H. H., 99
Leubner, G. W., 155, 156
Leuch, W. P., 45, 213, 309, 312, 313, 314, 320
Levinos, S., 179, 181, 182, 187, 190, 191, 192, 193
Levkoev, I. I., 320
Levy, M., 20, 41
Lewis, E. S., 315
Lewis, F. M., 177, 191
Lewis, J. M., 398
Liesegang, R. E., 75, 101
Lifschitz, I., 397
Light, W. A., 412, 418
Limmer, F., 400
Lind, E., 354, 412, 417, 418
Lindemeyer, R. B., 316
Lindquist, L. C., 157
Lindquist, R. M., 314, 316
Lindsey, R. V., 180, 192
Lippert, A. L., 43
Lithographic Technical Foundation, 89, 121, 353
Lithoplate, Inc., 134, 355
Lloyd, D. J., 99

Lobel, L., 92, 102
Loeffer, K. O., 399
Loening, E. E., 131
Logetronics, Inc., 400
Lohse, J. M., 189
Longdon, W., 313
Lopez, E. F., 313
Lothian, G. F., 399
Löwenthal, H., 68, 101
Lucius, M., 308
Luckey, G. W., 192
Lucy, F. A., 155
Luczak, M., 82, 101
Lumiere, A., 315
Lumiere, L., 86, 101, 288, 315, 317
Lumpkin, H. E., 189
Lupo, Jr., J. M., 63, 99
Lyman, H. T., 156
Lytle, D. B., 135

MacDonald, W. W., 41, 132
MacDonnel, L. R., 134
McCavley, C. E., 192
McCloskey, A. C., 43
McDonald, C. C., 190
McGavin, S., 99
McGraw, W. J., 189
McHugh, J. F., 419
McKnight, Jr. G. S., 130, 136
McLeish, W. L., 154
McMahon, H. O., 316
McNancy, J. T., 412, 418
McQuain, D. B., 400
McQueen, D. M., 396

Mache, G., 418
Maguire, R. J., 319
Maier, W., 311
Maillet, G., 92, 102
Mallison, H., 399
Mallory, F. B., 157
Mally, J. P., 336, 356
Malm, C. J., 138, 155
Manly, T., 49
Manning, A. B., 99
Marckwald, W., 399
Margerum, J. D., 399
Marks, E. C., 308
Marron, T. U., 314, 329, 355, 419

Marsden, E., 315
Martienssen, W., 13, 40
Martin, E. L., 165, 188 189
Martinez, M., 39, 45
Martinson, L. E., 133, 156
Marvel, C. S., 191, 193
Mason, E. N., 43, 213, 309
Mason, E. N. & Sons, Ltd., 43
Master Etching Machine Co., 131
Mastroianni, E. G., 312
Mathai, K. G., 43
Matheson, M. S., 177, 191
Matsumoto, S., 400
Maurer, K., 42, 70, 99
Maurer, R. D., 101
Maxcy, W. J., 319
Mayer, I. H., 68, 100
Mazanek, J. B., 130, 136
Mecherly, P. A., 310
Medalia, A. I., 190
Medved, D. B., 381, 399
Meigs, F. M., 134
Meisling, A. A., 70, 101
Meissner, W. L., 409, 418
Mellan, I., 327, 354, 355
Mellon, E. F., 59, 99, 101
Melnikov, N. W., 308
Melville, H. W., 192
Merkel, J. R., 192
Merrill, S. H., 147, 156, 157, 356
Mertle, J. S., 127, 132, 135
Mester, L., 317
Metz, F. I., 399
Michaelsen, J. D. 316
Michiels, M. J. S., 156
Mie, G., 42
Mihajlov, V. S., 193
Mikhalchenko, G. A., 397
Milborne, D. S., 36, 45
Miles, G. W., 44
Millard, F. W., 177, 191
Miller, A., 100
Miller, C. S., 403, 416, 419
Miller, H., 135
Miller, J. W., 134
Miller, L. J., 399
Miller, R. A., 417
Miller, R. E., 400, 409, 416, 418
Millich, F., 400

Milupo Jr., J., 100
Milyutinskaya, R. I., 192
Minnesota Mining and Manufacturing
   Co., 259, 313, 326, 404, 414, 419
Minsk, L. M., 131, 155, 156
Mittag, R., 319
Miyake, G., 42
Miyama Hajime, 191, 193
Miyashiro, J. J., 354
Mizuta, K., 134
Mizutani, Y., 193
Mochel, W. E., 188
Mohnhaupt, D. F. A., 416
Möler, K., 356
Monsen, G. L., 132
Moore, L. P., 43, 45
Moore, R. G. D., 204, 309, 355
Moore, W. M., 157
Moraw, R., 199, 219, 308
Morgan, C. R., 277, 316
Morgan, D. D., 157
Morgan, J. F., 311
Morgan, J. V., 41
Moritomo, K., 141, 155
Morrison, M., 313, 416
Mortimer, E. F., 50
Mosher, H. S., 399
Moskowitz, M. L., 355
Mounier, D., 317
Moureu, C., 294, 317
Mudrovčič, M., 192, 401
Mueller, F. W. H., 181, 182, 187, 190,
   191, 192, 193, 409
Mukaibo, T., 33, 44
Mullen, J. B., 312
Mullen, W. G., 43, 100, 136
Müller, R., 40, 418
Munder, J., 199, 219, 308, 356, 412,
   418
Murck, K., 133
Murray, A., 138, 141, 155, 156, 171,
   190, 418
Murray, H. D., 33, 44, 300, 309, 313,
   317, 318, 319
Murray, J. J., 84, 101, 132, 155, 156
Murray, M. H., 157
Mustafa, A., 139, 155

Nadeau, G. F., 135

Nagae, T., 15, 40
Nagamine, Y., 319
Nagdasar'yan, K. W., 192
Nagy, D. de, 130, 136
Nakagawa, Y., 196, 308, 318
Nakamura, N., 41
Nametkin, S. S., 308
Narasimhaswami, M. V., 399
National Cash Register Co., 190, 400, 406, 417
Neblette, C. B., 45
Nelson, H. H., 419
Nesmeyanov, A. N., 308
Neth, F. T., 316
Neuenhaus, H., 251, 295, 311
Neugebauer, W., 43, 117, 133, 155, 156, 157, 191, 263, 309, 314, 318, 328, 336, 352, 354, 355, 356, 357, 418
Neulipa, G. m. b. H., 313
Neuman, D. A., 131, 404, 416, 417
Neumann, F. W., 310, 311, 318
Neuroth, H., 315
New Jersey Zinc Company, 121
Newland, J. P., 99
Newman, A. L., 313
Newman, D. A., 100, 130, 136, 417, 419
Newman, D. J., 418
Nickerson, W. J., 192
Nicole, R., 313
Nièpce, J. N., 104, 137
Nieset, R. T., 280, 316
Nissl, F., 15, 40
Norman, D. J., 43, 213, 309, 313, 319
North, A. C. T., 99
Norton, C. A., 412, 419
Notley, N. T., 164, 188
Novak, S., 320
Nozoki, S., 142, 156

Obereigner, B., 354
O'Brien, Jr. B., 71, 73, 101
Ogden, F. F., 396
Olson, A. R., 154
O'Mara, E. A., 419
Omoto, R., 28, 43
Ono, K., 44
Oransky, R. L., 130, 136

Oriental Photo Industr. Co., 317
Orton, K. J. P., 308
O'Shaughnessy, M. T., 191
Osinski, E. D., 136
Osswald, D., 134, 356
Oster, G., 94, 102, 139, 155, 175, 179, 183, 184, 185, 191, 192, 193, 400
Oster, G. K., 94, 102, 179, 185, 191, 193
Ostlie, D. A., 416
Ostromislensky, I. I., 399
Ostwald, U., 128, 135
Otsu, T., 41
Overberger, C. G., 191
Owen, R., 403, 416, 417
Owens, J., 170, 173, 190
Oxford Paper Co., 135, 136
Ozalid Co., Ltd., 298, 305, 311, 312, 317, 418

Pakovich, I. A., 134
Paquin, L. J., 130, 136
Park, G. S., 190
Parker, C. A., 26, 43, 400
Parker, G. T., 309
Parker, R. B., 316
Parry, E., 299, 319
Partington, J. R., 102
Passailaigue, P., 399
Patat, F., 176, 191
Paterson, R. F., 132
Patterson, G. D., 41
Patterson, L. L., 131
Pauling, L., 40, 59, 99
Pedersen, C. J., 398
Pedlow, G. W., 310
Pelletier, S. W., 154
Pepe, L., 130, 136
Perikov, V. M., 45
Perkins, G. H., 130, 135, 136
Perrin, F. H., 68, 96, 100, 102
Peters, R. A., 17, 41
Peterson, E. J., 419
Peterson, M. L., 190
Peterson, W. D., 216, 263, 299, 307, 309, 310, 316, 318
Petrov, V. P., 320
Pfaff, M. E., 417
Pfoertner, K., 380, 398

Philips Company, 272
Philips Lamps Ltd., 354
Philips, N. V., 315, 316, 418
Philips, H., 99
Philpot, G. A., 156
Photo-Engraver's Research, Inc., 106
Pietsch, H., 400
Piper, C. W., 50
Plambeck, Jr. L., 161, 188
Pohl, R. W., 13, 40
Pointevin, A. L., 47, 50
Polgar, A., 290, 317, 394, 401
Polychrome Corp., 134
Ponton, S. M., 46
Pop, G., 313
Popovitski, A., 67, 100
Porter, A. S., 357
Porter, G. B., 43
Potapov, V. D., 133
Poudrier, D. C., 318
Pouradier, J., 61, 99
Powell, D. W., 43
Powers, A. J., 336, 356
Powers Chemco Inc., 100
Pratti, G., 185, 193
Prichard, G. O., 177, 191
Prichard, H. O., 177, 191
Pries, L. L., 99, 134
Printing, Packaging and Allied Trades
  Research Assoc., The, 100
Printy, J. O., 100, 319
Pruett, R. L., 43
Prüfer, H., 100
Pütter, R., 310

Quattrone, J. J., 417
Quoss, R. N., 417

Raaen, H. P., 190
Rabinowitch, E., 43
Raczynski, W. A., 417
Raek, M., 396
Ragan, R. O., 100
Raikhlin, V. S., 134
Rakos, M., 33, 44
Ramachanran, G. N., 99
Rampp, L., 316
Ramsperger, H. C., 175, 191
Rao, B. S. V. R., 399

Rao, E. L., 399
Rauner, F. J., 356, 418
Rauner, R. J., 156
Ravich, L. E., 307, 320
Ray, P. C., 399
Rebenstock, A., 123, 134, 191, 325,
  354, 356
Reboul, T. T., 42
Rechen, H. J. L., 397, 398
Reed, J. R., 312
Reed, R. F., 73, 86, 101, 132, 134
Regis, E. D., 308
Reichel, M. K., 117, 133, 272, 292,
  314, 315, 317, 318, 355
Reichert, J. S., 44
Reimann, P., 316
Reinhart, F., 42
Reiss, K., 356
Reitter, J. L., 418
Renfrew, M. M., 188
Reutov, O. A., 308
Reyes, Z., 314
Reynolds, A. P., 43, 135
Reynolds, G. A., 356
Reynolds, K., 314, 417
Rice, F. O., 176, 191
Rich, A., 99
Richard, L. E., 130, 136
Richards, G. N., 179, 191
Richards, L. M., 189, 190
Richey, G. T., 417
Richlin, I. M., 355
Richo Co. Ltd., 320
Richter, V., 96, 102
Riedel, L., 42
Rieger, P., 138, 155
Riess, K., 42
Rigley, J. T., 99
Rijssel van, T. W., 45
Rinke, H., 151, 156, 157
Ritter, W. T., 100
Ritzerfeld, G., 134, 397, 418, 419
Ritzerfeld, W., 134, 397, 418, 419
Roberts, H. L., 170, 190
Robertson, E. M., 155, 156, 335, 356,
  418
Robinson, P., 193
Robl, R., 397
Roblin, F., 189

Rodgers, J. L., 419
Roederer, E., 41
Roehrich, C., 101
Rogers, M. C., 132
Rohm and Haas Company, 165, 189
Röhrich, K., 318
Roman, P. A., 417
Romer, W., 82, 101
Roncken, H. W. H. M., 257, 309
Rooksby, H. P., 42
Rosati, I. F., 356, 418
Roscow, M., 396
Rosenberger, H. M., 329, 355
Rosenthal, F., 416
Roshkind, A. I., 419
Ross, H. G., 43
Rossell, R. E., 73, 77, 80, 101
Rossi, C., 45
Rössler, G., 41
Roth, C. B., 181, 187, 192, 193
Rotondo, R. J., 316
Rouse, E., 356
Rowell, G. S., 101
Royer, R. P., 313, 314, 317
Rubricius, F. I., 45
Ruff, O., 250, 311
Rupp, A. E., 133
Rupp, E., 101
Russell, J., 416
Russel, K. E., 189
Russel, R. B., 417
Rüst, E., 401
Rust, F. F., 190
Ruzicka, J., 107, 132
Ryskiewicz, E. E., 398
Rzmkowski, J., 43

Sachs, C. C., 181, 192
Sagura, J. J., 139, 155, 314, 334, 356, 359, 396, 417
Sahler, W., 407, 417, 418
Saito, E., 399
Sakurai, S., 309
Salvadori & Leperche, 313
Salzberg, H. K., 129, 136
Sanders, T. P. W., 257, 305, 309, 310, 312, 317, 319, 320
Sandford, R. S., 109, 132
Saner, W. R., 189

Santuppa, M., 190, 192
Sargent, D. E., 396
Saunders, K. H., 194, 307
Savitz, M. L., 157
Scanlan, R. J., 45
Schachowskoy, T., 101
Schaeffer, A., 314
Schäfer, W., 43, 318, 356
Scheibe, G., 399
Schellenberg, W., 148, 156, 157
Schenck, G. O., 192
Scherer, T., 356
Schiel, M., 100
Schieren, H. V., 45
Schleicher, L., 400, 416
Schlesinger, H., 311
Schloffer, F., 418
Schlotzhauer, A. T., 100, 404, 416, 417, 419
Schmidt, G. M. J., 399
Schmidt, J., 311
Schmidt, M. P., 28, 38, 43, 196, 201, 203, 208, 252, 261, 268, 295, 308, 309, 310, 311, 312, 313, 314, 315, 317, 318, 319, 323, 336, 354, 355, 356, 357, 401
Schmidt, R., 154
Schmidt, W. A., 396
Schmitz, H., 319
Schoemaker, C. J., 404, 416
Schoen, A., 17, 40, 41, 45, 131, 316, 396
Schoen, M., 311
Schönberg, A., 139, 155
Schönerer, F., 100
Schreiver, S. B., 99
Schröter, G. A., 138, 155
Schröter, W., 45, 199, 308
Schuler, F. W., 42, 43
Schuler, R. H., 191
Schulman, J. H., 42, 43
Schulte, J. W., 398
Schulze, H., 20, 41
Schwab, H., 400
Schwab, M., 15, 40
Schwartzchild, K., 5
Schwarz, G. S., 134
Schwarz, R., 43

Schwerin, A. K., 134, 177, 190, 191, 192, 193
Scott, H., 192
Sease, V. B., 319
Seaward, J. A., 419
Sedgwick, R., 419
Seifert, W. A., 316
Seliger, H. H., 43
Senefelder, A., 128
Senier, A., 399
Senti, F. R., 63, 99
Servoss, W. C., 399
Seven, R. P., 354
Severson, G. M., 64, 100
Seyewitz, A., 86, 101, 308, 314, 317
Seymour, M. W., 94, 100, 102
Shalit, H., 191
Shapiro, R., 128, 135
Sharp, F. W., 91, 102, 356
Shaw, W. G., 399
Sheberstov, V. I., 41
Shepheard, F. G. J., 399
Shepherd, J. V. R., 129, 136
Sheppard, S. E., 17, 18, 21, 40, 41, 42, 60, 70, 99, 117, 133
Sher, B. C., 131
Sherer, A. I., 107, 132
Shiraeff, D. A., 320
Shklover, F. Ya., 73, 101
Shoemaker, C. J., 314
Shoen, M., 250
Sickman, D. V., 175, 191
Siefken, W., 156
Silver, J. L., 181, 192
Simard, R. G., 377, 398
Simons, F. L., 129, 136
Simpson, W., 177, 191
Sims, J. C., Jr., 412, 419
Sincius, J. A., 190
Singh, B. K., 400
Singh, G., 399
Sisley, W. D., 170, 190
Sites, B. L., 193
Skiles, B. F., 398
Slater, B. J., 99
Slifkin, S. C., 40, 204, 298, 306, 307, 309, 310, 311, 313, 317, 318, 319, 320
Slimowicz, C. E., 310, 317

Smethurst, P. C., 45, 69, 70, 99, 101, 131
Smets, G., 186, 193
Smiles, S., 399
Smith, A. C., 147, 156, 157
Smith, D. A., 147, 156
Smith, G. W., 171, 190, 307, 320
Smith, H. A., 416
Smith, H. J., 393, 400
Smith, H. L., 400
Smith, J. G., 155, 156
Smith, K., 99, 131
Soga, N., 42
Sonderman, H. A., 102
Sorensen, D. P., 417
Sorensen, R. L., 189
Sorkin, J. L., 190
Sorrin, J. L., 319
Souers, C., 399
Spechler, D. S., 114, 133, 320
Spencer, D. A., 40
Spietschka, W., 318
Sponsler, O. L., 99
Sporer, A. H., 371, 397
Sprague, P. W., 397
Sprague, R. H., 39, 45, 362, 363, 396, 397, 398, 401, 407, 417
Spröngerts, E. W., 311, 318
Sprung, J. A., 396
Staehle, H. C., 131, 132, 133, 135, 136, 356, 401
Stahlhofen, P., 357
Staib Jr., L. A., 43, 416
Stanley, L. N., 309, 310, 311, 317, 318
Stanton, G. W., 170, 173, 190
Starck, C. B., 135
Stark, H. M., 41
Starostka, B., 82, 101
Starotin, L., 307
Stegonwalner, H., 312
Stein, V., 250, 311
Steinberger, F. K., 155
Steinert, H., 397
Stenger, E., 308
Steppan, H., 356
Stermitz, F. R., 157
Stewart, J. A., 398
Stiasny, E., 101
Stiehler, H., 69, 70, 101

Stobbe, H., 140, 155, 399
Stockmayer, W. H., 171, 190
Stoermer, R., 140, 155
Stookey, S. D., 22, 24, 25, 42, 43, 400
Stötzer, K., 68, 100
Straley, J. M., 308, 310, 311
Straub, E., 125, 134
Strauss, J., 132
Strauss, V., 131
Straw, D., 300, 306, 311, 319, 320
Streck, C., 317
Strecker, O., 124, 134
Streigh, P. B., 313
Stumpf, H. R., 356
Suchow, L., 41, 399
Suhr, H., 315
Sulich, J., 310, 313, 317, 318
Sullivan, H. H., 312
Sullivan, W. L., 44, 312
Sun, K. H., 42
Sury, J., 99
Süs, O., 38, 43, 44, 191, 261, 263, 266,
    309, 310, 311, 313, 314, 318, 325,
    336, 342, 354, 355, 356, 357, 417
Suttle, J. F., 398
Suzuki, M., 155
Suzuki, S., 15, 32, 40, 43, 71, 101
Swain, C. G., 171, 190
Swann, Jr., S., 191
Swan, Sir J., 48
Swanton, P. C., 193
Swayze, H. E., 132
Sweet, N. J., 133
Swoboda, T. J., 419
Symmes, E. M., 48, 99
Symons, M. C. R., 13, 40

Takagaki, S., 100
Takahashi, Y., 41
Takei, K., 15, 40
Talât-Erben, M., 177, 191
Talbot, W. H. F., 47
Tamblyn, J. W., 386, 400
Tanenbaum, A., 313, 314, 317
Taniyama, M., 193
Tashiro, M., 42
Taylor, E. W., 136
Taylor, H. A., 176, 191
Taylor, J. E., 371, 397

Taylor, N. W., 416
Tebbs, C. E., 132
Tede, K., 44
Tendeloo, H. J. C., 396
Thiebaut, R. P. J. G., 156
Thiele, J., 330, 355
Thimann, M., 132
Thode, W., 110, 133
Thom, J. A. 41
Thoma, W., 151, 156, 157
Thomiszer, H. J., 264, 314
Thommes, G. A., 188
Thomsen, D. L., 417
Thomson, F. D., 400
Thurlow, J. F., 136
Tien, J. M., 418
Time, Inc., 154, 165, 189
Timmerman, R., 134
Tinker, J. F., 417
Tobolsky, A. V., 169, 189, 190, 191
Toland, W. C., 100, 129, 134, 135
Tomanek, M., 155, 156, 157, 309, 310,
    352, 356, 357
Tomoda, Y., 21, 31, 41, 42, 44
Toppet, S., 186, 193
Torday, J., 299, 319
Tordoff, M., 170, 190
Tranchant, J. F. P., 270, 315
Trant, R. F., 100
Trapp, O. D., 191
Tregay, J. L., 313
Tritton, F. J., 91, 102, 134
Trojan, E. J., 356
Trojan, T. J., 311, 317
Trump, F. O., 312
Tsujimura, S., 33, 44
Tsunoda, T., 142, 156, 325, 354
Tubbs, M. R., 41
Tulagin, V., 417
Tumanov, N. N., 45
Tupis, C. K., 154, 157
Turner, J. L. F., 196, 308
Tyrrell, A., 309, 320
Tzalmova, A., 399

Uchida, K., 398
Uhlig, F., 123, 134, 357
Ulanov, M. S., 133
Ulrich, H., 370, 397

Unkauf, H. C., 311, 318, 319
Unruh, C. C., 135, 139, 147, 149, 150, 155, 156, 157, 356
Urbach, O. R., 419
Urbancik, J. J., 397
Uri, N., 190, 192, 193
Urry, W. H., 181, 192
Usvi, Y., 43

Vahtra, U., 316
Valenta, E., 91, 102
Vallen, M. M. P., 36, 45, 317
van Allen, J. A., 141, 155, 314, 334, 335, 356, 359, 396, 417
van Arkel, A. E., 40, 101
van Dam, M., 416
van der Grinten, F., 313
van der Grinten, K., 317
van der Grinten, K. J. J., 319
van der Grinten, L., 255, 289, 294, 309, 312, 313, 317
van der Grinten L., Chem. Fabriek, 309, 311, 312, 313, 314, 318, 319
van der Grinten L. P. F., 317, 319
van der Meulen, P. A., 16, 40, 41
van der Weel, W. H., 416, 418
van Dormael, A., 311
van Dusen, C. H., 133, 134, 135
van Loon, A., 309, 312
van Rensen, J., 312
van Rhijn, M. M., 317
van Rhijn, W. J., 318, 319
van Rijssel, T. W., 315
Vanselow, W., 16, 17, 40, 41, 309
Varahalu, K., 399
Vareine, J., 156
Vaughn, H. C., 132
Vaughan, P. A., 41
Vaughan, W. E., 190
Venkataraman, K., 310
Vierling, O., 399
Vincent, A. M., 355
Vogel, A. M., 417
Von Glahn, W. H., 308, 309, 310, 311, 314, 317, 318
von Meister, F. W., 255, 312, 318
von Poser, G., 201, 289, 308, 309, 315, 317, 401

Wadhams, W. H., 92, 102
Wagner, C. A., 400
Wagner, E., 94, 102
Wagner, E. W., 100, 319
Wagner, F., 116, 133
Wagner, H. B., 400
Wagner, H. M., 332, 355, 356
Wahl, A., 101
Wainer, E., 362, 365, 369, 396, 397
Walling, C., 191
Walther, R. J., 400
Warburg, J. C., 70, 101
Wark, H. A., 417
Warkentin, J., 191
Warman, H., 36, 45
Warren Co., S. D., 418
Wartman, T. G., 415, 416, 419
Watanabe, A., 193
Watson, H. E., 399
Watter, O., 82, 86, 97, 101, 124, 125, 134
Wayrynen, R. E., 408, 417
Webb, W. W., 26, 43
Weber, K., 192
Wedel, E., 419
Weegar, R. P., 317, 318, 319
Wehran, H. J., 41
Weingarten, A., 102
Weiser, H. B., 399
Weiss, J., 190, 193
Weissberger, A., 309
Weissenberger, W., 102
Weisser, H. R., 330, 355
Welch, W. J., 292, 317, 318
Wells, A. A., 40
Welsh, F. E., 399
Wendt, B., 154, 393, 395, 400, 401
Wensley, C. G., 53, 99
Werner, G., 203, 213, 309, 311, 315, 355, 357
Werner, R. L., 308
West, R. B., 43, 45, 268, 314
West, W., 155, 156, 192
Westcott, W. B., 129, 135
Wettermark, G., 399
Wettlauffer, W., 309
Weyde, E., 17, 41, 409, 418
Weyl, W. A., 42
Wheatley, C. C. H., 394, 401

Wheatley, C. W. C., 394, 401
White, K. F., 329, 355
White, L. A., 84, 101, 132
Whitlock, D. E., 31, 44
Whyzmuzis, P. J., 134
Wilde, F. G., 312
Wilders, J. H. A., 305, 309, 310, 312, 318, 319
Wildi, B. S., 417
Wilford, S. P., 43
Wilhelm, E. J., 133
Williams, J. L. R., 156, 157
Williams, R. J., 43
Williams, R. R., Jr., 192
Wilson, W. O., 44
Wingert, L. E., 417
Wintgen, R., 68, 101
Winzer, H., 319
Wistar, R., 216, 310
Woitach, P. T., 329, 354, 355, 356
Wojciak, W., 17, 40, 41
Wojtczak, J., 14, 40
Wolf, H., 415, 419
Wolfe, J., 319
Wolfson, K., 109, 132, 419
Wood, C. S., 157
Wood, L. J., 199, 308
Wood, W. H., 100, 122, 133, 134, 135
Woodham, E., 313
Woodward, D. W., 188, 319

Woolford, R. G., 193
Workman, W. R., 413, 417, 419
Worthe, P., 102
Worthen, S. V., 136
Wotherspoon, N., 192
Wright, J. F., 131, 155
Wyman, G. M., 154
Wu, C. S., 191

Yackel, E. C., 133, 379, 398, 413, 419
Yaeger, L. L., 103, 131
Yagi, M., 42
Yamada, Y., 132
Yamamoto, H., 308, 313
Yamashita, S., 308
Yamatani, K., 308
Yutzy, H. C., 413, 419

Zahn, R., 294, 310, 317, 322, 354, 355
Zandstra, P. J., 308
Zechnall, A., 92, 102
Zemp, R. R., 355, 398
Zerbst, R., 99, 131
Ziehm, A., 102
Zimmermann, W., 397
Zindler, W., 43, 316
Zollinger, H., 194, 219, 263, 307, 310, 314
Zschimmer, E., 42

SUBJECT INDEX

Acenaphthenes, 352
Acetamide, 139, 295
3-Acetamidophenol, 220
Acetanilide-*p*-disulfoxide, 382
Acethracene, 139
Acetic acid, 14, 20, 31, 39, 120, 125, 279, 376, 379, 410
Acetoacetamides, 303
4-(Acetoacetamido)benzene sulfonamide, 242
N-(β-Acetoacetaminoethyl)acetoacetamide, 243
Acetoacetanilide, 242, 266, 303
Acetoacetic acid -α-aminopyridine, 243
Acetoacetic acid, derivatives of, 242
Acetoacetic acid benzamide, 243
Acetoacetic acid-*o*-methylanilide, 243
N,N'-(Acetoacetyliminodiethylene)-diacetoacetamide, 243
Acetoin, 162
Acetone, 138
Acetonitriles, 215, 241
N-Acetonyl-pyridinium chloride, 247
Acetophenones, 145
Acetylacetonitrile, 241
1-Acetylamido-2-naphthol-5-sulfonic acid, 235
Acetyl chloride, 180
Acetyl radicals, 160
Acid fuchsine cyanide, 372, 375
Acid green 16-cyanide, 376
Acid violet 6B cyanide, 372, 374

Acridine, 379
Acridine yellow, 16
Acridones, 335
Acriflavin, 16, 184, 186
Acrylamide, 170, 173, 174, 182, 184, 186, 187, 262
Acrylate resins, 119, 138, 154
Acrylic acid, 121, 166, 179, 184, 277, 325
Acrylic acid esters, 164, 165
Acrylonitrile, 119, 173, 177, 180, 184, 186, 277, 332
Acyl disulfides, 167
Acyloin ethers, 162
Adipic acid, 148, 332
Agar-agar, 14, 361
Albertype, 51
Albumin, 47, 53, 55, 62, 66, 122, 125, 372
Aldehydes, 113
Alginates, 122, 130
Aliphatic amine, 121
Alkali diazotates, 217
Alkali iodates, 369
Alkali iodides, 369
Alkali-metal bromates, 33
Alkali-metal citrates, 94
Alkali-metal dichromates, 82
Alkali-metal ferrocyanides, 29
Alkali-metal halides, 13
Alkali-metal hydroxides, 33
Alkali-metal nitrates, 36

439

Alkali-metal oxalates, 36
Alkali-metal oxides, 22
Alkali-metal periodates, 369
Alkali-metal phosphate, 29
Alkali-metal silicate, 121, 326
Alkaline-earth halides, 14
Alkaline-earth iodates, 369
Alkaline-earth iodides, 369
Alkaline-earth periodates, 369
Alkyd resin lacquer, 114
Alkylacrylate copolymers, 150
Alkyl amines, 379
α-Alkylbenzoin, 163
Alkyl disulfides, 167
Alkyl iodides, 180
Alkyl malonamates, 244
σ-Alkyl xanthene esters, 168
Allyl alcohol, 186
Allyl chloroformate, 180
1-Allyl-3-β-hydroxethyl-2-thiourea, 295
Allyl isothiocyanate, 15
Allylselenourea, 15
Allylthiourea, 15, 185, 186, 294, 393, 395
Allyl-trichloromethanesulfenate, 170
Alumina, 121, 297, 298
  dyes laked with, 48
Aluminum, 127
Aluminum acetate, 131, 264
Aluminum chloride, 130
Aluminum hydroxide, 122
Aluminum oxide, 24, 361, 381
Aluminum plates, 120, 121, 124, 126
Aluminum powder, 294
Aluminum salts, 34
Aluminum selenide, 187
Aluminum silicate, 298
Aluminum sodium silicate, 48
Aluminum stearate, 142, 328
Aluminum sulfate, 131
Aluminum sulfide, 187
Aluminum telluride, 187
Amino acids, 56
  sulfur-containing, 56
Aminoaldehydes, 166
1-(3-Aminobenzamido)-4-napthol, 234
1-(3-Aminobenzamido)-7-napthol, 234
2-(3-Aminobenzamido)-5-napthol, 234
2-(4-Aminobenzamido)-5-napthol, 234

2-(3-Aminobenzamido)-7-napthol, 234
2-(4-Aminobenzamido)-7-napthol, 234
p-Aminobenzene diazosulfonate, 266
o-Aminobenzenes, derivatives of, 196
o-Aminobenzene thiol, 168
3-(N-3'-Aminobenzoyl)aminophenol, 220
3-(N-4'-Aminobenzoyl)aminophenol, 220
2-Amino-1-carbazidobenzene, 278
4"-Amino-2" carboxy-1"-N-phenyl-4, 4'-diamino-1,1'-diphenyl methane, diazotized, 323
p-Aminodialkylanilines, diazo derivatives of, 195, 380
N-(4-Amino-2,5-dibutoxyphenyl)ethyl-carbamate, diazonium sulfate of, 213
4-Amino-2,5-diethoxybenzene diazonium chloride, 323
p-Aminodiethylaniline hydrochloride, 166
1,2-Aminodihydroxybenzenes, diazotized, 380
1,4-Aminodihydroxybenzenes, diazotized, 380
1,2-Aminodihydroxynapthalenes, diazotized, 380
1,4-Aminodihydroxynapthalenes, diazotized, 380
p,p'-Amino(N,N-dimethylaniline), 366
p-Aminodiphenylamine, diazotized, 179, 195, 210, 271, 321, 380
4-Aminodiphenyl-4'-diazonium chloride, 290
1-Amino-2,5-dipropyl-1,4'-methyldiphenyl sulfide, diazotized, 328
4-Amino-1-ethoxybenzene chloroacetate, 407
N-4'-Amino-3'-ethoxyphenyl-(1')-thiomorpholine, diazotized, 210
Aminohydroquinone diethyl ether, 407
1,2-Aminohydroxybenzenes, diazotized, 380
1,4-Aminohydroxybenzenes, diazotized, 380
Aminohydroxynapthalenes, 252
1,2-Aminohydroxynapthalenes, diazotized, 380

1,4-Aminohydroxynapthalenes, diazotized, 380

2-Amino-5-hydroxynaphthalene-7-sulphonic acid, 252, 340

1-Amino-8-hydroxynaphthalene-3,6-sulfonic acid, 252

2-Amino-5-hydroxynaphthalene-7-sulfonic acid, monourea, 236

2-Amino-6-methylbenzothiazole, 406

4-Amino-1 (N-methyl-6-naphthalenetetrahydride-1,2,3,4)-aminobenzene, diazotized, 323

4-Amino-2-methylsulfonamido-4'-dimethylaminoazobenzene, diazotized, 271

o-Aminonaphthols, diazo derivatives of, 195

Aminonaphthol sulfonic acid, 360

p-Amino-phenacyl chloride, 180

m-Aminophenol, 37, 260, 403

m-Aminophenol and cyanuric chloride, condensation product of, 221

Aminophenols, 251, 365

o-Aminophenols, diazo derivatives of, 195

o-Aminophenol hydrochloride, 407

p-Aminophenol hydrochloride, 183

3-(Aminophenylsulfonylamino)phenol, 220

1'-Amino-4'-piperidyl-3'-benzoyl-1-amino-8-hydroxynaphthalene-3,6-disulfonic acid, 252

5-Aminoresorcinol and cyanuric chloride, condensation product of, 230

Ammonia, 12, 16, 35, 79, 89, 104, 118, 121, 122, 217, 252, 253, 272, 275, 379, 411

anhydrous, 219, 259

Ammonium acetate, 131, 259

Ammonium aluminum sulfate, 122

Ammonium arabate, 125

Ammonium benzenediazosulfonate, 177

Ammonium bicarbonate, 259

Ammonium carbonate, 259, 260, 263

Ammonium chloride, 127, 297

Ammonium chromate, 53

Ammonium compounds, quaternary, 31, 149

Ammonium dichromate, 36, 48, 51, 53, 71, 82, 83, 86, 92, 93, 97, 114, 121, 122, 125, 165

Ammonium ferric oxalate, 31

Ammonium ferrous oxalate, 33

Ammonium formate, 131, 259, 260

Ammonium molybdate, 264, 273

Ammonium nitrate, 36, 92

Ammonium nitroferricyanide, 29

Ammonium oxalate, 16, 38, 275

Ammonium persulfate, 36, 106, 174

Ammonium salts, 139

Ammonium thiocyanate, 409

Ammonium tungstate, 273

Ammonium zirconyl carbonate, 121

Amylopectin, 64

Amylose, 64

Anethole, 393

Anhydroaldehyde-amino compounds, diazo derivatives of, 195

Aniline, 92, 363, 364

diazo derivatives of, 37, 196

Aniline hydrochloride, 92, 194

Anils, 382

p-Anisidine, diazosulfonate of, 270

Anisoin ethyl ether, 162

Anthracene, 138, 143, 380

9-Anthracene-aldehyde acetal, 138

Anthracenes, sym-meso-di-substituted, 139

9-Anthraldehyde, 145

Anthraquinone, 144, 163, 164, 361, 396

2,7-Anthraquinone disulfonate, 201, 321

Anthraquinone dyes, 151

Anthraquinone sulfonic acid, 15, 187

Anthraquinone-2-sulfonic acid, 139

Anthrone, 142, 143, 144

9,10-Anthrylene-dipropionic acid, 1, 6-hexanediol derivatives of, 139

Antifogging agents, 117, 118

Antihalation layer, 161

Antimony, 413

Antimony compounds, 23

Antimony oxide, 22, 386

Antiseptic, 62, 122

Arabic acid, 64

Arabinogalactan, 125

1-Arabinose, 64
Aralkyl disulfides, 167
Arginine, 59
Aromatic azides, 330
Aroyl disulfides, 167
Arsenic oxide, 386
Arsine, 12
Aryl azides, 330
Aryl diazonium chlorides, 178, 194
Aryl diazosulfonates, 266, 269–270,
    274, 278, 291
Aryl diazosulfones, 267, 359
Aryl disulfides, 167
Aryl disulfinate, 267
Ascorbic acid, 14, 185, 186, 302
Asphaltum, 124
Auramine, 70, 379
Auramine G, 388
Auramine O, 379, 388
Aurin cyanide, 373
Autocoupling, 267
Autooxidation, 271
Avogadro's number, 2
4a-Azanaphthalenes, 335
Azides, organic, 330
4-Azidobenzalacetophenone-2-sulfonic
    acid, 331
2,6-di-(4'-Azidobenzal)-4-methylcyclo-
    hexanone, 335
1,2-di (4-Azidocinnamoyloxy)-ethane,
    332
Azido compounds, 113, 148, 330, 359
4'-Azido-4-azido-benzalacetophenone-2-
    sulphonic acid, 331
6-Azido-2-(4-Azidostyryl) benzimida-
    zole, 332
Azidobenzoic acid anhydride, 335
p-Azidobenzophenone, 332
p-Azidodiphenylamine carboxylic acid,
    330
4-Azido-β-methylstyrene-2-sulfonic acid
    sodium salt, 113
2-Azido-1,4-naphthalenedibenzenesul-
    fonamide, 333
β-(4-Azidophenoxy)ethanol, 335
2-(4'-Azidophenyl)acenaphthimidazole,
    334
2-(4'-Azidophenyl)-5(or 6)-methylben-
    zimidazole, 333

2-(4'-Azido-phenyl)-5-methyl-benzimi-
    dazole, 350
2-(4"-Azidophenyl)naptho-1',2' : 4,5-
    imidazole, 334
2-(4'-Azidophenyl)-naphtho-[1',2',4,5]-
    imidazole, 350
2-(4'-Azidophenyl)-6-phenylbenzimida-
    zole, 333
Azidophthalic acid anhydride, 335
3-Azidophthalic anhydride, 278
4-Azidophthalic anhydride, 278
Azido polymers, 335
Azido styrylarylazides, 330
Azidostyrylketones, 330
Azine dyes, 393
Azobenzene, 194
4-Azo-bis-cyanopentanoic acid, 178
1-Azo-bis-1-cyclohexanecarbonitrile,
    177, 178
α,α'-Azo-bis-isobutyronitrile, 177, 178
2-Azo-bis-2-methylbutyronitrile, 177,
    178
2-Azo-bis-2-methylheptonitrile, 178
2-Azo-bis-propane, 177, 178
2-Azo-bis-propionitrile, 178
Azo compounds, 137, 158
    as photopolymerization initiators,
    158, 175–180
Azo coupling, 215, 358
Azo dye formation, 215
Azo dye image, 411
Azo dyes, 48, 119, 215, 250, 358
Azomethane, photolytic decomposi-
    tion of, 175, 176
Azomethine dyes, 359
Azonitriles, 176
Azothioethers, heterocyclic, 177

Barbituric acid, 405
Barium hydroxide, 124, 265
Barium iodide, 14
Barium oxide, 22
Barium silicate, 24
Barium sulfate, 298
Baryta-coated papers, 298
Bentonite, 29
Benzalacetophenone, 149
Benzaldehyde, 145, 149, 150, 165
Benzaldehyde phenylhydrazone, 381

1,2-Benzanthraquinone, 144
2,3-Benzanthraquinone, 144, 163
1,9-Benzanthrone, 144
Benzanthrones, 396
Benzene, 138
1,3-Benzene disulfonyl chloride, 379
Benzene sulfonyl bromide, 379
Benzene sulfonyl chloride, 181
Benzil, 145, 162, 165
Benzil phenyl osazone, 381
Benzimidazole hydrochloride, 303
Benzoic acid, 379
Benzoin, 139, 161, 162, 165
Benzoin ethyl ether, 162
Benzoin methyl ether, 161, 162, 167
Benzoin propyl ether, 162
Benzophenone, 139, 145, 165, 304, 376
Benzophenone-N-[naphthoquinone-(1,
2)-diazide-(2)-4-sulfonyl]-hydra-
zine, 344
Benzoquinone, 144
Benzoquinone-(1,2)-diazide-(2)-4-
chlor-6(N-β-naphthyl)-sulfonamide,
349
Benzoquinone-(1,2)-diazide-(2)-4-(N-
ethyl-N-β-naphthyl)-sulfonamide,
348
Benzoquinone-(1,2)-diazide-(2)-4-sul-
fonic acid phenyl ester, 347
Benzoquinone-(1,4)-diazide-(4)-2-sul-
fonic acid-β-naphthylamide, 337
Benzotriazole, 117
Benzoylacenaphthenes, 142
1-Benzoylamino-4-amino-2,5-diethyl-
benzene, 407
4-Benzoylamino-2,5-diethoxyaniline, diazotized, 270
1-Benzoylamino-2,5-diethoxy-4-diazo-
benzene-N-sulfonic acid, 270
4-Benzoyl-amino-2,5-diethoxybenzene
diazonium chloride, 277
Benzoyl benzoate, 380
Benzoylguanide, 298
2-Benzoylmethylene-1-methyl-β-naph-
thothiazoline, 147, 335
N-Benzoyl-N'-[naphthoquinone-(1,2)-
diazide-(2)-5-sulfonyl]-hydrazide,
343
Benzoyl peroxide, 170, 171, 172

Benzyl alcohol, 376
α-Benzylbenzoin, 163
Benzyldithiocarbamic acid, 410
2,2'-Benzylidene-bis(5,5-dimethyl-1,3-
cyclohexanedione), 241
p,p'-Benzylidenebis(N,N-dimethylani-
line), 362
Beta-rays, 22
Benzyl isocyanate, 183
Benzyl salicylate, 377
Biguanide, 270, 271
Bimetallic plates, 127–128
4,4'-Biphenyl diamine, 362
N,N'-Bis(4-aminophenyl)bis-trimethy-
lenediamine, tetrazo compounds
of, 204
N,N'-Bis(4-aminophenyl) dimethylene-
diamine, tetrazo compounds of,
204
N,N'-Bis(4-aminophenyl)piperazine, tetrazo compounds of, 204
4,4'-Bis-naphthoquinone-(1'',4'')diazide-
(4'')-2''-(sulfonyl-amino)-diphenyl-
2,2'-disulfonic acid, 341
Bis-amide of benzoquinone-(1,4)-dia-
zide-(4)-2-carboxylic acid, 340
Bis-[n-(butylmethyl)thiocarbanyl] sulfide, 169
Bis-(carbethoxymethyl) ester of 1,4-
piperazine-bis-(carbodithoic acid),
168
Bis-[di-(β-chloroethyl)thiocarbanyl] sulfide, 169
1,5-Bis-(2,5-diethoxy-4-amino-phenyl-
thio)pentane, 213
Bis-(2,4-dihydroxyphenyl sulfoxide),
231
4,4'-Bis-dimethylamino-2''-chlorotriphe-
nylacetonitrile, 375
N,N'-Bis-1,2-ethyleneisophthalimide,
405
N,N'-Bis-furfuryl dithiooxamide, 410
N,N'-Bis-(5-hydroxy-7-sulfonic acid
naphthyl-(2)-urea, 341
Bis(2-methacrylamidoethyl)amine, 165
Bismuth hydride, 13
Bismuth nitrate, basic, 275
Bismuth oxychloride, 127

2,2′-Bis-(sulfo-p-methoxyanilido)-stilbene, 154
2,2′-Bis(naphtoquinone-(1″,4″)-diazide-(4″)-2″-(sulfonylamino)-diphenyl-4,4′-disulfonic acid, 341
N, N′-Bis(m-nitrobenzenesulfonyl)-N, N′-dichloroethylenediamine, 406
Bis-(tricyclohexyllead), 17
Bisphenol A, 262
Bitumen, 137
Biuret, 261
Bleaching agents, optical, 258
Bleaching of dyes, 17, 387–396
Bleaching solution, 39
Bleach-out dye papers, 395
  stability of, 395
Bleach-out process, 387–396
Blood albumin, 62, 122
Blueprint, 28–37
  color of, 35
  fading of, 35, 36
  marking and retouching solutions for, 33
  sensitizing solutions for, 29
  toning of, 37
Blueprinting, 28
Blueprint paper, bleeding of, 34
  contrast of, 31
  feathering of, 36
  precoat for, 29, 31
  printing latitude of, 35
  printing speed of, 31
  quality of, 35
  shelf-life of, 35, 36
  stabilization of, 34
Blueprint process, 27, 28–37
  monobath development of, 35
  semidry development of, 34
  two-bath development of, 35
Blue salt, 212
Blushed coatings, 402
Bolometers, 7
Borax, 104, 255, 272
Boric acid, 292
Borneol, 150
Borophosphoric acid, 296
Brilliant Green, 371
p-Bromacetanilide, 365
Bromal, 181

4-Brombiphenyl, 365
Bromide acceptors, 18
Bromide prints, 49
Bromine radical, 182
o-Bromoaniline, 362
4-Bromo-3,5-dihydroxybenzoic acid amide, 229
o-Bromo-N, N-dimethylaniline, 362
4′-Bromodiphenylamine-4-diazonium chloride, 325
Bromoform, 361
Bromoil process, 50
4-Bromoresorcinol, 224
N-Bromosuccinimide, 278, 365
Bronze powder, 294
Brownprint, 37–39, 294
  deterioration of, 39
  resolution of, 38
  shelf-life of, 39
Brunak solution, 121, 124
Brunak treatment, 123
Bunsen-Roscoe Law, 5, 31, 72
Butadiene acrylonitrile copolymer, 300
Butadiene styrene copolymer, 300
1, 4-Butane-diol, 139, 148
Butylanthraquinone, 163
2,2′-Butylidene-bis(5,5-dimethyl-1,3-cyclohexanedione), 240
Butyl peroxide, di-tert, 170
β-(p-tert-Butylphenoxy)ethyl alcohol, 376
1-n-Butyl-2-n-propylnaphtho-[1,2-α]-imidazole-7-yl-naphthoquinone-1,2-diazide-(1)carboxylic acid ester, 346
Butyroin, 162
Bytoxy radicals, 170

Cadmium acetate, 261
Cadmium chloride, 195
Cadmium compounds, 17, 34, 394
Cadmium formate, 261
Cadmium nitrate, 405
Cadmium oxalate, 188
Cadmium salts, 17, 34, 394
Cadmium selenide, 187
Cadmium stearate, 403
Cadmium sulfide, 17, 187
Cadmium telluride, 187

Caffeine, 257, 296
Calcium caseinate, 62
Calcium chloride, 125, 126, 128, 165
Calcium hydroxide, 55, 124
Calcium nitrate, 121, 327
Calcium resinate, 407
Calcium silicate, 29
Calcium stearate, 403
Camphor derivatives, 383
Capri blue, 379, 389
Caprolactam, 164, 332
  N-alkoxymethylated, 113
Caprylic acid, 376
Carbalkoxymethylene bis(*n*-propyl xanthene), 168
1-Carbazide-2:5-dihydroxybenzene, 278
2-Carbazido-1-naphthol, 278
1-Carbethoxy-2-keto-3, 4-dimethyl-6-bromo-3-azabenzanthrone, 144
Carbethoxymethyl-N, N-pentamethylene-dithiocarbamate, 168
Carbinol base of triphenylmethane dye, 367
Carbohydrates, 55, 82
Carbon black, 47, 96, 116, 123, 172, 409, 410, 411
Carbon dioxide, 7, 164
Carbon monoxide, 7
Carbon printing, 47–49
Carbon prints, 48
Carbon process, 48
Carbon tetrabromide, 181, 362, 364, 365, 366, 367, 368, 369, 370, 379, 396
Carbon tetrachloride, 180, 181, 364, 365
Carbon tetraiodide, 364
Carbon tissue, 49, 53, 108, 109, 113
Carbonyl compounds, as photopolymerization initiators, 158, 160–167
Carbowax, 130, 409
Carboxymethyl cellulose, sodium salt of, 66, 123, 129, 130, 298, 327, 328
Carboxymethyl-N, N-dimethyldithiocarbamate, 168
Carboxymethyl-ethers of phenol-aldehyde condensate, 337

Carboxymethylhydroxyethyl cellulose, 130
Carbro process, 50
Casein, 47, 55, 62, 122, 123, 129, 130, 131, 323
Catechin, 123
Catechol, 223, 409
  derivatives of, 223
  monohydroxyethylether of, 223
Cation-exchange resin, 293
Cellophane, 272, 299, 306, 408
Cellosolve, 126
Celluloid, 50, 128
Celulose, 128, 138, 323
  allylated, 141
  diazonium derivatives of, 179
  esterified, 141
  etherified, 394
  hydroxyallylated, 141
  hydroxyethyl, 130, 325
  incompletely acylated, 394
Cellulose acetate, 65, 128, 129, 147, 270, 276, 305, 366, 411, 412, 415
  saponified, 299
Cellulose acetate butyrate, 299, 403
Cellulose acetate citrate, 65
Cellulose acetate hydrogenphthalate, 164
Cellulose acetate phthalate, 65
Cellulose acetate succinate, 65
Cellulose alkyl ethers, 164
Cellulose *p*-amino-phenacyl ether, 179
Cellulose derivatives, 119
Cellulose esters, 138, 164, 299
Cellulose ethyl ether, 138
Cellulose gum, 122, 123
Cellulose nitrate, 119, 306, 366
Ceric behenate, 405
Ceric stearate, 405
Cerium chloride, 92
Cerium compounds, 23, 24, 34, 91, 386
Cerium hydroxide, 91
Cerium oxide, 22
Cerium salts, 23, 24, 34, 91, 386
Cerous fluoride, 361
Cesium fluoride, 13
Chain reaction, 8, 21, 159
Chalcone, 149, 150, 151

Chalcone-4,4′-bis-hydroxy acetic acid ethyl ether, 151
Chalcone-type compounds, 149–151
Chemical actinometers, 7
Chemical reactions, thermal requirements of, 3
Chloral, 181
Chloral hydrate, 180
Chlorine, 181
Chloroacetamide, 407
Chloroacetone, 180
Chloroacetyl chloride, 180
o-Chloroaniline, 362
Chloroanthraquinone, 144, 163, 365
o-Chlorobenzene diazocyanide, 274
p-Chlorobenzene diazocyanide, 274
N-Chlorobenzenesulfonanilide, 406
2-Chlorobutadiene, 180
1-Chlorocyclohexene, 180
4-Chloro-3, 5-dihydroxybenzoic acid amide, 229
Chloroform, 364
5-Chloro-6-hydroxy-1, 3-benzoxathiol-2-one, 247
α-Chloromethylnaphthalene, 172, 180
Chloromethyl naphthyl chloride, 180
Chloromethyl phosphorodichloridate, 378
1-Chloro-4-nitrobenzene, 365
p-Chlorophenol, 325
p-[*o*-Chlorophenylazo]-N, N-dimethylaniline, 386
p-Chlorophenyl-*p*-chlorobenzenesulfenate, 170
4-Chloro-*o*-phenylenediamine, 362
6-Chloro-quinoline-quinone-(3, 4)-diazide-(3), 344
4-Chlororesorcinol and acetaldehyde, condensation product of, 231
n-Chlorosuccinimide, 365
N-Chloro-*p*-toluenesulfonanilide, 406
Chromate ion, 82
  hydration of, 69
Chromates, 90, 321
  stability of, 90
Chrome alum, 36
Chrome green, 48
Chrome yellow, 48

Chromic acid, 67, 88, 89, 90, 125, 131, 165
Chromic chromate, 67, 70
Chromic ions, 62, 82
Chromic poisoning, 53
Chromic trioxide, 51
Chromium, 127
Chromium compounds, 394
Chromium hexacarbonyl, 381
Chromium hexamino compounds, 266
Chromium-manganese antimonides, 413
Chromium oxide, 67
Chromium oxychromate, 70
Chromium selenide, 187
Chromium sulfide, 187
Chromium telluride, 187
Chromous chloride, 164
Chrysene, 143
Cinnamic acid, 140, 141, 148, 150
Cinnamic acid derivatives, 140–149
Cinnamic acid-*p*-carboxyl acid dimethylester, 148
Cinnamic acid esters, 146
Cinnamide, 147
Cinnamoyl chloride, 141, 148
N-(Cinnamoylphenyl)urethane, 147
Cinnamoyl-polystyrene resins, 141
Cinnamylidene acetophenone, 141
Cinnamic acid-*p*-carboxyl acid dimethylester, 148
Cinnamylidenemalonic acid, 148
  diamides of, 148
Cinnamylidene methyl ethyl ketone, 141
Cis-trans isomerization, 137
Citric acid, 20, 25, 29, 31, 39, 120, 121, 125, 126, 267, 273, 292, 327, 369
Clay, 29, 130
Cloth, 28
Cobalt, trioxalato-complexes of, 26
Cobalt chloride, 91
Cobalt naphthenate, 407
Cobalt salts, 34, 91, 187, 409
Cold-top enamel, 104
Collagen, 55, 57
Collagen fibrils, 58
Collodion, 394
Collotype, 50–51

Colophony, 411
Copper, 127
 etching of, 111
Copper acetate, 14, 410
Copper compounds, 14–15, 37, 91, 126, 381, 395
Copper naphthenate, 172
Copper oxide, 386
Copper phthalocyanine, 380
Copper plate, 47, 104, 106, 107, 108
Copper salts, 14–15, 37, 91, 126, 381, 395
Copper sulfate, 91, 295
Copper sulfide, 26
Corn starch, 64, 298
Cotton organdy, 112
Counter etching, 121, 122, 124
Coupler, 39
Coupling, 215, 358
 mechanism of, 215
Coupling components, 215
 properties of, 219
 rate of, 216, 218
 reactivity of, 219
Coupling reaction, 215, 216
Covalent bonds, 159
Cronaking, 121
Cronak solution, 121, 124
Crosslinking, 160
Crosslinking agent, 161
Crotonic acid, 292
Crystal energy, 10, 11, 19, 69
Crystal violet, 14, 145, 294, 371, 379
Cumene hydroperoxide, 170
Cupric chloride, 91, 92, 106, 111, 127
Cupric salts, 14, 15
Cupric sulfate, 177
Cuprous bromide, 14
Cuprous chloride, 14, 111
Curie point, 412
Cyanacetamide, 242
Cyanacetanilide, 241
Cyanacetylamides, 241
Cyanacetylbenzylamide, 241
Cyanacetylthiourea, 242
Cyanacetylurea, 241
Cyanamide, 272
Cyanine dyes, 16, 142, 145, 151, 179, 369, 396

Cyanoacetic acid, 241
Cyanocarboxylic acid, 262
3-(α-Cyano-cinnamido-)phthalic anhydride, 147
4-(α-Cyano-cinnamido-)phthalic anhydride, 147
3-Cyano-4,5-dimethyl-5-hydroxy-3-pyrrolin-2-one, 410
Cyanogen, 32
Cyanohydrins, 275
1-Cyano-2-keto-3-methyl-6-bromo-3-azabenzanthrone, 144
Cyanuric acid, 378
Cyanuric chloride, 323, 378
Cycloalkyl disulfides, 167
Cyclobutane derivatives, 140
Cyclohexadiene, 361
Cyclohexanone, 327, 328
Cyclohexylacetoacetic acid amide, 243
Cyclohexylamine, 295
p-Cyclohexylaminobenzene diazonium chloride, 204
4-Cyclohexylbenzanthrone, 143
Cyclopentadiene, 361
Cyclopentadiene carboxylic acid, 251, 273
Cyclopentanone, 138
Cysteine, 394
Cystine, 394

Deep-etch plates, 124–126, 148
Deep-etch solution, 125, 126
Desensitizing gum, 123, 124
Desyl bromide, 181
Desyl chloride, 181
Developer, dye-forming, 166
Developing ink, deep-etch, 126
Dextran, 65, 125
Dextrin, 46, 65, 72, 258, 324, 329, 352, 372
Dextrose, 258
2, 4-Diacetoacetaminobenzene sulfonic acid, 243
2, 4-Diacetoacetaminotoluene, 244
Diacetoacetyl piperazine, 244
Diacetyl, 162, 177, 178
4,4′-Diacetylamino-2,2′-disulfanilidostilbene, 153
Diacetyl disulfide, 167

Diacetyl radicals, 160
Diacyl peroxides, 170
Dialdehydes, 51
3,5-Dialkoxy-*p*-phenylenediamine, 257
p-N,N-Dialkylaminoaniline, 322
Dialkyl peroxides, 170
4,4'-Diaminobenzophenone, 345
Diaminobenzophenone imides, 142
4,4'-Diaminodicyclohexylmethane, 165
Diaminodiphenyl carbinols, 142
4,4'-Diamino-diphenyl-2,2'-disulfonic acid, 340
4,4'-Diaminodiphenyl ketone, 145
Diaminodiphenyl ketones, 142
Diaminodiphenylmethane, 142, 362
4'',4'''-Diamino-2'',2'''-disulfo-1'',1'''-N, N-diphenyl-4,4'-diamino-1,1'-diphenyl, diazotized, 323
γ,γ'-Diaminopropylether, 148, 151
4,4'-Diaminostilbene-2,2'disulfonic acid, 258, 304
3,6-Diamino-thioxanthonium chloride, 391
Diammonium hydrogen phosphate, 125
Diammonium sodium ferricyanide, 29
p-Diamylaminobenzene diazonium chloride, 204
1,2-Dianilinoethylene, 362
Dianisidine, tetrazonium metal double salts of, 326
Dianthrone, 144
2,6-Di-(4'-azidobenzal)cyclohexanone, 334
4,4'-Diazidochalcone, 334
4,4'-Diazidodibenzalacetone, 332
Diazidodiphenylamine carboxylic acid, 330
Di-(4-azido-2'-hydroxybenzal)acetone-2-sulfonic acid, 331
1,3-Di-(4-azidophenyl)-2:3-propane-1-one, 332
4,4'-Diazidostilbene-α-carboxylic acid, 331
4,4'-Diazidostilbene-2,2'-disulfonic acid 330
4,4-Diazido-stilbene-2,2'-disulfonic acid anilide, 333
1-Diazo-4-alkylbenzylamino-3-alkoxy-benzene, 254

Diazoaminobenzene, 177, 203, 210, 212
morpholino derivatives of, 199, 210, 215
Diazo *m*-aminoesters, 213
Diazo-*o*-aminoesters, 213
Diazo *p*-aminoesters, 212
Diazoanhydride, 179
Diazobenzenes, substituted, 197, 202, 219
4,4'-Diazobenzophenone, 332
Diazobiguanides, 270
1-Diazo-2-carboxy-2-diethylaminobenzene, 204
1-Diazo-4-chloro-2, 5-diethoxybenzene, 203
Diazo compounds, 158, 175, 177, 194, 321, 380, 411
absorption spectrum of, 196
as photopolymerization initiators, 175–180
classification of, 201–214
double salts of, 195
light sensitivity of, 196
photolysis of, 196, 249
spectral sensitivity of, 201
stability of, 195
4-Diazo-2,5-dialkoxy acylanilides, 257
1-Diazo-3-dialkylamino-3-bromobenzenes, 204
1-Diazo-3-dialkylamino-3-chlorobenzene, 204
1-Diazo-3-dialkylamino-3-iodobenzenes, 204
3-Diazo, 5,7-dibromoindazole, 329
1-Diazo-2, 5-dibutoxybenzoylaminobenzene, 213, 256
1-Diazo-2,5-dichloro-4-benzylaminobenzene, 208
1-Diazo-2,5-dichloro-4-(N-methyl, N-cyclohexyl)-aminobenzene, 207
1-Diazo-2,5-diethoxy-4-acetoxyaminobenzene, 207
1-Diazo-2,5-diethoxybenzene, 202
1-Diazo-2,5-diethoxybenzoylaminobenzene, 212, 256
4'-Diazo-2',5'-diethoxy-5-phenyl-2-amino-4-imino-6-methyltriazine, 207
1-Diazo-4-diethylamino-3-chlorobenzene, 204

p-Diazodiethylaniline zinc chloride, 277

1-Diazo-4-(dihydroxyethyl)amino-3-methylbenzene, 204

1-Diazo-2,4-dimethyloxybenzene, 289

1-Diazo-2,5-dimethoxybenzene, 202

1-Diazo-2,4-dimethoxybenzene-5-sulfonic acid, 289

4-Diazo-2,5-dimethoxydiphenyl, 203

1-Diazo-2,5-dimethoxy-1-*p*-toluylmercaptobenzene, 256

1-Diazo-4-dimethylaminobenzene hydrofluoroborate, 321

1-Diazo-2-dimethylamino-3-chlorobenzene, 196

1-Diazo-4-dimethylamino-3-ethoxybenzene, 204

1-Diazo-2-dimethylamino-5-ethoxy-4-benzoylamine, 196

2-Diazo-3-dimethylaminotoluene, 196

p-Diazodimethylaniline zinc chloride, 277

1-Diazo-4,5-dimethyl-2-dimethylaminobenzene, 212

p-Diazodiphenylamine, 113, 293, 323, 324, 325
    photolysis of, 199

p-Diazodiphenylamine-formaldehyde condensate, 323, 324, 325

p-Diazodiphenylamine sulfate, 258, 277

3-Diazo-2,4-diphenyl-3H-pyrrolenine, 329

1-Diazo-4-ethoxybenzene, 202

4-Diazoethoxybenzene sulfonic acid, 201

1-Diazo-2-ethoxy-4-diethylaminobenzene, 204

4-Diazo-4'-ethoxydiphenylamine, 210

1-Diazo-4-ethylbenzylaminobenzene, 208

1-Diazo-4-ethylbenzyl-3-ethoxyaminobenzene, 208

p-Diazo-N-ethyl-N-(2-hydroxyethyl)aniline, 326

p-Diazoethylhydroxyethylaniline zinc chloride, 277

1-Diazo-4-ethylmercapto-2,5-diethoxybenzene, 213

Diazo-formaldehyde condensates, 324

Diazo hydroborofluorides, 195

Diazo hydroxides, 216, 217, 218

Diazoindiazoles, 329

Diazo mercaptobenzenes, 213

4-Diazomethoxybenzene sulfonic acid, 201

4-Diazo-2-methoxy-1-cyclohexylaminobenzene, *p*-chlorobenzenesulfonate of, 277

1-Diazo-4-methoxy-3-methylbenzene, 289

1-Diazo-3-methoxy-4-(N-n-propyl-N-cyclohexy)aminobenzene, 204

1-Diazo-4-methylamino-3-ethoxy-6-chlorobenzene, 207

1-Diazo-4-methylbenzylamino-2,5-diethoxybenzene, 208

1-Diazo-4-methylbenzylamino-3-ethoxybenzene, 208

1-Diazo-3-methyl-4-diethylanilide, 303

1-Diazo-3-methyl-4-monoethylaminobenzene, 204

4-Diazo-3-methyl-4-dimethylaniline sulfate, 321

1-Diazo-2-methyl-4-(N-methyl, N-hydroxypropyl)aminobenzene, 204

1-Diazo-3-methyl-4-monoethylaminobenzene, 204

p-Diazomonoethylaniline, 326

1-Diazo-3-monomethylnaphthylamine, 321

1-Diazo-3-morpholinoaminobenzene, 210, 215

1-Diazo-4-morpholino-2,5-dibutoxyaminobenzene, 210, 215

1-Diazo-4-morpholino-2,5-diethoxyaminobenzene, 210, 215

1-Diazo-4-morpholino-2,5-dimethoxyaminobenzene, 210, 215

1-Diazo-4-morpholino-2,5-dipropoxyaminobenzene, 210, 215

1-Diazo-4-morpholino-2-ethoxy-5-methoxyaminobenzene, 210, 215

1-Diazo-4-morpholino-3-methoxyaminobenzene, 210

2-Diazonaphthol-(1)-5-sulfochloride, 345

2-Diazo-1-naphthol-5-sulfonamide, 343

2-Diazo-1-naphthol-5-sulfonic acid, ester amide of, 270
2-Diazo-1-naphthol-5-sulfonic acid ethyl ether, 343
2-Diazo-1-naphthol-5-sulfonic acid methyl ether, 343
2-Diazo-1-naphthol-5-sulfonic acid naphthyl ether, 343
Diazonium chlorides, 178, 194
Diazonium chlorides, anhydrous, 200
Diazonium citrates, 194
Diazonium compounds, 158, 175, 177, 194, 321, 380, 411
Diazonium fluorborates, 178
Diazonium hydroxide, 179, 217
2-Diazonium-1-hydroxy-5-methyl-4-benzene sulfonic acid, 271
1-Diazonium-2-hydroxynaphthalene-4-sulfonic acid, 199, 272
Diazonium ion, 216
Diazonium oxalates, 194
Diazo oxides, 250, 251, 252, 278
1-Diazo-3-oxyethoxy-4-pyrrolidoneaminobenzene, 204
1-Diazo-4-oxyethylbenzyl-3,6-diethoxyaminobenzene, 208
1-Diazo-2-oxynaphthalene-4-sulfonate, 277
Diazophenol allyl ethers, light sensitivity of, 201
Diazophenol ethers, light sensitivity of, 201
Diazophenols, 250, 251, 252, 278
light sensitivity of, 201
9-(*p*-Diazophenyl)carbazole, 204
o-Diazoquinones, 342
Diazo quinonyl-sulfonamide, 278
Diazosulfonates, 266, 269–270, 274, 278, 291
Diazosulfones, 267, 359
Diazotate ion, 217
anti-Diazotates, 218
syn-Diazotates, 218
Diazotizable diamines, tetrazo derivatives of, 204
Diazotation, 194
1-Diazo-4-tolylmercapto-2,5-diethoxybenzene, 213, 256

4-Diazo-2,5,4'-triethoxydiphenyl, 203, 256
4-Diazo-2,3',6'-trimethoxy-2-dimethylaminobenzene, 196
Diazotype films, 305
resolving power of, 307
Diazotype material, base material for, 296
coating of, 300
manufacture of, 292–301
precoat for, 297
Diazotype microfilm, 259
Diazotype papers, applications of, 302–307
bleeding of, 295
Diazotype papers, coating of, 300–301
developing sheets for, 265
keeping properties of, 258, 301
positive-working, 251
sensitometric characteristics, 302
spectral sensitivity of, 198, 288
superfast, 199
thermal development of, 218, 259–267, 290
apparatus for, 264
Diazotype process, acid development of, 255
alkaline development of, 217, 255
copying machines for, 253
dry development of, 253
negative processes of, 267–282
one-component system of, 253
positive processes of, 249–267
quantum efficiency of, 197
quantum yield of, 199, 201
semiwet development of, 255, 258
two-component system of, 255
Diazotype processes, 194–320
Diazotype sensitizing solution, 292
Diazoxy radical, 179
Dibenzalacetone, 145
*o,o'*Di[benzoquinone-(1",2")-diazide-(2"),-4"-sulfonyl]-4,4'-dihydroxydiphenyl, 348
Dibenzothiophenone-5,5-dioxide sulfonic acid, 335
Dibenzoyl disulfide, 167
Dibornyl disulfide, 167
α,β-Dibromopropionaldehyde, 181

2,5-Dibutoxy-4-morpholino-1-benzene
diazonium chloride, 257
Di-*n*-butylamine, 262
p-Dibutylaminobenzene diazonium chloride, 204
Di-*n*-butyl disulfide, 167
1,4-Dicarbazido-2,3-dihydroxyfurane,
278
2,4-Dichlororesorcinol, 225
2,5-Dichloroaniline, 362
p-Dichlorobenzene, 365
2,4-Dichlorobenzoyl peroxide, 415
2,6-Dichloro-4-nitroaniline, 143
N,N'-Dichloro-N,N'-bis(*m*-nitrobenzene-sulfonyl)-ethylenediamine,
406
2,4-Dichlorophenol, 365
β-Dichloropropionaldehyde, 181
2,6-Dichloroquinone, 144
Dichromated albumin, 80, 87, 104
Dichromated-colloid layers, 46, 93
Dichromated-colloid layers, developers
for, 91
Dichromated colloids, 46–102, 321
afterhardening of, 68, 82
composition of the sensitizing solution, 51
dark reaction of, 68, 82–85
effect of colloid on, 88
effect of concentration on, 87
effect of humidity on, 86
effect of pH on, 83
effect of temperature on, 86
mechanism of, 88
desensitizing of, 94
hardening reaction of, 82, 89
light sensitivity of, 74, 91
effect of coating thickness of, 80
effect of dichromate concentration on, 74
effect of moisture on, 81
effect of pH on, 78
methods for increasing sensitivity of,
91–94
photochemical hardening of, 67
photochemical laws of, 71
printing speed of, 92
quantum yield of, 68, 72, 73
rate of hardening of, 89

sensitized layer of, 86
sensitizing solution of, 82
sensitometry of, 95–98
spectral sensitivity of, 71, 73
storage life of, 86, 90, 91, 95, 116
tanning theory of, 70
Dichromated-colloid solution, viscosity
of, 84, 85
Dichromated gelatin, 46, 51, 67, 72,
89, 112
Dichromated glue, 91, 104
Dichromated gum arabic, 64
Dichromate ion, 82
Dichromates, 90, 321
dermatitis of, 54
spectral absorption of, 71
Dichromic acid, 90
Dicinnamal-acetone, 140
Dicyandiamide, 262, 295, 297
Diethanolamine, 272
p-Diethoxyaminobenzene diazonium
chloride, 204
2,5-Diethoxy-4-chlorobenzene diazosulfonate, 270
2,5-Diethoxyphenol, 222
3,5-Diethoxyphenol, 223
N,N-Diethyl-N'-allylthiourea, 393
Diethylamidomonoethyl resorcinol
ether, 226
1-N,N-Diethylamino-4-amino-3-ethoxybenzene, diazo sulfonate of, 266
p-Diethylaminobenzene diazonium chloride, 204, 252, 293
β-Diethylamino-ethyl-polymethacrylate,
164
4-Diethylamino-2-hydroxy-1-diazobenzene, 270
1-Diethylamino-4-oxybenzene, 293
N,N-Diethylaniline, 362, 364
Diethylbenzene, 106
1,1'Diethylbenzidine, tetrazonium metal,
double salts of, 326
3,3'-Diethyl-4,5,4',5'-dibenzothia-carbocyanine bromide, 145
3,3'-Diethyl-4,5,4',5'-dibenzothiacyanine
iodide, 146
Diethyl maleate, 277
1,1-Difluoroethylene, 277

Diformyl-*p,p'*-diamino-dibenzoyl-4,4'-diaminostilbene-2,2'disulfonic acid, 382

Diguanidine disodium ferrocyanide, 29

6,6'-Dihexyl-3,3'iso-propylidene dioxy-diphenol, 230

Dihydrophenanthrene, 151

1,2-Dihydroxybenzene, 223

1,3-Dihydroxybenzene, 224

1,3 - Dihydroxybenzene - 6- chloro-4-sulfonic acid, 227

1,3 - Dihydroxybenzene - 4,6 - disulfonic acid, 226

1,3 - Dihydroxybenzene - 6-methyl-4-sulfonic acid, 227

1,3-Dihydroxybenzene-5-sulfonic acid, 227

3,5-Dihydroxybenzoic acid amide, 229

1,3-Dihydroxy-4-chlorobenzene, 224

1,3-Dihydroxy-5-chlorobenzene, 224

2,2-(4,4'-Dihydroxy-diphenyl) propane, 151

4,4'-Dihydroxy-1,1'-diphenylsulfone, 347

4,4'-Dihydroxy-3-methoxychalcone, 151

Dihydroxynaphthalenes, 303

1,5-Dihydroxynaphthalene, 239

2,3-Dihydroxynaphthalene, 237, 266, 303, 411

2,7-Dihydroxynaphthalene, 238

2,7-Dihydroxynaphthalene-3, 6-disulfonic acid, 239

2,8-Dihydroxynaphthalene-3, 6-disulfonic acid, 239

5,7-Dihydroxynaphthalene-2-(N-β-hydroxyethyl sulfonamide), 242

2,7-Dihydroxy-1-naphthalene-methanesulfonic acid, 239

2,3-Dihydroxynaphthalene mono-N-dimethylamino(β)ethyl ether, 238

2,3-Dihydroxynaphthalene monoglycollic acid ether, 238

1,6 - Dihydroxynaphthalene - 3 - sulfonic acid, 239

1,8 - Dihydroxynaphthalene - 3 - sulfonic acid, 240

2,3 - Dihydroxynaphthalene - 6 - sulfonic acid, 238, 250, 296, 303

2,7-Dihydroxynaphthalene-3-sulfonic acid, 239

2,8 - Dihydroxynaphthalene - 6 - sulfonic acid, 238

Dihydroxy-2-naphthanilide, 303

bis-(2,4-Dihydroxyphenyl sulfide), 231

p-Dihydroxypropylaminobenzene diazonium chloride, 204

3,4-Dihydroxytetraphenylmethane, 404

2,6-Dihydroxytoluene, 227

3,5-Dihydroxytoluene, 227

4,5-Dihydroxytoluene, 223

1,2',4'-Diimino-1',2',3',4'-tetrahydro-1', 3',5' - triazino - 7- hydroxy-naphthalene, 236

Diisopropylbenzene thiol, 168

Diketones, 240

Dilauroyl disulfide, 167

3,3'-Dilauryloxacyanine perchlorate, 146

Dimerization, 140

5,6 - dimethoxy -1- methyl-2- methylthio-benzothiazolium methosulfate, 167

2,5-Dimethoxyphenol, 222

2,5-Dimethoxy-4-phenylazoaniline, 386

6,8-Dimethoxy-quinoline-quinone-(3,4)-diazide-(3), 344

p-Dimethylaminobenzene diazonium chloride, 204, 250, 252

p-Dimethylaminobenzhydrol, 150

p, p'-Dimethylaminobenzophenone, 145

7-Dimethylamino-8-methoxy-3-oxo-di-hydro-1,4-thiazine-6-diazonium chloride, 277

1-Dimethylaminomethyl-2-hydroxy-3, 6-dimethylbenzene, 222

1-Dimethylamino-4-naphthalene diazonium fluoroborate, 277

p-[*p*-Dimethylamino phenylazo]acetanilide, 386

4-[4-(*p*-Dimethylaminophenyl)-1,3-butadienyl]quinoline, 368

4-*p*-Dimethylaminostyrylquinoline, 367, 368

N, N-Dimethylaniline, 362, 370

Dimethylanilinium ion, 217

Dimethyl-2-azo-bis-isobutyrate, 178

o, o'-Dimethylbenzidine, tetrazonium metal double salts of, 326

5,5-dimethyl-1,3-cyclohexanedione, 240
Dimethyl disulfide, 167
N, N'-Dimethyldithiocarbamate, 168
2,4-Dimethyl-3-ethoxycarbonyl-5-t-butoxycarbonyl-pyrrole, 264
Dimethyl formamide, 151
Dimethylglyoxime, 409
Dimethyl ketene-cyanoisopropylimine, 177
2,5-Dimethyl-4-morpholinomethylphenol, 248
N,N-Dimethyl-α-naphthylamine chlorohydrate, 370
1',3-Dimethyl-6-nitrothia-2'-cyanine iodide, 146
Dimethylolurea, 130
2,4-Dimethyl-1-penten-3-one, polymer of, 278
N,N'-Dimethylphenylazoaniline, 366
N,N-Dimethyl-p-phenylenediamine, 362
Dimethylpolysiloxane, 404
Dimethyl sulfoxide, 372
2,7-Dimethyl-3,6-tetraethyldiamino-9-cyanoselenoxanthonium chloride, 392
6,6'-Dimethyl-3,3'-trimethylene dioxydiphenol, 230
N,N-Di-[naphthoquinone-(1,2)-diazide-(2)-5-sulfonyl]-aniline, 349
p-Dinitrobenzene, 143
4,6-Dinitrobenzene-2,1-diazo oxide, 194
2,4-Dinitrobenzenesulfenyl chloride, 379
2,2'-Dinitrobenzidine-di-oxamic acid, 359
3,3'-Di (p-nitrobenzyl) oxacarbocyanine iodide, 146
2-(2',4'-Dinitrobenzyl)pyridine, 382
4,4'-Dinitro-2,2'-disulfanilidostilbene, 152
4,4'-Dinitro, 2,2'-bis-(sulfo-m-chloroanilido)stilbene, 153
3, 3'-Di(p-nitrophenyl)thiacarbocyanine iodide, 145
6,6'-Dinitro-o-tolidine-dioxamic acid, 359
Dioctyl sodium sulfosuccinate, 106
Dioctyl sulfosuccinate, 31
m, m-Dioxydiphenol, 303

Dioxynaphthalene, derivatives of, 237
2,3-Dioxynaphthalene monooxyethyl ether, 238
Dipentamethylenethiuram disulfide, 169
N,N'-Dipentamethylenethiuram monosulfide, 169
Dipentamethylenethiuram tetrasulfide, 169
Diphenyl, 249, 257
derivatives of, 233
Diphenylamine, 362, 363, 370
Diphenylamine-carbontetrabromide system, 366
Diphenylamine-carbontetrabromide systems, spectral sensitivity of, 366
Diphenyl-p-amino esters, diazo derivatives of, 213
2,3-Diphenylanthraquinone, 163
Diphenyl-dimethyl fulgide, 382
Diphenyl disulfide, 167
Diphenylmethane dyes, 393
Diphenylnitrosamine, 407
Di-p-phenylol-2: 2-propane, 148
Diphenyltriketone, 162
1-N,N-Dipropylamino-4-amino-3-ethoxybenzene, diazo sulfonate of, 267
Dipthaloylnaphthalenes, 142
Diresorcyl sulfide, 303
Diresorcyl sulfoxide, 303
Dissociation energy, 158
Dissociation, thermal, 158
2,2'-Disulfanilidostilbene, 152
Disulfoxides, 382
Dithiocarbamates, 168
Dithiooxamide, 410
Dithizone derivatives, 384
1,4-Ditoluido-anthraquinone blue, 409
Ditolyl disulfide, 167
Divinyl benzene, 182
Divinyl formal, 361
Double transfer, 48
Dow Etch process, 105, 106
Dragon's blood, 105
Dried milk, 122
"Dual Spectrum" process, 414
Durol black, 409
"Dycril" photopolymer plates, 164, 165
Dye absorption, 86

Dye cyanides, 371
Dye images, 37
Dyes,
  bleaching of, 17, 387–396
  leuco bases of, 22, 370–380
  photochemical destruction of, 358
  photochemical formation of, 358
  photoreducible, as photopolymeriza-
    tion initiators, 94, 184–187
Dye-sensitized photopolymerization,
  mechanism of, 185

Egg albumin, 62, 104, 113, 122
Einstein-Bohr law, 3
Einstein unit, 2, 3
Ektalith process, 129
Ektafax process, 411
Ektagraph process, 113
Eletrolytic etching, 106
Electromagnetic engraving system, 107
Electromagnetic radiations, 1
Electromagnetic spectrum, 2
Electron affinity, 10, 11, 12
Encapsulation, 384, 407
Endothermic compounds, 20
Endothermic reaction, 8
Endothermic systems, 18
Energy of activation, 90
Eosin, 94, 175, 184
Epichlorohydrin, 148
Epichlorohydrin-bisphenol resin, 327
Epoxy resin, 327
Epoxy resins, esterified with cinnamoyl
  chloride, 148
  esterified with sorbitol, 148
Equivalent, photochemical, 6
Erythrosin, 70, 94, 175, 184, 391, 413
Etching, 105, 108
Etching ink, 105
Etching process, 47
Etching solution, 47, 124
Ethanedial, 122
Ethanolamine, 36, 121
1-Ethoxybenzene-4-sulfonic acid, 266
Ethyl acetoacetate, 247
Ethyl acrylate, 118, 277
Ethyl alcohol, 376
Ethyl 4-aminocinnamate, 147
2-Ethylaminonaphthalene, 370

1-Ethylamino-4-diazonaphthalene, 270
2-Ethyl-anthraquinone, 361
Ethyl-2-benzothiazylsulfenate, 170
Ethyl celulose, 403, 404, 410
Ethyl cyanacetate, 247
Ethyl cyanine, 94
N,N-Ethylene-bis-acetoacetamide, 243
Ethylene chloride, 165
Ethylenediaminotetraacetic acid, 94
Ethylene dichloride, 327
N,N'-Ethylene-dimethylol cyclic urea,
  129
Ethylene dioxy-5,5'-resorcinol, 329
Ethylene glycol, 148, 295
Ethylene glycol acetal, 166
Ethylene glycol monoethylether, 126
Ethylene glycol monomethyl ether, 147
Ethylene oxide, 181
N,N'-ethylene thiourea, 172
Ethylene/vinyl cinnamate copolymers,
  147
Ethyl green cyanide, 373
1-Ethyl-2(p-hydroxyethoxystyryl)quino-
  linium iodide, 335
6 - Ethyl - 4-hydroxy-1-methyl-2(1)pyri-
  done, 245
Ethyl-12-hydroxystearate, 150
Ethyl malonamate, 244
6-Ethylpyronone, 244
1-Ethyl-2-(β-styryl)quinolinium iodide,
  335
S-Ethylthiodiphenylamine sulfonium
  perchlorate, 352
Ethyl-trichloromethanesulfenate, 170
Ethyl urea, 263, 264
Ethyl violet, 94
Europium salts, 386
Exothermic reaction, 8

Farmer's reducer, 116, 276
Ferric ammonium citrate, 26, 28, 29,
  30, 173, 278
Ferric ammonium oxalate, 26, 30, 36,
  38, 173, 275
Ferric ammonium tartrate, 30, 173
Ferric chloride, 25, 28, 30, 47, 92,
  106, 107, 109, 111, 126, 127, 131,
  175, 177, 395
Ferric citrate, 26, 30

Ferric ferrocyanide, 27
Ferric gallate, 404
Ferric guanidine oxalate, 36
Ferric hydroxide, 32, 111
Ferric oxalate, 16, 26, 30, 32, 36, 37, 75, 201
Ferric perchlorate, 125
Ferric potassium citrate, 30
Ferric potassium oxalate, 30
Ferric salts, 22, 25, 27, 37, 129, 187, 275
Ferric salts, photoreduction of, 39
Ferric sodium oxalate, 30
Ferric stearate, 404, 409, 410
Ferric sulfate, 25, 28, 110
Ferric tartrate, 26
Ferrioxalate actinometer, 27
Ferro-gallic process, 27
Ferrotype plate, 108
Ferrous ammonium oxalate, 38, 178
Ferrous chloride, 25, 111, 395
Ferrous ferricyanide, 33, 36
Ferrous ferrocyanide, 32, 33, 36
Ferrous oxalate, 32, 38, 174
Ferrous sulfate, 40
Ferrous sulfate developer, 17
Ferrous tartrate, 15
Films, hand-cut, 112
Fish glue, 46, 53, 62, 66, 113, 119
Fixing solution, 118
Flavinduline O, 389
Fluoboric acid, 195
Fluorescein, 175, 390
Fluorescence, 5, 185
4-Fluororesorcinol, 225
Fluosulfonates, 195
Fog inhibitors, 117
Formaldehyde, 61, 116, 130, 138, 295, 297, 323, 326
Formaldehyde condensation products of β-naphthalene sulfonic acid, 195
Formaldehyde naphthalenesulfonic acid, polymerized, 269
Formamide disulfite, 107
Formazans, 384
4-Formyl-acetophenone polyvinyl acetal, 166
4-Formyl-benzophenone polyvinyl acetal, 166

p-Formylcinnamic acid acetal of polyvinyl alcohol, 148
Free radicals, 5, 158, 159, 361
Fulgides, 382
Fumaric acid, 31, 38, 137
Furfural, 138
2-Furfuraldehyde, 149
Furfuryl alcohol, 325

d-Galactose, 64
Gallic acid, 27, 28, 404
Gamma rays, 2, 19, 20, 25, 71, 379, 380
Gelatin, 14, 17, 19, 20, 27, 28, 39, 40, 46, 47, 55–62, 66, 83, 91, 103, 108, 114, 119, 125, 181, 276, 295, 298, 322, 324, 331, 336, 372, 380, 384, 394, 407
  gelation of, 60, 61
  hardening of, 61
  hydrolysis of, 60
  isoelectric point of, 56, 61
  melting point of, 61, 62
  pigmented, 48
  setting point of, 61
  silver halide emulsions, quantum yield of, 20
  swelling of, 59, 60
  thiolated, 187
  viscosity of, 60
  water absorption of, 59
Gelatin size, 29
Gelatin sol, 61
Gelatin stencil, 47
Gelatin subbing, 115
Gelatino-mercury iodide emulsion
Gelation, 84
Gelatose, 76
Glass, alkali metal borosilicate, 386
Glass cloth, 28
Glass, photochromic, 386
  photosensitive, 22–25
Gluconic acid, 255, 405
Glucose, 21, 28, 116, 255, 292, 294
d-Glucuronic acid, 64
Glue, 103, 107, 114, 276, 331
  animal, 28, 55, 372
  photoengraving, 83
  photogravure's, 125

Glutamic acid, 59
Glutaric acid, 257
Glycerol, 48, 51, 113, 125, 258, 295, 410
Glycerol dimethacrylate, 165
Glycine, 56
Glycol, 15, 125, 410
Glycol acetate, 125
Glyoxylic acid, 174
Gold, 24
Gold chloride, 18, 172
Gold salts, 22, 37, 273
Gold toning, 22
Graft polymerization, 179, 180
Graining, 120, 124
Graphite, 413
Gravure plates, 154
Gravure tissue, 108
Grotthus-Draper law, 3, 71, 380
Guanidine, 261
Guanidine carbonate, 31
Guanidine oxalate, 36
Guanidine salt of dioctylsulfonic acid ester, 31
Guanidinium trichloroacetate, 407
Gum arabic, 46, 53, 55, 64, 83, 87, 104, 119, 121, 123, 124, 125, 126, 131, 147, 324, 325, 327, 331, 337, 352, 407
Gumming, 124
Gums, vegetable, 372

H-acid, 252
Halftones, 47, 48
Halogen compounds, as photopolymerization initiators, 180–183
Halosulfuryl compounds, 181
Hammett's equation, 171, 219
Heat of activation, 3
Heat of dissociation, 10, 11, 12
Heat of formation, 9, 10, 12, 13, 19
Heat of sublimation, 10, 11, 12
Heat-sensitive papers, 402
Heliotype, 51
Helvetia green cyanide, 375
Hematin, 123
Hematoxylin, 123
Heptylbiguanide, 298
Heptylguanide, 298

Hexachlorobenzene, 365
Hexachloroethane, 365, 380, 396
Hexafluoboric acid, sodium salt of, 337
Hexafluosilicic acid, sodium salt of, 337
Hexafluotitanic acid, sodium salt of, 337
Hexa-β-hydroxyethyl-p-rosaniline cyanide, 375
Hexamethylenediamine, 332
Hexamethylenediamine adipate, 165
Hexamethylenetetramine, 34, 260, 262, 404
Hexamine cobaltic chloride, 26
Hurter-Driffield characteristic curve, 96
Hydrazine, 174
α-Hydrocarbo-substituted acyloins, 163
Hydrochloric acid, 27, 33, 56, 106, 111, 120, 126, 161, 194, 410
Hydrofluoric acid, 24, 120, 121, 126, 329
Hydrogen bromide, 8, 9
   photolysis of, 8
Hydrogen chloride, 8, 9, 115
Hydrogen compounds, 12
Hydrogen flouride, 9
Hydrogen halides, 9
   dissociation energy of, 9
   photolysis of, 9
Hydrogen iodide, 7, 8, 9
Hydrogen iodide, photolysis of, 7
Hydrogen peroxide, 33, 35, 54, 57, 170, 174. 252, 271, 379, 396
Hydrogen selenide, 12
Hydrogen sulfide, 12
Hydrogen telluride, 12
Hydroquinone, 15, 38, 49, 93, 115, 147, 172, 178, 365
   derivatives of, 232
Hydroquinone monoethyl ether, 232
Hydrotype process, 50
Hydroxyacetic acid, 125
ω-Hydroxyalkoxyacetophenones, 150
1-Hydroxy-8-aminonaphthalene-6-sulfonic acid, 240
p-Hydroxybenzal acetophenone, 151
1-Hydroxybenzene-4-diazonium borofluoride, 274

p-Hydroxybenzene diazonium chloride, 271

1-Hydroxybenzene-2-diazonium fluorosulfonate, 274

1-Hydroxybenzene-5-diazonium-4-sulfonic acid-6-carboxylic acid, 274

Hydroxybenzoic acid, 376

6-Hydroxy-1, 3-benzoxathiol-2-one, 247

m-Hydroxybenzyl alcohol, 222

β-Hydroxy-butyric aldehyde, 104

4-Hydroxy-5-(2, 4-diamino-phenylazo) benzenesulfonic acid, 413

1-Hydroxy-2-diazo-4-benzene sulfonic acid, 271

1-Hydroxy-2-diazoniumbenzene-4-sulfonic acid, 321

Hydroxy-1-diazonium-2-methyl-6-benzene-4-sulfonic acid, 272

o-Hydroxydiphenyl, 233

4-(*β*-Hydroxyethoxy)acetophenone, 150

4'(*β*-Hydroxyethoxy)-chalcone, 149

N-Hydroxyethyl-N'-allythiourea, 394

Hydroxyethyl cellulose, 130, 325

3-(2-Hydroxyethyl)-5-(4-dimethylamino-benzylidene)-rhodamine, 139

Hydroxyethyl-2-heptadecenyl glyoxalidine, 279

N-Hydroxyethyl-4-oxyquinolone-2, 245

N-*β*-Hydroxyethyl-*α*-resorcylamide, 225

3-(2-Hydroxyethyl)-rhodamine, 139

Hydroxyl ammonium chloride, 379

Hydroxylbenzophenone, 361

Hydroxyl radical, 182, 185

2-Hydroxy-4-methoxy benzophenone, 377

4-Hydroxy-2-methylbenzimidazole, 247

2-Hydroxymethyl-1',2',4,5-naphthimidazole, 295

2-Hydroxy-4-Methylphenyl glutaric acid, 222

2-Hydroxy-5-methylthiophene-4-carboxylic acid, 246

1-Hydroxynaphthalene, 234

2-Hydroxynaphthalene, 235

7-Hydroxynaphthalene-1-acetoacetic acid amide, 243

7-Hydroxynaphthalene-1-biguanidine, 236

2-Hydroxynaphthalene-6,8-disulfonic acid, 236

2-Hydroxynaphthalene-3,6-disulfonic acid, 235

2-Hydroxynaphthalene-4-sulfonic acid, 235

2-Hydroxynaphthalene-6-sulfonic acid, 235

2-Hydroxynaphthalene-7-sulfonic acid, 236

7'-Hydroxy-1',2',4,5,-naphthimidazole, 349

2-Hydroxy-1-naphthoic acid, 405

3-Hydroxy-2-naphthoic acid diethanolamide, 237

2-Hydroxynaphthoic acid diethylene amide, 237

3-Hydroxy-2-naphthoic acid ethanolamide, 237

7-Hydroxynaphtho-1',2',4, 5-imidazole, 247, 345

3-Hydroxy-oxanilic acid, 220

4-Hydroxyphenol thiourea, 221

o-Hydroxyphenyl propionic acid, 221

Hydroxyproline, 56, 57, 58, 62

4-(*γ*-Hydroxypropoxy)acetophenone, 150

Hydroxy pyridones, 245

5-Hydroxy-3-pyrrolin-2-one, 408

8-Hydroxyquinoline, 409

12-Hydroxystearate, 150

1-Hydroxy-3-sulfanylnaphthalene, 234

3-Hydroxythiophene-5-carboxylic acid, 246

3-Hydroxythiophene-5-carboxylic acid anilide, 246

3-Hydroxythiophene-5-carboxylic acid methylester, 246

Hypsochromatic shift, 296

Hystidine, 56

Imino acids, 56

p-Iminoquinone-diazides, 338

p,*p*'-Iminylidenebis(N,N-dimethylaniline), 362

Indenecarboxylic acid, 342

Indicator dye, 407

Indoaniline dyes, 359

Indole, 363

Indoline-benzopyrylospiran, derivatives
 of, 385
Indoxyl, 276
Induction period, 187
Inertia, 96, 97
Infrared radiation, 2, 4, 15, 402
Ink, lithographic, 51, 119
Ink receptivity, 122
Inorganic compounds, 1, 12–27
 stability of, 9
Intaglio image, 47
Intaglio offset, 124
Iodine, 181, 361
Iodine compounds, 138
Iodoform, 138, 181, 361, 365
2-Iodo-5-nitrothiophene, 353
4-Iodoresorcinol, 224
Ion-exchange resins, 64, 125
Ionic crystals, 10
Ionization, 5
Ionization energy, 10, 11, 14
Ionization potential, 5
Iron compounds, bis(aromatic hydro-
 carbon), 26
Iron-gold system, 37
Iron-mercury system, 37
Iron oxide, 108
Iron processes, 27
Iron salts, 22, 25, 27, 37, 129, 187,
 275
Iron-silver system, 37–39, *see* Brown-
 print
6-Isobutyl-4-hydroxy-2(-1)pyridone,
 245
ρ-Isocyanatobenzal acetophenone, 151
β-Isocyanatoethyl acrylate, 151
Isoimidazoles, diazo derivatives of, 329
Isonitrosoacetylacetone, 28
ω-Isonitroso-ω-cyano-2,4-dimethylaceto-
 phenone, 28
Isonitrosopropionylacetone, 28
Isopropanol amines, 107
Isopropyl alcohol, 126
Isopyrazoles, diazo derivatives of, 329
β-Isotruxillic acid, 140
Itaconic acid, 31, 293

J-acid, 252

Kallitype, 39
Kaolin, 48
Kerosene, 410
Ketoaldehydes, 51
2-Keto-3-azabenzanthrone, 144
3-Keto-1,2-diazabenzanthrone, 144
2-Keto-3-methyl-1,3-diazabenzanthrone,
 144
Kodak Photo Resist, 140, 141
 spectral sensitivity of, 146
"K-Tin" plastic plate, 129

Lacquer, deep-etch, 126
Lacquers, nonblinding, 123
Lactic acid, 125, 128, 273
Lactose, 294
Lanthanum hydroxide, 91
Lanthanum salts, 91
Larchwood, 125
Latent image, 15, 18, 20, 273
1-Lauryl-2-(2'-[1-hydroxy]-naphthyl)
 benzimidazole-5-sulfonic acid, 322
Lauryl methacrylate, 172
Lauroyl peroxide, 172
Lead, 127
Lead acetate, 17, 261
Lead arsenite, 17
Lead compounds, 17, 22
Lead formate, 17, 261
Lead iodide, 17, 138
Lead oxalate, 17
Lead sulfate, 17
Lead sulfide, 17, 26
Lead sulfite, 116
Lead tert-butyl mercaptide, 168
Lecithin, 409
Lenticular films, 39
Leuco base of triphenylmethane dyes,
 367
Leuco crystal violet, 367, 368
Leuco cyanides, 370
Leuco dyes, 94, 370–380
 light-sensitive, spectral sensitivity of,
 377
Leuco malachite blue, 406
Leuco phthalocyanine, 380
Leuco sulfuric acid ester of a vat dye,
 37
Leuco uranine, 379

Lichtdruck, 51
Light, absorption of, 3
Light green SF cyanide, 374
Light quanta, 1, 2, 159
Light sensitivity, 6, 11
Lignin, 297
Lignosulfonic acid, 327
Lithium bromide, 125
Lithium floride, 13
Lithium metasilicate glass, 24
Lithium silicate, 24
Lithographic ink, 124
Lithographic plate making, 119
Lithographic plates, 39, 62, 63, 66, 86, 119–131, 139, 147, 148, 150, 151, 173, 366, 369, *see also*: Printing plates, Bimetallic and trimetallic, 127–128; Paper and plastic, 128–131; Deep-etch, 124–126, 148; Surface plates, 120–124
 phosphate treatment of, 122
Lithographic stone, 121
Lithomat plates, 129
Lysine, 59

Magnesium chloride, 92, 125
Magnesium diacrylate, 165
Magnesium hydroxide, 29
Magnesium nitrate, 122
Magnesium plates, 104, 106
Magnesium salts, 34
Magnesium silicate, 29, 107
Magnesium stearate, 403
Maize starch, 298
Malachite green, 94, 145, 294, 371, 379, 415
Malachite green cyanide, 377
Maleic acid, 31, 38, 137, 405
Maleic acid anhydride, 366
 copolymers of, 139, 150
Malic acid, 125
Manganese, trioxalato-complexes of, 26
Manganese compounds, 22
Manganese salts, 34, 394
Manganese sulfate, 91
Mannitol, 258
Mariotype, 49
Melamine aldehyde resin, 121
Melamine formaldehyde resin, 130

Mendola's blue, 389
Mercaptans, 168, 361
Mercaptobenzenes, 257
2-Mercaptobenzimidazole, 168
2-Mercaptobenzothiazole, 168
2-Mercaptobenzoxazole, 168
2-Mercapto-5-chlorobenzoxazole, 168
2-Mercaptonaphthoxazole, 168
2-Mercapto-4-phenylbenzothiazole, 168
2-Mercapto-4-tolylbenzimidazole, 168
Mercuric bis-dithizonate, 384
Mercuric chloride, 16, 187, 275, 395
Mercuric compounds, 15, 377
Mercuric orthoarsenate, 17
Mercuric oxalates, 17, 188
Mercuric oxide, 15
Mercuric phenyl mercaptide, 168
Mercuric stearate, 404
Mercuric sulfate, 175
Mercuric sulfite, 17
Mercuric tert-butyl mercaptide, 168
Mercurous azide, 17
Mercurous carbonate, 17
Mercurous chromate, 17
Mercurous citrate, 15
Mercurous formate, 17
Mercurous halide, 17
Mercurous iodide, 15, 16, 17
Mercurous molybdate, 17
Mercurous nitrate, 15, 272
Mercurous orthoarsenite, 17
Mercurous oxalate, 15, 16, 17
 thermal decomposition of, 16
Mercurous phosphate, 17
Mercurous sulfate, 17
Mercurous tartrate, basic, 15
Mercurous tungstate, 17
Mercury ammonium oxalate, 15
Mercury salts, 15–17, 37, 360, 381
Mercury selenide, 187
Mercury sulfide, 26, 187
Mercury telluride, 187
Mercury vapor, 93
Merocyanine dyes, 369, 396
Metal alkyls, 158
Metal-diazonium process, 272–276
 resolving power of, 275
 spectral sensitivity of, 274
Metal mercaptides, 168

Metal oxides, 183
Metal screens, 112
Metanilic acid, 270
Methacrylamide, 170
m-Methacrylamidobenzaldehyde, 167
m-Methacrylamido-α-cinnamaldehyde, 167
5-Methacrylamido-1-methylquinaldinium methosulfate, 167
o-Methacrylamidophenol, 167
p-Methacrylamidophenol, 167
Methacrylate copolymers, 150
Methacrylic acid, 121, 166, 173, 179, 184, 325
Methacrylic acid esters, 165
Methacryloylaminoacetaldehyde, 166
p-Methacrylyloxybenzaldehyde, 167
o-Methoxy-*p*-aminodiphenylamine, diazonium metal salts of, 326
4-Methoxybenzaldehyde, 150
p-Methoxybenzene diazocyanide, 274
m-Methoxybenzene diazonium fluoroborate, 278
p-Methoxybenzene thiol, 168
2-Methoxycarbazole-3-diazonium bromide, 325
4-Methoxycinnamaldehyde, 141
4-Methoxy-1-dihydronaphthalene, 405
4-Methoxy-4'-(β-hydroxy-ethoxy)chalcone, 150
N-Methoxy-methyl-polyhexamethyleneadipamide, 165
1-Methoxynaphthalene-4-sulfonic acid, 266
4-Methoxy-1-naphthol, 410, 413
p-Methoxyphenol, 164
N-Methoxyphenyl-4-oxyquinolone-2, 245
1-Methoxy-4-propenylbenzene, 393
Methyl acrylate, 177, 119, 277
p-Methylallylaminobenzene diazonium chloride, 204
Methylamine, 92
Methylamino ethane sulfonic acid, 272
Methylaminonaphthimidazole, diazotized, 268
2-Methylamino-4-phenyl-5-bromothiazole, 407

2-Methylanthraquinone, 163
N-(4'-methyl-benzenesulfonyl)-imino-2, 5-diethoxybenzoquinone-(1, 4)-diazide-4, 338
α-Methylbenzoin, 163
2-Methylbenzothiazole, 368
3-Methyl-2-benzothiazolinone-1'-hydroxy-2'-naphthoylhydrazone, 406
Methyl cellulose, 69, 324, 372
1-Methyl-2,4-diaminobenzene, 358
3-Methyl-1,3-diaza-1,9-benzanthrone, 144
2-Methyl-4-diethylaminobenzene diazophenylsulfone, 267
1-Methyl-ω-dimethylamino-2-hydroxynaphthalene, 237
1-Methyl-2(2,4-dinitrobenzyl)-pyridinium *p*-toluene-sulfonate, 407
N-Methyldiphenylamine, 362
N,N'-Methylene-bis-acrylamide, 164, 165, 174, 182, 187
Methylene blue, 94, 175, 184, 294, 389, 394, 395, 404
Methylene bridge, 323
Methylene chloride, 151
α-Methyleneglutaric acid, 293
5-Methyl-5-ethyl-1, 3-cyclohexanedione, 240
Methyl ethyl ketone, 148
Methyl ethyl ketone peroxide, 172
3-Methyl-6-ethyl-4-morpholinomethylphenol, 248
1-Methyl-3-hydroxy-4-acetylamidobenzene, 221
Methyl-*p*-hydroxy benzoate, 122
7-Methyl-4-hydroxybenzotriazole, 248
1-Methyl-4'-hydroxyethoxystilbazolium methosulfate, 335
6-Methyl-4'-hydroxy-1-(β-hydroxy)-ethyl-2(1)-pyridone, 245
6-Methyl-4-hydroxy-2(1)pyridone, 245
4,4',4''-Methylidenetris(N,N-dimethylaniline), 362
4,4',4''-Methylidenetris-(N,N-dimethylaniline), 364
3-Methylindole, 364
3-Methyl-6-isopropyl-4-morpholinomethylphenol, 248

2-Methyl-5-isopropyl-4-morpholino methylphenol, 248
Methyl malonamate, 244
Methyl methacrylate, 150, 180
2-Methyl-6-methoxybenzoselenazole, quaternary salts of, 247
Methyl-2-(N-methylbenzothiazolylidene) dithioacetate, 148
1-Methyl-ω-(methylmethylcarboxyamino)-2-naphthol, 237
1-Methyl-8-nitronaphthalene, 322
N-Methylol acrylamide, 183
N-Methyl-4-oxyquinolone-2, 245
Methyl-N, N-pentamethylenedithiocarbamate, 168
1-Methyl-2-phenyl-indone, 370
Methylphenylpyrazolone, 252
Methyl polymethacrylate, 277
3-Methyl-5-pyrazolone, 246
3-Methylpyrazolone, 266
3-(3'Methyl-pyrazolone-5)benzene sulfonamide, 242
6-Methylpyronone, 244
β-2-Methyl-quinolyl-(5)-acrylic acid, 292
4-(4'-β-Methylstyryl)pyridine, 113
3'-Methyl-spiro (2H-1-β-naphthopyran-2:2[2'H-1'-benzopyran]), derivatives of, 385
S-Methylthio-di-α-naphthylamine sulfonium perchlorate, 352
2-Methyl-4,5,6,7-tetrachloro-benzotriazole, 378
2-Methylthiobenzothiazole, methomethsulfate, quaternary salt of, 167
m,m'-1-Methyltrimethylene dioxydiphenol, 229
Methylvinyl-ether/maleic-anhydride copolymer, 327
Methyl violet, 86, 145, 371
3-Methyl-10-(9'-xanthylidene)-anthrone, 385
Metol, 38, 272
Metol-hydroquinone developer, 18
Michler's ketone, 147
Mineral oil, 410
Molecular compounds, 403
Molecular rearrangement, 137
Molybdenum carbonyl, 172

Molybdenum compounds, 21, 22, 394
Molydbenum hexacarbonyl, 381
Molybdic acid, 21
Monel metal, 120
Mono-dithizone mercuric chloride, 384
Monohydric phenols, 220
Monomer, 158
Monomethine dyes, 370
Monoperoxyphthalic acid, 403
Morpholine, 272
Morpholine citrate, 295
1-Morpholinoacetylamino-7-naphthol, 248
4-Morpholinobenzene diazonium chloride, 267
o-Morpholinobenzene diazonium chloride, 294
4-Morpholino-2, 5-dialkoxyanilines, 303
Mucochloric acid, 164

Napthalene, 143
Napthalene-2,1-diazo-oxide-4-sulfonic acid, 250
Naphthalene-1, 2-diazo-oxide-4-sulfonic acid, 251
Naphthalene-β-diazo-N-sulfonic acid, sodium salt of, 270
Naphthalenedisulfonic acid, 292
1,5-Naphthalenedisulfonic acid, 293
2,6-Naphthalenedisulfonic acid, 293
2,7-Naphthalenedisulfonic acid, 293
Naphthalene green V-cyanide, 376, 378
Naphthalenemonosulfonic acid, 292
β-Naphthalene-sulfonyl chloride, 181
Naphthalenetrisulfonic acid, 273
Naphthalene-1,3,6-trisulfonic acid, 292, 293
Naphthaline black, 116
1',2',4,5-Naphthimidazole, substituted, 256
Naphthoic acid, derivatives of, 237
Naphthol, 116
β-Naphthol, 187, 258, 273, 328
Naphtholate ions, 217
Naphthols, 217, 234
1,2-Naphthoquinone, 144
1,4-Naphthoquinone, 163, 361
Naphthoquinone-1,2-diazide-(2)-phenyl sulfone-(4), 345

Naphthoquinone-(1, 2)-diazide-(2)-5-sulfo acid cyclohexyl ester, 343
Naphthoquinone-(1, 4)-diazide-(4)-2-sulfochloride, 340
Naphthoquinone-(1, 2)diazide-(2)-4-sulfochloride, 349
Naphthoquinone-1, 2-diazide-(2)-5-sulfochloride, 347
Naphthoquinone-(1, 2)-diazide sulfonic acid, 342
Naphthoquinone-(1, 4)-diazide-(4)-2-sulfonic acid, 341
p-Naphthoquinonediazide sulfonic amide, 337
Naphthoquinone-(1, 2)-diazide-(2)-sulfonic acid chloride-(5), 350
Naphthoquinone-(1, 2)-diazide-(2)-5-sulfonic acid ester of 4'-hydroxy-diphenyl-4-azo-β-naphthol, 346
Naphthoquinone-(1, 2)-diazide-(2)-4-sulfonic acid ester of 7'-hydroxy-2-ethyl-N-(*n*-propyl)-naphtho-1', 2':4, 5-imidazole, 347
Naphthoquinone-1, 2-diazide-(2)-4-sulfonic acid *p*-tolyester, 348
p-Naphthoquinonediazide sulfonic ester, 337
1-[Naphthoquinone-(1',2')-diazide-(2')-5'-sulfonyl]3, 5-dimethyl pyrazole, 344
2-(Naphthoquinone-(1, 2)-diazide-(2)-sulfonyloxy-5-monohydroxy-(1)-anthraquinone, 351
β-Naphthoquinone sulfonic acid, 28
1, 2-Naphthoquinonesulfonic acid, 290
2-Naphtho-6-sulfonic acid, 219
Naphthylamine, 260, 362, 364
2-Naphthylamine-6-sulfonic acid, 219
α-Naphthylamino camphor, 384
Naphthyl-*p*-amino esters, diazo derivatives of, 213
N-α-Naphthylhydroxylamine, 359
α-Naphthyl thiol, 168
β-Naphthyl thiol, 168
Natural Gums, 63
Neoprene latex, 119
Nickel, 127
Nickel chloride, 92
Nickel nitrate, 58

Nickel oxalate, 405
Nickel salts, 34, 91, 187, 409
Nickel stearate, 410
Nickel sulfate, 294, 295
Nickel sulfide, 26
Nigrosine, 174, 411
Nital treatment, 122
Nitric acid, 63, 106, 121, 122, 125, 272
5-Nitroacenaphthene, 352
4-Nitro-3-aldehyde phenyl carbonate, 322
5-Nitro-2-aminotoluene, 143
m-Nitroaniline, 143
p-Nitroaniline, 143
o-Nitroanisol, 143
m-Nitroanisole, 143
p-Nitroanisole, 143
3-Nitroanthranilic acid, diazotized, 328
Nitroaryl compounds, 142
Nitrobenzaldehyde, 379
o-Nitrobenzaldehyde, 137
Nitrobenzene, 143
p-Nitrobenzenediazonium-*p*-chlorobenzenesulfonate, 177
o-Nitrobenzenesulfenyl chloride, 379
p-Nitrobenzenesulfonyl chloride, 379
6-Nitrobenzimadazole, 117
6-Nitrobenzimidazole, sulfonation product of, 117
6-Nitrobenzopyrazole, 117
6-Nitrobenzotriazole, 117
6-Nitro-5-benzoylacenaphthene, 352
p-Nitrobenzyl cyanide, 241
o-Nitrobenzylidenedulcitol, 322
o-Nitrobenzylindeneglycerin, 322
p-Nitrobromobenzene, 143
Nitrocellulose, 65, 114, 126, 299
4-Nitro-2-chloroaniline, 143
2-Nitrocinnamaldehyde, 141
4-Nitrocinnamaldehyde, 141
p-Nitrodiphenyl, 143
o-Nitrodiphenylether, 143
Nitrofluorenes, 142
Nitrogen, 51
Nitrogen iodide, 21
Nitrogen oxides, 39
o-Nitromandelic acid, 275
p-Nitromandelic acid, 275

Nitromannitol, 379
4-Nitro-4'-methoxy-2-sulfanilidostilbene, 153
1-Nitro-8-methylnaphthalene-4-sulfonic acid, 322
1-Nitronaphthalene-8-carboxylic acid, 322
1-Nitronaphthalene-3-disulfonic acid, 322
1-Nitronaphthalene-2-sulfonic acid, 322
1-Nitronaphthalene-8-sulfonic acid, 322
Nitrones, 359
m-Nitrophenol, 143
Nitrophenols, 139
o-Nitrosobenzoic acid, 137
4-Nitroso-3-carboxy phenyl carbonate, 322
N-Nitroso-N-(*p*-diethylaminophenyl)-urea, 358
Nitroso-β-naphthol, 28
N-Nitroso-N-phenyl stearamide, 358
β-Nitrostyrene, 143
4-Nitro-2-sulfanilidostilbene, 152
5-Nitro-2-thienyl-o-carboxyphenyl sulfide, 353
Nitrothiophene derivatives, 353
Nylon, 112, 154, 165, 409, 411

Octanedione-2, 3, 162
Octyl alcohol, 325
Offset duplicating, 39
Oil of lavender, 138
Oil, vegetable, 410
Oils, drying, 138
Oleotype, 50
Opal blue, 379
Optical brighteners, 297
Optical sensitizer, 16, 70, 94, 141, 182,
Organic colloids, 39, 54–67
Oxalic acid, 7, 15, 16, 20, 21, 25, 28, 29, 31, 36, 120, 292, 380, 394, 405
photolysis of, 27
Oxalo-molybdic acid, 394
Oxaluric acid, 262
Oxazine dyes, 393
p-Oxazolidinoaniline, diazonium salt of, 204
Oximes, 137

3-Oxo-7-dialkylaminobenzothiazine diazonium borofluoride, 278
4-Oxo-1, 4-diazanaphthalenes, 335
Oxonium dyes, 393
5-Oxo-1-phenyl-2-pyrazoline-3-carboxylic acid, 247
2-Oxopropylene bis(methyl xanthene), 168
4-Oxo-1-thia-3a, 7-diazaindenes, 335
Oxycellulose, 130
4-Oxydiphenylamine, 293
Oxyglutin, 67
4-Oxyquinolones, 245
Ozalid process, 252
Ozobrome process, 49, 50
Ozotype, 49, 50

Palladiotype, 37
Palladium chloride, 18
Palladium salts, 18, 22, 37, 172
Paper, glassine, 299, 408
transparentizing, 48
waterproofed, 129
Paper litho plates, 128–131
Paraffin, chlorinated, 278
Paraffin oil, 48
Paraffin wax, 139, 265
Paraformaldehyde, 323
Pararosaniline, 379
Parrafin, halogenated, 361
Passivating agent, 107
Pentachlorophenol, 62, 122
Pentanedione-2, 3, 162
Pentennic acid, 292
Peptide chain, 84
Perfluoroazomethane, 177
Periodic acid, 361
Peroxides, 29, 170, 173
as photopolymerization initiators, 158, 170–172
Petroleum ether, 407
Phenacyl bromide, 180
Phenanthrene, 143, 151
Phenanthrenequinone, 139, 163, 164
Phenol, 37, 67, 122, 216, 217, 361
Phenolate ion, 216
Phenol-formaldehyde resin, 124, 181, 326
sulfonated, 323

Phenolic resin, 181
    sulfonated, 293
Phenoxide ion, 216, 217
Phenoxyacetic acid, 379
β-Phenylanthraquinone, 144
Phenylazo-*n*-butyl sulfone, 279
4-Phenylazodiphenylamine, 366, 386
Phenylbenzene thiol, 168
Phenylbiguanidine, 296
1-Phenylbutane dione-1, 2, 162
Phenyldiazonium chloride, 195
Phenyl-*m*-diisocyanate, 183
p-Phenylene diacrylic acid, 151
p-Phenylenediamine, 322, 359
    diazotized, 303, 326
m,m' -(*p*-Phenylene-dimethylenedioxy)-
    diphenol, 230
Phenylglyoxal, 162
N-Phenylhydroxylamine, 359
Phenyl *p*-hydroxybenzoate, 377
Phenyl isocyanate, 183
1-Phenyl-3-methyl-5-pyrazolone, 246
Phenylmethylpyrazolene sulfonic acid,
    328
Phenyl-2-naphthylnitrosamine, 407
Phenylnitromethane, 383
Phenylphosphonic acid, 296
Phenylphosphorodichloridates, 378
6-Phenylpyronone, 244
7 - Phenyl - quinoline-quinone-(3,4)-dia-
    zide-(3), 344
N-Phenyl-α-resorcylamide, 225
3-Phenyl-s p i r o(2H, 1-benzopyran-2,2'
    [2'H, 1'-benzopyran]), derivatives
    of, 385
3-(N-Phenylsulfanyl)-1-naphthol, 234
Phenylsulfinic acid, 296
1-(Phenylsulfonyl-2-styrylethylene, 352
Phloroglucide, 234
Phloroglucinol, 93, 219, 232, 252, 257,
    258, 260, 266, 303, 365, 407, 411
Phloroglucinol and cyanuric chloride,
    condensation product of, 232
Phloroglucinol monocarboxylic acid al-
    kyl esters, 232
Phloroglucinol monoethyl ether, 232
Phosphine, 12
Phosphomolybdic acid, 21, 377
Phosphorescence, 5, 185

Phosphoric acid, 34, 36, 56, 120, 122,
    124, 125, 147, 292, 323, 325, 328,
    334, 337, 342, 352
Phosphorus, red, 164
Phosphotungstic acid, 21, 22, 48, 363,
    377, 395
Phosphotungstomolybdic acid, 377
Phosphotungstous acid, 22
Photochemical equivalence, Law of,
    5, 7
Photochemical laws, 3–8, 71–74
Photochemical process, primary, 6, 7
    secondary, 7
Photochromic glass, 386
Photochromism, 380–386
    dark reaction of, 381
Photoelectric cells, 7
Photoengraving, 47, 53, 104–107
Photogelatin, 51
Photoglyphy, 47
Photographic developer, 115
Photographic resist, 65, 66, 71, 103–
    104, 140, 141, 173, 179, 183, 366
Photogravure, 53, 107–112
Photogravure plates, 47
Photolithographic plates, 39, 62, 66,
    119–131, 139, 147, 148, 150, 151,
    173, 366, 369
Photolithography, 47, 53, 119–131
Photomat plates, 129
Photomechanical printing processes, 46,
    103–136
Photon, 2, 160
Photopolymerization, photomultiplica-
    tion effect, 160
Photopolymerization initiators, 160–
    188
    azo and diazo compounds, 158, 175–
    180
    carbonyl compounds, 158, 160–167
    halogen compounds, 180–183
    peroxides, 170–172
    photoreducible dyes, 184–187
    sulfur compounds, 167–170
Photopolymerization processes, 158–
    193
Photoreducible dyes, 94, 184–187
Photoresists, 65, 66, 71, 103, 140, 141,
    173, 179, 183, 366

Photosensitive glass, 22–25
  development temperature of, 23
Photostaining, 25
Photostencils, 113
Photothermographic systems, 15, 16, 17, 20
Phototropic images, 21, 380–386
Phthalaldehyde, 139
Phthalazinone, 405
Phthalein dyes, 16, 393
Phthalic anhydride, 148
Phthalocyanine dyes, 48
Phthalocyanines, 380
Physical developer, 18, 38
4-Picoline, 149
Pigment images, 49
Pigment papers, 82, 86, 108
Pinatype green, 94
Pinatype process, 50
Piperic acid, 171
Piperidine, 171
Piperidinium trichloroacetate, 407
Piperine, 171
Piperite, 171
Pivaloin ethyl ether, 162
Planck's constant, 2
Plastic metaphosphate, 31
Plastolith plates, 129
Plates, *see* Lithographic plates
Platinic chloride, 47
Platinotype, 37
Platinum salts, 37, 126, 273
Polyacrylamide, 186, 325, 332
  methylolated, 130
Polyacrylic acid, 131, 325, 327, 338
Polyacrylic acid esters, 411
Polyalkylene ether glycol polyurethane, 164
Polyalkylene oxide, 379
Polyamides, 66, 113, 148, 151, 154, 165, 324
  N-alkoxymethylated, 113
Polycarbonate, 183
Polycarbonate film, 299
Polychlorophene, 164
Polyester base, glass-filled, 299
Polyethyl acrylate, 119
Polyethylene, 139, 278, 366, 411, 412
Polyethylene glycol, 164, 265, 328, 409

Polyethylene glycol dimethacrylate, 161
Polyethylene oxides, 164
Polyethylene terephthalate, 108, 166, 278, 300, 305
Polyethylene terephthalate sebacate, 166
Polyhexamethylene adipamide, 164
Polymer, definition of, 158
Polymerization, thermal initiators for, 158
Polymethacrylic acid, 298, 327, 338, 415
Polymethine dyes, 395
Polymethyl acrylate, 119
Polymethyl isopropenyl ketone, 370
Polymethylmethacrylate, 366
Polynuclear· quinones, 163
Polypetide bonds, 56
Polypetide chain, 54, 63
Polyphenols, chlorinated, 410
Polyphenylmethane carbinols, 366
Polyphenylmethane dyes, 369
Polysaccharide, 125
Polysaccharide carboxyether, 130
Polystyrene, 120, 276, 277, 297, 298, 362, 366, 402, 411
  acylation of, 141
  brominated, 365
Polystyrene latex, 119, 130
Polytetrafluoroethylene, 254, 264, 414
Polytetramethylene cinnamalidenemalonate, 148
Polyvinyl acetals, 165, 166, 380
Polyvinyl acetate, 36, 66, 113, 265, 276, 298, 299, 361, 369
Polyvinyl acetate-3-azido-phthalate, 335, 409
Polyvinyl acetate-vinyl sorbate, 164
Polyvinyl acetophenone, 149
Polyvinyl alcohol, 14, 31, 66, 69, 72, 103, 105, 113, 114, 119, 122, 123, 125, 129, 130, 138, 141, 150, 151, 165, 166, 167, 187, 276, 290, 295, 298, 322, 323, 324, 361, 372, 380, 394
Polyvinyl-aral-acetophenones, 149
Polyvinylbenzene sulfonate, 149
Polyvinyl benzophenone, 150
Polyvinyl butyral, 16, 66, 299, 323

Polyvinyl chloride, 20, 277, 278, 366, 409
Polyvinyl chloride/polyvinyl acetate copolymer, 119
Polyvinyl-*p'*-chlorobenzophenone, 150
Polyvinyl cinnamate, 141, 142, 143, 147, 149
Polyvinyl cinnamate phthalate, 147
Polyvinyl cinnamate succinate, 147
Polyvinyl ester acetal, 164
Polyvinyl formal, 325
Polyvinylidene chloride, 277, 366
Polyvinyl-*p*-methoxybenzophenone, 150
Polyvinylmethylsulfonate, 149
Polyvinyl-2-naphthophenone, 150
Polyvinylpyridine, 164
Polyvinylpyrrolidone, 66, 108, 328, 332
Polyvinyl sulfonates, 149
Polyvinyltolyene sulfonate, 149
Post-Cronak treatment, 123
Post-Nital treatment, 123
Potassium alum, 121, 131
Potassium bicarbonate, 303
Potassium borate, 258
Potassium chloride, 114
Potassium chloroplatinite, 37
Potassium chromate, 52, 53
Potassium citrate, 94
Potassium cyanide, 371, 377
Potassium dichromate, 31, 33, 36, 46, 47, 48, 52, 53, 71, 97, 108, 125, 271
Potassium ferricyanide, 29, 31, 32, 34, 49, 116
Potassium ferrocyanide, 27, 32, 33, 34, 38, 93, 116, 328
Potassium halides, 18
Potassium malonate, 261
Potassium 1, 2-naphthoquinone-4-sulfonate, 358
Potassium oxalate, 16, 29, 33, 37
Potassium oxide, 24
Potassium permanganate, 303
Potassium persulfate, 172
Potassium sodium hexametaphosphate, 31
Potassium thiocyanate, 58
Potassium zirconium fluoride, 121

Potato starch, 64
Primuline dyes, 201
Primuline process, 294
Printed-circuit, manufacture of, 24, 103
Printing-out papers, 91
Printing, planographic, 124
Printing process, planographic, 119, 124
Printing plates, 51, 65, 138, 146, 148, 152, 161, 166, 181, 183, 187; *see also* Lithographic plates
diazo sensitizers for, 321–330
presensitized, 128, 321–357
Print-out image, 15, 16, 17, 91, 115
Process glue, 53, 62; *see also* Glue
Proline, 56, 62
Propionic acid, 376
Propylamine, 262
6-Propylpyronone, 244
Proteins, 55, 62, 82
Protocatechuic acid, 405, 409
Protofibril, 57
Prussian blue, 33, 37, 48
Prussian blue toning, 22
Purpurogallin, 350
Pyperidine, 92
Pyranthrone, 143
Pyrax, 92
Pyrazolones, 246
Pyridine, 90, 92, 149
Pyridine dichromate, 90, 92
β-(α-Pyridyl-acrylic acid, 292
Pyridyl mercuric acetate, 62, 122
N-3-Pyridylsydnone, 383
Pyrocatechol, 404
Pyronones, 244
Pyrrolenines, diazo derivatives of, 329

Quanta, 1
Quantum efficiency, 6, 179, 197
Quantum energy, 9
Quantum theory, 2
Quantum yield, 6, 7, 20, 21, 27, 175, 177, 178, 186, 199, 201
Quinoline, 92
Quinoline-quinone-(3, 4)-diazide-(3), 344
Quinoline-quinone(3, 4)-diazide-(3)-6-sulfonic acid phenyl ester, 344

Quinone, 115, 415
Quinone-1, 2-diazide, 323
o-Quinone diazide of 1-amino-2-phenanthrol, 346
o-Quinone diazide sulfonic acid, hydroxy-(1,2,1',2')-pyridobenzimidazole esters of, 342
Quinone diazides, 250, 251, 252, 278; *see* Diazophenols
o-Quinone diazides, 339
p-Quinone diazides, 336
Quinone hydrochloride, 361
p-Quinone-iminodiazides, photolysis of, 200
Quinones, 141, 142, 163
Quinoquinoline hydrochloride, anhydrous, 383
Quinoxaline, 92

Radiant energy, 1
Rare-earth salts, 91
Rayon, 112
Red ochre, 48
Redox systems, 173, 175
Red potash, 29
Reflex copying, 282–291
Reflex exposure ratio, 283
Relative humidity, 81, 82, 86, 108, 123
Relief image, 24, 39, 46, 103, 116, 165, 171, 172, 174, 182, 183, 187
positive, 118
Relief images, colored, 166, 167, 174
Resinotype, 50
Resorcinol, 37, 93, 219, 224, 252, 258, 265, 266, 273, 407
derivatives of, 224
monoether of, 303
Resorcinol-*o*-acetic acid, 226
Resorcinol and acetaldehyde, condensation product of, 231
Resorcinol and arabinose, condensation product of, 231
Resorcinol and formaldehyde, condensation product of, 231
Resorcinol and phosgen, reaction product of, 231
Resorcinol monoacetate, 226

Resorcinol mono-N(β-aminoethyl) carbamate, 226
Resorcinol monobenzoate, 361
Resorcinol monocarbazate, 226
Resorcinol mono-N'N-diethyl carbamate, 226
Resorcinol monoethyl carbonate, 226
Resorcinol monomethylether, 226
Resorcinol-3-sulfonic acid, 294
α-Resorcylamide, 225
1,3,5-Resorcylic acid amide, 228
1,3,5-Resorcylic acid anilide, 228
1,2,5-Resorcylic acid ethanolamide, 228
1,3,5-Resorcylic acid ethanolamide, 228
1,2,4-Resorcylic acid methyl ester, 228
Reticles, 25
Reticulation, 50, 51
Reubeanic acid, 405
Reversal images, 118, 280
resolving power of, 119
l-Rhamnose, 64
Rhodamine B, 94, 175, 379, 390
Rhodamine compounds, hydroxyalkyl derivatives of, 139
Rhodium chloride, 18
Rhoduline blue 6GA, 145
Riboflavine, 184, 185
Rice starch, 64, 298
Rose bengal, 94, 175, 184
Rotargo film, 108
Rotary press, 108
Rotofilm, 108
Rotogravure, 108
R-salt, 235
Rubber, 278
cyclized, 407
Rubber latex, 119
Rubidium iodide, 13
Ruthenium chloride, 18

Saccharin, 405
Salicylic acid, 376
Salicylidene aniline, 382
Sandblasting, 107, 120
Saponin, 296
Saran latex, 119
Sarcosine, 272

Schaeffer salt, 235
Schwarzschild coefficient, 72
Schwarzschild's law, 72
Scotophores, 380
Scumming, 147
Selenoxanthonium dyes, 393, 395
Semiquinone radical, 185
Sensitized reactions, 5
Sensitizer, 5
Sensitizing dyes, 16, 70, 94, 141, 182
Sepia image, diazotype, 303
Sepia prints, brownprint, 37
Shellac, 46, 65, 71, 104, 125
   dichromated, 142
Silica, 29, 36, 297, 298, 381
Silicic acid, 332
Silicomolybdic acid, 21, 377
Silicon dioxide, 187
Silicotungstic acid, 21, 377
Silk, 112
Silk-screen process, 39, 66, 112–114
Silver acetate, 171
Silver amide, 21
Silver anthranilate, 20
Silver azide, 21
Silver behenate, 405, 409, 410, 413
Silver benzamidoxime, 20
Silver benzene sulfinate, 20, 183
Silver benzoate, 20
Silver bromide, 17, 18, 19
Silver carbide, 21
Silver carbonate, 39
Silver chloride, 18, 19, 20, 114, 115,
   116, 118, 386
Silver cinnamate, 20
Silver citrate, 39, 183
Silver compounds, 18–21, 24, 377; *see*
   Silver salts
Silver ferrocyanide, 116
Silver fluoride, 18
Silver fulminate, 21
Silver glutardiamidoxime, 20
Silver halide, 114, 181, 187, 386
Silver halides, heat of formation of, 19
Silver halide emulsion, 57, 113, 158,
   174, 181, 379, 409, 413
Silver images, amplication of, 172
Silver imide, 21
Silver iodide, 15, 16, 18, 19, 21, 94

Silver malondiamidoxime, 20
Silver molybdate, 19, 20
Silver nitrate, 17, 18, 21, 37, 38, 39,
   114, 171, 272 273, 275
   ammoniacal solution of, 116, 139
Silver oxalate, 16, 20, 188
   thermal decomposition of, 16
Silver phthalate, 20
Silver salicylate, 20
Silver salts, 20, 37, 129, 181, 187, 273,
   360, 361; *see* Silver compounds
Silver succindiamidoxime, 20
Silver sulfide, 26
Silver sulfinate, 20
Silver sulfite, 188
Silver sulfosalicylate, 20
Silver tartrate, 39
Silver thiosemicarbazide, 20
Silver titanate, 20
Silver *p*-toluene sulfinate, 20
Silver toning, 22
Silver tungstate, 19, 20
Single transfer, 48
Sizing, 29
Sodalite, 381
Sodium acetate, 63, 255, 261, 272, 353
Sodium alginate, 297
Sodium aluminate, 130
Sodium aluminum silicate, 381
Sodium azide, 332
Sodium benzoate, 62, 122
Sodium bisulfite, 54, 266
Sodium carbonate, 89, 113, 115, 255,
   352
Sodium carboxymethyl cellulose, 66,
   123, 129, 130, 298, 327, 328
Sodium caseinate, 297
Sodium chloride, 14, 15, 16, 381
Sodium chloroaurate, 37
Sodium chloropalladite, 37
Sodium chromate, 53
Sodium citrate, 29
Sodium cyanide, 377
Sodium decyl sulfate, 20
Sodium 4,4′-diazidostilbene-2,2′-disul-
   fonate, 332
sodium dichromate, 52, 53, 97
Sodium dioctyl phosphate, 20

Sodium *p*-ethoxybenzene diazosulfon- ate, 270
Sodium 2-ethylhexene sulfonate, 20
Sodium ethyl oxalacetate, 247
Sodium fluoride, 264
Sodium formaldehyde-sulfo-oxalate, 394
Sodium formate, 29
Sodium heptadecyl sulfate, 20
Sodium hexametaphosphate, 114, 119
Sodium hydrosulfite, 15, 258
Sodium hydroxide, 37, 89, 381
Sodium hyposulfite, 39
Sodium iodide, 15
Sodium lauryl sulfate, 20
Sodium lead thiosulfate, 17
Sodium metabisulfite, 303
Sodium metaborate, 326
Sodium molybdate, 21
Sodium 1, 5-naphthalene disulfonate, 292
Sodium 1-(or 2-)naphthalenesulfonate, 293
Sodium 1: 2-naphthoquinone-2-diazide-5-sulfonate, 278
Sodium nitrite, 18, 31, 34, 194
Sodium oxalate, 63
Sodium oxide, 22
Sodium pentasulfide, 48
Sodium persulfate, 106
Sodium phosphate, 255, 326
  secondary, 264, 293
Sodium phosphomolybdate, 326
Sodium silicate, 325, 327
Sodium silicomolybdate, 326
Sodium stannite, 21
Sodium sulfide, 116
Sodium sulfite, 36, 93, 115, 131, 174, 182, 258, 269
Sodium thiosulfate, 15, 16, 17, 38, 116, 118, 172, 272
Sodium triphosphate, 322
Sodium tungstate, 19, 21
Soluble blue cyanide, 374
Sorbitol, 148, 255, 258
Soybean, 122
Spectral sensitization, 3
Spectral sensitizer; *see* Optical sensitizer

Spectrum, electromagnetic, 1, 2
  visible, 1
Spiroindone, 404, 410
Staging, 109
Stainless steel, 127
Stainless steel plates, 120, 124
Stannic chloride, 195
Stannous chloride, 164, 185, 187, 303
Starch, 55, 64, 151, 297, 298, 361
  acid hydrolysis of, 65
  acid modified, 130
  chlorinated, 130
  dichromated, 47
  hydroxyl ether of, 130
  methylation of, 65
  oxidized, 130
Starch acetate, 130
Stearic acid, 377
Stearylamine, 265
Steel plates, 47, 127
Stencil, 112
Stencil printing, 112
Stibine, 13
Stilbene, 151
Stilbene compounds, 151–154, 335
Stilbene derivatives, 382
Stripping film, 108
Strontium hydroxide, 124
Strontium iodide, 14
Strontium oxalate, 188
Strontium sulfite, 188
Styrene, 184
Styrene-butadiene copolymer, 130
Styrene/maleic-anhydride copolymer, 147, 149, 150, 297, 300, 327
Styryl dyes, 368, 407
Styryl dye bases, 366, 367
Succinic acid, 257
Succinonitrile, 408
Sudan blue, 409
Sugar, 31, 46, 48
Sulfamic acid, 279
2-Sulfanilido-9-methylene-fluorenes, 352
Sulfenates, 170
Sulfenyl halides, 379
Sulfinic acid, 359
Sulfobenzaldehyde/4-formylbenzophe-none polyvinyl acetal, 166

2 -(3-Sulfobenzoylmethylene)-1-methyl-
β-naphthothiazoline, 335
Sulfocinnamic acid, 292
Sulfohydrazides, 322
6-Sulfo-2-hydroxy-3-naphthalenecar-
boxylic acid, 292
5-Sulfo-N-methylanthranilic acid, 292
Sulfomethylcellulose, 327
Sulfonamides, 242
Sulfonated cumarone indene resin, 195
Sulfonated polybenzyl resin, 195
Sulfones, unsaturated, 352
Sulfonic acid, 115
Sulfonyl halides, 379
1-p-Sulfophenyl-3-methyl-5-pyrazolone,
246
5-Sulfosalicylic acid, 292
Sulfur chloride pentafluoride, 170
Sulfur compounds, as photopolymeriza-
tion initiators, 158, 167–170
Sulfur dioxide, 15, 25
Sulfuric acid, 27, 36, 52, 56, 120, 121,
126, 323
Sulfurous acid, 395
Sulfuryl chloride, 180, 181
Support, temporary, 50
Surface plates, 63, 120–124
desensitizing solution for, 123, 124
developing ink for, 123, 124
Sydones, 383
Syneresis, 61, 89
Synthetic resins, 65
Syrian asphalt, 104

Tannic acid, 27, 28, 124, 395
Tannin, 395
Tanning processes, 39–40
Tapioca starch, 64
Tartaric acid, 15, 20, 25, 31, 38, 121,
148, 258, 272, 292, 327
Teflon, 264
Tellurium compounds, 15
Temperature-sensitive papers, 402
Tenebrescent substances, 380
Terephthalal -4,4′-dinitro-2,2′disulfanili-
doditoluene, 153
Terphenyls, hydrogenated, 410
1,2,3,4-Tetrabrombutane, 365
Tetrabromo-o-cresol, 365

Tetrabromophenolphthalein, 365
1,2,3,4-Tetrachlorobenzene, 365
1,2,3,5-Tetrachlorobenzene, 365
N-(2,3,4,6-Tetrachorobenzyl)-p-phenyl-
enediamine, diazotized, 329
Tetrachlorobisphenol A, 405
Tetrachlorobisphenol A/diethanola-
mine, 403
Tetrachloroquinone, 415
Tetrachlortetrahydronaphthalcne, 365
Tetrachromates, 90
Tetrachloroketodihydronaphthalene,
383
p,p′-Tetraethyldiaminodiphenylketone,
145
Tetraethyl lead, 187
Tetraethylthiuram monosulfide, 169
Tetrafluoroethylene, 170
Tetrahydrofurfuryl alcohol, 294
1,2,3,4-Tetrahydronaphthalene, 337
2,2′4,4′-Tetrahydroxydiphenyl, 233
3,3′,5,5′-Tetrahydroxydiphenyl, 233
4,4′,6,6′-Tetrahydroxydiphenyl, 234
Tetraisopropylthiuram monosulfide, 169
N,N,N′,N′,-Tetrakis (2-hydroxypro-
pyl)ethylene diamine, titanium
ester of, 376
Tetrakis(2-hydroxypropyl)ethylene diamine-iso-propyl titanate, 376
Tetramethyl ammonium chloride, 262
p,p′,-Tetramethyldiaminobenzophen-
one, 145
3,6-Tetramethyldiamino-9-cyano-thio-
xanthonium chloride, 391
p,p′-Tetramethyldiamino diphenyl-4-
anilinonaphthyl methane, 362
p,p′-Tetramethyldiaminodiphenylketone,
145
p,p′-Tetramethyldiamino-diphenylme-
thane, 362
1,2,5,8-Tetramethyl-3,6-diamino-selen-
oxanthonium chloride, 392
Tetramethylthiuram disulfide, 169
Tetramethylthiuram monosulfide, 169
Tetramethylthiuram tetrasulfide, 169
Tetraphenyl-dihydrotriazine, 383
Tetrazo-N,N′-bis(4 - aminophenyl)alky-
lenediamines, 295
Thallic oxalate, 18

Thallium bromide, 18
Thallium nitrate, 187
Thallous bromide, 18
Thallous bromide emulsion, 18
Thallous chloride, 18
Thallous iodide, 18
Thallous nitrate, 175
Theophylline, 296
Thermo-Fax process, 291
Thermographic copying papers, 403
   chemical papers, 404
   resolving power of, 408
   single component papers, 403
   transfer sheets for, 409
Thermographic images, 405
Thermographic recording papers, 402
Thermography, 402–416
Thermopiles, 7
Thiazine dyes, 141, 201, 393
Thioacetamide, 365
Thioacridones, 335
Thiobarbituric acid, 247
Thiocarbamic acid, 294
Thiocarbanilide, 406
Thiocarbonic acids, 294
o-Thiocresol, 168
p-Thiocresol, 168
Thioflavine TCN, 390
Thioglycolic acid, 294
Thioindoxyl, 275
Thiolated gelatin, 187
Thiol polymers, 187
Thiols, 168, 365
Thionine, 184
Thionyl chloride, 181
Thiophene derivatives, 246
Thiophenol, 168
Thiosemicarbazide, silver salt of, 20
Thiosinamine, 15, 185, 186, 294, 393, 395
Thiourea, 27, 93, 107, 172, 186, 261, 267, 294, 393, 365, 405, 409
Thioxanthonium dyes, 393, 395
Thiuram derivatives, 169
Thorium chloride, 92
Three-dimensional images, 24, 172; *see* Relief images
Thymol, 62, 122
Tin compounds, 23, 258

Tin oxide, 386
Titanium dioxide, 48, 175, 187, 299, 403
Titanium lactate, 187
Titanium potassium oxalate, 296
Titanium salt, 394
Titanium sodium citrate, 296
Titanium sodium tartrate, 296
p-Toluene diazocyanide, 274
p-Toluene sulfonyl chloride, 181
β-Toluenesulfonyl chloride, 180
p-Toluene sulfonic acid ester of polyvinyl alcohol, 149
p-Toluidine, 362, 364
Toluidine toner, 327
Tolu-*p*-quinone, 144
o-Tolylbenzene thiol, 168
Tolyoin, 162
1-(*p*-Tolylsulfonyl)-2-(2-methoxystyryl ethylene, 352
Topping powder, 105
Trácing cloth, 114
Tracing paper, 114
Transition metal complexes, 25–40
Transition metals, 25
4,4′,4′-Triamino-3-methyltriphenylacetonitrile, 372
p,p′,p″-Triamino-*o*-methytriphenyl methane, 362
4,4′,4″Triaminotriphenylacetonitrile, phenylacetonitrile, 373
4, 4′, 4″-Triaminotriphenylacetonitrile, 372
p,p′,p″-Triaminotriphenyl carbinol, 362
p,p′,p″-Triaminotriphenyl methane, 362
Triarylmethane dyes, 377
Triarylmethyl leuco nitriles, 371
Triazene dyes, 407
Triazoles, diazo derivatives of, 329
Tribromoacetophenone, 368, 379
Tributyl phosphate, 376
Trichlorethylene, 141, 411
Trichloroacetic acid, 122, 261
Trichromates, 90
Triethanolamine, 94, 147, 260
2,5,4′-Triethoxydiphenyl-4-diazonium oxalate, 255
Triethylamine, 279
Triethylbenzylcyanurate, 378

Triethylene glycol diacrylate, 164
Triethyl phosphate, 376
Trifluoracetic acid, 122
Trihydroxybenzenes, 232
2,3,4-Trihydroxybenzothenone-naphtho-
  quinone - (1,2)-diazide-(2)-5-sulfo-
  nic acid ester, 351
2,4,4'-Trihydroxydiphenyl, 233
3,3',5-Trihydroxydiphenyl, 233
Trihydroxyethylamine oxalate, 36
1,3,5-Trihydroxy-2-methylbenzene, 232
1,2,3-Triketohydrindene, 407
Trimetallic plates, 127–128
Trimethoxyboroxine, 378
Trimethylbenzylammonium hydroxide,
  31
m, m'-Trimethylene dioxydiphenol, 229
1,1,3 - Trimethylindolino -6'-nitro-8'-me-
  thoxybenzo-pyrylospiran, 385
Trimethyl phenyl ammonium chloride,
  262
1, 3, 3 - Trimethylspridobenzopyranindo-
  line, 406
1:3:3 - Trimethyl-spiro-2(H-1'-benzopy-
  ran-2':2'-indoline, derivatives of,
  385
Trimethyl starch, 65
2,4,6-Trinitroaniline, 143
Triphenylamine, 362
Triphenylformazane, 384
1,2,3-Triphenylguanidine, 362
Triphenylmethane, 370
Triphenylmethane dye, leuco base of,
  367
Triphenylmethane dyes, 142, 145, 151,
  201, 363, 370, 371, 379, 393, 395,
  407
  carbinol base of, 367
Triphenyl phosphate, 410
Tripropoxyboroxine, 378
Tris(ethyl acetoacetato)albumin, 161
Trisodium phosphate, 342, 357
Tropocollagen, 58
True-to-scale process, 39
α-Truxillic acid, 140
Tungsten compounds, 394
Tungsten hexacarbonyl, 381
Tungstic acid, 21
Turnbull's blue, 32, 33

Turpentine, 123
Turquoise blue, 94
Tyndall effect, 60
Tyrosine, 56, 59

Ultramarine, 48
Ultraviolet absorber, 35
Ultraviolet rays, 2, 4, 16, 97
Unsaturated compounds, 137–157
Uranium compounds, 22, 34, 36, 394
Uranium nitrate, 38
Uranium salts, 22, 34, 36, 394
Uranyl nitrate, 164
Uranyl salts, 7, 187
Urea, 64, 128, 139, 261, 262, 263,
  266, 291, 294, 295, 406
Urea-formaldehyde resin, 66, 129, 130,
  299
Urea of *m*-aminophenol, 221
Urea peroxide, 33
Utocolor, 387, 393
Utopaper, 387

Valeric acid, 376
γ-Valerolactone, 299
Vanadium, salt of, 22, 394
Vanadium compounds, 22, 394
Vanadium pentoxide, 31
Van Dyke prints, 37, 294; *see* Brown-
  print
Velour charbon, 49
Vesicular process, 179, 276–282
  resolution of, 282
  spectral sensitivity of, 279
Victoria blue, 145, 371, 388
Vinyl acetate, 150, 184, 186, 277
Vinyl acetate/crotonic acid copolymer,
  300
Vinyl acetate/maleic acid copolymer,
  66, 147, 300
Vinyl acetophenone, 150
N-Vinylamine, 369
p-Vinylbenzaldehyde   ethylene   glycol
  acetal, 166
Vinyl benzalacetophenone polymers,
  150
p-Vinylbenzene-sulfonamidobenzalde-
  hyde ethylene glycol acetal, 166

N-Vinylcarbazole, 181, 369
Vinyl chloride. 277, 361
Vinyl copolymers, 66
Vinylidene chloride, 277, 361
Vinylidene chloride/acrylonitrile co-
polymer, 277
Vinylidene chlorofluoride, 277
Vinylidene compounds, polymerization
of, 187
N-Vinylimide, 369
Vinyl lacquers, 126
Vinyl methyl ether/maleic anhydride,
66, 270. 276, 326, 337
N-Vinylphthalimide. 369
Vinyl polymers, 66
Vinyl propionate. 150
N-Vinylpyrrole, 369

Wash-off process. 114–118
Water, photo-oxidation of, 27
Waxoline red, 147
Wetting agents, 20, 31, 38
Wheat starch, 64
Whiteprinting, 302
Wipe-on plates, 353

Xanthene dyes, 186, 393
Xanthoxonium dyes, 393
Xanthylidene-anthrone, derivatives of,
385
X-rays, 2, 13, 20, 369, 379, 380, 381

Xylene, 147
Xylene blue VS cyanide, 373
Xylene sulfonyl chloride, 181

Yellow ochre, 25, 48

Zein, 65
Zinc, 127
Zinc acetate, 261, 361
Zinc behenate, 403
Zinc chloride, 125, 130, 294, 295
complex with diazonium chlorides,
195
Zinc compounds, 17, 34, 381
Zinc formate, 261
Zinc oxalate, 188
Zinc oxide, 175, 188, 365, 394
Zinc phosphate, 35
Zinc plates, 87, 104, 106, 120, 124,
147
Zinc salts, 17, 34, 381
Zinc selenide, 187
Zinc silicate, 29
Zinc sulfide, 17, 187
Zinc sulfite, 188
Zinc telluride, 187
Zirconium acetate, 131
Zirconium dioxide, 187
Zirconium hexafluoride, 327
Zirconium salts, 29, 34